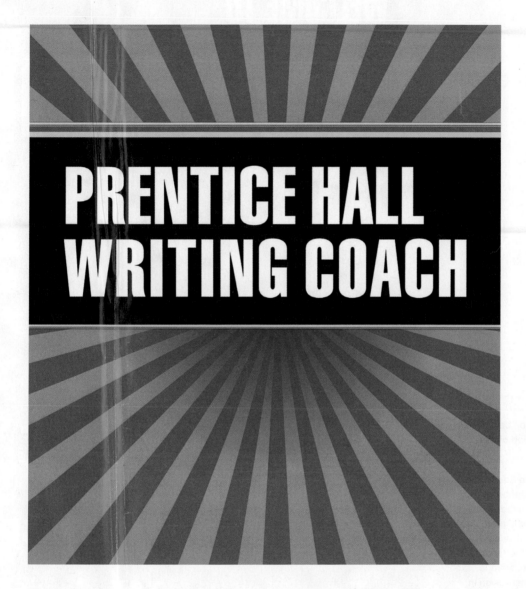

PRENTICE HALL
WRITING COACH

PEARSON

Upper Saddle River, New Jersey
Boston, Massachusetts
Chandler, Arizona
Glenview, Illinois

WRITING COACH

WELCOME TO Writing COACH

Seven Great Reasons to Learn to Write Well

Acknowledgments appear on page R50, which constitute an extension of this copyright page.

PEARSON

0-13-253142-9
978-0-13-253142-9
18 V057 15

1 Writing is hard, but hard is **rewarding**.

2 Writing helps you **sort things out**.

3 Writing helps you **persuade** others.

4 Writing makes you a **better reader**.

5 Writing makes you **smarter**.

6 Writing helps you get into and through **college**.

7 Writing **prepares you** for the world of work.

AUTHORS

Program Authors

Jeff Anderson

Jeff Anderson has worked with struggling writers and readers for almost 20 years. His works integrate grammar and editing instruction into the processes of reading and writing. Anderson has written articles in NCTE's *Voices from the Middle, English Journal*, and *Educational Leadership.* Anderson won the NCTE Paul and Kate Farmer Award for his *English Journal* article on teaching grammar in context. He has published two books, *Mechanically Inclined: Building Grammar, Usage, and Style into Writer's Workshop* and *Everyday Editing: Inviting Students to Develop Skill and Craft in Writer's Workshop* as well as a DVD, *The Craft of Grammar.*

Grammar gives me a powerful lens through which to look at my writing. It gives me the freedom to say things exactly the way I want to say them.

Kelly Gallagher

Kelly Gallagher is a full-time English teacher at Magnolia High School in Anaheim, California. He is the former co-director of the South Basin Writing Project at California State University, Long Beach. Gallagher is the author of *Reading Reasons: Motivational Mini-Lessons for the Middle and High School, Deeper Reading: Comprehending Challenging Texts 4–12, Teaching Adolescent Writers,* and *Readicide.* He is also featured in the video series, *Building Adolescent Readers.* With a focus on adolescent literacy, Gallagher provides training to educators on a local, national and international level. Gallagher was awarded the Secondary Award of Classroom Excellence from the California Association of Teachers of English—the state's top English teacher honor.

The best swimmers swim the most; the best writers write the most. There's only one way to become a good writer: write!

Contributing Authors

Evelyn Arroyo

Evelyn Arroyo is the author of **A+RISE,** Research-based Instructional Strategies for ELLs (English Language Learners). Her work focuses on closing the achievement gap for minority students and English language learners. Through her publications and presentations, Arroyo provides advice, encouragement, and practical success strategies to help teachers reach their ELL students.

Your rich, colorful cultural life experiences are unique and can easily be painted through words. These experiences define who you are today, and writing is one way to begin capturing your history. Become a risk-taker and fall in love with yourself through your own words.

When you're learning a new language, writing in that language takes effort. The effort pays off big time, though. Writing helps us generate ideas, solve problems, figure out how the language works, and, above all, allows us to express ourselves.

Jim Cummins, Ph.D.

Jim Cummins is a Professor in the Modern Language Centre at the University of Toronto. A well-known educator, lecturer, and author, Cummins focuses his research on bilingual education and the academic achievement of culturally diverse students. He is the author of numerous publications, including **Negotiating Identities: Education for Empowerment in a Diverse Society.**

Grant Wiggins, Ed.D.

Grant Wiggins is the President of Authentic Education. He earned his Ed.D. from Harvard University. Grant consults with schools, districts, and state education departments; organizes conferences and workshops; and develops resources on curricular change. He is the co-author, with Jay McTighe, of **Understanding By Design,** the award-winning text published by ASCD.

I hated writing as a student—and my grades showed it. I grew up to be a writer, though. What changed? I began to think I had something to say. That's ultimately why you write: to find out what you are really thinking, really feeling, really believing.

Concepts of grammar can sharpen your reading, communication, and even your reasoning, so I have championed its practice in my classes and in my businesses. Even adults are quick to recognize that a refresher in grammar makes them keener— and more marketable.

Gary Forlini

Gary Forlini is managing partner of the School Growth initiative **Brinkman—Forlini—Williams,** which trains school administrators and teachers in Classroom Instruction and Management. His recent works include the book **Help Teachers Engage Students** and the data system **ObserverTab** for district administrators, **Class Acts: Every Teacher's Guide To Activate Learning**, and the initiative's workshop **Grammar for Teachers**.

CONTENTS IN BRIEF

WRITING

> *Writing without grammar only goes so far. Grammar and writing work together. To write well, grammar skills give me great tools.*

CORE WRITING CHAPTERS

GRAMMAR

GRAMMAR GAME PLAN

Find It FIX IT **20** **Major Grammatical Errors and How to Fix Them**

> Grammar without writing is only a collection of rules, but when these rules are put into action as I write, the puzzle comes together.

CORE GRAMMAR CHAPTERS

STUDENT RESOURCES

Handbooks

Glossaries

Writing COACH

How to Use This Program

This program is organized into two distinct sections: one for WRITING and one for GRAMMAR.

In the **WRITING** section, you'll learn strategies, traits, and skills that will help you become a better writer.

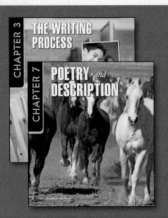

In the **GRAMMAR** section, you'll learn the rules and conventions of grammar, usage, and mechanics.

What DIGITAL writing and grammar resources are available?

The Writing Coach Online boxes will indicate opportunities to use online tools.

In **Writing,** use the **Interactive Writing Coach™** in two ways to get personalized guidance and support for your writing.

- Paragraph Feedback and
- Essay Scorer

WRITING COACH

Online
www.phwritingcoach.com

Interactive Writing Coach™

- Choosing from the Topic Bank gives you access to the Interactive Writing Coach™.
- Submit your writing and receive instant personalized feedback and guidance as you draft, revise, and edit your writing.

WRITING COACH

Online
www.phwritingcoach.com

Grammar Tutorials
Brush up on your grammar skills with these animated videos.

Grammar Practice
Practice your grammar skills with Writing Coach Online.

Grammar Games
Test your knowledge of grammar in this fast-paced interactive video game.

In **Grammar,** view grammar tutorials, practice your grammar skills, and play grammar video games.

What will you find in the WRITING section?

Writing Genre

Each chapter introduces a different **writing genre.**

Learn about the key characteristics of the **genre** before you start writing.

Focus on a single form of the genre with the **Feature Assignment**.

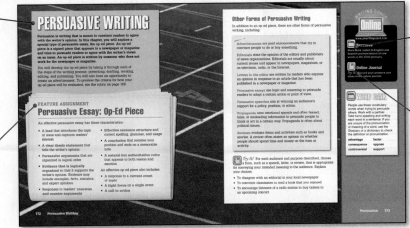

Writing Coach Online

- View the **Word Bank** words in the eText glossary, and hear them pronounced in both English and Spanish.

- Use your **Online Journal** to record your answers and ideas as you respond to *Try It!* activities.

Mentor Text and Student Model

The **Mentor Text** and **Student Model** provide examples of the genre featured in each chapter.

Use the **Mentor Text** to see how a professional crafted a piece of writing.

Review the **Student Model** as a guide for composing your own piece.

Writing Coach Online

- Use the **Interactive Model** to mark the text with Reader's and Writer's Response Symbols.

- Listen to an audio recording of the **Mentor Text** or **Student Model**.

The **Topic Bank** provides prompts for the **Feature Assignment.**

Choose from a bank of topics, or follow steps to find an idea of your own.

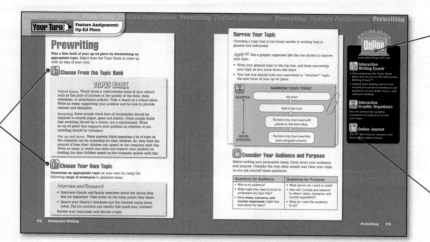

Writing Coach Online

- As you narrow your topic, get the right type of support! You'll find three different forms of graphic organizers— one model, one with step-by-step guidance, and one that is blank for you to complete.

- Use *Try It!* ideas to practice new skills. Use *Apply It!* activities as you work on your own writing.

Whether you are working on your essay drafts online or with a pen and paper, an **Outline for Success** can get you started.

Consult this **outline** for a quick visual specific to the writing task assigned in each chapter.

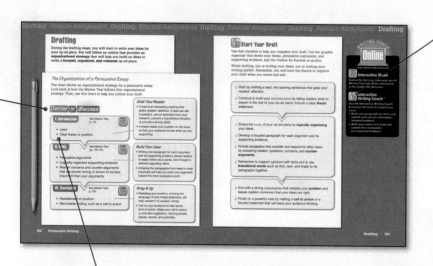

Follow the bulleted suggestions for each part of your draft, and you'll be on your way to success.

Writing Coach Online

- Start with just a paragraph and build up to your essay draft, or if you are ready, go straight to submitting your essay. The choice is yours!

You can use the **Revision RADaR** strategy as a guide
for making changes to improve your draft.

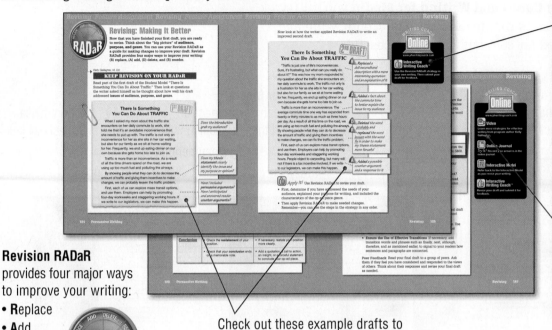

Revision RADaR
provides four major ways
to improve your writing:
- **R**eplace
- **A**dd
- **D**elete
- **R**eorder

Check out these example drafts to
see how to apply **Revision RADaR.**

Writing Coach Online
- With **Interactive Writing Coach™**, submit your paragraphs and essays multiple times. View your progress in your online writing portfolio. Feel confident that your work is ready to be shared in peer review or teacher conferencing.
- View **videos** with strategies for writing from program author **Kelly Gallagher.**

In the editing stage, **What Do You Notice?** and
Mentor Text help you zoom in on powerful sentences.

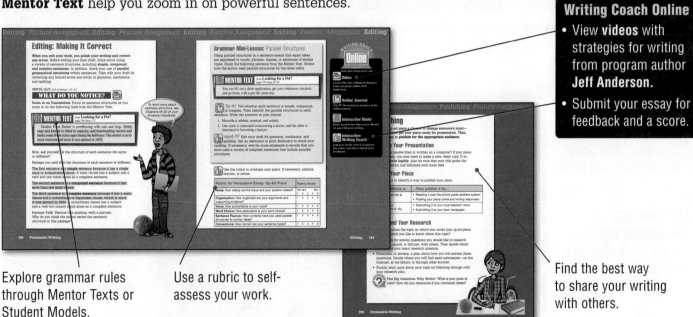

Writing Coach Online
- View **videos** with strategies for writing from program author **Jeff Anderson.**
- Submit your essay for feedback and a score.

Explore grammar rules
through Mentor Texts or
Student Models.

Use a rubric to self-
assess your work.

Find the best way
to share your writing
with others.

How do end-of-chapter features help you apply what you've learned?

21st Century Learning

In **Make Your Writing Count** and **Writing for Media** you will work on innovative assignments that involve the 21st Century life and career skills you'll need for communicating successfully.

Make Your Writing Count

Work collaboratively on project-based assignments and share what you have learned with others. Projects include:

- Debates
- TV Talk Shows
- News Reports

Writing for Media

Complete an assignment on your own by exploring media forms, and then developing your own content. Projects include:

- Blogs
- Storyboards
- Documentary Scripts
- Multimedia Presentations

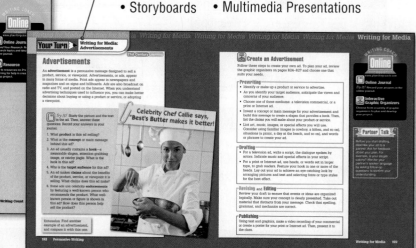

Test Prep

The **Writing for Assessment** pages help you prepare for important standardized tests.

SAT/PSAT PREP ACT Notice these icons that emphasize the types of writing you'll find on high-stakes tests.

Use **The ABCDs of On-Demand Writing** for a quick, memorable strategy for success.

Writing Coach Online
Submit your essay for feedback and a score.

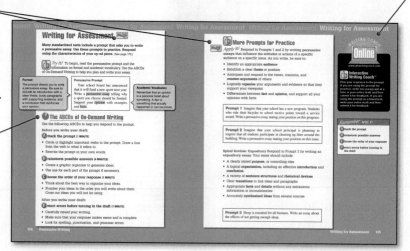

What will you find in the GRAMMAR section?

The **Find It/Fix It** reference guide helps you fix the **20** most common errors in student writing.

Study each of the 20 common errors and their corrections, which are clearly explained on each page.

Follow cross-references to more instruction in the grammar chapters.

Review the **Check It** features for strategies to help you avoid these errors.

Each grammar chapter begins with a **What Do You Notice?** feature and **Mentor Text.**

Use the **Mentor Text** to help you zoom in on powerful sentences. It showcases the correct use of written language conventions.

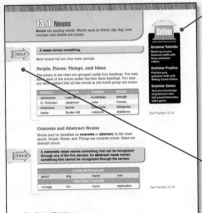

Writing Coach Online
The **Writing Coach Online** digital experience for Grammar helps you focus on just the lessons and practice you need.

Use the grammar section as a quick reference handbook. Each **grammar rule** is highlighted and numbered.

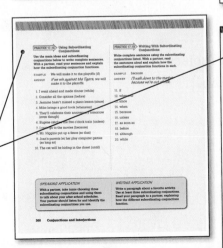

Try **Practice** pages and **Test Warm-Ups** to help you check your progress.

WRITING

WRITING GAME PLAN

WRITING COACH

Online

www.phwritingcoach.com

All content available online
- Interactive Writing Coach™
- Interactive Graphic Organizer
- Interactive Models
- Online Journal
- Resources
- Video

WRITING

Connect to the Big Questions

- **What do you think?**
  What challenges change us most?

- **Why write?**
  What should we put in and leave out to be accurate and honest?

Connect to the Big Questions

- **What do you think?**
  In the conflict between people and nature, what does it take to win?

- **Why write?**
  What can fiction do better than nonfiction?

www.phwritingcoach.com

All content available online
- Interactive Writing Coach™
- Interactive Graphic Organizer
- Interactive Models
- Online Journal
- Resources
- Video

WRITING

CHAPTER 7 | Poetry and Description

118

Connect to the Big Questions

- **What do you think?**
  What makes an experience memorable?

- **Why write?**
  How does one best convey feelings through words on a page?

Connect to the Big Questions

- **What do you think?**
  What can we learn from the past?

- **Why write?**
  What should we tell and what should we describe to make information clear?

WRITING COACH

Online

www.phwritingcoach.com

All content available online

- Interactive Writing Coach™
- Interactive Graphic Organizer
- Interactive Models
- Online Journal
- Resources
- Video

WRITING

Connect to the Big Questions

• **What do you think?**
What kinds of community service have the most impact?

• **Why write?**
What is your point of view? How will you know if you've convinced others?

Connect to the Big Questions

- **What do you think?**
  What should we read?

- **Why write?**
  What should you write about to make others interested in a text?

www.phwritingcoach.com

All content available online
- Interactive Writing Coach™
- Interactive Graphic Organizer
- Interactive Models
- Online Journal
- Resources
- Video

WRITING

Connect to the Big Questions

- **What do you think?**
  Should we study extreme environments?

- **Why write?**
  Do you understand your subject well enough to write about it? How will you find out what all the facts are?

Connect to the Big Questions

- **What do you think?**
  What is the best way to communicate about what we see?

- **Why write?**
  What do daily workplace communications require of format, content, and style?

WRITING COACH
Online

www.phwritingcoach.com

All content available online
- Interactive Writing Coach™
- Interactive Graphic Organizer
- Interactive Models
- Online Journal
- Resources
- Video

GRAMMAR

WRITING COACH

Online

www.phwritingcoach.com

All content available online
- Grammar Tutorials
- Grammar Practice
- Grammar Games

GRAMMAR

WRITING COACH
Online
www.phwritingcoach.com

All content available online
- Grammar Tutorials
- Grammar Practice
- Grammar Games

GRAMMAR

USAGE

MECHANICS

WRITING COACH

Online

www.phwritingcoach.com

All content available online

• Grammar Tutorials
• Grammar Practice
• Grammar Games

GRAMMAR

WRITING COACH

Online

www.phwritingcoach.com

All content available online
- Grammar Tutorials
- Grammar Practice
- Grammar Games

STUDENT RESOURCES

NONFICTION NARRATION *Personal Narrative* FICTION NARRATION *Tall*

Essay PERSUASION *Editorial* RESPONSE TO LITERATURE *Critical Review*

Friendly Letter,. Letter of Complaint NONFICTION NARRATION *Personal Na*

EXPOSITION *Cause-and-Effect Essay* PERSUASION *Editorial* RESPONSE TO

WRITING *Letter of Request, Friendly Letter, Letter of Complaint* NONFICTIO

rse Poem and Lyric Poem EXPOSITION *Cause-and-Effect Essay* PERSUA

search Report WORKPLACE WRITING *Letter of Request, Friendly Letter, Le*

ATION Tall Tale POETRY *Free Verse Poem and Lyric Poem* EXPOSITION

view RESEARCH *Informational Research Report* WORKPLACE WRITING *Le*

Writing

CHAPTER 1

YOU, THE WRITER

Why Do You Write?

Writing well is one of the most important life skills you can develop. Being a good writer can help you achieve success in school and beyond. Most likely, you write for many reasons. You write:

To Share

You probably often write to **share** your experiences with others. Writing can be an easy way to **reach out** to people and connect with them.

To Persuade People

Writing can also be an effective way to **persuade** people to consider your opinions. For example, you may find it's easier to convince someone of your point of view when you've effectively organized your thoughts in an essay or a letter.

To Inform

Another reason to write is to **inform**. Perhaps you want to tell an audience how you built your computer network or how you finally got your e-mail to function properly.

To Enjoy

Personal fullfillment is another important motivation for writing, since writing enables you **to express** your thoughts and feelings. In addition, writing can also help you recall an event, or let you escape from everyday life.

Fortunately, writing well is a skill you can learn and one that you can continue to improve and polish. This program will help you improve your writing skills and give you useful information about the many types of writing.

What Do You Write?

Writing is already an important part of your everyday life. Each day is full of opportunities to write, allowing you to capture, express, think through and share your thoughts and feelings, and demonstrate what you know. Here are some ways you might write.

- Recording thoughts in a journal
- Texting friends or posting on social networking sites
- E-mailing thank-you notes to relatives
- Creating lists of things to do or things you like
- Writing research reports, nonfiction accounts, fiction stories, and essays in school

How Can You Find Ideas?

The good news is that ideas are all around you. You just need to be aware of the rich resources that are available.

By Observing

Observing is a good way to start to find ideas. Did you see anything interesting on your way to school? Was there something unusual about the video game you played last night?

By Reading

Reading is another useful option— look through newspaper articles and editorials, magazines, blogs, and Web sites. Perhaps you read something that surprised you or really made you feel concerned. Those are exactly the subjects that can lead to the ideas you want to write about.

By Watching

Watching is another way to get ideas— watch online videos or television programs, for example.

❝ Writer to Writer ❞

I write when I want to be heard or connect. Writing lets me be a vital part of my community and reach outside it as well. All the while, I get to be me—my unique self.

—Jeff Anderson

How Can You Keep Track of Ideas?

You may sometimes think of great writing ideas in the middle of the night or on the way to math class. These strategies can help you remember those ideas.

Start an Idea Notebook or a Digital Idea File

Reserving a small **notebook** to record ideas can be very valuable. Just writing the essence of an idea, as it comes to you, can later help you develop a topic or essay. A **digital idea file** is exactly the same thing—but it's recorded on your computer, cell phone, or other electronic device.

Keep a Personal Journal

Many people find that keeping a **journal** of their thoughts is helpful. Then, when it's time to select an idea, they can flip through their journal and pick up on the best gems they wrote— sometimes from long ago.

Maintain a Learning Log

A **learning log** is just what it sounds like—a place to record information you have learned, which could be anything from methods of solving equations to computer shortcuts. Writing about something in a learning log might later inspire you to conduct further research on the same topic.

Free Write

Some individuals find that if they just let go and write whatever comes to mind, they eventually produce excellent ideas. **Free writing** requires being relaxed and unstructured. This kind of writing does not require complete sentences, correct spelling, or proper grammar. Whatever ends up on the paper or on the computer screen is fine. Later, the writer can go back and tease out the best ideas.

How Can You Get Started?

Every writer is different, so it makes sense that all writers should try out techniques that might work well for them. Regardless of your writing style, these suggestions should help you get started.

Get Comfortable

It's important to find and create an environment that encourages your writing process. Choose a spot where you'll find it easy to concentrate. Some writers prefer quiet. Others prefer to work in a room with music playing softly.

Have Your Materials Ready

Before starting to write, gather all the background materials you need to get started, including your notes, free writing, reader's journal, and portfolio. Make sure you also have writing tools, such as a pen and paper or a computer.

Spend Time Wisely

Budgeting your available writing time is a wise strategy. Depending on your writing goal, you may want to sketch out your time on a calendar, estimating how long to devote to each stage of the writing process. Then, you can assign deadlines to each part. If you find a particular stage takes longer than you estimated, simply adjust your schedule to ensure that you finish on time.

◀ October ▶						
SUNDAY	MONDAY	TUESDAY	WEDNESDAY	THURSDAY	FRIDAY	SATURDAY
		1 Start Research	2 Finish Research	3 Write Outline	4	5
6	7	8 Finish First Draft	9 Finish Revising	10 Finish Proof-reading	11	12
13	14 DUE DATE	15	16	17	18	19
20	21	22	23	24	25	26
27	28	29	30	31		

How Do You Work With Others?

If you think of writing as a solitary activity, think again. Working with others can be a key part of the writing process.

Brainstorming

Brainstorming works when everyone in a group feels free to suggest ideas, whether they seem commonplace or brilliant.

Cooperative Writing

Cooperative writing is a process in which each member of a group concentrates on a different part of an assignment. Then, the group members come together to discuss their ideas and write drafts.

Peer Feedback

Peer feedback comes from classmates who have read your writing and offered suggestions for improvements. When commenting, it's important to provide constructive, or helpful, criticism.

21st Century Learning

Collaborate and Discuss

In **collaborative writing,** each group member takes a role on a writing project. The goal is to work and rework the writing until all members feel they have produced the best result.

Possible Roles in a Collaborative Writing Project

LEADER
Initiates the discussion by clearly expressing group goals and moderates discussions

FACILITATOR
Works to move the discussion forward and clarify ideas

COMPROMISER
Works to find practical solutions to differences of opinion

LISTENER
Actively listens and serves to recall details that were discussed

Using Technology

Technology allows collaboration to occur in ways that were previously unthinkable.

- By working together on the Internet, students around the world have infinite opportunities to collaborate online on a wide-range of projects.

- Collaboration can range from projects that foster community cooperation, such as how to improve debates during local elections, to those that increase global awareness, such as focusing on how to encourage more recycling.

- Being able to log in and to contribute to media, such as journals, blogs, and social networks, allows you to connect globally, express your views in writing, and join a world-wide conversation.

Where Can You Keep Your Finished Work?

A **portfolio,** or growing collection of your work, is valuable for many reasons. It can serve as a research bank of ideas and as a record of how your writing is improving. You can create a portfolio on a computer or in a folder or notebook. You'll learn more about managing a portfolio in chapter 3.

A **Reader's Journal,** in which you record quotes and ideas from your reading, can also be used to store original ideas. Your journal can be housed on a computer or in a notebook.

Reflect on Your Writing

Analyzing, making inferences, and drawing conclusions about how you find ideas can help you become a better, more effective writer. Find out more about how you write by asking yourself questions like these:

- Which strategies have I found most effective for finding good ideas for writing?

- What pieces of writing represent my best work and my weakest work? What do the pieces in each group have in common?

Partner Talk

With a partner, talk about your collaborative writing experiences. Be sure to share your responses to such questions as these: What project did you work on as a collaborative effort? What did you learn that you might not have discovered if you were developing a writing project by yourself?

CHAPTER 2

TYPES of WRITING

Genres and Forms

Genres are types, or categories, of writing.

- Each genre has a specific **purpose,** or goal. For example, the purpose of persuasive writing is to convince readers to agree with the writer's point of view.
- Each genre has specific **characteristics.** Short stories, for example, have characters, a setting, and a plot.

In this chapter, you will be introduced to several genres: nonfiction narratives, fiction narratives, poetry and descriptive writing, expository writing, persuasive writing, responses to literature, and workplace writing.

Forms are subcategories of genres that contain all the characteristics of the genre plus some unique characteristics of their own. For example, a mystery is a form of short story. In addition to plot, characters, and setting, it has a mystery to be solved.

Selecting Genres

In some writing situations, you may need to select the correct genre for conveying your intended meaning.

- To **entertain,** you may choose to write a short story or a humorous essay.
- To **describe** an emotion, writing a poem may be best.
- To **persuade** someone to your point of view, you may want to write a persuasive essay or editorial.

Each genre has unique strengths and weaknesses, and your specific goals will help you decide which is best.

Nonfiction Narration

Nonfiction narratives are any kind of literary text that tells a story about real people, events, and ideas. This genre of writing can take a number of different forms but includes well-developed conflict and resolution, interesting and believable characters, and a range of literary strategies, such as dialogue and suspense. Examples include Mark Twain's "Cub Pilot on the Mississippi" and Annie Dillard's "An American Childhood."

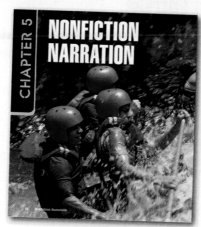

Personal Narratives

Personal narratives tell true stories about events in a writer's life. These types of writing are also called **autobiographical essays.** The stories may tell about an experience or relationship that is important to the writer, who is the main character. They have a clearly defined focus and communicate the reasons for actions and consequences.

Biographical Narratives

In a **biographical narrative,** the writer shares facts about someone else's life. The writer may describe an important period, experience, or relationship in that other person's life, but presents the information from his or her own perspective.

Blogs

Blogs are online journals that may include autobiographical narratives, reflections, opinions, and other types of comments. They may also reflect forms such as expository writing, and they may include other media, such as photos, music, or video.

Diary and Journal Entries

Writers record their personal thoughts, feelings, and experiences in **diaries** or **journals.** Writers sometimes keep diaries and journals for many years and then analyze how they reacted to various events over time.

Eyewitness Accounts

Eyewitness accounts are nonfiction writing that focus on historical or other important events. The writer is the narrator and shares his or her thoughts about the event. However, the writer is not the main focus of the writing.

Memoirs

Memoirs usually focus on meaningful scenes from writers' lives. These scenes often reflect on moments of a significant decision or personal discovery. For example, many modern U.S. presidents have written memoirs after they have left office. These memoirs help the public gain a better understanding of the decisions they made while in office.

Reflective Essays

Reflective essays present personal experiences, either events that happened to the writers themselves or that they learned about from others. They generally focus on sharing observations and insights they had while thinking about those experiences. Reflective essays often appear as features in magazines and newspapers.

Try It! With a small group, discuss which of the narrative nonfiction forms would be the best choice for each of these purposes. For each, identify two ideas you would expect the writing to address. Discuss your ideas and report your decisions.

- To tell about seeing a championship kite-flying tournament
- To write about one of the first astronauts to walk in space
- To record personal thoughts about a favorite teacher

Fiction Narration

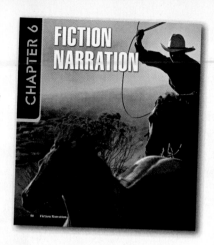

Fiction narratives are literary texts that tell a story about imagined people, events, and ideas. They contain elements such as characters, a setting, a sequence of events, and often, a theme. As with nonfiction narratives, this genre can take many different forms, but most forms include well-developed **conflict** and **resolution.** They also include **interesting and believable elements** and a range of **literary strategies,** such as dialogue and suspense. Examples include Toni Cade Bambara's "Raymond's Run" and O. Henry's "A Retrieved Reformation."

Realistic Fiction

Realistic fiction portrays invented characters and events in everyday situations. Because the focus is on everyday life, realistic fiction often presents problems that many people face and solutions they devise to solve them.

Fantasy Stories

Fantasy stories stretch the imagination and take readers to unreal worlds. Animals may talk, people may fly, or characters may have superhuman powers. Good fantasy stories manage to keep the fantastic elements believable.

Historical Fiction

Historical fiction is about imaginary people living in real places and times in history. Usually, the main characters are fictional people who know and interact with famous people and participate in important historical events.

Mystery Stories

Mystery stories present unexplained or strange events that characters try to solve. These stories are often packed full of suspense and surprises. Some characters in mystery stories, such as Sherlock Holmes, have become so famous that many people think of them as real people.

Myths and Legends

Myths and **legends** are traditional stories, told in cultures around the world. They were created to explain natural events that people could not otherwise explain or understand. They may, for example, tell about the origin of fire or thunder. Many myths and legends include gods, goddesses, and heroes who perform superhuman actions.

Science Fiction

Science fiction stories tell about real and imagined developments in science and technology and their effects on the way people think and live. Space travel, robots, and life in the future are popular topics in science fiction.

Tall Tales

You can tell a **tall tale** from other story types because it tells about larger-than-life characters in realistic settings. These characters can perform amazing acts of strength and bravery. One very famous hero of tall tales is Pecos Bill, who could ride just about anything—even a tornado!

Try It! Think about what you've read about narrative fiction and narrative nonfiction genres. Then, discuss in a group which **genre** would be best if you were planning a first draft and had these purposes in mind. Select the correct genre for conveying your intended meaning to your audiences. Then, identify two or three ideas that you would expect to include in a first draft. Be sure to explain your choices.

- To tell about a Texas rancher who can lasso lightning
- To share a true story about a famous person
- To tell the story of your most exciting day at school

Poetry and Description

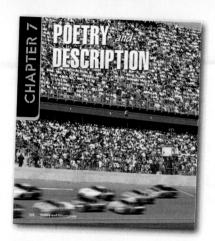

Poetry and other kinds of descriptive literature express ideas and feelings about real or imagined people, events, and ideas. They use rhythm, rhyme, precise language, and sensory details—words that appeal to the senses—to create vivid images. In addition, they use figurative language—writing that means something beyond what the words actually say—to express ideas in new, fresh, and interesting ways.

Structural elements, such as line length and stanzas, also help the poet express ideas and set a mood. Some examples of poetry include Eleanor Farjeon's "Cat!" and Langston Hughes's "Harlem Night Song."

Ballad

A **ballad** is a form of lyric poetry that expresses the poet's emotions toward someone or something. Ballads rhyme, and some have refrains that repeat after each stanza, which makes them easy to translate into songs.

In many places, traditional folk ballads were passed down as oral poems or songs and then later written. Some ballads tell about cultural heroes. Other ballads tell sad stories or make fun of certain events.

Free Verse

Free verse is poetry that has no regular rhyme, rhythm, or form. Instead, a free verse poem captures the patterns of natural speech. The poet writes in whatever form seems to fit the ideas best. A free verse poem can have almost anything as its subject.

Think about an example of fiction that you've especially enjoyed reading. Then, choose a partner and report your choices to each other. Be sure to explain what made the fiction piece so enjoyable, interesting, or exciting.

Prose Poem

A **prose poem** shares many of the features of other poetry, but it takes the form of prose, or non-verse writing. Therefore, a prose poem may look like a short story on a page.

Sonnet

The **sonnet** is a form of rhyming lyric poetry with set rules. It is 14 lines long and usually follows a rhythm scheme called iambic pentameter. Each line has ten syllables and every other syllable is accented.

Haiku

Haiku is a form of non-rhyming poetry that was first developed in Japan hundreds of years ago. Typically, the first line has five syllables, the second line has seven syllables, and the third line has five syllables. Haiku poets often write about nature and use vivid visual images.

Other Descriptive Writing

Descriptive writing includes descriptive essays, travel writing, and definition essays.

- **Descriptive essays** often use words that involve the senses to create a clear picture of a subject.
- A **travel essay** uses sensory words to describe a place.
- A **definition essay** can draw on a writer's emotional experience to describe something abstract, like friendship or happiness.

  Description can be used in other types of writing. For example, a short story may include strong description.

Try It! Now that you've learned more about poetry and description, discuss which specific **genre** would be best for each of these purposes. Select the correct genre for conveying your intended meaning to your audiences. Then, identify two or three types of information that you would want to include in a first draft. Be ready to explain your thinking.

- To tell about a trip to a beach in Mexico
- To describe a drop of rain
- To tell the story of a character who lives in the wilderness

Exposition

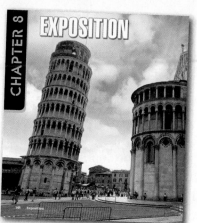

Exposition is writing that seeks to communicate ideas and information. It relies on facts to inform or explain.

- Effective expository writing includes effective introductory paragraphs, body paragraphs, and concluding paragraphs.

- In addition, good expository writing uses a variety of sentence structures and rhetorical devices—deliberate uses of language for specific effects.

Examples of expository writing include Richard and Joyce Wolkomir's "Sun Sucker's and Moon Cursers" and Maryann Mott's "USDA Fights Invasive Fire Ants With Flies."

Analytical Essay

An **analytical essay** explores a topic by supplying relevant information in the form of facts, examples, reasons, and valid inferences to support the writer's claims.

- An **introductory paragraph** presents a thesis statement, the main point to be developed.

- The **body of the essay** provides facts about the topic, using a variety of sentence structures and transitions.

- The **concluding paragraph** sums up ideas.

Compare-and-Contrast Essay

A **compare-and-contrast** essay explores similarities and differences between two or more things for a specific purpose. As with other expository essays, the compare-and-contrast essay offers clear, factual details about the subject.

Cause-and-Effect Essay

A **cause-and-effect essay** traces the results of an event or describes the reasons an event happened. It is clearly organized and gives precise examples that support the relationship between the cause and effect.

Writer to Writer

Expository forms can shape my thinking and help my writing jell. I find the expository patterns clarifying my thoughts and filling in gaps that I may have otherwise missed.

—Jeff Anderson

> **Partner Talk**
>
> Choose a different partner this time. Discuss a poem that you've read in class. Share your thoughts about the poem and describe what made the piece successful.

Classification Essay

In a **classification essay,** a writer organizes a subject into categories and explains the category into which an item falls.

- An effective classification essay **sorts** its subjects—things or ideas—into several categories.
- It then offers **examples** that fall into each category. For example, a classification essay about video games might discuss three types of video games—action, adventure, and arcade.
- The essay might conclude with a statement about how the items classified are different or about how they are similar.

Problem-Solution Essay

A **problem-solution essay** presents a problem and then offers solutions to that problem. This type of essay may contain opinions, like a persuasive essay, but it is meant to explain rather than persuade.

- An effective problem-solution essay presents a clear statement of the problem, including a summary of its causes and effects.
- Then, it proposes at least one realistic solution and uses facts, statistics, or expert testimony to support the solution.
- The essay should be clearly organized, so that the relationship between the problem and the solution is obvious.

Pro-Con Essay

A **pro-con essay** examines arguments for and against an idea or topic.

- It has a topic that has two sides or points of view. For example, you might choose the following as a topic: Is it right to keep animals in zoos?
- Then, you would develop an essay that tells why it's good to keep animals in zoos, as well as why it's harmful to keep animals in zoos.
- It's important to be sure to give a clear analysis of the topic.

Newspaper and Magazine Articles

Newspaper and **magazine articles** offer information about news and events. They are typically factual and do not include the writer's opinions. They often provide an analysis of events and give readers background information on a topic. Some articles may also reflect genres other than the analytical essay, such as an editorial that aims to persuade.

Internet Articles

Articles on the **Internet** can supply relevant information about a topic.

- They are often like newspaper or magazine articles but may include shorter sentences and paragraphs. In addition, they include more visuals, such as charts and bulleted lists. They may also reflect genres other than analytical essays.

- It's always wise to consider the source when reading Internet articles because only the most reputable sources should be trusted to present correct facts.

On-Demand Writing

Because essay questions often appear on school tests, knowing how to write to **test prompts**, especially under time limits, is an important skill.

Test prompts provide a clear topic with directions about what should be addressed. The effective response to an essay demonstrates not only an understanding of academic content but also good writing skills.

Try It! Think about what you've learned about expository writing and consider the other genres you've discussed. Then, discuss in a group which **genre** would be best if you were planning a first draft with these purposes in mind. Select the correct genre for conveying your intended meaning to your audiences. Then, identify two or three key ideas that you would want to include in a first draft. Be sure to explain your choices.

- To weigh the benefits of two kinds of pets
- To imagine what life would be like on the moon

Partner Talk

Share your experiences with writing expository essays with a partner. Talk about strategies that worked well for you, as well as those that weren't as successful. Be sure to include your analysis of why certain strategies worked better than others.

Persuasion

Persuasive writing aims to influence the attitudes or actions of a specific audience on specific issues. A strong persuasive text is logically organized and clearly describes the issue. It also provides precise and relevant evidence that supports a clear thesis statement. Persuasive writing may contain diagrams, graphs, or charts. These visuals can help to convince the reader. Examples include "The Trouble With Television"; Susan B. Anthony's "On Woman's Right to Suffrage"

Persuasive Essays or Argumentative Essays

A **persuasive essay** or **argumentative essay** uses logic and reasoning to persuade readers to adopt a certain point of view or to take action. A strong persuasive essay starts with a clear thesis statement and provides supporting arguments based on evidence. It also anticipates readers' counter-arguments and responds to them as well.

Persuasive Speeches

Persuasive speeches are presented aloud and aim to win an audience's support for a policy, position, or action. These speeches often appeal to emotion and reason to convince an audience. Speakers sometimes change their script in order to address each specific audience's concerns.

Editorials

Editorials state the opinion of the editors and publishers of news organizations. Editorials usually present an opinion about a current issue, starting with a clear thesis statement and then offering strong supporting evidence.

Op-Ed Pieces

An **op-ed, or opposite-editorial, piece** is an essay that tries to convince readers to agree with the writer's views on an issue. The writer may not work for the publication and is often an expert on the issue or has an interesting point of view.

Letters to the Editor

Readers write **letters to editors** at print and Internet publications to express opinions in response to previously published articles. A good letter to the editor gives an accurate and honest representation of the writer's views.

Reviews

Reviews evaluate items and activities, such as books, movies, plays, and music, from the writer's point of view. A review often states opinions on the quality of an item or activity and supports those opinions with examples, facts, and other evidence.

Advertisements

Advertisements in all media—from print to online sites to highway billboards—are paid announcements that try to convince people to buy something or do something. Good advertisements use a hook to grab your attention and support their claims. They contain vivid, persuasive language and multimedia techniques, such as music, to appeal to a specific audience.

Propaganda

Propaganda uses emotional appeals and often biased, false, or misleading information to persuade people to think or act in a certain way. Propaganda may tap into people's strongest emotions by generating fear or attacking their ideas of loyalty or patriotism. Because propaganda appears to be objective, it is wise to be aware of the ways it can manipulate people's opinions and actions.

Try It! Think about what you have learned about exposition, description, and persuasion. Form a group to discuss and draw conclusions about which **genres** would be best if you were planning a first draft with each of these intentions in mind. Select the correct genre for conveying your intended meaning to your audiences. Then, identify two or three types of information that you would want to include in a first draft.

- To explain how an event happened
- To describe a beautiful landscape
- To encourage teens to buy teeth-whitening toothpaste

Partner Talk

Share your experiences with various types of persuasive texts with a partner. Talk about the types of persuasive text that you think are most effective, honest, and fair. Be sure to explain your thinking.

Responses to Literature

Responses to literature analyze and interpret an author's work. They use clear **thesis statements** and **evidence from the text using embedded quotations to support the writer's ideas.** They also evaluate how well authors have accomplished their goals. Effective responses to literature extend beyond literal analysis to evaluate and discuss how and why the text is effective or not effective.

Critical Reviews

Critical reviews evaluate books, plays, poetry, and other literary works. Reviews present the writer's opinions and support them with specific examples. The responses may analyze the aesthetic effects of an author's use of language in addition to responding to the content of the writing.

Compare-and-Contrast Essays

Compare-and-contrast essays explore similarities and differences between two or more works of literature. These essays provide relevant evidence to support the writer's opinions.

Letters to Authors

Readers write **letters to authors** to share their feelings and thoughts about a work of literature directly.

Blog Comments

Blog comments on an author's Web site or book retailer pages let readers share their ideas about a work. Readers express their opinions and give interpretations of what an author's work means.

 *Try It!* As a group, decide which **genre** would be most appropriate if you were planning a first draft for each of these purposes. Select the correct genre for conveying your intended meaning to your audiences. Then, identify two or three key questions that you would want to answer in a first draft.

- To tell an author why you think her book is excellent
- To write an opinion about a newspaper article
- To imagine how a certain landform came to be

> **Partner Talk**
>
> Interview your partner about his or her experiences writing interpretative responses. Be sure to ask questions such as these:
>
> - How did you support your opinion of the author's work?
> - How did you choose evidence, such as quotes, to support your analysis or opinion?

Research Writing

Research writing is based on factual information from outside sources. Research reports organize and present ideas and information. They present evidence in support of a clear thesis statement.

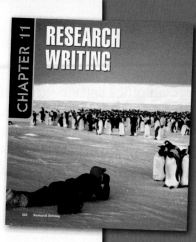

Research Reports and Documented Essays

Research reports and **documented essays** present information and analysis about a topic that the writer has studied. Start with a clear thesis statement. Research reports often include graphics and illustrations. Documented essays are less formal research writing that show the source of every fact, quote, or borrowed idea in parentheses.

Experiment Journals and Lab Reports

Experiment journals and **lab reports** focus on the purposes, procedures, and results of a lab experiment. They often follow a strict format that includes dates and specific observation notes.

Statistical Analysis Reports

A **statistical analysis report** presents numerical data. Writers of this type of report must explain how they gathered their information, analyze their data, tell what significance the findings may have, and explain how these findings support their thesis.

Annotated Bibliographies

An **annotated bibliography** lists the research sources a writer used. It includes the title, author, publication date, publisher, and brief notes that describe and evaluate the source.

Try It! Discuss which kinds of reports you might write if you were planning a first draft for these purposes. **Select the correct form** for conveying your intended meaning to your audiences. Then, identify two or three key questions that you would want to answer in a first draft. Explain your choices.

- To accompany a project you plan to enter in a science fair
- To write about a poll taken to predict the results of an election

Share with a partner the kinds of research writing you've done in school. Explain which projects you've enjoyed and why.

Workplace Writing

Workplace writing is writing done on the job or as part of a job, often in an office setting. It usually communicates details about a particular job or work project. This type of writing features organized and accurately conveyed information and should include reader-friendly formatting techniques, such as clearly defined sections and enough blank space for easy reading.

Business Letters and Friendly Letters

A **business letter** is a formal letter written to, from, or within a business. It can be written to make requests or to express concerns or approval. For example, you might write to a company to ask about job opportunities. Business letters follow a specific format that includes an address, date, formal greeting, and closing.

In contrast, a **friendly letter** is a form of correspondence written to communicate between family, friends, or acquaintances. For example, you might write a thank-you note for a gift.

Memos

Memos are short documents usually written from one member of an organization to another or to a group. They are an important means of communicating information within an organization.

E-mails

E-mail is an abbreviation for "electronic mail" and is a form of electronic memo. Because it can be transmitted quickly allowing for instant long-distance communication, e-mail is a very common form of communication that uses a computer and software to send messages.

Forms

Forms are types of workplace writing that ask for specific information to be completed in a particular format. Examples include applications, emergency contact information forms, and tax forms.

Instructions

Instructions are used to explain how to complete a task or procedure. They provide clear, step-by-step guidelines. For example, recipes and user manuals are forms of instructions.

Project Plans

Project plans are short documents usually written from one member of an organization to another. They outline a project's goals and objectives and may include specific details about how certain steps of a project should be achieved.

Résumés

A **résumé** is an overview of a person's experience and qualifications for a job. This document lists a person's job skills and work history. Résumés can also feature information about a person's education.

College Applications

College applications are documents that ask for personal information and details about someone's educational background. College administrators use this information to decide whether or not to accept a student.

Job Applications

Job applications are similar to résumés in that they require a person to list work experience and educational background. Most employers will require a completed job application as part of the hiring process.

Try It! As a group, discuss which form of workplace writing would be best for each of these purposes. Select the correct form for conveying your intended meaning to your audiences. Identify two or three types of information you would expect to include in a first draft.

- To inform the company that made your cell phone that it does not work properly
- To prepare information about your qualifications for a job search
- To create a plan for your group assignment in science class

Partner Talk

Share with a partner your experience with workplace and procedural writing. For example, have you ever written instructions, created a résumé, or completed a job application? What do you find are particular challenges with this type of writing?

Writing for Media

The world of communication has changed significantly in recent years. In addition to writing for print media such as magazines and books, writers also write for a variety of other **media,** in forms such as:

- Scripts for screenplays, video games, and documentaries
- Storyboards for graphic novels and advertisements
- Packaging for every kind of product
- Web sites and blogs

Scripts

Scripts are written for various media, such as documentaries, theater productions, speeches, and audio programs. Movies, television shows, and video games also have scripts.

- A good script focuses on a clearly expressed or implied **theme** and has a specific **purpose.**
- It also contains interesting details, which contribute to a definite **mood or tone.**
- A good script also includes a clear **setting,** **dialogue,** and well-developed **action.**

Blogs

Blogs address just about every purpose and interest. For example, there are blogs about local issues, pets, or food.

Advertisements

Advertisements are designed to persuade someone to buy a product or service. Advertisements use images, words, and music to support their message. Writers write the content of advertisements. In addition, they may help create music and design the sound and the images in the ad.

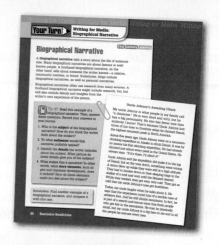

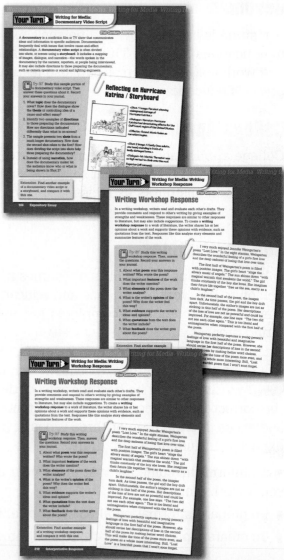

Creating Multimedia Projects

A **multimedia project** or presentation uses sound, video, and other media to convey a point or entertain an audience. No matter what type of project you choose as your own multimedia project, it is important to follow these steps:

- Decide on the project's **purpose** and your target **audience.**

- Choose **media** that will effectively convey your **message.**

- **Plan** your presentation. Will you work alone or with a partner or group? If you work with others, how you will assign the tasks?

- What **equipment** will you need? Will you produce artwork, record audio, and take photographs? Should you produce a storyboard to show the sequence of details in your presentation? Be sure to allow enough time to produce the text and all the other elements in your project.

- Keep the **writing process** in mind. There should be working and reworking along the way.

- **Assess** the progress of the project as you work. Ask questions, such as: Does my project incorporate appropriate writing genres? Will the presentation interest my audience? Have I kept my purpose in mind?

- **Rehearse!** Before presenting your project, be sure to do several "practice runs" to weed out and correct any errors.

- Keep an electronic record of your presentation for future reference.

- After your presentation, have others assess the project. Their critique will help you to do an even better job next time!

Reflect on Your Writing

Learning more about the different types of writing can help you focus on the characteristics of each type so you can keep improving your own writing. Think about what you've learned in Chapter 2 as you answer these questions:

- What type of writing most interests you?
- What type of writing do you think is most useful? Why?

Partner **Talk**

Share with a partner your experience with writing for media or multimedia projects. Have you created a Web site or contributed to one? Have you had to complete multimedia projects for a class assignment or for a personal project on which you worked? Talk about how writing for media presents different challenges from more traditional writing and how you have dealt with those challenges.

CHAPTER 3

THE WRITING PROCESS

Writing Traits

Good writing has specific qualities, or traits. In this chapter you will learn about these traits and how to use rubrics to evaluate them. You will also learn how to apply traits during the stages of the writing process.

Ideas

Good writing sends a strong message or presents a clear "angle" or point of view on a subject. It is also informative. The ideas are well developed, or explained with examples and other details.

Organization

A well-organized paper has an obvious plan. You will want to make sure that your ideas move from sentence to sentence and paragraph to paragraph in a logical way. For example, events in a story often appear in the order in which they occurred.

Voice

Voice is the combination of word choice and personal writing style that makes your writing unique. Voice connects a reader to the writer. It can show your personality or "take" on a story.

Word Choice

Your choice of words can help you achieve your purpose. Precise word choice means choosing the word that says exactly what you mean to say. Vivid word choice involves choosing words that create pictures for readers, describing how a subject looks, sounds, smells, and so on.

Sentence Fluency

Good writing is like a song—it has fluency, or a rhythm and a flow. By varying sentence patterns, writers ensure that the rhythm of their writing stays interesting.

Conventions

By following the rules of spelling, capitalization, punctuation, grammar, and usage, you help readers understand your ideas.

Overview of Writing Traits	
Ideas	• Significant ideas and informative details • Thorough development of ideas • Unique perspective or strong message
Organization	• Obvious plan • Clear sequence • Strong transitions
Voice	• Effective word choice • Attention to style
Word Choice	• Precise, not vague, words • Vivid, not dull, words • Word choices suited to audience and purpose
Sentence Fluency	• Varied sentence beginnings, lengths, and structures • Smooth sentence rhythms
Conventions	• Proper spelling and capitalization • Correct punctuation, grammar, usage, and sentence structure

WRITING COACH

Online

www.phwritingcoach.com

 Online Journal

Try It! Record your answers and ideas in the online journal. You can also record and save your answers and ideas on pop-up sticky notes in the eText.

" Writer to Writer "

Good writing is a symphony of traits—all coming together to make the paper sing.

—Kelly Gallagher

Rubrics and How To Use Them

You can use rubrics to evaluate the traits of your writing. A rubric allows you to score your writing on a scale in different categories. You will use a six-point rubric like this to help evaluate your writing in chapters 5–12.

Writing Traits	Rating Scale					
Ideas: How interesting, significant, or original are the ideas you present? How well do you develop ideas?	Not very 1	2	3	4	5	Very 6
Organization: How logically is your piece organized? Do your transitions, or movements from idea to idea, make sense?	1	2	3	4	5	6
Voice: How authentic and original is your voice?	1	2	3	4	5	6
Word Choice: How precise and vivid are the words you use? To what extent does your word choice help achieve your purpose?	1	2	3	4	5	6
Sentence Fluency: How well do your sentences flow? How strong and varied is the rhythm they create?	1	2	3	4	5	6
Conventions: How correct is your punctuation? Your capitalization? Your spelling?	1	2	3	4	5	6

Each trait appears in the first column. The rating scale appears in the second column. The higher your score for a trait, the better your writing exhibits that trait.

Using a Rubric on Your Own

A rubric can be a big help in assessing your writing while it is still in process. Imagine you've just started writing a piece of narrative fiction. You know that narrative fiction should have characters, a setting, and a conflict and resolution. You can check the rubric as you write to make sure you are on track. For example, you may use the rubric and decide that you have not developed the conflict well. You can revise to improve your writing and get a better score.

Narrative Fiction Elements	Rating Scale					
	Not very					Very
Interesting characters	1	2	3	4	5	6
Believable setting	1	2	3	4	5	6
Literary strategies	1	2	3	4	5	6
Well-developed conflict	1	2	3	4	5	6
Well-developed resolution	1	2	3	4	5	6

 Try It! If you checked your story against the rubric and rated yourself mostly 1s and 2s, what actions might you want to take next?

Using a Rubric With a Partner

In some cases, building your own rubric can help you ensure that your writing will meet your expectations. For example, if your class has an assignment to write a poem, you and a partner might decide to construct a rubric to check one another's work. A rubric like the one shown here can help point out whether you should make any changes. Extra lines allow room for you to add other criteria.

Poetry Elements	Rating Scale					
	Not very					Very
Good sensory details	1	2	3	4	5	6
Colorful adjectives	1	2	3	4	5	6
	1	2	3	4	5	6
	1	2	3	4	5	6
	1	2	3	4	5	6

 Try It! What other elements might you add to the rubric?

Using a Rubric in a Group

It is also helpful to use a rubric in a group. That way you can get input on your writing from many people at the same time. If the group members' ratings of your piece are similar, you will probably have an easy time deciding whether to make changes. If the responses vary significantly, you might want to discuss the results with the group. Then, analyze what led to the differing opinions and make careful judgments about what changes you will make.

WRITING COACH

Online

www.phwritingcoach.com

Online Journal

Try It! Record your answers and ideas in the online journal. You can also record and save your answers and ideas on pop-up sticky notes in the eText.

What Is the Writing Process?

The five steps in the writing process are prewriting, drafting, revising, editing, and publishing. Writing is a process because your idea goes through a series of changes or stages before the product is finished.

Study the diagram to see how moving through the writing process can work. Remember, you can go back to a stage in the process. It does not always have to occur in order.

Prewriting

In prewriting, you will:
- Explore ideas
- Choose a purpose and an audience
- Gather details
- Sequence ideas

Drafting

In drafting, you will:
- Put ideas down
- Develop a thesis or controlling idea
- Structure ideas in a sustained way

In publishing, you will:
- Produce a final polished copy of your writing
- Share your writing

Revising

In revising, you will:
- Re-read draft to see what works and what does not
- Use a rubric to evaluate
- Analyze what you want to change or improve
- Make changes

Publishing

In the editing phase, you will:
- Check the accuracy of facts
- Correct errors in spelling, grammar, usage, and mechanics

Editing

Why Use the Writing Process?

Writing involves careful thinking, which means you will make changes as you write. Even professional writers don't just write their thoughts and call it a finished work of art. They use a process. For example, some writers keep going back to the revising stage many times, while others feel they can do the revision in just one step. It is up to each writer to develop the style that works best to produce the best results.

You might find that the writing process works best for you when you keep these tips in mind:

- Remember that the five steps in the writing process are equally important.
- Think about your audience as you plan your paper and develop your writing.
- Make sure you remember your topic and stick to your specific purpose as you write.
- Give your writing some time to "rest." Sometimes it can be good to work on a piece, walk away, and look at it later, with a fresh eye and mind.

The following pages will describe in more detail how to use each stage of the writing process to improve your writing.

WRITING COACH

Online
www.phwritingcoach.com

Online Journal
Try It! Record your answers and ideas in the online journal. You can also record and save your answers and ideas on pop-up sticky notes in the eText.

66 Writer to Writer 99

Writing process gives us the freedom to write like mad, tinker like an engineer, evaluate like a judge—playing different roles at different stages. Most importantly it gives us the freedom to get our words out of our heads and into the world.

—Jeff Anderson

Prewriting

Prewriting

Drafting

Revising

Editing

Publishing

No matter what kind of writing you do, planning during the prewriting stage is crucial. During prewriting, you determine the topic of your writing, its purpose, and its specific audience. Then, you narrow the topic and gather details.

Determining the Purpose and Audience

What Is Your Purpose?

To be sure your writing communicates your ideas clearly, it is important to clarify why you are writing. Consider what you want your audience to take away from your writing. You may want to entertain them, or you may want to warn them about something. Even when you write an entry in a private journal, you're writing for an audience—you!

Who Is Your Audience?

Think about the people who will read your work and consider what they may already know about your topic. Being able to identify this group and their needs will let you be sure you are providing the right level of information.

Choosing a Topic

Here are just a few of the many techniques you can use to determine an appropriate topic.

- **Brainstorm**
  You can brainstorm by yourself, with a partner, or with a group. Just jot down ideas as they arise, and don't rule out anything. When brainstorming in a group, one person's idea often "piggybacks" on another.

- **Make a Mind Map**
  A mind map is a quick drawing you sketch as ideas come to you. The mind map can take any form. The important thing is to write quick notes as they come to you and then to draw lines to connect relationships among the ideas.

- **Interview**

  A fun way to find a writing topic is to conduct an interview. You might start by writing interview questions for yourself or someone else. Questions that start with *what*, *when*, *why*, *how*, and *who* are most effective. For example, you might ask, "When was the last time you laughed really hard?" "What made you laugh?" Then, conduct the interview and discover the answers.

- **Review Resources and Discuss Ideas**

  You can review resources, such as books, magazines, newspapers, and digital articles, to get ideas. Discussing your initial ideas with a partner can spark even more ideas.

Narrowing Your Topic

Once you have settled on a topic idea you really like, it may seem too broad to tackle. How can you narrow your topic?

- **Use Graphic Organizers**

  A graphic organizer can help narrow a topic that's too broad. For example, you might choose "Animals" as a topic. You might make your topics smaller and smaller until you narrow the topic to "The Habitat of Emperor Penguins."

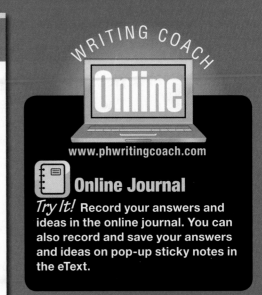

WRITING COACH

Online

www.phwritingcoach.com

Online Journal

Try It! Record your answers and ideas in the online journal. You can also record and save your answers and ideas on pop-up sticky notes in the eText.

❝ Writer to Writer ❞

Put something down. Anything. Then, magic will happen.

—Jeff Anderson

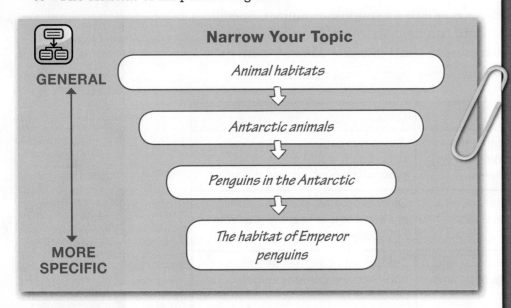

Narrow Your Topic

GENERAL

MORE SPECIFIC

Animal habitats

Antarctic animals

Penguins in the Antarctic

The habitat of Emperor penguins

Prewriting (continued)

Prewriting

Drafting

Revising

Editing

Publishing

- **Use Resource Materials**
  The resource materials you use to find information can also help you narrow a broad topic. Look up your subject online in an encyclopedia or newspaper archive. Scan the resources as you look for specific subtopics to pursue.

Gather Details

After you decide on a topic, you will want to explore and develop your ideas. You might start by looking through online resources again, talking with people who are knowledgeable about your topic, and writing everything you already know about the topic. It will be helpful to gather a variety of details. Look at these types:

- Facts
- Statistics
- Personal observations
- Expert opinions

- Examples
- Descriptions
- Quotations
- Opposing viewpoints

After you have narrowed your topic and gathered details, you will begin to plan your piece. During this part of prewriting, you will develop your essay's thesis or controlling idea—its main point.

As you plan your piece, you can use a graphic organizer. Specific kinds of graphic organizers can help structure specific kinds of writing. For example, a pro-con chart like this one can clarify the reasons for and against an idea.

Pro	Con
Adding funds to the school music budget would allow more students to learn to play instruments.	Giving more money to the music department would mean other programs would get less money.
Research shows that music helps the brain become more flexible.	Other programs, such as sports, are important in keeping students physically healthy.
Band members could stop selling gift-wrap materials at holiday time.	The school board has already approved the current budget allocations.

Drafting

In the drafting stage, you get your ideas down. You may consult an outline or your prewriting notes as you build your first draft.

Prewriting
Drafting
Revising
Editing
Publishing

The Introduction

Most genres should have a strong introduction that immediately grabs the reader's attention and includes the thesis. Even stories and poems need a "hook" to grab interest.

Try It! Which of these first sentences are strong openers? Read these examples of first sentences. Decide which ones are most interesting to you. Explain why they grab your attention. Then, explain why the others are weak.

- Have you ever wondered what it would be like to wake up one morning to find you're someone else?
- There are many ways to paint a room.
- Autumn is a beautiful season.
- On Sunday, we went to the store.
- When I woke up that morning, I had no idea that it would be the best day of my life.

The Body

The body of a paper develops the main idea and details that elaborate on and support the thesis. These details may include interesting facts, examples, statistics, anecdotes or stories, quotations, personal feelings, and sensory descriptions.

The Conclusion

The conclusion typically restates the thesis and summarizes the most important concepts of a paper.

WRITING COACH

Online

www.phwritingcoach.com

Online Journal

Try It! Record your answers and ideas in the online journal. You can also record and save your answers and ideas on pop-up sticky notes in the eText.

Revising: Making It Better

Prewriting

Drafting

Revising

Editing

Publishing

No one gets every single thing right in a first draft. In fact, most people require more than two drafts to achieve their best writing and thinking. When you have finished your first draft, you're ready to revise.

Revising means "re-seeing." In revising, you look again to see if you can find ways to improve style, word choice, figurative language, sentence variety, and subtlety of meaning. As always, check how well you've addressed the issues of purpose, audience, and genre. Carefully analyze what you'd want to change and then go ahead and do it. Here are some helpful hints on starting the revision stage of the writing process.

Take a Break

Do not begin to revise immediately after you finish a draft. Take some time away from your paper. Get a glass of water, take a walk, or listen to some music. You may even want to wait a day to look at what you've written. When you come back, you will be better able to assess the strengths and weaknesses of your work.

Put Yourself in the Place of the Reader

Take off your writer's hat and put on your reader's hat. Do your best to pretend that you're reading someone else's work and see how it looks to that other person. Look for ideas that might be confusing and consider the questions that a reader might have. By reading the piece with an objective eye, you may find items you'd want to fix and improve.

Read Aloud to Yourself

It may feel strange to read aloud to yourself, but it can be an effective technique. It allows you to hear the flow of words, find errors, and hear where you might improve the work by smoothing out transitions between paragraphs or sections. Of course, if you're more comfortable reading your work aloud to someone else, that works, too.

Share Your Work to Get Feedback

Your friends or family members can help you by reading and reacting to your writing. Ask them whether you've clearly expressed your ideas. Encourage them to tell you which parts were most and least interesting and why. Try to find out if they have any questions about your topic that were not answered. Then, evaluate their input and decide what will make your writing better.

Use a Rubric

A rubric might be just what you need to pinpoint weaknesses in your work. You may want to think about the core parts of the work and rate them on a scale. If you come up short, you'll have a better idea about the kinds of things to improve. You might also use a rubric to invite peer review and input.

Partner Talk

After a group revision session, talk with a partner to analyze each other's feelings on how the session went. Discuss such issues as these: Did the group adhere to the ground rules? What suggestions could you and your partner make to improve the next session?

21st Century Learning

Collaborate and Discuss

When presenting and sharing drafts in the revision stage with a small group, it may be wise to set some ground rules. That way, the group is more likely to help each other analyze their work and make thoughtful changes that result in true improvements.

Here are some suggestions for reviewing drafts as a group:

- Cover the names on papers the group will review to keep the work anonymous.
- Print out copies for everyone in the group.
- Show respect for all group members and their writing.
- Be sure all critiques include positive comments.
- While it is fine to suggest ways to improve the work, present comments in a positive, helpful way. No insults are allowed!
- Plan for a second reading with additional input after the writer has followed selected suggestions.

Revision RADaR

Prewriting

Drafting

Revising

Editing

Publishing

The Revision RADaR strategy, which you will use throughout this book, is an effective tool in helping you conduct a focused revision of your work.

You can use your Revision RADaR to revise your writing. The letters **R**, **A**, **D**, and **R** will help you remember to **r**eplace, **a**dd, **d**elete, and **r**eorder.

To understand more about the Revision RADaR strategy, study the following chart.

R	**A**	**D** and	**R**
Replace . . .	**Add . . .**	**Delete . . .**	**Reorder . . .**
• Words that are not specific • Words that are overused • Sentences that are unclear	• New information • Descriptive adjectives and adverbs • Rhetorical or literary devices	• Unrelated ideas • Sentences that sound good, but do not make sense • Repeated words or phrases • Unnecessary details	• So most important points are last • To make better sense or to flow better • So details support main ideas

R Replace

You can strengthen a text by replacing words that are not specific, words that are overused, and sentences that are unclear. Take a look at this before and after model.

BEFORE
I kicked the soccer ball hard into the goal.

AFTER
With amazing power, I slammed the soccer ball into the goal.

Apply It! **How did the writer replace the overused word *kicked*? What other replacement do you see? How did it improve the text?**

 Add

You can add new information, descriptive adjectives and adverbs, and rhetorical or literary devices to make your piece more powerful. Study this before and after model.

BEFORE
I was happy when I won the award.
AFTER
I was beyond thrilled when I won the Science Fair award.

Apply It! **How did the second sentence make you feel, compared with the first? Explain. What information was added to the second sentence?**

 Delete

Sometimes taking words out of a text can improve clarity. Analyze this before and after model.

BEFORE
I knew the test would be difficult, so I should have studied harder for the test before the test day.
AFTER
I knew the test would be difficult, so I should have studied harder for it.

Apply It! **Describe the revision you see. How did taking out unnecessary repetition of the word *test* help the sentence flow more naturally?**

 Reorder

When you reorder, you can make sentences flow more logically.

BEFORE
Today, I have band practice, but yesterday I didn't.
AFTER
I didn't have band practice yesterday, but today I do.

Apply It! **Which of the models flows more logically? Why?**

Revision RADaR (continued)

Read the first draft of the Student Model—a review of the novel *End Game.* Think about how you might use your Revision RADaR to improve the text in a second draft.

Kelly Gallagher, M. Ed.

Prewriting
Drafting
Revising
Editing
Publishing

KEEP REVISION ON YOUR RADaR

End Game Fails to Thrill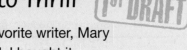

I like detective stories. So when my favorite writer, Mary O'Reilly, published a new detective novel, I bought it. Unfortunately, the novel, *End Game,* was incredibly disappointing.

In the story, an online video gamer disappears. A detective, Katherine, tries to track down the missing man through gaming Web sites. But here's where O'Reilly really messed up. It's clear that she didn't research the technology involved in online gaming. For example: "Katherine waited while her dial-up modem connected her to the virtual world."

The cheesy and ridiculous dialogue made my reading experience even worse. The errors in the book were bad enough! For example, the suspect says to Katherine, "I'm gonna get you, copper!" Now, this is the year 2010. A modern-day criminal would never use such outdated, silly lines. Instead of making the story exciting, the dialogue made it laughably bad.

O'Reilly has written many great books. My favorites were *On the High Seas* and *Danger in Denver.* They were great. I loved them! But I think it's time for O'Reilly to put down her pen. She clearly doesn't have what it takes any more to be a great writer. And as for *End Game*...don't waste your money!

Is my introduction interesting? Does it grab my readers' attention?

Have I fully analyzed and explained my examples from the text?

Is my information logically ordered?

Is my information relevant to the thesis? Have I included only necessary information?

After writing a draft, the student asked questions like these:

- What could I **replace**?
- What could I **add**?
- What words might I **delete**?
- Should I **reorder** anything?

The student writer created this second draft.

End Game Fails to Thrill

The suspense and high-paced action in detective stories are so thrilling! I simply can't get enough of these books. So when my favorite writer, Mary O'Reilly, published a new detective novel, I ran to the store to buy my copy. Unfortunately, the novel, *End Game,* was incredibly disappointing.

In the story, an online video gamer disappears. A detective, Katherine, tries to track down the missing man through gaming Web sites. But here's where O'Reilly really messed up. It's clear that she didn't research the technology involved in online gaming. For example: "Katherine waited while her dial-up modem connected her to the virtual world." Dial-up modems aren't fast enough to do serious online gaming!

Although the errors in the book were bad enough, the cheesy and ridiculous dialogue made my reading experience even worse. For example, the suspect says to Katherine, "I'm gonna get you, copper!" Now, this is the year 2010. A modern-day criminal would never use such outdated, silly lines. Instead of making the story exciting, the dialogue made it laughably bad.

I think it's time for O'Reilly to put down her pen. She clearly doesn't have what it takes any more to be a great writer. And as for *End Game*…don't waste your money!

R *Replaced dull first line with a more engaging opening.*

A *Added a sentence to better explain to my audience why the information from the text was incorrect.*

R *Reordered text so that the information about the errors connected the ideas in the second and third paragraphs.*

D *Deleted unnecessary information.*

Try It! What other words did the writer replace? Add? Delete? Reorder?

WRITING COACH

Online

www.phwritingcoach.com

Online Journal

Try It! Record your answers and ideas in the online journal. You can also record and save your answers and ideas on pop-up sticky notes in the eText.

Partner Talk

Work with a partner to come up with a list of words that describe detective stories. For example, you might use "high-paced action" or "thrilling." Then discuss the value of using more specific words in your writing.

Editing: Making It Correct

Prewriting

Drafting

Revising

Editing >

Publishing

Editing is the process of checking the accuracy of facts and correcting errors in spelling, grammar, usage, and mechanics. Using a checklist like the one shown here can help ensure you've done a thorough job of editing.

Editing Checklist

Task	Ask Yourself
Check your facts and spelling	❑ Have I checked that my facts are correct? ❑ Have I used spell check or a dictionary to check any words I'm not sure are spelled correctly?
Check your grammar	❑ Have I written any run-on sentences? ❑ Have I used the correct verbs and verb tenses? ❑ Do my pronouns match their antecedents, or nouns they replace?
Check your usage	❑ Have I used the correct form of irregular verbs? ❑ Have I used object pronouns, such as *me*, *him*, *her*, *us*, and *them* only after verbs or prepositions? ❑ Have I used subject pronouns, such as *I*, *he*, *she*, *we*, and *they* correctly—usually as subjects?
Check for proper use of mechanics	❑ Have I used correct punctuation? ❑ Does each sentence have the correct end mark? ❑ Have I used apostrophes in nouns but not in pronouns to show possession? ❑ Have I used quotation marks around words from another source? ❑ Have I used correct capitalization? ❑ Does each sentence begin with a capital letter? ❑ Do the names of specific people and places begin with a capital letter?

Using Proofreading Marks

Professional editors use a set of proofreading marks to indicate changes in a text. Here is a chart of some of the more common proofreading marks.

	Proofreader's Marks
(b.f.)	boldface
⌐	break text start new line
(Caps)	capital letter
⌒	clos e up
ℓ	deletes
a /	insert ∧ word
⌐/	insert ∧ comma
= /	insert ∧ hyphen
+ /	insert le t er
⊙ /	insert period ∧
(ital)	italic type
(Stet)	let stand as is
(l.f.)	lightface
(l.c.)	Lower case letter
⌐	move left
⌐	move right
⌐¶	new paragraph
(rom)	roman type
	run text up
(sp)	spell out whole word
	transpo es

www.phwritingcoach.com

Online Journal

Try It! Record your answers and ideas in the online journal. You can also record and save your answers and ideas on pop-up sticky notes in the eText.

USING TECHNOLOGY

Many word processing programs have automatic spelling and grammar checks. While these tools can be helpful, be sure to pay attention to any suggestions they offer. That's because sometimes inappropriate substitutes are inserted automatically!

Editing: Making It Correct (continued)

Prewriting

Drafting

Revising

Editing

Publishing

WRITE GUY *Jeff Anderson, M. Ed.*

WHAT DO YOU NOTICE?

Using an editing checklist is a great way to check for correct grammar. However, using a checklist is not enough to make your writing grammatically correct. A checklist tells you what to look for, but not how to correct mistakes you find. To do that, you need to develop and apply your knowledge of grammar.

Looking closely at good writing is one way to expand your grammar know-how. The *What Do You Notice?* feature that appears throughout this book will help you zoom in on passages that use grammar correctly and effectively.

As you read this passage, from "Jobs for Kids," zoom in on the sentences in the passage.

> I have a paper route. After school, I deliver newspapers on my bike to my neighbors. I love this job because I get exercise, and I get to be outside.

Now, ask yourself: *What do you notice about the sentences in this passage?*

Maybe you noticed that the writer uses sentences of varying lengths and with different structures.

After asking a question that draws your attention to the grammar in the passage, the *What Do You Notice?* feature provides information on a particular grammar topic. For example, following the passage and question, you might read about simple and complex sentences, which are both used in the passage.

The *What Do You Notice?* feature will show you how grammar works in actual writing. It will help you learn how to make your writing correct.

Online Journal

Try It! Record your answers and ideas in the online journal. You can also record and save your answers and ideas on pop-up sticky notes in the eText.

Jobs for Kids

I like having my own money. That way, I can buy things I want and can also save money for my future. But here's the problem: How can we, as kids, make money? There are many types of jobs for kids, but each job has pluses and minuses.

I have a paper route. After school, I deliver newspapers on my bike to my neighbors. I love this job because I get exercise, and I get to be outside. This job isn't for everyone, though. Some kids have a lot of after-school activities, so they don't go straight home. Because papers have to be delivered on time, this can be challenging.

A friend of mine babysits because she has fun with and loves taking care of children. To be a babysitter, you have to find out if your state has a law about how old you have to be before you can babysit. You also have to be a patient, responsible person who is good with children. Finally, it helps to know first-aid, just in case a child gets injured.

My brother does yard work for neighbors. He rakes leaves, weeds gardens, and mows lawns. He loves to be outside and doesn't mind getting dirty. However, there are certain safety issues involved. For example, you have to know how to handle a lawnmower properly and wear protective gear.

What type of job is right for you? What are your interests? Get creative, and start making some money!

❝ Writer to Writer ❞

If I wonder how to write any kind of writing, I look at models— well-written examples of the kind of writing I want to do. Models are the greatest how-to lesson I have ever discovered.

—Jeff Anderson

Try It! Read "Jobs for Kids." Then, zoom in on two more passages. Write a response to each question in your journal.

1. What do you notice about the pronouns (*you, he*) in the fourth paragraph?

2. How does the writer use transitions, such as the word *finally*, to connect ideas in the third paragraph?

Publishing

Prewriting

Drafting

Revising

Editing

Publishing

When you publish, you produce a final copy of your work and present it to an audience. When publishing you'll need to decide which form will best reach your audience, exhibit your ideas, show your creativity, and accomplish your main purpose.

To start assessing the optimal way to publish your work, you might ask yourself these questions:

- What do I hope to accomplish by sharing my work with others?
- Should I publish in print form? Give an oral presentation? Publish in print form and give an oral presentation?
- Should I publish online, in traditional print, or both?
- What specific forms are available to choose from?

The answers to most of these questions will most likely link to your purpose for writing and your audience. Some choices seem obvious. For example, if you've written a piece to contribute to a blog, you'll definitely want to send it electronically.

Each publishing form will present different challenges and opportunities and each will demand different forms of preparation. For example, you may need to prepare presentation slides for a speech, or you may want to select music and images if you will be posting a video podcast online.

Ways to Publish

There are many ways to publish your writing. This chart shows some of several opportunities you can pursue to publish your work.

Genre	Publishing Opportunities	
Narration: Nonfiction	• Blogs • Book manuscript • Audio recording	• Private diary or journal entries • Electronic slide show
Narration: Fiction	• Book manuscript • Film	• Audio recording • Oral reading to a group
Poetry and Description	• Bound collection • Visual display	• Audio recording • Oral reading to a group
Exposition and Persuasion	• Print or online article • Web site • Slide show • Visual display	• Film • Audio recording • Oral reading or speech
Response to Literature	• Print or online letters • Visual displays	• Blogs • Slide show
Research Writing	• Traditional paper • Print and online experiment journals	• Multimedia presentation

Reflect on Your Writing

Think about what you learned in Chapter 3 as you answer these questions:

- What did you learn about the writing process?
- What steps in the writing process do you already use in your writing?
- Which stage do you think is the most fun? Which one may be most challenging for you? Explain.

WRITING COACH

Online

www.phwritingcoach.com

Online Journal

Try It! Record your answers and ideas in the online journal. You can also record and save your answers and ideas on pop-up sticky notes in the eText.

Partner Talk

Discuss the chart on this page with a partner. If there are ways to publish that neither of you has ever tried, talk about how you might go about experimenting with those forms.

SENTENCES, PARAGRAPHS, *and* COMPOSITIONS

Good writers know that strong sentences and paragraphs help to construct effective compositions. Chapter 4 will help you use these building blocks to structure and style excellent writing. It will also present ways to use rhetorical and literary devices and online tools to strengthen your writing.

The Building Blocks: Sentences and Paragraphs

A **sentence** is a group of words with two main parts: a subject and a predicate. Together, these parts express a complete thought.

A **paragraph** is built from a group of sentences that share a common idea and work together to express that idea clearly. The start of a new paragraph has visual clues—either an indent of several spaces in the first line or an extra line of space above it.

In a good piece of writing, each paragraph supports, develops, or explains the main idea of the whole work. Of course, the traits of effective writing—ideas, organization, voice, word choice, sentence fluency, and conventions—appear in each paragraph as well.

Writing Strong Sentences

To write strong paragraphs, you need strong sentences. While it may be your habit to write using a single style of sentences, adding variety will help make your writing more interesting. Combining sentences, using compound elements, forming compound sentences, and using subordination all may help you make your sentences stronger, clearer, or more varied.

Combine Sentences

Putting information from one sentence into another can make a more powerful sentence.

BEFORE	Basketball is a fun game. It takes a lot of skill and practice.
AFTER	Basketball, which takes a lot of skill and practice, is a fun game.

Use Compound Elements

You can form compound subjects, verbs, or objects to help the flow.

BEFORE	Students enjoy many different hobbies. Some play sports. Some write poetry. Some paint.
AFTER	Students enjoy many different hobbies, such as playing sports, writing poetry, and painting.

Form Compound Sentences

You can combine two sentences into a compound sentence.

BEFORE	Some people enjoy skateboarding. It can be a dangerous hobby.
AFTER	Some people enjoy skateboarding, but it can be a dangerous hobby.

Use Subordination

Combine two related sentences by rewriting the less important one as a subordinate clause.

BEFORE	Horseback riding allows you to be outside in the fresh air. That is good for you.
AFTER	Horseback riding allows you be outside in the fresh air, which is good for you.

Writing Strong Paragraphs

If all the sentences in a paragraph reflect the main idea and work together to express that idea clearly, the result will be a strong paragraph.

Express Your Main Idea With a Clear Topic Sentence

A **topic sentence** summarizes the main idea of a paragraph. It may appear at the beginning, middle, or end of a paragraph. It may even be unstated. When the topic sentence comes at the beginning of a paragraph, it introduces the main idea and leads the reader naturally to the sentences that follow it. When it appears at the end of a paragraph, it can draw a conclusion or summarize what came before it. If the topic sentence is unstated, the rest of the paragraph must be very clearly developed, so the reader can understand the main idea from the other sentences.

Think about the topic sentence as you read this paragraph.

There is no question that computer skills are necessary to have today. Without these skills, it will be difficult to get a college degree and find a good job. Most assignments in college must be done on a computer. Much research in college is done on the Internet, and many libraries have switched from a paper card catalog to a digital catalog. In addition, many companies won't hire someone who has no computer skills. After all, if you can't send e-mails and create important documents in word processing programs, how will you be able to properly do many jobs?

 Try It! Look back at the sample paragraph to answer these questions.

1. What is the topic sentence?

2. Does the topic sentence introduce the main idea or draw a final conclusion? Explain.

3. What makes this topic sentence strong?

Write Effective Supporting Sentences

A clear topic sentence is a good start, but it needs to be accompanied by good details that support the paragraph's main idea. Your supporting sentences might tell interesting facts, describe events, or give examples. In addition, the supporting sentences should also provide a smooth transition, so that the paragraph reads clearly and logically.

Think about the topic sentence and supporting details as you read this paragraph.

Owning a dog can be hard work, but it is well worth it! A dog owner must be very responsible and take good care of her pet. She has to feed and walk the dog every day and bathe it regularly. Every dog also needs a lot of play time with its owner! All of this takes a great deal of time and energy. However, a dog can be your best friend. It will love you and protect you, and sometimes make you laugh! Plus, what could be better than snuggling up with a sweet, loving dog?

 Try It! Look at the paragraph and answer these questions.

1. What is the topic sentence of the paragraph?

2. Do you think it's an effective topic sentence? Why or why not?

3. What supporting details does the writer provide?

4. If you were the writer, what other supporting details might you add to strengthen the paragraph?

WRITING COACH
Online
www.phwritingcoach.com

Online Journal

Try It! Record your answers and ideas in the online journal. You can also record and save your answers on pop-up sticky notes in the eText.

Include a Variety of Sentence Lengths, Structures, and Beginnings

To be interesting, a paragraph should include sentences of different lengths, types, and beginnings. Similarly, if every sentence has the same structure—for example, article, adjective, noun, verb—the paragraph may sound boring or dry.

Collaborate and Discuss

With a group, study this writing sample.

> On the night of the school concert, I didn't think I'd survive my stage fright. My hands felt cold and clammy, and a lump was stuck in my throat. A trickle of sweat slipped between my shoulder blades and down my back. I was so nervous! As the band began playing the opening notes of the first song and I stepped up to the microphone, the glare of the bright lights blinded me. I closed my eyes, took a deep breath, and belted out the song without even thinking. When the song was over, the audience responded with deafening applause. I had done it!

Discuss these questions about the paragraph.

1. What is the topic sentence? How does it draw in the reader?

2. What details support the topic sentence of the paragraph?

3. Point out some examples of varying sentence lengths and beginnings.

4. What examples can you find of sentences with a variety of sentence structures?

Partner Talk

Work with a partner to take another look at the writing sample on this page. Talk about what you think the writer did well. Then, discuss what might make the paragraph even stronger.

USING TECHNOLOGY

It's often better to use the tab key, rather than the space bar, to indent a paragraph. Using the tab key helps to ensure that the indents in all paragraphs will be uniform.

Composing Your Piece

You've learned that the building blocks of writing are strong sentences and paragraphs. Now it's time to use those building blocks to construct a composition. While the types of writing vary, most types have a definite structure with clearly defined parts.

The Parts of a Composition

Writers put together and arrange sentences and paragraphs to develop ideas in the clearest way possible in a composition. Some types of writing, such as poetry and advertisements, follow unique rules and may not have sentences and paragraphs that follow a standard structure. However, as you learned in Chapter 3, most compositions have three main sections: an introduction, a body, and a conclusion.

I. Introduction

The introduction of a composition introduces the focus of the composition, usually in a thesis statement. The introduction should engage the reader's interest, with such elements as a question, an unusual fact, or a surprising scene.

II. Body

Just as supporting statements develop the ideas of a topic sentence, the body of a composition develops the thesis statement and main idea. It provides details that help expand on the thesis statement. The paragraphs in the body are arranged in a logical order.

III. Conclusion

As the word implies, the conclusion of a composition concludes or ends a piece of writing. A good way to ensure the reader will remember your thesis statement is to restate it or summarize it in the conclusion. When restating the thesis, it's usually most effective to recast it in other words. Quotations and recommendations are other ways to conclude a composition with memorable impact. The conclusion should provide a parting insight or reinforce the importance of the main idea.

> **" Writer to Writer "**
>
> **Strong, varied sentences and unified paragraphs are the building blocks of effective writing.**
>
> **—Kelly Gallagher**

Rhetorical and Literary Devices

Like any builders, good writers have a set of tools, or devices, at their fingertips to make their writing interesting, engaging, and effective. Writers can use the rhetorical devices of language and their effects to strengthen the power of their style. This section presents some tools you can store in your own writing toolbox to develop effective compositions.

Sound Devices

Sound devices, which create a musical or emotional effect, are most often used in poetry. The most common sound devices include these:

- **Alliteration** is the repetition of consonant sounds at the beginning of words that are close to one another.

  Example: The sweet sound of singing swam in the breeze.

- **Assonance** is the repetition of vowel sounds in words that are close to one another.

  Example: We see shells on the beach, by the sea.

- **Consonance** is the repetition of consonants within or at the end of words.

  Example: The doctor checked the sick patient at three o'clock.

Structural Devices

Structural devices determine the way a piece of writing is organized. Rhyme and meter are most often used to structure poetry, as are stanzas and many other structural devices.

- **Rhyme** is the repetition of sounds at the ends of words. Certain poetry forms have specific rhyme schemes.
- **Meter** is the rhythmical pattern of a poem, determined by the stressed syllables in a line.
- **Visual elements**, such as stanzas, line breaks, line length, fonts, readability, and white space, help determine how a piece of writing is read and interpreted. These elements can also affect the emotional response to a piece.

Other Major Devices

You can use these devices in many forms of writing. They help writers express ideas clearly and engage their readers.

Device	Example
Figurative language is writing that means something beyond what the words actually say. Common forms of figurative language include these: • A **simile** compares two things using the words *like* or *as*. • A **metaphor** compares two things by mentioning one thing as if it is something else. It does not use *like* or *as*. • **Personification** gives human characteristics to a non-human object.	*His voice sounded like nails on a chalkboard.* *The trapeze artist was a bird in flight.* *The sun smiled down on us.*
Hyperbole is exaggeration used for effect.	*I felt stronger than a superhero!*
Irony is a contradiction between what happens and what is expected.	In a famous story, a wife cuts her hair to buy her husband a watch fob, and he sells his watch to buy her combs.
Paradox is a statement that contains elements that seem contradictory, but could be true.	Mother Teresa said, "…if you love until it hurts, there can be no more hurt, only more love."
An **oxymoron** is word or phrase that seems to contradict itself.	The movie was seriously funny!
A **symbol** is an object that stands for something else.	The American flag is often considered a symbol of freedom.
An **allegory** is a narrative that has a meaning other than what literally appears.	Some say the story of the sinking ship is an allegory for the effects of pride.
Repetition (or tautology) occurs when content is repeated, sometimes needlessly—for effect.	The band's song was loud, loud and far too long.

WRITING COACH

Online

www.phwritingcoach.com

Online Journal

Try It! Record your answers and ideas in the online journal. You can also record and save your answers on pop-up sticky notes in the eText.

USING TECHNOLOGY

Most word processing programs have a built-in thesaurus tool. You can use the thesaurus to find descriptive words that can often substitute for weaker, overused words.

Partner Talk

There are many online tools that can help you strengthen your writing. For example, you can search for examples of figurative language and sound devices. Then you can model your own writing after the samples. Just be sure that you don't plagiarize or copy the written work of others.

Using Writing Traits to Develop an Effective Composition

You read about rubrics and traits in Chapter 3. Now it's time to look at how they function in good writing.

Ideas

A good writer clearly presents and develops important information, a strong message, and original ideas.

As you read the sample, think about the ideas it presents.

Achoo!

Achoo! The common cold can be a major downer. Who wants to be home with a runny nose and sore throat? It happens more often than you might think, though. According to the Mayo Clinic, students can get as many as six to ten colds a year! If you understand the causes of the common cold and take precautions, you can successfully avoid catching a cold.

A common cold is caused by a virus. Many different viruses could be responsible for your runny nose, but all of them have one thing in common: they're very contagious. A common-cold virus can spread in the air when a sick person coughs, sneezes, or even talks.

Once you know how colds spread, you can see that avoiding a cold is fairly easy, if you follow some simple rules. Wash your hands often. Keep doorknobs and countertops clean. Don't share drinking glasses or silverware. Most importantly, avoid being around sick people. If you do happen to catch a cold, sneeze or cough into your elbow to help keep your cold from spreading to others. No one likes to be sick!

Try It! Think about ideas in the writing sample as you answer this question.

What is the writer's message? List three details that clearly convey or give support for this message.

Organization

A well-organized composition flows easily from sentence to sentence and paragraph to paragraph. It clearly shows relationships between ideas. The paper also avoids needless repetition.

Think about organization as you reread "Achoo!" on page 56.

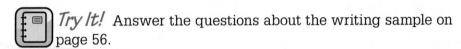 **Try It!** Answer the questions about the writing sample on page 56.

1. Which sentence introduces the topic of the piece?
2. Why must the second paragraph appear before the third?
3. List three details in the third paragraph. Explain how each supports the first sentence in the paragraph.

Voice

Voice is the individual "sound" of a writer's writing, reflecting the writer's personality or perspective. A successful paper has a definite voice expressing the writer's individuality.

Read the writing sample. Think about voice as you read.

> I'll never forget the day my parents got home with 4-month-old Liang. I was sitting on the couch, waiting for them. My stomach was doing flip-flops. Then Mom and Dad walked through the door, carrying this little bundle wrapped in a blanket. Mom sat on the couch with me and introduced me to my new brother. I expected him to totally freak out— to scream and cry. Instead, he just looked up at me with his big, brown eyes and smiled. His tiny hand reached out and grabbed my finger. He had a pretty strong grip!
>
> I found out that while babies are sometimes loud, smelly, and drooly, all of that stuff didn't matter. I loved my little brother, and I couldn't wait till he grew up, so I could teach him how to use that strong grip to hold a football!

 **Try It!** Consider the writer's voice as you answer this question.

Which words and phrases give you a clear sense of the writer's personality and perspective? Explain.

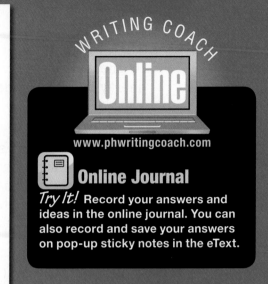

WRITING COACH

Online

www.phwritingcoach.com

Online Journal

Try It! Record your answers and ideas in the online journal. You can also record and save your answers on pop-up sticky notes in the eText.

Partner Talk

Analyze the composition about colds on page 56 with a partner. Discuss how well it might score on the traits of ideas and organization—from ineffective (1), to somewhat effective (2), to fairly effective (3), to effective (4), to highly effective in parts (5), to highly effective throughout (6).

Word Choice

By choosing words with precision, good writers give their writing energy and help readers picture exactly what they are talking about. Think about word choice as you read these two drafts:

> Bob got into Ted's car. As he sat down, he realized he was hearing something familiar. "That's right," Ted said. "I finally put our stuff on CD. It sounds so nice on this system!"

> Bob climbed over chrome fittings into Ted's customized SUV. As Bob eased into the leather-upholstered seat, he recognized the crunching guitar chords that came crashing through the car stereo's speakers. "That's right," Ted said. "I finally mixed our band's songs down to a CD. They sound so crisp on this system!"

 Try It! Answer these questions about the two drafts.

1. List two vague or imprecise words in the first draft.

2. What do the precise words in the second draft help you understand?

Sentence Fluency

In the best writing, sentences have rhythm. They flow smoothly when read aloud, rather than sounding awkward. To control rhythm, good writers use a variety of sentence structures. Think about the rhythm of the writer's sentences as you read this draft:

> After six years of weekly lessons, I can say I have done my best to master the cello. I may not have been good enough for the All-County Orchestra last year, but this year will be different. This year, my dedication will pay off!

 Try It! Respond to this prompt about the draft.

Describe the rhythm of the sentences in the passage.

Conventions

If a piece of writing reflects a good command of spelling, capitalization, punctuation, grammar, usage, and sentence structure, it is much more likely to communicate clearly to readers.

Pay attention to spelling, capitalization, punctuation, grammar, usage, and sentence structure as you read this first draft.

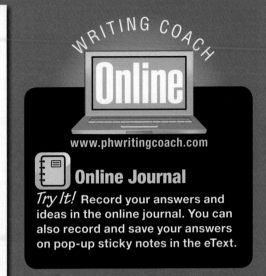

If your an action-movie fan, you have to run—not walk— to see *Welcome to Mars!* This movie is non-stop action, from start to finish. Me and my friend were blown away by the battle scenes, special effects, and suspense.

The movie has a great message, too: Understanding can lead to peace. In one very tense moment, the lead scientist on Mars is captured by aliens. I was so sure they would kill her! Instead, she stayed with them learning their language and to learn, their ways of life. This led to peace between the humans and the aliens.

Now, read this section of the reviewer's second draft.

If you're an action-movie fan, you have to run—not walk— to see *Welcome to Mars!* This movie is non-stop action, from start to finish. My friend and I were blown away by the battle scenes, special effects, and suspense.

The movie has a great message, too: Understanding can lead to peace. In one very tense moment, the lead scientist on Mars is captured by aliens. I was so sure they would kill her! Instead, she stayed with them, learning their language and their ways of life. This led to peace between the humans and the aliens.

Try It! Answer these questions about both drafts.

1. What errors in convention did the writer correct in the second draft?
2. Why is the next-to-last sentence easier to read in the second draft?

Using Interactive Writing Coach

As you learned in Chapter 3, you can use rubrics and your Revision RADaR to check how well your paragraphs and essays read. With Writing Coach, you also have another tool available to evaluate your work: the Interactive Writing Coach.

The Interactive Writing Coach is a program that you can use anywhere that you have Internet access. Interactive Writing Coach functions like your own personal writing tutor. It gives you personalized feedback on your work.

The Interactive Writing Coach has two parts: **Paragraph Feedback** and **Essay Scorer**.

- Paragraph Feedback gives you feedback on individual paragraphs as you write. It looks at the structure of sentences and paragraphs and gives you information about specific details, such as sentence variety and length.

- Essay Scorer looks at your whole essay and gives you a score and feedback on your entire piece of writing. It will tell you how well your essay reflects the traits of good writing.

This chart shows just a few questions that Paragraph Feedback and Essay Scorer will answer about your writing. The following pages explain Paragraph Feedback and Essay Scorer in more detail.

Sentences	• Are sentences varied in length?
	• Do sentences have varied beginnings?
	• Which sentences have too many ideas?
	• Are adjectives clear and precise?
	• Is the sentence grammatically correct?
	• Is all spelling correct in the sentence?
Paragraphs	• Does the paragraph support its topic?
	• Does the paragraph use transitions?
	• Does the paragraph contain the right amount of ideas and information?
Compositions	• Does the essay reflect characteristics of the genre?
	• Does it demonstrate the traits of good writing?
	• Is the main idea clear?
	• Is the main idea well supported?
	• Is the essay cohesive—does it hold together?

Interactive Writing Coach and the Writing Process

You can begin to use Essay Scorer during the drafting section of the writing process. It is best to complete a full draft of your essay before submitting to Essay Scorer. (While you are drafting individual paragraphs, you may want to use Paragraph Feedback.) Keep in mind, however, that your draft does not need to be perfect or polished before you submit to Essay Scorer. You will be able to use feedback from Essay Scorer to revise your draft many times. This chart shows how you might use the Interactive Writing Coach and incorporate Essay Scorer into your writing process.

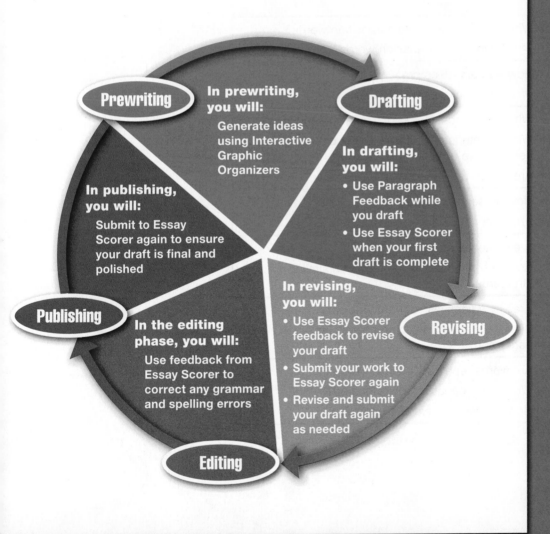

Prewriting

In prewriting, you will:
Generate ideas using Interactive Graphic Organizers

Drafting

In drafting, you will:
- Use Paragraph Feedback while you draft
- Use Essay Scorer when your first draft is complete

In publishing, you will:
Submit to Essay Scorer again to ensure your draft is final and polished

In revising, you will:
- Use Essay Scorer feedback to revise your draft
- Submit your work to Essay Scorer again
- Revise and submit your draft again as needed

Revising

Publishing

In the editing phase, you will:
Use feedback from Essay Scorer to correct any grammar and spelling errors

Editing

Paragraph Feedback With Interactive Writing Coach

Paragraph Feedback assesses the ideas and topic support for each paragraph you write. You can enter your work into Paragraph Feedback one paragraph at a time. This makes it easy to work on individual paragraphs and get new feedback as you revise each one. Here are some things that Paragraph Feedback will be able to tell you.

Overall Paragraph Support	• Does the paragraph support the main idea? • Which sentences do not support the main idea?
Transitions	• Which sentences contain transition words? • Which words are transition words?
Ideas	• How well are ideas presented? • Which sentences have too many ideas?
Sentence Length and Variety	• Which sentences are short, medium, and long? • Which sentences could be longer or shorter for better sense or variety? • Are sentences varied?
Sentence Beginnings	• How do sentences begin? • Are sentence beginnings varied?
Sentence Structure	• Are sentence structures varied? • Are there too many sentences with similar structures?
Vague Adjectives	• Are any adjectives vague or unclear? • Where are adjectives in sentences and paragraphs?
Language Variety	• Are words repeated? • Where are repeated words located? • How can word choice be improved?

Essay Scoring With Interactive Writing Coach

Essay Scorer assesses your essay. It looks at the essay as a whole, and it also evaluates individual paragraphs, sentences, and words. Essay Scorer will help you evaluate the following traits.

Ideas	• Are the ideas significant or original? Is a clear message or unique perspective presented? • Is the main idea clearly stated? • Is the main idea supported by informative details?
Organization	• Is the organization logical? • Is the introduction clear? Is the conclusion clear? • What transitions are used, and are they effective?
Voice	• Does the writing have a unique, individual "sound" showing the personality or perspective of the writer? • Does the tone match the audience and purpose?
Word Choice	• Are precise words used? • Are vivid words used? • Do the word choices suit the purpose and audience?
Sentence Fluency	• Are sentence beginnings, lengths, and structures varied? • Do the sentences flow smoothly?
Conventions	• Is spelling correct? • Is capitalization used properly? • Is all punctuation (ending, internal, apostrophes) accurate? • Do subjects and verbs agree? • Are pronouns used correctly? • Are adjectives and adverbs used correctly? • Are plurals formed correctly? • Are commonly confused words used correctly?

Whenever you see the Interactive Writing Coach icon, you can go to Writing Coach Online and submit your writing, either paragraph by paragraph or as a complete draft, for personalized feedback and scoring.

www.phwritingcoach.com

Interactive Writing Coach™

Interactive Writing Coach provides support and guidance to help you improve your writing skills.

• Select a topic to write about from the Topic Bank.
• Use the interactive graphic organizers to narrow your topic.
• Go to Writing Coach Online and submit your work, paragraph by paragraph or as a complete draft.
• Receive immediate, personalized feedback as you write, revise, and edit your work.

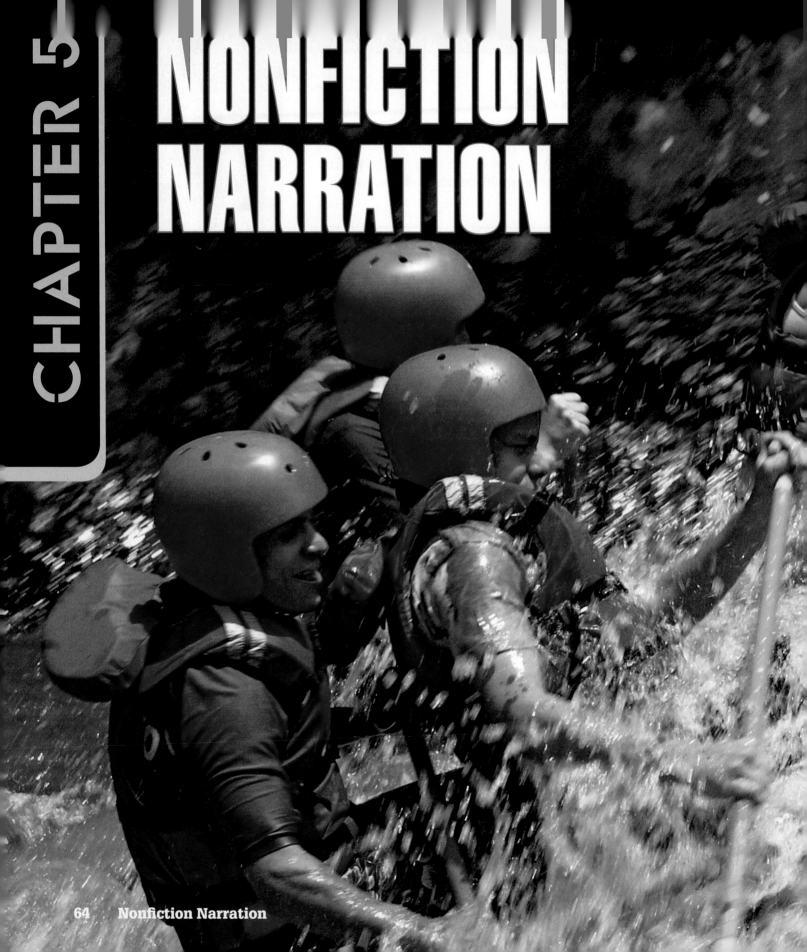

CHAPTER 5

NONFICTION NARRATION

What Do You Remember?

What interesting events have happened in your life? What makes these events special?

To tell a story about an event, you will need to remember details of the experience. Using vivid details to describe your memories will make them more interesting to others.

Try It! Think about a recent event in your life. What story could you tell about that event?

Take notes as you consider these questions. Then participate in an extended discussion with a partner. Take turns expressing your ideas and feelings about the event you chose. As you listen to your partner's story, see if you can answer the questions listed here.

- What happened?
- Where were you and who was there?
- How did you feel during the experience?
- What did you see, smell, touch, taste, or hear?

What's Ahead

In this chapter, you will review two strong examples of a personal narrative: a Mentor Text and a Student Model. Then, using the examples as guidance, you will write a personal narrative of your own.

WRITING COACH

www.phwritingcoach.com

Online Journal

Try It! Record your answers and ideas in the online journal.

You can also record and save your answers and ideas on pop-up sticky notes in the eText.

Connect to the Big Questions

Discuss these questions with your partner:

1 What do you think? What challenges change us most?

2 Why write? What should we put in and leave out to be accurate and honest?

NARRATIVE NONFICTION

Narrative nonfiction is writing that tells a true story. In this chapter, you will explore a special type of narrative nonfiction that is all about you—a personal narrative. A personal narrative is a true story about *your* life. It allows you to share your experience in a deeper way, telling not only what happened to you but also how you felt about it and what it meant to you. Not only can you entertain, move, and inform your readers, you can also gain new insight into your own experience.

You will develop your personal narrative by taking it through each of the steps of the writing process: prewriting, drafting, revising, editing, and publishing. You will also have an opportunity to use your writing skills to create a diary entry for a blog. To preview the criteria for how your personal narrative will be evaluated, see the rubric on page 83.

FEATURE ASSIGNMENT

Narrative Nonfiction: Personal Narrative

An effective nonfiction narrative has these characteristics:

- A **clearly defined focus** that shows the point of the narrative

- A **sequence of events** in chronological, or time, order

- Details that reflect on, or think back about, the importance of **decisions, actions,** and/or **consequences**

- A **plot** with **a conflict** and **resolution,** or a problem and its solution

- **Specific details** and **dialogue**, to help readers connect to the characters

- A **specific** and **consistent point of view,** or a single character's or the writer's perspective

- Effective **sentence structure** and **correct spelling, grammar, and usage**

A personal narrative also includes:

- The writer as the main character, or person at the center of the narrative

- Vivid images and a clear description of feelings

Other Forms of Narrative Nonfiction

In addition to a personal narrative, there are other forms of narrative nonfiction writing, including:

Biographical narratives are stories that share facts about someone else's life.

Blogs are comments that writers share in online forums. They may include personal narratives, opinions, and other types of comments. Blogs often invite other writers to respond online, too. They usually are not thought of as "permanent" writing.

Diary entries, which are highly personal, include experiences, thoughts, and feelings. The audience, however, is private, unless writers choose to share their diary entries.

Narrative essays use personal narratives to illustrate or support a main idea.

Memoirs focus on an important person or event from the writer's own life. Book-length memoirs by famous people are often quite popular because they offer insight into public events.

Reflective essays present personal experiences, either events that happened to the writers or that the writers learned about from others. Reflective essays stand out because they do more than tell a story: They also share the writer's thoughts about those experiences. Reflective essays often appear as features in magazines and newspapers.

Try It! For each audience and purpose described, choose a form, such as a blog, diary entry, or reflective essay, that is appropriate for conveying your intended meaning to the audience. Explain your choices.

- To tell and share your feelings about meeting a national political figure
- To tell online friends about one of your accomplishments
- To remind yourself, for the future, what it was like to go to your first concert

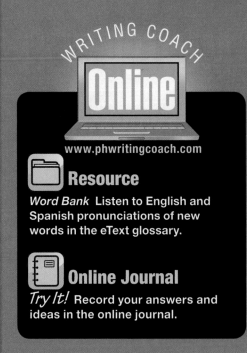

WRITING COACH

Online

www.phwritingcoach.com

Resource

Word Bank Listen to English and Spanish pronunciations of new words in the eText glossary.

Online Journal

Try It! Record your answers and ideas in the online journal.

WORD BANK

People often use these basic and content-based vocabulary words when they talk about narrative nonfiction writing. Work with a partner. Take turns saying each word aloud. Then, write a sentence using each word. If you are unsure of the meaning of a word, use the Glossary or a dictionary to check the definition.

conflict	perspective
consequences	resolution
dialogue	sensory

Learn From Experience

 Read the personal narrative on pages 68–69. As you read, take notes to develop your understanding of basic sight and English vocabulary. Then, read the numbered notes in the margins to learn about how the author presented his ideas.

Answer the *Try It!* questions online or in your notebook.

---

1 The introduction has a **clearly defined focus.** This helps readers anticipate what the narrative will be about and sparks interest in reading more.

Try It! Think about the situation the author describes and his reaction to it. What is the focus of the narrative?

2 The author uses **chronological order** to tell his story. By putting events in the order in which they happened, he makes the story easy to follow.

Try It! Which phrases let you know that the story is in chronological order? Quote two.

3 The author's **conflict,** or problem, builds in this section.

Try It! How would you describe the conflict? Is it between the narrator and someone else or within the narrator himself? Explain.

Extension Find another example of a personal narrative, and compare it with this one.

The Day I Threw the Trivia Bowl

by Robert Siegel

I have a confession to make: I threw the Trivia Bowl. The year was 1988. The place, eleventh grade.

1 In 1988, as an academically advanced (read: geeky) sixteen-year-old, my primary objective in life was the
5 maintenance of my low profile among classmates. I did not want to stick out in any way, especially for anything that had even the faintest whiff of dorkery.

Problem was, I happened to be the captain of a formidable four-man Trivia Bowl team that was to represent the school
10 at the countywide Trivia Bowl competition.

For a boy prone to nightmares of academic achievement-related mockery, this was not good.

2 The night before the Trivia Bowl, I was freaking. I imagined that if we won, they would proudly announce
15 it over the intercom to the entire school during homeroom. This is what they did whenever someone did something notable. I imagined all the kids pointing and laughing at the trivia dork. This prospect terrified me beyond words.

And yet, another part of me desperately wanted to win
20 the Trivia Bowl. I loved trivia and, even more, I loved winning at stuff. It was a terrible dilemma.

2 The day of the competition comes. We burst out of the gate strongly. . . . What is the capital of Nepal? Kathmandu. What is the largest animal that has ever lived? The blue whale.
25 By the end of the first round, we were in second place and, thanks to a furious late run, had momentum squarely on our side. I was excited, but all the while in the back of my mind, I was imagining that dreaded homeroom announcement.

3 Things go even better (or worse) in Round Two. We
30 take the lead. As the competition heads toward the finish, it becomes clear that it's a two-team race. Us versus our hated rivals from Massapequa. We go back and forth, trading blows like Foreman and Ali.

It all comes down to one question. If we get it right, we
35 win; if we miss, they have the chance to answer for the win.

"Who shot Robert F. Kennedy?"

Uh-oh. I know it.

No one else on my team knows. They all look at
me expectantly. I am well-known amongst them as the
40 assassination expert. They assume I will blurt out the answer,
which, of course, is Sirhan B. Sirhan. I hem and haw. *What's
going on?* they are clearly wondering. *Rob doesn't know?*
After what seems like an eternity, I give my answer.

"Jack Ruby?"

45 "I'm sorry; that's not correct."

Massapequa pounces and gets it right. My teammates
and I watch as they hold aloft the 1988 Trivia Bowl trophy
in sweet victory.

The whole ride home, I wrestled with my decision to
50 blow the Trivia Bowl. ❹ I felt terrible about what I did, but
at least I would avoid homeroom humiliation. Right?

Wrong. The next morning in homeroom:

"Congratulations to eleventh-graders Robert Siegel,
Mark Roth, Adam Frankel and Dan Eckert for their valiant
55 effort yesterday in the countywide Trivia Bowl competition,
in which they placed second."

Not only was I a dork, I was a losing dork.

❺ The moral of the story is, if you're ever in a Trivia
Bowl, don't throw it. Either way, they're gonna announce it
60 in homeroom, so you might as well win.

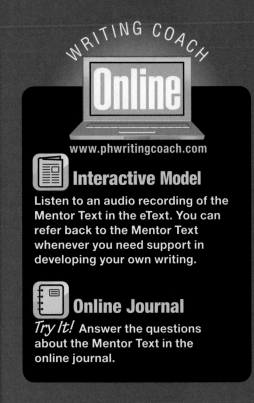

WRITING COACH

Online

www.phwritingcoach.com

📰 Interactive Model

Listen to an audio recording of the Mentor Text in the eText. You can refer back to the Mentor Text whenever you need support in developing your own writing.

📓 Online Journal

Try It! **Answer the questions about the Mentor Text in the online journal.**

❹ The author gives readers a laugh by reminding them why he threw the Trivia Bowl, then telling what happened as a **consequence**.

Try It! How does the author feel as a result of throwing the Trivia Bowl? Which sentences give you insight into how he feels?

❺ The writer provides a moral that serves as the **resolution** of the story.

Try It! What moral does the narrator state? Explain why he came to that conclusion. What insights do you as a reader gain from reading this narrative?

STUDENT MODEL

Personal Narrative

With a small group, take turns reading the Student Model aloud. As you read, practice newly acquired vocabulary by correctly producing the word's sound. Think about how story elements, such as dialogue and vivid details, help to fully develop the writer's experience. Also, think about how the theme and structure of the narrative are expressed.

 ## Use a Reader's Eye

Now, reread the Student Model. On your copy of the Student Model, use the Reader's Response Symbols to react to what you read.

Reader's Response Symbols

+ **I like where this is going.**

− **This isn't clear to me.**

? **What will happen next?**

! **Wow! That is really cool/weird/ interesting!**

 ## Partner Talk

With a partner, discuss your ideas and opinions about which lines you thought best conveyed the writer's experience.

My Heart

by Zachary Landow

It is just a routine doctor visit, no different than those of past check-ups on my heart. The doctor comes in. The words seem to fall out of his mouth like boulders fall off a cliff: "This is what's wrong."
5   I am looking at the results of my heart test. My stomach feels as if it shriveled up. "This will require a procedure," he says, and then my mind just goes crazy. *Bad, bad, bad.* Although the doctor's mouth is moving, nothing comes out. Mom asks, "Are you
10 okay?" I want to say no, but my mouth is frozen. I'm shaking, thinking about what is to come.

Boston? We have to go to Boston? "Yes," Mom says, "Boston." Why there? "Because that is where you will get the best treatment. It will be a
15 family trip. You'll have lots of fun." Yeah, right.

Days later, I read the big green sign out of my car window: *Welcome to Massachusetts.* The few days we spend in Boston fly by, and then, all too soon, it is time. We go to the hospital.

20 Will it hurt? "No."

Are you sure? "Positive," the lady from the hospital continually reassures me.

I thought about what the doctor had told me yesterday: "…So that is how the procedure will go.
25 Um…Zachary, you should leave now. I need to go over the risks of this procedure. You don't need to hear this. It will only make you more nervous."

There are minutes to go, and I feel my heart pumping. They say music helps. Although it doesn't
30 help, I still lie there on the bed, listening to my MP3

1

player. A nurse taps my shoulder. It's time to go.

In the surgery room, I see a giant Red Sox flag. It will loom over me while the doctor works. The nurse tells me, "After this, you will always have
35 a little piece of the Red Sox in your heart." As a New York fan, I laugh. I'm given the anesthesia, which will put me to sleep for the procedure. I start to feel very, very sleepy. My eyelids flutter. *Sweet dreams,* I think, and I'm out.

40 Everything is moving around. I don't know what is up or down, left or right. Then someone asks how I feel. I say "fine" as the moving things settle down. "Am I okay?" I mumble.

"It went perfectly," the doctor says. I'm in the
45 clear, and I can go home.

I guess now there *will* always be a little piece of the Red Sox in me. I can't wait to get home to tell my friends. This will be a big hit with them!

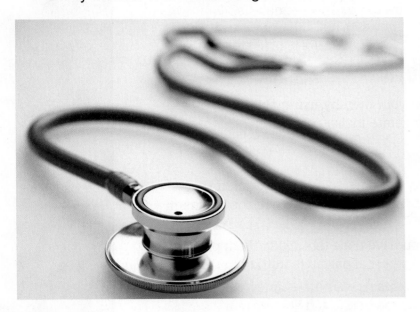

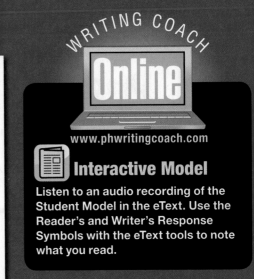

WRITING COACH

Online

www.phwritingcoach.com

 Interactive Model

Listen to an audio recording of the Student Model in the eText. Use the Reader's and Writer's Response Symbols with the eText tools to note what you read.

Use a Writer's Eye

Now, evaluate the narrative as a writer. On your copy of the Student Model, use the Writer's Response Symbols to react to what you read. Identify places where the student writer uses the characteristics of an effective personal narrative.

Writer's Response Symbols
E.S. **Engaging story**
C.R. **Clear, well-developed conflict and resolution**
B.C. **Believable characters**
S.D. **Specific and vivid details**

Your Turn

**Feature Assignment:
Personal Narrative**

Prewriting

Plan a first draft of your personal narrative **by choosing a topic based** on your own experiences. You may select from the Topic Bank or come up with an idea of your own.

Choose From the Topic Bank

TOPIC BANK

A Time to Remember Think about an unforgettable day you had with a friend. Tell the story of this experience, reflecting on your reactions to it then and now.

What a Trip! Think of a memorable trip you have taken somewhere such as the beach, a relative's home, a big city, or even the supermarket. Write a description of the trip and the place you visited. Tell why the trip was memorable.

Firsts Think about a "first" in your life—the first time you rode a bicycle, and so on. Write a personal narrative that explains that event and how you felt. Make sure to use specific details.

Choose Your Own Topic

Determine an appropriate topic on your own **by using the following range of strategies** to generate ideas.

Question and Remember

- Jot down notes about stories you have told about yourself that impressed others or made them laugh. Would one of these make a good personal narrative?

- Ask family members what you have done that made them proud or happy. Look for ideas for a personal narrative in their answers.

- Remember and list turning points in your life—times when something about you changed forever. Could you write a narrative about what happened?

Review your responses and choose a topic.

Narrow Your Topic

If your topic is too broad, readers might miss the meaning of the events in your personal narrative. A narrative with **a clearly defined focus** will help readers to share your experience and insight.

Apply It! Use a graphic organizer like the one shown to narrow your topic.

- Record your general topic—your broadest story idea—in the top box. Then, narrow your topic as you move down the chart.
- Your final box should hold your narrowest story idea, the new focus of your personal narrative.

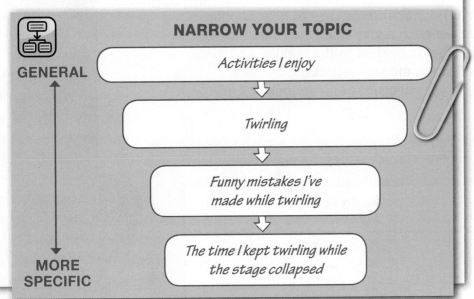

NARROW YOUR TOPIC

GENERAL

- Activities I enjoy
- Twirling
- Funny mistakes I've made while twirling
- The time I kept twirling while the stage collapsed

MORE SPECIFIC

Consider Your Audience and Purpose

Before writing, think about your audience and purpose. Consider how others will respond to your writing as you ask yourself these questions.

Questions for Audience	Questions for Purpose
• What should I tell my audience about myself? • What background information will they need? • What do I want them to learn from my writing?	• Why am I writing this personal narrative? What do I want to show, explain, or teach? • What point will this story make? How will I develop a clearly defined focus to make this point?

Record your answers in your writing journal.

www.phwritingcoach.com

Interactive Writing Coach™

- Choosing from the Topic Bank gives you access to the Interactive Writing Coach™.
- Submit your writing and receive instant personalized feedback and guidance as you draft, revise, and edit your writing.

Interactive Graphic Organizers

Use the interactive graphic organizers to help you narrow your topic.

Online Journal

Try It! Record your answers and ideas in the online journal.

Plan Your Piece

You will use a graphic organizer like the one shown to describe your characters and setting, and to plan the details for the beginning, middle, and end of your narrative. When it is complete, you will be ready to write your first draft.

Develop Your Focus To develop a clearly defined **focus** for your personal narrative, think about what you learned from the experience or what you want your audience to learn. In a personal narrative, your focus should be on the importance of the experience and what it taught you.

Map Out Your Story Use the graphic organizer to help develop a draft that tells what happened in a way readers can understand. Tell what happened first, what happened in the middle, and what happened at the end. Remember to reflect on, or think back about, the reasons for your **decisions** and **actions** as well as their **consequences**.

Plan Your Story

Characters:	Me, my twirling coach, and football fans
Setting:	The football field at halftime
Beginning (Introduce the problem.)	
Middle (Tell how the problem got worse.)	The crowd gasped, but I didn't hear it. I was having trouble keeping my balance. The stage was collapsing!
End (Tell how the problem was resolved and why events were important.)	

Gather Details

To bring their personal narratives to life, writers usually focus on these literary elements. Look at these examples:

- **Characters/Dialogue:** *"Teresa," Coach Sandy asked, "would you do your routine for the twirling show at halftime next week?"*

  "Um, okay, I guess," I said nervously.

- **Setting:** *At halftime, a sea of faces turned to the temporary stage at the end of the sunny field.*

- **Vivid Details:** *I was so nervous! I broke out into a clammy, cold sweat, and I felt as if I couldn't swallow.*

- **Suspense:** *The crowd gasped, but I didn't hear it. I was concentrating too hard on catching a high toss. Why was I having so much trouble keeping my balance?*

Try It! Read the Student Model excerpt and identify how the author's opening engages the readers' interest and clearly defines the focus.

Online

www.phwritingcoach.com

Interactive Graphic Organizers

Use the interactive graphic organizers to help you create a plan for your writing.

Interactive Model

Refer back to the Interactive Model in the eText as you plan your writing.

STUDENT MODEL   from **My Heart**
page 70; lines 5–11

> My stomach feels as if it shriveled up. "This will require a procedure," he says, and then my mind just goes crazy. *Bad, bad, bad.* Although the doctor's mouth is moving, nothing comes out. Mom asks, "Are you okay?" I want to say no, but my mouth is frozen. I'm shaking, thinking about what is to come.

Apply It! Review the elements that narrative nonfiction writers often use. Decide how your gathered story details will make those elements clear.

- Choose details that will help readers to experience what you saw and felt and to understand the **focus** of your writing.
- Select details that support your reflections on your **decisions** and **actions** and that make their **consequences** clear.
- Add each detail to the correct part of your graphic organizer.

Drafting

During the drafting stage, you will start to write your ideas for your personal narrative. You will follow an outline that provides an **organizational strategy,** or plan, that will help you **build on the ideas** from your graphic organizer to write a **focused, organized, and coherent** personal narrative—one in which all the ideas work together.

The Organization of a Nonfiction Narrative

The chart shows an organizational strategy for a nonfiction narrative. Look back at how the Mentor Text follows this organizational strategy. Then, use this chart to help you outline your draft.

Outline for Success

I. Beginning

See Mentor Text, p. 68.

- Clearly defined focus
- Details about the writer

II. Middle

See Mentor Text, pp. 68–69.

- Plot line with conflict
- Reflections on decisions, actions, and/or consequences
- Specific details about characters' movement, expressions, and feelings

III. End

See Mentor Text, p. 69.

- Resolution
- Consequences of actions

Grab Your Reader

- A personal narrative should focus on a specific series of events.
- Personal details about the writer help to focus the topic, establish the setting, and set the scene for the conflict to come.

Develop Your Plot

- Readers are better able to follow a narrative if the events are told in chronological order.
- The conflict, or problem, is what gets readers interested in a narrative. It may affect one, some, or all of the characters.
- Vivid details about the characters, setting, and action help readers feel as though they are part of the story.

Wrap It Up

- The resolution of a story tells how the problem was solved or how events ended it.
- The end of a personal narrative clearly shows how the events that took place affected the writer.

Start Your Draft

Use this checklist to help you with your draft. Use the graphic organizer that shows the beginning, middle, and end of your narrative, and the Outline for Success as guides.

While drafting, aim at writing your ideas, not on making your writing perfect. Remember, you will have the chance to improve your draft when you revise and edit.

√ Start by drafting an attention-getting **opening** sentence.

√ Establish your **setting** and characters. Use vivid details to help your readers connect with the characters.

√ Continue your **beginning** by creating a clearly defined **focus** and connecting with readers in a way that makes them want to keep reading.

√ Use chronological order to develop the **middle** of your personal narrative. Present a series of plot events that show reasons for the **conflict** and actions, and the problem that the conflict creates.

√ Include **dialogue** in order to fully develop the plot and the characters.

√ Use **suspense** to keep your readers interested in the story's events.

√ Keep the narrative interesting by including **vivid images** and specific details to describe the characters, setting, and action.

√ At the **end** of your narrative, show the **resolution**—how the conflict worked out.

√ Finish in a way that **reflects** on your decisions and actions and how they affected you and others.

WRITING COACH

Online

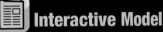
www.phwritingcoach.com

Interactive Model

Outline for Success View pop-ups of the Mentor Text referenced in the Outline for Success.

Interactive Writing Coach™

Use the Interactive Writing Coach to receive the level of support you need:
• Write one paragraph at a time and submit each one for immediate, detailed feedback.
• Write your entire first draft and submit it for immediate, personalized feedback.

Revising: Making It Better

Now that you have finished your first draft, you are ready to revise. Think about the "big picture" of audience, purpose, and genre. You can use Revision RADaR as a guide for making changes to improve your draft. Revision RADaR provides four major ways to improve your writing: (R) replace, (A) add, (D) delete, and (R) reorder.

Kelly Gallagher, M. Ed.

KEEP REVISION ON YOUR RADaR

Read part of the first draft of the Student Model "My Heart." Then, look at questions the writer asked himself as he thought about how well his draft **addressed issues of audience, purpose, and genre**.

My Heart

1ˢᵀ DRAFT

It is just a routine doctor visit, no different than those of past check-ups on my heart. The doctor comes in. The words seem to fall out of his mouth like boulders fall off a cliff. My stomach feels bad. "This will require a procedure," he says, and then my mind just goes crazy. *Bad, bad, bad.* Although the doctor's mouth is moving, nothing comes out. Mom asks, "Are you okay?" I want to say no, but my mouth is frozen. I'm shaking, thinking about what is to come.

Boston? We have to go to Boston? "Yes," Mom says, "Boston. It will be a family trip. You'll have lots of fun." Yeah, right.

Days later, I read the big green sign out of my car window: *Welcome to Massachusetts.* We go to the hospital after spending a few days in Boston.

*A narrative should have a clearly defined **focus**. Can readers tell what is happening and why?*

*Is "My stomach feels bad" a **vivid image** that will help my audience share my experience?*

*Have I included the **reasons for actions** in my narrative? Will it be clear to my audience why I have to go to Boston?*

*Have I created enough **suspense** and accurately described my emotions here?*

Now, look at how the writer applied Revision RADaR to write an improved second draft.

My Heart

2ND DRAFT

It is just a routine doctor visit, no different than those of past check-ups on my heart. The doctor comes in. The words seem to fall out of his mouth like boulders fall off a cliff: "This is what's wrong." I am looking at the results of my heart test. My stomach feels as if it shriveled up. "This will require a procedure," he says, and then my mind just goes crazy. *Bad, bad, bad.* Although the doctor's mouth is moving, nothing comes out. Mom asks, "Are you okay?" I want to say no, but my mouth is frozen. I'm shaking, thinking about what is to come.

Boston? We have to go to Boston? "Yes," Mom says, "Boston." Why there? "Because that is where you will get the best treatment. It will be a family trip. You'll have lots of fun." Yeah, right.

Days later, I read the big green sign out of my car window: *Welcome to Massachusetts.* The few days we spend in Boston fly by, and then, all too soon, it is time. We go to the hospital.

A *Added sentences to make the problem clear*

R *Replaced a vague description with a vivid image*

A *Added sentences to tell the reason for the decision*

R *Reordered details and*

A *added phrases such as <u>all too soon</u> and <u>it is time</u> to show how nervous I was and to create suspense*

Apply It! Use Revision RADaR to revise your draft after rethinking how well questions of purpose, audience, and genre have been addressed.

- First, determine if you have created a clearly defined **focus** that indicates your purpose, considered how well the audience will react to your story, and included the characteristics of the narrative nonfiction genre.

- Also check to see that your narrative clearly reflects on the reasons for **decisions**, **actions**, and **consequences**.

- Then apply Revision RADaR to make your writing better. Remember—you can use the steps in Revision RADaR in any order.

Look at the Big Picture

Use the chart to evaluate how well each section of your personal narrative addresses **purpose, audience, and genre.** When necessary, use the suggestions in the chart to revise your narrative.

Section	Evaluate	Revise
Beginning	• Check the **opening sentences** of your narrative. Do they grab your readers' attention?	• Add a question, a quotation, or some other detail that makes readers curious.
	• Consider your **focus;** if it is clearly defined, readers will understand the topic and connect with you as the writer.	• Ask yourself, "Why would I want to read this story?" The answer may help you sharpen your focus.
Middle	• Make sure that the plot of your narrative presents a **conflict**—a problem that readers will understand and care about.	• Add or replace details to show why the problem matters to you, the writer and main character. If it matters to you, it should matter to readers.
	• Make sure that you have included enough dialogue and created enough **suspense.**	• Add dialogue and phrases that set up suspense where possible to help your readers connect with your characters and stay interested in your story.
	• Review details about characters, setting, and action. Could any **images** be more vivid, specific, and interesting?	• Add or replace details, or images, so that readers can "see," or "hear" the actions. Make them feel that they are part of the story!
End	• Make sure that your narrative has a **resolution** that shows how the conflict worked out.	• Add or replace details to show how the problem was solved or how events ended it.
	• Underline **consequences of actions** and **decisions** in the narrative and make sure you have clearly reflected on their importance.	• Add a detail that answers the question "So what?" about the outcome and makes one more connection with your readers.

Focus on Craft: Sentence Variety

In a personal narrative, one way to express your ideas is by varying the length and types of sentences you use.

- In a **simple sentence,** one subject and its verb form a main, or independent, clause that expresses one idea: *The cat runs quickly.*

- In a **compound sentence,** two main clauses express two equal ideas: *The cat runs quickly, but the dog is faster.*

- A **complex sentence** has two clauses, but one is a main clause and the other is a subordinate clause, showing that one idea is less important than the other: *Although the dog chased the cat, the cat was able to escape.* Read these sentences from the Student Model.

 **STUDENT MODEL** from **My Heart**
pages 70–71; lines 28–31

> There are minutes to go, and I feel my heart pumping. They say music helps. Although it doesn't help, I still lie there on the bed, listening to my MP3 player.

 Try It! Now, ask yourself these questions:

- Which sentence is simple? Compound? Complex?

- Would the first sentence be better if it read "There are minutes to go. I feel my heart pumping."? Explain.

WRITING COACH

www.phwritingcoach.com

 Video

Learn more strategies for effective writing from program author Kelly Gallagher.

 Online Journal

Try It! Record your answers in the online journal.

 Interactive Model

Refer back to the Interactive Model as you revise your writing.

 Interactive Writing Coach™

Revise your draft and submit it for feedback.

Fine-Tune Your Draft

Apply It! Use the revision suggestions to prepare your final draft after rethinking how well questions of **audience, purpose, and genre** have been addressed.

- **Use a Variety of Sentences** Raise your readers' interest level by using a variety of sentence structures.

- **Include Vivid Images** Add or replace details so that readers can easily imagine the setting, characters, and action.

Teacher, Peer, or Family Feedback Ask your teacher, a peer, or a family member if the focus of your personal narrative is clear. Think about the feedback you receive and revise your final draft as needed.

Editing: Making It Correct

Before editing your final draft, think about using a variety of sentence structures, including **simple, compound, and complex sentences,** as well as keeping a **consistent verb tense** throughout your narrative. Then, edit your draft by correcting any errors in **grammar, mechanics, or spelling.**

WRITE GUY *Jeff Anderson, M. Ed.*

WHAT DO YOU NOTICE?

Zoom in on Conventions Focus on sentence structures as you zoom in on these lines from the Student Model.

>  **STUDENT MODEL** from **My Heart**
> page 70; lines 8–10
>
> Although the doctor's mouth is moving, nothing comes out. Mom asks, "Are you okay?" I want to say no, but my mouth is frozen.

Now, ask yourself: *Is the structure of each sentence the same or different?*

Perhaps you said that the structure of each sentence is different.

The first sentence is a **complex** sentence because it has a main, or independent, clause and a subordinate, or dependent, clause. A subordinate clause has a subject and a verb, but it cannot stand alone as a complete sentence. Which clause in the sentence is the subordinate clause? How do you know?

The second sentence is a **simple** sentence because it has a single main clause. Remember that a main clause has a subject and a verb and can stand alone as a complete sentence.

The third sentence is a **compound** sentence because it has two main clauses that could each stand alone as its own sentence. They are joined by a conjunction.

Partner Talk Discuss this question with a partner: *Why do you think the author varied the sentence structure in this passage?*

To learn more about sentence structure, see Chapter 20 of your Grammar Handbook.

Grammar Mini-Lesson: Consistent Tenses

To learn more, see page 284.

There are three main verb tenses: past *(He went there yesterday)*, present *(He goes there every day)*, and future *(He will go there later)*. If everything in your narrative happens in the past, it is very important to use accurate and consistent verb tenses when writing the narrative. Using a consistent verb tense helps your readers to follow the sequence of events in your story.

Read these sentences from the Mentor Text. Notice how the author uses a consistent verb tense in the sentences.

 MENTOR TEXT from **The Day I Threw the Trivia Bowl**
page 68; lines 20–21

> I loved trivia and, even more, I loved winning at stuff. It was a terrible dilemma.

Try It! In your journal, write a short paragraph about what you did before you arrived at school today. In the paragraph, include at least one simple, compound, and complex sentence, and underline the subordinate clause in your complex sentence. Be sure to use a consistent verb tense throughout your paragraph.

 Apply It! Edit your draft for **grammar, mechanics, and spelling.** If necessary, revise sentences to use a variety of sentence structures and a consistent verb tense.

Use the rubric to evaluate your narrative. If necessary, rethink, rewrite, or revise.

WRITING COACH

Online

www.phwritingcoach.com

 Video

Learn effective editing techniques from program author Jeff Anderson.

 Online Journal

Try It! Record your answers in the online journal.

 Interactive Model

Refer back to the Interactive Model as you edit your writing.

 Interactive Writing Coach™

Edit your draft. Check it against the rubric and then submit it for feedback.

Rubric for Nonfiction Narration: Personal Narrative	Rating Scale
Ideas: How focused is your narrative on a single, important event?	Not very Very 1 2 3 4 5 6
Organization: How logical is your sequence of events?	1 2 3 4 5 6
Voice: How authentic and engaging is your voice?	1 2 3 4 5 6
Word Choice: How vivid and specific is your word choice?	1 2 3 4 5 6
Sentence Fluency: How well have you used a variety of sentence structures?	1 2 3 4 5 6
Conventions: How correct is your verb tense?	1 2 3 4 5 6

Publishing

Take your turn in the spotlight by publishing your personal narrative! First, get your narrative ready for presentation. Then, choose a way to publish it for the appropriate audience.

Wrap Up Your Presentation

Is your narrative handwritten? If so, you may need to make a new, clean copy. Be sure to **write legibly.** Also be sure that your title grabs the reader's attention and indicates your topic.

Publish Your Piece

Use the chart to identify a way to publish your personal narrative.

If your audience is...	...then publish it by...
Students or adults at school	• Posting it on your school Web site • Submitting it to a school essay contest • Collecting class essays and publishing an anthology
People outside of your school	• Reading it aloud and recording it as a podcast • Posting it as part of a blog on an appropriate topic

 Reflect on Your Writing

Now that you are done with your personal narrative, read it over and use your writing journal to answer these questions. Use specific details to describe and explain your reflections. Increase the specificity of your details based on the type of information requested.

- Which parts of your narrative were the hardest to write? Which were easiest? Why?

- What did you discover about your experience from writing?

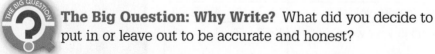 **The Big Question: Why Write?** What did you decide to put in or leave out to be accurate and honest?

Manage Your Portfolio You may wish to include your published personal narrative in your writing portfolio. If so, consider what this piece reveals about your writing and your growth as a writer.

21st Century Learning

MAKE YOUR WRITING COUNT

Tell the Key Events of a Narrative Through Images

Personal narratives tell about important events in the writers' lives. Capture your audience's imagination by creating a bulletin-board collage or electronic **photo album** based on a personal narrative.

With a group, choose a narrative to illustrate. As you work through the group process, pause at each step to analyze and evaluate your ideas about your work. Publish your work as a series of text and graphics, either on a bulletin-board collage or as a **multimedia presentation**.

Here's your action plan.

1. Set goals and choose roles, such as image researcher, caption writer, and presenter.

2. Select the personal narrative you could retell best through images. Decide what distinct perspective the images should convey.

3. Plan your collage by summarizing events and giving suggestions for images.

   - Gather images from magazines, the Internet, or your own collections, or create your own images. Make sure the images tell a coherent and focused story.

   - Write text captions for each image.

   - Arrange the images and text in a collage, creating a title or header.

   - If you plan to create a multimedia slide show, research options on the Internet. Many free services allow you to create slide shows using digital images.

4. Present your final product to the class.

Listening and Speaking Divide your illustrated personal narrative into sections to be read aloud while your class views the collage or Web album. As you rehearse your readings, give each reader feedback about volume, pacing, and intonation. As a group, share your reasoning for selecting scenes and creating illustrations.

WRITING COACH

Online

www.phwritingcoach.com

Online Journal
Reflect on Your Writing Record your answers and ideas in the online journal.

Resource
Link to resources on 21st Century Learning for help in creating a group project.

Your Turn ▶ **Writing for Media: Diary Entry for a Blog**

Diary Entry for a Blog

A **diary** is a personal record of your thoughts and events in your life. You may keep it in order to help you analyze events or to let you reflect on and remember them later. Some people choose to share diary entries on a **blog**—a Web site on which a person shares feelings, ideas, and opinions. Your diary entry, however, will be shorter and less formal than a personal narrative. Online writing is often briefer and more direct than other types of writing. It is very public, and it should not include any information that the writer wants to keep private.

Try It! Read this diary entry. Then, answer these questions. Record your answers in your journal.

1. How can you tell that this diary entry is part of a **blog?**

2. Who is the **audience** for the diary entry?

3. What is the **topic** or focus of the diary entry? How does the writer define her focus?

4. What do you think is the **purpose** of the diary entry?

5. Does the writer clearly explain the importance of the **actions and consequences** she describes? What do these reflections tell you about the writer and what she learned from her experience?

6. How would you describe the diary entry's **mood,** or the overall feeling created by or shown in the writing? Explain.

Extension Find another example of a diary entry for a blog, and compare it with this one.

Tanya's Blog

The Best News Ever

posted 8/15/2011, 4:30 P.M.

I just got into the High School for Fine Arts! See, I've been making art since I was little, only I didn't really think of it as art. When I was younger, I just drew wild pencil lines and glued on wads of tissue paper. As I got older, the lines turned into sketches, and instead of tissue paper, I used cloth, leaves, plastic wrap—all kinds of things.

I always loved art class, but I never showed my weird pencil-and-object compilations to anyone outside my family. They didn't look like anything I had seen in any art book, and I was afraid people would laugh.

Well, I finally showed a few of my best ones to Mr. Robinson, my art teacher. The next thing I knew he was helping me fill out an application form.

Then, I took the bus across town and showed my work to a panel of teachers. I was so nervous I almost fainted!

Today a letter from the school came in the mail. It started, "I am pleased to inform you . . . ." I'll never doubt myself or be afraid to share my artwork with others again!

Create a Diary Entry for a Blog

Follow these steps to create your own diary entry for a blog. To plan your diary entry, review the graphic organizers on pages R24–R27 and choose one that suits your needs.

Prewriting

- Select an experience that you want to share. You might want to share a funny story, some good news, or an experience that was out of the ordinary.

- Identify your target audience. Think about who might read your diary entry. Will they understand what happened?

- Think about what you want to tell your audience, and make sure that you clearly define your focus.

- List or map out the events of your diary entry—its beginning, middle, and end.

- Fill in the details; for example, note things that you or others said and how you felt as the events were happening.

Drafting

- Use chronological, or time, order to recount the events. When writing a blog, you will have varied audiences, so be sure to explain any background information the reader may need to know.

- Write a narrative that reflects on what you did, what decisions you made, and the results of your actions. Be sure to tell readers why the decisions, actions, and consequences were important.

- Keep paragraphs short, but include details or comments that your audience will appreciate and to which they will be able to connect.

Revising and Editing

- Review your draft to ensure that your narrative is complete and interesting. Look for places to add specific words and vivid images.

- Review the tone of the diary entry. You may want to make your writing more informal and friendly, or less so.

- Check that spelling, grammar, and mechanics are correct.

Publishing

Post your diary entry to a blog. Don't forget to label your post with the date and time.

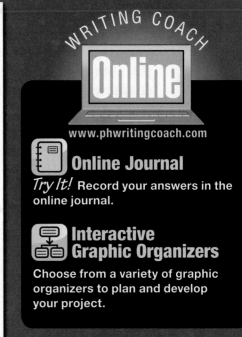

WRITING COACH

Online

www.phwritingcoach.com

Online Journal

Try It! Record your answers in the online journal.

Interactive Graphic Organizers

Choose from a variety of graphic organizers to plan and develop your project.

 **Partner Talk**

Before you start drafting, explain your diary entry to a partner. Be specific and detailed in your explanation. Ask for his or her opinion about your plan. For example, are you telling the whole story? Are your details interesting and descriptive?

Writing for Assessment

Many standardized tests include writing prompts. Use these prompts to practice. Your narratives should have the same characteristics as your personal narrative. (See page 66.)

 Try It! Read the prompt and the information on format and academic vocabulary. Then, write a **personal narrative** by using the ABCDs of On-Demand Writing.

Format

The prompt directs you to write a *personal narrative.* Make sure that you keep a clearly defined focus through your narrative's beginning, middle, and end.

Narrative Nonfiction Prompt

Think about a time you took part in a contest or competition. Write a personal narrative about this experience, reflecting on your reactions to it then and now. Use vivid images and dialogue to bring your story to life.

Academic Vocabulary

Remember that *vivid images* help describe something in a way that makes it seem real, such as "the snowflakes melted in my mouth like cotton candy." *Dialogue* is a conversation between characters.

The ABCDs of On-Demand Writing

Use the following ABCDs to help you respond to the prompt.

Before you write your draft:

A ttack the prompt [1 MINUTE]

- Circle or highlight important verbs in the prompt. Draw a line from the verb to what it refers to.
- Rewrite the prompt in your own words.

B rainstorm possible answers [4 MINUTES]

- Create a graphic organizer to generate ideas.
- Use one for each part of the prompt if necessary.

C hoose the order of your response [1 MINUTE]

- Think about the best way to organize your ideas.
- Number your ideas in the order you will write about them. Cross out ideas you will not be using.

After you write your draft:

D etect errors before turning in the draft [1 MINUTE]

- Carefully reread your writing.
- Make sure that your response makes sense and is complete.
- Look for spelling, punctuation, and grammar errors.

 **More Prompts for Practice**

Apply It! Respond to Prompts 1 and 2 by writing **personal narratives** with a clearly defined **focus.** As you write, be sure to:

- Identify an appropriate **audience** for your intended **purpose**
- Use a graphic organizer, such as a beginning-middle-end chart, to structure your ideas
- Fully develop the **characters** in your narrative, including yourself, through the use of dialogue
- Use vivid **images** to bring your story to life for your audience
- Reflect on the importance of or reasons for **decisions, actions,** and their **consequences**

> **Prompt 1** Everyone feels sad sometimes. Think about a time you felt sad. What did you do to feel better? Write a personal narrative about this time and what you did to help yourself change your mood.

> **Prompt 2** Think about a time when you received a big surprise. It might have been a gift, a party, or an unexpected event. Write a personal narrative about your surprise and how you felt about it.

More Strategies for Writing for Assessment

- Consider several possible topics and quickly list details that you might use in your response. Then, choose the topic for which you have the strongest ideas.
- If you do not understand any words in the prompt, use context clues to help you determine the meaning of any unfamiliar words.
- Be sure to follow the ABCDs for writing to a prompt. Planning is an important part of writing. Don't just start writing right away.
- Make sure to reread your piece after you have completed it. This will give you time to find and correct errors. If you are in a timed situation, be sure to leave enough time for this step.

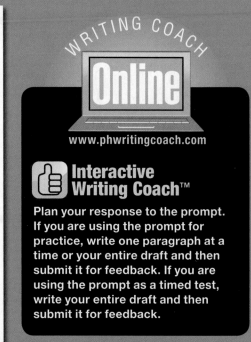

WRITING COACH

Online

www.phwritingcoach.com

Interactive Writing Coach™

Plan your response to the prompt. If you are using the prompt for practice, write one paragraph at a time or your entire draft and then submit it for feedback. If you are using the prompt as a timed test, write your entire draft and then submit it for feedback.

Remember **ABCD**

A ttack the prompt

B rainstorm possible answers

C hoose the order of your response

D etect errors before turning in the draft

CHAPTER 6

FICTION NARRATION

What's the Story?

What is happening in the photograph? What story can you tell about what happened shortly before this photograph was taken?

Many stories have realistic settings. Believable details about setting, such as the prairie in the early morning, help get the reader interested and add to the story. Conflict is also important. Conflict is a challenge or problem the main character faces.

Try It! Think about what might have happened in the moments before the photograph was taken. Take notes as you consider these questions. Then participate in an extended discussion with a partner. Take turns expressing your ideas and feelings about the people, events, and ideas pictured.

- Why is this person lassoing horses?
- What is the setting of this story?
- How does this cowgirl feel?
- Is this a normal day for this person or an extraordinary one? Why do you think that?

Review your notes. Use your notes to tell a story about the cowgirl. Be sure to use details to make your story believable.

What's Ahead

In this chapter, you will review two strong examples of a fiction story: a Mentor Text and a Student Model. Then, using the examples as guidance, you will write a fiction story of your own.

 Connect to the Big Questions

Discuss these questions with your partner:

1 **What do you think?** In the conflict between people and nature, what does it take to win?

2 **Why write?** What can fiction do better than nonfiction?

SHORT STORY

A short story is a made-up, or fictional, tale with a beginning, middle, and end. In this chapter, you will write a special type of short story called a tall tale. A tall tale is a short story in which characters perform amazing acts of strength, bravery, or even silliness. Often, tall tales explain how the main character solves a problem by doing something wild and fantastic that normal people could never do.

You will develop a tall tale by taking it through each of the steps of the writing process: prewriting, drafting, revising, editing, and publishing. You will also have an opportunity to use your tall tale to write a dramatic scene. To preview the criteria for how your tall tale will be evaluated, see the rubric on page 111.

FEATURE ASSIGNMENT

Short Story: Tall Tale

An effective and imaginative short story has these characteristics:

- **A believable setting** created through the use of **sensory details**

- **An engaging plot**, or storyline, with conflict and **well-paced action** that **sustains**, or keeps, **reader interest**

- One or more **well-developed, interesting characters**

- A **range of literary strategies and devices**, such as dialogue and interesting comparisons, to enhance the **style and tone**

- **Effective sentence structure** and correct spelling, grammar, and usage

A tall tale also usually includes:

- Larger-than-life **characters**

- An action-packed **plot** with an interesting climax, or high point of interest and suspense

- A resolution in which the main character resolves the conflict, or problem, in a remarkable way

Other Forms of Short Stories

In addition to tall tales, there are other forms of short stories, including:

Fantasy stories stretch the imagination and take readers to unreal worlds. Animals may talk, people may fly, or characters may have superhuman powers.

Historical fiction tells about imaginary people living in real places and times in history. Usually, the main characters are fictional people who know and interact with famous people in history and participate in important historical events.

Mystery stories focus on unexplained or strange events that one of the characters tries to solve. These stories are often full of suspense and surprises.

Myths and legends are traditional stories that different cultures have told to explain natural events, human nature, or the origins of things. They often include gods and goddesses from ancient times and heroes who do superhuman things.

Realistic fiction portrays invented characters and events in everyday life that most readers would find familiar.

Science fiction stories focus on real or imagined developments in science and technology and their effects on the way people think and live. Space travel, robots, and life in the future are popular topics for science fiction.

Try It! For each audience and purpose described, choose a story form, such as a mystery, myth, or historical fiction, that is appropriate for conveying your intended meaning to the audience. Explain your choices.

- To describe how detectives figure out who committed a crime
- To show readers what it was like to live during the westward expansion of settlers in the United States
- To explain how the desert was formed

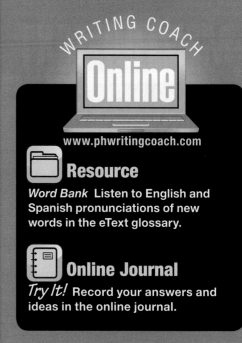

WRITING COACH

Online

www.phwritingcoach.com

Resource

Word Bank Listen to English and Spanish pronunciations of new words in the eText glossary.

Online Journal

Try It! Record your answers and ideas in the online journal.

WORD BANK

People use these words when they talk about writing short stories. Work with a partner. Take turns using each word in a sentence. If you are unsure of the meaning of a word, use the Glossary or a dictionary to check the definition.

device	realistic
fantastic	sensory
imaginative	suspense

MENTOR TEXT   Tall Tale

Learn From Experience

 Read the tall tale on pages 94–97. As you read, take notes to develop your understanding of basic sight and English vocabulary. Then, read the numbered notes in the margins to learn about how the author presented his ideas.

Answer the *Try It!* questions online or in your notebook.

---

1 The tale is told in the third-person **point of view.** An outside observer, and not Paul Bunyan, narrates the story, telling what happened.

> *Try It!* How might the tale change if it were told in the first person by Paul Bunyan?

2 Though the events in the tale are imaginary, it has a **specific, believable setting**—North Dakota.

> *Try It!* What is the effect of setting the tale in a real place?

3 Tall tales are known for their **hyperbole,** or outrageous exaggeration. This **literary device** helps make the tale "tall," or filled with fantastic objects and deeds.

> *Try It!* Give an example of hyperbole from the paragraph. What effect does the hyperbole have on your perceptions as a reader?

Extension Find another example of a tall tale, and compare it with this one.

How Paul Bunyan Cleared North Dakota

Told by Dell J. McCormick

1 Soon after Paul had finished digging the St. Lawrence River he received a letter from the King of Sweden. It seems that the King had heard of Paul Bunyan through Ole the Big Swede. He wanted Paul to cut down all the trees in North Dakota so the Swedes could settle there and farm the land. The King wrote that he wanted this job done in one month so the farmers could plant their grain at once. All the trees were to be cut up and made into toothpicks for the Swedish army.

2 When this huge job was finished, all the Swedes in North America were to settle in the New Kingdom of North Dakota and farm the land. This was about the largest job that Paul ever attempted. He soon gathered his men together and started moving his camp to North Dakota. When they all arrived, he built the largest camp the world had ever seen.

3 The bunks in the new sleeping quarters were eighteen decks high and the men in the top bunks had to get up an hour earlier in the morning in order to get down to breakfast on time. The dining room was longer than ever, and the boy that drove the salt and pepper wagon around the tables would only be halfway around by nightfall. He would stay overnight at the other end and drive back the next day.

Paul had to finish the job in one month, so he hired the Seven Axemen. They were famous woodsmen and could cut down trees faster than anyone except Paul himself.

4 They were all cousins, and each was named Frank. It was very confusing, because every time Paul shouted "Frank!" all the Seven Axemen would drop their work and
30 run over to see what he wanted.

5 The Seven Axemen used great double-bitted axes that an ordinary man could not lift. When the axes became dull they would start a round, flat rock rolling down the hillside and run beside it holding the blades of their axes
35 against the rock until they were sharp again.

4 This paragraph captures the **tone** of the tale, or the author's attitude toward the subject.

Try It! How would you describe the tone? Light? Serious? Something else? Explain.

5 Tall tales always include larger-than-life characters, such as the Seven Axemen. The characters perform amazing acts of strength, bravery, or even silliness.

Try It! How are the Seven Axemen larger than life? What characters in film and contemporary literature that you know seem similar to the Seven Axeman?

6 The story's **conflict,** or central problem, begins at this point. Many obstacles stand in the way of Paul Bunyan's success.

Try It! What problem delays the work? Is the problem believable or another example of hyperbole?

7 **Literary devices** make the tale more interesting. The author uses **figurative language** here to help readers imagine the thick fog.

Try It! To what is the fog compared?

8 The author uses vivid **details** to make the fog come to life.

Try It! Which details help you imagine the fog?

9 The author uses **dialogue,** or conversation between characters, to move the plot along.

Try It! What plan is revealed in the dialogue?

No matter how fast they worked, the huge job was always being delayed. **6** Paul began to have bad luck. First, Babe the Blue Ox lost his heavy iron shoes in a swamp, and a new mine had to be opened to get enough iron to make him
40 a new set.

7 Next came the great fog that covered the earth like a blanket. It was so thick that the fish in the river couldn't tell where the water left off and the fog began. They swam around in the fog and got lost among the trees in the forest.
45 When the fog disappeared, thousands of small fish were left in the woods many miles from the nearest stream.

8 The Seven Axemen had to chop a tunnel in the fog from the kitchen to the dining room so the cooks could serve food. The fog even got into the coffee and made it
50 so weak the men wouldn't drink it. At night the men had to sleep with mosquito netting over their heads to keep the tadpoles from getting in their ears.

Finally the fog went away, but all the blankets and shirts were so wet it took fourteen days to dry them out.
55 At last all the trees were cut down and split into toothpicks, but still the King of Sweden wasn't satisfied. He wrote Paul another letter which said, "My farmers will not be able to till the soil with all the stumps," and the farmers refused to settle in the new Kingdom of North Dakota.
60 **9** Paul called Johnnie Inkslinger into the office and said, "You are good at solving problems. What are we going to do about the stumps?" Johnnie Inkslinger thought and thought for seven days and nights.

"We will send for several large fire hoses and flood the
65 ground with water," said Johnnie Inkslinger finally. "Babe the Blue Ox, as you all know, doesn't like to get his feet wet, for that gives him a cold in the head.

"With water all over the ground, he will walk on the stumps. He is so heavy his huge hoofs will drive the stumps
70 into the ground."

The men did as Johnnie said. They covered the whole country with water. Babe roamed all over North Dakota, stepping very carefully from stump to stump to avoid getting his feet wet. His heavy weight drove the stumps six feet underground.

The King of Sweden was finally satisfied, and to this day there isn't a single tree or stump in the whole state of North Dakota.

www.phwritingcoach.com

Interactive Model

Listen to an audio recording of the Mentor Text in the eText. You can refer back to the Mentor Text whenever you need support in developing your own writing.

Online Journal

Try It! **Answer the questions about the Mentor Text in the online journal.**

 In the **resolution,** the conflict is resolved, and the theme of the tale is made clear.

Try It! Explain how the conflict is resolved. What fact about North Dakota and its culture in this time period does the tale attempt to explain?

STUDENT MODEL Tall Tale

With a small group, take turns reading this Student Model aloud. Watch for the amazing feats the main character does to solve a problem.

 ## Use a Reader's Eye

Now, reread the Student Model. On your copy of the Student Model, use the Reader's Response Symbols to react to what you read.

> **Reader's Response Symbols**
>
> **+** **This is a good description.**
>
> **–** **This isn't clear to me.**
>
> **!** **This is really cool/weird /interesting!**
>
> **?** **What will happen next?**

 ### Partner Talk

Participate in an extended discussion with a partner. Express your opinions and share your responses to the Student Model. Pay close attention to how the writer builds his plot action.

The Amazing Memory Man

by Stefan Williams

Nathan slammed his social studies book closed and put his head on his desk. A large stack of papers slid to the floor and scattered. He sighed. There was no way he could remember
5 all the names and dates for the big test.

"I'm going to flunk the test," he said. "My memory is like Swiss cheese."

P.J., Nathan's big brother, looked across the room at Nathan and said, "If only you were the Amazing
10 Memory Man, eh?"

Nathan answered, "Memory Man? What is that— some new computer program?"

P.J. closed his book. "Are you telling me you never heard of Memory Man?"

15 Nathan shook his head. His brother was a real know-it-all.

"Look, P.J., I really need to study," Nathan said. "I don't have time for another one of your stories."

P.J. said, "This is a true story, Nathan. Memory Man
20 could remember anything. He once memorized every emperor in the Roman Empire and the years each one of them ruled."

"Really?" Nathan asked. He opened his book.

"For real, Nate. Memory Man had a special power
25 to remember anything. In fact, he once used his memory to save our city from certain disaster."

"How could a good memory save a city?" Nathan asked.

1

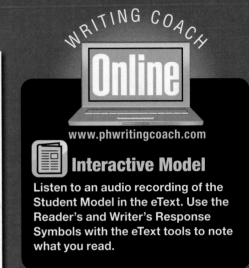

WRITING COACH

Online

www.phwritingcoach.com

Interactive Model

Listen to an audio recording of the Student Model in the eText. Use the Reader's and Writer's Response Symbols with the eText tools to note what you read.

30 "Well, back in the day, his dad worked at the city phone-book factory. One afternoon, Memory Man was waiting at the factory for his dad to give him a ride, and his dad was late. To pass the time, Memory Man began reading a typewritten copy of the new city directory."

35 "So what? Is there a point to this story?" asked Nathan.

"Sure," P.J. answered. "That night, there was a fire in the factory. Flames shot from the roof, and thick, black smoke poured from the windows. Nobody 40 was hurt, but the only copy of the new directory burned up. All the new telephone numbers and addresses were gone. Everybody was super-upset."

"How did they ever solve their problem?" Nathan asked.

45 P.J. smiled and said, "Memory Man had memorized the entire phone book and told the factory all the names, numbers, and addresses. Just a few weeks later, the new phone books were ready. I heard all about it from my friend Bill. His grandfather 50 went to school with Memory Man. Even better, Bill's grandfather told us Memory Man's secret."

Nathan looked surprised. "How did he do it? If I only knew, I could ace all my tests!"

P.J. shook his head. "I forgot."

Use a Writer's Eye

Now, evaluate the piece as a writer. On your copy of the Student Model, use the Writer's Response Symbols to react to what you read. Identify places where the student writer uses characteristics of an effective tall tale.

Writer's Response Symbols	
R.D.	**Realistic and believable dialogue**
S.D.	**Vivid sensory details that appeal to the senses, create imagery, or suggest mood**
W.C.	**Well-developed, interesting character**
E.S.	**Engaging story**

2

**Feature Assignment:
Tall Tale**

Prewriting

Plan a first draft of your tall tale **by determining an
appropriate topic.** You can select from the Topic Bank or come
up with an idea of your own.

Choose From the Topic Bank

TOPIC BANK

Taming Nature Think about the power of nature. Hurricanes, tornados,
and earthquakes can cause terrible damage. Imagine if these disasters
could be stopped before any damage is done. Write a tall tale about a
character who tames an element in nature.

Saving the World Imagine saving the world from a disastrous
event, such as a meteor hurtling toward Earth. Write a tall tale
about a character who saves the world from a global threat.

Helping People Skyscrapers, bridges, and other structures are everyday
things to us now, but that was not always true. Think about some of
the problems these types of structures help solve. Write a tall tale about
a character who builds an amazing structure that helps many people.

Choose Your Own Topic

Determine an appropriate topic on your own by using the
following **range of strategies** to generate ideas.

Tap into Personal Interests and Discuss

- Think about topics that make you curious. About what events,
  structures, or customs do you wonder? Note topics that
  interest you.

- With a group of friends, discuss some problems that need to be
  solved. Brainstorm for wild or silly solutions for these problems.

Review your responses and choose a topic.

Narrow Your Topic

If the topic for your tall tale is too broad, you may end up with a wandering story line that is hard for your readers to follow.

Apply It! Use a graphic organizer like the one shown to narrow your topic.

- Write the main topic of your tall tale in the top box. Narrow your topic as you move down the chart.
- Your last box should hold your narrowest topic, the main focus of your story.

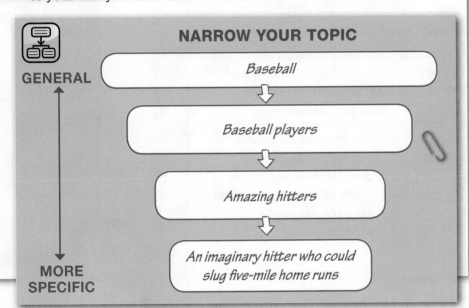

NARROW YOUR TOPIC

GENERAL

Baseball

Baseball players

Amazing hitters

An imaginary hitter who could slug five-mile home runs

MORE SPECIFIC

 # Consider Your Audience and Purpose

Before writing, think about your audience and purpose. Consider the views of others as you ask yourself these questions.

Questions for Audience	Questions for Purpose
• Who is my audience? • What kinds of story lines will they find engaging?	• Why am I writing the story? To make my audience laugh? Think? • How will I hold my audience's interest? What devices can I use?

Record your answers in your writing journal.

Plan Your Piece

You will use the graphic organizer to plan your plot, develop characters and setting, and identify details. When it is complete, you will be ready to write your first draft.

Organize Your Tall Tale Use a graphic organizer to plan a **plot with well-paced action; a specific, believable setting; and interesting characters**. Consider how each of these elements will help sustain, or keep, readers' interest.

Develop Your Tall Tale

Main character and his or her amazing accomplishment	*Sam ("Slugger") Smith was the most amazing hitter baseball has ever seen.*
Beginning • *A specific, believable setting* • *Interesting characters* • *A problem or goal*	• *The story takes place in a baseball stadium.* • *Sam Smith is an amazing young player with a problem.* • *He and his manager don't get along.*
Middle *Keep readers interested by using well-paced action to create an engaging story line. Include:* • *Events that build suspense about the problem* • *Characters' thoughts and actions* • *The climax, when the problem reaches a crisis point*	
End • *What happens to solve the problem* • *The main, lasting results of the character's action*	• *After hitting a ball five miles, Sam becomes a legend.*

Gather Details

To make the audience want to keep reading, develop interesting characters and a believable setting through the use of **sensory details.** Writers use sensory details that appeal to the senses of:

- **Sight:** *The bright green grass sparkled in the sun.*
- **Sound:** *Hear the crashing sound of the bat hitting the ball!*
- **Taste:** *He savored the icy sweetness of the orange juice.*
- **Smell:** *Spicy, tangy aromas floated from the concession stand.*
- **Touch:** *A soft, warm breeze ruffled her hair.*

Writers also use a **range of literary strategies and devices to enhance the style and tone** of a story. Look at these examples.

- **Dialogue:** *"Hey, Sam, you're late," shouted the manager. "No, I'm not!" Sam replied.*
- **Suspense:** *It was the top of the ninth with two outs. The Middleton Monsters were losing. Sam walked up to the plate.*
- **Interesting Comparisons:** *As he walked toward the plate, Sam felt as frightened and alone as a child on his first day of school.*

Try It! Read the Student Model excerpt and identify which kinds of sensory details describe the setting.

WRITING COACH

Online

www.phwritingcoach.com

Interactive Graphic Organizers

Use the interactive graphic organizers to help you create a plan for your writing.

Interactive Model

Refer back to the Interactive Model in the eText as you plan your writing.

STUDENT MODEL from **The Amazing Memory Man** page 98; lines 1–5

Nathan slammed his social studies book closed and put his head on his desk. A large stack of papers slid to the floor and scattered. He sighed. There was no way he could remember all the names and dates for the big test.

 Apply It! Review the types of sensory details and literary strategies a short story writer can use. Then write at least one sensory detail or literary device for each section of your story.

- Use **sensory details** that help create a realistic setting.
- Include strategies and devices that will improve the **style and tone** of your imaginative story.
- Then, add these details to your graphic organizer.

Drafting

During the drafting stage, you will start to write your ideas for your tall tale. You will follow an outline that provides an **organizational strategy** that will help you **build on ideas to create a focused, organized, and coherent** tall tale.

The Organization of a Short Story

The chart shows an organizational strategy for a short story. Look back at how the Mentor Text follows this organizational strategy. Then, use this chart to help you outline your draft.

Outline for Success

I. Beginning
See Mentor Text, p. 94.

- Setting and characters
- Conflict or problem

Set the Scene
- Sensory details can be used to set the scene and bring characters to life by showing what the characters do, say, or feel.
- Introducing the story's conflict, or the problem that must be faced, will make readers want to read on.

II. Middle
See Mentor Text, pp. 94–96.

- Plot with well-paced action
- Climax when the suspense is at its highest point

Build Suspense
- An interesting plot includes a series of events that make the conflict stronger and build toward the climax.
- The climax of a story is the point at which the conflict reaches its most difficult point— Will the character succeed or fail?

III. End
See Mentor Text, p. 97.

- Resolution
- The results of the character's action

Wrap It Up
- A satisfying resolution shows how the problem is solved and ties up loose ends.
- Tall tales often end by describing something permanent that remains as evidence of the events.

Start Your Draft

Use this checklist to help you complete your draft. Use the graphic organizer that shows the beginning, middle, and end, and the Outline for Success as guides.

While drafting, aim at writing your ideas, not on making your writing perfect. Remember, you will have the chance to improve your draft when you revise and edit.

√ Start drafting with the opening of your imaginative story. Describe the setting and interesting characters. Include amazing details about the character that will **sustain reader interest.**

√ Continue by introducing the conflict, or problem, that the character must face.

√ Create an engaging story line by building suspense, or curiosity about what will happen next. Use vivid **sensory details** to help readers feel what the characters feel and to communicate a believable setting.

√ Use **literary strategies** and devices including dialogue and interesting comparisons in similes, metaphors, and hyperboles to enhance style and tone.

√ Keep the action moving at a good **pace** and focused on the conflict. Describe events in time order, building to the climax.

√ Finish by describing what happens after the main character **solves** the problem and by showing the result of his or her actions.

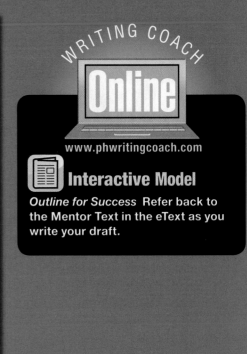

WRITING COACH

Online
www.phwritingcoach.com

Interactive Model
Outline for Success Refer back to the Mentor Text in the eText as you write your draft.

Revising: Making It Better

Now that you have finished your first draft, you are ready to revise. Think about the "big picture" of **audience, purpose, and genre**. You can use the Revision RADaR strategy as a guide for making changes to improve your draft. Revision RADaR provides four major ways to improve your writing: (R) replace, (A) add, (D) delete, and (R) reorder.

Kelly Gallagher, M. Ed.

KEEP REVISION ON YOUR RADAR

Read part of the first draft of the Student Model "The Amazing Memory Man." Then look at questions the writer asked himself as he thought about how well this draft addressed issues of audience, purpose, and genre.

Memory Man

1ST DRAFT

Nathan closed his social studies book and put his head on his desk. There was no way he could remember all the names and dates for the big test.

"I'm going to flunk the test," Nathan said. "My memory is really lousy."

P.J., Nathan's big brother, looked across the room at Nathan and said, "If only you were filled with special powers like the Amazing Memory Man, eh?"

Nathan snorted. "Memory Man? What is that—some new computer program?"

P.J. closed his world history book. "Are you telling me you never heard of Memory Man?"

Nathan shook his head. His brother was a real know-it-all.

"For real, Nate. Memory Man had a special power to remember anything."

Does my opening capture attention and introduce the setting with sensory detail?

Does this dialogue hold my audience's attention and develop my characters?

Is the action well paced and does it build toward a tall tale?

Now look at how the writer applied Revision RADaR to write an improved second draft.

WRITING COACH

Online

www.phwritingcoach.com

Video

Learn more strategies for effective writing from program author Kelly Gallagher.

Memory Man   2ND DRAFT

Nathan slammed his social studies book closed and put his head on his desk. A large stack of papers slid to the floor and scattered. He sighed. There was no way he could remember all the names and dates for the big test.

> **A** Added sensory details to grab readers

"I'm going to flunk the test," he said. "My memory is like Swiss cheese."

> **R** Replaced dialogue with specific details to describe the problem in a more engaging way

P.J., Nathan's big brother, looked across the room at Nathan and said, "If only you were the Amazing Memory Man, eh?"

Nathan snorted. "Memory Man? What is that—some new computer program?"

> **D** Deleted the unnecessary words <u>filled with special powers like</u>

P.J. closed his book. "Are you telling me you never heard of Memory Man?"

Nathan shook his head. His brother was a real know-it-all.

"Look, P.J., I really need to study," Nathan said. "I don't have time for another one of your stories."

P.J. said, "This is a true story, Nathan. Memory Man could remember anything. He once memorized every emperor in the Roman Empire and the years each one of them ruled."

> **A** Added more action and details to pace the plot more effectively

Apply It! Use your Revision RADaR to revise your draft.

- First, determine if you have engaged your audience, made the conflict or problem clear, and included the characteristics of a short story.

- Then apply the Revision RADaR strategy to make needed changes. Remember—you can use the steps in the strategy in any order.

Look at the Big Picture

Use the chart and your analytical skills to evaluate how well each section of your tall tale addresses **audience, purpose, and genre**. When necessary, use the suggestions in the chart to revise your piece.

Section	Evaluate	Revise
Beginning	• Check the **opening**. Will it grab readers' attention and make them want to read more?	• Introduce an interesting or outlandish characteristic of your main character.
	• Introduce the **problem.**	• Describe what problem the main character must handle.
	• Introduce a specific **setting**.	• Add sensory details to describe a believable setting where the action takes place.
Middle	• Check that the **action** is well-paced and the **plot** makes sense.	• Show events in time order, building up to the climax, to help create an engaging story line.
	• Make sure that literary strategies and **devices** are used to create the style and tone you want.	• Reorder details as necessary to better build suspense. Add dialogue or interesting comparisons to sustain reader interest.
End	• Check that **loose ends** of the story are tied up.	• Answer questions such as *What happened then? What did the characters do after the problem was solved?*
	• Make sure you described the **results** of the main character's actions.	• Explain what the character did and how it turned out.

Focus on Craft: Vivid Images

Writers use **vivid images,** or word pictures, to help readers hear, see, taste, feel, and smell the setting, characters, and action in a story. They also use images to set a mood and tone. For example, the image of trees shimmering in the sun creates a pleasant mood, while trees thrashing in the wind creates a violent, frightening mood.

Think about vivid images as you read these sentences from the Student Model.

 **STUDENT MODEL** from **The Amazing Memory Man**
page 99; lines 37–39

"That night, there was a fire in the factory. Flames shot from the roof, and thick, black smoke poured from the windows..."

 Try It! Now, ask yourself these questions. Record your answers in your journal.

- Does the second sentence create a vivid picture of the scene for you? Why or why not?
- Would the second sentence be more engaging if it read "There were flames and smoke. They came out the windows."? Explain.

Fine-Tune Your Draft

Apply It! Use the revision suggestions to prepare your final draft **after rethinking how well questions of purpose, audience, and genre have been addressed**.

- **Ensure Vivid Images** Substitute vivid images for vague or boring words and phrases.
- **Confirm Consistent Point of View** Make sure that the same person, or voice, tells the whole story.
- **Check Internal and External Coherence** Make sure that ideas, sentences, and paragraphs are organized in a logical sequence and that they flow easily.

Peer Feedback Read your final draft to a group of peers. Ask if you have included **an engaging story line**. Think about their responses and revise your final draft as needed.

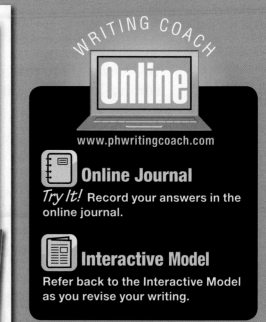

WRITING COACH

Online

www.phwritingcoach.com

Online Journal

Try It! Record your answers in the online journal.

Interactive Model

Refer back to the Interactive Model as you revise your writing.

Editing: Making It Correct

You may want to read through your work several times when editing, looking for different errors each time.

Before editing your draft, make sure each **pronoun** has a clear **antecedent,** or a clearly stated person, place, or thing that the pronoun later replaces.

WRITE GUY *Jeff Anderson, M. Ed.*

WHAT DO YOU NOTICE?

Zoom in on Conventions Focus on the use of pronouns as you read these lines from the Mentor Text.

 **MENTOR TEXT** from **How Paul Bunyan Cleared North Dakota** pages 95–96; lines 31–35, 71–72

> The Seven Axemen used great double-bitted axes that an ordinary man could not lift. When the axes became dull they would start a round, flat rock rolling down the hillside and run beside it holding the blades of their axes against the rock until they were sharp again…. The men did as Johnnie said. They covered the whole country with water.

To learn more about pronoun-antecedent agreement, see Chapter 23 of your Grammar Handbook.

Now ask yourself: *Which highlighted section of text contains a vague pronoun reference?*

- The first highlighted section of text contains two vague pronoun references. It is unclear as to whom or what the pronoun *they* is referring both times in the second sentence. The sentence should read: *When the axes became dull, the Axemen would start a round, flat rock rolling down the hillside and run beside it holding the blades of their axes against the rock until the blades were sharp again.* When the pronoun *they* is removed in both cases, it is clear who (the Axemen) is doing the action and what (the blades) is receiving the action.

- The second highlighted section of text has correct pronoun-antecedent usage. Since only one group of people, *the men,* is mentioned in the first sentence, the pronoun *they* clearly takes the place of that antecedent. There is no way that the pronoun could refer to any other group of people.

Grammar Mini-Lesson: Antecedents

To learn more, see Chapter 23.

In some complex sentences, a **relative pronoun** (*that, which, who, whom,* and *whose*) begins a subordinate clause that describes something in the main clause. For example: *She likes the cat* that *sits in the window*. Commonly, the **antecedent** comes right before the relative pronoun. Notice how the author uses a relative pronoun *(that)* and its antecedent *(job)* in the Mentor Text.

 **MENTOR TEXT** from **How Paul Bunyan Cleared North Dakota** page 94; lines 12–13

This was about the largest job that Paul ever attempted.

Try It! Underline each pronoun and identify its antecedent. If the pronoun-antecedent relationship is vague, then rewrite the sentence for clarity. Write the answers in your journal.

1. Janelle put the bowl on the table, and it immediately tipped over.
2. Janelle got out her sister's bowl, and she put it on the table.
3. Janelle put the bowl, which immediately tipped over, on the table.

Apply It! Edit your draft for **grammar, mechanics, and spelling.** Make sure that your **pronouns,** including relative pronouns, have correctly identified antecedents.

Use the rubric to evaluate your piece. If necessary, rethink, rewrite, or revise.

Rubric for Short Story: Tall Tale	Rating Scale					
Ideas: How well have you developed your characters and plot?	Not very					Very
	1	2	3	4	5	6
Organization: How clearly organized is the sequence of events in your story?	1	2	3	4	5	6
Voice: How well does your style engage the reader?	1	2	3	4	5	6
Word Choice: How effective is your word choice in creating vivid images?	1	2	3	4	5	6
Sentence Fluency: How well have you developed coherence in your writing?	1	2	3	4	5	6
Conventions: How correct are your pronouns and antecedents?	1	2	3	4	5	6

 Video
Learn effective editing techniques from program author Jeff Anderson.

www.phwritingcoach.com

 Online Journal
Try It! Record your answers in the online journal.

 Interactive Model
Refer back to the Interactive Model as you edit your writing.

Publishing

Share your tall tale with others by publishing it. First, get the story ready to present. Then choose a way to **publish your work for an appropriate audience.**

Wrap Up Your Presentation

Is your story handwritten or written on a computer? If your story is written on a computer, you may be tempted to choose a fancy or unusual font, or type style. Instead, make sure the font you choose is easily readable. Also be sure to add a title to your story.

Publish Your Piece

Use this chart to identify a way to publish your written work.

If your audience is...	...then publish it by...
Students or adults at your school	• Recording a dramatic reading of your story as a podcast and making it available for download • Submitting it to an online literary magazine for young people • Posting it to a Web site with illustrations and background sound effects
Younger children at the local library	• Making it into a puppet show • Drawing large, colorful illustrations to use as you read it aloud

 ## Reflect on Your Writing

Now that you are done with your tall tale, read it over and use your writing journal to answer the following questions. Use specific details to describe and explain your reflections. Increase the specificity of your details based on the type of information requested.

- What do you like best about your final story? Explain.
- What might you do differently the next time you write? Why?
- What purpose do you think tall tales serve? Explain.

 The Big Question: Why Write? What can fiction do better than nonfiction?

Manage Your Portfolio You may wish to include your published tall tale in your writing portfolio. If so, consider what this piece reveals about your writing and your growth as a writer.

MAKE YOUR WRITING COUNT

Make a Comic Book Based on a Tall Tale

Tall tales are stories about larger-than-life characters. Many comic books contain elements of tall tales, complete with heroic characters, comical dialogue, and adventure. Tell a tall tale in comic-book form.

As a group, produce a **comic book** as a **multimedia presentation.** A multimedia presentation blends text, graphics, and sound. Present your comic book by reading it aloud while showing the printed pages or by using presentation software, including audio files.

Here's your action plan.

1. Choose roles, such as artist, writer, reader, and editor.

2. Review your peers' tall tales and choose one as the basis for your comic book.

3. Identify the scenes to illustrate. Your comic should include the following:

   - A series of drawings, or frames, that illustrate the characters and action
   - Speech bubbles with dialogue
   - Narrative text containing background or description, below each frame

4. Conduct online research to learn how to use technology to create or publish comic books.

5. Check your comic book for layout and edit the text.

6. Present each member of the class with a copy of your comic so they can follow along as you read it aloud, or share the comic using presentation software.

Listening and Speaking As a group, practice your presentation. Give one another feedback on volume, pacing, and tone. Use specific details to describe and explain your ideas. Increase the specificity of your details based on the type of information requested or that you are delivering. Whether you record your comic book's sound elements or give a live presentation to the class, keep your peers' feedback in mind.

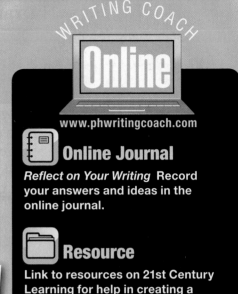

WRITING COACH

Online

www.phwritingcoach.com

Online Journal

Reflect on Your Writing Record your answers and ideas in the online journal.

Resource

Link to resources on 21st Century Learning for help in creating a group project.

**Writing for Media:
Dramatic Scene**

Dramatic Scene

A **dramatic scene** is a story written to be performed by actors on stage or on film. The purpose of a dramatic scene is generally to entertain. Dramatic scenes are written as scripts, with lines for each character and stage directions telling actors how to speak and move. Like other stories, they have a setting, characters, plot, and well-paced action.

Try It! Study the example of a dramatic scene. Then, answer these questions. Record your answers in your journal.

1. At what **audience** is this scene most likely aimed?

2. Is the story line of "The Bell of the Ball" engaging? Explain why or why not.

3. What is the **purpose** of "The Bell of the Ball"?

4. How would you describe the **pace of the action**?

5. Which **character** is most interesting to you? Why?

Extension Find another example of a dramatic scene, and compare it with this one.

The Bell of the Ball

[Two cats are wildly batting a ball around the floor. The ball has a loud, annoying bell in it. It creates quite a racket. A sleepy old dog lies in the corner, with one eye open, watching the game.]

CAT 1. It's MY ball! [hits it with his paw. It bounces off a chair leg.]

CAT 2. [chasing the ball] NO! It's mine!

[Dog groans and tries to get comfortable.]

CAT 1. Mine, from my birthday. [slams the ball under the table]

CAT 2. [gets the ball and slides it into the kitchen] That was my birthday! It's MY ball.

[Dog snorts.]

CAT 1. [from the kitchen. The bell jingles wildly.] Well if it's yours, how come I have it now?

CAT 2. [hissing and screeching, dashes into kitchen] MINE!!

[Dog looks up.]

CAT 2. [slams the ball. It bounces off the wall and toward the corner where the dog is.] Ha ha! You can't get it!

DOG. [matter-of-factly opens huge jaws. Ball rolls right into his mouth. Makes swallowing sound.] Glmph.

Create a Dramatic Scene

Follow these steps to create your own dramatic scene. To plan your dramatic scene, review the graphic organizers on pages R24–R27 and choose one that suits your needs.

Prewriting

- Identify and narrow a topic. Then think about your target audience. What reaction do you want them to have?

- Invent characters for your scene. Think about how they talk. How will what they say define their character?

- Invent a setting for your scene. What will the setting look like? Think about how the setting is important to the story.

- Outline the story line, the beginning, middle, and end of your scene. What is the main conflict and how will it be resolved?

Drafting

- Use a script form to draft your scene.

- Draft an opening that grabs your audience.

- Introduce the characters and create a specific, believable setting.

- Develop an engaging story line with well-paced action through the beginning, middle, and end.

- Use a range of literary strategies and devices, such as dialogue and suspense, to enhance the style and tone.

Revising and Editing

- Review your draft to make sure events are organized logically. Make sure the conflict, or problem, is clear.

- Use the Revision RADaR strategy to improve your draft.

- Check that spelling, grammar, and mechanics are correct.

Publishing

- Read through your scene with classmates, and then rehearse the scene and perform it for the class.

- You may also want to record your performance using video and post it on an Internet video site. You can also post a link to your video on a social networking site.

WRITING COACH

Online

www.phwritingcoach.com

 **Online Journal**

Try It! Record your answers in the online journal.

Interactive Graphic Organizers

Choose from a variety of graphic organizers to plan and develop your project.

Partner Talk

Before you start drafting, describe your dramatic scene to a partner. Ask for feedback about your ideas. For example, will your story hold readers' interest? Monitor your partner's spoken language by asking follow-up questions to confirm your understanding.

Writing for Assessment

Use these prompts to practice writing short stories on demand.
Make sure your responses include the characteristics on page 92.

Try It! Read the **short story** prompt and the information on
format and academic vocabulary. Then write a tall tale by following
instructions in the ABCDs of On-Demand Writing.

Format

The prompt directs you to
write a *short story*. Begin by
introducing the characters
and conflict, develop the
plot in the middle, and tell
how the conflict turned out
in the end.

Short Story Prompt

Write an imaginative short story set
in the past about a character who created
a certain landform, such as the Rocky
Mountains or the Colorado River. Use
dialogue and other literary devices in
your story.

Academic Vocabulary

Remember that *dialogue*
is conversation between
characters. A *literary device*
is a technique, such as
metaphor, that creates
meaning.

The ABCDs of On-Demand Writing

Use the following ABCDs to help you respond to the prompt.

Before you write your draft:

Ⓐttack the prompt [1 MINUTE]

- Circle or highlight important verbs in the prompt. Draw a line
  from the verb to what it refers to.
- Rewrite the prompt in your own words.

Ⓑrainstorm possible answers [4 MINUTES]

- Create a graphic organizer to generate ideas.
- Use one for each part of the prompt if necessary.

Ⓒhoose the order of your response [1 MINUTE]

- Think about the best way to organize your ideas.
- Number your ideas in the order you will write about them.
  Cross out ideas you will not be using.

After you write your draft:

Ⓓetect errors before turning in the draft [1 MINUTE]

- Carefully reread your writing.
- Make sure that your response makes sense and is complete.
- Look for spelling, punctuation, and grammar errors.

More Prompts for Practice

Apply It! Respond to Prompts 1 and 2 by writing imaginative **short stories** that **sustain the reader's interest**. As you write, be sure to:

- Identify an **appropriate audience**
- Establish a clear **plot focus**
- Develop logical and **well-paced action** and an **engaging story line**
- Create a specific, believable **setting** through the use of **sensory details**
- Develop **interesting characters**
- Use **literary strategies and devices** to enhance your **style and tone**

> **Prompt 1** Write a short story about a character who has a unique pet that helps the character achieve greatness. Develop an engaging story with a cohesive plot through beginning, middle, and end.

> **Prompt 2** Write a short story about a character who suddenly discovers that he or she has super powers. What does the character decide to do with his or her powers?

Spiral Review: Narrative Respond to Prompt 3 by writing a **diary entry**. Make sure your diary entry reflects all of the characteristics described on page 66, including:

- A clearly defined focus
- Reflections on **decisions** and their consequences
- Reflections on **actions** and their consequences

> **Prompt 3** Think about a day that you will never forget. It could have been a great day or an awful day, a funny day or a touching day. Write a diary entry about that day. Use your narrative skills to tell why the day is so memorable.

WRITING COACH

Online

www.phwritingcoach.com

Interactive Writing Coach™

Plan your response to the prompt. If you are using the prompt for practice, write one paragraph at a time or your entire draft and then submit it for feedback. If you are using the prompt as a timed test, write your entire draft and then submit it for feedback.

Remember **ABCD**

Attack the prompt

Brainstorm possible answers

Choose the order of your response

Detect errors before turning in the draft

CHAPTER 7

POETRY *and* DESCRIPTION

What Do You See?

People see different things when they look at something. Some people may look at this photograph and see cars. Others may look at it and see excitement or courage.

People also use different words to describe what they see. Words can be a powerful way to capture a moment or feeling.

Try It! Describe the photograph. Remember, you might describe the actual image or you might describe how it makes you feel.

Take notes as you consider these questions. Then participate in an extended discussion with a partner. Take turns expressing your ideas and feelings.

- What do you actually see?
- What emotions does this photograph make you feel?
- What would you feel if you were at the race?

Review the notes you wrote. Use your notes to write a paragraph about what you see in this photograph.

What's Ahead

In this chapter, you will review some strong examples of poems: Mentor Texts and Student Models. Then, using the examples as guidance, you will write a poem of your own.

WRITING COACH

Online

www.phwritingcoach.com

Online Journal

Try It! Record your answers and ideas in the online journal.

You can also record and save your answers and ideas on pop-up sticky notes in the eText.

Connect to the Big Questions

Discuss these questions with your partner:

1 What do you think? What makes an experience memorable?

2 Why write? How do we best convey feelings through words on a page?

POETRY AND DESCRIPTION

In this chapter, you will focus on writing a poem. Poetry uses language in imaginative and musical ways to express ideas and feelings. Poems are shorter than most other written works, and so poets must choose their words carefully. Description is vital to poetry, as it is to most other kinds of writing. Sensory details and vivid, precise language help readers see, hear, smell, taste, or feel what the writer wants to share with them.

You will develop a poem by taking it through each stage of the writing process: prewriting, drafting, revising, editing, and publishing. To preview the criteria for how your poem will be evaluated, see the rubric on page 137. You will also have an opportunity to write a blog entry that is a profile of a natural place.

FEATURE ASSIGNMENT

Poem

An effective poem has these characteristics:

- A specific **focus** on a subject—an event, idea, person, place, or thing

- **Poetic techniques** that create a powerful poem

- **Figurative language** that creates imaginative descriptions

- **Graphic elements** that strengthen the poem's meaning

- Precise **word choice** and **vivid imagery** that allow the reader to see what the poet describes

- **Effective sentence structure** and correct spelling, grammar, and usage

A lyric poem also has these characteristics:

- A strong focus on the poet's feelings about the subject

- No specific form—free verse, or a more structured form with rhyme and meter

A free verse poem also has these characteristics:

- Language meant to reflect the patterns of natural speech

- No specific meter or rhyme scheme

- No specific length

Forms of Poetry and Description

There are many forms of poetry and description, including:

Ballads are poems that tell stories and are often meant to be sung. Ballads have a rhyme scheme and use meter, or a strong, regular rhythm.

Descriptive essays use precise images and details to help readers imagine a person, place, thing, or event. Like all essays, they include an introduction, body, and conclusion.

Free verse is poetry that imitates the rhythms of everyday speech. Freed of set rhythm and rhyme patterns, free verse uses figurative language and sound devices to convey ideas and feelings.

Haiku are three-line poems that originated in Japan. The first and last lines of haiku have five syllables, while the middle line has seven syllables.

Lyric poems are poems expressing the speaker's feelings about a certain person, place, thing, or event. Lyric poems can use rhyme and meter or can be free verse.

Prose poems look like prose (the text that you would find in a story or essay), but use poetic techniques to create memorable descriptions.

Sonnets are highly structured 14-line poems. One type, the English sonnet, is made up of three four-line stanzas and a final couplet, or two rhyming lines. In each stanza, alternating lines rhyme.

Try It! For each audience and purpose described, choose a poetic form, such as a sonnet or ballad, that is appropriate for conveying your intended meaning to the audience. Explain your choices.

- To describe to other travelers a place you once visited
- To tell your parents on a special family occasion how much they mean to you
- To tell classmates the story of a well-known event, using verse

WRITING COACH

Online

www.phwritingcoach.com

Resource

Word Bank Listen to English and Spanish pronunciations of new words in the eText glossary.

Online Journal

Try It! Record your answers and ideas in the online journal.

WORD BANK

People often use these basic and content-based vocabulary words when they talk about poetic or descriptive writing. Work with a partner. Take turns saying each word aloud. Then write one sentence using each word. If you are unsure of the meaning of a word, use the Glossary or a dictionary to check the definition.

convey	repetition
emotion	rhythm
precise	technique

MENTOR TEXT

Free Verse and Lyric Poems

Learn From Experience

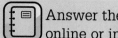 After reading the free verse and lyric poems on pages 122–123, read the numbered notes in the margins to learn about how the poets presented their ideas.

Answer the *Try It!* questions online or in your notebook.

---

1 The **precise word choice** creates **vivid images** of the speaker's childhood. **Figurative language** adds to the effect.

Try It! How does the poem's literal and figurative language affect the reader?

2 The poet uses **graphic elements** to draw attention to three phrases by indenting them.

Try It! Read aloud lines 25–27. How does the position of the phrases on the page affect the way you read them?

3 In the last line of the poem, the tone changes from light and happy to serious. The serious tone reveals the speaker's **feelings** about growing older.

Try It! How does the speaker feel about growing older? Explain.

Extension Find other examples of poems, and compare them with these.

Old Man

by Jimmy Santiago Baca

1 My heart was once an elementary
school-building hall
during class change, filled
with a hundred excited voices.
5 Fragrance of soap on my cheeks,
t-shirt blue jelly spotted, I ran
to see evening softball games,
whiffing scent of rain in the air.
The earth smelled of the new pair
10 of shoes mother wore
as we stood in our driveway
and waved at father
roaring away in his bright red Mack,
gone for another
15 three-week haul.

Each tree was a green lit window
I used as a marker when walking in the dark, when
I stayed out too late, and found myself alone.

Earth was a mask, breathing
20 through small holes in rocks, alive,
and each evening mist swirled out dialogues
of eternities I would live.
Dawn was a white soaring torch,
that left my name a fossil
25 **2**   as I became a wheel,
                                    a lizard,
                                    a roadrunner—

3 I do not want to become an old man.

April Rain Song

by Langston Hughes

Let the rain kiss you
4 Let the rain beat upon your head with silver liquid drops
Let the rain sing you a lullaby
The rain makes still pools on the sidewalk
5 The rain makes running pools in the gutter
The rain plays a little sleep song on our roof at night
5 And I love the rain.

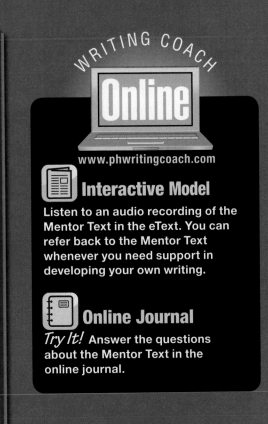

WRITING COACH

Online

www.phwritingcoach.com

Interactive Model

Listen to an audio recording of the Mentor Text in the eText. You can refer back to the Mentor Text whenever you need support in developing your own writing.

Online Journal

Try It! Answer the questions about the Mentor Text in the online journal.

4 The **vivid imagery** and precise **word choice** help create a picture of the rain.

Try It! To which of the fives senses do these images appeal? What feelings do they create in you as you read them? Explain.

5 The statement in the last line shows the speaker's **feelings** about rain.

Try It! Which words and phrases in the poem show and support the speaker's statement? Explain.

STUDENT MODEL

Free Verse and Lyric Poems

With a small group, take turns reading each Student Model aloud. As you read, practice newly acquired vocabulary by correctly producing the word's sound. You may also want to take a look at the Poet's Toolbox on page 129. Look for evidence in the poem to support your understanding.

Use a Reader's Eye

Now, reread the Student Models. On your copy of the Student Models, use the Reader's Response Symbols to react to what you read.

Reader's Response Symbols

+ **I can picture this.**

− **This image could be stronger.**

? **I wonder what this means.**

! **This is cool!**

Express your opinions, ideas, and feelings about the Student Models to a partner. Discuss responses that were the same for both of you, as well as responses that were different.

The Bluest Blue

A free verse poem by Jaqui Nguyen

The bluest blue I've ever seen was this flower,
    lobelia.
You usually spot them on the edges of gardens,
    glowing blue carpets in front of taller blooms.
5 The blossoms are small and delicate, but
    there's nothing delicate about that color.
Intense blue—
    deep, but not all the way to purple.
They are so blue,
10   they almost shine like water.
If lobelia had a scent,
    it would be the smell of blueberry
    muffins, hot from the oven.
If they made a sound,
15   it would be a long, sweet blues
    note from a clarinet.
But lobelia don't make a sound or have a smell.
They just concentrate, super hard,
    on being blue
20   blue
    blue.

1

Memory Sparks

A lyric poem by Jake Melendez

When I was young, one winter night,
I heard a fireplace log go *SNAP*—
So loud it gave me such a fright
And woke my grandpa from his nap.
5   I jumped, but Lito said to me,
"That noise comes from a sunny day
Felt long ago by the living tree—
A beam of sunlight stored away.
Just as this log recalls the sun,
10   So we recall our own bright days,
And even when a good time's done,
Its happy memory stays and stays."
And now I know what Lito knew:
That something good is never lost.
15   We keep its memory strong and true,
       A sunbeam in a time of frost.

2

WRITING COACH

Online

www.phwritingcoach.com

Interactive Model

Listen to an audio recording of the Student Models in the eText. Use the Reader's and Writer's Response Symbols with the eText tools to note what you read.

Use a Writer's Eye

Now, evaluate each poem as a writer. On your copies of the Student Models, use the Writer's Response Symbols to react to what you read. Identify places where the student writers use characteristics of an effective poem.

Writer's Response Symbols

R.R. Rhythm or rhyme (if present) fits poem's form

S.D. Effective use of sound devices

F.L. Figurative language conveys a mood

I.D. Images and details appeal to the senses

Prewriting

Plan a first draft of your poem by deciding which form of poetry
you want to write—a free verse, lyric, or other type of poem. Then,
choose an appropriate topic. Select a topic from the Topic Bank
or come up with an idea of your own.

Choose From the Topic Bank

TOPIC BANK

American Role Model Write a poem to describe someone from
the United States, from the present or past, whom you see as a
good role model for today's young people.

Family Member or Caretaker Write a poem about a member of
your family or someone else who takes care of you. Describe this
person so that even readers can picture him or her.

The Place Where You Live Write a poem to describe the place
where you live. Your poem might focus on just one aspect of the
place, or it may give readers an overall impression of it.

Choose Your Own Topic

Determine an appropriate topic on your own by using the
following **range of strategies** to generate ideas.

Brainstorm, Trade, and Read

- Work with a partner to brainstorm for possible subjects for your
  poem. List people, places, natural features, events, and objects.
- Trade lists with your partner. Circle the topics on his or her list
  that interest you. Then, read your own list again to see what
  your partner liked. Star the topics that seem the most promising.
- Look through a literature book or poetry collection to get ideas
  from topics published poets chose.

Review your responses and choose a topic.

Narrow Your Topic

Effective poems are concentrated and focused. Narrow your topic to help you find something you can describe in precise detail.

Apply It! Use a graphic organizer like the one shown to narrow your topic.

- Write your general topic in the top box, and keep narrowing your topic as you move down the chart.

- Your last box should hold your narrowest or "smallest" topic—the focus of your poem.

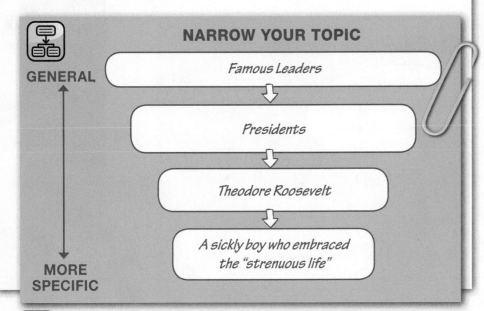

NARROW YOUR TOPIC

GENERAL

Famous Leaders

Presidents

Theodore Roosevelt

A sickly boy who embraced the "strenuous life"

MORE SPECIFIC

 # Consider Your Audience and Purpose

Before writing your poem, think about your audience and purpose. Consider the views of others as you ask yourself these questions.

Questions for Audience	Questions for Purpose
• Who will read my poem? My teacher? My classmates? A family member? Someone else? • What will my readers need to know to understand my poem?	• Why am I writing? Do I want to entertain my readers, share an idea or feeling, or achieve some other purpose? • What kinds of poetic techniques will help me fulfill my purpose?

Record your answers in your writing journal.

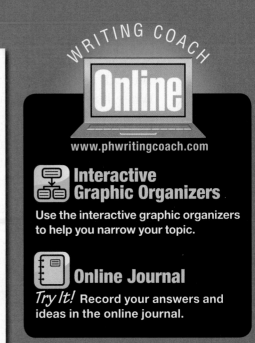

WRITING COACH

Online

www.phwritingcoach.com

Interactive Graphic Organizers

Use the interactive graphic organizers to help you narrow your topic.

Online Journal

Try It! Record your answers and ideas in the online journal.

Plan Your Poem

You will use a graphic organizer like this one to develop your ideas. When it is complete, you will be ready to write your first draft.

Develop Ideas To focus your poem, go over your notes and choose the central idea or emotion that best fulfills your purpose. Then, write a clear statement of your topic, theme, or controlling idea in the graphic organizer.

Express Ideas Use the graphic organizer to identify ideas, feelings, and sensory details about sights, sounds, tastes, smells, and touch. Choose the details that best communicate your topic.

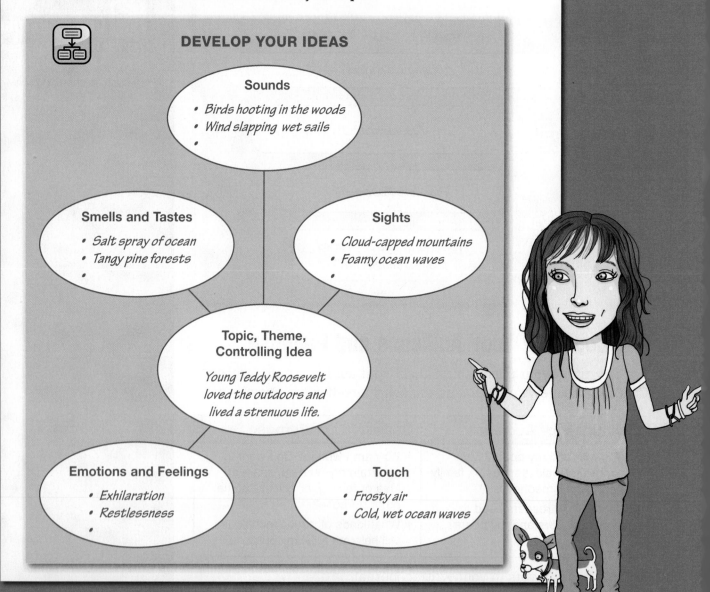

DEVELOP YOUR IDEAS

Sounds
- Birds hooting in the woods
- Wind slapping wet sails

Smells and Tastes
- Salt spray of ocean
- Tangy pine forests

Sights
- Cloud-capped mountains
- Foamy ocean waves

Topic, Theme, Controlling Idea

Young Teddy Roosevelt loved the outdoors and lived a strenuous life.

Emotions and Feelings
- Exhilaration
- Restlessness

Touch
- Frosty air
- Cold, wet ocean waves

Poet's Toolbox

Poets **use a variety of poetic techniques, figurative language, and graphic elements** like these to make their ideas vivid and clear.

Figurative Language is writing that means something beyond what the words actually say.	
Simile: comparison using *like* or *as*	*Like a young wolf, Teddy Roosevelt roamed the woods.*
Metaphor: comparison made by saying that one thing is something else	*The forest was his library.*
Personification: human characteristics applied to non-human objects	*The mountains called to Teddy.*
Symbols add depth and insight to poetry.	
An object that stands for something else	*To Teddy, the birds were symbols of freedom.*
Sound Devices create a musical or emotional effect.	
Alliteration: repetition of consonant sounds at the beginning of nearby words	***W**aves **w**ashed and **s**prayed the **s**ails of the **b**oy's **b**oat.*
Assonance: repetition of vowel sounds in nearby words	*He **would** have lived in the **woods** if he **could**.*
Consonance: repetition of consonants in the middle or at the end of words	*He woul**d** have live**d** in the woo**ds** if he coul**d**.*
Structural Elements help build the framework for poetic language.	
Rhyme: repetition of sounds at the ends of lines of poetry	*Young **Teddy learned a lesson we** should **know**.* *Each challenge makes our spirits **grow!***
Meter: rhythmical pattern of a poem. It is determined by stressed syllables in a line. Some forms of poetry have specific patterns of stressed syllables.	*Young **Ted**dy **learned** a **les**son **we** should **know**.* (Stressed syllables in poetry are marked with a ´, while unstressed syllables are marked with a ˘.)
Graphic Elements position the words on the page.	
Arrangement of words on a page	capital letters, line spacing, and line breaks

Apply It! Review the ideas and details you added to your prewriting graphic organizer. Decide what techniques from the Poet's Toolbox you would like to use in your poem.

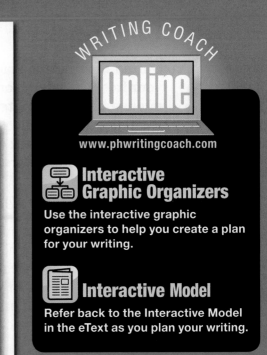

WRITING COACH
Online
www.phwritingcoach.com

Interactive Graphic Organizers
Use the interactive graphic organizers to help you create a plan for your writing.

Interactive Model
Refer back to the Interactive Model in the eText as you plan your writing.

Drafting

During the drafting stage, you will start to write your ideas for your free verse, lyric, or other type of poem you choose. First, **choose an appropriate organizational strategy** based on the form of poem you choose to write. Then, **build on the ideas** that you developed in your graphic organizer to write a **focused, organized,** and **coherent** poem.

Drafting a Free Verse Poem or Lyric Poem

Each poetic form has specific characteristics, or details that are specific to the form. You will write your poem using these characteristics, the techniques from the Poet's Toolbox, and the notes you developed in your graphic organizer. These charts give the characteristics of each form. Review the characteristics. Then, answer the questions in the right column as you draft your poem.

Free Verse Poem Characteristics	Questions to Answer While Drafting
• Number of lines varies • Number of stanzas varies • No meter is used; follows natural patterns of speech • Rhyme not often used • Poetic techniques used • Feelings or emotions conveyed • Story or narrative may be developed • Vivid descriptions presented	• How long do I want my poem to be? **Tip:** You do not have to decide upon an *exact* number of stanzas and lines right now. • What poetic techniques and sound devices will I use? • What feelings or emotions will I express? • How will I make my descriptions vivid?

Lyric Poem Characteristics	Questions to Answer While Drafting
• Number of lines varies • Stanzas may be used, but they are not required • Rhyme scheme may be used, but it is not required • Meter (regular rhythm) may be used, but it is not required • Poetic techniques used • Feelings or emotions conveyed • Vivid descriptions presented	• How many lines will I write? Will I use stanzas? • How will I position various lines and words? • What feelings or emotions will I express? • How will I make my descriptions vivid? • Will my poem rhyme? If so, what words will I rhyme in each stanza? **Tip:** Consult a rhyming dictionary and thesaurus. • Will my poem use a regular meter? **Tip:** Try out different rhythms as you write. If you have a beat in mind, you will find it easier to write lines that fit it. • What poetic techniques will I use?

Start Your Draft

Writing poetry is different than creating most other genres. The process is more open. Use the graphic organizer that shows your topic, ideas, and sensory details, and the Poet's Toolbox as guides, but be ready to experiment with your draft.

While developing your poem, aim at writing your ideas, not on making your writing perfect. Remember, you will have the chance to improve your poem when you revise and edit.

WRITING COACH

Online

www.phwritingcoach.com

Interactive Model
Refer back to the Mentor Text in the eText as you write your draft.

Before You Write

√ Choose the **poetic form** you want to use—free verse poem, lyric poem, or another poetic form.

√ Review the **poetic traditions** of your poetic form that are listed in Drafting a Free Verse Poem or Lyric Poem. Make sure you use these characteristics when you write your draft.

√ State or imply the **theme, topic,** or **controlling idea.** It does not have to be apparent in each line, but it should be clear in the poem as a whole.

√ Include your ideas from prewriting. If a feeling, emotion, sensory detail, or other idea does not seem to work, you may decide not to keep it in your poem.

While You Write

√ Use **poetic techniques** to support your ideas. If a technique does not seem to work, try another.

√ Use **figurative language,** such as similes, metaphors, and personification, in your poem. Figurative language will keep your writing interesting.

√ Use **sensory details** in your poem, to make your poem come alive to your readers.

√ Use **graphic elements,** such as line and stanza breaks, to signal changes in ideas.

Revising: Making It Better

Now that you have finished your draft, you are ready to revise. Think about the "big picture" of **audience, purpose, and genre.** You can use Revision RADaR as a guide for making changes to improve your draft. Revision RADaR provides four major ways to improve your writing: (R) replace, (A) add, (D) delete, and (R) reorder.

Kelly Gallagher, M. Ed.

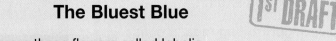

KEEP REVISION ON YOUR RADAR

Read part of the first draft of the Student Model "The Bluest Blue." Then look at questions the writer asked herself as she thought about how well her draft addressed issues of audience, purpose, and genre.

The Bluest Blue

1ST DRAFT

There are these flowers called lobelia.

You usually spot them on the edges of gardens.

Blue carpets in front of taller blooms.

The blossoms are small and delicate, but

there's nothing delicate about that color.

They are so blue,

they almost shine like water.

Intense blue—

deep, but not all the way to purple.

> *Did I state or hint at my **central idea or feeling?***

> *Does this **description** help my audience picture what I'm writing about?*

> *Does the order of these lines develop my **central idea or feeling?***

Now look at how the writer applied Revision RADaR to write an improved second draft.

The Bluest Blue

2ND DRAFT

The bluest blue I've ever seen was this
    flower, lobelia.
You usually spot them on the
    edges of gardens,
    glowing blue carpets in front of taller
    blooms.
The blossoms are small and delicate, but
    there's nothing delicate about that color.
    Intense blue—
    deep, but not all the way to purple.
They are so blue,
    they almost shine like water.

R *Replaced the first line to establish the idea of the bluest blue right away*

A *Added the sensory detail <u>glowing</u> to strengthen my image*

A *Reordered these lines to better develop my central idea by ending the stanza with the dramatic image of flowers shining like water*

WRITING COACH

Online

www.phwritingcoach.com

Video

Learn more strategies for effective writing from program author Kelly Gallagher.

Apply It! Now, revise your draft after rethinking how well questions of **purpose, audience, and genre have been addressed.**

- First, reread your poem and determine whether you have used **poetic techniques, figurative language,** and **graphic elements** effectively to express your ideas and feelings.

- Then apply your Revision RADaR to make needed changes. Focus especially on revising to **ensure precise word choice** and **vivid images.** Remember—you can use the steps in Revision RADaR in any order.

Look at the Big Picture

Use the chart and your analytical skills to evaluate how well each section of your poem **addresses purpose, audience, and genre.** When necessary, use the suggestions in the chart to revise your poem.

	Evaluate	Revise
Topic and Sensory Details	• Check that your **controlling idea** or theme is clear.	• Identify the idea or feeling you want most to convey. Add a word, phrase, or image to emphasize your theme.
	• Make sure that your **sensory details** all support the controlling idea or theme.	• Replace sensory details that do not support the controlling idea with new details that help paint a clearer picture.
	• Consider your **audience**. Who will be reading the poem?	• Adapt your language to your audience.
Poetic Techniques	• Check your usage of the poetic techniques **meter** and rhyme, if you have decided to include them.	• Use a rhyming dictionary to find better rhymes. Tap out the rhythm and reorder words to fix any awkward spots.
	• Make sure to include effective **sound devices**.	• Read your poem aloud. Then use a dictionary or thesaurus to find words to substitute to create better assonance or alliteration.
	• Make sure your **figurative language** and word choices help convey your meaning and purpose.	• Replace boring or vague words with figurative language, vivid words, and sensory details.
Graphic Elements	• Check that your **stanzas** are a good length for your rhyme, meter, and meaning.	• If you are writing free verse, make sure the stanza divisions, line breaks, and positions of words help express your meaning.

Focus on Craft: Vivid Images

Imagery is writing that appeals directly to the senses of sight, hearing, smell, taste, and touch. **Vivid images** enable readers to connect more powerfully with what the writer is describing. The best images are original and precise, fresh and unexpected. Carefully chosen images can enhance the mood of descriptive writing. Consider the difference between a voice like "scratchy sandpaper" and one like "a crystal bell."

Think about the use of vivid images as you read these lines from the Student Model.

 **STUDENT MODEL** from **The Bluest Blue,** page 124, lines 11–16

> If lobelia had a scent,
>   it would be the smell of blueberry
>   muffins, hot from the oven.
> If they made a sound,
>   it would be a long sweet blues
>   note from a clarinet.

 Try It! Now, ask yourself these questions:

- What image of the lobelia is created in the first three lines?
- How would your impression of the lobelia change if the last three lines of the stanza read: "If they made a sound, it would be the sound of distant thunder"?

Fine-Tune Your Draft

Apply It! Use the revision suggestions to prepare your final draft.

- **Use Poetic Devices** Use **precise word choice** to add **figurative language** and **vivid images** that will replace words and phrases that do not enhance the poem.
- **Fine-Tune Graphic Elements** Make sure that the line and stanza breaks keep your meaning clear.

Teacher Feedback Read your poem aloud to your teacher. Ask if you have created vivid images. Think about your teacher's response and revise your final draft as needed.

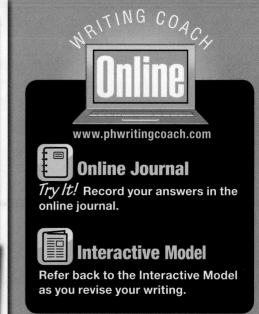

WRITING COACH

Online

www.phwritingcoach.com

Online Journal
Try It! Record your answers in the online journal.

Interactive Model
Refer back to the Interactive Model as you revise your writing.

Editing: Making It Correct

Editing your draft means polishing your work and correcting errors. You may want to read through your work several times, looking for different errors and issues each time.

As you edit your work, think about your use of **participial, appositive, adjectival,** and **adverbial phrases.** Keep in mind that these phrases act as modifiers and help to create vivid images. Then, edit your draft by correcting any errors in **grammar, mechanics, and spelling.**

WRITE GUY *Jeff Anderson, M. Ed.*

WHAT DO YOU NOTICE?

Zoom in on Conventions Focus on phrases as you zoom in on these lines from the Mentor Text.

> To learn more about phrases as modifiers, see Chapter 19 of your Grammar Handbook.

 **MENTOR TEXT** | from **Old Man**
page 122; lines 6, 12–13

and waved at father
roaring away in his bright red Mack,…

Earth was a mask, breathing through small holes in rocks…

Now, ask yourself: *How do the highlighted phrases make the writing more vivid?*

Perhaps you said that the phrases add descriptive details.

The second line contains a **participial phrase** beginning with the participle *roaring*. A participle is a verb form that is often used as an adjective. A participial phrase is a group of words that starts with a participle and acts as an adjective in a sentence. The participial phrase *roaring away in his bright red Mack* modifies *father*.

Also notice in the third and fourth lines the **participial phrase** beginning with the participle *breathing*. This participial phrase modifies *Earth*.

Partner Talk Discuss this question with a partner: *Why do you think the author included descriptive phrases in these sentences?*

Grammar Mini-Lesson: Phrases as Modifiers

An **adjectival phrase** is a prepositional phrase that modifies a noun or pronoun. An **adverbial phrase** is a prepositional phrase that modifies a verb, an adjective, or an adverb. Both kinds of phrases can create vivid images. Notice how the prepositional phrases act as modifiers in the Student Model.

 **STUDENT MODEL** from **Memory Sparks**
page 125; lines 6, 16

> "That noise comes from a sunny day...
>
> A sunbeam in a time of frost.

Try It! Use each italicized phrase in a sentence so that it functions as indicated in each numbered item. Write the sentences in your journal.

1. participial phrase: *sweating under the noon sun*
2. appositive phrase: *the smartest student in school*
3. adjectival phrase: *in the dentist's office*
4. adverbial phrase: *over the high wall*

Apply It! Edit your draft for **grammar, mechanics, and spelling.** Make sure you have placed modifying phrases close to the words they modify.

Use the rubric to evaluate your piece. If necessary, rethink, rewrite, or revise.

Rubric for Poetry: Free Verse or Lyric Poem	Rating Scale
Ideas: How well do your ideas develop your poem's subject or controlling idea?	Not very Very 1 2 3 4 5 6
Organization: How clearly are your ideas organized?	1 2 3 4 5 6
Voice: How effectively do you use figurative language and poetic techniques to create a unique voice?	1 2 3 4 5 6
Word Choice: How vivid are the images your words create?	1 2 3 4 5 6
Sentence Fluency: How effective is the rhythm and sound of your poem?	1 2 3 4 5 6
Conventions: How correct is your punctuation, capitalization, and spelling for the form you have chosen?	1 2 3 4 5 6

To learn more, see Chapter 19.

WRITING COACH

 Online

www.phwritingcoach.com

 Video
Learn effective editing techniques from program author Jeff Anderson.

 Online Journal
Try It! Record your answers in the online journal.

Interactive Model
Refer back to the Interactive Model as you edit your writing.

Publishing

A poem is meant to be shared with others. First, get your poem ready for presentation. Then, choose a way to **publish your work for appropriate audiences**.

Wrap Up Your Presentation

Is your poem handwritten or written on a computer? If it is handwritten, you may need to make a new, clean copy. If so, be sure to **write legibly**. Also be sure that your title grabs the reader's attention and indicates your poem's topic.

Publish Your Piece

Use this chart to help you find a way to publish your poem.

If your audience is...	...then publish it by...
Members of your family	• Making a video recording of yourself reading it, adding images or music, and creating DVD copies for each family member • Printing out copies for each family member, and sending them through the mail to surprise them
Teachers and classmates at your school	• Putting together a student anthology, and printing, illustrating, and distributing it • Posting it on a class or school blog

 ## Reflect on Your Writing

Now that you have finished your poem, read it over and use your writing journal to answer these questions.

- Do you feel that your poem accurately expresses your feelings about your topic? Explain.
- Which images do you think are the most vivid? Which ones are weaker? How can you improve your images next time?
- How does writing a poem help you appreciate other poets' work?

The Big Question: Why Write? How do we best convey feeling through words on a page?

Manage Your Portfolio You may wish to include your published poem in your writing portfolio. If so, consider what it reveals about your writing and your growth as a writer.

MAKE YOUR WRITING COUNT

Turn a Poem Into a Music Video

Poetry uses language to express feelings. Many poems are set to music and turned into songs. Express your feelings and moods in a creative new way by using a poem as the basis for a **music video**.

With a group, choose one of your peers' poems to turn into a music video. Set the poem to music. Then, create a storyboard—a series of sketches showing the visual elements of each video scene. Share your music "video" in a live or video-recorded **multimedia presentation** including sound, the poems' text, and graphics.

Here's your action plan.

1. Choose roles, such as writer, composer, director, and performers.

2. With your group, analyze the mood and language in your poems. Choose one to turn into a music video.

3. Compose music or choose a familiar song that suits the poem. Record the song, if possible.

4. Find example storyboards online. Then, create one, including:

   - Sketches of each frame, or scene
   - Text under each frame to explain the action or visuals and note the corresponding lyrics

5. Practice performing the actions shown in the storyboard, with music. If your storyboard calls for still images, figure out how to include them in the recorded or live performances.

6. Present your performance of the music "video" as an actual video, or perform it live for the class or school.

Listening and Speaking As you rehearse your video, work together to provide feedback to the group about volume, pacing, tone, and gestures. Incorporate the feedback you received during rehearsal as you record your video or perform it live. If you are performing the "video" in a live presentation, be sure to share the storyboard with your class.

WRITING COACH

Online

www.phwritingcoach.com

Online Journal

Reflect on Your Writing Record your answers and ideas in the online journal.

Resource

Link to resources on 21st Century Learning for help in creating a group project.

Your Turn

**Writing for Media:
Profile of a Natural Place**

Profile of a Natural Place

21st Century Learning

A **profile of a natural place** is a type of descriptive writing that focuses on a natural setting, such as a mountain, river, beach, or forest. Writers of profiles attempt to describe a place so coherently and vividly that readers can picture it in their minds. Writers must choose effective sensory details and organize them carefully, often using spatial order to describe what a person would see if they walked through the place. You may have read a profile in a travel brochure or on a travel blog.

Try It! Study the sample travel blog entry that is a profile of a natural place. Then, answer these questions. Record your answers in your journal.

1. What **natural place** is the writer describing?

2. What seems to be the writer's overall **feeling** about this place?

3. An effective profile includes specific **sensory details** in the description of the place. What specific details are included in this profile?

4. Writers often use **spatial order** to organize profiles. How does this writer describe what you might see if you walked through the caverns?

5. A **profile** might be helpful when planning a film or special event that will take place in a natural setting. What kinds of films or events do you think these caverns might be appropriate for, and why?

Extension Find another example of profiles of natural places, and compare it with this one.

The Caverns by Lisa Flannigan

September 27, morning tour

The Caverns are an impressive network of underground limestone caves, several miles long, like a series of rooms. The ceilings swoop from a height of ten feet to four. For most of the passageways, however, I am able to walk upright. Long, thin stalactites drip down from the ceilings, while sturdier stalagmites rise up from the floor, almost like frozen, long-necked extraterrestrials craning their pointy, eyeless heads.

The layout of each chamber is different. Some are large, open spaces, while others are shaped like bent figure eights lying on their sides, the walls widening, then closing in, turning, and widening again.

Everything I see has been created by water from an ancient river. I can still hear the occasional echoing *drip* of liquid at work, creating stalactites and stalagmites. In fact, the acoustics in the larger chambers are amazing. The tour guide explained that several enterprising people have even organized concerts for music lovers brave enough to walk into this natural auditorium that lurks 30 feet below Earth's surface.

Create a Profile of a Natural Place

Follow these steps to create your own blog entry describing a natural place. To plan your description, review the graphic organizers on pages R24–R27 and choose one that suits your needs.

Prewriting

- Identify the place to be described.

- Target a specific audience—travelers who would like to visit the location. Then answer these questions: What are the main features of the place? What will your readers find interesting about it? What do they need to know to plan their activity?

- Brainstorm for sensory details you can use to create a specific, believable setting. These details should help the reader imagine how the place looks, smells, sounds, and feels.

Drafting

- Format the profile as a travel blog entry.

- First, write a head identifying the place.

- Then, present your profile information, with the most significant details presented clearly. Consider using spatial order to organize your profile.

- As you write, aim for a clear, vivid style to appeal to your audience. Use a conversational tone to express your ideas and feelings about the place.

Revising and Editing

- Review your draft to ensure that the description is logically organized and the details and images are specific.

- Take out details that do not serve your purpose or that might confuse the reader.

- Check that spelling, grammar, and mechanics are correct.

Publishing

Add a multimedia element to your blog entry. Include images with captions of your natural place, some of the text that describes the place, and background music. Then present it to your class.

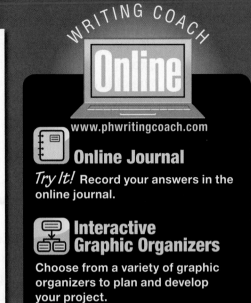

WRITING COACH

Online

www.phwritingcoach.com

Online Journal

Try It! Record your answers in the online journal.

 **Interactive Graphic Organizers**

Choose from a variety of graphic organizers to plan and develop your project.

Partner Talk

Before you start drafting, describe the place to a partner. Use specific details to describe and explain your ideas. Increase the specificity of your details based on the type of information you are delivering. Ask for feedback about the description. For example, can your partner picture what you are describing?

Writing for Assessment

Writing a good poem can take a lot of practice. You can use the prompts on this page to practice. Your responses should include the characteristics on page 120.

Try It! To begin, read the **poetry** prompt and the information on format and academic vocabulary. Then, use the ABCDs of On-Demand Writing to help you plan and write your poem.

Format

The prompt directs you to write a *poem*. Consider the format of the poem you will write and develop a controlling idea that addresses the prompt.

Poetry Prompt

Think about the street on which you live. Decide on the impression that you want to create of your street. Then write a poem describing your street and your feelings about it. Use poetic techniques, graphic elements, and figurative language.

Academic Vocabulary

Remember that *poetic techniques* are the tools poets use to create a musical quality, emphasize words, or enhance rhythm. *Graphic elements* are the visual elements that make a poem look a certain way. *Figurative language* is writing that is not meant to be taken literally.

The ABCDs of On-Demand Writing

Use the following ABCDs to help you respond to the prompt.

Before you write your draft:

Attack the prompt [1 MINUTE]

- Circle or highlight important verbs in the prompt. Draw a line from the verb to what it refers to.
- Rewrite the prompt in your own words.

Brainstorm possible answers [4 MINUTES]

- Create a graphic organizer to generate ideas.
- Use one for each part of the prompt if necessary.

Choose the order of your response [1 MINUTE]

- Think about the best way to organize your ideas.
- Number your ideas in the order you will write about them. Cross out ideas you will not be using.

After you write your draft:

Detect errors before turning in the draft [1 MINUTE]

- Carefully reread your writing.
- Make sure that your response makes sense and is complete.
- Look for spelling, punctuation, and grammar errors.

More Prompts for Practice

Apply It! Respond to Prompt 1 by writing a **poem.** As you write, be sure to:

- Identify your **audience**
- Choose your poetic form and use **graphic elements,** such as lines breaks and stanzas, appropriate to it
- Establish a clear **central idea** or **theme**
- Use **poetic techniques** to develop ideas
- Include **figurative language,** such as similes and metaphors, to make your writing interesting and lively

Prompt 1 Human relationships are a source of great inspiration to many poets. Think about your best friend, and write a poem about him or her. You might describe your friend's appearance and personality or tell about something he or she did.

Spiral Review: Narrative If you choose to write a diary entry in response to Prompt 2, make sure your **personal narrative** reflects the characteristics described on page 66.

Prompt 2 Write a diary entry about a day you'll never forget. Include details about the importance of your decisions and actions.

Spiral Review: Short Story If you choose to write an imaginative **short story** that retains reader interest in response to Prompt 3, make sure it reflects the characteristics on page 92, including: well-paced **action** and an engaging **story line,** sensory details to describe specific settings, interesting characters, and a range of **literary strategies and devices** to enhance the style and tone.

Prompt 3 Sports events can be very exciting, and sometimes surprising! Write a short story about characters who are in or attend a sports event. Be sure to fully describe the people and the events that take place to create an engaging story.

WRITING COACH

Online

www.phwritingcoach.com

Interactive Writing Coach™

Plan your response to the prompt. If you are using the prompt for practice, write one paragraph at a time or your entire draft and then submit it for feedback. If you are using the prompt as a timed test, write your entire draft and then submit it for feedback.

Remember **ABCD**

A ttack the prompt

B rainstorm possible answers

C hoose the order of your response

D etect errors before turning in the draft

EXPOSITION

CHAPTER 8

How Can You Explain This?

What do you know about buildings and how they are built? What ideas and information about buildings could you share with others?

Information can be presented many ways. For example, you can compare two things, you can discuss causes and effects, or you can present a problem and a solution.

Try It! Imagine that you wanted to talk about the causes and effects of the leaning tower shown in the photo. What details might you discuss?

Take notes as you consider these questions. Then participate in an extended discussion with a partner. Take turns expressing your ideas and feelings.

- What might have caused the building to lean?
- What effects do you think the leaning building has on people?
- What details would you use to give information about this building?

Review the ideas you wrote to identify a statement of cause-and-effect. Then, explain your topic to your partner.

What's Ahead

In this chapter, you will review two strong examples of an expository essay: a Mentor Text and a Student Model. Then, using the examples as guides, you will write an analytical essay in the cause-and-effect form.

Connect to the Big Questions

Discuss these questions with your partner:

1 What do you think? What can we learn from the past?

2 Why write? What should we tell and what should we describe to make information clear?

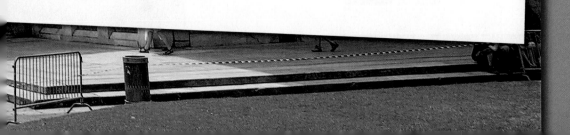

EXPOSITORY ESSAY

An expository essay explains a topic by providing facts, quotations, and other details about it. In this chapter, you will learn to write a type of expository essay known as a cause-and-effect essay. A cause-and-effect essay explains the reasons behind or results of a particular event or situation. Although a cause-and-effect essay can include opinions, like a persuasive essay, its main purpose is to explain rather than to persuade.

You will develop your cause-and-effect essay by taking it through each of the steps of the writing process: prewriting, drafting, revising, editing, and publishing. You will also have an opportunity to create a documentary video script. To preview the criteria for how your cause-and-effect essay will be evaluated, see the rubric on page 163.

FEATURE ASSIGNMENT

Expository Essay: Cause-and-Effect Essay

An effective expository essay has these characteristics:

- An **effective introduction** and **conclusion**

- A **clearly stated purpose and controlling idea,** or **thesis**

- A **variety of sentence structures** and **rhetorical devices,** such as rhetorical questions and analogies

- **Transitions** to link paragraphs

- **Clear, logical organization**

- **Facts, quotations**, and **other types of details** that support the explanations

- **No extraneous information,** or information that is not relevant, or **inconsistencies,** or facts that don't agree with one another

- Ideas that are **accurately synthesized**, or combined, from **several sources**

A cause-and-effect essay also includes:

- A **thesis** or **controlling idea** that states a cause-and-effect relationship

- A clear explanation of **causes** and/or **effects**

Other Forms of Expository Essays

In addition to the cause-and-effect essay, there are other forms of expository writing, including:

Classification essays organize a subject into categories or explain the category into which an item falls.

Compare-and-contrast essays explore similarities and differences between two or more things, people, places, or ideas.

Newspaper and magazine articles that are printed or published on the Internet supply relevant information about a particular topic by analyzing the topic's elements. They may also reflect genres other than expository essays (for example, persuasive writing or narrative nonfiction writing).

Pro-con essays examine the arguments for and against a particular action or decision.

Problem-solution essays identify a problem and explain one or more ways to solve it.

Try It! For each audience and purpose described, choose a form, such as a pro-con essay or a problem-solution essay, that is appropriate for conveying your intended meaning to your audience. Explain your choices.

- To explain to a parent how soccer and football are alike and how they are different
- To help a student understand the categories into which languages are grouped
- To help club members see the benefits and drawbacks of a particular decision

MENTOR TEXT
Expository Essay

Learn From Experience

 After reading the expository essay on pages 148–149, read the numbered notes in the margins to learn about how the author presented her ideas. Later you will read a Student Model, which shares these characteristics and also has the characteristics of a cause-and-effect essay.

Answer the *Try It!* questions online or in your notebook.

---

1 The introduction has a clearly stated **controlling idea,** or thesis.

Try It! What is the controlling idea of this essay? Based on the controlling idea, what do you think is the author's purpose in writing this article? What message does she hope to convey?

2 The author uses a **variety of sentence structures.**

Try It! Rewrite these sentences using only simple sentences. Which version is easier to read?

3 A **quotation** from a student involved in micro-lending supports the explanation of the process and adds interest.

Try It! How would the effect be different without the quotation?

Extension Find another example of an expository essay, and compare it with this one.

Big Changes from Small Change

by Kathleen Thompson

1 If you think only banks can make business loans, you should talk to the students of Bellevue High School in Bellevue, Washington. During the 2008–2009 school year, they made more than a thousand loans to small businesses.
5 These were loans, not gifts. The money will be repaid with interest. Each loan was only about $150, but that can go a long way in Haiti or the Dominican Republic. These students are helping people move out of poverty while learning about business and managing money.

The Student Lenders

10 The Bellevue students make their loans through an organization called Esperanza International. **2** A similar student group in Las Vegas, the Meadows School MicroBank, makes their loans through Kiva. Kiva is a not-for-profit group in San Francisco. Both Esperanza and Kiva
15 make only micro-loans, sums of money that seem very small to most of us. Those small sums, however, can build businesses and change lives in some parts of the world, including the United States.

For the students who become involved in these micro-
20 lending groups, there are many rewards. Of course, they get the satisfaction of helping others. They also learn a great deal about business. To begin, the students have to raise the money they are going to lend. They learn how to make presentations to businesses and others who might
25 help finance their project. Then they have to choose a reputable organization, such as Esperanza or Kiva, through which to make their loans. With Kiva, students can read loan applications online and decide to whom they will lend money. **3** "We are able to know the names and see the
30 faces of the people receiving the loans," student Justin Blau explained to *Edutopia* magazine. "I love that."

A Great Idea

The whole idea of micro-lending began thirty years ago with a man named Muhammad Yunus, the founder of the
35 Grameen Bank. He started lending very small sums to people who were trying to build businesses in Bangladesh. These people could not get loans from anyone else. The amount they needed was too small for most banks to be interested. The people were also considered bad credit risks.

40 These are very small businesses. For example, one business involved just one woman making clothes who needed a sewing machine. Once that woman had the money for a machine, though, she was able to increase her income. Then she could feed her family and possibly send
45 her children to school. A January 2010 article in *Time* magazine says of Yunus, "His great discovery was that even with few assets, these entrepreneurs repaid on time. Grameen and microfinance have since become financial staples of the developing world. . . ."

50 ❹ **Help in America**

There is now a group that provides micro-loans to businesses in Appalachia, one the U.S.'s poorer regions. Appalachian Community Enterprises, Inc. (ACE) gives small businesses, some owned by teens, sums from $500
55 to $35,000. These are larger loans than most of those made in developing countries. ❺ This is because the U.S. economy is different. ❺ However, these loans are small compared to the business loans made by most banks. Like the first Grameen loans, they are given to people that most
60 commercial banks would not lend.

So, from funding loans to receiving loans, young people in the United States are involved in one of the most original and effective business movements of our time. Students like those at Bellevue High and Meadows School
65 are making a difference in people's lives while learning business skills they will need later in their own lives.

WRITING COACH

Online

www.phwritingcoach.com

Interactive Model

Listen to an audio recording of the Mentor Text in the eText. You can refer back to the Mentor Text whenever you need support in developing your own writing.

Online Journal

Try It! Answer the questions about the Mentor Text in the online journal.

❹ The author uses headings to create clear, logical **organization** in her article.

Try It! How do headings make it easier for an audience to find information? How do headings affect the audience's reading experience?

❺ The author uses **transitions** to link details and ideas.

Try It! How do the transitions help you understand the relationships between the ideas?

STUDENT MODEL Cause-and-Effect Essay

With a small group, take turns reading this Student Model aloud. As you read, identify the cause-and-effect relationships, and decide whether the causes and effects are clear.

 ## Use a Reader's Eye

Now, reread the Student Model. On your copy of the Student Model, use the Reader's Response Symbols to react to what you read.

Reader's Response Symbols

+ **Aha! That makes sense to me.**

– **This isn't clear to me.**

? **I have a question about this.**

! **Wow! That is cool/weird/ interesting.**

Rain, Rain, Go AWAY!

by Elinora Rafael

Every Saturday in the summer, my mom lets me stop on the way home from the park to buy peaches at the farmers' market. This year, though, I had to buy a lot fewer peaches—because they
5   cost so much more! What made the price go up? The rainy weather has caused the prices of not just peaches but most fruits and vegetables to soar.

Plants need sunlight to produce flowers, or blossoms. When it rains too much, the peach
10   trees have fewer blossoms that turn into fruit. Mr. Montez, the farmer who sells me peaches, explained the problem to me: "When it rains, not only do fewer peach blossoms form, but the rain knocks off some of the blossoms. Fewer
15   blossoms mean fewer peaches. And with fewer peaches, I have to charge more for the ones I sell. Otherwise, I couldn't earn a living."

Having fewer peaches isn't the only reason that Mr. Montez has had to raise prices. He is
20   also paying more this year to rent his stall at the farmers' market. Carla Leone, who runs the farmers' market, had to raise stall rent because the market has 25 percent fewer farmers this year than last. "It's because of the rain," she said. "Fruit
25   growers are lucky—they have some fruit to sell, even though it's less than usual. But quite a few vegetable farmers had their crops washed out

1

entirely. Those farmers simply didn't show up this year." Obviously, with fewer farmers renting space,
30 Ms. Leone has to charge those who are there more money in order to keep the market going.

According to the newspaper, prices for fruits and vegetables have also gone up at area supermarkets. When it's so rainy that local farmers have smaller
35 crops or no crops at all, the supermarkets have to buy fruits and vegetables from much farther away. The stores pay more due to higher shipping costs. Because of this, they have to charge customers more to make money and stay in business.

40 All in all, the rainy summer has meant a big increase in the price of most fruits and vegetables. My family still eats them because they're delicious and important for our health. However, we've had to be a lot more careful about how much we buy!

2

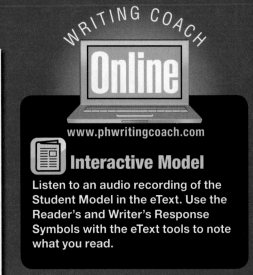

WRITING COACH
Online
www.phwritingcoach.com

 **Interactive Model**

Listen to an audio recording of the Student Model in the eText. Use the Reader's and Writer's Response Symbols with the eText tools to note what you read.

Use a Writer's Eye

Now, evaluate the essay as a writer. On your copy of the Student Model, use the Writer's Response Symbols to react to what you read. Identify places where the student writer uses characteristics of an effective cause-and-effect essay.

Writer's Response Symbols	
C.T.	**Clearly stated thesis**
I.C.	**Effective introduction and conclusion**
R.D.	**Good use of rhetorical devices and sentence structures**
S.E.	**Effective supporting evidence**

Your Turn

Feature Assignment: Cause-and-Effect Essay

Prewriting

Plan a first draft of your cause-and-effect essay **by determining an appropriate topic.** You can select from the Topic Bank or come up with an idea of your own.

Choose From the Topic Bank

TOPIC BANK

Historical Event Think about events you have been studying in your social studies class. Which event interests you the most? Write an essay about the causes and effects of this event.

Role Models Role models are people who show us how to be our best selves. They may have character traits we admire, like courage or intelligence. They may be people who are famous or people who are members of our own families. Think about the people who are role models for you. Write an essay in which you identify one of your role models and explain the influence this role model has had on your life.

Test Prep Think about a test you took in another class. Think about how you prepared for it and about how you performed on the test. Write an essay in which you explain how you prepared for this test and describe the effects of your test preparation.

Choose Your Own Topic

Choose a topic on your own by using the following **range of strategies** to generate ideas.

Brainstorm

- Brainstorm about interesting situations or events in nature. List your ideas.

Review your responses and choose a topic.

Narrow Your Topic

Some topics are too broad to cover in a cause-and-effect essay. By narrowing your topic, you can focus on presenting a manageable number of causes or effects.

Apply It! Use a graphic organizer like the one shown to narrow your topic to an appropriate length.

- Write your general topic in the top box, and keep narrowing as you move down the chart.
- Your last box should hold your narrowest topic, which will be the controlling idea of your cause-and-effect essay.

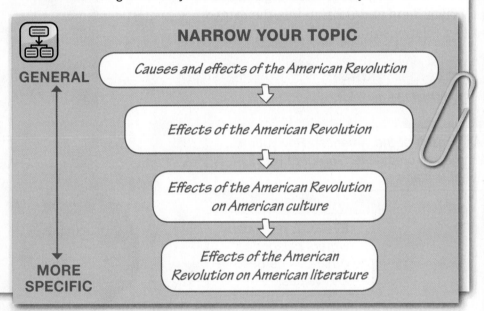

NARROW YOUR TOPIC

GENERAL

Causes and effects of the American Revolution

⇩

Effects of the American Revolution

⇩

Effects of the American Revolution on American culture

⇩

Effects of the American Revolution on American literature

MORE SPECIFIC

Consider Your Audience and Purpose

Before writing, think about your audience and purpose. Consider how your writing will convey the intended meaning to this audience.

Questions for Audience	Questions for Purpose
• Who is my audience? • What questions might the audience have about my topic?	• How might I make the causes and effects clear to my audience? • What point about the cause-and-effect relationships do I want to make?

Record your answers in your writing journal.

WRITING COACH

www.phwritingcoach.com

Interactive Writing Coach™

- **Choosing from the Topic Bank gives you access to the Interactive Writing Coach™.**
- **Submit your writing and receive instant personalized feedback and guidance as you draft, revise, and edit your writing.**

Interactive Graphic Organizers

Use the interactive graphic organizers to help you narrow your topic.

Online Journal

Try It! **Record your answers and ideas in the online journal.**

Plan Your Essay

You will use a graphic organizer to state your thesis and organize your causes and effects. When it is complete, you will be ready to write your first draft.

Develop a Clear Thesis Evaluate your ideas and information to develop a clear thesis, or **controlling idea**. Your thesis should make a general statement about the cause-and-effect relationships in your essay. Write your thesis at the top of a graphic organizer like the one shown.

Logically Organize Your Facts and Details List causes or effects you plan to discuss in boxes on your graphic organizer by logically organizing appropriate facts and details. Use the arrows to show the cause-and-effect relationships.

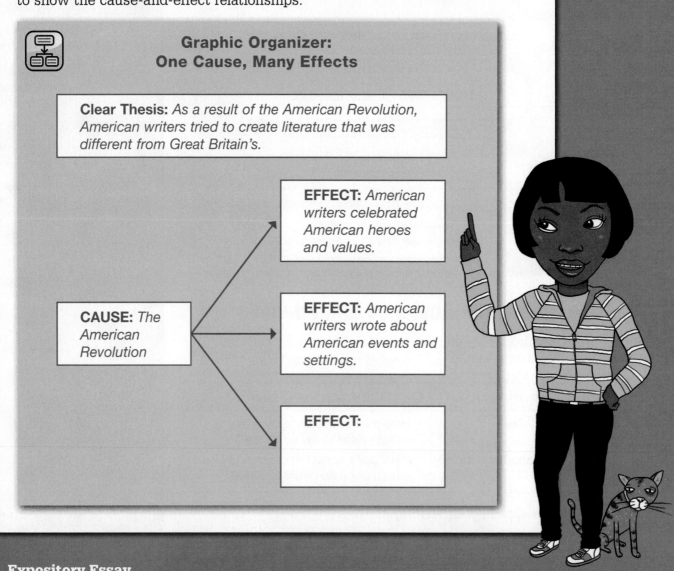

**Graphic Organizer:
One Cause, Many Effects**

Clear Thesis: *As a result of the American Revolution, American writers tried to create literature that was different from Great Britain's.*

CAUSE: *The American Revolution*

EFFECT: *American writers celebrated American heroes and values.*

EFFECT: *American writers wrote about American events and settings.*

EFFECT:

Gather Details

To explain causes and effects, look at these examples of details you might use.

- **Facts:** *Before the American Revolution, most American books were published in Great Britain.*

- **Examples:** *Washington Irving's "Rip Van Winkle" tells of a man who goes to sleep before the Revolution and wakes up years later in a changed world.*

- **Quotations:** *"Proceed, great Chief, with virtue on thy side"—Phillis Wheatley, "To His Excellency, General Washington"*

- **Personal Experiences:** *When I visited Wisconsin, I saw places described in Longfellow's epic poem The Song of Hiawatha.*

Try It! Read this Student Model excerpt. Then identify and take notes about which kinds of details the author used to support her ideas.

WRITING COACH

Online

www.phwritingcoach.com

Interactive Graphic Organizers

Use the interactive graphic organizers to help you create a plan for your writing.

Interactive Model

Refer back to the Interactive Model in the eText as you plan your writing.

> **STUDENT MODEL** from **Rain, Rain, Go Away!**
> page 150; lines 21–24
>
> Carla Leone, who runs the farmers' market, had to raise stall rent because the market has 25 percent fewer farmers this year than last. "It's because of the rain," she said.

 Apply It! Review the types of support an expository essay can present. Think about examples of each you might use in discussing the causes or effects that support your thesis.

- Decide which **facts and details** best support your thesis. Eliminate details that are **extraneous,** or not relevant.

- Be sure to review information from a **variety of sources.** Then, identify any **inconsistencies,** or differences among the sources. Finally, **synthesize ideas** from different sources by deciding what key points to include.

- Identify one or two details that could help make your **introduction** and **concluding paragraph** more effective. Sometimes a quotation or a personal experience can help capture reader attention.

Drafting

During the drafting stage, you will start to write your ideas for your cause-and-effect essay. You will follow an outline that provides an **appropriate organizational strategy** that builds on ideas and that will help you write a **focused, organized**, and **coherent** cause-and-effect essay.

The Organization of an Expository Essay

The chart provides an organizing structure for an expository essay. As you adapt it for your particular cause-and-effect essay, be sure to keep in mind your audience and purpose.

Outline *for* Success

I. Introduction
See Mentor Text, p. 148.

- Attention-grabbing opening
- Controlling idea or thesis

II. Body
See Mentor Text, pp. 148–149.

- Causes and/or effects that support the thesis
- Logical organization of facts and details

III. Conclusion
See Mentor Text, p. 149.

- Restatement of controlling idea or thesis
- Memorable ending

Grab Your Reader

- Rhetorical questions, interesting quotations, personal experiences, or other strong details can quickly capture an audience's attention.
- A thesis statement is a general statement about the cause-and-effect relationships you will discuss in your essay.

Develop Your Ideas

- Causes and effects are supported by appropriate facts, examples, quotations, and details that explain or illustrate them.
- If an essay is about many unrelated causes or effects, one paragraph can be devoted to each, arranged from least important to most important.
- If an essay is about a chain reaction, in which one cause has an effect that causes another effect and so on, chronological, or time, order will be most effective.

Wrap It Up

- In the conclusion, the thesis is restated in a powerful or interesting way.
- Rhetorical devices, such as analogies or rhetorical questions, often help to make ideas memorable.

 **Start Your Draft**

Use this checklist to help you complete your draft. Use the graphic organizer with your causes and effects, and the Outline for Success as guides.

While drafting, aim at writing your ideas, not on making your writing perfect. Remember, you will have the chance to improve your draft when you revise and edit.

√ Start with **opening** sentences to capture your reader's attention.

√ Continue building an effective **introduction** by including a thesis, or **controlling idea,** that makes a general statement about the cause-and-effect relationships you will be discussing.

√ Develop the **body** of your cause-and-effect essay by providing causes or effects that support your thesis.

√ Accurately **synthesize,** or pull together as a whole, ideas from several sources, and choose facts and details to include. Make sure there are no inconsistencies among your details and omit any extraneous, or irrelevant, details.

√ Make sure your essay is **logically organized** by using chronological order or by devoting one paragraph to each and arranging them in order of importance.

√ Use a variety of sentence structures, or a mix of sentence lengths, and **rhetorical devices,** such as rhetorical questions and analogies, to make your writing lively and interesting.

√ Include **transitions** to link paragraphs and ideas.

√ End with an effective **concluding paragraph** that restates your **thesis** in an interesting way.

√ Use a **rhetorical device** to make your ending memorable.

WRITING COACH

Online

www.phwritingcoach.com

 **Interactive Model**

Outline for Success View pop-ups of the Mentor Text referenced in the Outline for Success.

Interactive Writing Coach™

Use the Interactive Writing Coach to receive the level of support you need:
- Write one paragraph at a time and submit each one for immediate, detailed feedback.
- Write your entire first draft and submit it for immediate, personalized feedback.

Revising: Making It Better

Now that you have finished your first draft, you are ready to revise. Think about the "big picture" of **audience, purpose, and genre.** You can use Revision RADaR as a guide for making changes to improve your draft. Revision RADaR provides four major ways to improve your writing: (R) replace, (A) add, (D) delete, and (R) reorder.

Kelly Gallagher, M. Ed.

KEEP REVISION ON YOUR RADaR

Read part of the first draft of the Student Model "Rain, Rain, Go Away!" Then look at questions the writer asked herself as she thought about how well her draft addressed issues of audience, purpose, and genre.

Rain, Rain, Go Away!

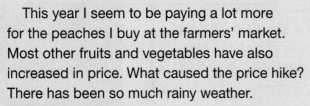

This year I seem to be paying a lot more for the peaches I buy at the farmers' market. Most other fruits and vegetables have also increased in price. What caused the price hike? There has been so much rainy weather.

Plants need sunlight to produce flowers, or blossoms. In the shade many plants still grow, but most of them make far fewer flowers. When it rains so much, the peach trees produce fewer blooms to turn into fruit. Mr. Montez, the man with the peaches, explained that he has to charge more when he cannot grow as much.

Having fewer peaches isn't the only reason that Mr. Montez has had to raise prices. He is also paying more this year to rent his stall at the farmers' market. Carla Leone runs the farmers' market. She had to raise rental costs. The market has about 25 percent fewer farmers this year than last.

*Does the introduction grab my audience and clearly state my **thesis**, or **controlling idea?***

*Is this detail relevant to the cause-and-effect relationships, or is it **extraneous** information?*

*Will my **audience** understand this statement, or should I make it clearer?*

*How can I **vary** sentence structures to avoid so many short, choppy sentences and make the cause-and-effect relationship clearer?*

Now look at how the writer applied Revision RADaR to write an improved second draft.

Rain, Rain, Go AWAY!

2ND DRAFT

Every Saturday in the summer my mom lets me stop on the way home from the park to buy peaches at the farmers' market. This year, though, I had to buy a lot fewer peaches—because they cost so much more! What made the price go up? The rainy weather has caused the prices of not just peaches but most fruits and vegetables to soar.

Plants need sunlight to produce flowers, or blossoms. When it rains too much, the peach trees have fewer blossoms that turn into fruit. Mr. Montez, the farmer who sells me peaches, explained the problem to me: "When it rains, not only do fewer peach blossoms form, but the rain knocks off some of the blossoms. Fewer blossoms mean fewer peaches. And with fewer peaches, I have to charge more for the ones I sell. Otherwise, I couldn't earn a living."

Having fewer peaches isn't the only reason that Mr. Montez has had to raise prices. He is also paying more this year to rent his stall at the farmers' market. Carla Leone, who runs the farmers' market, had to raise stall rent because the market has 25 percent fewer farmers this year than last.

R Replaced a boring opening with a personal anecdote to make the introduction more effective

A Added a thesis that made a clearer general statement of my topic that shows a cause-and-effect relationship

D Deleted information not relevant to the cause-and-effect relationship

R **A** Replaced general wording with precise language. Added a quotation to help my audience better understand the cause-and-effect relationship

R Reordered and combined three sentences to vary sentence structures and make the cause-and-effect relationship clearer

*Apply It!* Use your Revision RADaR to revise your draft.

- Include all the appropriate characteristics of the expository essay genre, using details that address the needs of your purpose and audience.

- Then use the Revision RADaR strategy to make needed changes. Remember—you can use the steps in any order.

Look at the Big Picture

Use the chart and your analytical skills to evaluate how well each section of your cause-and-effect essay **addresses purpose, audience,** and **genre**. When necessary, use the suggestions in the chart to revise your essay.

Section	Evaluate	Revise
Introduction	• Be sure your **opening** grabs reader attention.	• Add a quotation, a rhetorical question, or another strong detail to create an effective introduction.
	• Make sure your **thesis**, or controlling idea, is clearly stated.	• Add a statement that sums up the cause-and-effect relationship in your essay.
Body	• Make sure you have accurately **synthesized** ideas from several sources.	• Reread your sources to see whether or not they are consistent with the main point of your essay.
	• Check that you clearly identified **causes** and **effects**.	• Add transitions such as *because* and *as a result* to clarify causes and effects and to link paragraphs.
	• Check that you have **logically organized** appropriate facts and details.	• Reorder causes and effects in chronological order to show time or sequence, or in order of importance.
	• Review information to make sure your ideas will be clear to your **audience**.	• Replace vague language with more precise language, or add appropriate facts and other details, such as quotations.
	• To ensure internal and external **coherence,** or the logical flow of the text, underline information that supports your thesis.	• Delete extraneous details and resolve any inconsistencies to make sure your text flows well.
	• Check that you have used a variety of **sentence structures.**	• Break or combine sentences to vary their structures.
Conclusion	• Check that you have restated your thesis and summed up **main** ideas.	• Rewrite to sum up all your main points.
	• Make sure that your essay ends on a **memorable** note.	• Add rhetorical devices, such as rhetorical questions or analogies, to make the ending more effective.

Focus on Craft: Effective Transitions

Your writing will be smoother if you use clear **transitions**, words and phrases that show the connections between ideas. Transitions can indicate different types of relationships between words, phrases, or sentences—cause and effect, comparison or contrast, and so on. Transitions that indicate a cause include *because, since, as,* and *for.* Transitions that indicate an effect include *as a result, therefore, so,* and *consequently.*

Look for transitions as you read these sentences from the Student Model.

 **STUDENT MODEL** from **Rain, Rain, Go Away!**
page 151; lines 37–39

> The stores pay more due to higher shipping costs. Because of this, they have to charge customers more to make money and stay in business.

Try It! Now, ask yourself these questions. Record your answers in your journal.

- What kind of relationship does the transition *due to* signal?
- What other transition do the sentences contain, and what kind of relationship does it signal?

Fine-Tune Your Draft

Apply It! Use these revision suggestions to prepare your final draft **after rethinking how well questions of purpose, audience, and genre have been addressed**.

- **Use Effective Transitions** It is important that the ideas within and between all the sentences and paragraphs follow a logical flow. To ensure this **internal and external coherence,** use transitions between sentences and paragraphs to clarify relationships between ideas.

- **Use Consistent Point of View** Your personal opinions, observations, and anecdotes should be in the first person.

Teacher Feedback After submitting your final draft for teacher review, revise it in response to his or her feedback.

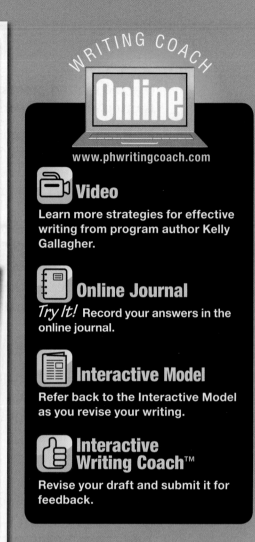

WRITING COACH

Online

www.phwritingcoach.com

Video
Learn more strategies for effective writing from program author Kelly Gallagher.

Online Journal
Try It! Record your answers in the online journal.

Interactive Model
Refer back to the Interactive Model as you revise your writing.

Interactive Writing Coach™
Revise your draft and submit it for feedback.

Editing: Making It Correct

Use the editing process to polish your work and correct errors. It is often helpful to work with a partner when editing your drafts.

As you edit, think about whether or not you have used **transitions** effectively. A transition is a word, phrase, clause, or sentence that creates a relationship between ideas. Then, correct any factual errors and errors in **grammar, mechanics, and spelling.**

WRITE GUY *Jeff Anderson, M. Ed.*

WHAT DO YOU NOTICE?

Zoom in on Conventions Focus on transitions as you zoom in on these sentences from the Student Model.

STUDENT MODEL from **Rain, Rain, Go Away!**
page 151; lines 37–44

The stores pay more due to higher shipping costs. Because of this, they have to charge customers more to make money and stay in business.

All in all, the rainy summer has meant a big increase in the price of most fruits and vegetables. My family still eats them because they're delicious and important for our health. However, we've had to be a lot more careful about how much we buy!

Now ask yourself: *How do transitions make the relationship between ideas clear?*

Perhaps you said the transition *Because of this* makes clear the cause-and-effect relationship between the first two sentences. Or maybe you noticed the transition *All in all,* which shows a sequential relationship between the last paragraph and those that came before it. Finally, the transition *However* indicates a contrast between ideas in the last two sentences.

Partner Talk Discuss this question with a partner: *What other transitions could the author have used to express the same relationships?*

> To learn more about sentence beginnings, see Chapter 20.

Grammar Mini-Lesson:
Commas With Transitions

To learn more, see Chapter 25.

Most transitions should be set off from the rest of the sentence by **commas.** The comma may be omitted after a short **introductory transition** if the sentence is clear without it. Notice how a comma sets off the transition *Because of this* in the Student Model.

 **STUDENT MODEL** from **Rain, Rain, Go Away!**
page 151; lines 37–39

The stores pay more due to higher shipping costs. Because of this, they have to charge customers more to make money and stay in business.

 Try It! Copy the passage into your journal. Identify the transitions and indicate if any commas need to be added.

The American Revolution also revolutionized American literature. In the past writers in the Thirteen Colonies had imitated British models. Now writers turned to American settings and themes.

 Apply It! **Edit your draft for grammar, punctuation, capitalization, and spelling errors.** Use a dictionary or other resource to check your spelling. Make sure that you have used commas after introductory structures, such as transitions.

Use the rubric to evaluate your essay. If necessary, rethink, rewrite, or revise.

Rubric for Expository Writing: Cause-and-Effect Essay	Rating Scale					
Ideas: How well do you present the cause-and-effect relationship?	Not very					Very
	1	2	3	4	5	6
Organization: How well is information organized to support your ideas?	1	2	3	4	5	6
Voice: How well do you engage the reader?	1	2	3	4	5	6
Word Choice: How clearly do your words convey your specific ideas?	1	2	3	4	5	6
Sentence Fluency: How effectively do you use transitions?	1	2	3	4	5	6
Conventions: How correct is your usage of commas with transitions?	1	2	3	4	5	6

WRITING COACH

Online

www.phwritingcoach.com

 Video
Learn effective editing techniques from program author Jeff Anderson.

 Online Journal
Try It! Record your answers in the online journal.

 Interactive Model
Refer back to the Interactive Model as you edit your writing.

 Interactive Writing Coach™
Edit your draft. Check it against the rubric and then submit it for feedback.

Publishing

Give your cause-and-effect essay a chance to inform people. Get it ready for presentation. Then, choose a way to **publish it for the appropriate audience.**

Wrap Up Your Presentation

Now that you have finished your draft, add the final details. Choose images to add to the final draft of your expository essay to provide readers with visual support of the evidence you presented. Also be sure to add a title to your essay.

Publish Your Piece

Use the chart to identify a way to publish your essay.

If your audience is...	...then publish it by...
Classmates and others at your school	• Submitting it to your school newspaper or Web site • Organizing a group reading of the class's essays
Your local community	• Submitting it to a local newspaper • Reading and discussing your ideas on a local radio station
The larger community	• Posting it online and inviting responses • Entering it in a regional or national essay contest

 ## Extend Your Research

Think more about the topic on which you wrote your cause-and-effect essay. What else would you like to know about this topic?

- Brainstorm for several questions you would like to research and then consult, or discuss, with others. Then, decide which question is your major research question.

- Formulate, or develop, a plan about how you will answer these questions. Decide where you will find more information—on the Internet, at the library, or through other sources.

- Finally, learn more about your topic by following through with your research plan.

 The Big Question: Why Write? What should we tell and what should we describe to make information clear?

21st Century Learning

MAKE YOUR WRITING COUNT

Conduct a Seminar Based on an Expository Essay

A cause-and-effect essay analyzes a topic in depth. A seminar is a class that focuses on one very specific topic. Conduct a **seminar** for a small group of students to learn about a topic in depth.

With a group, choose one cause-and-effect essay on which to base a seminar. Your group will then conduct the seminar to teach more about the topic. Prepare a **multimedia presentation** by including **text, graphics,** and **sounds,** such as news clips, as props for use during the discussions. You may decide to video-record it, and show it to a larger audience.

Here's your action plan.

1. Choose roles, such as researcher, graphics designer, and moderator.

2. Then, meet to judge each cause-and-effect essay. Decide which one would work best as the basis of a seminar.

3. Plan a 15-minute seminar. Each group member should prepare to discuss in depth one cause and/or effect from the essay.

   - Do additional research to find more information on the causes and effects.

   - Create at least one visual, such as a flowchart, using spreadsheet software or poster paper. Find sound clips to enhance the presentation on the Internet or make your own.

   - Prepare an agenda. As a group, go over the order of the points you will cover and the rules you will follow in the seminar.

4. Sitting in a circle, begin your seminar. Video-record your discussion, or have the class act as silent observers.

Listening and Speaking During the planning stage, meet with your group to discuss which information from the essay to include in the seminar. Listen actively to suggestions about how to show the cause-effect relationship visually. During your seminar, work as a team to present information logically. Work to elaborate on one another's comments, to make the seminar as informative as possible.

WRITING COACH

Online

www.phwritingcoach.com

Online Journal

Extend Your Research Record your answers and ideas in the online journal.

Resource

Link to resources on 21st Century Learning for help in creating a group project.

 **Your Turn**

Writing for Media: Documentary Video Script

21st Century Learning

A **documentary** is a nonfiction film or TV show that communicates ideas and information to specific audiences. Documentaries frequently deal with issues that involve cause-and-effect relationships. A **documentary video script** is often divided into shots, or scenes using a **storyboard**. It includes a mapping of images, dialogue, and narration—the words spoken in the documentary by the narrator, reporters, or people being interviewed. It may also include directions to those preparing the documentary, such as camera operators or sound and lighting engineers.

Try It! Study this sample portion of a documentary video script. Then answer these questions about it. Record your answers in your journal.

1. What **topic** does the documentary cover? How does the dialogue show the **thesis** or controlling idea of a cause-and-effect essay?

2. Identify two examples of **directions** to those preparing the documentary. How are directions indicated differently than what is on-screen?

3. The sample presents two **shots** from a much longer documentary. How does the second shot relate to the first? How does dividing the script into shots help those preparing the documentary?

4. Instead of using **narration,** how does the documentary maker let the audience know who or what is being shown in Shot 2?

Extension Find another example of a documentary video script or a storyboard, and compare it with this one.

Reflecting on Hurricane Katrina / Storyboard

`<Shot 1 Image:` Pan shot showing widespread damage of Hurricane Katrina.`>`

`<Dialogue>` Narrator: Hurricane Katrina had devastating effects for the Gulf Coast region of the United States.

`<Effects>` Sound: Music fades as narration begins.

`<Shot 2 Image:` A family (two adults, one teen) standing in front of a badly damaged home.`>`

`<Dialogue>` Mr. Martin: The water was so high we had to climb onto the roof.

Reporter (off camera): How did you survive?

Mrs. Martin: A helicopter and rescue workers came and took us up one at a time.

`<Effects>` Scrolling caption beneath image: The Martin family, New Orleans, Louisiana

Create a Documentary Video Script

Follow these steps to create your own video script and storyboard for a documentary for a **specific audience**. To plan your script, review the graphic organizers on R24–R27 and choose one that suits your needs.

Prewriting

- Choose a topic that involves causes or effects and is an idea that you would like to investigate.
- Gather details by researching various sources, and conducting on-site investigations or interviews.
- After examining your information, develop a controlling idea that makes a general statement about the cause-and-effect relationships in your documentary.

Drafting

- Draft your video script into ten or more shots drawn from the information you gathered. Put the shots in chronological order when appropriate.
- Add narration, or words spoken by a narrator, to express your thesis or controlling idea and other key points. Also, use narration or captions to clarify what each shot shows and also to help smooth the transitions between shots.
- Give your documentary a catchy title that points to its content.

Revising and Editing

- Check that your dialogue is accurate and your directions and narration are clear.
- Make sure that the shots are logically organized, with smooth transitions, so that the flow of information is clear.
- Add directions to include music or other effects.

Publishing

Produce the actual documentary for which you wrote the script on video, or have classmates read your script and offer suggestions for improvement.

WRITING COACH

Online
www.phwritingcoach.com

Online Journal
Try It! Record your answers in the online journal.

Interactive Graphic Organizers

Choose from a variety of graphic organizers to plan and develop your project.

Partner Talk

Explain your topic to a partner. Ask what questions or concerns he or she might have on the topic of your documentary, and take notes about his or her responses. Monitor your partner's spoken language by asking follow-up questions to confirm your understanding.

Writing for Assessment

Many tests include a prompt that asks you to write an expository essay. Your responses should include most of the same characteristics as your cause-and-effect essay. (See page 146.)

 Try It! To begin, read the **expository essay** prompt and the information on format and academic vocabulary. Use the ABCDs of On-Demand Writing to help you plan and write your essay.

Format

A cause-and-effect *expository essay* includes a clear introduction, body paragraphs with supporting facts and details, and a conclusion.

Expository Prompt

Write an expository essay about the effects of peer pressure. Examine how peer pressure sometimes causes people to behave or think and what the effects of such pressure might be.

Academic Vocabulary

Remember that a *cause* is an event that creates an *effect*, or result. When you write a cause-and-effect essay, describe how one cause has a certain effect, which in turn has another effect, and so on.

The ABCDs of On-Demand Writing

Use the following ABCDs to help you respond to the prompt.

Before you write your draft:

A ttack the prompt [1 MINUTE]

- Circle or highlight important verbs in the prompt. Draw a line from the verb to what it refers to.
- Rewrite the prompt in your own words.

B rainstorm possible answers [4 MINUTES]

- Create a graphic organizer to generate ideas.
- Use one for each part of the prompt if necessary.

C hoose the order of your response [1 MINUTE]

- Think about the best way to organize your ideas.
- Number your ideas in the order you will write about them. Cross out ideas you will not be using.

After you write your draft:

D etect errors before turning in the draft [1 MINUTE]

- Carefully reread your writing.
- Make sure that your response makes sense and is complete.
- Look for spelling, punctuation, and grammar errors.

More Prompts for Practice

Apply It! Respond to Prompts 1 and 2 by writing multi-paragraph **expository essays** according to these guidelines.

- Grab readers' attention with an **effective introductory paragraph** that states a clear thesis, or **controlling idea,** and ends with a memorable **concluding paragraph**.

- **Organize** appropriate facts and details logically.

- Include information from a variety of sources. **Synthesize** information by looking for key ideas that overlap into each one.

- Be sure to eliminate **inconsistencies** and extraneous, or unnecessary, information.

- Use a variety of **sentence structures** and **rhetorical devices** to help make your writing interesting.

- Use clear **transitions** to link paragraphs and ideas.

> **Prompt 1** Think about the effects of a particular type of pollution—such as pollution from factories or from cars—in your community or in the world. Write an essay in which you explore the causes and effects of this type of pollution.

> **Prompt 2** Think about the effects of the media's portrayal of celebrities. How do the media portrayals affect the celebrities' careers, and the general public? Write a cause-and-effect essay in which you explore the effects of the media's portrayal of celebrities.

Spiral Review: Poetry Respond to Prompt 3 by writing a **poem**. Make sure your poem reflects all the characteristics described on page 120, including **poetic techniques, figurative language,** and **graphic elements**.

> **Prompt 3** Think about a memorable storm that you experienced. Write a poem describing the storm and its effect on you or others.

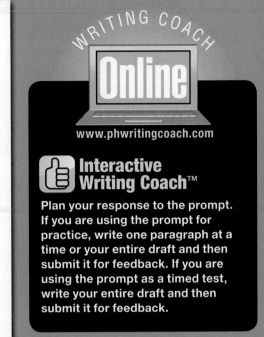

WRITING COACH

Online
www.phwritingcoach.com

Interactive Writing Coach™

Plan your response to the prompt. If you are using the prompt for practice, write one paragraph at a time or your entire draft and then submit it for feedback. If you are using the prompt as a timed test, write your entire draft and then submit it for feedback.

Remember **ABCD**

Attack the prompt

Brainstorm possible answers

Choose the order of your response

Detect errors before turning in the draft

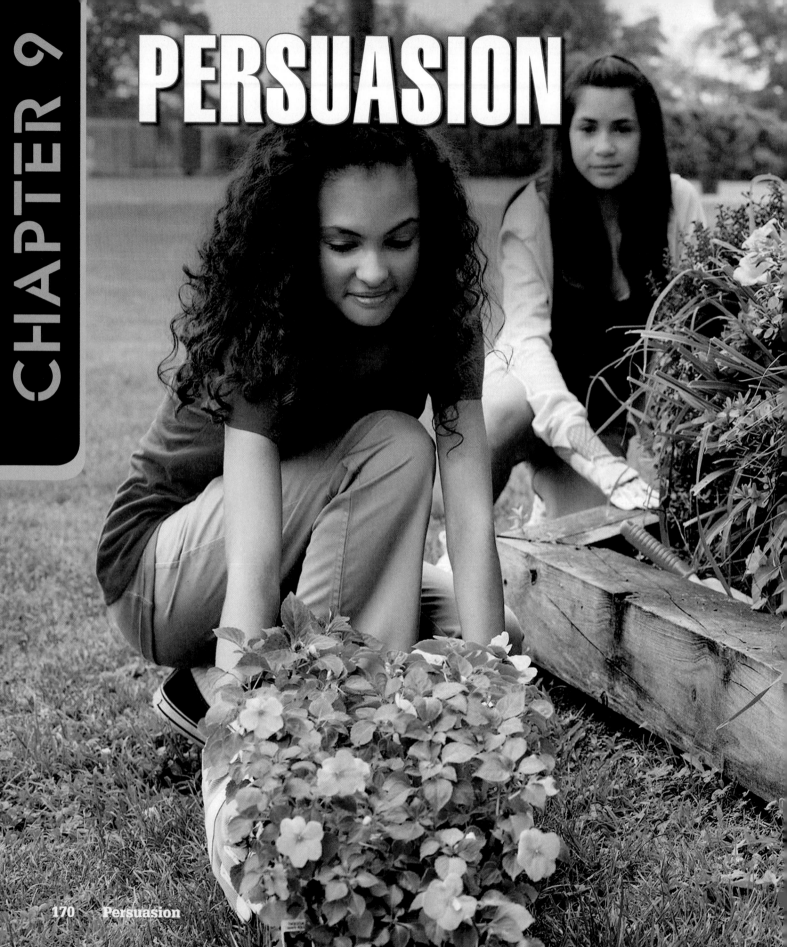

CHAPTER 9

PERSUASION

What Do You Think?

The photo shows teenagers working to better their community. People have different feelings on whether or not teenagers should be required to do community service.

You probably have an opinion on this topic. You may want to convince someone to share your opinion. When you use words to convince people, you are using persuasion.

Try It! List reasons why teenagers should or should not be required to do community service. Consider these questions as you participate in an extended discussion with a partner. Take turns expressing your ideas and feelings.

- What are the benefits of teenagers doing community service?

- What are some of the reasons why teenagers should not have to do community service?

- What should teenagers be doing instead of community service?

Review the list you made. Choose a position on the issue by deciding which side to take. Write a sentence that states which position, or side, you will take. Then, take turns talking about your ideas and positions with a partner.

What's Ahead

In this chapter, you will review two strong examples of a persuasive essay: a Mentor Text and a Student Model. Then, using the examples as guidance, you will write a persuasive essay of your own.

WRITING COACH

Online

www.phwritingcoach.com

Online Journal

Try It! Record your answers and ideas in the online journal.

You can also record and save your answers and ideas on pop-up sticky notes in the eText.

Connect to the Big Questions

Discuss these questions with your partner:

1 **What do you think?** What kinds of community service have the most impact?

2 **Why write?** What is your point of view? How will you know if you've convinced others?

PERSUASIVE WRITING

Persuasive writing is intended to convince an audience to agree with a specific position or idea. In this chapter, you will explore a particular type of persuasive essay, the editorial. An editorial is an opinion piece written by a newspaper or magazine editor to try to persuade readers to agree with the views expressed in the article. Because it represents the views or positions of the newspaper or magazine as a whole, it is not signed by an author.

You will develop your editorial by taking it through each step of the writing process: prewriting, drafting, revising, editing, and publishing. You will also have an opportunity to create a letter to the editor. To preview the criteria for how your editorial will be evaluated, see the rubric on page 189.

FEATURE ASSIGNMENT

Persuasive Essay: Editorial

An effective persuasive essay has these characteristics:

- A **clear thesis or position statement** that expresses the writer's opinion

- **Persuasive arguments** that are organized in an effective, logical order. Arguments should consider others' views and anticipate readers' concerns.

- **Evidence that is logically organized** so that it supports the writer's opinion. Evidence may include examples, facts, statistics, and expert opinions.

- Responses to readers' **concerns and counter-arguments**

- A **conclusion** that restates your position and ends on a memorable note with a call to action

- **Effective sentence structure** and correct spelling, grammar, and usage

An editorial may also include:

- A **lead** that introduces the topic or issue and captures readers' interest

- A **natural but authoritative voice** that appeals to both reason and emotion

Other Forms of Persuasive Writing

In addition to the editorial, there are other forms of persuasive writing, including:

Advertisements are paid public notices that try to persuade people to do or buy something.

Critical reviews summarize, analyze, and evaluate items and activities such as books, movies, and music. Reviews provide information, like the strengths and weaknesses of a movie, that helps readers make choices.

Letters to the editor communicate the opinions of the readers of a newspaper or magazine. Readers may write in response to a specific situation or to an article that was published.

Op-ed pieces are signed editorials that express the opinion of the author, who may or may not work for the newspaper or magazine in which the piece appears.

Persuasive essays use logic and reasoning to convince readers to adopt a certain action or point of view.

Persuasive speeches aim at winning an audience's support for a policy, position, or action.

Propaganda is biased, false, or misleading information presented through emotional appeals. The goal of propaganda is to influence people to think or act in a certain way, typically about political issues.

Try It! For each audience and purpose described, choose a form, such as a speech, letter, or review, that is appropriate for conveying your intended meaning to the audience. Explain your choices.

- To persuade classmates to vote for you for student council
- To convince neighbors to hire you to mow their lawns
- To encourage community members to clean up litter in the neighborhood during a Community Cleanup campaign

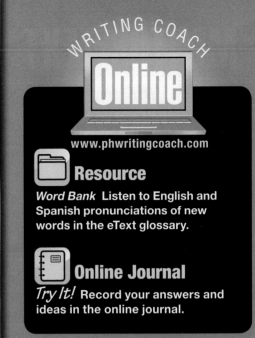

MENTOR TEXT — Editorial

Learn From Experience

 Read the editorial on pages 174–175. As you read, take notes to develop your understanding of basic sight and English vocabulary. Then, read the numbered notes in the margins to learn about how the author presented ideas.

Answer the *Try It!* questions online or in your notebook.

---

❶ The introduction contains **language that appeals to both emotion and reason.**

Try It! Which sentences contain language that stirs up strong feelings in you? Which sentences state ideas that seem especially well thought out, or reasonable?

❷ The **thesis** states the editorial's position on graduated licensing laws.

Try It! What three risk factors does the editorial say that graduated licensing laws need to address?

❸ Subheads help create a **logically organized argument.**

Try It! How do this subhead and the other two subheads relate to the risk factors stated in the thesis? How does this structure help organize the editorial logically?

Extension Find another example of an editorial, and compare it with this one.

A Few Limits on Teenage Drivers Could Save Their Lives

❶ To parents with teenagers, the 16th birthday is a time of both relief and fear. Relief that their children can help out with driving chores. Fear that they could be injured or killed in an auto accident.

5 On an average day in the USA, 10 teens die in accidents involving teen drivers. Three factors—inexperience, night driving and distractions caused when other teens are riding in the car—all compound the problem, the USA TODAY analysis shows.

10 This rite of passage need not be so deadly. Simple "graduated licensing" laws, which place conditions on young drivers, already are saving hundreds of lives a year. Forty-six states have them.

But during the past few years, states stopped passing new 15 restrictions. Not one imposes conditions to address all three risk factors, according to the analysis by USA TODAY and the Insurance Institute for Highway Safety. **❷** The number of teen highway deaths would likely plummet if all states addressed all three factors.

20 **❸** **Age restrictions** Many states allow youths to receive learner's permits at 15, which often leads to a full license when they turn 16. This makes little sense. New data from the Insurance Institute show that driving at age 16 is riskier than driving at 17, 18 or 19—and the fatal crash rate for 25 16-year-olds is five times that of drivers 20 and older.

Inexperience is clearly one factor. Another possible explanation emerges from brain-scan research. The region of the brain that weighs risk matures more slowly than previously thought—generally after the teenage years.

30 Postponing the learner's permit process until age 16 and then requiring at least six months of permit-restricted

Wednesday, February 20   **14**

licensure to age 17, and that state has the nation's lowest death rates for 16-year-olds. In Britain, teens can't drive
35 until they reach 17. In Germany, the driving age is 18.

Nighttime conditions. ❹ Although 38 states impose night-driving restrictions on young drivers, most are weak. Half of the limits don't start until midnight. Barring teen driving after 9 p.m., until the driver reaches the age of 18,
40 would cover the times when teens are most likely to crash, according to the Institute.

Passenger limits. A teen driver's risk of dying more than doubles when two or more male passengers are present. A restriction that limits young drivers to just one passenger, until age 18,
45 would remove distractions that contribute to deadly crashes.

❺ Some critics argue that laws prohibiting unrestricted driving until age 18 only push up the accident rates for 18-year-olds. They are simply wrong. The Institute data show the extra years of maturity make a difference.

50 Others note—accurately—that while the number of deaths caused by 16-year-old drivers has declined, the number per 16-year-old driver has not. Restrictions are simply keeping them from the roads. Still, lives are saved, despite relatively weak laws.

55 Yes, new conditions create inconveniences for parents and teens, including highly responsible new drivers. And new laws don't guarantee compliance. They can, however, fortify rules parents set themselves. Considering the daily carnage on the nation's roads, inconvenience would seem to
60 be a small price for greater safety and peace of mind.

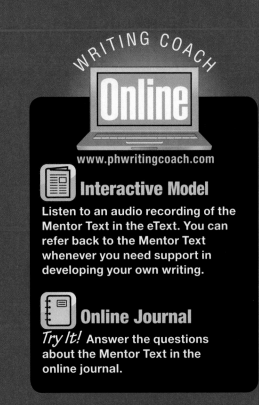

WRITING COACH

Online

www.phwritingcoach.com

Interactive Model

Listen to an audio recording of the Mentor Text in the eText. You can refer back to the Mentor Text whenever you need support in developing your own writing.

Online Journal

Try It! Answer the questions about the Mentor Text in the online journal.

❹ At this point and others, the editorial's position is supported with **sound reasoning, facts, and details**.

Try It! Give an example of a fact presented to support the editorial's position. What reason is given to explain why banning teen driving after 9 P.M. might save lives?

❺ The editorial includes **statements that consider and respond to the views of others**.

Try It! Give examples of two times when the editorial gives other people's views about the issue. How does the editorial rebut, or argue against, these opposing views?

STUDENT MODEL · Editorial

With a small group, take turns reading this Student Model aloud. As you read, practice newly acquired vocabulary by correctly producing the word's sound. Also note the information, strength, and quality of evidence in the text. Ask yourself if the writer provides adequate evidence to support his position and make his argument credible.

Use a Reader's Eye

Now, reread the Student Model. On your copy of the Student Model, use the Reader's Response Symbols to react to what you read.

Reader's Response Symbols

+   I strongly agree with this.

–   I strongly disagree with this.

?   I have a question about this.

!   Wow! That is cool/weird/ interesting.

Partner Talk

Share your responses to the Student Model with a partner. Discuss responses that were the same for both of you, as well as those that were different.

Texting Troubles

by Dylan Ruiz

I've been having a lot of pain in my thumbs lately so I went to the doctor. He told me it was due to texting! I began to notice how texting affects me and my classmates. In addition to affecting our
5   health, texting causes disruptions at school and fighting and hard feelings among teens. We can prevent the negative effects of texting by using good judgment and limiting how many texts we send.

Students need to remember that texting does
10   not make us who we are. Certainly, texting makes us feel connected. However, frequent texting is not a good measure of our connections with others. The number of texts we send and receive is less important than sharing our thoughts
15   and feelings with friends and loved ones.

Texting also takes away some of our independence, which is something I never want to happen. When we text questions to peers and parents about things we could figure out for
20   ourselves, we definitely become dependent on those people. We need to think for ourselves!

Do you remember the golden rule we learned when we were kids? "Treat others as you want to be treated." We should think about that rule when we
25   text: Text others as you would like them to text you. Texting is a less personal way of communicating, so it's easier to bully with a text. Cruel messages can hurt people. Showing people private messages that someone sent you can destroy that person's
30   reputation. Also, threats—even when they're meant as a joke—can get you into trouble with the police. We need to be positive with our text messaging to avoid trouble and to avoid hurting others.

1

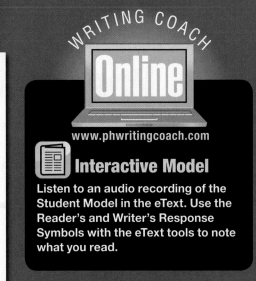

WRITING COACH

Online

www.phwritingcoach.com

Interactive Model

Listen to an audio recording of the Student Model in the eText. Use the Reader's and Writer's Response Symbols with the eText tools to note what you read.

35 Texting also causes distractions at school. We miss a lot of what our teachers are telling us when we sneak out phones to text. Teachers have noticed a connection between texting in class and failing grades, so we need to reserve texting for social times. Resist temptation by keeping

40 your cell phone in your locker or at home.

Finally, we need to turn off our cell phones occasionally to rest our minds and bodies. The Nielsen Company says the average teen sends and receives 2,272 text messages per month! This

45 constant disruption of our cell phones going off makes it difficult to relax and also makes us restless and anxious. Chatting with friends is important, but texting late at night means we don't get enough sleep. According to the American Medical

50 Association, a lack of sleep can cause irritability, inability to concentrate, or even hallucinations!

We need to avoid the negative effects of texting. Limit texting to give your thumbs a rest and allow for down time. Limit where and when you text to

55 get enough sleep and focus on classes. Use good judgment. Think about what you text to protect your and others' privacy and avoid hurting people. We all need to recognize our worth beyond the cell phone and truly think before we hit *send*.

Use a Writer's Eye

Now, evaluate the piece as a writer. On your copy of the Student Model, use the Writer's Response Symbols to react to what you read.

Writer's Response Symbols	
C.T.	**Clearly stated thesis**
P.A.	**Good persuasive arguments**
S.E.	**Effective supporting evidence**
C.A.	**Good responses to readers' counter-arguments**

2

Your Turn ▷ **Feature Assignment:**
Editorial

Prewriting

Plan a first draft of your editorial **by determining an appropriate topic.** You can select from the Topic Bank or come up with an idea of your own.

 Choose From the Topic Bank

TOPIC BANK

Self-Expression Some people argue that freedom of expression ends at the school entrance. Choose an issue involving self-expression, such as school uniforms or the rights of school newspapers. Write an editorial expressing your position on the issue you selected.

School Sports Programs Many people consider sports programs valuable to the school experience. Write an editorial in which you explain whether or not you think it is important for students to participate in sports programs at their schools.

Magazine Clothing Ads Some people believe that magazine clothing ads are harmful to teenagers because they present unrealistic images that don't reflect the average person. Write an editorial in which you explain your position on this issue.

 Choose Your Own Topic

Determine an appropriate topic on your own by using a **range of strategies** to generate ideas.

Personal Interests and Discussion

- Read a current magazine or newspaper and look for articles that interest you. Identify and list two or three controversial issues. Keep a careful record of any outside sources that you use.

- Take notes and write several key points about each issue.

- Discuss these issues with others and take notes on their counter-arguments. Which issue do you want to take a stand on?

Review your responses and choose a topic.

Narrow Your Topic

Choosing a topic that is too broad will result in writing that is unfocused and confusing.

Apply It! Use a graphic organizer like the one shown to narrow your topic.

- Write your general topic in the top box and keep narrowing your topic as you move down the chart.
- In the last box, write your narrowest, or "smallest" topic, the new focus of your editorial.

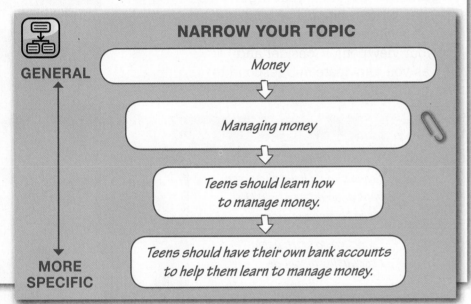

NARROW YOUR TOPIC

GENERAL

Money

↓

Managing money

↓

Teens should learn how to manage money.

↓

Teens should have their own bank accounts to help them learn to manage money.

MORE SPECIFIC

Consider Your Audience and Purpose

Before writing, think about your audience and purpose. Consider how your writing will convey the intended meaning to an audience. **Consider and respond to the views of others** as you ask yourself these questions.

Questions for Audience	Questions for Purpose
• Who is my audience?	• What is my viewpoint about my topic?
• What information do they need to understand my topic?	• How can I anticipate and answer reader concerns and counter-arguments?
• What concerns and counter-arguments might they have about my topic?	• What do I want my audience to do?

Record your answers in your writing journal.

Plan Your Piece

You will use the graphic organizer to state your thesis, organize your arguments, and identify details. When it is complete, you will be ready to write your first draft.

Develop a Clear Thesis To stay focused as you write your draft, establish a clear thesis using your notes as a guide. Your thesis should be a single sentence that sums up your position. Add your thesis to a graphic organizer like the one shown.

Logically Organize Your Arguments Organize your arguments from least to most important. Then write them, using complete sentences, in a graphic organizer. Include evidence that is logically organized to support your viewpoint. Consider and respond to the views of others as you anticipate and respond to reader concerns and counter-arguments.

Develop Your Persuasive Arguments

Clear Thesis	*Teens should have their own bank accounts to help them learn to manage money.*
First Persuasive Argument	*Teens would learn basic accounting methods.*
Supporting Evidence/ Details	
Second Persuasive Argument	*Teens would learn how to budget and make wise spending choices.*
Supporting Evidence/ Details	
Reader's Counter-arguments	*Teens may spend all their money.*
Responses to Counter-arguments	

Gather Details

To provide evidence for their arguments, writers use many kinds of details. Look at these examples.

- **Logical Reasoning:** *Money kept in an account is less accessible, so kids have time to think before withdrawing funds.*

- **Expert Opinion:** *Banker Maria Rose says, "It is important for teens to learn how to use a checking account."*

- **Personal Observations:** *Having a bank account helped me save for larger purchases.*

- **Example:** *High school senior Ethan Kane used a bank account to save money for his first car.*

Also, as you gather evidence, be sure to **differentiate between fact and opinion.**

- A **fact** is something that can be proven.

- An **opinion** is a belief based on a person's judgment. An opinion cannot be proven, but it can be supported by facts.

Try It! Read the Student Model excerpt and identify which type of detail the author used to support his argument.

WRITING COACH

Online

www.phwritingcoach.com

Interactive Graphic Organizers

Use the interactive graphic organizers to help you create a plan for your writing.

Interactive Model

Refer back to the Interactive Model in the eText as you plan your writing.

> **STUDENT MODEL** from **Texting Troubles**
> page 177; lines 41–47
>
> Finally, we need to turn off our cell phones occasionally to rest our minds and bodies. The Nielsen Company states the average teen sends and receives 2,272 text messages per month! This constant disruption of our cell phones going off makes it difficult to relax and also makes us restless and anxious.

Apply It! Review the types of evidence writers use to support persuasive writing. Identify at least one detail for each argument to add to your graphic organizer.

- Review your details to **differentiate between fact and opinion.** Support opinions with facts, and check that facts are reliable.

- Consider the quality and amount of evidence you have gathered. If necessary, collect more factual details before you draft.

- Make sure that **evidence is logically organized to support your viewpoint.** Add the details to your graphic organizer.

Drafting

During the drafting stage, you will start to write your ideas for your editorial. You will follow an outline that provides an **organizational strategy** that will help you **build on ideas** to write a **focused, organized, and coherent** editorial.

The Organization of a Persuasive Essay

The chart shows an organizational strategy for a persuasive essay. Look back at how the Mentor Text follows this organizational strategy. Then, use this chart to help you outline your draft.

Outline for Success

I. Introduction

See Mentor Text, p. 174.

- Lead
- Clear thesis or position

Grab Your Reader

- An interesting lead will grab your reader's attention. You can use a quote or an anecdote from your research, present an interesting example, or reveal a startling statistic.
- A clear thesis statement will help your audience understand your position.

II. Body

See Mentor Text, pp. 174–175.

- Persuasive arguments
- Logically organized supporting evidence
- Reader concerns and counter-arguments that are proven wrong or shown to be less significant than your arguments

Build Your Case

- Each paragraph should have its own argument and supporting evidence.
- Counter-arguments are reasons that others may have to prove your argument wrong. By including and refuting these and other opposing concerns, you can make your argument even stronger.

III. Conclusion

See Mentor Text, p. 175.

- Restatement of position
- Memorable ending, such as a call to action

Wrap It Up

- Restating your position means echoing the language of your thesis to help cement it in readers' minds.
- To end on a convincing note, you might urge your audience to take specific action. For example, you might suggest that they participate in an activity.

 **Start Your Draft**

Use this checklist to help you complete your draft. Use the graphic organizer that shows your thesis, persuasive arguments, and supporting evidence, and the Outline for Success as guides.

While drafting, aim at writing your ideas, not on making your writing perfect. Remember, you will have the chance to improve your draft when you revise and edit.

√ Start by drafting a **lead,** the opening statement that grabs your readers' attention.

√ Continue to develop your **introduction** by letting readers know what to expect in the rest of your editorial. Include a clear **thesis statement**.

√ Shape the **body** of your editorial by developing a focused paragraph for each argument and its supporting evidence. This will help to **logically organize** your ideas and writing.

√ Consider and respond to the views of others by including reader concerns or **counter-arguments** and your responses to them.

√ Remember to differentiate between **fact** and **opinion** and to support opinions with facts.

√ To build coherence, or a logical flow and focus to your writing, use **transition words** such as *first, therefore, furthermore,* and *finally* to tie paragraphs together.

√ End with a strong **conclusion** that restates your **position.**

√ Use **powerful language** to finish on a memorable note.

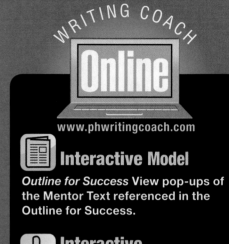

WRITING COACH

Online

www.phwritingcoach.com

Interactive Model

Outline for Success View pop-ups of the Mentor Text referenced in the Outline for Success.

Interactive Writing Coach™

Use the Interactive Writing Coach to receive the level of support you need:
• Write one paragraph at a time and submit each one for immediate, detailed feedback.
• Write your entire first draft and submit it for immediate, personalized feedback.

Revising: Making It Better

Now that you have finished your first draft, you are ready to revise. Think about the "big picture" of **audience, purpose, and genre**. You can use the Revision RADaR strategy as a guide for making changes to improve your draft. Revision RADaR provides four major ways to improve your writing: (R) replace, (A) add, (D) delete, and (R) reorder.

Kelly Gallagher, M. Ed.

KEEP REVISION ON YOUR RADaR

Read part of the first draft of the Student Model "Texting Troubles." Then look at questions the writer asked himself as he thought about how well his draft addressed issues of audience, purpose, and genre.

Texting Troubles

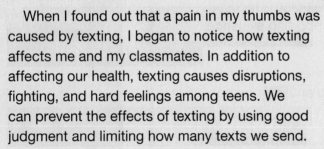

1ST DRAFT

When I found out that a pain in my thumbs was caused by texting, I began to notice how texting affects me and my classmates. In addition to affecting our health, texting causes disruptions, fighting, and hard feelings among teens. We can prevent the effects of texting by using good judgment and limiting how many texts we send.

Students need to remember that texting does not make us who we are. Certainly, texting makes us feel connected. However, frequent texting is not a good measure of our connections with others. Texting also takes away some of our independence, which is something I never want to happen. When we text questions to peers and parents about things we could figure out for ourselves, we definitely become dependent on those people. We need to think for ourselves!

*Does the **introduction** include a **lead** that grabs my attention?*

*Does my **thesis statement** clearly identify the issue and my purpose or opinion?*

*Have I answered reader **counter-arguments**?*

*Have I **logically organized** my ideas?*

Now look at how the writer used Revision RADaR to write an improved second draft.

Texting Troubles

2ND DRAFT

I've been having a lot of pain in my thumbs lately so I went to the doctor. He told me it was due to texting! I began to notice how texting affects me and my classmates. In addition to affecting our health, texting causes disruptions at school and fighting and hard feelings among teens. We can prevent the negative effects of texting by using good judgment and limiting how many texts we send.

R Replaced *boring lead with a livelier version*

A Added *the word* <u>negative</u> *to make my position clearer*

Students need to remember that texting does not make us who we are. Certainly, texting makes us feel connected. However, frequent texting is not a good measure of our connections with others. The number of texts we send and receive is less important than sharing our thoughts and feelings with friends and loved ones.

A Added *a response to a possible counter-argument*

Texting also takes away some of our independence, which is something I never want to happen. When we text questions to peers and parents about things we could figure out for ourselves, we definitely become dependent on those people. We need to think for ourselves!

R Reordered *ideas by creating a new paragraph*

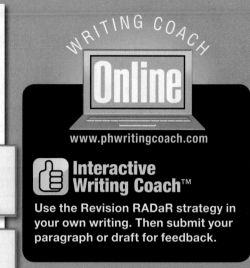

WRITING COACH

Online

www.phwritingcoach.com

Interactive Writing Coach™

Use the Revision RADaR strategy in your own writing. Then submit your paragraph or draft for feedback.

Apply It! Use your Revision RADaR to revise your draft.

- First, determine if you have addressed the needs of your audience, explained your purpose for writing, and included all the genre characteristics for an editorial.
- Then, apply your Revision RADaR to make changes. Remember, you can use the steps in the strategy in any order.

Look at the Big Picture

Use the chart and your analytical skills to evaluate how well each section of your editorial addresses **purpose**, **audience**, and **genre**. When necessary, use the suggestions in the chart to revise your piece.

Section	Evaluate	Revise
Introduction	• Check the **lead**. Will it grab readers' attention and inspire them to read on?	• Your lead will be more interesting with an example, anecdote, or statistic.
	• Make sure that the **thesis** clearly identifies the issue and states your viewpoint.	• You should use clear, direct language to state your issue and opinion.
Body	• Check that you have clearly defined your **persuasive arguments** and organized them in a logical way to support your viewpoint.	• Place weaker arguments before the strongest argument, ending with your most convincing idea.
	• Underline details that offer **supporting evidence**. Draw a line from each detail to the argument it supports.	• Details should be in the same paragraph as the argument that they support. Delete unnecessary repetitions and unimportant information.
	• Check that supporting evidence differentiates between fact and opinion and provides facts to **support opinions**.	• Facts, such as statistics and examples, strengthen your arguments and back up your opinion.
	• Check that you have anticipated reader concerns and **counter-arguments** and that you have responded to each.	• Details can strengthen your responses to readers' views and help make your argument more persuasive than others.
Conclusion	• Check the **restatement** of your position.	• The restatement of your position should match your thesis.
	• Check that you used **powerful language** that appeals to emotion and reason.	• A quotation or a strong, authoritative statement can make sure your writing will influence the attitudes and actions of a specific audience about your specific issue.

Focus on Craft: Effective Transitions

Using **effective transitions** is an important way to show how sentences and paragraphs are connected. Transitions, such as *therefore*, *next*, or *finally*, link evidence and arguments so that persuasive writing is logically organized. Transition words and phrases such as *however* or *in contrast* signal the connection between the author's position and counter-arguments.

Think about effective transitions as you read the following sentences from the Student Model.

 **STUDENT MODEL** from **Texting Troubles**
page 176; lines 10–13

> Certainly, texting makes us feel connected. However, frequent texting is not a good measure of our connections with others.

 Try It! Now, ask yourself these questions. Record your answers in your journal.

- What connection does the transition word *However* show between the two sentences?
- What other words or phrases could you substitute for *However*?

Fine-Tune Your Draft

Apply It! Use the revision suggestions to write your final draft **after rethinking how well questions of purpose, audience, and genre have been addressed.**

- **Use Effective Transitions** Add transition words and phrases to connect sentences and paragraphs.
- **Use Precise Words** Substitute specific words for vague or overly general words. Precise words make persuasive writing stronger because they convey the author's exact intended meaning. For example, change *biggest* to *most important* or *bad* to *negative*.

Peer Feedback Read your final draft to a group of your peers. Ask if you have considered and responded to the views of others. Think about your peers' feedback and revise your final draft as needed.

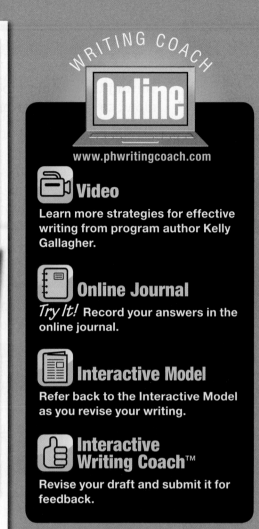

WRITING COACH

Online

www.phwritingcoach.com

Video
Learn more strategies for effective writing from program author Kelly Gallagher.

Online Journal
Try It! Record your answers in the online journal.

Interactive Model
Refer back to the Interactive Model as you revise your writing.

Interactive Writing Coach™
Revise your draft and submit it for feedback.

Editing: Making It Correct

During the editing process, it may be helpful to read your draft aloud to listen for errors.

Before editing, think about the **variety of complete sentences** in your draft, and how **parallel structures** can be used in your sentences. Also think about the **proper placement of modifiers,** such as adjectives and adverbs. Then correct any factual errors and errors in **grammar, mechanics, and spelling.**

WRITE GUY *Jeff Anderson, M. Ed.*

WHAT DO YOU NOTICE?

Zoom in on Conventions Focus on the placement of modifiers as you zoom in on these sentences from the Student Model.

> **STUDENT MODEL** from **Texting Troubles**
> page 177; lines 34–39
>
> Texting also causes distractions at school. ...Teachers have noticed a connection between texting in class and failing grades, so we need to reserve texting for social times.

Now, ask yourself: *Do each of the highlighted modifiers come before or after the words they modify?*

Perhaps you said that some of the modifiers come before and some after the words they modify.

Most adjectives come before the nouns they modify, as in the phrases *failing grades* and *social times.*

Adjectival phrases typically come after the words they modify. The adjectival phrase *at school* follows *distractions,* the noun it modifies, just as the adjectival phrase *in class* follows *texting,* the word it modifies.

For clarity, it is best to place modifiers close to the words they modify. For example, the second sentence could have been: *Teachers have noticed in class a connection between texting and failing grades.* In that case, a reader might think that any texting, rather than *texting in class,* causes failing grades.

Partner Talk Discuss this question with a partner: *Why did the author place modifiers close to the words they modify?*

> To learn more about properly placed modifiers, see Chapter 20.

To learn more, see chapter 20.

Grammar Mini-Lesson: Parallel Structures

Parallel structures can add clarity and persuasive force to writing. Using **parallel structures** in complete sentences, or sentences with both a subject and predicate, means that equal ideas are expressed in words, phrases, and clauses of similar types. Notice how the Student Model uses parallel structure.

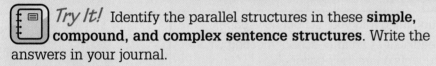

STUDENT MODEL from **Texting Troubles**
page 176; lines 6–8

We can prevent the negative effects of texting by <u>using good judgment</u> and <u>limiting how many texts we send.</u>

 Try It! Identify the parallel structures in these **simple, compound, and complex sentence structures**. Write the answers in your journal.

1. Texting can be harmful, distracting, and isolating.
2. I do not text in class, and I do not text while driving.
3. The teachers and the principal agree that students should not text in school, unless an emergency occurs.

 Apply It! **Edit your draft for grammar, mechanics, and spelling.** Ensure that you have used a variety of complete sentences with parallel structures and **properly placed modifiers**.

 Use the rubric to evaluate your piece. If necessary, rethink, rewrite, or revise.

WRITING COACH

www.phwritingcoach.com

 Video
Learn effective editing techniques from program author Jeff Anderson.

 Online Journal
Try It! Record your answers in the online journal.

 Interactive Model
Refer back to the Interactive Model as you edit your writing.

 Interactive Writing Coach™
Edit your draft. Check it against the rubric and then submit it for feedback.

Rubric for Persuasive Essay: Editorial	Rating Scale
Ideas: How clearly are the issue and your position stated?	Not very Very 1 2 3 4 5 6
Organization: How organized are your arguments and supporting evidence?	1 2 3 4 5 6
Voice: How authoritative is your voice?	1 2 3 4 5 6
Word Choice: How persuasive is your word choice?	1 2 3 4 5 6
Sentence Fluency: How correctly have you used parallel structures to convey ideas?	1 2 3 4 5 6
Conventions: How correct are your sentence types?	1 2 3 4 5 6

Publishing

Give your editorial a chance to change someone's mind—publish it! First, get your editorial ready for presentation. Then, choose a way to **publish it for the appropriate audience.**

Wrap Up Your Presentation

If your editorial is handwritten, you may need to make a new, clean copy. If so, be sure to **write legibly.**

Publish Your Piece

Use the chart to identify a way to publish your editorial.

If your audience is...	...then publish it by...
Students or adults at school	• Submitting it to your school newspaper • Reading it at an after-school meeting where students share their editorials • Posting it online and inviting responses
People in your neighborhood or city	• Posting it on the community bulletin board at your public library • Submitting it to your town newspaper

 ## Extend Your Research

Think more about the topic on which you wrote your editorial. What else would you like to know about this topic? As you record your thoughts, use specific details to describe and explain your ideas. Increase the specificity of your details based on the type of information.

- Brainstorm for several questions you would like to research and then consult, or discuss, with others. Then decide which question is your major research question.

- Formulate, or develop, a plan about how you will answer these questions. Decide where you will find more information—on the Internet, at the library, or through other sources.

- Finally, learn more about your topic by following through with your research plan.

 The Big Question: Why Write? What is the point? How did you determine whether you made it successfully?

MAKE YOUR WRITING COUNT

Use an Editorial for an Interview

People who write editorials for a living are often the same "pundits" seen in TV interviews, expressing strong opinions on controversial issues. Communicate your opinion to a wider audience by producing a **video-recorded interview.**

With a group, choose one editorial to use as the basis for an interview. Your group will work together to write questions and answers about the topic in the editorial. Present your TV-style interview live for the class, or video-record it.

Here's your action plan.

1. Choose roles, such as interviewer, interviewee, and videographer.

2. With your group, judge each editorial and decide which one would work best as an interview.

3. Watch news interviews on television to establish criteria for your work. For example, notice the style and tone of the language the people use in the context of the interview. Then, create the interview.

   - Use the editorial and any meeting notes to write the questions the interviewer will ask. Also include a brief introduction that tells the audience the topic.

   - Work as a team to write the answers for the interviewee.

   - Conduct online research to find answers to questions not covered in the editorial.

   - Help the interviewer and interviewee practice their lines.

4. Present the interview to the class, either live or on video.

Listening and Speaking As your group practices the interview, keep track of the amount of time it takes to complete it. Adjust the number and length of questions and answers accordingly. Pay attention to how the formality of the language you use influences your listeners' understanding.

WRITING COACH

Online

www.phwritingcoach.com

Online Journal

Extend Your Research Record your answers and ideas in the online journal.

Resource

Link to resources on 21st Century Learning for help in creating a group project.

21st Century Learning

Letter to the Editor

Letters to the editor are letters sent by readers to the editor of a newspaper or magazine about an issue of concern. Readers may comment on current events or respond to previously published stories or opinions. Letters to the editor must be brief and to the point, so they focus on a single subject. Because they reflect the reactions of readers, the letters are often written in a forceful, passionate tone. The language is sometimes witty or sarcastic. Editors reject letters that are offensive or contain poor grammar.

Try It! Study this letter to the editor. Then, answer these questions. Record your answers in your journal.

1. What is the main **message** of this letter?

2. Who is the true **target audience** for this letter?

3. The opening statement in a letter to the editor usually contains a **lead** to hook the reader's attention. What is the writer's opening statement?

4. What is the writer's **position** or **opinion** on the issue?

5. What do you notice about the **organization** of the letter?

6. What **arguments** does the writer present?

7. Like an editorial, a letter to the editor must include **evidence** to support the author's arguments, such as facts, statistics, or expert testimony. What evidence does the author present?

8. Letters to the editor often have short, punchy **concluding** statements. How does the author conclude this letter?

Extension Find another example of a letter to the editor on an important issue, and compare it with this one.

To the Editor,

Your article "Park Sell-Off Passes Committee," published on September 18, raised more questions than it answered.

In the past, your paper has covered the City Council in great detail. However, this was not done in discussing a proposal to sell parts of Central Park. How much of the park would be sold? How much money would be raised? What say will citizens have in the matter? These questions affect everyone in our community. However, your reporter said only, "Details of the deal are still being discussed."

I rely on the *Times* to help me discover the truth. But after reading your article, I wonder: Is the park proposal really a sell-off, or have the *Times* and the City Council sold out the citizens of Lakeview?

Miguel Figueroa

Lakeview Resident

Create a Letter to the Editor

Follow these steps to create your own letter to the editor. To plan your letter, review the graphic organizers on pages R24–R27 and choose one that suits your needs.

Prewriting

- Choose a topic and determine your opinion on the issue. To help you clarify your ideas, explain them to a classmate.
- Write a clear thesis statement that identifies your position.
- Identify your target audience. Anticipate and respond to the views, concerns, and counterarguments of your audience.
- Identify two arguments to support your opinion.
- Gather evidence to support each of your arguments.
- Decide what you want the audience to do.

Drafting

- Write a short, punchy lead that gets straight to the point. Focus your position statement on one or two key points. If you refer to a previously published item, like a news story, include its headline and date of publication.
- In your arguments, direct criticism toward the views of others, not the individuals. Add a personal twist with a story based on experience. If necessary, choose your strongest argument to keep the letter short.
- Conclude with a call to action, perhaps asking people to speak out, contact an organization, or change their habits.

Revising and Editing

Review your draft to ensure your ideas are well organized. Make sure your opening statement is clearly presented and delete irrelevant information that distracts from your viewpoint. Also check that spelling, grammar, and mechanics are correct.

Publishing

Type up and print your letter to the editor. Share it with your class or send it to your school newspaper.

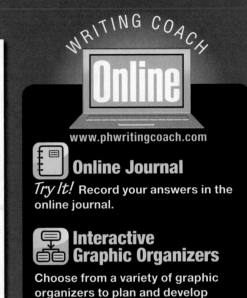

WRITING COACH

Online

www.phwritingcoach.com

Online Journal

Try It! **Record your answers in the online journal.**

Interactive Graphic Organizers

Choose from a variety of graphic organizers to plan and develop your project.

Partner Talk

Before you start drafting, discuss your letter with a partner. Ask for feedback about your arguments. For example, which argument is strongest? Use specific details to describe and explain your ideas. Increase the specificity of your details based on the type of information you are delivering.

Writing for Assessment SAT PREP ACT

Many standardized tests include a prompt that asks you to write a persuasive essay. You can use the prompts on these pages to practice. Your responses should include the same characteristics as your editorial. (See page 172.)

 Try It! To begin, read the **persuasive** prompt and the information on format and academic vocabulary. Use the ABCDs of On-Demand Writing to help you plan and write your essay.

Format

A *persuasive essay* includes a clear thesis, body paragraphs with supporting evidence, and a conclusion that restates your position.

Persuasive Prompt

What hobby would you recommend? Write a persuasive essay describing it and why others should try it. Support your opinion with examples and facts.

Academic Vocabulary

An *opinion* is a personal judgment. A *fact* can be proven. Be sure to differentiate between fact and opinion.

The ABCDs of On-Demand Writing

Use the following ABCDs to help you respond to the prompt.

Before you write your draft:

A ttack the prompt [1 MINUTE]

- Circle or highlight important verbs in the prompt. Draw a line from the verb to what it refers to.
- Rewrite the prompt in your own words.

B rainstorm possible answers [4 MINUTES]

- Create a graphic organizer to generate ideas.
- Use one for each part of the prompt if necessary.

C hoose the order of your response [1 MINUTE]

- Think about the best way to organize your ideas.
- Number your ideas in the order you will write about them. Cross out ideas you will not be using.

After you write your draft:

D etect errors before turning in the draft [1 MINUTE]

- Carefully reread your writing.
- Make sure that your response makes sense and is complete.
- Look for spelling, punctuation, and grammar errors.

More Prompts for Practice

Apply It! Respond to Prompts 1 and 2 by writing **persuasive essays** that **influence a specific audience**. As you write, be sure to:

- Identify an **appropriate audience**
- Establish a **clear thesis** or position
- Consider and respond to the **views of others**
- **Logically organize** your arguments and evidence so they support your viewpoint
- Differentiate between **fact and opinion**
- Anticipate and answer **readers' concerns** and **counter-arguments**

> **Prompt 1** A local animal rescue group needs funding for a campaign to give pet food to owners who might otherwise send their pets to already overcrowded shelters. Write a persuasive essay convincing people to donate money to this cause.

> **Prompt 2** Your technology class has been studying how multimedia is shaping the future, which is the subject of a new exhibit at the Museum of Science and Industry. Write a persuasive essay to convince your principal to allow students to go on a field trip to the museum.

Spiral Review: Expository Respond to Prompt 3 by writing a **compare-and-contrast essay**. Make sure your essay reflects all of the characteristics described on page 146, including:

- Effective **introductory** and **concluding paragraphs**
- A clearly stated purpose or **controlling idea**
- **Logical organization** with appropriate facts and details, and no extraneous information or inconsistencies
- An accurate **synthesis** of ideas from several sources
- A variety of **sentence structures, rhetorical devices**, and **transitions** to link paragraphs.

> **Prompt 3** Choose a celebrity and write a composition that compares and contrasts your life with what you think that celebrity's life is like.

WRITING COACH

Online

www.phwritingcoach.com

 Interactive Writing Coach™

Plan your response to the prompt. If you are using the prompt for practice, write one paragraph at a time or your entire draft and then submit it for feedback. If you are using the prompt as a timed test, write your entire draft and then submit it for feedback.

Remember **ABCD**

A ttack the prompt

B rainstorm possible answers

C hoose the order of your response

D etect errors before turning in the draft

CHAPTER 10

RESPONSE *to* LITERATURE

What Do You Think?

Authors have purposes for writing. Some authors write to inform. Some write to entertain. Others write to persuade.

Part of being an active reader is analyzing the author's purpose. You think about the author's purpose and use details to show how the author achieves that purpose.

Try It! Think about your favorite book. What do you think the author was trying to communicate by writing this book? Consider these questions as you participate in an extended discussion with a partner. Take turns expressing your ideas and feelings.

- How did you feel when reading this book?
- How did the author achieve his or her purpose?
- Do you think the author did a good job achieving his or her purpose? Why or why not?
- What details support your answer?

What's Ahead

In this chapter, you will review two strong examples of an interpretative response essay: a Mentor Text and a Student Model. Then, using the examples as guides, you will write an interpretative response essay of your own.

Connect to the Big Questions

Discuss these questions with your partner:

1 What do you think? What should we read?

2 Why write? What should you write about to make others interested in a text?

INTERPRETATIVE RESPONSE

An interpretative response is a reader's written reaction to an author's work. When you write an interpretative response, you analyze an author's work. You examine text elements and features. You discuss what the work communicated to you. You state your opinions about the work and support your opinions with details from the text. In this chapter, you will explore a special kind of interpretative response, the critical review.

You will develop your critical review by taking it through each of the steps of the writing process: prewriting, drafting, revising, editing, and publishing. You will also have an opportunity to create a writing workshop response to a poem. To preview the criteria for how your critical review will be evaluated, see the rubric on page 215.

FEATURE ASSIGNMENT

Interpretative Response: Critical Review

An effective interpretative response has these characteristics:

- A strong, interesting **focus or thesis statement**

- A **summary of important features** of the work

- **Sustained evidence** from the text, including **quotations when appropriate,** to defend and support ideas

- **Analysis of story elements,** such as character, plot, setting, and theme

- **Ideas** that demonstrate personal insights and opinions

- **Effective sentence structure** and correct spelling, grammar, and usage

A critical review also includes:

- A thesis explaining the writer's analysis and view of the author's work

- An explanation for why the writer chose to review the author's work

Other Forms of Interpretative Response

In addition to a critical review, there are other forms of interpretative response, including:

Blog comments share readers' ideas about an author's work. Readers express their opinions and discuss their understanding of what an author's work means. Comments may be posted on an author's Web site or on the Web site of an online bookstore. Some readers have their own pages on which they write blogs.

Comparison essays explore similarities and differences between two or more works of literature. For example, a comparison essay may compare how main characters in two stories handle a similar problem.

Letters to authors offer reader feedback about books, plays, poetry, and other written works. Letters may be mailed to an author through his or her publishing company or submitted to the author's Web site. These interpretative works present the writer's opinions and support them with specific examples.

Response to literature essays analyze and interpret an author's work. These kinds of essays examine what an author states directly and indirectly and what those statements mean. Response to literature essays also evaluate how well an author has accomplished what he or she has set out to do.

Try It! For each audience and purpose described, choose a form, such as a comparison essay or a letter to an author, that is appropriate for conveying your intended meaning to the audience. Explain your choices.

- To point out to a teacher key differences between two novels
- To exchange ideas with other readers about a book of poetry
- To explain to an author why her latest book is her best yet

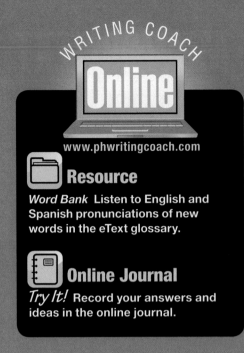

WRITING COACH

Online

www.phwritingcoach.com

📁 **Resource**

Word Bank Listen to English and Spanish pronunciations of new words in the eText glossary.

📔 **Online Journal**

Try It! Record your answers and ideas in the online journal.

WORD BANK

An affix is a word part that can be used to change the meaning of a root word. Affixes can be added to the beginning of the word as a prefix or at the end of the word as a suffix. For example, the suffix *-er* changes the word *dance* to *dancer*. Think about root words and affixes as you review these vocabulary words.

Work with a partner. Take turns using each word in a sentence. If you are unsure of the meaning of a word, use the Glossary or a dictionary to check the definition.

analysis	**evaluate**
develop	**interpret**
effective	**theme**

MENTOR TEXT   Critical Review

Learn From Experience

 After reading the critical review on pages 200–201, read the numbered notes in the margins to learn about how the author presented her ideas.

Answer the *Try It!* questions online or in your notebook.

① The question helps **focus** the critical review on one aspect of Anne Frank's writing: her reasons for becoming a writer.

Try It! How does asking a question help get readers involved in the critical review and its focus?

② By answering the opening question, the author helps **organize the details** in the review.

Try It! What two answers to the question does the review give? How does the question in lines 23–24 expand on the opening question?

③ The review **analyzes** story elements, such as **character** and **setting,** in the context of a diary.

Try It! What does the reviewer mean by calling the diary a character that "never really becomes a character"? How could it help Frank become a character?

From Anne Frank: A Hidden Life

by Mirjam Pressler

① What made [Anne Frank] write? **②** She wanted to keep a diary, but that is not unusual in adolescent girls, and teenagers of her time probably kept diaries more often than teenagers today. So there is nothing
5 out of the ordinary about a girl sitting at a desk, leaning over the paper, blushing as she confides her secrets to her diary. However, it is obvious that Anne Frank wanted more than just a safe place for her secrets. **②** She enjoyed writing for its own sake; it was a way to depict herself—a way to paint
10 a verbal picture of herself and her place in the world. . . .

Anne Frank enjoyed writing and found it a challenge. She tended to write well-rounded stories with a beginning, a middle, and an end. . . . She never gave in to the obvious temptation for someone in her difficult position to write in
15 an exaggerated way.

② However, that still does not explain her growing passion for writing. Later on, it became almost an obsession. If she had simply liked narrative writing for its own sake, she would have concentrated more on the stories she wrote
20 for *Tales from the Secret Annex.* But even after August 1943, when she had begun writing stories and was feeling very enthusiastic about them, she did not neglect her diary. **②** Where did she get this passion for what is, after all, a very lonely pursuit?
25 The reason is fairly obvious: for her, writing was not lonely at all. **③** Anne made her diary into a person; she made it "you," someone to talk to, "Kitty," the real friend she had wanted for so long. It was an extremely "literary" approach to adopt. Many children think up imaginary
30 friends on whom they project their wishes and longings, but they do not very often make the imaginary friend into a literary character. However, this isn't exactly true. "Kitty"

never really becomes a character in Anne Frank's writing. We hear hardly anything about her; instead, she enables Anne Frank to become a literary character herself. . . .

However, even this original way of coping with her need for intimacy and company would not in itself make Anne Frank a writer. ❹ To be a writer, you must have the desire (and of course the ability) to portray yourself, giving form to your life, your ideas, and your needs, intensifying them so that you can put them down on paper. Anne Frank's mastery of that ability, despite her youth, must surely have been partly due to her situation. Her world had to be small enough to fit into the Secret Annex, its few rooms, the hallway, and the attic. The immediate surroundings of the Annex, which offered a little variety, at least at first, were confined to the firm's offices, and Anne could only occasionally look out at the world beyond through a crack in the curtains. The few people she saw through binoculars or walking along the street had to replace not only the whole city but also school outings, trips, everything. Her only glimpse of natural beauty consisted of the leaves and flower spikes of the chestnut tree outside the window, a few clouds passing by, a seagull. ❺ She created nature inside her head; a little moonlight now and then aroused her romantic feelings—and what really made her a writer was this ability to create wide-ranging emotions out of relatively small incidents and then describe them.

WRITING COACH

Online

www.phwritingcoach.com

📰 **Interactive Model**
Listen to an audio recording of the Mentor Text in the eText. You can refer back to the Mentor Text whenever you need support in developing your own writing.

📓 **Online Journal**
Try It! Answer the questions about the Mentor Text in the online journal.

❹ Because the author's focus is on what made Frank a writer, the author gives her **personal insights** and **judgments** instead of providing evidence from the text.

Try It! What does the author say it takes to become a writer? Do you agree with her? Explain.

❺ The **conclusion** brings the reader full circle by providing another answer to the opening question.

Try It! According to the review, what made Anne Frank write?

Extension Find another example of a critical review, and compare it with this one.

STUDENT MODEL   Critical Review

Ray Bradbury's "The Drummer Boy of Shiloh"

With a small group, take turns reading this Student Model aloud. Look for evidence in the text that supports your understanding of the review. As you read, think about the author's purpose and the audience for which she is writing.

Use a Reader's Eye

Now, reread the Student Model. On your copy of the Student Model, use the Reader's Response Symbols to react to what you read.

Reader's Response Symbols

+   I agree with this point.

–   This isn't clear to me.

?   I have a question about this.

!   Well said!

Partner Talk

Participate in an extended discussion with a partner. Express your opinions and share your responses to the Student Model. Discuss the author's analysis and her use of supporting quotations.

Ray Bradbury's "The Drummer Boy of Shiloh"

by Anna Lehman

Ray Bradbury's "The Drummer Boy of Shiloh" is a short story that leaves readers thinking about the tragedy of war. Even though no one dies during the story, it's a sad tale all the same. By focusing
5   on just two characters, Bradbury paints a grim picture of what it was like to fight in the Civil War.

The main character is 14-year-old Joby, a Civil War drummer boy. It's the night before the battle of Shiloh, and Joby can't sleep. He's
10   been with the army only three weeks. He's never been in a battle before, and he's scared. He realizes that drummers carry no weapons, so they can't even fight back. "I got only a drum," he thinks, "two sticks to beat it, and no shield."

15   During the night, a man walks by and hears Joby crying. It turns out that the man is the army general. He stops to talk with Joby. He tells the boy that he cried, too, thinking about what's ahead.

The general talks about how young, innocent
20   soldiers will get shot. He fears they will end up in Owl Creek, "just floating, at sundown tomorrow, not caring where the current takes them." He says the sad truth the soldiers will learn is that "men actually die in war."

25   Joby listens, wondering why the general is telling him this. The general then explains why Joby's job is so important. The drummer boy is "the heart of the army," he tells him. He sets the pace for

1

the men. A "sure, steady, ever faster" drumbeat
30 will carry the soldiers forward. It will give them
courage. Without it, the battle "would be more than
a slaughter, it would be murderous nightmare."

When the general leaves, Joby feels a little calmer.
The general has built up his courage. Joby now feels
35 that he has a key part to play in the coming battle.

Even though Joby seems more at ease, the story
has a lingering sadness. The general's talk of death
and bloodshed, and Joby's fear of the next day's
battle, leave the reader uneasy. A young boy may
40 die the next day, along with many other soldiers.

2

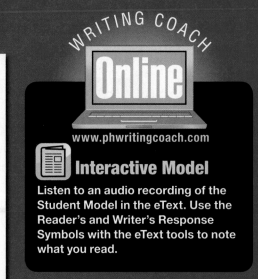

WRITING COACH

Online

www.phwritingcoach.com

Interactive Model

Listen to an audio recording of the
Student Model in the eText. Use the
Reader's and Writer's Response
Symbols with the eText tools to note
what you read.

Use a Writer's Eye

Now, evaluate the piece as a writer. On
your copy of the Student Model, use the
Writer's Response Symbols to react to
what you read. Identify places where the
student writer uses characteristics of an
effective critical review.

Writer's Response Symbols	
C.T.	**Clearly stated thesis**
I.A.	**In-depth analysis**
S.E.	**Effective supporting evidence**
E.Q.	**Effective quotations**

 **Feature Assignment: Critical Review**

Prewriting

Plan a first draft of your critical review **by determining an appropriate topic.** You can select from the Topic Bank or come up with an idea of your own.

 ## Choose From the Topic Bank

> ### TOPIC BANK
>
> **Response to Two Stories** Read "Thank You M'am" by Langston Hughes and "The Story-Teller" by Saki. In your review, compare how the authors reveal theme in each story. Detail what is similar and what is different about the way each accomplishes conveying his message.
>
> **Response to Poetry** Poets often use symbolism in their poetry. Think about a poem you've read where the poet has used symbols or symbolism to communicate ideas to the reader. Write a critical review of the poem in which you discuss the meaning of one symbol the poet uses.
>
> **Response to a Short Story** Think about a short story in which the setting has been important to the plot. Write a critical review of the short story in which you discuss why the setting is important to the story.

 ## Choose Your Own Topic

Determine an appropriate topic on your own by using the following **range of strategies** to generate ideas.

> ### *Thought and Discussion*
>
> - Think about a book or story that made you laugh or cry. Consider the reasons for your reaction. Compare your feelings with those of another student.
>
> Review your responses and choose a topic.

Narrow Your Topic

If you choose a topic that is too broad, your writing will not have a clear focus.

Apply It! Use a graphic organizer like the one shown to narrow your topic.

- Write your general topic in the first box, and narrow your topic as you move down the chart.
- Your last box should hold your narrowest or "smallest" topic, the new focus of your critical review.

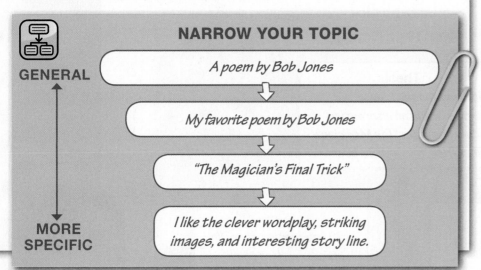

NARROW YOUR TOPIC

GENERAL

A poem by Bob Jones

My favorite poem by Bob Jones

"The Magician's Final Trick"

I like the clever wordplay, striking images, and interesting story line.

MORE SPECIFIC

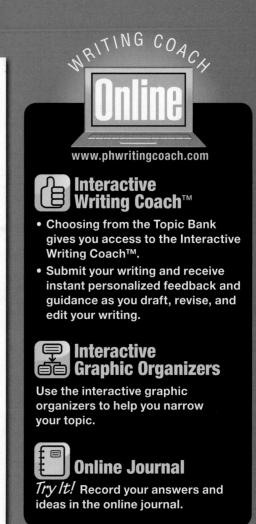

WRITING COACH

Online

www.phwritingcoach.com

Interactive Writing Coach™

- Choosing from the Topic Bank gives you access to the Interactive Writing Coach™.
- Submit your writing and receive instant personalized feedback and guidance as you draft, revise, and edit your writing.

Interactive Graphic Organizers

Use the interactive graphic organizers to help you narrow your topic.

Online Journal

Try It! Record your answers and ideas in the online journal.

Consider Your Audience and Purpose

Before writing, think about your audience and purpose. Consider how your writing will convey your intended meaning to this audience.

Questions for Audience	Questions for Purpose
• Who will read my critical review? My teacher? My classmates?	• What do I want my readers to know about the work I am reviewing?
• What will my audience need to know to understand my ideas?	• What ideas and feelings do I want to convey in my review?

Record your answers in your writing journal.

Plan Your Piece

You will use a graphic organizer like the one shown to state your thesis, organize your ideas, and identify details. When it is complete, you will be ready to write your first draft.

Develop Your Thesis Think about your reaction to the author's work. State your feelings and thoughts in a **clear thesis**. Add your thesis statement to a graphic organizer.

Logically Organize Your Supporting Evidence Use a graphic organizer to help you organize **sustained evidence** from the text, including **quotations** when appropriate.

Develop Your Response

Thesis
Striking images, clever wordplay, and an interesting story line make "The Magician's Final Trick" my favorite poem.

Idea
- *Strong images create emotion.*

Evidence
- *The poet compares the magician's temper to a "hurricane in a bottle."*
-

Idea
- *An interesting story line makes readers think.*

Evidence
- *The poet ...*
-

Idea
- *Clever wordplay keeps readers engaged.*

Evidence
- *The poet plays on words with this line:*
-

Gather Details

To support their ideas, writers **provide sustained evidence from the text**, such as the types of details in these examples.

- **Quotations:** *"'I've saved my best trick for last,' he cried, and vanished with a pop!"*

- **Details:** *The magician doesn't want to commit a crime, but he feels he has no choice: "Bills to pay and mouths to feed, and Houdini I'm not!"*

- **Examples:** *The magician's hair was "gray as a winter sky." The light in his eyes "burned dimly, like dying embers."*

- **Relevant Information and Judgments:** *The magician is not a bad person. He is just a tired old man who feels he has run out of options.*

- **Personal Insights:** *The magician has been honest his whole life, and he deeply regrets what he feels he must do. Most people, even me, have regretted a decision from time to time.*

Try It! Read the Student Model excerpt and identify the evidence that the author uses to support her ideas.

 **STUDENT MODEL** from **Ray Bradbury's "The Drummer Boy of Shiloh"** page 202; lines 9–14

> He's been with the army only three weeks. He's never been in a battle before, and he's scared. He realizes that drummers carry no weapons, so they can't even fight back. "I got only a drum," he thinks, "two sticks to beat it, and no shield."

Apply It! Review the types of supporting evidence that can be used in a critical review. Then, identify and write one piece of relevant evidence of each type.

- Review your evidence to make sure it clearly supports your thesis. Be sure to include one or more pieces of each kind of sustained evidence from the text.

- Add your supporting evidence to your graphic organizer. Remember that your goal is to write a response that is logically organized with appropriate details from the text.

- Be sure to make clear how your evidence supports your ideas and arguments to show personal insights and understanding of the text.

WRITING COACH

Online

www.phwritingcoach.com

Interactive Graphic Organizers

Use the interactive graphic organizers to help you create a plan for your writing.

Interactive Model

Refer back to the Interactive Model in the eText as you plan your writing.

Drafting

During the drafting stage, you will start to write your ideas for your critical review. You will follow an outline that provides an **organizational strategy** that will help you build on ideas to write a **focused, organized, and coherent** critical review.

The Organization of an Interpretative Response

The chart shows an organizational strategy for an interpretative response. Look back at how the Mentor Text follows this organizational strategy. Then, use this chart to help you outline your draft.

Outline for Success

I. Introduction
See Mentor Text, p. 200.

- Strong opening paragraph
- Name of the work and the author
- Clear thesis

II. Body
See Mentor Text, pp. 200–201.

- Introduction to and summary of the work
- Evidence from the text
- Analysis of elements
- Personal insights

III. Conclusion
See Mentor Text, p. 201.

- Strong concluding paragraph
- Restatement of thesis
- Explanation of the significance of main points

Grab Your Reader

- An interesting opening can make a strong statement, ask a question, or refer to a character or event in the author's work.
- Both the work about which you are writing and its author should be identified.
- The thesis statement focuses on your overall ideas about the text. The rest of your response will support your thesis.

Develop Your Ideas

- The important features of the work should be briefly summarized.
- Evidence from the text, including quotations and other examples, should support your ideas about the text.
- An analysis of story elements includes your thoughts of character, plot, setting, and theme.
- Your ideas and arguments should show your personal insights and judgments.

Wrap It Up

- Briefly restating your thesis in slightly different wording reinforces your point.
- An explanation of the significance of your thesis or main points will leave readers with a clear understanding of your ideas and feelings.

Start Your Draft

Use this checklist to help you complete your draft. You will use the graphic organizer that shows your thesis and supporting evidence, and the Outline for Success as guides.

While drafting, aim at writing your ideas, not on making your writing perfect. Remember, you will have the chance to improve your draft when you revise and edit.

√ Start with a strong **opening** that will grab your reader's interest.

√ Your **introduction** should identify the story, poem, or other work about which you're writing, as well as the **author** of the work.

√ Present your **thesis** statement.

√ The **body** of your review should use an appropriate **organizational strategy** that demonstrates the writing skills for multi-paragraph essays. (See page 146.)

√ Be sure to also include a brief **summary** of key features of the work.

√ Your ideas and opinions should show your understanding of the text and be supported with **sustained evidence** from the text, including quotations.

√ Include an **analysis of story elements** that relate to your ideas, such as themes or specific plot events.

√ In your **conclusion**, restate or **paraphrase** your thesis.

√ End with a strong **final statement** that clearly expresses your thoughts and feelings about the work.

WRITING COACH

www.phwritingcoach.com

Interactive Model

Outline for Success View pop-ups of the Mentor Text referenced in the Outline for Success.

Interactive Writing Coach™

Use the Interactive Writing Coach to receive the level of support you need:
• Write one paragraph at a time and submit each one for immediate, detailed feedback.
• Write your entire first draft and submit it for immediate, personalized feedback.

Revising: Make It Better

Now that you have finished your first draft, you are ready to revise. Think about the "big picture" **of audience, purpose, and genre**. You can use the Revision RADaR strategy as a guide for making changes to improve your draft. Revision RADaR provides four major ways to improve your writing: (R) replace, (A) add, (D) delete, and (R) reorder.

Kelly Gallagher, M. Ed.

KEEP REVISION ON YOUR RADaR

Read part of the first draft of the Student Model "Ray Bradbury's 'The Drummer Boy of Shiloh.'" Then, look at questions the writer asked herself as she thought about how well her draft **addressed issues of audience, purpose, and genre.**

Ray Bradbury's "The Drummer Boy of Shiloh"

The general talks about how soldiers will get shot. Some of them may end up as bodies in Owl Creek. It's sad but true. The fact of the matter is that men get killed when they fight in a war.

Joby listens, wondering why the general is telling him this. The general then explains why Joby's job is so important. The drummer boy plays a key part during battle. When the drummer beats the drum, the soldiers hear it. A fast beat encourages the men. A slow beat doesn't. If the drummer doesn't do what he's supposed to, the battle "would be more than a slaughter, it would be murderous nightmare."

When the general leaves, Joby feels a little calmer. Joby seems more at ease.

Have I used sustained evidence from the text?

Have I gone beyond a summary to analyze the story?

Do my ideas show insights and understanding of the text?

Now look at how the writer applied Revision RADaR to write an improved second draft.

Ray Bradbury's "The Drummer Boy of Shiloh"

The general talks about how young, innocent soldiers will get shot. He fears they will end up in Owl Creek, "just floating, at sundown tomorrow, not caring where the current takes them." He says the sad truth the soldiers will learn is that "men actually die in war."

R *Replaced more general language with quotations from the text*

A *Added the words young, innocent to provide more detail*

Joby listens, wondering why the general is telling him this. The general then explains why Joby's job is so important. The drummer boy is "the heart of the army," he tells him. He sets the pace for the men. A "sure, steady, ever faster" drumbeat will carry the soldiers forward. It will give them courage. Without it, the battle "would be more than a slaughter, it would be murderous nightmare."

A *Added quotations from the text to develop story analysis*

D *Deleted unnecessary last sentence*

When the general leaves, Joby feels a little calmer. The general has built up his courage. Joby now feels that he has a key part to play in the coming battle.

A *Added two sentences to expand analysis of story elements.*

 Apply It! Use Revision RADaR to revise your draft.

- First, ask yourself: Have I addressed the needs of my audience, made clear my purpose for writing, and included the characteristics of the interpretative response genre?

- Then, apply the Revision RADaR strategy to make needed changes. Remember—you can use the steps in the strategy in any order.

Look at the Big Picture

Use the chart and your analytical skills to evaluate how well each section of your critical review addresses **purpose, audience, and genre**. When necessary, use the suggestions in the chart to revise your piece.

Section	Evaluate	Revise
Introduction	• Check the **opening.** It should grab readers' interest and make them want to continue reading. Introduce the title and author of the work to which you are responding.	• Make your opening more interesting by writing a strong first sentence or referring to a key event in the author's work. Add the title and author's name.
	• Make sure the **thesis** clearly expresses the focus of your response.	• Reread your review, keeping your thesis in mind. Your thesis should reflect your main idea about your response to the author's work. If it doesn't, revise your thesis.
Body	• Make sure that you have briefly **summarized** the work.	• Skim the author's work to make sure you have covered all the key features of the plot.
	• Make sure that you have included **sustained evidence** from the text to defend and support ideas. Use quotations from the text when appropriate.	• Add more supporting evidence as needed. Look for examples, details, and quotations in the text to support your ideas. Review the writing skills for multi-paragraph essays and revise as needed. (See page 146.)
	• Check that you've included ideas and arguments that show your personal **insights** and judgments of the text.	• Think about the meaning of the work. Convey your understanding to readers by basing your conclusions on specific elements of the text.
	• Make sure you have included an **analysis of story elements,** such as character, plot, setting, and theme.	• Add specific information about story elements to develop and support your main ideas.
Conclusion	• Check the **restatement** of your thesis.	• If necessary, discuss your restatement with a partner and ask for revision suggestions.
	• Check that your conclusion leaves readers with a clear **understanding** of your thoughts.	• Add a final statement that sums up your ideas about the work.

Focus on Craft: Consistent Point of View

Your audience will be confused if you do not have a **consistent point of view** throughout your critical review. Some critical reviews are written in the first-person point of view, using words such as *I* and *we*. Other reviews are written in second-person point of view, using words such as *you* and *your*, while still others are written in third-person point of view, using words such as *he*, *she*, and *it*.

Think about point of view as you read these sentences from the Student Model.

 STUDENT MODEL from **Ray Bradbury's "The Drummer Boy of Shiloh"** page 202; lines 1–6

Ray Bradbury's "The Drummer Boy of Shiloh" is a short story that leaves readers thinking about the tragedy of war. Even though no one dies during the story, it's a sad tale all the same. By focusing on just two characters, Bradbury paints a grim picture of what it was like to fight in the Civil War.

 Try It! Now, ask yourself these questions:

- Which point of view does the author of the Student Model use? Why might that be a good choice for a critical review?
- Why might a change in point of view confuse readers?

 Fine-Tune Your Draft

Apply It! Use the revision suggestions to prepare your final draft after **rethinking how well questions of purpose, audience, and genre have been addressed**.

- **Use a Consistent Point of View** Avoid changing your point of view within paragraphs or from one paragraph to the next.
- **Use a Variety of Sentence Structures** Check that you have a mix of sentence types, from simple sentences with one main clause to compound sentences with two main clauses to more complex types.

Peer Feedback Read your final draft to a group of peers. Ask if you have provided enough **evidence from the text** to defend and support ideas in your interpretive response. Listen carefully and revise your final draft as needed.

WRITING COACH

Online

www.phwritingcoach.com

 Video
Learn more strategies for effective writing from program author Kelly Gallagher.

 Online Journal
Try It! Record your answers in the online journal.

 Interactive Model
Refer back to the Interactive Model as you revise your writing.

 Interactive Writing Coach™
Revise your draft and submit it for feedback.

Editing: Making It Correct

Editing your draft means polishing your work and correcting errors. You may want to read through your work several times, looking for different errors and issues each time.

As you edit, check that your sentences contain **consistent verb tenses**. You may need to use the **perfect tense** and **progressive tense** to show that actions are taking place over a period of time. Then edit your final draft for errors in **grammar, mechanics, and spelling**.

WRITE GUY *Jeff Anderson, M. Ed.*

WHAT DO YOU NOTICE?

Zoom in on Conventions Focus on perfect and progressive tense verbs as you zoom in on this sentence from the Mentor Text.

> **MENTOR TEXT** from **Anne Frank: A Hidden Life**
> page 200; lines 20–22
>
> But even after August 1943, when she had begun writing stories and was feeling very enthusiastic about them, she did not neglect her diary.

Now, ask yourself: *When do the two actions in the clause "when she had begun writing stories and was feeling very enthusiastic about them" occur?*

Perhaps you said that the two actions happened in the past over a period of time.

Perfect tenses are made by adding a form of the verb *have* to the participle of the main verb. *Had begun* is past perfect. It adds the helping verb *had* to *begun*, the past participle of *begin*. It shows an action that started in the past and was completed.

Progressive tenses are made by adding a form of the verb *be* to the *-ing* form of the main verb. *Was feeling* is past progressive. The verb *was* is added to the *-ing* form of *feel*. This tense shows that the action was taking place over a period of time.

Partner Talk Discuss this question with a partner: *How does verb tense help readers understand a sequence of events?*

> To learn more about perfect and progressive verb tenses, see Chapter 21.

Grammar Mini-Lesson: Consistent Tenses

To learn more, see Chapter 21.

It is important to use **consistent tenses** so that readers understand the sequence of events. However, when you are writing sentences with more than one clause or complete action, you may need to use varied tenses to express sequence: *In the past, Nicole has been too busy to run for office, but this year she will be campaigning.* Notice how the Mentor Text uses consistent tenses.

 MENTOR TEXT from **Anne Frank: A Hidden Life**
page 200; lines 11–12

> Anne Frank enjoyed writing and found it a challenge. She tended to write well-rounded stories . . .

 Try It! Identify the verb tenses in each sentence. Write the answers in your journal.

1. By the time Anita arrived at the party, the guests had eaten all the food. (complex sentence)

2. Adam was buying more paint, but we had already finished painting. (compound sentence)

 Apply It! **Edit your draft for grammar, mechanics, and spelling.** If necessary, revise some sentences to make sure you have used a variety of complete sentences that include consistent tenses.

Use the rubric to evaluate your piece. If necessary, rethink, rewrite, or revise.

Rubric for Interpretative Response: Critical Review	Rating Scale					
Ideas: How well does your response present a focused statement about the work?	Not very					Very
	1	2	3	4	5	6
Organization: How clearly organized is your analysis?	1	2	3	4	5	6
Voice: How well have you engaged the reader and sustained his or her interest?	1	2	3	4	5	6
Word Choice: How clearly do your words state your views?	1	2	3	4	5	6
Sentence Fluency: How well have you used a consistent point of view in your writing?	1	2	3	4	5	6
Conventions: How correct is your use of consistent verb tenses?	1	2	3	4	5	6

WRITING COACH

Online

www.phwritingcoach.com

Video

Learn effective editing techniques from program author Jeff Anderson.

 Online Journal

Try It! Record your answers in the online journal.

Interactive Model

Refer back to the Interactive Model as you edit your writing.

 Interactive Writing Coach™

Edit your draft. Check it against the rubric and then submit it for feedback.

Publishing

Share your critical review with others—publish it! First, get your review ready for presentation. Then, choose a way to publish it for appropriate audiences.

Wrap Up Your Presentation

Now that you have finished your draft, add the final details. Include page numbers on each page of your final draft. Also be sure to add a title to your review that grabs your audience's attention and indicates the topic.

Publish Your Piece

Use the chart to identify a way to publish your critical review.

If your audience is...	...then publish it by...
People in your town or city	• Submitting it to a local newspaper • Submitting it to a local bookstore • Posting it to a community Web site
Students or teachers at school	• Submitting it to your school Web site • Reading it aloud in English class • Posting your piece online and inviting comments

 ## Extend Your Research

Think more about the topic on which you wrote your critical review. What else would you like to know about this topic?

- Brainstorm for several questions you would like to research and then consult, or discuss, with others. Then decide which question is your major research question.

- Formulate, or develop, a plan about how you will answer these questions. Decide where you will find more information—on the Internet, at the library, or through other sources.

- Finally, learn more about your topic by following through with your research plan.

 The Big Question: Why Write? What should you write about to make others interested in a text?

MAKE YOUR WRITING COUNT

Build an Advertisement for Fiction or Poetry

When a new book comes out, the publisher advertises it in the media. Hone your business skills by creating an **advertisement** for a work of fiction or poetry that you think is worth "selling."

In a group, turn a critical review into an advertisement. Analyze print and nonprint examples of book ads, radio ads, e-mails from online booksellers, or Web pages. Note the common elements of all media book advertisements: title, author, and selling points. Then, choose either print or nonprint media for your ad.

www.phwritingcoach.com

Online Journal

Extend Your Research Record your answers and ideas in the online journal.

Resource

Link to resources on 21st Century Learning for help in creating a group project.

Here's your action plan.

1. Choose roles, such as copy writer, illustrator, and presenter.

2. Choose a critical review to turn into an advertisement.

3. Use catchy phrases and appealing graphics as you work together to create your ad.

   - Highlight the selling points of the work.
   - Include a short excerpt from the story or poem to attract potential buyers.
   - Look online for critics' comments about the work that you could include in your ad.
   - For visual media, display the title and author of the story, and create a "cover" to include in the ad.

4. As a group, discuss the arrangement of your ad elements.

5. Present the ad to the school and see who might want to "buy" the product.

Listening and Speaking As you work with your group, take turns making suggestions for adding selling points. If your ad involves only print and visual media, explain your choices in the presentation. If it involves audio, for example, a radio ad or an online video, present your ad to the class. Listen actively during the presentations of other groups, and give constructive feedback.

Your Turn

Writing for Media: Writing Workshop Response

Writing Workshop Response

In a writing workshop, writers read and evaluate each other's drafts. They provide comments and respond to other's writing by giving examples of strengths and weaknesses. These responses are similar to other responses to literature, but may also include suggestions. To create a **writing workshop response** to a work of literature, the writer shares his or her opinions about a work and supports these opinions with evidence, such as quotations from the text. Responses like this analyze story elements and summarize features of the work.

Try It! Study this writing workshop response. Then, answer the questions. Record your answers in your journal.

1. About what **poem** was this response written? Who wrote the poem?

2. What important **features** of the work does the writer mention?

3. What **elements** of the poem does the writer analyze?

4. What is the writer's **opinion** of the poem? Why does the writer feel this way?

5. What **evidence** supports the writer's ideas and opinion?

6. What **quotations** from the text does the writer include?

7. What **feedback** does the writer give about the poem?

Extension Find another example of a writing workshop response, and compare it with this one.

I very much enjoyed Jennifer Weingarten's poem "Lost Love." In the eight stanzas, Weingarten describes the wonderful feeling of a girl's first love and the deep sadness of losing that love over time.

The first half of Weingarten's poem is filled with positive images. The girl's heart "sings the silvery music of angels." The sun shines down "with magical warmth that awakens the world." The girl thinks constantly of the boy she loves. She imagines their future life together "free as the sea, merry as a child's laughter."

In the second half of the poem, the images turn dark. As time passes, the girl and the boy drift apart. Unfortunately, the author's images are not as striking in this half of the poem. Her descriptions of the loss of love are not as powerful and could be improved. For example, one line says: "The two did not see each other again." This is too literal and unimaginative when compared with the first half of the poem.

Weingarten perfectly captures a young person's feelings of love with beautiful and imaginative language in the first half of the poem. However, she should revise her descriptions of loss in the second half of the poem by making better word choices. This will make the tone of the poem more even, and the poem as a whole more interesting. Still, "Lost Love" is a heartfelt poem that I won't soon forget.

Create a Writing Workshop Response to a Poem

Follow these steps to create your own writing workshop response to a poem. To plan your response, review the graphic organizers on pages R24–R27 and choose one that suits your needs.

Prewriting

- Choose a poem about which you have strong feelings.
- Think about the content of the poem. How does the poem express the poet's feelings? Does the poem describe a place or an event? Does it tell a story?
- Think about key elements of the poem, such as theme, rhyme, rhythm, and imagery. Which ones stand out in your mind? Why?
- Carefully review the poem and decide what kind of feedback you will give. Are any parts of the poem confusing to you? Should the author's word choices be revised? Are specific images striking?
- Consider what quotations from the poem you might include.

Drafting

- Begin with a strong opening. It should grab your readers' interest and express your main idea.
- Summarize important features of the poem and consider what you might say about the poem's key elements.
- Defend and support your ideas and opinions with sustained evidence from the text. Include quotations when appropriate.
- End with a strong statement that sums up your feelings.

Revising and Editing

Review your draft to ensure that your ideas are logically organized. Check that you have described and explained your ideas with specific details and examples. Look to see if you have presented your evidence in a clear and persuasive way. Finally, check that spelling, grammar, and mechanics are correct.

Publishing

Post your response on a school Web site, and invite classmates to read it and comment on it. Check the site regularly to see when others have posted responses to your ideas.

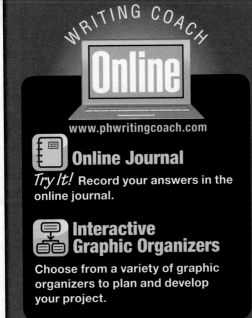

WRITING COACH

Online

www.phwritingcoach.com

Online Journal

Try It! Record your answers in the online journal.

Interactive Graphic Organizers

Choose from a variety of graphic organizers to plan and develop your project.

Partner Talk

Before you start drafting, explain your planned response to a partner, and ask for feedback. For example, ask whether you've included enough evidence to support your ideas and opinions. Monitor your partner's spoken language by asking follow-up questions to confirm your understanding.

Writing for Assessment

You may be asked to respond to an **interpretative response** prompt. Use the prompts on these pages to practice. Your responses should include the characteristics on page 198.

 Try It! To begin, read the prompt and the information on format and academic vocabulary. Use the ABCDs of On-Demand Writing to help you write your essay.

Format

The prompt directs you to write an *interpretative response* to a story, book, or poem. Make sure to create a fully developed introduction, body, and conclusion.

Interpretative Response Prompt

Write an interpretative response that is a critical review of a short story, book, or poem you have read. Analyze the work and offer personal insights. Support your analysis and insights with details from the text.

Academic Vocabulary

Remember that an *analysis* of a story, book, or poem is a study of its elements and parts. Your *insights* into a work are key points you make that show your understanding of the text.

The ABCDs of On-Demand Writing

Use the following ABCDs to help you respond to the prompt.

Before you write your draft:

A ttack the prompt [1 MINUTE]

- Circle or highlight important verbs in the prompt. Draw a line from the verb to what it refers to.
- Rewrite the prompt in your own words.

B rainstorm possible answers [4 MINUTES]

- Create a graphic organizer to generate ideas.
- Use one for each part of the prompt if necessary.

C hoose the order of your response [1 MINUTE]

- Think about the best way to organize your ideas.
- Number your ideas in the order you will write about them. Cross out ideas you will not be using.

After you write your draft:

D etect errors before turning in the draft [1 MINUTE]

- Carefully reread your writing.
- Make sure that your response makes sense and is complete.
- Look for spelling, punctuation, and grammar errors.

 **More Prompts for Practice**

Apply It! Respond to Prompts 1 and 2 by writing **interpretative responses** that demonstrate the use of **writing skills for a multi-paragraph essay.** (See page 146.) As you write, be sure to:

- Express the main idea of your response in a clear thesis statement
- Introduce the title and author of the work to which you are responding and summarize important features of the work
- Include **sustained evidence from the text,** including **quotations**
- Present ideas that show personal insights and judgments, and understanding of the text

Prompt 1 Write a composition that compares and contrasts two characters from two different books or short stories.

Prompt 2 Write a composition that interprets a theme, or big idea, in a short story, book, or poem you have read.

 Spiral Review: Persuasive Respond to Prompt 3 by writing a **persuasive essay.** Make sure your essay reflects all of the characteristics described on page 172, including:

- **A clear thesis or position**
- **Consideration of and response to the views of others,** as well as **answers reader concerns and counter-arguments**
- Evidence **that is logically organized to support the author's viewpoint**
- **Differentiation between fact and opinion**

Prompt 3 Some parents want to limit the amount of homework teachers can assign to students each week. Teachers argue that the amount of homework is necessary. What is your view? Write a composition to persuade the school board to agree with your view.

WRITING COACH

Online

www.phwritingcoach.com

Interactive Writing Coach™

Plan your response to the prompt. If you are using the prompt for practice, write one paragraph at a time or your entire draft and then submit it for feedback. If you are using the prompt as a timed test, write your entire draft and then submit it for feedback.

Remember **ABCD**

A ttack the prompt

B rainstorm possible answers

C hoose the order of your response

D etect errors before turning in the draft

CHAPTER 11

RESEARCH WRITING

What Do You Want To Know?

How do people find out more information about interesting topics? They do research. Research writing is a way to gather, organize, and present information in a report that others can read.

One of the first steps of research writing is to identify a topic that interests you and then formulate open-ended research questions. Open-ended research questions ask what you want to find out about the topic. For example, if you want to find out more about penguins, you would first decide what you want to know about them.

Try It! Take a few minutes to brainstorm for some things you may want to know about the penguins in the photograph. List your answers to these questions as you participate in an extended discussion with a partner. Take turns expressing your ideas and feelings.

- What do you want to know about the penguins?
- What do you want to know about how the penguins live?
- What do you want to know about where this photograph was taken?

Review your list of questions with a partner. Compare lists to determine if any questions overlap or if you can build off each other's ideas. Then, discuss where you would go to research answers to your questions.

What's Ahead

In this chapter, you will review a strong example of an informational research report. Then, using the example as guidance, you will develop your own research plan and write your own informational research report.

 Online Journal

Try It! Record your answers in the online journal.

You can also record and save your answers and ideas on pop-up sticky notes in the eText.

 **Connect to the Big Questions**

Discuss these questions with your partner:

1 What do you think? Should we study extreme environments?

2 Why write? Do you understand your subject well enough to write about it? How will you find out what all the facts are?

RESEARCH WRITING

Research writing is a way to gather information from various sources, and then evaluate, organize, and synthesize that information into a report for others to read. In this chapter, you will write an informational research report that conveys what you have learned about a topic that interests you. Before you write, you will search for information about your topic in different kinds of sources. You will evaluate the information you find, choose the best facts and details for your report, and organize your ideas so that you can clearly communicate them to your audience.

You will develop your informational research report by taking it through each of the steps of the writing process: prewriting, drafting, revising, editing, and publishing. You will also have an opportunity to use your informational research report in an oral or multimedia presentation that uses text, graphics, and other images to share what you have learned. To preview the criteria on which your research report will be evaluated, see the rubric on page 247.

FEATURE ASSIGNMENT

Research Writing: Informational Research Report

An effective informational research report has these characteristics:

- **A clear topic sentence,** or thesis statement, that explains the conclusions of the research and how those **conclusions** will be supported with evidence

- **Quotations** from—as well as **summaries** or **paraphrases** of—research findings, based on reliable and accurate **primary and secondary sources**

- **Clearly organized evidence,** in the form of **relevant facts and details,** that explains the topic and the writer's conclusions

- **Graphics,** such as charts, maps, or illustrations, that help explain the research

- Proper **documentation** of sources that shows where the writer found information

- **Effective sentence structure,** and correct spelling, grammar, and usage

Other Forms of Research Writing

In addition to an informational research report, there are other forms of research writing, including:

Biographical profiles give specific details about the life and work of a real person. The person may be living or dead, someone famous, or someone familiar to the writer.

Consumer information reports provide information about consumer products and services—including data on price, components, and usability—often comparing different brands and models of similar products and services.

Documentaries are filmed reports about a specific topic or issue. These multimedia presentations use spoken and written text as well as photographs, videos, music, and other sound effects.

Historical reports give in-depth information about a past event or situation. These reports have a narrow topic and may discuss causes and effects.

I-Search reports blend informational and personal writing. In an I-search report, you tell the story of your research and investigations, including the dead-ends and small victories, in addition to presenting the results of your research.

Scientific reports analyze information and data concerning a current, past, or future scientific issue or problem. An **experiment** or **lab report** describes a scientific experiment, including observations and conclusions.

Try It! For each research report described, brainstorm for possible topics with others. Then, consult with others to decide on and write a major research question for each topic. As you write, keep your audience and purpose in mind.

- A consumer report on a technology product made by two competing manufacturers
- A biographical profile of a person of historical importance
- A documentary to raise awareness about a serious issue, such as global warming

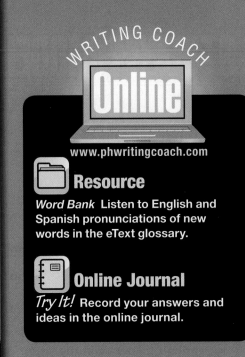

WORD BANK

People use these basic and content-based words when they talk about writing that reports information. Work with a partner. Take turns saying and writing each word in a sentence. If you are unsure of the meaning of a word, use the Glossary or a dictionary to check the definition.

determine	research
explanation	summarize
fact	support

STUDENT MODEL

Informational Research Report

Use a Reader's Eye

Read the Student Model on pages 226–229. On your copy of the Student Model, use the Reader's Response Symbols to react to what you read.

> ### Reader's Response Symbols
>
> √ **OK. I understand this. It's very clearly explained.**
>
> ? **I don't follow what the writer is saying here.**
>
> ✛ **I think the writer needs more details here.**
>
> − **This information doesn't seem relevant.**
>
> ! **Wow! That is cool/weird/interesting.**

Learn From Experience

Read the numbered notes in the margins as you reread the Student Model to learn how the writer presents ideas.

Answer the *Try It!* questions online or in your notebook.

---

1 The header and pagination follow the approved **formatting** for the first page of a document.

2 The topic sentence or **thesis statement** of a research paper explains the main idea or **conclusion** the writer has drawn from her research and how it will be supported by evidence.

3 The writer **marshals evidence** to explain the topic—how railroads shaped the United States.

Try It! What is the topic of the report? What is the purpose and intended audience?

---

1 Scholder 1

1 Vanessa Scholder
Ms. W. Martin
American Studies
5 November 2009

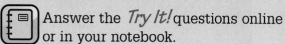

1 Tracks Across a Nation: How the Railroad Shaped and United America

"Today, far more Americans are likely to live near a highway or an airport than a railroad track. Yet the railroad helped define the United States," argues railroad historian Elinor Posen (Message to the author). In fact, many experts
5 claim that the railroad transformed the United States into a unified nation. **2** The railroad not only made communication, business, and travel between the coasts possible; it also shaped the country and helped it mature into a great nation.

3 After the Revolutionary War, people, goods, and news
10 could be transported in the United States only by horse or by boat. Both forms of transportation were expensive and often dangerous. As a result, says historian Sarah H. Gordon, by 1800 "more than two-thirds of the American people lived within fifty miles of the Atlantic Ocean, and
15 they had almost no contact with settlers" who had moved to the frontier (14). The Erie Canal made moving people and goods easier, but political leaders thought that trains might provide better transportation.

Between 1830 and 1845, railroads sprang up in the
20 Northeast. They were built for passengers, not for goods, and were rarely longer than 100 miles ("History of Railroads and Maps"). Once the government offered funding and land for the railroads, however, the states east of the Mississippi River were soon crisscrossed with tracks (see figure 1).
25 Travelers paid two cents per mile to travel anywhere in

Scholder 2

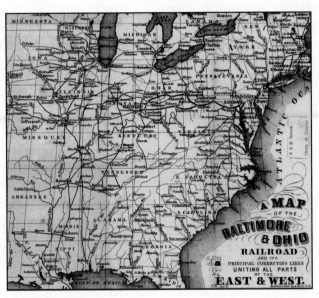

④ Figure 1. This map shows how the Baltimore and Ohio Railroads connected the states east of the Mississippi during the mid-1800s. Originally from A. Hoen & Co. LC Railroad Maps of Baltimore, MD, circa 1860 (Library of Congress: Washington, DC 1977; No. 338; print).

the eastern U.S. in fewer than three days (Stover 24). Yet despite great progress, political divisions between the North and the South would soon derail the railroad.

30 The Civil War erupted in 1861, and it affected the railroad. During the war, construction on railroads slowed. The government had no money to fund them, and most workers were fighting in the war. Yet, President Abraham Lincoln believed that the railroad could unite the country. ⑤ In 1862, he signed the Pacific Railroad Act. It gave two companies,
35 the Union Pacific and the Central Pacific, permission to build a transcontinental track that would connect the western territories to the states in the east ("Chronological History"). In turn, the railroad was crucial to ending the war. The North used its superior railroads to move troops and supplies
40 efficiently. The South was at a disadvantage; it had a smaller and less reliable rail system (Stover 28–29). After 1865, the country was reunited politically. Soon it would be united geographically by the railroad.

The building of the transcontinental railroad was a race
45 against time. It began in 1863, and the last spike—a special one made of gold—was driven on May 10, 1869, at

④ This **map** is relevant to the written explanation of how the railroads expanded in the United States before 1860.

Try It! How do the map and figure reference help you to find and understand the information? Explain.

⑤ The writer **summarizes her findings**, and tells events in chronological order.

Try It! Why is it helpful to readers for writers to put events in the order in which they took place?

STUDENT MODEL

Informational Research Report (*continued*)

Scholder 3

6 The writer follows accepted formats for including **parenthetical citations.**

7 Here the writer provides **relevant reasons** for her conclusions.

Try It! What conclusions does the writer support with her evidence?

8 The writer follows accepted formats by setting off the long quotation and by framing it to fit into the flow of ideas.

Try It! What does the quotation tell you about the impact of the railroads on the West?

9 **Evidence** shows that the railroads had an impact on the culture of the West.

Try It! Do you think the facts the writer provides are convincing and help support her conclusion? Why or why not?

10 The Works Cited list provides proper citations by listing publication information for each source used to write the report. The **formatting** of the list follows the MLA style manual.

Try It! Study the Works Cited list on page 229. How does it help readers to list sources in alphabetical order?

Extension Locate one of the sources from the Works Cited page, and write a brief synopsis of it in your own words.

Promontory Summit, Utah **6** (Mintz). For the first time, a person could board a train in New York and reach California within a week. **7** The completion of the railroad
50 led to the opening of the West for business, travel, and settlement. People poured in. As a result, the railroad's impact on the landscape and culture of the Western half of the country was undeniable. As historian James P. Ronda points out:

55   **8** Half a century after engines touched pilot to pilot at Promontory, Utah, to complete the first transcontinental railroad, the imprint of the Iron Road was nearly everywhere in the American West. Some enthusiastic real estate promoters and railway officials even claimed
60 that the railroads invented the West—or at least the national image of the West. (44)

    Towns and cities sprang up around the newly built railroad stations (see figure 2). They grew quickly as immigrants and settlers arrived by train. The look of the western towns changed,
65 too, as sturdy building materials could be shipped easily from the northeast, and sod houses were replaced with wooden and brick structures. In addition, the land was reshaped to allow the railroads through. Bridges were built over rivers. Tunnels

Figure 2. Passenger train at depot of Hannover Junction, PA, circa 1860, from Hirst D. Milhollen and Donald H. Mugridge, *Civil War Photographs, 1861–1865* (Library of Congress: Washington, DC 1977; No. 0187; print).

Scholder 4

were carved through mountains (Ronda 44–51).

70 Just as important as the physical changes were the cultural ones. ❾ For the first time, people from all over the country could move easily and form new, diverse communities. They could communicate quickly, too, thanks to the telegraph poles built along the railroad tracks. Sadly, though, the rise of the railroad ruined many Native 75 American communities. For example, the trains took over Pawnee land in Nebraska, leaving the people no way to earn a living (Gordon 155). Other Native Americans attacked the trains until government troops were brought in to stop them. Due to the rise of populations and the fall of 80 Native American culture, says historian Steven Mintz, "the 1890 census would declare that the American frontier had disappeared. The railroad was a major cause" (7).

The development of the railroad had a major impact on the United States geographically and culturally. It 85 united the country by connecting its different regions and opening channels of communication and business. After the completion of the transcontinental railroad, our nation spread out and became prosperous. Eventually, it would become one of the world's superpowers, thanks in part to the railroad.

---

❿ Works Cited

"Chronological History." *Union Pacific: Building America.* Union Pacific Railroad Company, 2009. Web. 2 Nov. 2009.

Gordon, Sarah H. *Passage to Union: How the Railroads Transformed American Life, 1829–1929.* Chicago: Ivan R. Dee, 1996. Print.

"History of Railroads and Maps." *American Memory: Railroad Maps, 1828–1900.* Library of Congress, 1998. Web. 1 Nov. 2009.

Mintz, Steven. "Building the Transcontinental Railroad." *Digital History.* U of Houston, 2007. Web. 2 Nov. 2009.

Posen, Elinor. Message to the author. 5 Nov. 2009. E-mail.

Ronda, James P. "The West the Railroads Made." *American Heritage* 58.4 (2008): 44–51. Print.

Stover, John F. *The Routledge Historical Atlas of the American Railroads.* New York: Routledge, 1999. Print.

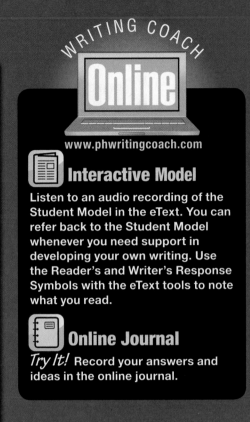

WRITING COACH

Online

www.phwritingcoach.com

Interactive Model

Listen to an audio recording of the Student Model in the eText. You can refer back to the Student Model whenever you need support in developing your own writing. Use the Reader's and Writer's Response Symbols with the eText tools to note what you read.

Online Journal

Try It! Record your answers and ideas in the online journal.

Use a Writer's Eye

Now go back to the beginning of the Student Model and evaluate the piece as a writer. On your copy of the Student Model, use the Writer's Response Symbols to react to what you read. Identify places where the student writer uses characteristics of an effective informational research report.

Writer's Response Symbols

T.S.   Clear thesis statement

S.E.   Supporting evidence

R.G.   Relevant graphic

D.S.   Proper documentation of sources

Prewriting

Begin to plan a first draft by choosing a topic. You can select from the Topic Bank or come up with an idea of your own.

 ## Choose From the Topic Bank

TOPIC BANK

GPS What is the global positioning system? Research the development of GPS and its common uses. How does it work? How has it impacted society or daily life?

Colonial Innovations Research technological or scientific innovations of colonial times, such as the steamboat, cotton gin, or Bessemer steel process. How did the new technology change how people lived? How did it affect the future of the United States?

Then and Now Compare what people knew about Earth, space, and the universe in colonial times to what we know today. What myths and misconceptions have been cleared? What questions are still unsolved?

 ## Choose Your Own Topic

Determine an appropriate topic of your own by using **the following range of strategies** to generate ideas.

Brainstorm and Browse

- **Consult** with a partner to **brainstorm for** and **decide upon a list of topics** that interest you.

- **Formulate major research questions** about your topics. Circle key words in your questions. Use your key words and phrases as you browse the resources in the library.

- Do a **preliminary search** on the Internet, using the same key words and phrases. Work with your partner to decide which topics provide results that interest you most.

- Review your work and choose a topic.

Formulate Your Research Question

A broad, general topic is almost impossible to research well and cover thoroughly. Plan to do some preliminary research in order to narrow your topic and then formulate a major research question.

Apply It! Use a printed or online graphic organizer.

- Write your general topic in the top box, and keep narrowing your topic with research questions as you move down the chart.

- Your last box should hold your narrowest or "smallest" research question. This will be the focus of your research report. As you research, you may need to **narrow your topic or broaden it** based on the information you find.

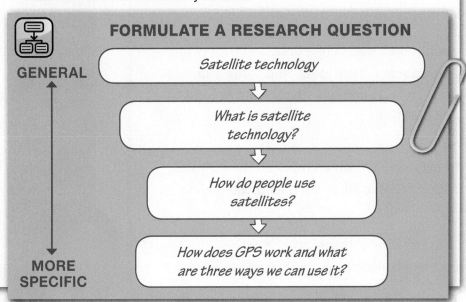

FORMULATE A RESEARCH QUESTION

GENERAL

Satellite technology

What is satellite technology?

How do people use satellites?

How does GPS work and what are three ways we can use it?

MORE SPECIFIC

Consider Your Audience and Purpose

Before researching, think about your audience and purpose. Consider the views of others as you ask yourself these questions.

Questions About Audience	Questions About Purpose
• Who will read my report? My teacher? My classmates?	• Why am I writing my report? To inform? To interest my audience in my topic?
• What does my audience probably already know about my topic? What new information will readers need?	• How do I want my audience to respond to the conclusions I draw?
• What background information will I have to provide for my readers?	• How do I feel about my topic? Enthusiastic? Skeptical?

Record your answers in your writing journal.

WRITING COACH Online

www.phwritingcoach.com

Interactive Writing Coach™

- Choosing from the Topic Bank gives you access to the Interactive Writing Coach™.
- Submit your writing paragraph by paragraph and receive detailed feedback and guidance as you draft, revise, and edit your writing.

Interactive Graphic Organizers

Use the interactive graphic organizers to help you narrow your topic.

Online Journal

Record your answers and ideas in the online journal.

Make a Research Plan

Once you have written your major research question, you are ready to make a research plan. As part of your plan, you will create a timeline for finishing your report. You also will find and evaluate sources of information.

Find Authoritative, Objective Sources You will need to **compile data,** or gather information, from a variety of sources. Make sure the sources you plan to use are related to the topic you are researching and not out of date. Use a variety of **advanced search strategies** including electronic databases, card catalogues, and search engines to locate resources. Look at these tips:

Print Resources

- Find print resources in libraries and bookstores.
- Use encyclopedias, magazines, newspapers, and trade journals.
- Search for print resources using electronic databases or with help from the reference librarian.

Electronic Resources

- Find electronic resources using search engines on the Internet.
- Choose only authoritative, reliable sites, such as those ending in:
  .edu (educational institution)
  .gov (government group)
  .org (not-for-profit organizations; these may be biased)
- If you are not sure that a site is reliable and unbiased, do not use it.

Interviews With Experts

- Interview an expert.
- Set up a short meeting in person, by e-mail, or by telephone.
- Record the interview and take good notes.

Multimedia and Other Resources

- Watch movies about your topic.
- Listen to podcasts or seminars related to the topic.
- Search for relevant photos, diagrams, charts, and graphs.

Evaluate Your Sources Do not assume that all sources of information on your topic are useful, good, or trustworthy. Use the checklist on page 233 to evaluate sources of information you find. The more questions that you can answer with a yes, the more likely you should use the source.

Checklist for Evaluating Sources

Does the source of information:

❑ Contain **relevant** information that answers your research questions?

❑ Provide **facts** and not just unsupported, **subjective** opinions?

❑ Give facts and details at a level you can understand?

❑ Tell all sides of a story so that it is **unbiased?**

❑ Provide **authoritative** and **accurate** information written or compiled by experts?

❑ Have a recent **publication date,** indicating it is up-to-date?

Online Journal

Record your answers and ideas in the online journal.

Partner Talk

Review your sources with a partner. Discuss why one source is more useful than another. Explain your reasons.

Distinguish Between Types of Sources As you research, you will discover two kinds of sources: primary sources and secondary sources. Your teacher may require that you use both.

- A **primary source** is an **original or first-hand source of information,** such as a letter, diary, or legal document. For example, a treaty signed by Jefferson is a primary source.

- A **secondary source** is one that **synthesizes and interprets information** from primary sources. For example, an American history textbook is a secondary source. When you read a secondary source, be aware that you are reading a writer's ideas about a subject.

Apply It! Create and follow a **written research plan** and timeline with steps that you apply to obtain and evaluate information and to prepare your report. After you have done some research in reference works and completed some additional advanced text searches, create a written research plan. List at least four sources, including print and electronic resources, of information that you plan to use.

- Work with your teacher to determine the due dates for finishing each step: research, thesis statement drafting, and final report.

- For each source you plan to use, record full **bibliographic information** using a standard format.

- Use the checklist to explain if each source is **reliable and valid.**

- Identify whether each source is primary or secondary.

Modify Your Plan After you begin to research and investigate a topic, you may find that you need to **narrow or broaden your research question**. If you cannot find answers to a research question, you may decide to **refocus** or change the emphasis of your topic.

Collect and Organize Your Data

For your informational research report, you will need to use **multiple sources** of information. Notes will help you remember and keep track of your sources and information. Different forms of notes include handwritten notes on note cards, typed notes in an electronic document, and a learning log summarizing what you know and still need to know about your topic.

Keep Track of Multiple Sources You can create a card for each source, and give each its own number. Write the full bibliographic information for the source, including the author, title, city of publication, publisher, and copyright date. The example shown is from the Student Model. It matches MLA style used in the Works Cited on page 229.

Take Notes When you take notes on a source, follow these guidelines.

- Note only **relevant information**—facts and details you might use to answer your research question.

- Look for larger thematic patterns or constructs in the information you investigate. **Categorize** the notes using headings that sum up the theme, or main idea, of each group of notes.

- When you **paraphrase information,** be sure to use your own words. It is acceptable to use abbreviations in your notes.

- If you want to quote someone, enclose the exact words in large quotation marks. They will remind you that these are someone else's words —not your own.

Apply It! Take notes on information that is relevant to your research questions and topic. Effectively **organize the information** from different sources on note cards into categories by theme or sub-topic. Organizing notes this way can help you to make connections between data and to see big ideas. Paraphrase the information, or summarize it your own words. If you want to quote, copy the original, using quotation marks.

Source 1

Gordon, Sarah H. *Passage to Union: How the Railroads Transformed American Life, 1829-1929.* Chicago: Ivan R. Dee, 1996. Print.

Notes From Source 1

Transportation in U.S. before trains @ 1800

- *Roads, stagecoaches, sailboats*

- *"More than two-thirds of the American people lived within fifty miles of the Atlantic Ocean, and they had almost no contact with settlers who had crossed the Allegheny Mountains." (p. 14)*

Avoid Plagiarism

Plagiarism is the use of another person's words or ideas as your own, without documenting the source of the information. Plagiarism is a serious error with severe consequences. Do not plagiarize.

Careful Note-taking Matters You can accidentally set yourself up to plagiarize by not taking good notes. The student who wrote this note card made two mistakes. She followed the original source too closely, and she did not include the page on which she found the information.

> In Nebraska the Pawnees… suffered a fate that cannot be described in brief. As they lost more and more land, they also lost their wealth and dignity.

Original Source

Notes From Source 5

Trains and Native Americans

In Nebraska, the Pawnee people suffered a fate that can't be described. They lost more and more land, and they also lost their wealth and dignity.

Plagiarized Notes

Use these strategies to avoid plagiarizing your sources.

- **Paraphrase** Restate information from a source using your own words. Here's how: Read a passage, think about what it means, and then write it as you might explain it to a friend.

- **Summarize** Use your own words to identify the most important ideas in a long passage. A summary should be shorter than the original passage. It should cover only the big ideas, not the supporting details.

- **Direct Quotation** Use a writer's exact words and give credit to the **source**. Enclose the exact words in quotation marks, and indicate who said it and where it's from. (See page 247.)

Try It! Look at the *Notes From Source 5* in the example. Highlight the parts that are plagiarizing rather than paraphrasing the original. Now, write a new note based on the original source. Be sure to avoid plagiarizing the content.

WRITING COACH

Online

www.phwritingcoach.com

Online Journal

Record your answers and ideas in the online journal.

Partner Talk

Review taking notes with a partner. Explain why each of these is important:

- Citing valid and reliable sources
- Making a source card for each source
- Writing a source card number on each note card
- Using your own words to summarize ideas
- Printing large quotation marks for direct quotations

Document Your Sources

When you write a research report, you need to cite all **researched information** that is not common knowledge, and cite it **according to a standard format**.

Works Cited On the Works Cited page at the end of your report, list all the sources that you used to write your report. Do not include sources you looked at but did not use. Follow the format shown in a standard style manual, such as that of the Modern Language Association (MLA) or American Psychological Association (APA). Your teacher will tell you which standard format style you should use.

Look at the example citations shown. Use these and the MLA Style for Listing Sources on page R16 as a guide for writing your citations. Pay attention to formatting, including italics, abbreviations, and punctuation.

Book

Author's last name, author's first name followed by the author's middle name or initial (if given). *Full title of book.* City where book was published: Name of publisher, year of publication. Medium of publication.

Stover, John F. *The Routledge Historical Atlas of the American Railroads.* New York: Routledge, 1999. Print.

Interview or Correspondence (letter or e-mail)

Author's last name, author's first name followed by the author's middle name or initial (if given). Description of correspondence, interview, or message. Date of exchange. Type of communication.

Posen, Elinor. Message to the author. 5 Nov. 2009. E-mail.

Web Page

Author's last name, author's first name followed by author's middle name or initial (if given) OR name of group that sponsors the page (if given). "Name of page." *Name of site.* Publisher, institution, or sponsor OR N.p. if none given, date page was posted OR n.d. if none given. Medium of publication. Date you accessed the page.

"History of Railroads and Maps." *American Memory: Railroad Maps, 1828–1900.* Library of Congress, 1998. Web. 1 Nov. 2009.

Parenthetical Citations A parenthetical citation is a quick reference to a source listed on the Works Cited page. These citations give the author's last name or a book or article title and the page number on which the information is located. Look at this sample citation from the Student Model.

 **STUDENT MODEL** from **Tracks Across a Nation: How the Railroad Shaped and United America** pages 226–227; lines 25–26

> Travelers paid two cents per mile to travel anywhere in the eastern U.S. in fewer than three days (Stover 24).

When the author's name is not given, use a word(s) from the title:

> Between 1830 and 1845, railroads sprang up in the Northeast. They were built for passengers, not for goods, and were rarely longer than 100 miles ("History of Railroads and Maps").

Try It! Use MLA style to create a short Works Cited page based on the sources described.

- A book by James E. Vance, Jr., titled *The North American Railroad*. It was published in Baltimore in 1995 by the publisher The Johns Hopkins University Press.

- A magazine article called "The Engineers." The article appeared in *Trains* magazine in December of 2003. It starts on page 36 but continues on page 52.

- A Web page called "Early Passenger Trains" from American-Rails.com. The author, publisher, and date are not available. The writer looked at the page on November 20, 2010.

Critique Your Research Process

At every step in the research process, be ready to change your plan. If you can't find enough information to write your thesis statement, try **broadening your research question**. If you have too much information, try **narrowing your research question**. Remember to stick to your timeline. Once you've found the answers to your research question, you're ready to start drafting your paper.

Apply It! Write an entry for the Works Cited page for every source you have used to prepare your research report. Format your sources correctly using the MLA style or the style your teacher has directed you to use. Confirm that you have researched enough information to begin writing your draft.

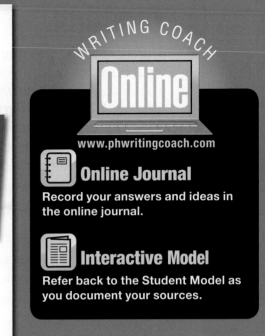

> **Partner Talk**
>
> Work with a partner to discuss research sources. What sources do you like? What hasn't been reliable? Monitor your partner's spoken language by asking follow-up questions to confirm your understanding.

Drafting

During the drafting stage, you will start to write your ideas for your research report. You will write a **clear topic sentence,** or thesis statement. You will follow an outline that provides an **organizational strategy** that will help you write a **focused, organized, and coherent research report.** As you write your draft or prepare your notes for an oral presentation, remember to keep your audience in mind.

The Organization of an Informational Research Report

The chart shows an organizational strategy for a research report. Look back at how the Student Model follows this same strategy. Then, create a detailed outline using the template on page R26. Refer to your work and the Outline for Success as you draft.

Outline for Success

I. Introduction — See Student Model, p. 226.

- Interesting opening expert quotation or attention-grabbing anecdote
- Thesis statement that draws clear conclusions

II. Body — See Student Model, pp. 227–228.

- Synthesis of information from a variety of sources
- Summaries and paraphrases of findings
- Evidence and reasons that support conclusions
- Graphics and illustrations to explain concepts

III. Conclusion — See Student Model, p. 229.

- Restatement of thesis
- A final thought or interesting insight

Introduce Your Thesis Statement

- A quotation, story, question, or interesting fact will grab the reader's attention.
- A **clear thesis statement** is often the last sentence in the introduction. It answers your research question.

Support Your Thesis Statement

- Categorizing your notes thematically can help you to see what you have learned about similar ideas that support your thesis.
- A well-ordered report arranges information in a logical order, such as chronological or cause-and-effect.
- A strong body paragraph clearly identifies a key idea and supports it with evidence, including facts, statistics, examples, and quotations from your notes.
- Using relevant graphics or images helps convey information visually.

Add a Final Thought

- For a strong conclusion, restate your thesis in the final paragraph.
- Suggesting an interesting or thought-provoking idea helps leave a memorable impression.

Start Your Draft

Use the checklist below to help complete your draft. Use your specific thesis statement; your detailed outline that shows your topic sentences and supporting evidence; and the Outline for Success as guides.

While drafting, aim at writing your ideas, not on making your writing perfect. Remember, you will have the chance to improve your draft when you revise and edit.

√ Open your **introduction** with an attention-getting quotation, anecdote, or expert opinion.

√ Include a clearly worded **thesis statement** based on the conclusions you've drawn about your research question.

√ Draft the paper's **body** one paragraph at a time. Remember, body paragraphs must explain your thesis. Use the body of your paper to present reasons and evidence based on your research.

√ Begin each paragraph with a topic sentence that gives a strong supporting reason for your thesis statement.

√ Marshal the evidence you have collected and organized, and explain your topic.

√ Include conclusions you draw from your research. Summarize or paraphrase your research findings in a systematic way so readers can understand. Remember to give relevant, logical reasons for your conclusions.

√ Prepare a **concluding paragraph** that sums up or restates your thesis or adds a final, interesting thought.

WRITING COACH

Online

www.phwritingcoach.com

Interactive Model

Outline for Success View pop-ups of Student Model selections referenced in the Outline for Success.

Interactive Writing Coach™

Submit your draft one paragraph at a time and receive immediate, detailed feedback.

Provide and Document Evidence

While you are drafting, you will provide **evidence** to support your thesis and related claims. Your **claims** are an important part of your **analysis** of your topic. They are your opinions or understanding of information connected to your thesis, stated from your **point of view**. Be careful to differentiate between your opinions and ideas and those of other people. Follow an accepted format to **document** the words and ideas of other people when you provide evidence.

Give Facts and Statistics Facts are convincing evidence because they can be proven true. Statistics, or facts stated in numbers, are also convincing when they come from authoritative and up-to-date sources. Document facts and statistics that are not common knowledge or that could not be found in most sources about a topic.

Give Examples Make abstract or complicated ideas easier to understand by providing examples. You do not need to document examples from personal experience or observations. You do need to document examples from a particular source.

Quote Authorities Direct quotations from experts are also convincing evidence. Make sure a quotation fits smoothly into your paragraph, and use your own words to identify the expert as shown in the example from the Student Model.

 **STUDENT MODEL** from **"Tracks Across a Nation: How the Railroad Shaped and United America"** page 226; lines 12–16

As a result, says historian Sarah H. Gordon, by 1800 "more than two-thirds of the American people lived within fifty miles of the Atlantic Ocean, and they had almost no contact with settlers" who had moved to the frontier (14).

Remember these guidelines:

- Only quote if you must use an expert's exact words.
- Do not quote if paraphrasing is just as clear.
- Separate and inset a quote of four lines or more.
- Be sure to punctuate quotes correctly. (See page 247.)
- Follow quotes with a proper parenthetical citation.

Apply It! Draft a paragraph for your research report. Your paragraph should include facts, examples, a quotation, and citation. Remember to explain and correctly format your quotations and citations to avoid interrupting the flow of your ideas.

Use Graphics and Illustrations

You can present evidence in graphics and other visuals as well as in words. While you are drafting, consider how you can create a diagram or other types of graphics to help your audience understand ideas in your report. Be sure to refer to the figure in your text. Then, label your visuals with a figure or table number, caption, and source citation for the data. If you copy an existing graphic, you will need permission from the copyright holder to publish your work outside of school.

- **Photographs** Use a photograph to help your audience picture how something looks. If you insert a photograph in your report, include a caption, or brief sentence explaining what the photo shows.

- **Charts, Tables, and Graphs** These graphics provide data in a more visual way. Give each a title that tells what it shows. Include a complete citation for the source of information you used to create the chart, table, or graph below.

Table 1. This timeline shows early railroad developments based on information compiled from the *Union Pacific: Building America* Web site.

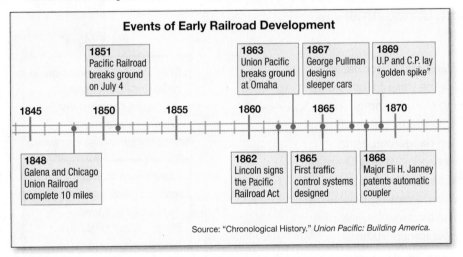

Events of Early Railroad Development

| 1851 Pacific Railroad breaks ground on July 4 | 1863 Union Pacific breaks ground at Omaha | 1867 George Pullman designs sleeper cars | 1869 U.P and C.P. lay "golden spike" |

1845 · 1850 · 1855 · 1860 · 1865 · 1870

| 1848 Galena and Chicago Union Railroad complete 10 miles | 1862 Lincoln signs the Pacific Railroad Act | 1865 First traffic control systems designed | 1868 Major Eli H. Janney patents automatic coupler |

Source: "Chronological History." *Union Pacific: Building America.*

- **Maps** Maps can provide geographical information visually. Be sure to include a legend and a compass rose with your map, in addition to the figure number, caption, and source.

Apply It! Consider the best way to present your findings in a meaningful format. Brainstorm for two graphics that you can use in your report.

- Identify the type of information each graphic would explain.
- Find or create the two graphics, and add them to your report to present your findings in the most meaningful way.
- Document your sources of the information.

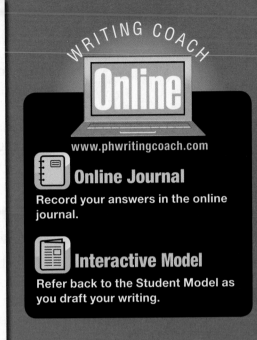

WRITING COACH

Online

www.phwritingcoach.com

Online Journal

Record your answers in the online journal.

Interactive Model

Refer back to the Student Model as you draft your writing.

Partner Talk

Get together with a partner and participate in an extended discussion to evaluate each graphic that you want to include in your research report. Express your opinions and explain to your partner why you have chosen each graphic.

Revising: Making It Better

Now that you have finished your first draft, you are ready to revise. Think about the "big picture" of **audience, purpose, and genre.** You can use the Revision RADaR strategy as a guide for making changes to improve your draft. Revision RADaR provides four major ways to improve your writing: (R) replace, (A) add, (D) delete, and (R) reorder.

Kelly Gallagher, M. Ed.

KEEP REVISION ON YOUR RADAR

Read part of the first draft of the Student Model "Tracks Across a Nation: How the Railroad Shaped and United America." Then, look at questions the writer asked herself as she thought about how well her draft addressed issues of audience, purpose, and genre.

from Tracks Across a Nation: How the Railroad Shaped and United America

After the Revolutionary War, people, goods, and news could be transported in the United States only by horse or by boat. Although the government had helped develop a system of toll roads, the roads were unpaved, slow and often dangerous. Both forms of transportation were expensive and often dangerous. So in 1800 most people lived near the ocean. Later, the Erie Canal made moving people and goods easier, but political leaders thought that trains might provide better transportation.

Once the government offered funding and land for the railroads, however, the states east of the Mississippi River were soon crisscrossed with tracks. But before then, between 1830 and 1845, a few railroads sprang up in the northeast. They were built for passengers only and were only 100 miles long ("History of Railroads and Maps"). People paid money to go anywhere in the east part of the country in days (Stover 24).

Is all of the information relevant? Does the evidence support my thesis statement?

Have I marshaled enough evidence to support my thesis? Have I documented my sources according to the correct format?

Have I presented my information in a logical order?

Is my language as strong and direct as it can be?

Now look at how the writer applied Revision RADaR to write an improved second draft.

Tracks Across a Nation: How the Railroad Shaped and United America

2ND DRAFT

After the Revolutionary War, people, goods, and news could only be transported in the United States by horse or by boat. Both forms of transportation were expensive and often dangerous. As a result, says historian Sarah H. Gordon, by 1800 "more than two-thirds of the American people lived within fifty miles of the Atlantic Ocean, and they had almost no contact with settlers" who had moved to the frontier (14). The Erie Canal made moving people and goods easier, but political leaders thought that trains might provide better transportation.

Between 1830 and 1845, railroads sprang up in the Northeast. They were built for passengers, not for goods, and were rarely longer than 100 miles ("History of Railroads and Maps"). Once the government offered funding and land for the railroads, however, the states east of the Mississippi River were soon crisscrossed with tracks (see figure 1). Travelers paid two cents per mile to travel anywhere in the eastern U.S. in fewer than three days (Stover 24).

D *Deleted irrelevant sentence about toll roads; the next sentence tells readers that both roads and sailing had disadvantages*

A *Added a quotation and citation from an expert that explains why people lived by the ocean*

A *Added the transition As a result to link transportation and how people lived*

R *Reordered sentences to show chronological order of events*

R *Replaced weak verb and vague nouns*

A *Added specific details about how much money and how many days*

WRITING COACH

Online

Video

Learn more strategies for effective writing from program author Kelly Gallagher.

Interactive Writing Coach™

Use the Revision RADaR strategy in your own writing. Then, submit your draft paragraph by paragraph for feedback.

Apply It! Use your Revision RADaR to revise your draft.

- First, ask yourself if you have met your readers' needs. Have you explained your ideas clearly and systematically? Check for **internal coherence** by tracking whether your ideas make sense within each paragraph and sentence. Also check for **external coherence** by making sure the entire report flows logically.

- Then, apply Revision RADaR to make needed changes. Remember—you can use the steps in the strategy in any order.

Look at the Big Picture

Use the chart and your analytical skills to evaluate how well each section of your informational research report addresses **purpose, audience, and genre.** When necessary, use the suggestions in the chart to revise your piece.

Section	Evaluate	Revise
Introduction	• Make sure that your **opening paragraph** gets readers' attention. It should make them want to learn about your topic.	• Add a funny or unusual anecdote (brief story) or an interesting quotation to build interest.
	• Check that you have a clear thesis statement that tells what **major research question** your paper will answer.	• Strengthen the language of your clear thesis statement to answer your research question.
Body	• Make sure each body paragraph focuses on one **major idea** and uses **marshalled evidence** to explain the topic.	• Add a topic sentence to each paragraph. Add supporting evidence to weaker paragraphs.
	• Check that the reasons and evidence you use to support your conclusions are **relevant** to the topic.	• Remove information that does not support your conclusions.
	• Review your draft to decide whether you present your findings in a **systematic** way, such as categorized by theme or sub-topic.	• Reorder sentences and paragraphs to present information in a logical way. • Use transitional words to connect ideas.
	• Make sure that you have used graphics when a visual can best illustrate the data.	• Convert data into graphics or pick up existing graphics to present your findings in the most meaningful format.
	• Make sure that you have **documented** quotations and facts that are not common knowledge.	• Cite your sources, using an accepted format, such as parenthetical citation, to avoid interrupting the flow of ideas.
Conclusion	• Check that your conclusion returns to your **thesis statement.**	• Add a restatement of your thesis, and remind readers how your main points relate to that key idea.
	• End with an insight or leave the reader with a memorable thought.	• Add a sentence about what you learned or how you feel about your topic.
Works Cited/ Bibliography	• Include a reference list that follows an **accepted format** and style specified by your teacher.	• List all the sources you used in your paper under the Works Cited. Check a style manual for the correct format.

Focus on Craft: Sentence Variety

Improve the style of your writing by varying your sentence beginnings and sentence structures. A paragraph in which all the sentences begin with a noun and a verb may be dull for your readers. By starting some sentences with words, phrases, or clauses, and by mixing in sentences that are compound or complex, you can create an interesting rhythm that keeps readers engaged in your writing.

Think about sentence variety as you read these sentences from the Student Model.

STUDENT MODEL | from **Tracks Across a Nation: How the Railroads Shaped and United America** page 229; lines 83–89

> The development of the railroad had a major impact on the United States geographically and culturally. It united the country by connecting its different regions and opening channels of communication and business. After the completion of the transcontinental railroad, our nation spread out and became prosperous. Eventually, it would become one of the world's superpowers, thanks in part to the railroad.

Try It! How does starting the third sentence with a phrase ("After the completion . . .") affect the paragraph? How does starting the last sentence with the word *Eventually* affect its rhythm? How is the final sentence different from the first two? Record your answers in your journal.

Fine-Tune Your Draft

Apply It! Use these revision suggestions to prepare your final draft.

- **Vary Your Sentences** Begin some sentences with words, phrases, or clauses instead of with the subject and its verb. Use a variety of sentence structures in your paragraphs. Mix simple sentences with compound sentences (two independent clauses joined by a conjunction—*and, but, or*) and complex sentences (a sentence that contains a subordinate clause).

- **Improve Your Transitions** Use transitional words and phrases such as *also* and *as a result* to help link ideas and connect sentences and paragraphs.

Teacher and Family Feedback Share your draft with your teacher or a family member. Carefully review the comments you receive. Then, revise your final draft as needed.

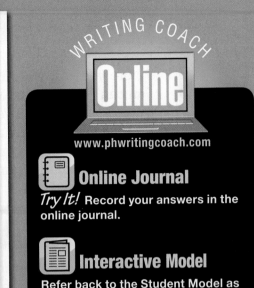

WRITING COACH

Online

www.phwritingcoach.com

Online Journal

Try It! Record your answers in the online journal.

Interactive Model

Refer back to the Student Model as you revise your writing.

Interactive Writing Coach™

Revise your draft and submit it paragraph by paragraph for feedback.

Editing: Making It Correct

Before you edit your final draft, take time to think about how you can improve the way you have paraphrased, summarized, quoted, and cited all your researched information. **Then, edit your draft using a** style manual to accurately document sources and format the materials, **including quotations. Finally, edit your draft for errors in** grammar, mechanics, and spelling.

WRITE GUY *Jeff Anderson, M. Ed.*

WHAT DO YOU NOTICE?

Zoom in on Conventions Focus on quotations as you zoom in on these lines from the Student Model.

 **STUDENT MODEL**

from **Tracks Across a Nation**
page 226; lines 1–5

> "Today, far more Americans are likely to live near a highway or an airport than a railroad track. Yet the railroad helped define the United States," argues railroad historian Elinor Posen (Message to the author). In fact, many experts claim that the railroad transformed the United States into a unified nation.

Now, ask yourself this question: *How has the writer integrated the quotation and citation into the writing to maintain a flow of ideas?*

Perhaps you noted that the writer used these helpful techniques to blend the quotation with the paragraph:

- The writer has properly punctuated a direct quotation within the text.
- The writer follows the quotation with a phrase that identifies the source and tells why she is an expert.
- The writer has properly cited the source, using correct format and punctuation.

Partner Talk Discuss this question with a partner: *How does the writer make sure that the quotation fits in with the rest of the paragraph?*

To learn more about integrating quotations, see Grammar Game Plan Error 18, page 290.

Grammar Mini-Lesson: Punctuation

To learn more, see Chapter 25.

Punctuating Quotations With Citations Quotations follow specific rules for punctuation. Study these sentences from the Student Model. Notice how the writer punctuates a quotation with its citation.

 **STUDENT MODEL** from **Tracks Across a Nation: How the Railroads Shaped and United America** page 229; lines 79–82

> Due to the rise of populations and the fall of Native American culture, says historian Steven Mintz, "the 1890 census would declare that the American frontier had disappeared. The railroad was a major cause" ("Building").

Try It! Decide whether these quotations are punctuated properly and have correct citation formatting. Correct the punctuation where necessary. Write the answers in your journal.

1. John F. Stover suggests that until railroad travel, the speed of transportation was unchanged for thousands of years because "the speed of a horse was . . . the maximum speed of land travel" (Stover 10)

2. According to a comment from a railroader's blog "the age of the railroad isn't over. It just hasn't been rediscovered yet. (*RRCrossing. Blog.com*)"

Apply It! Edit your draft for grammar, mechanics, and spelling. If necessary, rewrite sentences to ensure you've integrated, punctuated, and cited quotations properly.

Use the rubric to evaluate your piece. If necessary, rethink, rewrite, or revise.

Rubric for Informational Research Report	Rating Scale					
Ideas: How focused and clearly supported is your thesis statement?	Not very 1	2	3	4	Very 5	6
Organization: How logical is the progression of ideas?	1	2	3	4	5	6
Voice: How clearly have you expressed your conclusions about your research question?	1	2	3	4	5	6
Word Choice: How effectively does your word choice develop and support your thesis statement?	1	2	3	4	5	6
Sentence Fluency: How well have you varied sentences?	1	2	3	4	5	6
Conventions: How correctly are your sources formatted?	1	2	3	4	5	6

WRITING COACH

 Online

www.phwritingcoach.com

 Video
Learn effective editing techniques from program author Jeff Anderson.

 Online Journal
Try It! Record your answers in the online journal.

 Interactive Model
Refer back to the Student Model as you edit your writing.

Interactive Writing Coach™
Edit your draft and check it against the rubric. Submit it paragraph by paragraph for feedback.

Publishing

It is time to share your research report. When you've finished your final draft, **publish it for an appropriate audience.**

Wrap Up Your Presentation

Your teacher may require you to turn in a typed report. Follow the guidelines provided. Create a cover sheet, table of contents, and a Works Cited list. Also be sure to add a lively title that indicates the topic of the report.

Publish Your Piece

Use the chart to brainstorm for ways to publish your research report for an appropriate audience. You may decide to circulate or post a written report or share an oral report or **multimedia presentation.**

If your audience is...	...then publish it by...
Students or teachers at school	• Displaying your written report in the school library or media center • Posting your report on your class or school Web page
A local group or club with a special interest in your topic	• Giving a multimedia presentation at a club meeting and answering questions about your findings • Posting your paper on a Web site related to the group or club and inviting comments

 Reflect on Your Writing

Now that you are done with your informational research report, read it over and use your writing journal to answer these questions.

- Which parts of preparing your research report were the most fun? Which parts were more difficult?
- What will you do differently the next time?
- What important things have you learned about research writing?

The Big Question: Why Write? Did you understand your subject well enough to write about it? How did you find out what all the facts were?

Manage Your Portfolio Consider including your published informational research report in your writing portfolio. If so, consider what this piece reveals about your writing and your growth as a writer.

MAKE YOUR WRITING COUNT

Explore a Topic by Planning a Web Site

Research reports provide an in-depth look at their topics. Share with your audience the wealth of information in your research report by creating a **Web site**.

A Web site is a type of Internet document. It can have an unlimited number of interconnected pages. Each page may contain text, graphics, images, sounds, and links to other Web pages. Plan a Web site based on one of your peers' reports. Then, produce a **multimedia presentation,** including text, graphics, images, and sound. Share a mock-up of your Web site or an actual Web site.

Here's your action plan.

1. With your group, assign roles and deadlines.

2. Choose a research report that interests the whole group.

3. View informational Web sites. Notice how the pages interlink.

4. Work together to plan a mock Web site. In your Web site, plan to:

   - Identify a clear topic

   - Include 3 to 5 Web pages based on the research report

   - Use available technology to deliver information through images, audio and/or video, and text

   - Show links between pages and to other Web sites

5. Edit your pages. If possible, use Web authoring tools to create the Web site.

6. Rehearse your presentation. Present your mock-up—including audio or video clips on the side—or a complete Web site.

Listening and Speaking As a group, discuss how best to present your Web site. Practice your presentation, using visuals and sounds. Ask listeners for feedback. During the presentation, remember to incorporate your peers' feedback on the sound and visual elements of your Web site.

WRITING COACH

Online

www.phwritingcoach.com

Online Journal

Reflect on Your Writing Record your answers and ideas in the online journal.

Resource

Link to resources on 21st Century Learning for help in creating a group project.

Your Turn

**Writing for Media:
Observation Report**

Observation Report

An **observation report** is an opportunity to evaluate a speaker and his or her presentation. In this assignment, you will get to evaluate a special "event," such as a guest speaker in class or a student-led assembly. First, you will formulate questions. Next, you will do some research to gather information about the topic of the instruction. Then you'll observe the event, take notes, and write an observation report in a **blog.** Link your parenthetical citations to the bibliography.

📓 *Try It!* Study the excerpt from the observation report on this page. Then, answer the questions. Record your answers in your journal.

1. What **event** does the observation report cover?

2. What is the writer's **purpose?** Who is the intended audience?

3. An observation report evaluates a presenter and the audience at work. What observations does this report share?

4. What other information do you want to know? What other **questions** would you expect the report to answer?

5. Is the writer **fair** to the presenter and students he observed? How can you tell?

6. What suggestions would you make to the writer for **improving** this observation report?

Observation Report

Class: Earth Science
Presenter: Mrs. Beatrice Cohen,
        local organic farmer
Evaluator: Robbie Gutierrez
Date of Observation: March 6, 2010

QUESTIONS AND RESEARCH PLAN

My main questions were: *Why is compost important? How does it work?* I did some research and found out that composting is when food and other plant materials are mixed together and allowed to decompose so that they will turn into a rich soil called compost (Pleasant 24). I also learned that layering ingredients in a compost pile is the key to its success ("Outdoor").

OBSERVATIONS

• What was the classroom event? What were the speaker's objectives?

Ms. Cohen demonstrated how to make and use a compost pile. The objectives were to build a compost pile and to work effectively in teams.

INSTRUCTOR OBSERVATIONS

▪ How well did the speaker present the information?

Ms. Cohen used a slide show to tell what compost is and how to make it. Next, she used real materials to show making compost. Then she put students in teams to create their own compost.

▪ Was the speaker engaged with the audience?

Ms. Cohen stopped often to ask if students had any questions. She also had volunteers summarize the steps. As students worked, she walked around the room, asking questions and making comments.

STUDENT OBSERVATIONS

▪ Were the students interested in the activity? Did they participate actively?

Students worked together well. They asked questions when necessary and offered feedback during the team work.

OVERALL EVALUATION

▪ What was the most effective or interesting part of the presentation? How could the speaker have improved it?

The demonstration was good because it showed exactly how to build a compost pile. Ms. Cohen should have explained why compost is important.

Create an Observation Report

Follow these steps to create your own **observation report**. To plan your observation report, review the graphic organizers on pages R24–R27 and choose one that suits your needs.

Prewriting

- Find out about a school event that you would like to observe. Think about the topics it addresses. Choose one that is interesting and get permission to observe.

- Be sure to identify the target **audience** for your observation report. Are you writing to **inform** the speaker about his or her performance or to inform others?

- Brainstorm for specific questions about the event to answer as you observe. Consult with others to formulate major research questions that are fair and wide-ranging.

- It's important to formulate a **research plan**. What specific research question will you try to answer?

- Prepare to write the formal research section of your report. This will set up your observation. Follow the steps in your plan to **gather information** from **relevant sources** to build necessary context and share the ideas of experts.

- After some preliminary research in reference works and additional texts, create a **written plan** for more specific resources, including print and electronic sources. You may need to **broaden or narrow** your research question in order to produce better results. Refine your plan as needed.

- As you obtain information, **evaluate** your sources. Make sure they are **relevant, valid,** and **up-to-date.** Check elements such as publication date and point of view. Document **bibliographic information** according to a standard format.

- To plan for the direct observation section of your report, think about how you will **take notes** during your observation. Consider using note cards to create a list of questions.

- As you take notes, **paraphrase** or **summarize** information. If you use a **direct quotation**, enclose it in big quotation marks to avoid plagiarism.

- Consider the ways your observation supports or contradicts your formal research. Prepare to share your ideas with your audience. Categorize your notes according to themes or subtopics in order to make connections and see big ideas.

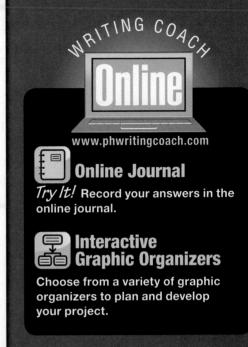

WRITING COACH

Online

www.phwritingcoach.com

Online Journal

Try It! Record your answers in the online journal.

Interactive Graphic Organizers

Choose from a variety of graphic organizers to plan and develop your project.

Partner Talk

Ask a partner to review your research plan. Discuss:

- The difference between plagiarism and paraphrasing
- The importance of citing valid and reliable sources
- Why one source is more useful than another

Your Turn ▶ **Observation Report** (*continued*)

Drafting

- To help present your findings in a meaningful way, organize your questions and observation notes under subject headings. For example, under the heading *Instructor Observations,* put all your comments about the speaker's performance. Then, start writing sentences and paragraphs.

- Be sure to list key information at the top of your report, including the name of the event and the date. Also list your name and the date of the observation.

- An effective report is concise and logical. It draws conclusions, summarizes, and paraphrases the findings in a **systematic** and organized way.

- Marshal the evidence you have collected and organized to support your conclusions and explain the topic. Include specific **details** about the event and provide relevant reasons for the conclusions you have drawn about it. Include helpful **visuals,** such as photographs, charts, or video of the event.

- If you use someone else's words, be sure to put them in **quotation marks** to avoid plagiarism.

- Acknowledge your **sources,** as needed, in context or in a credits section. Avoid interrupting the flow of the report. Use accepted formats for integrating quotations and citations.

Revising

Use Revision RADaR techniques as you review your draft carefully.

- **Replace** general terms with vivid details and unclear explanations with precise ideas.

- **Add** specific details or missing information to support your argument.

- **Delete** information that does not support your argument.

- **Reorder** sentences and paragraphs to present ideas clearly and logically.

Read aloud your observation report to make sure it reads smoothly. Vary sentence beginnings and length. Tie ideas and sentences together with transition words, such as *first, however,* and *next.*

Editing

Now take time to check your observation report carefully before your publish it. Focus on each sentence and then on each word. Look for these kinds of errors:

- Incomplete sentences or sentence fragments
- Inconsistent verb tense
- Spelling mistakes
- Misuse of commonly confused words
- Missing punctuation marks
- Improper citations and quotations

As you edit your report, be sure you follow an accepted format for integrating quotations and citations into your text to maintain a flow of ideas.

Publishing

- Publish your observation report by submitting it to the school newspaper.
- Get permission to post an electronic version of your report on the school's Web site.
- With your classmates, compile and design an anthology of observations. Print it for display in the guidance counselor's office or post an electronic version on the appropriate page of your school's Web site.

> **Extension** Find another example of an observation report and compare it with the one you are writing.

WRITING COACH

Online

www.phwritingcoach.com

 Online Journal

Record your answers in the online journal.

 Interactive Graphic Organizers

Choose from a variety of graphic organizers to plan and develop your project.

Partner Talk

Before you finalize your observation report, ask a partner to check it carefully. Proofread each other's reports for accurate citation of sources. Make sure that the sources of direct quotations, additional background information, and graphics are accounted for.

Writing for Assessment

Many tests include a prompt that asks you to write or critique a research plan. Use these prompts to practice. Respond using the characteristics of your informational research report. (See page 224.)

 Try It! Read the prompt carefully, and then create a **research plan.** List all of the actions you will take to research this topic. Tell where you will look for sources and how you will evaluate them. Be as specific as you can. Use the ABCDs of On-Demand Writing to help you plan and write your research plan.

Format

Write your *research plan* in the form of an outline. List and number each step you must take in the order you would take it. Some steps may have more than one part.

Research Plan Prompt

Write a research plan about a person, battle, or event related to World War II. Your plan should include (1) a narrowed research topic and question, (2) a list of possible sources ideas, (3) the intended audience, and (4) the steps you'll take in a time-line. [30 minutes]

Academic Vocabulary

Before you locate sources, formulate questions about your topic. Then, consider the types of sources you may use. Think about how you may need to *narrow* your topic based on what your sources support. Organize your thoughts before writing by creating a list.

The ABCDs of On-Demand Writing

Use these ABCDs to help you respond to the prompt.

Before you write your draft:

A ttack the prompt [1 MINUTE]

- Circle or highlight important verbs in the prompt. Draw a line from the verb to what it refers to.
- Rewrite the prompt in your own words.

B rainstorm for possible answers [4 MINUTES]

- Create a graphic organizer to generate ideas.
- Use one for each part of the prompt if necessary.

C hoose the order of your response [1 MINUTE]

- Think about the best way to organize your ideas.
- Number your ideas in the order you will write about them. Cross out ideas you will not be using.

After you write your draft:

D etect errors before turning in the draft [1 MINUTE]

- Carefully reread your writing.
- Make sure that your response makes sense and is complete.
- Look for spelling, punctuation, and grammar errors.

More Prompts for Practice

Apply It! **Critique the research plan** in Prompt 1. In a written response, report on your ideas and make specific suggestions to improve each research plan. Consider these questions:

- Is there a **narrow topic**? Is it appropriate for the **audience** and **purpose**?
- Is the writer planning to find enough **varied sources**?
- Does the research plan say anything about **evaluating** sources?

> **Prompt 1** Elijah wrote this research plan. Evaluate it for what he did well and what needs improvement.
>
> *My Topic:* I am going to write a research plan about homeschooling because I'm curious to know if it is as effective as going to a school.
>
> *My Research:* I will look at education journals to find out who homeschools and why. I will also interview a friend who is homeschooled and her parents.
>
> *My Writing:* I will research the first week. Write a draft the second week. Revise and edit the third week.

Spiral Review: Narrative If you choose to write a **nonfiction narrative** in response to Prompt 2, make sure your story reflects the characteristics described on page 66.

> **Prompt 2** Think about a time you took an action or made a tough decision. Use specific details to tell about the events leading up to the action or decision, and explain what the experience meant to you.

Spiral Review: Response to Literature If you choose to write a **response to literature** in response to Prompt 3, make sure it reflects all of the characteristics on page 198, including: a clear, strong **thesis statement**; **details** that are focused, organized and coherent; **evidence** from the text, using quotations; and an **analysis** of story elements, such as character and theme.

> **Prompt 3** Recall an expository or literary text you have read with a powerful theme or message. Write an essay that identifies what you learned from the text. Explain how the author revealed it through actions and dialogue.

WRITING COACH

Online

www.phwritingcoach.com

Interactive Writing Coach™

Plan your response to the prompt. If you are using the prompt for practice, write one paragraph at a time or your entire draft and then submit it for feedback. If you are using the prompt as a timed test, write your entire draft and then submit it for feedback.

Remember **ABCD**

Attack the prompt

Brainstorm for possible answers

Choose the order of your response

Detect errors before turning in the draft

CHAPTER 12

WORKPLACE WRITING

What's Ahead

In this chapter, you will learn how you can write workplace documents, including business letters and how-to essays. You will also learn how to write other practical forms of writing, including friendly letters. All of these functional documents should present organized information that is accurately conveyed, or written, and presented in a reader-friendly format.

Characteristics of Writing

Effective workplace and practical writing has these characteristics:

- **Information** that is clear, concise, and focused
- A clear **purpose** and intended **audience**
- **Formal, polite** language
- **Reader-friendly formatting techniques,** such as sufficient white or blank space and clearly defined sections
- Correct **grammar, punctuation,** and **spelling** appropriate to the form of writing

Forms of Writing

Forms of workplace writing include:

How-to essays are used to explain how something works or how to do something. These essays are written in a step-by-step format.

Letters of complaint are formal correspondence written to a business, newspaper, or other organization. They are written to express criticism or dissatisfaction with an item, service, or issue.

Letters of request are formal letters written to a business or outside organization and stating a request.

Memos are short documents usually written from one member of a group or organization to another or to another group. They assume some background on the topic.

Other forms of practical writing include:

Friendly letters are informal correspondence written to a relative, friend, or acquaintance. They can be written for various reasons, including to ask how someone is doing or just to say hello.

 Try It! For each audience and purpose described, select the appropriate form, such as letter of request, friendly letter, how-to essay, or letter of complaint. Explain your choices.

- To ask about events at a local museum
- To reach out to a pen pal in another country

WRITING COACH

Online

www.phwritingcoach.com

 Resource

Word Bank Use the eText glossary to learn more about these words.

 Online Journal

Try It! Record your answers and ideas in the online journal.

 **Connect to the Big Questions**

Discuss these questions:

1 What do you think? What is the best way to communicate about what we see?

2 Why write? What do daily workplace communications require of format, content, and style?

WORD BANK

These vocabulary words are often used with workplace writing. Use the Glossary or a dictionary to check the definitions.

address	explanation
connection	support

STUDENT MODEL
Letter of Request

Learn From Experience

 After reading the letter of request on this page, read the numbered notes in the margin to learn about how the writer presented his ideas.

Try It! Record your answers and ideas in the online journal.

---

1 The letter uses conventional **business letter formatting:**
- writer's complete address
- full date including day, month, and year
- recipient's complete address
- formal salutation
- closing with signature

2 Notice that a colon is placed after the **salutation** of a business letter.

3 In the **first sentence,** the writer **makes a request.** From the first sentence, the purpose of the letter is clear.

4 The bulleted list of questions is **clear, concise, and focused.** Writers are more likely to get the results they want when their request is clear.

Try It!
- Why is it important to include a return address on a business letter?
- What kind of impression do you think the writer made by following standard business letter format?
- Is there anything about the letter you would change? Explain.

Extension Play the role of recipient of the letter and write a response to the sender.

---

1 Ben Baxter
1285 Maple Ave.
Newport, IN 47966

1 March 24, 2010

1 Ms. Nancy Brennan
Director of Admissions
Indiana University
Bloomington, IN 47405

2 Dear Ms. Brennan:

3 I am writing to inquire about admissions requirements at Indiana University. As an eighth-grader, I am looking ahead so that I can map out my high school class selections.

It would be helpful if I could get answers to the following questions:

4 • How many semesters of high school English, math, history, and science are required?
- Is there a foreign language requirement?
- Would taking advanced placement classes in high school help me get accepted to the university?

Thank you very much for your help. I look forward to hearing from you.

1 Sincerely,

Ben Baxter

Ben Baxter

 **Feature Assignment: Letter of Request**

Prewriting

- Plan a first draft of your **letter of request.** You can select from the Topic Bank or come up with an idea of your own.

Work Rules There are rules for when and where teenagers can work. Write to the U.S. Department of Labor to request information about the rules and regulations that apply to teenagers.

Volunteer Effort Suppose that you are interested in volunteering for a local organization. Write a letter to the organization of your choice, requesting information about its volunteer programs and requirements.

- Brainstorm for a list of things that your audience will need to know about you and your purpose for writing the letter.

- Find the accurate contact information for the letter's recipient in a telephone directory or online resource.

 ## Drafting

- **Request information** using reader-friendly formatting techniques, including all of the features of business letters and language that suits a **business context**.

- Organize the information so that the purpose is clearly stated.

- Accurately convey information by double-checking your facts.

 ## Revising and Editing

Review your draft to ensure that information is presented accurately and concisely. Ask yourself if the purpose of your letter is clearly identified and addressed.

Publishing

- If you plan to mail the letter, print the letter on paper suitable for business correspondence.

- If you plan to e-mail the letter, attach your letter to a message as a Portable Document Format (PDF).

www.phwritingcoach.com

 Interactive Model

Listen to an audio recording of the Student Model.

 Online Journal

Try It! Record your answers and ideas in the online journal.

 Interactive Writing Coach

Submit your writing and receive personalized feedback and support as you draft, revise, and edit.

 Video

Learn strategies for effective revising and editing from program authors Jeff Anderson and Kelly Gallagher.

Partner Talk

Read your final draft to a partner. Ask him or her if the request is clearly stated in the beginning of the letter.

STUDENT MODEL | Friendly Letter

Learn From Experience

 After reading the friendly letter on this page, read the numbered notes in the margin to learn about how the writer presented her ideas. As you read, take notes to develop your understanding of basic sight and English vocabulary.

Try It! Record your answers and ideas in the online journal.

---

1 The writer uses a **conventional friendly letter format:** date line followed by salutation. Notice that a comma is placed after the salutation of a friendly letter. Some writers also include their address, before the date line.

2 The writer **supports ideas** with **clear details,** such as specific activities she has been doing at camp.

3 The language in the letter is casual but clear. Friendly letters are less formal than business letters.

4 The writer ends with an appropriate **closing.** She might use a less personal closing if the letter were for someone outside her family.

Try It!

- In what ways is a friendly letter like a business letter?
- In what ways is it different?

---

1 June 30, 2010

Dear Mom and Dad,

I'm so happy that when I asked if I could go to Camp Echo with Jean and Frankie, you said yes! We are having the best time. This camp is even better than I imagined it would be.

Every day we're up just after sunrise. I know you probably have trouble believing that, but it's true! There are so many activities I want to fit into a single day, it's easy to get up in the morning. **2** So far, I have been horseback riding, swimming, and playing baseball almost every day.

I've been trying some new things, too. **2** This camp has an amazing archery range, and I think you would be surprised at how good I've gotten. I've done loads of arts and crafts, and every night we end up around the campfire singing songs.

3 Even though I am enjoying camp, I do miss home—a little. How are Mickey and Mags? I hope Tom is giving them a good walk every day as he said he would. I'm looking forward to seeing everyone in two weeks, when camp ends.

4 Love,

Krissy

Krissy

Feature Assignment:
Friendly Letter

Prewriting

- Plan a first draft of your **friendly letter.** You can select from the Topic Bank or come up with an idea of your own.

Good Times Write a friendly letter to a relative, inviting him or her to attend a party. Include details about the time, place, and reason for the party.

Say Hello Suppose that you had a classmate who moved to another state. Write a friendly letter to him or her, telling what's been going on at school since he or she left.

- Brainstorm for a list of ideas you would like to include in your letter. Consider opinions you might share or information you might request.

- Use a telephone directory or online resource to find the accurate contact information for the letter's recipient.

Drafting

- Use reader-friendly formatting techniques, including all the features of a friendly letter.

- Use a familiar salutation that matches your relationship with the recipient.

- **Organize** the information so that your purpose is clear.

- Accurately convey information by double-checking your ideas.

 ## Revising and **Editing**

Review your draft to ensure that information is presented accurately and concisely. Ask yourself if the **purpose and audience** for your letter are clearly identified and addressed.

Publishing

- If you plan to mail the letter, print the letter or write it neatly on paper or stationery suitable for the recipient.

- If you plan to e-mail the letter, confirm the correct e-mail address and attach your letter to a message as a PDF.

 Interactive Model

Listen to an audio recording of the Student Model.

 Online Journal

Record your answers and ideas in the online journal.

 Interactive Writing Coach

Submit your writing and receive personalized feedback and support as you draft, revise, and edit.

 Video

Learn strategies for effective revising and editing from program authors Jeff Anderson and Kelly Gallagher.

Work with a partner to edit your letter. Ask for feedback about spelling, punctuation, and vocabulary. Then, read your partner's letter with similar questions in mind.

STUDENT MODEL
Letter of Complaint

Learn From Experience

 After reading the letter of complaint on this page, read the numbered notes in the margin to learn about how the writer presented his ideas.

Try It! Record your answers and ideas in the online journal.

❶ The writer uses conventional business letter format, including writer's address, date, recipient's address, formal salutation, and closing.

❷ The writer begins by giving **background information** that helps the reader understand the problem. This creates a more positive tone than beginning with the complaint.

❸ Here, the writer **states the complaint** clearly but **politely.**

❹ In this **clear and concise statement,** the writer explains how he would like the problem solved.

Try It!
- Why is it important to keep a positive tone in a complaint letter?
- What are some examples of polite language that the writer uses?

Extension Inferring from the letter's tone, consider the way a recipient might respond. Use the letter's tone to help you distinguish fact from opinion. Write a response from the recipient that summarizes the complaint and responds to the original writer's attitude.

---

❶ Mike Valesquez
13 S. Addison St.
Chicago, IL 60613

❶ September 9, 2010

❶ Mr. John Russell
Chairman, City Council
2437 S. Michigan Ave.
Chicago, IL 60616

❶ Dear Mr. Russell:

❷ As you know, the streets around Addison Elementary School are really busy. The traffic makes it hard for us kids to ride our bikes to school safely. Last fall, the city council voted to create bike lanes in the school neighborhood. Bike lanes would definitely make the streets safer for us.

❸ More than a year has passed, and we still do not have the bike lanes. When you visited our school last year, you said you really wanted to help us. I believe you still do.

❹ Please let me know when we can expect work to begin on the bike lanes. I appreciate your help in answering this question, and I look forward to hearing from you.

Sincerely,

Mike Valesquez

Mike Valesquez

Your Turn **Feature Assignment: Letter of Complaint**

Prewriting

- Plan a first draft of your **letter of complaint.** You can select from the Topic Bank or come up with an idea of your own.

TOPIC BANK

Raise Awareness Write a letter to the editor of your local newspaper with a complaint about an unsafe condition in your neighborhood or community. Include suggested solutions to the problem.

Consumer Complaint Write a letter to a company expressing a concern you have about a product it manufactures.

- Brainstorm for a list of things that your letter's recipient will need to know about you and the complaint you are registering.

- Find the accurate contact information for the letter's recipient in a telephone directory or online resource.

Drafting

- Use a formal salutation that matches your relationship with the recipient. Use the correct formatting for a business letter.

- Include organized information that clearly states your opinion. As you write, use formal language appropriate for a business context.

- Accurately convey information by double-checking your facts.

Revising and Editing

Review your draft to ensure that information is presented accurately and concisely. Read your final draft to your teacher or a classmate. Ask if you have clearly registered a complaint. Think about the **feedback you received and revise** as needed.

Publishing

- If you plan to mail the letter, print the letter or write it neatly on paper or stationery suitable for the recipient.

- If you plan to e-mail the letter, confirm the correct e-mail address and attach your letter to a message as a PDF.

WRITING COACH

Online
www.phwritingcoach.com

 Interactive Model
Listen to an audio recording of the Student Model.

 Online Journal
Try It! Record your answers and ideas in the online journal.

 Interactive Writing Coach
Submit your writing and receive personalized feedback and support as you draft, revise, and edit.

 Video
Learn strategies for effective revising and editing from program authors Jeff Anderson and Kelly Gallagher.

Partner Talk
Work with a partner to revise your letter. Ask for feedback on the content and organization of the information. Is your complaint clear? Is it well-supported?

MAKE YOUR WRITING COUNT

Present a Research Report for Taking Action

Letters help people communicate important information to specific audiences. Both formal and informal letters may involve the seeds for activities or ideas that will help classmates learn more. Make a **research report** and presentation that might inspire a positive call to action if supported by research.

With a group, **brainstorm** for several topics from among your work in this chapter. Have a discussion with others to **decide upon a topic** that will be helpful to someone thinking about taking action to improve your community. Work together to **formulate an open-ended research question** that will help you produce a report about the topic. Consider topics like traffic safety, environmental concerns, and ways to increase volunteerism. Conduct some **preliminary research** in reference works and search additional texts to make sure that your question is a good one.

Group members should **consult** one another and **critique the process** as they work, and be prepared to adjust as needed. Remember that a research report should:

- State a specific thesis
- Meet the needs of audience and purpose
- Express a clear point of view
- Provide supporting evidence
- Present ideas in a logical way
- Document sources using correct formatting

Organize a Take-Action Day to present your research results to students in your school. Share the information you have gathered in a **multimedia presentation** that uses graphics, images, and sound. You may use posters and other displays or an electronic slide show that uses presentation software.

21st Century Learning

Here's your action plan.

1. Research takes time. In a group, make a plan for several group meetings. Set objectives and choose roles for each member.

2. Work together to develop a written research plan that includes:

   - Obtaining and evaluating a variety of sources, including a range of **print and electronic sources** as well as data and **quotations from experts**

   - **Categorizing notes** by theme or sub-topic to see big ideas

   - **Using a standard format to record bibliographic information** for all notes and sources

   - Checking elements such as publication date and point of view to ensure that your sources are **reliable and valid**

3. Discuss your findings. **Evaluate the sources,** discussing the importance of citing valid and reliable sources. Reject sources that are biased or dated and explain why they aren't useful. Work together to create a **clear thesis statement.**

4. Outline the content of the report. Assign sections of the outline to each group member. You may need to **narrow or broaden your research question** and research further before you write a draft.

5. Work together to write a draft by compiling collected data and using the **marshalled**—collected and organized—evidence to explain the topic. As a group, discuss the difference between **plagiarism** and **paraphrasing.** Use the proper style for acknowledging sources and for integrating **quotations** and **citations** without interrupting the flow of ideas.

6. Revise and edit to ensure that the thesis statement is supported by **evidence.** Be sure your report **states relevant reasons for conclusions** and **summarizes** your findings in a systematic way.

7. Add audio and visuals and present it in a **meaningful format.**

8. Present your report to students, counselors, and teachers.

Listening and Speaking Practice the presentation in front of another group or each other. Listen to questions or comments from the audience to help you make improvements. When you present, speak clearly and confidently to your audience.

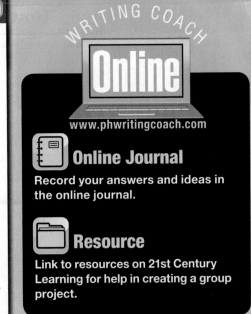

WRITING COACH

Online

www.phwritingcoach.com

Online Journal
Record your answers and ideas in the online journal.

Resource
Link to resources on 21st Century Learning for help in creating a group project.

Your Turn → **Writing for Media:
How-To Essay**

How-To Essay

Multimedia presentations are frequently used in schools, in the workplace, at conferences, and online. They are an effective way to present information to a wide audience. Multimedia presentations use a combination of text, images, music, charts, graphics, and animation. They allow people to share information on a variety of topics. Slide shows allow the presenter to share only key points in text while giving an oral presentation.

A multimedia presentation is a good way to share a **how-to essay.** The presenter can provide information to the audience one point at a time, helping the audience to focus. Often, printed versions of the presentation are also given to the audience for reference.

Try It! Study the slides on this page. Then, answer the questions. Record your answers in your journal.

1. How does the **title slide** communicate the purpose of the how-to essay?

2. How do the **images** help the reader, or audience, follow along?

3. Is the amount of **text** per slide reader-friendly? Explain.

4. What do you think the **presenter** should say as each slide is shown?

Extension Find another example of a multimedia presentation, and compare it with this one.

How to Make a Fruit Salad

Step 1: Choose 3-4 kinds of your favorite fruit

Step 2: Wash fruit and peel it, if necessary

Step 3: Cut fruit into 1-inch pieces

Step 4: Toss all fruit pieces together in a large bowl

Create a How-To Essay

Follow these steps to create your own multimedia slide show that features a **how-to essay.** To plan your presentation, complete an online or printed graphic organizer. See pages R24–R27 to choose an appropriate format.

Prewriting

- Brainstorm for a list of steps for a procedure that you could present in a how-to essay using a **multimedia** slide show.
- Choose the procedure you think is best. Make a list of the steps involved in the procedure.
- Consider the needs of your specific **audience.** What does the audience already know about the procedure? What does the audience need to know? What is the **purpose** of your slide show?

Drafting

- Divide your procedure into slides. Each slide should contain only a small amount of text. This will allow the audience to focus on one step of the procedure at a time.
- Number the steps and order them according to what is done first, second, next, and so on. Include details to explain the reason for each step.
- Write a script for the oral presentation. Organize the information to support the content of each slide.
- Add **graphics, images,** and **sound** to slides to make your presentation easier to understand. Choose colors and backgrounds that make the **text** easy for the audience to read.

Revising and **Editing**

- As you revise, review each slide to be sure that its content correctly matches each section of your oral presentation.
- Check that the design of your slides makes them easy to read.
- Double-check the accuracy of information on your slides.
- Check spelling and grammar.

Publishing

- Present your slide show to your class or another audience.
- Speak clearly and allow time for your audience to ask questions.

WRITING COACH

www.phwritingcoach.com

Online Journal

Try It! Record your answers and ideas in the online journal.

Interactive Graphic Organizers

Use the graphic organizers to plan your multimedia presentation.

 **Partner Talk**

Before publishing, practice your presentation with a partner. Ask your partner if he or she understands how to complete the procedure you've described. Monitor your partner's spoken language by asking follow-up questions to confirm your understanding.

Writing for Assessment

Many standardized tests include a prompt that asks you to write a procedural text. Use these prompts to practice. Respond using the characteristics of a how-to essay. (See pages 266–267.)

 Try It! Read the **procedural text** prompt and the information on the format and academic vocabulary. Use the ABCDs of On-Demand Writing to help you plan and write your response.

Format

The prompt directs you to write a *procedural text*. Describe the purpose of the text in the first section. Be sure to include steps with organized information such as a numbered list or visuals.

Procedural Text Prompt

Your grandmother wants to set up a page on a social network site. She wants written instructions to review. Write a procedural text that includes stepped-out instructions for logging on and using a social networking site. [30 Minutes]

Academic Vocabulary

A procedural text is a kind of text that tells somebody how to perform a task. *Stepped-out instructions* have numbered lists that provide details in the order they are used.

The ABCDs of On-Demand Writing

Use the following ABCDs to help you respond to the prompt.

Before you write your draft:

Attack the prompt [1 MINUTE]

- Circle or highlight important verbs in the prompt. Draw a line from the verb to what it refers to.
- Rewrite the prompt in your own words.

Brainstorm possible answers [4 MINUTES]

- Create a graphic organizer to generate ideas.
- Use one for each part of the prompt if necessary.

Choose the order of your response [1 MINUTE]

- Think about the best way to organize your ideas.
- Number your ideas in the order you will write about them. Cross out ideas you will not be using.

After you write your draft:

Detect errors before turning in the draft [1 MINUTE]

- Carefully reread your writing.
- Look for spelling, punctuation, and grammar errors.
- Make sure that your response makes sense and is complete.

More Prompts for Practice

 Apply It! Respond to Prompt 1 by writing a **procedural text.** As you write, be sure to:

- Consider what your **audience** knows and needs to know
- **Organize** information into steps or paragraphs
- **Define** any terms that your audience may not know

> **Prompt 1** Your friend wants to learn a skill from your favorite sport or activity. Choose a skill like shooting a free throw, casting a fishing line, or throwing a curve ball and write a procedural text that includes stepped-out instructions on executing the skill.

Spiral Review: Expository If you choose to respond to Prompt 2, write a compare-and-contrast **expository essay.** Make sure your essay reflects the characteristics described on page 146.

> **Prompt 2** After-school activities are an important part of an educational experience. Write an expository essay that compares and contrasts two different activities you could recommend to a new student in your school.

Spiral Review: Research Plan If you choose to respond to Prompt 3, write a **critique of the research plan.** Make sure your critique evaluates all of the characteristics described on page 224. Your critique should determine if the research plan:

- Contains a **narrowed topic,** and is appropriate for the **audience**
- Includes enough **primary and secondary sources,** and says something about **evaluating** sources

> **Prompt 3** Julianna wrote the following research plan. Explain what she did well and what needs improvement.
> *My Topic:* How the railway system helped America grow.
> *My Research:* I'm going to search the Internet, talk to the reference librarian, and look for print sources. I know that the development of the railway led to the destruction of many Native American cultures, so I will look for first-hand accounts from Native Americans to show the downside of building the railway system.
> *My Drafting:* After a few days of research, I will write my draft.

WRITING COACH

Online

www.phwritingcoach.com

Interactive Writing Coach™

Plan your response to the prompt. If you are writing the prompt for practice, write one paragraph at a time or your entire draft and submit it for feedback. If you are using the prompt for a timed test, write your entire draft and submit it for feedback.

Remember **ABCD**

Attack the prompt

Brainstorm possible answers

Choose the order of your response

Detect errors before turning in the draft

OUNS AND PRONOUNS *Concrete and Abstract Nouns* VERBS *Transitive Ve*
Adverb? CONJUNCTIONS AND INTERJECTIONS *Subordinating Conjunct*
ositive Phrases EFFECTIVE SENTENCES *Combining Sentence Parts* PUNCT
rbs ADJECTIVES AND ADVERBS *Interogative Adjectives* PREPOSITIONS
nctions BASIC SENTENCE PARTS *Subjects and Predicates* PHRASES AND
NCTUATION NOUNS AND PRONOUNS *Concrete and Abstract Nouns* VE
ONS *Preposition or Adverb?* CONJUNCTIONS AND INTERJECTIONS *Subo*
ND CLAUSES *Appositive Phrases* EFFECTIVE SENTENCES *Combining Sente*
RBS *Transitive Verbs* ADJECTIVES AND ADVERBS *Interogative Adjective*

Grammar

Find It FIX IT

This handy guide will help you find and fix errors in your writing!

Grammar Game Plan

20 Major Grammatical Errors and How to Fix Them

1

Using the Wrong Word

GAME PLAN Use the right words to make your writing clear. Make sure your words say exactly what you mean them to say.

CLARIFY MEANING Do not confuse the meanings of words with similar spellings. Also, words with similar definitions can have important shades of meaning. Check that words you found in a thesaurus are used correctly.

I will put the clothes ~~in~~ ∧into the laundry basket.

Are you going to ~~refute~~ ∧refuse her offer?

SPELL-CHECK ERRORS Computer spell-checkers often correct a misspelling with a different, similarly spelled word. Be sure to proofread your work carefully to catch these errors. In each of the following examples, the word with a strikethrough represents an inappropriate spell-checker correction.

Why did you ~~recline~~ ∧decline the invitation?

The ~~intention~~ ∧invention Betsy entered into the contest seems the most helpful.

Tech Tip

Be your own "spell-checker"! Proofread! Your computer's spell-checker will not identify every misspelling or incorrectly used word.

LEARN MORE
- **See Chapter 20, Effective Sentences, pages 455–459**
- **See Writing Coach Online**

 *Check It*

Use a current or completed draft of your work to practice using words correctly.

✓ **READ carefully.** Take the time to read your draft closely. For a double-check, have someone else read your work.

✓ **IDENTIFY possible mistakes.** Mark any difficult or commonly misused words in your draft.

✓ **USE a dictionary.** If you are not sure of a word's meaning, look it up in a dictionary.

Find It/FIX IT

2

Missing Comma After Introductory Element

Tech Tip

Remember to add commas to introductory elements that you cut and paste from different parts of a sentence or paragraph.

LEARN MORE
- See Chapter 25, Punctuation, pages 559, 562
- See Writing Coach Online

GAME PLAN Place a comma after the following introductory elements in your work.

WORDS Place a comma after introductory words.

Greetings, welcome to our conference.

William, do you have time to help me?

PHRASES Place a comma after introductory prepositional phrases. If the prepositional phrase has only two words, a comma is not necessary.

Upon arrival at the arena, we looked for our seats.

During the family dinner, my dog sat under the table.

Before long we had arrived at our destination.

CLAUSES Introductory adverbial clauses should be followed by a comma.

Unless it snows, we won't be able to go sledding.

When I found out she was going to be late, I changed the reservation.

✔ Check It

Use a current or completed draft of your work to practice placing commas after introductory clauses.

✔ **SCAN your draft.** Look for introductory words, phrases, and clauses.

✔ **IDENTIFY missing commas.** Mark sentence starters that might need a comma.

✔ **USE your textbook.** Check the grammar section of your textbook if you are not sure whether or not to use a comma.

GAME PLAN Provide complete citations for borrowed words and ideas. Use the citation style (such as MLA) that your teacher recommends.

MISSING CITATIONS Cite sources of direct quotes and statistics. Remember–when in doubt, cite the source.

Professor Williams claims, "The book is an original copy"ᴧ(James 14).

Mr. Kenneth says that 12 percent of the cases are unsolvableᴧ(Kenneth 18).

INCOMPLETE CITATIONS Make sure your citations include complete source information. This information will vary depending on the source and the citation style. It often includes the author's name, the source's title, and the page numbers.

The artist has been called "the best sculptor of his time" (ᴧBurbury 7).

At state colleges, nearly 90 percent of all seniors graduate (Wheatonᴧ32).

Tech Tip

When researching for an assignment on the Internet, be sure to use only reputable sources that cite their information. Then, use the correct citation style for Internet sources, which often includes the Web site URL and date visited.

LEARN MORE
- See Chapter 11, Research Writing, pages 234–237
- See Writing Coach Online

 **Check It**

Use a current or completed draft of your work to practice documenting your sources.

✔ **REVIEW your notes.** Look for borrowed words and ideas such as quotations, statistics, and other facts.

✔ **USE a style guide.** Check the correct format for your citations in the style guide your teacher recommends.

4

Vague Pronoun Reference

Tech Tip

It is important to proofread your work after you cut and paste text. You may have inserted vague pronoun references while moving text and making new sentences.

LEARN MORE

- See Chapter 6, Fiction Narration, pages 110–111
- See Writing Coach Online

GAME PLAN Create clear pronoun-antecedent relationships to make your writing more accurate and powerful.

VAGUE IDEA Pronouns such as *which*, *this*, *that*, and *these* should refer to a specific idea. To avoid vague references, try changing a pronoun to an adjective that modifies a specific noun.

Mrs. Jones taught a star pupil and one whom she knew had potential. These ∧students are the reason she loves teaching.

UNCLEAR USE OF *IT*, *THEY*, AND *YOU* Be sure that the pronouns *it*, *they*, and *you* have a clearly stated antecedent. Replacing the personal pronoun with a specific noun can make a sentence clearer.

Danny asked for a new bike and a helmet. I̶t̶ ∧The helmet will help him be safe.

The teachers asked the administrators i̶f̶ t̶h̶e̶y̶ c̶o̶u̶l̶d̶ ∧to help with the conference scheduling.

When y̶o̶u̶ ∧bakers make bread, yeast is often needed.

✓ Check It

Use a current or completed draft of your work to practice identifying vague pronoun references.

✓ **READ** carefully. Read your draft slowly to locate pronouns.

✓ **IDENTIFY** possible errors. Mark any vague pronoun references.

✓ **REVISE** your draft. Rewrite sentences with vague pronoun-antecedent relationships.

5

Spelling Error

GAME PLAN Spelling errors can change the meaning of a sentence. Proofread your work after spell checking to be sure you have used the correct words.

SPELL-CHECK ERRORS Computer spell-checkers often replace misspelled words with others close in spelling but different in meaning. Proofread your work carefully to correct these errors.

My favorite book begins with a scene that takes place in a ~~place~~ palace.

The ~~princes~~ princess in the story has an elaborate ball gown.

HOMOPHONES Words that are pronounced the same but have different spellings and meanings are called homophones. Check that you have used the correct homophones to convey your meaning.

The team is ~~band~~ banned from competition because of misconduct.

I will compete in ~~too~~ two events during the track meet.

Tech Tip

Proper nouns are not checked by a computer spell-checker. Proofread to make sure that you have spelled people's names correctly.

LEARN MORE
- **See Chapter 20, Effective Sentences, pages 455–459**
- **See Writing Coach Online**

✔ *Check It*

Use a current or completed draft of your work to practice spelling words correctly.

✔ **READ** carefully. Read your draft word by word looking for spelling errors.

✔ **IDENTIFY** possible mistakes. Mark any incorrect words or words that are misspelled.

✔ **USE** a dictionary. If you are not certain how to spell a word or think a homophone has been used incorrectly, check a dictionary.

6

Punctuation Error With a Quotation

Tech Tip

If you cut and paste quotations, remember to copy the taglines to make sure you have included all of the correct punctuation marks with direct quotations.

LEARN MORE

- See Chapter 25, Punctuation, pages 575–586
- See Writing Coach Online

GAME PLAN Quotation marks are used to identify direct quotations. Correct punctuation helps to identify quotations and relate them to your work.

DIRECT AND INDIRECT QUOTATIONS A direct quotation is enclosed in quotation marks. Indirect quotations do not need quotation marks.

Noelle's dad said, **"**Your dance recital was fantastic.**"**

Noelle's dad said her dance recital was fantastic.

QUOTATION MARKS WITH OTHER PUNCTUATION When commas or periods end a quotation, the punctuation goes inside the quotation marks. Question marks and exclamation marks go either inside or outside the quotation marks, depending on the sentence structure.

The football coach said, **"**Next Friday is your most important game of the season**."**

"We will win the game**!"** exclaimed the team captain.

Did he say, **"**We won't win the game**"?**

✓ Check It

Use a current or completed draft of your work to practice punctuating quotations correctly.

✓ **READ** carefully. If you used indirect quotations, make sure you did not put them in quotation marks.

✓ **IDENTIFY** direct quotations. Mark each direct quotation in your work. Is each quotation punctuated correctly?

✓ **REVISE** your sentences. Correct all punctuation errors in your quotations.

GAME PLAN Before you insert a comma, think about how your ideas relate to one another. Make sure the comma is necessary.

APPOSITIVES If an appositive is essential to the meaning of a sentence, it is *not* set off by commas.

The belongings of the Egyptian pharaoh, Tutankhamun, are on display at the history museum.

PARTICIPIAL PHRASES If a participial phrase is essential to the meaning of a sentence, it should *not* be set off by commas.

The exhibit, displaying Egyptian pharaohs, related to what the students were learning in class.

ADJECTIVAL CLAUSES Essential adjectival clauses should *not* be set off by commas.

The museum, that has a lot of exhibits about history, is my favorite to visit.

Tech Tip

Remember to add or delete commas as needed when you cut and paste and move text.

LEARN MORE
- **See Chapter 25, Punctuation, pages 560–563**
- **See Writing Coach Online**

✔ *Check It*

Use a current or completed draft of your work to practice correctly punctuating essential elements.

✔ **SCAN** Mentor Texts. Notice how professional writers use commas.

✔ **IDENTIFY** essential elements. Did you incorrectly use commas to indicate these elements?

✔ **REVISE** your sentences. Delete any commas that set off essential elements.

8

Unnecessary or Missing Capitalization

Tech Tip

Sometimes word processors will automatically capitalize any word that follows a period, even if the period is part of an abbreviation. Proofread carefully for incorrectly capitalized words.

LEARN MORE

- See Chapter 26, Capitalization, pages 606–626
- See Writing Coach Online

GAME PLAN Follow the rules of capitalization. For example, capitalize proper nouns, the first word of a sentence, and titles of works of art.

PROPER NOUNS Names, geographical locations, and organizations are examples of nouns that should be capitalized.

Alaska covers the most area of any state in the United States.

Many Americans have visited the White House.

I plan to attend the lecture at Eastville Historical Society.

TITLES OF WORKS OF ART The first and last words and all other key words in the titles of books, poems, stories, plays, paintings, and other works of art are capitalized.

Will we read *The Diary of Anne Frank* this year in English class?

Did you ever read *Alice's Adventures in Wonderland*?

✓ Check It

Use a current or completed draft of your work to practice correctly capitalizing words.

✓ **SCAN** your draft. Look for words that are capitalized.

✓ **IDENTIFY** errors in capitalization. Mark words that might be capitalized incorrectly.

✓ **USE** your textbook. Check the grammar section of your textbook if you are not sure if a word should be capitalized.

GAME PLAN Make sure there are no missing words in a text so that your ideas flow smoothly and are clear to readers.

ARTICLES To make sure that ideas flow smoothly, you must proofread your work. A missing word, even a missing article (*a, an, the*), can confuse a reader.

 Julian lost his sandal when he was running to catch
∧the bus!

KEY IDEAS When copying and pasting text, you might miss moving a word in a sentence. If that word is part of the main idea of the sentence, your meaning could be lost.

 Bridgette was ecstatic when she received the ∧lead role in the local musical.

I thought that Jill was a better ∧singer, but Bridgette was a better actress.

Use a current or completed draft of your work to practice proofreading.

✔ **READ** carefully. Read your draft word by word to make sure that you did not leave out a word.

✔ **IDENTIFY** unclear sentences. Mark any sentences you find that do not make sense. Are they unclear because of a missing word?

✔ **REVISE** your sentences. Add words to your sentences to make the meaning clear.

Tech Tip

When cutting and pasting sentences, you may use the same word twice by mistake. Proofread to be sure your sentences read correctly.

LEARN MORE
- See Editing sections in the writing chapters
- See Writing Coach Online

Find It / FIX IT

10

Faulty Sentence Structure

Tech Tip

Be careful when you cut one part of a sentence and paste it in another. Remember to check that the new sentence structure is correct.

LEARN MORE

- See Chapter 20, Effective Sentences, pages 460–462
- See Writing Coach Online

GAME PLAN Sentences should express complex ideas clearly. Use parallel, or similar, stuctures to make your writing clear.

WORDS IN A SERIES Check that the words you use in a series have parallel structure.

Sledding, ~~to ski~~ ∧skiing, and ice skating are fun activities to do with friends when it snows.

After school I have to study, eat, and ~~relaxing~~∧relax.

COMPARISONS In writing comparisons, be sure to compare a phrase with the same type of phrase. Also, compare a clause with the same type of clause.

My younger sister says that it's too cold that she forgot her gloves, and∧that she wants to get home quickly.

Channel 4 News says it will start to rain at noon, and ~~3 P.M. is when~~ Channel 6 News says it will start to rain∧at 3 P.M.

✔ Check It

Use a current or corrected draft of your work to practice writing using parallel structures.

✔ **SCAN** Mentor Texts. Notice how professional writers present complex ideas.

✔ **IDENTIFY** possible mistakes. Mark any sentences that have faulty parallelism.

✔ **REVISE** your sentences. Rewrite any sentences that do not have correct sentence structure.

GAME PLAN Use commas to set off nonessential elements of sentences.

APPOSITIVE If an appositive is not essential to the meaning of a sentence, it should be set off by commas.

Hawaii,∧a small state in area,∧is one of two states not part of the contiguous United States.

PARTICIPIAL PHRASE A participial phrase not essential to the meaning of a sentence is set off by commas.

Hawaii,∧ratified as a state in 1950,∧is the most recent state to be admitted to the Union.

ADJECTIVAL CLAUSE Use commas to set off an adjectival clause if it is not essential to the meaning of a sentence.

Hawaii,∧which is in the Pacific Ocean,∧has several active volcanoes.

Tech Tip

When you cut part of a sentence and paste it to another, be sure to include the correct punctuation. Proofread these sentences carefully.

LEARN MORE
- See Chapter 25, Punctuation, pages 560–563
- See Writing Coach Online

✔ *Check It*

Use a current or completed draft of your work to practice using commas correctly with nonessential elements.

✔ **SCAN** Mentor Texts. Notice how professional writers use commas to set off nonessential elements.

✔ **IDENTIFY** nonessential elements. Did you use commas to indicate these words, phrases, or clauses?

✔ **REVISE** your sentences. Use commas to set off nonessential elements.

12

Unnecessary Shift in Verb Tense

LEARN MORE
- See Chapter 20, Effective Sentences, pages 464–465
- See Writing Coach Online

GAME PLAN Use consistent verb tenses in your work. Shift tenses only to show that one event comes before or after another.

ACTIONS OCCURRING AT THE SAME TIME Use consistent tenses to show actions that occur at the same time.

I ran to the soccer ball, and I ~~kick~~ ∧kicked it into the goal.

The cat scurries up the tree and ~~looked~~ ∧looks down at the dog.

ACTIONS OCCURRING AT DIFFERENT TIMES If actions occur at different times, you can switch from one tense to another. You may use a time word or phrase to show the shift in tense.

Last year we spent a week in Hawaii; next year we ~~spent~~ ∧are spending a week in Arizona.

My aunt ordered dinner two hours ago, and now we ~~waited~~ ∧are waiting for it to be delivered.

 **Check It**

Use a current or completed draft of your work to practice using consistent tenses.

✓ **SCAN** Mentor Texts. Notice how professional writers use consistent tenses within a sentence.

✓ **IDENTIFY** possible mistakes. Mark any unnecessary shift in verb tense within a sentence.

✓ **USE** your textbook. Consult the grammar section of your textbook if you are not sure that have used consistent tenses.

GAME PLAN Use a comma before a coordinating conjunction to separate two or more main clauses in a compound sentence.

MAIN CLAUSES Place a comma before a coordinating conjunction (e.g. *and, but, or, nor, yet, so, for*) in a compound sentence.

Jillian is learning to play the drums,ₐand she wants to join the marching band.

Mr. Gould is applying to be the new vice principal,ₐbut he doesn't have much experience.

BRIEF CLAUSES The main clauses in some compound sentences are brief and do not need a comma if the meaning is clear.

He has a dog and she has a cat.

SINGLE WORDS Commas should *not* be used to separate single words that are joined by a conjunction.

Bella found a hat, and glove on the sidewalk.

He was strict, but nice when he taught his class.

✔️ *Check It*

Use a current or completed draft of your work to practice using commas in compound sentences.

✔ **SCAN** your draft. Look for compound sentences.

✔ **IDENTIFY** missing commas. Mark any compound sentences that should be punctuated with a comma.

✔ **REVISE** your sentences. Add commas before coordinating conjunctions to separate main clauses.

Tech Tip

Be careful when you create a compound sentence by cutting and pasting from different parts of a sentence or paragraph. Remember to include a comma to separate the main clauses.

LEARN MORE
- See Chapter 25, Punctuation, pages 554, 557
- See Writing Coach Online

14

Unnecessary or Missing Apostrophe

Tech Tip

Proofread your draft carefully. Not all computer grammar checkers will point out incorrect uses of apostrophes.

LEARN MORE

- **See Chapter 22, Using Pronouns, pages 504, 507**
- **See Chapter 25, Punctuation, pages 593–597**
- **See Writing Coach Online**

GAME PLAN Use apostrophes correctly to show possession.

SINGULAR NOUNS To show the possessive case of most singular nouns, add an apostrophe and *-s*.

 The student assembly took place in the school's gym.

PLURAL NOUNS Add an apostrophe to show the possessive case for most plural nouns ending in *-s* or *-es*. For plural nouns that do not end in *-s* or *-es*, add an apostrophe and *-s*.

 The girls' clothes were being washed.

Those gentlemen's manners are always perfect.

POSSESSIVE PRONOUNS Possessive pronouns (e.g., *his, hers, its, our, their*) show possession without the use of an apostrophe. Do not confuse *its* with *it's*. The word *its* shows possession, but the word *it's* means "it is."

 ~~His'~~ His friend heard the old car approaching before he could see it because of ~~it's~~ its loud engine!

✓ Check It

Use a current or completed draft of your work to practice showing possession.

✓ **SCAN** Mentor Texts. Notice when professional writers use apostrophes to indicate possession.

✓ **IDENTIFY** possible mistakes. Mark all the apostrophes in your draft. Did you use them correctly to show possession?

✓ **REVISE** your sentences. Make sure to delete any apostrophes you used with possessive pronouns.

15

Run-on Sentence

GAME PLAN Use correct punctuation to avoid run-on sentences. A run-on sentence is two or more sentences punctuated as if they were a single sentence.

FUSED SENTENCE A fused sentence contains two or more sentences joined with no punctuation. To correct a fused sentence, place a period or an end mark between the main clauses.

Juliet wants to go sailing ~~today the~~ today. The weather is perfect.

Why did he go for a walk after ~~dinner he~~ dinner? He said he wanted to finish his homework.

RUN-ON SENTENCE Place a comma and a coordinating conjunction between main clauses to avoid run-on sentences.

By the time we arrived at the concert, it was almost half over, but we got to hear the best songs.

LEARN MORE
- See Chapter 20, Effective Sentences, pages 447–450
- See Writing Coach Online

 **Check It**

Use a current or completed draft of your work to practice correcting run-on sentences.

✔ **SCAN** your draft. Look for run-on sentences.

✔ **IDENTIFY** missing punctuation. Mark sentences that might need a period or an end mark to separate main clauses.

✔ **REVISE** your sentences. When correcting fused sentences, vary your sentence structure.

LEARN MORE
- **See Chapter 20, Effective Sentences, pages 447–450**
- **See Chapter 25, Punctuation, pages 554–555**
- **See Writing Coach Online**

GAME PLAN Use correct punctuation to avoid comma splices. A comma splice happens when two or more complete sentences are joined only with a comma.

PERIOD Replace the comma with a period (and capitalize the following word) to separate two complete thoughts.

 Robin called to say she couldn't make it to my basketball game, ~~we~~ We knew she had an essay to finish.

SEMICOLON Replace the comma with a semicolon if the ideas are similar.

 Cameron won a stuffed animal at the fair, ; he gave it to his sister.

COORDINATING CONJUNCTION A comma splice can be corrected by placing a coordinating conjunction (e.g., *and, or, but, yet, nor*) after the comma.

 Kate thought she was the first one to finish the race, but she saw Tom waiting at the finish line!

✔ *Check It*

Use a current or completed draft of your work to practice correcting comma splices.

✔ **READ** carefully. Take time to read your draft carefully. Have someone else read your work for a double-check.

✔ **IDENTIFY** possible mistakes. Mark any comma splices you find.

✔ **REVISE** your sentences. Fix comma splices in different ways to vary your sentence structure.

GAME PLAN Check that pronouns agree with their antecedents in number, person, and gender. When the gender is not specified, the pronoun must still agree in number.

GENDER NEUTRAL ANTECEDENTS When gender is not specific, use *his or her* to refer to the singular antecedent.

Each of the three siblings had ~~their~~ ∧his or her own room.

OR, NOR, AND When two or more singular antecedents are joined by *or* or *nor*, use a singular personal pronoun. Use a plural personal pronoun when two or more antecedents are joined by *and*.

I think Carlos <u>or</u> Henry will get an A on ~~their~~ ∧his project.

Jenny <u>and</u> Kate are finishing ~~her~~ ∧their group science project.

INDEFINITE PRONOUNS A plural personal pronoun must agree with a plural indefinite pronoun. A singular personal pronoun must agree with a singular indefinite pronoun.

<u>Both</u> of the twins gave ~~his~~ ∧their old toys to charity.

<u>One</u> of the singers sang ~~their~~ ∧her song without any accompaniment from the band.

Check It

Use a current or completed draft of your work to practice pronoun-antecedent agreement.

✔ **READ** carefully. Take time to read your draft carefully. For a double-check, have someone else read your work.

✔ **IDENTIFY** possible mistakes. Mark any pronouns that do not agree with their antecedents in a sentence.

✔ **USE** your textbook. Check the grammar section of your textbook if you are not sure whether your pronouns and antecedents agree.

Tech Tip

Be careful when you cut and paste text from one sentence to another. Check that the pronouns agree with the antecedents in the new sentences you create.

LEARN MORE
• See Chapter 23, Making Words Agree, pages 525–529
• See Writing Coach Online

18

Poorly Integrated Quotation

LEARN MORE

- See Chapter 25, Punctuation, pages 575–583
- See Writing Coach Online

GAME PLAN Quotations should flow smoothly into the sentence that surrounds them. Add information to explain and link quotes to the rest of your work.

QUOTE IN A SENTENCE Prepare the reader for the information contained in the quote by introducing the quote's idea.

The author∧provides many details of the weather on the day the main event took place: "It was cool and sunny, with only a slight breeze" (Thompson 17).

Chad claims∧that his music teacher is the best teacher he has had: "With no other teacher have I learned so much in a few months."

QUOTE AS A SENTENCE Place an introductory phrase before or after a quotation that stands alone. In most cases, this phrase should identify the quote's author or speaker.

∧According to the mayor, "The town has recovered a great deal from when last year's tornado hit" (Jenson 8).

Use a current or completed draft of your work to practice integrating quotations.

✓ **SCAN Mentor Texts.** Notice how professional writers integrate quotations into their work.

✓ **IDENTIFY quotes.** Mark each quote in your work. Does each quote flow smoothly with the surrounding sentence?

✓ **REVISE your sentences.** Add information as needed to explain and introduce quotes.

GAME PLAN Use hyphens correctly in your writing, including with compound words and compound adjectives.

COMPOUND WORDS Hyphens can connect two or more words that are used as one compound word. Some compound words do not require a hyphen. Check a current dictionary if you are not sure about hyphenating a word.

The ~~fortyyearold~~ forty-year-old man doing the ~~cross-word~~ crossword puzzle is my dad.

Her ~~brotherinlaw~~ brother-in-law knows the new ~~congress-man~~ congressman.

COMPOUND ADJECTIVES A compound adjective that appears before a noun should be hyphenated. Remember not to hyphenate a compound proper noun acting as an adjective. Also, do not hyphenate a compound adjective that has a word ending in *-ly*.

The ~~bushy tailed~~ bushy-tailed dog belongs to my cousin.

The dog's ~~happily-wagging~~ happily wagging tail always makes me laugh.

My friends and I prefer ~~South-American~~ South American cooking.

Tech Tip

The automatic hyphenation setting in word processors causes words at the end of a line of text to hyphenate automatically. Be sure that this setting is turned off when you are writing an essay.

LEARN MORE
- See Chapter 25, Punctuation, pages 587–592
- See Writing Coach Online

Use a current or completed draft of your work to practice hyphenating words.

✓ **IDENTIFY** possible errors. Mark any compound adjectives before a noun that are not hyphenated.

✓ **REVISE** your sentences. Add a hyphen to words that should be hyphenated.

✓ **USE** a dictionary. Check a dictionary if you are not sure if a word should be hyphenated.

Find It/FIX IT

20

Sentence Fragment

Tech Tip

Sometimes, when you cut text from a sentence and paste it to another, you may miss cutting the whole sentence. Make sure you have both a subject and a verb in the new sentences.

LEARN MORE
- See Chapter 20, Effective Sentences, pages 442–446
- See Writing Coach Online

GAME PLAN Use complete sentences when writing. Make sure you have a subject and a complete verb in each and that each sentence expresses a complete thought.

LACKING A SUBJECT OR VERB A complete sentence must have a subject and a verb.

Shelly is going to the science museum tomorrow. ~~And~~ ∧She will get to see all of the new exhibits.

Susie∧was leaving her house when she heard the phone ring.

SUBORDINATE CLAUSE A subordinate clause cannot stand on its own as a complete sentence because it does not express a complete thought.

The class trip was cancelled.~~After~~ ∧after we had already signed our permission slips.

Timmy called his mom to pick him up from soccer practice. ~~Before~~ ∧before it was rescheduled.

✓ Check It

Use a current or completed draft of your work to practice writing complete sentences.

✔ **SCAN** your draft. Look for incomplete sentences.

✔ **IDENTIFY** missing words. Mark sentences that have missing subjects or verbs.

✔ **REVISE** your sentences. Rewrite any sentences that are missing subjects or verbs, or are subordinate clauses standing on their own.

CHAPTER 13

NOUNS and PRONOUNS

Use a balance of nouns and pronouns in your writing to help you create sentences that flow smoothly.

WRITE GUY *Jeff Anderson, M.Ed.*

WHAT DO YOU NOTICE?

Focus on nouns and pronouns as you zoom in on sentences from "The Adventure of the Speckled Band" by Arthur Conan Doyle.

MENTOR TEXT

> Sherlock Holmes ran her over with one of his quick, all-comprehensive glances.
>
> "You must not fear," said he soothingly, bending forward and patting her forearm.

Now, ask yourself the following questions:

- How do you know that the personal pronouns *his* and *he* refer to Sherlock Holmes?

- How can you tell whether the personal pronoun *you* refers to Holmes or to the woman identified as *her*?

You can tell that *he* and *his* refer to Sherlock Holmes because those are the personal pronouns used for males, and Holmes is the only male the narrator mentions. The personal pronoun *you* must refer to the woman because Holmes is the speaker. If he were speaking of himself, he would say *I* instead.

Grammar for Writers Writers use personal pronouns to create sentences that readers can understand and follow. Check that you matched nouns and pronouns correctly in your writing.

Is the pizza for you or her?

That's an easy one! It's for me.

13.1 Nouns

Nouns are naming words. Words such as *friend*, *sky*, *dog*, *love*, *courage*, and *Seattle* are nouns.

RULE 13.1.1

A noun names something.

Most nouns fall into four main groups.

People, Places, Things, and Ideas

The nouns in the chart are grouped under four headings. You may know most of the nouns under the first three headings. You may not have realized that all the words in the fourth group are nouns.

PEOPLE	PLACES	THINGS	IDEAS
veterinarian	Lake Mead	bumblebee	strength
Dr. Robinson	classroom	collar	honesty
Americans	kennel	motorcycle	willingness
leader	Bunker Hill	notebook	obedience

Concrete and Abstract Nouns

Nouns may be classified as **concrete** or **abstract.** In the chart above, *People, Places,* and *Things* are concrete nouns. *Ideas* are abstract nouns.

RULE 13.1.2

A concrete noun names something that can be recognized through any of the five senses. An abstract noun names something that cannot be recognized through the senses.

CONCRETE NOUNS			
pencil	dog	tractor	river
ABSTRACT NOUNS			
courage	fun	honor	exploration

WRITING COACH

Online
www.phwritingcoach.com

Grammar Tutorials
Brush up on your Grammar skills with these animated videos.

Grammar Practice
Practice your grammar skills with Writing Coach Online.

Grammar Games
Test your knowledge of grammar in this fast-paced interactive video game.

See Practice 13.1A

See Practice 13.1B

Collective Nouns

A few nouns name groups of people or things. A *pack*, for example, is "a group of dogs or other animals that travel together." These nouns are called **collective nouns.**

> A **collective noun** names a group of people or things.

See Practice 13.1C

13.1.3 RULE

COLLECTIVE NOUNS		
club	herd	army
troop	orchestra	committee
class	team	group

Count and Non-count Nouns

Nouns can be grouped as **count** or **non-count** nouns.

> **Count nouns** name things that can be counted. **Non-count nouns** name things that cannot be counted.

13.1.4 RULE

COUNT NOUNS	NON-COUNT NOUNS
orange	thunder
bench	rice
street	grass

Count nouns can take an article and can be plural.

EXAMPLE   a bench   the bench   three benches

Non-count nouns do not take an indefinite article (*a* or *an*) and cannot be plural:

EXAMPLES   We cut the grass on Saturday.
(*not* We cut *a* grass on Saturday.)

She needs clothing for the vacation.
(*not* She needs clothing**s** for the vacation.)

See Practice 13.1D

Read the sentences. Then, write the nouns in each sentence.

EXAMPLE   The powerful body of the lion gives it a proud appearance.

ANSWER   *body, lion, appearance*

1. The camels are a popular attraction at the zoo.

2. Many scientists find oceans fascinating to study.

3. Most pets offer love to their owners.

4. Some people like only certain types of flowers.

5. Jamal's friends are coming to his house to see a movie.

6. A dictionary is a kind of reference book.

7. We invited Hector to play golf.

8. Kevin and Louisa walked near the ocean.

9. Lyle bought milk at the store.

10. Martin needs new shoes for playing basketball.

Read the sentences. Then, write the nouns in each sentence, and label each one *concrete* or *abstract*.

EXAMPLE   Josie sometimes behaves foolishly despite her cleverness.

ANSWER   *Josie* — concrete
cleverness — abstract

11. We saw some crabs scuttling across the sand.

12. Dad always reminds us of the importance of self-respect.

13. Sometimes a herd of buffalo grazes near that road.

14. The senator vowed to work toward equality.

15. The teacher showed no enthusiasm for my idea.

16. The detective only wanted to discover the truth.

17. Justice is an important principle in a democracy.

18. My friend showed her sympathy by sending a card.

19. Jason has always had a terrible fear of insects.

20. Leslie often uses humor to hide her discomfort.

SPEAKING APPLICATION

Tell a partner about a sporting event you've watched. Your partner should listen for and name three nouns that you use.

WRITING APPLICATION

Use sentence 18 as a model, and write three more sentences that each contain two concrete nouns and one abstract noun.

PRACTICE 13.1C **Finding Collective Nouns**

Read the pairs of nouns. Each pair includes one collective noun. Write the collective noun.

EXAMPLE   squad, men

ANSWER   *squad*

1. panel, judges
2. crew, pilot
3. family, parent
4. professor, faculty
5. person, audience
6. band, guitarist
7. jury, peer
8. face, crowd
9. bunch, flower
10. singer, choir

PRACTICE 13.1D **Identifying Count and Non-count Nouns**

Read the sentences. Then, list the count and non-count nouns. One sentence has only count nouns.

EXAMPLE   A player must have endurance to play soccer well.

ANSWER   *Count noun — player*
Non-count nouns — endurance, soccer

11. Water quickly filled the boat.
12. My little brother has great fun with his toy airplane.
13. We watched the lightning from the safety of the porch.
14. The group of friends went to the game together.
15. He always says there is no excuse for boredom.
16. That dog is not getting enough nutrition.
17. His intelligence was obvious to the teacher.
18. Right now the refrigerator is in storage.
19. Mom's wisdom is a gift that I value.
20. Travel is one leisure activity the whole family enjoys.

SPEAKING APPLICATION

With a partner, take turns describing a vacation or day trip you enjoyed. Your partner should listen for and name at least one collective noun, one count noun, and one non-count noun.

WRITING APPLICATION

Use sentence 20 as a model, and write two more sentences that each contain one non-count noun and two count nouns.

Recognizing Compound Nouns

Some nouns are made up of two or more words. *Classroom* is a **compound noun** made up of *class* and *room*.

RULE 13.1.5

> A **compound noun** is one noun made by joining two or more words.

Compound nouns are written in three different ways: as single words, as hyphenated words, and as two or more separate words.

COMPOUND NOUNS		
SINGLE WORDS	HYPHENATED WORDS	SEPARATE WORDS
crossbar	by-product	dinner jacket
firefighter	right-hander	pole vault
thunderstorm	middle-distance	pen pal
classroom	mother-in-law	chief justice

See Practice 13.1E

Using Common and Proper Nouns

All nouns can be divided into two large groups: **common nouns** and **proper nouns.**

RULE 13.1.6

> A **common noun** names any one of a class of people, places, things, or ideas. A **proper noun** names a specific person, place, thing, or idea.

Common nouns are not capitalized. Proper nouns are always capitalized.

COMMON NOUNS	PROPER NOUNS
inventor	Alexander Graham Bell
village	Tarrytown
story	"The Tell-Tale Heart"
organization	American Red Cross
idea	Germ Theory of Disease

See Practice 13.1F

PRACTICE 13.1E > Identifying Compound Nouns

Read the sentences. Then, write the compound nouns, and draw a line between the words that make up each compound noun. One sentence has two compound nouns.

EXAMPLE   We won the game because of good teamwork.

ANSWER   *team| work*

1. Gigi wants to be a famous songwriter.
2. There was a car accident near the high school.
3. The baseball got lost in the tall grass.
4. Please stop by the post office on your way to the store.
5. Ellie's aunt drives a tractor-trailer for a living.
6. Pedro's self-confidence grew after he made his first two baskets.
7. All the cheerleaders arrived at the game early.
8. The jet stream has an influence on weather and climate.
9. An earthquake is a sudden movement of the earth's crust.
10. The greenhouse is full of thriving houseplants.

PRACTICE 13.1F > Using Common and Proper Nouns

Read the sentences. Then, rewrite them, replacing the underlined words with proper nouns.

EXAMPLE   The trailer for that movie was funny.

ANSWER   *The trailer for Marley and Me was funny.*

11. I have read almost every book by this author.
12. The science program at the school is very good.
13. Juanita is moving to that street next month.
14. The athlete I admire most is that player.
15. We will meet at a theater to see the dance performance.
16. During the vacation, Carly got to see the famous bridge.
17. My grandmother has been receiving that newspaper for many years.
18. Jenna read a short story for her literature class.
19. The exhibit has several paintings by a famous artist.
20. Have you ever seen that national monument?

SPEAKING APPLICATION

With a partner, take turns describing your town or city. Your partner should listen for two compound nouns and two proper nouns.

WRITING APPLICATION

Write three sentences. In your sentences, include at least one compound noun, one common noun, and one proper noun.

13.2 Pronouns

Pronouns are words that take the place of nouns. They are used rather than repeating a noun again and again. Pronouns make sentences clearer and more interesting.

WRITING COACH

Online

www.phwritingcoach.com

Grammar Tutorials

Brush up on your Grammar skills with these animated videos.

Grammar Practice

Practice your grammar skills with Writing Coach Online.

Grammar Games

Test your knowledge of grammar in this fast-paced interactive video game.

> A **pronoun** is a word that takes the place of a noun or a group of words acting as a noun.

Imagine, for example, that you are writing about Uncle Mike. If you were using only nouns, you might write the following sentence:

WITH NOUNS Uncle Mike was late because **Uncle Mike** had to make **Uncle Mike's** mashed potatoes.

WITH PRONOUNS Uncle Mike was late because **he** had to make **his** mashed potatoes.

Sometimes a pronoun takes the place of a noun in the same sentence.

EXAMPLES My sister opened **her** presents first.
                    pronoun

Many people say finding a hobby has helped **them**.
                                                            pronoun

A pronoun can also take the place of a noun used in an earlier sentence.

EXAMPLES My sister ate her soup first. **She** was hungry.
                                                    pronoun

Visitors must take off their shoes. **They** can then put on slippers.
                                                        pronoun

A pronoun may take the place of an entire group of words.

EXAMPLE Trying to make our family's recipe was hard work. **It** took a lot of time.
             pronoun

Antecedents of Pronouns

The word or group of words that a pronoun replaces or refers to is called an **antecedent.**

> An **antecedent** is the noun (or group of words acting as a noun) to which a pronoun refers.

RULE 13.2.2

EXAMPLES

The **doctors** described how **they** performed **their**
     antecedent   pronoun   pronoun
jobs.

Finally, the **doctor** spoke. **She** seemed to think
            antecedent   pronoun
the patient was fine.

How Michael was saved is amazing. **It** is a story
           antecedent   pronoun
that he'll tell often.

Although **she** was a pediatrician, **Tara** also
         pronoun   antecedent
diagnosed adults.

See Practice 13.2A

Some kinds of pronouns do not have any antecedent.

EXAMPLES

Everyone at the party knew the truth.
indefinite pronoun

Who cooked the food?
interrogative pronoun

See Practice 13.2B

The pronouns *everyone* and *who* do not have a specific antecedent because their meaning is clear without one.

Pronouns

PRACTICE 13.2A > Recognizing Pronouns and Antecedents

Read the sentences. Then, write each pronoun and its antecedent.

EXAMPLE   The park has closed its gates for the day.

ANSWER   *its, park*

1. Many people say they have seen strange objects in the sky.

2. When Tamesa read *Oliver Twist* for the first time, she cried.

3. Jamal called his mother as soon as the karate class was over.

4. That tree is colorful, but it only blooms for a few weeks each year.

5. Serena, would you give your speech now?

6. The four boys walked to the gate with their tickets in hand.

7. Because of his injury, the dancer could not perform.

8. If she had wanted to, Cheryl could have won the spelling bee.

9. Jerome said, "I would like to read a book about space travel."

10. Arthur C. Clarke entertains readers, but he suggests ideas to them, too.

PRACTICE 13.2B > Supplying Pronouns for Antecedents

Read the sentences. Then, write each sentence, filling in the blank with the appropriate pronoun. Correctly identify and underline the antecedent of the pronoun you supply.

EXAMPLE   Mom, could _____ please give the boys a ride?

ANSWER   <u>Mom</u>, could you please give the boys a ride?

11. "_____ fixed the DVD player," said Ann.

12. Since Phoebe moved, _____ has been getting better grades.

13. "Girls, _____ will have to clean up this mess right now," commanded Ms. Chavez.

14. Bryant tried to call his mother, but _____ was not in the office.

15. The brothers joined the team as soon as _____ could.

16. The book is not as difficult as _____ first chapter suggests.

17. The Garcias said _____ would volunteer at the food bank.

18. Uncle Gene donated _____ used clothing to charity.

19. Somehow Amy managed to lose _____ clarinet.

20. According to Dad, all dogs can behave well if _____ are trained properly.

SPEAKING APPLICATION

Tell a partner about a movie you saw recently. Have your partner listen for and name at least two pronouns and their antecedents.

WRITING APPLICATION

Write three sentences about animals. Use at least one pronoun and antecedent in each sentence. Circle each pronoun and draw an arrow to the antecedent.

302   Nouns and Pronouns

Recognizing Personal Pronouns

The pronouns used most often are **personal pronouns**.

> **Personal pronouns** refer to (1) the person speaking or writing, (2) the person listening or reading, or (3) the topic (person, place, thing, or idea) being discussed or written about.

The first-person pronouns *I, me, my, mine, we, us, our,* and *ours* refer to the person or persons speaking or writing.

EXAMPLES **I** like the latest edition of the book.

Please hand **us** the china plates.

The second-person pronouns *you, your,* and *yours* refer to the person or persons spoken or written to.

EXAMPLES **You** should see that movie.

Your DVD player isn't working.

The third-person pronouns *he, him, his, she, her, hers, it, its, they, them, their,* and *theirs* refer to the person, place, thing, or idea being spoken or written about.

EXAMPLES **He** wants to watch the inaugural speech.

They wrote letters to the new president.

Some personal pronouns show possession. Although they can function as adjectives, they are still identified as personal pronouns because they take the place of possessive nouns.

EXAMPLES **Joe's** nutrition book will be published soon.
possessive noun

His recipes in the book are delicious.
possessive pronoun

The chart on the next page presents the personal pronouns.

PERSONAL PRONOUNS		
	SINGULAR	PLURAL
First person	I, me, my, mine	we, us, our, ours
Second person	you, your, yours	you, your, yours
Third person	he, him, his, she, her, hers, it, its	they, them, their, theirs

See Practice 13.2C

Reflexive and Intensive Pronouns

The ending *-self* or *-selves* can be added to some pronouns to form **reflexive** or **intensive pronouns.** These two types of pronouns look the same, but they function differently within a sentence.

REFLEXIVE AND INTENSIVE PRONOUNS		
	SINGULAR	PLURAL
First person	myself	ourselves
Second person	yourself	yourselves
Third person	himself, herself, itself	themselves

RULE 13.2.4

A reflexive pronoun directs the action of the verb toward its subject. Reflexive pronouns point back to a noun or pronoun earlier in the sentence.

A reflexive pronoun is essential to the meaning of a sentence.

REFLEXIVE   **Tara** helped **herself** to some cookies.
                 noun   reflexive pronoun

They made **themselves** homemade cookies.
pronoun   reflexive pronoun

See Practice 13.2D

RULE 13.2.5

An intensive pronoun simply adds emphasis to a noun or pronoun in the same sentence.

An intensive pronoun is not essential to the meaning of the sentence.

INTENSIVE   The mayor **herself** attended the carnival.

PRACTICE 13.2C ▷ **Recognizing Personal Pronouns**

Read the sentences. Then, write the personal pronouns in each sentence.

EXAMPLE   Carlos thought he would enjoy his vacation.

ANSWER   *he, his*

1. Mason brushed his cat's fur carefully.

2. At the game, we supported our team by cheering loudly.

3. Will you please close the door?

4. José decided he would practice his soccer skills.

5. Rosa could see her dog standing at the bowl eating its food.

6. The students wanted to perform a skit, so first they wrote a script.

7. My brother would sell his car, but it is not worth much.

8. The Johnsons bought their house in 1998, and they are still happy with it.

9. Mr. Montoya made us tacos and rice.

10. I believe you left your jacket in the car, Josh.

PRACTICE 13.2D ▷ **Supplying Reflexive and Intensive Pronouns**

Read the sentences. Write the reflexive or intensive pronoun that completes each sentence.

EXAMPLE   The audience members prepared _____ for an exciting performance.

ANSWER   *themselves*

11. Luis _____ can do several card tricks.

12. The cellist gave _____ a stage name.

13. Viewers found for _____ a new kind of hero in Captain Kirk.

14. Wonder Woman could not fly by _____.

15. I _____ can't understand why more people don't recycle.

16. The researchers _____ are unsure about the results.

17. Dan is sick, so I may have to finish the project _____.

18. The actors treated _____ to snacks at the opening night party.

19. Marianne gave _____ a chance to catch her breath.

20. Fix _____ a sandwich and let's go!

SPEAKING APPLICATION

Tell a partner a funny story about your family. Your partner should listen for and name at least two personal pronouns.

WRITING APPLICATION

Write three sentences, using a reflexive or an intensive pronoun in each.

Demonstrative Pronouns

Demonstrative pronouns point to people, places, and things, much as you point to them with your finger.

RULE
13.2.6

> A **demonstrative pronoun** points to a specific person, place, or thing.

There are two singular and two plural demonstrative pronouns.

DEMONSTRATIVE PRONOUNS			
SINGULAR		**PLURAL**	
this	that	these	those

This and *these* point to what is near the speaker or writer. *That* and *those* point to what is more distant.

NEAR   **This** is where I keep my videos.

These are my favorite bands to listen to.

FAR   Is **that** the road to take?

Those are my smoothies!

See Practice 13.2E

Using Relative Pronouns

Relative pronouns are connecting words.

RULE
13.2.7

> A **relative pronoun** begins a subordinate clause and connects it to another idea in the same sentence.

There are five relative pronouns.

RELATIVE PRONOUNS				
that	which	who	whom	whose

The chart on the next page gives examples of relative pronouns connecting subordinate clauses to independent clauses. (See Chapter 19 to find out more about relative pronouns and clauses.)

INDEPENDENT CLAUSES	SUBORDINATE CLAUSES
Here is the recipe	that Bonnie lost.
Ricky bought our old computer,	which needs repairs.
She is a teacher	who has an unusual gift.
Is this the child	whom you saw earlier?
He is the one	whose car has a new stereo.
Here is the restaurant	that was described in the article.
Charlie found his ball	that was under the table.

See Practice 13.2F
See Practice 13.2G
See Practice 13.2H

Interrogative Pronouns

To interrogate means "to ask questions."

> An **interrogative pronoun** is used to begin a question.

13.2.8 RULE

All five interrogative pronouns begin with *w*.

INTERROGATIVE PRONOUNS				
what	which	who	whom	whose

Most interrogative pronouns do not have antecedents.

EXAMPLES **What** did the principal say?

Which is the best place to invest money?

Who wants to see a movie?

From **whom** will you receive the best directions?

See Practice 13.2I

Whose was the best cake at the taste test?

Indefinite Pronouns

RULE 13.2.9

> An **indefinite pronoun** refers to a person, place, thing, or idea that is not specifically named.

EXAMPLES   **Everything** is ready for our trip to Europe.

Everyone really wants to see Rome first.

Anyone can afford to travel by bus.

Something fell off the table when I bumped it.

Among its other uses, an indefinite pronoun functions as an adjective or as the subject of a sentence. If it functions as an adjective, it is called an indefinite adjective.

ADJECTIVE   **Both** girls want to be veterinarians.

SUBJECT   **Both** want to be veterinarians.

A few indefinite pronouns can be either singular or plural, depending on their use in a sentence.

INDEFINITE PRONOUNS			
SINGULAR		**PLURAL**	**SINGULAR OR PLURAL**
another	much	both	all
anybody	neither	few	any
anyone	nobody	many	more
anything	no one	others	most
each	nothing	several	none
either	one		some
everybody	other		
everyone	somebody		
everything	someone		
little	something		

See Practice 13.2J

PRACTICE 13.2E **Identifying Demonstrative Pronouns**

Read the sentences. Then, write the demonstrative pronoun and the noun to which it refers.

EXAMPLE   Isn't that an interesting painting?

ANSWER   *that, painting*

1. That was an important decision you made.

2. This is the largest stadium in the state.

3. Are these the shoes you were asking me about?

4. Skis are expensive, so be careful with those!

5. That is not the movie I would have chosen.

6. "I'd like to try some of that," said Brandon, pointing to the salad.

7. My advice to you is this: Be patient.

8. "May I please see those?" Janelle asked, looking at the earrings.

9. Are these the treats you want to buy for the dog?

10. Those are the instructions for the printer.

PRACTICE 13.2F **Supplying Relative Pronouns**

Read the sentences. Then, write the correct relative pronoun (e.g., *whose, that, which*) for each sentence.

EXAMPLE   She bought some shoes _____ matched her purse.

ANSWER   *that*

11. One leader _____ our country will never forget is George Washington.

12. I could not find a dress _____ fit properly.

13. The woman _____ writes that column is not a journalist.

14. These sandals, _____ I wear often, are very comfortable.

15. Ernesto, _____ is bringing the dip, has not arrived yet.

16. Can you find a frame _____ will fit this photo?

17. Consuela is the girl _____ pen I borrowed.

18. The singer _____ we liked best sang two solos.

19. Solar panels, _____ harness the sun's energy, are good for the environment.

20. The birds _____ we saw at the lake were herons.

SPEAKING APPLICATION

With a partner, take turns describing a favorite hobby. Use at least one demonstrative pronoun and one relative pronoun (e.g., *whose, that, which*), and ask your partner to identify them.

WRITING APPLICATION

Write three sentences using relative pronouns (e.g., *whose, that, which*). Read your sentences aloud to a partner. Have your partner identify each relative pronoun.

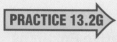

PRACTICE 13.2G Recognizing Clauses Beginning With Relative Pronouns

Read each sentence. Then, write the subordinate clause that begins with a relative pronoun.

EXAMPLE   Helaine gave her brother the toy that he wanted.

ANSWER   *that he wanted*

1. Ms. Garcia praised the drawing that I made.

2. The deadline is Thursday, which is just a week away.

3. Do you know whose umbrella this is?

4. Everyone laughed at the dog that was riding on the elephant.

5. This store attracts buyers who are thrifty.

6. Sally was the one whom I invited to the party.

7. My dog leaves footprints everyplace that he walks.

8. Sam cheers for the team whose uniforms are red and gold.

9. The wall that I climbed was more than ten feet high.

10. The color guard lowered the flag to honor the senator who died yesterday.

PRACTICE 13.2H Identifying Relative Pronouns

Read each sentence. Then, write the relative pronoun and the word to which it refers.

EXAMPLE   I found the bracelet that I lost several weeks ago.

ANSWER   *that, bracelet*

11. The fire was caused by an old wire, which was frayed.

12. I chose the kitten whose fur was the brightest orange.

13. The rainstorm forced the principal to cancel the picnic that we had planned.

14. Selena invited everyone whom she knew to the party.

15. I am looking for the person who lost this watch.

16. The waves broke over the levee that was built to protect the beach.

17. Use *an* before words that begin with a vowel.

18. Benjamin Franklin wrote many sayings that we still use today.

19. Denora requested pancakes, which are her favorite food.

20. Are you the customer who wanted to try on these shoes?

SPEAKING APPLICATION

With a partner, take turns describing a school event. Your partner should listen for and name three relative pronouns.

WRITING APPLICATION

Write three sentences with relative pronouns. Underline the pronouns you use.

PRACTICE 13.2I > **Identifying Interrogative Pronouns**

Read the sentences. Then, write the interrogative pronoun in each sentence.

EXAMPLE What is the largest species of bird?

ANSWER *What*

1. Who took you to the museum?
2. Whose is the cellphone with the red holder?
3. To whom should we send the package?
4. Which is the jacket you got for your birthday?
5. What is the yogurt flavor you like best?
6. Who left his backpack lying on the floor?
7. What does that symbol on your cap represent?
8. Whom did you sit with at the game?
9. Which is the best dish to order here?
10. Whom will you get to help with the forms?

PRACTICE 13.2J > **Supplying Indefinite Pronouns**

Read the sentences. Then, write an appropriate indefinite pronoun for each sentence.

EXAMPLE _____ of my friends are going to see a professional basketball game tomorrow.

ANSWER *Some*

11. _____ of the actors did not know their lines.
12. Has _____ eaten the rest of the soup?
13. _____ of the host's hints proved helpful.
14. A _____ of us are going surfing next week.
15. Carmen finally asked _____ for directions.
16. _____ of these books are slightly damaged.
17. _____ has to pay an entry fee this time.
18. _____ in the audience laughed at the comedian.
19. I will see the movie with _____ from my family.
20. The teacher encouraged _____ of the students to study.

SPEAKING APPLICATION

With a partner, take turns using interrogative pronouns to ask questions about a school event. Your partner should listen for and name the interrogative pronoun in each question.

WRITING APPLICATION

Write two questions beginning with interrogative pronouns. Write a sentence with an indefinite pronoun to answer each question.

Test Warm-Up

DIRECTIONS
Read the introduction and the passage that follows. Then, answer the questions to show that you can use and understand the function of relative pronouns in reading and writing.

Simon wrote this paragraph for his social studies class. Read the paragraph and think about the changes you would suggest as a peer editor. When you finish reading, answer the questions that follow.

The Flag Was Still There

(1) Francis Scott Key is the person which wrote the words of "The Star-Spangled Banner." (2) He was a lawyer who's home was in Washington, D.C. (3) During the War of 1812, he traveled to Baltimore. (4) It was 40 miles from Washington. (5) There, he witnessed a battle taking place at Fort McHenry in Baltimore harbor. (6) The British shelled the fort with hundreds of rockets that lit up the night. (7) Key was thrilled the next morning when he saw the giant American flag still flying over Fort McHenry. (8) He wrote a poem to express his joy that the flag was still there.

1 What change, if any, should be made in sentence 1?

  A Add a comma after *person*

  B Change *which* to **who**

  C Replace the period with a question mark

  D Make no change

2 What change, if any, should be made in sentence 2?

  F Replace *who's* with **whose**

  G Delete the apostrophe in *who's*

  H Add a comma after *lawyer*

  J Make no change

3 What is the BEST way to combine sentences 3 and 4?

  A During the War of 1812, he traveled to Baltimore, and it was 40 miles from Washington.

  B During the War of 1812, he traveled to Baltimore when it was 40 miles from Washington.

  C During the War of 1812, he traveled to Baltimore, which was 40 miles from Washington.

  D During the War of 1812, he traveled 40 miles from Washington to Baltimore.

4 What change, if any, should be made in sentence 6?

  F Change *with* to **which**

  G Change *that* to **who**

  H Add a comma after *rockets*

  J Make no change

VERBS

Use strong verbs to convey actions in clear and powerful ways in your writing.

CHAPTER 14

WRITE GUY *Jeff Anderson, M.Ed.*

WHAT DO YOU NOTICE?

Seek out the verbs as you zoom in on this sentence from the story "Who Can Replace a Man?" by Brian Aldiss.

MENTOR TEXT

> When he swung suddenly to face them as they loomed over him, they saw that his countenance was ravaged by starvation.

Show that you can use and understand the function of verbs by answering the following questions. Discuss your answers with a partner.

- Which words are action verbs in this sentence?
- Which words make up a verb phrase in this sentence?

Swung, loomed, saw, and *was ravaged* are action verbs; they describe the specific actions of *he* or *they* in the sentence. The words *was* and *ravaged* form the verb phrase *was ravaged.* The word *was* is a helping verb, and the word *ravaged* is the main verb.

Grammar for Writers Writers can use action verbs to add dimension to their writing. Choose action verbs that bring your sentences to life and that help readers picture scenes as they unfold.

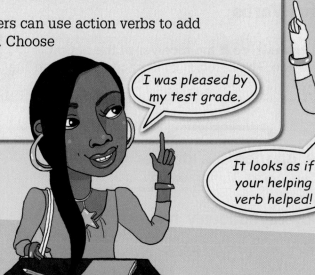

I was pleased by my test grade.

It looks as if your helping verb helped!

14.1 Action Verbs

Verbs such as *walk, sailed, played, migrate, raced, crossed, learn,* and *arrive* all show some kind of action.

RULE **14.1.1**

> An **action verb** tells what action someone or something is performing.

EXAMPLES   Tara **carries** all her science books.

The old truck **chugged** into the garage.

I **believe** it's hurricane season.

Joshua **remembered** to bring the script.

The verb *carries* explains what Tara did with the books. The verb *chugged* tells what the truck did. The verb *believe* explains my action about the hurricane season. The verb *remembered* explains Joshua's action with the script.

Some actions, such as *carries* or *chugged,* can be seen. Some actions, such as *believe* or *remembered,* cannot be seen.

Using Transitive Verbs

RULE **14.1.2**

> An action verb is **transitive** if the receiver of the action is named in the sentence. The receiver of the action is called the **object** of the verb.

EXAMPLES   Bonnie **opened** the **drawer** with difficulty.
               verb   object

The bicyclist suddenly **hit** a **pothole**.
                        verb   object

WRITING COACH

Online

www.phwritingcoach.com

Grammar Tutorials
Brush up on your Grammar skills with these animated videos.

Grammar Practice
Practice your grammar skills with Writing Coach Online.

Grammar Games
Test your knowledge of grammar in this fast-paced interactive video game.

See Practice 14.1A

In the first example, *opened* is transitive because the object of the verb—*drawer*—names what Bonnie opened. In the second example, *hit* is transitive because the object of the verb—*pothole*—tells what the bicyclist hit.

Using Intransitive Verbs

> An action verb is **intransitive** if there is no receiver of the action named in the sentence. An intransitive verb does not have an object.

14.1.3 RULE

EXAMPLES

The conference call **began**.

The motorcyclist **raced** through the traffic jam.

The teaching staff **gathered** in the teachers' lounge.

My doorbell **rang** at midnight!

Some action verbs can be transitive or intransitive. You need to determine if the verb has an object or not.

TRANSITIVE VERB   Chuck **painted** the **garage door**.

INTRANSITIVE VERB   The student **painted** in art class.

TRANSITIVE VERB   Jody **sang** a funny **song**.

INTRANSITIVE VERB   The chorus **sang** on stage.

TRANSITIVE VERB   Will **flew** his small **plane**.

See Practice 14.1B   INTRANSITIVE VERB   The small plane **flew** over the bridge.

PRACTICE 14.1A > Finding Action Verbs

Read the sentences. Then, write each action verb.

EXAMPLE   Ants live in colonies and dig
           underground.

ANSWER   *live, dig*

1. Athletes from many countries compete in the Olympics.

2. The band marched onto the field and played the national anthem.

3. Jason wonders about getting into college.

4. The subway pulled away from the platform.

5. Rosa bought a handmade basket and filled it with dried flowers.

6. Sometimes Aunt Lucy thinks of her lost cat and cries.

7. Chop the onions into small pieces.

8. I dream of a bright future for all children.

9. Brianna opened the door for her little brother.

10. Plants use carbon dioxide and produce oxygen.

PRACTICE 14.1B > Identifying Transitive and Intransitive Verbs

Read the sentences. Write each verb and label it *transitive* or *intransitive*.

EXAMPLE   New York City offers many
           attractions for tourists.

ANSWER   *offers* — transitive

11. During World War II, Japan cooperated with Germany.

12. Brenda took a trip to Arizona with her family.

13. Vendors usually sell pretzels at baseball games.

14. Each boy named his favorite sport.

15. My brother ran in the 100-yard dash.

16. The game lasted for almost two hours.

17. Please explain your actions to the principal.

18. The dog slept peacefully on the floor all morning.

19. After a long train ride, we reached the village.

20. Receiving loud applause, the dancer grinned broadly.

SPEAKING APPLICATION

Tell a partner about a form of exercise you enjoy. Your partner should listen for and name at least two transitive verbs and two intransitive verbs.

WRITING APPLICATION

Write two sentences with transitive verbs and two sentences with intransitive verbs.

14.2 Linking Verbs

Some widely used verbs do not show action. They are called **linking verbs.**

RULE 14.2.1

A **linking verb** is a verb that connects a subject with a word that describes or identifies it.

EXAMPLES

IDENTIFIES

Joshua **was** an army **soldier**.
subject / linking verb / predicate nominative

IDENTIFIES

The **winners** of first place **were** **Heather and I**.
subject / linking verb / predicate nominative

DESCRIBES

We **were** extremely **tired** after our workout.
subject / linking verb / predicate adjective

Recognizing Forms of *Be*

In English, the most common linking verb is *be.* This verb has many forms.

FORMS OF *BE*		
am	can be	has been
are	could be	have been
is	may be	had been
was	might be	could have been
were	must be	may have been
am being	shall be	might have been
are being	should be	must have been
is being	will be	shall have been
was being	would be	should have been
were being		will have been
		would have been

Linking Verbs 317

Using Other Linking Verbs

Several other verbs also function as linking verbs. They connect the parts of a sentence in the same way as the forms of *be*. In the sentence below, *calm* describes *father*.

EXAMPLE   Her **father** **remained** **calm** after the news.
            subject   linking verb   predicate
                                        adjective

OTHER LINKING VERBS		
appear	look	sound
become	remain	stay
feel	seem	taste
grow	smell	turn

Action Verb or Linking Verb?

Some verbs can be used either as linking verbs or action verbs.

LINKING   **The sky looked black.**
           (*Looked* links *sky* and *black.*)

ACTION   **The reporter looked at the sky.**
           (The reporter performed an action.)

LINKING   **The puppy grew impatient.**
           (*Grew* links *puppy* and *impatient.*)

ACTION   **The gardener grew flowers.**
           (The gardener performed an action.)

To test whether a verb is a linking verb or an action verb, replace the verb with *is, am,* or *are.* If the sentence still makes sense, then the verb is a linking verb.

EXAMPLE   **The puppy is impatient.**
                       linking verb

See Practice 14.2A
See Practice 14.2B
See Practice 14.2C
See Practice 14.2D

PRACTICE 14.2A **Identifying Action Verbs and Linking Verbs**

Read the sentences. Write the verb in each sentence, and label it either *action* or *linking*.

EXAMPLE   Marcus turned pale at the accident site.

ANSWER   *turned*— linking

1. My uncle in Indiana grows vegetables in his garden.

2. The teams stayed in a hotel near the stadium.

3. Those burritos look delicious and healthful.

4. For some reason Lupita remains cheerful all the time.

5. Sometimes a rash appears on his face.

6. Heather looked through the binoculars.

7. The lawyer appears very calm and confident.

8. That orange smells delightful.

9. Dad tasted the peach for me.

10. Suddenly, the sky became darker.

PRACTICE 14.2B **Using *Be* and Other Linking Verbs**

Read the pairs of words below. For each pair of words, write a sentence that uses a linking verb to connect them.

EXAMPLE   plane   late

ANSWER   *Because of snow, the plane was late.*

11. server   happy

12. they   early

13. Dickens   writer

14. plan   excellent

15. sauce   salty

16. actress   daughter

17. sister   athlete

18. children   afraid

19. painting   work

20. runner   exhausted

SPEAKING APPLICATION

With a partner, take turns describing a special meal you have had. Your partner should listen for and name at least one action verb and one linking verb.

WRITING APPLICATION

Write one sentence using *taste* as a linking verb and another sentence using it as an action verb. Then do the same with one of these verbs: *smell, stay, look,* or *grow.*

PRACTICE 14.2C Identifying Action Verbs and Linking Verbs

Read the sentences. Write the verb in each sentence, and label it either *action or linking*. Some sentences may contain two verbs.

EXAMPLE Felix hopes to play on the varsity squad next year.

ANSWER *hopes* — action

1. The fire seemed to be burning out of control.
2. Five firefighters rushed into the building.
3. They pointed hoses toward the flames and sprayed streams of water on them.
4. The floors were almost too hot to walk on.
5. Slowly, the water calmed the raging fire.
6. The firefighters felt confident that the worst was over.
7. A large crowd gathered outside of the burning building.
8. Many people grew anxious during the next several minutes.
9. They worried about their possessions inside the building.
10. The crowd cheered for the firefighters as they safely completed their task.

PRACTICE 14.2D Using Action Verbs and Linking Verbs in Sentences

Read each sentence. Then, write your own sentence using the same action verb or linking verb.

EXAMPLE The young child seemed very unhappy.

ANSWER *The puppy seemed lonely by itself.*

11. The mechanic inspected the car carefully.
12. The bride felt nervous before her wedding.
13. Honore's skin turned bright red from the sun.
14. The frightening ordeal was finally over.
15. A dull light appeared in the sky.
16. Your answer appears incorrect.
17. The police dog smelled the suitcase.
18. Those muffins smell wonderful.
19. We all turned to face the flag.
20. The crowd remained quiet and composed.

SPEAKING APPLICATION

With a partner, take turns describing a movie you both saw recently. Your partner should listen for and name two action verbs and two linking verbs you use.

WRITING APPLICATION

Write one sentence using *appear* as an action verb and another sentence using it as a linking verb. Then do the same with two of these verbs: *become, sound, remain, feel*.

Test Warm-Up

DIRECTIONS
Read the introduction and the passage that follows. Then, answer the questions to show that you can use and understand action verbs and linking verbs in reading and writing.

Leanne wrote this story about her day at the beach. Read the story and think about the changes you would suggest as a peer editor. When you finish reading, answer the questions that follow.

Too Much Sun

(1) Everyone in my family love the beach. (2) We go almost every weekend and lie out on the sand for hours. (3) Last weekend, the sun was really hot. (4) I didn't put on enough sunscreen for protection. (5) Then I fell asleep for a long time. (6) My skin seemed to bake in the sun until it was very red. (7) Luckily, my sister woke me up by rubbing more sunscreen on my back. (8) It sounded as if she really "had my back."

1 What change, if any, should be made in sentence 1?

  A Change *everyone* to **every one**

  B Change *my* to **our**

  C Change *love* to **loves**

  D Make no change

2 What is the BEST way to combine sentences 3 and 4?

  F Last weekend, the sun was really hot, so I didn't put on enough sunscreen for protection.

  G Last weekend, the sun was really hot when I didn't put on enough sunscreen for protection.

  H Last weekend, the sun was really hot, and I didn't put on enough sunscreen for protection.

  J Last weekend the sun was really hot, I didn't put on enough sunscreen for protection.

3 The meaning of sentence 6 can be clarified by changing the word *was* to —

  A remained

  B turned

  C felt

  D stayed

4 The meaning of sentence 8 can be clarified by changing the word *sounded* to —

  F seemed

  G was

  H became

  J remained

14.3 Helping Verbs

Sometimes, a verb in a sentence is just one word. Often, however, a verb will be made up of several words. This type of verb is called a **verb phrase**.

RULE 14.3.1

> **Helping verbs** are added before another verb to make a **verb phrase.**

Notice how these helping verbs change the meaning of the verb *jump.*

EXAMPLES   jump   **might have** jumped

had jumped   **should have** jumped

will have jumped   **will be** jumping

Recognizing Helping Verbs

Forms of *Be* Forms of *be* are often used as helping verbs.

SOME FORMS OF *BE* USED AS HELPING VERBS	
HELPING VERBS	**MAIN VERBS**
am	growing
has been	warned
was being	told
will be	reminded
will have been	waiting
is	opening
was being	trained
should be	written
had been	sent
might have been	played

See Practice 14.3A

Other Helping Verbs Many different verb phrases can be formed using one or more of these helping verbs. The chart below shows just a few.

HELPING VERBS	MAIN VERBS	VERB PHRASES
do	remember	do remember
has	written	has written
would	hope	would hope
shall	see	shall see
can	believe	can believe
could	finish	could finish
may	attempt	may attempt
must have	thought	must have thought
should have	grown	should have grown
might	win	might win
will	jump	will jump
have	planned	have planned
does	want	does want

Sometimes the words in a verb phrase are separated by other words, such as *not* or *certainly*. The parts of the verb phrase in certain types of questions may also be separated.

WORDS SEPARATED

He **could** certainly **have come** today.

This **has** not **occurred** to me before.

Aunt Grace **has** certainly not **learned** how to cook!

She **had** certainly **written** a long term paper.

Did you ever **expect** to see a full eclipse?

When **will** we **arrive** at the hotel?

Did you ever **expect** the cake to be so good?

Carolyn **must** not **have taken** the test.

Would you ever **want** to go to Europe?

See Practice 14.3B

PRACTICE 14.3A Identifying Helping and Main Verbs

Read the sentences. Write *main verb* if the underlined verb is a main verb. Write *helping verb* if it is a helping verb.

EXAMPLE   Our cat, Sophie, <u>has been</u> living with us for eight years.

ANSWER   *helping verb*

1. They <u>have</u> often hiked to the top of the mountain.

2. Alisa <u>went</u> to the hockey game on Tuesday night.

3. What time are you <u>going</u> to the Earth Day festival?

4. Yes, he did <u>explain</u> his project to the teacher.

5. Rosita <u>could have</u> won first place.

6. The clerk carefully <u>wrapped</u> the vase for shipping.

7. The singers are <u>preparing</u> for the concert.

8. The speaker <u>has been</u> delayed because of traffic.

9. A walk in the park <u>is</u> a pleasant experience.

10. Zach <u>is</u> bringing his tennis racquet.

PRACTICE 14.3B Using Verb Phrases

Read the verb phrases. Use each verb phrase in an original sentence.

EXAMPLE   have been decorating

ANSWER   *The girls have been decorating their room.*

11. has arrived

12. will help

13. has asked

14. have been saving

15. may wish

16. should have gone

17. must have disagreed

18. have been studying

19. could hear

20. was reaching

SPEAKING APPLICATION

With a partner, take turns telling a brief story about a pet or other animal. Your partner should listen for and name at least two verb phrases.

WRITING APPLICATION

Write three sentences about your favorite school subject. Use a verb phrase in each sentence.

ADJECTIVES and ADVERBS

Use adjectives and adverbs in your descriptions to help your readers create mental pictures as they read.

WRITE GUY *Jeff Anderson, M.Ed.*

WHAT DO YOU NOTICE?

Watch for adjectives and adverbs as you zoom in on these sentences from Maya Angelou's autobiography, *I Know Why the Caged Bird Sings.*

MENTOR TEXT

> Her sounds began cascading gently. I knew from listening to a thousand preachers that she was nearing the end of her reading, and I hadn't really heard, heard to understand, a single word.

Now, ask yourself the following questions:

- Which words do the adverbs *gently* and *really* modify?
- Which word is an adjective that describes an amount, and which noun does it modify?

The adverb *gently* modifies *cascading,* telling readers in what way the words were spoken. The adverb *really* modifies *heard* and describes to what extent Angelou heard the words. The adjective *thousand* modifies *preachers.* A thousand is probably an exaggeration, but it creates a vivid picture for the reader.

Grammar for Writers To craft memorable descriptions, writers carefully select adjectives and adverbs. Before choosing an adjective or adverb, ask yourself if and how it will help your reader see what you are describing.

Is truly an adverb?

Yes, truly is truly an adverb.

325

15.1 Adjectives

Adjectives are words that make language come alive by adding description or information.

Adjectives help make nouns more specific. For example, *car* is a general word, but a *red two-door car* is more specific. Adjectives such as *red* and *two-door* make nouns and pronouns clearer and more vivid.

RULE 15.1.1

> An **adjective** is a word that describes a noun or pronoun.

Adjectives are often called *modifiers*, because they modify, or change, the meaning of a noun or pronoun. You can use more than one adjective to modify a noun or pronoun. Notice how *dress* is modified by each set of adjectives below.

EXAMPLES   **old-fashioned** dress

new **black** dress

women's **evening** dress

sparkly **blue** dress

Adjectives answer several questions about nouns and pronouns. They tell *What kind? Which one? How many?* or *How much?* Numeral adjectives, such as *eleven*, tell exactly how many. In the chart below, notice how adjectives answer these questions.

WHAT KIND?	WHICH ONE?	HOW MANY?	HOW MUCH?
brick house	that judge	one daffodil	no time
white flowers	each answer	both trees	enough raisins
serious argument	those books	several jars	many hobbies
colorful shirts	this student	four books	some cars

Adjective Position An adjective usually comes before the noun it modifies, as do all the adjectives in the chart on the previous page. Sometimes, however, adjectives come after the nouns they modify.

EXAMPLES

The publishing world, **complex** and **serious**,
is sometimes very fast-paced.

The subway platform, **crowded** and **dark**,
frightened us.

Colors, **vivid** and **bold**, filled the walls of the room.

Adjectives that modify pronouns usually come after linking verbs. Sometimes, however, adjectives may come before the pronoun.

AFTER

She was **shy** and **quiet**.

He is **anxious** and **hopeful**.

She is **talkative**.

BEFORE

Timid yet **confident**, **she** walked into the class.

Peaceful and **happy**, **she** sat on a park bench.

Intelligent and **hardworking**, **she** always did
well on exams.

See Practice 15.1A
See Practice 15.1B

PRACTICE 15.1A ▷ Identifying Adjectives

Read the sentences. Then, write each adjective and list the question it answers. (*What kind? Which one? How many? How much?*)

EXAMPLE   Put some dip in that bowl, please.

ANSWER   *some* — How much?
that — Which one?

1. A large man stepped from the red truck.

2. Few people could climb to the top of those mountains.

3. Leanne, tired from cleaning, took a long nap on the couch.

4. Bernice wore a wide-brimmed hat with a green cotton ribbon.

5. Several citizens have complained about that dangerous intersection.

6. Each artist sold two portraits at the outdoor festival.

7. Jan made four calls to the company but received no help.

8. They packed the antique posters in a large box.

9. We saw many birds in the three days we spent at that cabin by the lake.

10. This sculpture has a smooth surface and little detail.

PRACTICE 15.1B ▷ Identifying Adjectives and Words They Modify

Read the sentences. Then, write the adjectives and the words they modify.

EXAMPLE   The many colors of fall were featured in the beautiful photograph.

ANSWER   *many, colors*
beautiful, photograph

11. A cheerful girl skipped across the field.

12. That rude, thoughtless comment was inappropriate.

13. The tall receiver reached for the pass and made a great catch.

14. The third attempt to break the record was successful.

15. The horse, muscular and graceful, trotted around the ring.

16. Sometimes I enjoy the cold, brisk days of winter.

17. Serena received a bouquet of fresh flowers.

18. This state boasts many natural wonders.

19. The lake, sparkling and clear, looked refreshing.

20. That young woman is a talented violinist with the local symphony.

SPEAKING APPLICATION

Tell a partner about a piece of artwork you like. Have your partner listen for and name at least four adjectives and the words they modify.

WRITING APPLICATION

Write three sentences about your favorite season. Use at least one adjective in each sentence.

Articles

Three frequently used adjectives are the words *a, an,* and *the.*
They are called **articles.** Articles can be **definite** or **indefinite.**
Both types indicate that a noun will soon follow.

> *The* is a **definite article.** It points to a specific person, place, thing, or idea. *A* and *an* are **indefinite articles.** They point to any member of a group of similar people, places, things, or ideas.

15.1.2 RULE

DEFINITE	Mr. Halpern is **the** one to see. (a specific person)
	Go into **the** house, and I'll meet you. (a specific place)
	I want to drive **the** new car. (a specific thing)
INDEFINITE	I want to see **a** concert. (any concert)
	Please take **an** envelope. (any envelope)
	You should ask **a** friend to go with you. (any friend)

A is used before consonant sounds. *An* is used before vowel sounds. You choose between *a* and *an* based on sound. Some letters are tricky. The letter *h,* a consonant, may sound like either a consonant or a vowel. The letters *o* and *u* are vowels, but they may sometimes sound like consonants.

USING *A* AND *AN*	
***A* WITH CONSONANT SOUNDS**	***AN* WITH VOWEL SOUNDS**
a black wallet	an endangered species
a happy occasion (*h* sound)	an honest friend (no *h* sound)
a one-lane road (*w* sound)	an old car (*o* sound)
a Union general (*y* sound)	an umbrella (*u* sound)
a jeep	an egg
a pear	an individual
a universal remote (*y* sound)	an angry horn

See Practice 15.1C

PRACTICE 15.1C > **Identifying Definite and Indefinite Articles**

Read the sentences. Then, write the articles and label them *definite* or *indefinite*.

EXAMPLE   Uncle Ian used a metal detector to find the watch.

ANSWER   *a* — indefinite
          the — definite

1. Most of the research can be done at the downtown library.
2. A treasure is said to be hidden in the cave.
3. A family of ducks was trying to cross the street.
4. Have you seen the senator yet?
5. Randall bought a new hockey stick and a helmet.
6. Our science teacher explained the theory well.
7. The alley leading to the parking lot is blocked off.
8. Read the book on the Vietnam War, and then write a report.
9. We spent an entire week working on the social studies project.
10. Tracy is hoping for an island vacation or a luxury cruise.

SPEAKING APPLICATION

Tell a partner what chores you are responsible for at home. Your partner should listen for and name two definite articles and two indefinite articles.

WRITING APPLICATION

Use sentence 3 as a model, and write two more sentences that each contain one indefinite article and one definite article.

Using Proper Adjectives

A **proper adjective** begins with a capital letter. There are two types of proper adjectives.

> A **proper adjective** is (1) a proper noun used as an adjective or (2) an adjective formed from a proper noun.

15.1.3 RULE

A proper noun used as an adjective does *not* change its form. It is merely placed in front of another noun.

PROPER NOUNS	USED AS PROPER ADJECTIVES
Chicago	the Chicago skyline (*Which* skyline?)
Florida	Florida wetlands (*Which* wetlands?)
December	December weather (*What kind* of weather?)

When an adjective is formed from a proper noun, the proper noun will change its form. Notice that endings such as *-n, -ian,* or *-ese* have been added to the proper nouns in the chart below or the spelling has been changed.

PROPER NOUNS	PROPER ADJECTIVES FORMED FROM PROPER NOUNS
America	American history (*Which kind* of history?)
Japan	Japanese cities (*Which* cities?)
Norway	Norwegian legends (*Which* legends?)
Inca	Incan empire (*Which* empire?)
Florida	Floridian sunset (*Which* sunset?)

See Practice 15.1D

Using Nouns as Adjectives

Nouns can sometimes be used as adjectives. A noun used as an adjective usually comes directly before another noun and answers the question *What kind?* or *Which one?*

NOUNS	USED AS ADJECTIVES
shoe	a shoe salesperson (*What kind* of salesperson?)
waterfowl	the waterfowl refuge (*Which* refuge?)
court	a court date (*What kind* of date?)
morning	a morning appointment (*What kind* of appointment?)

Using Compound Adjectives

Adjectives, like nouns, can be compound.

RULE 15.1.4

> A **compound adjective** is made up of more than one word.

Most **compound adjectives** are written as hyphenated words. Some are written as combined words, as in "a *runaway* horse." If you are unsure about how to write a compound adjective, look up the word in a dictionary.

HYPHENATED	COMBINED
a well-known actress	a featherweight boxer
a full-time job	a freshwater lake
snow-covered mountains	a sideways glance
one-sided opinions	heartbreaking news
so-called experts	a nearsighted witness

See Practice 15.1E

PRACTICE 15.1D > Using Proper Adjectives

Read the sentences. Then, rewrite each sentence to include a proper adjective before the underlined noun.

EXAMPLE   Carmen enjoyed the <u>play</u>.

ANSWER   *Carmen enjoyed the Shakespearean play.*

1. That store carries some expensive <u>antiques</u>.
2. My neighbor adopted a <u>cat</u>.
3. My mother collects <u>jewelry</u>.
4. Last week we learned about <u>explorers</u>.
5. The dancers performed traditional <u>dances</u>.
6. Aunt Carol invited us to her house for a <u>feast</u>.
7. We saw many <u>tourists</u> in Italy.
8. I'd like a book about the fashions of the <u>era</u>.
9. Meet me in the library after <u>class</u>.
10. Jason enjoys studying ancient <u>coins</u>.

PRACTICE 15.1E > Recognizing Nouns Used as Adjectives

Read the sentences. Write the noun, proper noun, or compound noun used as an adjective. Then, write the noun that the adjective modifies.

EXAMPLE   Dad used a whole bag of Idaho potatoes in the soup.

ANSWER   *Idaho, potatoes*

11. The evening sky was laced with orange and pink.
12. We spent the second day of our trip driving across the California desert.
13. Piano music could be heard from the street.
14. You will find the subway station just three blocks from here.
15. Isn't Texas toast much thicker than regular toast?
16. The students constructed a wire-mesh statue of Abraham Lincoln.
17. The art festival will be held at the park near the river.
18. Jenna sighed when she first saw the lovely lakeside cabin.
19. The January temperatures were unusually mild that year.
20. All of the grade-seven teachers calmly led their students out of the building.

SPEAKING APPLICATION

Tell a partner about a country you would like to visit. Have your partner listen for and name two nouns used as adjectives, as well as one proper adjective.

WRITING APPLICATION

Write sentences using each of the following as adjectives: a noun, a compound noun, and a proper noun. Then, write one sentence using a proper adjective.

Using Pronouns as Adjectives

Pronouns, like nouns, can sometimes be used as adjectives.

RULE 15.1.5

A pronoun becomes an adjective if it modifies a noun.

EXAMPLES   We saw the dress on **this** side of the mall.

Which store has the nicest dress?

In the first example, the demonstrative pronoun *this* modifies *side*, and in the second example, the interrogative pronoun *which* modifies *store*.

Using Possessive Nouns and Pronouns as Adjectives

The following personal pronouns are often **possessive adjectives:** *my, your, her, his, its, our,* and *their*. They are adjectives because they come before nouns and answer the question *Which one?* They are pronouns because they have antecedents.

EXAMPLES

In the first example, *their* is an adjective because it modifies *hands*. At the same time, it is a pronoun because it refers to the antecedent *children*.

In the second example, *its* is an adjective because it modifies *computers*. The word *its* is also a pronoun because it refers to the antecedent *library*.

Note About Possessive Nouns Possessive nouns function as adjectives when they modify a noun.

EXAMPLES   The slide is in the **Browns'** backyard.

The **cat's** tail is orange and white.

See Practice 15.1F
See Practice 15.1G

Using Demonstrative Adjectives

This, that, these, and *those*—the four demonstrative pronouns—can also be **demonstrative adjectives.**

PRONOUN   We bought **that** .

ADJECTIVE   **That** man is the new principal.

PRONOUN   Why did you buy **these** ?

ADJECTIVE   **These** children are waiting for frozen yogurt.

Using Interrogative Adjectives

Which, what, and *whose*—three of the interrogative pronouns—can be **interrogative adjectives.**

PRONOUN   **Which** is your favorite dish?

ADJECTIVE   **Which** sauce do you like the best?

PRONOUN   **Whose** is that?

ADJECTIVE   **Whose** poodle can that be?

Using Indefinite Adjectives

A number of indefinite pronouns—*both, few, many, each, most,* and *all,* among others—can also be used as **indefinite adjectives.**

PRONOUN   I ordered one of **each** .

ADJECTIVE   **Each** student gets to choose.

PRONOUN   I don't need **any** .

ADJECTIVE   I don't need **any** advice.

See Practice 15.1H
See Practice 15.1I

Recognizing Possessive Nouns and Pronouns Used as Adjectives

Read the sentences. Then, write the possessive noun or pronoun used as an adjective in each sentence.

EXAMPLE   The club treasurer understands her responsibilities.

ANSWER   *her*

1. Everyone found the dancers' performance inspiring.

2. Did you call your cousin last night?

3. I will share my sandwich with you if you like.

4. The Jacksons' house is the one on the corner.

5. Lily's mother goes to yoga class twice a week.

6. Jada and Lewis will give their presentation on ancient Rome.

7. I think that book is about Lincoln's presidency.

8. The boy finally found his backpack near the bus stop.

9. Our dance last weekend was a big success.

10. The puppy knocked over its water bowl and made a mess.

Identifying Possessive Nouns and Pronouns Used as Adjectives

Read each sentence. Write the possessive noun or pronoun used as an adjective. Then, write the noun the adjective modifies. Some sentences have more than one answer.

EXAMPLE   Haden's friends planned a surprise party for him.

ANSWER   *Haden's, friends*

11. Sheryl was chosen to be the committee's spokesperson.

12. We all cheered when she made her speech.

13. A turtle's shell protects it from harm.

14. The bullfighter waved a red cape to get the bull's attention.

15. The ant lost its freedom, becoming trapped in the spider's web.

16. The twins' mother came to take them home.

17. A fierce tiger paced inside its cage in the zoo.

18. We all appreciate Thomas Edison's invention, the lightbulb.

19. His face was covered with two weeks' growth of beard.

20. The storm's intensity increased throughout the evening.

SPEAKING APPLICATION

With a partner, take turns describing a concert or play you have seen. Have your partner listen for and name at least one possessive noun and one possessive pronoun used as an adjective.

WRITING APPLICATION

Write four sentences about the ocean. In your sentences, use at least one possessive noun used as an adjective and one possessive pronoun used as an adjective.

PRACTICE 15.1H > **Identifying Demonstrative, Interrogative, and Indefinite Adjectives**

Read the sentences. Then, write the adjective in each sentence and label it *demonstrative, interrogative,* or *indefinite.*

EXAMPLE   This marvel of geology attracts tourists from across the country.

ANSWER   *This*— demonstrative

1. Could you hand me one of those pears, please?

2. Which poem are you going to recite in class?

3. This watch was a gift from a friend.

4. Both students gave presentations.

5. There are many acts auditioning for the show.

6. What kind of music do you like most?

7. I need to organize these books and then dust the shelves.

8. Have you made some necklaces to give as gifts?

9. Whose sculptures will be on display at the gallery?

10. Each child made a mobile to take home.

PRACTICE 15.1I > **Using Demonstrative, Interrogative, and Indefinite Adjectives in Sentences**

Read the words. Then, write a sentence in which you use each word as the type of adjective indicated in parentheses.

EXAMPLE   which (interrogative)

ANSWER   *Which road should we take to the cabin?*

11. that (demonstrative)

12. any (indefinite)

13. several (indefinite)

14. those (demonstrative)

15. some (indefinite)

16. what (interrogative)

17. both (indefinite)

18. which (interrogative)

19. this (demonstrative)

20. whose (interrogative)

SPEAKING APPLICATION

With a partner, take turns asking directions to a restaurant in your town. The partner should listen for and name at least one demonstrative, one interrogative, and one indefinite adjective you use.

WRITING APPLICATION

Write a brief paragraph about a time you received a big surprise. Use at least one demonstrative, one interrogative, and one indefinite adjective in your paragraph.

Test Warm-Up

DIRECTIONS
Read the introduction and the passage that follows. Then, answer the questions to show that you can use and understand demonstrative, interrogative, and indefinite adjectives in reading and writing.

Alonzo wrote this paragraph for his science class. Read the paragraph and think about the changes you would suggest as a peer editor. When you finish reading, answer the questions that follow.

Vegetables to the Rescue

(1) Believe it or not, vegetables can help cure all diseases.
(2) Some vegetables contain antioxidant vitamins and minerals.
(3) This antioxidants help reduce the amount of cholesterol in our bodies.
(4) Cholesterol buildup can lead to heart attacks or strokes. (5) Broccoli is one vegetable. (6) It has many important healthful properties.
(7) Broccoli contains several special compound that help build and repair cells. (8) These cells are then strong enough to fight off attacks by cancer cells.

---

1 The meaning in sentence 1 can be clarified by changing the word ***all*** to —

  A few

  B each

  C both

  D many

2 What change, if any, should be made in sentence 3?

  F Change ***This*** to **These**

  G Change ***amount*** to **number**

  H Change ***bodies*** to **body**

  J Make no change

3 What is the BEST way to combine sentences 5 and 6?

  A Broccoli is one vegetable that has each important healthful properties.

  B Broccoli is the vegetable that has many important healthful properties.

  C Broccoli is one vegetable that has an important healthful property.

  D Broccoli is one vegetable that has many important healthful properties.

4 What change, if any, should be made in sentence 7?

  F Change ***contains*** to **contain**

  G Change ***several*** to **few**

  H Change ***compound*** to **compounds**

  J Make no change

15.2 Adverbs

Adverbs can modify three different parts of speech. They make the meaning of verbs, adjectives, or other adverbs more precise.

15.2.1 RULE

> An **adverb** modifies a verb, an adjective, or another adverb.

Although adverbs may modify adjectives and other adverbs, they generally modify verbs.

Using Adverbs That Modify Verbs

Adverbs that modify verbs will answer one of these four questions: *Where? When? In what way? To what extent?* These adverbs are also known as *adverbs of place, adverbs of time, adverbs of manner,* and *adverbs of degree.*

ADVERBS THAT MODIFY VERBS			
WHERE?	**WHEN?**	**IN WHAT WAY?**	**TO WHAT EXTENT?**
push upward	will leave soon	works carefully	hardly ate
fell there	comes daily	speaks well	really surprised
stay nearby	swims often	chews noisily	almost cried
go outside	exhibits yearly	acted willingly	partly finished
is here	report later	walk quietly	nearly won
jump away	come tomorrow	smiled happily	fully agree
drove down	went yesterday	moved gracefully	totally oppose

Negative adverbs, such as *not, never,* and *nowhere,* also modify verbs.

EXAMPLES   Heather **never** **arrived** at the dinner.
                        adverb   verb

He **could** **not** **answer** the judge.
     verb   adverb   verb

Continuing to argue **had led** **nowhere**.
                              verb   adverb

See Practice 15.2A

Using Adverbs That Modify Adjectives

An adverb modifying an adjective answers only one question:
To what extent?

> **When adverbs modify adjectives or adverbs, they answer the question *To what extent?***

ADVERBS THAT MODIFY ADJECTIVES	
very upset	extremely tall
definitely wrong	not hungry

EXAMPLE   The snow can be **very beautiful**.

The adverb *very* modifies the adjective *beautiful.*

EXAMPLE   The mountain is **extremely snowy**.

The adverb *extremely* modifies the adjective *snowy.*

Adverbs Modifying Other Adverbs

When adverbs modify other adverbs, they again answer the question *To what extent?*

ADVERBS MODIFYING ADVERBS	
traveled less slowly	move very cautiously
lost too easily	lived almost happily

EXAMPLE   Owls are **hardly ever** seen in the daytime.

The adverb *hardly* modifies the adverb *ever.*

EXAMPLE   When writing, my hand cramps **too quickly**.

The adverb *too* modifies the adverb *quickly.*

See Practice 15.2B

PRACTICE 15.2A > Identifying How Adverbs Modify Verbs

Read the sentences. Write the adverb in each sentence and list the question it answers. (*When? Where? In what way? To what extent?*)

EXAMPLE   To get to the stadium, turn right at the light.

ANSWER   *right*— In what way?

1. Harriet Tubman was known everywhere along the Underground Railroad.

2. Tanya opened the door to the barn cautiously.

3. The engine sputtered and then stopped.

4. Approval for the Brooklyn Bridge was finally given in 1869.

5. The cat napped quietly on the back of the couch.

6. She immediately called the police about the robbery.

7. Silently, the cougar leapt from the rock.

8. Jason has almost finished the jigsaw puzzle.

9. Gina and Alexis played soccer outside.

10. The new school is nearly completed.

PRACTICE 15.2B > Recognizing Adverbs and Words They Modify

Read the sentences. Write the word that each underlined adverb modifies. Then, write whether that word is a *verb*, an *adjective*, or an *adverb*.

EXAMPLE   Jake <u>expertly</u> applied the glue to the fabric.

ANSWER   *applied*— verb

11. My little sister is learning to speak <u>more</u> clearly.

12. The running back's movements seemed <u>rather</u> sluggish.

13. We tried to catch the hamster, but it was moving <u>too</u> fast.

14. The beef stew simmered <u>slowly</u> on the stove.

15. Caleb gave the teacher his term paper <u>late</u>.

16. At the awards ceremony, Consuela seemed <u>slightly</u> upset.

17. The police officers approached the building <u>quite</u> cautiously.

18. My brother <u>quickly</u> swept the front porch.

19. The dance team purchased an <u>almost</u> new CD player.

20. My mother speaks Portuguese <u>extremely</u> well.

SPEAKING APPLICATION

With a partner, take turns describing the ideal pet. Your partner should listen for three adverbs and tell what words the adverbs modify.

WRITING APPLICATION

Write three sentences about birds. In the first sentence, use an adverb that modifies a verb. In the second sentence, use an adverb that modifies an adjective. In the third, use an adverb that modifies another adverb.

Finding Adverbs in Sentences

Adverbs can be found in different places in sentences. The chart below shows examples of possible locations for adverbs. Arrows point to the words that the adverbs modify.

LOCATION OF ADVERBS IN SENTENCES	
LOCATION	**EXAMPLE**
At the beginning of a sentence	Carefully, she approached the puppy.
At the end of a sentence	She approached the puppy carefully.
Before a verb	She carefully approached the puppy.
After a verb	She tiptoed silently toward the puppy.
Between parts of a verb phrase	She had carefully approached the puppy.
Before an adjective	The puppy was always quiet.
Before another adverb	The puppy whined rather quietly.

Conjunctive adverbs **Conjunctive adverbs** are adverbs that join independent clauses. (See Chapter 17 for more about conjunctive adverbs.)

EXAMPLES Her computer broke; **therefore** , she couldn't finish
her essay.
conjunctive adverb

Tara bought a new outfit at the mall; **however** ,
she forgot to take the tags off.
conjunctive adverb

See Practice 15.2C

Adverb or Adjective?

Some words can function as adverbs or as adjectives, depending on their use in a sentence.

> If a noun or pronoun is modified by a word, that modifying word is an **adjective.** If a verb, adjective, or adverb is modified by a word, that modifying word is an **adverb.**

15.2.3 RULE

An adjective will modify a noun or pronoun and will answer one of the questions *What kind? Which one? How many?* or *How much?*

An adverb will modify a verb, an adjective, or another adverb and will answer one of the questions *Where? When? In what way?* or *To what extent?*

ADVERB MODIFYING VERB	Teachers **work** **hard**.
	verb adverb
	When the puppies reached the door, they **stepped** **inside**.
	verb adverb
ADJECTIVE MODIFYING NOUN	Teachers accomplish **hard** **tasks**.
	adjective noun
	This is the **right** **spot** to see the sun rise over the mountains.
	adjective noun

While most words ending in *-ly* are adverbs, some are not. Several adjectives also end in *-ly*. These adjectives are formed by adding *-ly* to nouns.

ADJECTIVES WITH -LY ENDINGS	a **lovely** dress
	a **costly** meal
EXAMPLES	At the mall we found a **lovely** dress.
	Eating out is fun, but that was a **costly** meal.

See Practice 15.2D

PRACTICE 15.2C Locating Adverbs

Read the sentences. Then, write each adverb and the word or words it modifies.

EXAMPLE I have often wondered about that run-down building.

ANSWER *often, have wondered*

1. Usually I finish my homework before dinner.
2. Many fans arrived at the game early.
3. My friend Harriet is a very kind person.
4. These candied yams are especially delicious.
5. The home team was defeated rather easily by the visitors.
6. The little child spoke too softly to be heard.
7. Jeanette has made this gravy awfully thick.
8. Serena awoke early on the day of the spelling bee.
9. She squinted because the sun was shining so brightly.
10. Please order the tickets soon.

PRACTICE 15.2D Recognizing Adverbs and Adjectives

Read the sentences. Then, write whether each underlined word is an *adjective* or an *adverb*.

EXAMPLE I worked <u>hard</u> to pass the test.

ANSWER *adverb*

11. When it rains, we eat lunch <u>inside</u>.
12. The batter swung at an <u>inside</u> pitch.
13. Sam eats breakfast before his <u>early</u> class.
14. Please try to arrive <u>early</u> on Saturday.
15. The highway runs too <u>far</u> from our house.
16. That's Kai in the <u>far</u> corner.
17. We are planning to move in the <u>near</u> future.
18. He came <u>near</u> as I walked away.
19. The students studied for their <u>weekly</u> quiz.
20. I receive the magazine <u>weekly</u>.

SPEAKING APPLICATION

With a partner, take turns telling about a typical evening at your home. Your partner should listen for and name at least three adverbs.

WRITING APPLICATION

Use sentences 19 and 20 as models, and write one sentence in which *weekly* is used as an adjective and one sentence in which *weekly* is used as an adverb.

PREPOSITIONS

Build meaning into your sentences by using prepositions to create relationships between words.

CHAPTER 16

WRITE GUY *Jeff Anderson, M.Ed.*

WHAT DO YOU NOTICE?

Spot the prepositions as you zoom in on these sentences from the essay "Science and the Sense of Wonder" by Isaac Asimov.

MENTOR TEXT

> Should I stare lovingly at a single leaf and willingly remain ignorant of the forest? Should I be satisfied to watch the sun glinting off a single pebble and scorn any knowledge of a beach?

Now, ask yourself the following questions:

- In the two prepositional phrases that begin with the preposition *of*, what are the objects of the prepositions?

- In the two prepositional phrases that contain the word *single*, what are the prepositions and their objects?

In the phrase *of the forest*, *forest* is the object of the preposition. The noun *beach* is the object of the preposition in the phrase *of a beach*. In the phrase *at a single leaf*, the preposition is *at* and the object is *leaf*. In the phrase *off a single pebble*, the preposition is *off* and the object is *pebble*.

Grammar for Writers Choosing one preposition over another can change the meaning of a sentence. Use prepositions in your writing that convey the meaning you intend.

I need to study before tomorrow's test.

Well, definitely not after it!

16.1 Prepositions

Prepositions function as connectors, relating one word to another within a sentence.

WRITING COACH

Online

www.phwritingcoach.com

Grammar Tutorials
Brush up on your Grammar skills with these animated videos.

Grammar Practice
Practice your grammar skills with Writing Coach Online.

Grammar Games
Test your knowledge of grammar in this fast-paced interactive video game.

They allow a speaker or writer to express the link between separate items. **Prepositions** can convey information about location, time, or direction or provide details.

RULE 16.1.1

> A **preposition** relates the noun or pronoun following it to another word in the sentence.

EXAMPLES **The flower fell onto the surface of the counter.**
preposition   noun   preposition   noun

The puppy ran across the patio and
preposition   noun

hid inside his doghouse.
preposition   noun

In the first example, the flower fell where? (onto the surface) It was the surface of what? (the counter) In the second example, the puppy ran where? (across the patio) The puppy hid where? (inside his doghouse)

FIFTY COMMON PREPOSITIONS				
about	behind	during	off	to
above	below	except	on	toward
across	beneath	for	onto	under
after	beside	from	opposite	underneath
against	besides	in	out	until
along	between	inside	outside	up
among	beyond	into	over	upon
around	but	like	past	with
at	by	near	since	within
before	down	of	through	without

See Practice 16.1A

346   **Prepositions**

Compound Prepositions Prepositions consisting of more than one word are called **compound prepositions.** Some of them are listed in the chart below:

COMPOUND PREPOSITIONS		
according to	by means of	instead of
ahead of	in addition to	in view of
apart from	in back of	next to
aside from	in front of	on account of
as of	in place of	on top of
because of	in spite of	out of

Because prepositions have different meanings, using a particular preposition will affect the way other words in a sentence relate to one another. In the first sentence, for example, notice how each preposition changes the relationship between *parade* and *City Hall.*

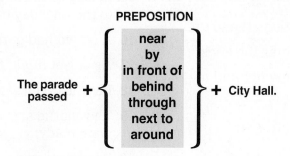

In this sentence, the preposition changes the relationship between *girls* and *gym.*

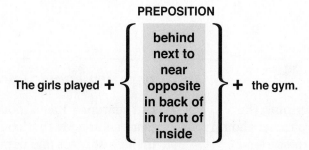

See Practice 16.1B

PRACTICE 16.1A > Identifying Prepositions

Read the sentences. Then, write the preposition in each sentence.

EXAMPLE   Our dog runs from the house when he hears the bathwater running.

ANSWER   *from*

1. The plants are on the porch.

2. Where are the photos from our vacation?

3. The boat chugged along the wide river.

4. We can ask Mrs. Lopez about the math test.

5. During the winter we often go skiing.

6. We found the teddy bear underneath the child's blankets.

7. The boys strolled into the pizza parlor.

8. The traffic snaked slowly through the town.

9. Before dinner Sara always walks the dogs.

10. After all the excitement, I could not find my suitcase.

PRACTICE 16.1B > Identifying Compound Prepositions

Read the sentences. Then, write the compound preposition in each sentence.

EXAMPLE   The flight was canceled because of the storm.

ANSWER   *because of*

11. The flower seeds can be found next to the gardening tools.

12. I'd like a salad instead of fries, please.

13. In spite of the trouble, we arrived at the train station in time.

14. According to the book jacket, this is the story of an adventure at sea.

15. Keeley gave her sister a nice gift in addition to the birthday card.

16. A crowd had gathered in front of the building.

17. As of last night, the concert was canceled.

18. Put the dog treats on top of the refrigerator.

19. The shuttle arrived ahead of time, but we were ready.

20. Darren started the game in place of the usual point guard.

SPEAKING APPLICATION

With a partner, take turns describing the street on which you live. Your partner should listen for and name at least three different prepositions.

WRITING APPLICATION

Use sentence 1 as a model, and write three more sentences that contain prepositions. Include at least one compound preposition in your sentences.

Prepositions Used in Sentences

A preposition is never used by itself in a sentence. Instead, it appears as part of a phrase containing one or more other words.

> **A preposition** in a sentence always introduces a **prepositional phrase.**

16.1.2 RULE

Prepositional Phrases

A **prepositional phrase** is a group of words that begins with a preposition and ends with a noun or pronoun. The noun or pronoun following the preposition is the **object of the preposition.**

Some prepositional phrases contain just two words—the preposition and its object. Others are longer because they contain modifiers.

EXAMPLES

during school
preposition   object

from the **White House**
preposition   object

in place of the old, used **sneakers**
preposition   object

inside the warm, new **house**
preposition   object

with time
preposition object

See Practice 16.1C
See Practice 16.1D
See Practice 16.1F

according to the new **manager**
preposition   object

Prepositional phrases convey information about location, time, or direction or provide details. (See Chapter 23 to learn about prepositional phrases and their influence on subject–verb agreement.)

Preposition or Adverb?

Some words can be used either as prepositions or as adverbs. The following chart lists some examples. When the word is used as a preposition, it begins a prepositional phrase and is followed by the object of the preposition. If the word has no object, it is probably being used as an adverb.

PREPOSITION OR ADVERB		
above	inside	outside
after	nearby	past
around	opposite	underneath
before	out	within

PREPOSITION The broken glass was **outside** the cabinet.

ADVERB The woman saw the broken glass **outside**.

PREPOSITION She appeared **before** the committee.

ADVERB She had not seen that **before**.

PREPOSITION The girl ran **past** the classroom door.

ADVERB The teacher walked **past** quickly.

PREPOSITION She sat **inside** the salon.

ADVERB Please go **inside** tomorrow.

PREPOSITION The teacher sat **behind** the students.

ADVERB The student lingered **behind**.

PREPOSITION The book was on the shelf **above** the table.

ADVERB Confetti fell on them from **above**.

See Practice 16.1E
See Practice 16.1G
See Practice 16.1H

PRACTICE 16.1C > **Recognizing Prepositional Phrases**

Read the sentences. Write the prepositional phrase in each sentence, and underline the object of the preposition.

EXAMPLE   Beyond that small mountain range is a Hopi reservation.

ANSWER   *Beyond that small mountain <u>range</u>*

1. The postal carrier left a box outside the house.

2. The puppy wriggled under the heavy blankets.

3. The package warned consumers of many dangers.

4. You will see a stained-glass window near the front door.

5. What are those weeds growing between the fence slats?

6. Three deer could be seen grazing by the road.

7. She looked beautiful in her new outfit.

8. In spite of his concerns, Mr. Grant mailed the letter.

9. In front of my aunt's house stands a large, old maple tree.

10. June tried to see ahead of the traffic but could not spot anything.

PRACTICE 16.1D > **Distinguishing Prepositions and Prepositional Phrases**

Read the sentences. Write the prepositional phrases. Then, underline the preposition in each phrase.

EXAMPLE   Because of the heavy traffic, the Garcias arrived late.

ANSWER   *<u>Because of</u> the heavy traffic*

11. Use the large baking dish for that casserole.

12. The dog was so excited that he ran into the wall.

13. According to the label, this dish soap is highly concentrated.

14. The trampoline in the backyard has had much use.

15. The dirty towels are on top of the washing machine.

16. Scott threw the ball toward first base.

17. Without your help, we never could have succeeded.

18. Jumping off the high dive can be frightening.

19. Let's have pancakes instead of scrambled eggs.

20. The girls took a long hike through the woods.

SPEAKING APPLICATION

Tell a partner how you usually celebrate your birthday. Your partner should listen for and name at least three prepositional phrases.

WRITING APPLICATION

Use sentence 16 as a model, and write three more sentences that each contain a prepositional phrase.

PRACTICE 16.1E > Distinguishing Prepositions and Adverbs

Read the sentences. Label each underlined word *preposition* or *adverb*.

EXAMPLE   Greg picked up the rock and looked <u>underneath</u>.

ANSWER   *adverb*

1. Nina jogged <u>through</u> the park on her way home from school.

2. If you can't get through the gate, just go <u>around</u>.

3. The tourists had to travel <u>along</u> the main road for three more miles.

4. Janelle gets nervous whenever a storm comes <u>near</u>.

5. We watched the parade go <u>by</u>.

6. Wiggling its tiny body, the puppy tried to slip <u>through</u> the door.

7. I called to her, but she ran <u>outside</u>.

8. A festive crowd had gathered <u>near</u> the parade route.

9. Sam found a lot of dust <u>behind</u> the couch.

10. Please walk <u>along</u> quietly until you reach the ticket counter.

PRACTICE 16.1F > Supplying Prepositions and Prepositional Phrases

Read the sentences. Then, expand each sentence by adding a prepositional phrase that begins with a preposition of your choice, or use one of these prepositions: *in, for, on, of, by, from, with, into, between, through, about.*

EXAMPLE   The hamster is running.

ANSWER   *The hamster is running on its exercise wheel.*

11. The dog is trying to climb.

12. We make breakfast and then get dressed.

13. Kevin likes pizza.

14. We found the perfect camping site.

15. Karli works every day.

16. Dad promised to help us.

17. Several rows of pansies were planted.

18. One of the ushers smiled.

19. The softball game has been postponed.

20. The parking lot is full.

SPEAKING APPLICATION

Tell a partner a story about your best friend. Your partner should listen for and name at least one preposition and one adverb that could also be used as a preposition.

WRITING APPLICATION

Write a sentence that contains a preposition. Then write a second sentence that uses the same word as an adverb.

PRACTICE 16.1G > Identifying Prepositions and Adverbs

Read each sentence. Write one word to fill the blank and complete each sentence. Then, write whether the word is used as a preposition or as an adverb.

EXAMPLE   When the bell rang, everyone came _____.

ANSWER   *inside* — adverb

1. Propelled by the wind, the sailboat sped _____ the lake.

2. The witness said she had never seen the defendant _____.

3. The banners flying _____ the stadium represented the five team championships.

4. The clumsy waiter slipped and fell _____, spilling food everywhere.

5. It was so cold _____ that even my dog didn't want to go for a walk.

6. Danielle wore the medal proudly _____ her neck.

7. We drove _____ your house last night, but you weren't home.

8. The lake is so large that it takes 30 minutes to paddle _____.

9. Using his new telescope, he scanned the stars _____.

10. The passengers waited patiently to pass _____ security.

PRACTICE 16.1H > Writing Sentences With Prepositions and Adverbs

Read each word below. Then, following the directions in parentheses, write a sentence using the word as a preposition or an adverb.

EXAMPLE   down (adverb)

ANSWER   *The clown slipped on a banana peel and fell down.*

11. across (preposition)

12. outside (adverb)

13. past (preposition)

14. nearby (adverb)

15. above (preposition)

16. beneath (adverb)

17. beside (preposition)

18. inside (adverb)

19. over (adverb)

20. over (preposition)

SPEAKING APPLICATION

With a partner, take turns describing a scene from a scary movie. Your partner should listen for and name two prepositions and two adverbs you use.

WRITING APPLICATION

Write a paragraph describing the rules of a sport. Use at least five prepositions. Then, underline each preposition and indicate whether it is used as an adverb or as an introduction to a prepositional phrase.

Test Warm-Up

DIRECTIONS
Read the introduction and the passage that follows. Then, answer the questions to show that you can use and understand prepositions and adverbs in reading and writing.

Stewart wrote this story about a ride in a hot-air balloon. Read the story and think about the changes you would suggest as a peer editor. When you finish reading, answer the questions that follow.

Sailing Away

(1) Shelby was nervous and excited as she sat inside the basket suspended below. (2) Soon she would be sailing across the sky and through the clouds. (3) The balloon pilot climbed outside to gather more gear. (4) Shelby was glad the balloon was held steady by strong ropes around. (5) Suddenly, a powerful gust of wind struck the balloon, pulling the ropes free. (6) The balloon and Shelby were now airborne. (7) Luckily, Shelby remembered how to release air from the balloon and bring it.

1 How should sentence 1 be revised?

A Shelby was nervous and excited inside as she sat inside the basket suspended below the mountains.

B Shelby was nervous and excited as she sat below the basket suspended below.

C Above Shelby was nervous and excited as she sat inside the basket.

D Shelby was nervous and excited as she sat inside the basket suspended below the balloon.

2 What change, if any, should be made in sentence 2?

F Change *across* to **nearby**

G Change *through* to **after**

H Change *across* to **before**

J Make no change

3 The meaning of sentence 4 can be clarified by changing the adverb ***around*** to —

A through

B underneath

C past

D opposite

4 What change, if any, should be made in sentence 7?

F Insert the adverb **down** after ***it***

G Change *from* to **around**

H Change *how* to **where**

J Make no change

CHAPTER 17

CONJUNCTIONS *and* INTERJECTIONS

Use conjunctions to show relationships between ideas in your writing; add interjections to affect the mood.

WRITE GUY *Jeff Anderson, M.Ed.*

WHAT DO YOU NOTICE?

Search for conjunctions as you zoom in on this sentence from the essay "The Trouble With Television" by Robert MacNeil.

MENTOR TEXT

> Literacy may not be an inalienable human right, but it is one that the highly literate Founding Fathers might not have found unreasonable or even unattainable.

Now, ask yourself the following questions:

- Why does the author use the coordinating conjunction *but*?
- How does the use of *or* differ from the use of *but* in the sentence?

The author uses a comma followed by *but* to connect two sentences. The first sentence is *literacy may not be an inalienable human right,* and the second is *it is one that the highly literate Founding Fathers might not have found unreasonable or even unattainable.* The use of *or* differs from the use of *but* because *or* connects two adjectives, *unreasonable* and *unattainable.*

Grammar for Writers Conjunctions help writers show relationships between ideas. Use conjunctions in your writing to infuse variety and interest.

Should I put the conjunction here or there?

I think you need one here and there.

17.1 Conjunctions

Conjunctions are like links in a chain: They help you join words and ideas.

WRITING COACH

Online

www.phwritingcoach.com

Grammar Tutorials
Brush up on your Grammar skills with these animated videos.

Grammar Practice
Practice your grammar skills with Writing Coach Online.

Grammar Games
Test your knowledge of grammar in this fast-paced interactive video game.

RULE 17.1.1

> A **conjunction** connects words or groups of words.

Conjunctions fall into three groups: **Coordinating conjunctions, correlative conjunctions,** and **subordinating conjunctions.**

Coordinating Conjunctions

RULE 17.1.2

> **Coordinating conjunctions** connect words of the same kind, such as two or more nouns or verbs. They can also connect larger groups of words, such as prepositional phrases or even complete sentences.

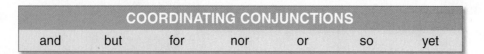

COORDINATING CONJUNCTIONS						
and	but	for	nor	or	so	yet

In the following examples, notice the coordinating conjunctions that connect the highlighted words.

Connecting Nouns	My dad and his boss met for lunch to close the deal.
Connecting Verbs	They brought my soup but forgot to bring the salad.
Connecting Prepositional Phrases	Put the vegetables onto the table or into the basket.
Connecting Two Sentences	The roast was still in the oven, yet it was time to eat.

See Practice 17.1A

Correlative Conjunctions

Correlative conjunctions are *pairs* of words that connect similar kinds of words or groups of words.

CORRELATIVE CONJUNCTIONS		
both . . . and	neither . . . nor	whether . . . or
either . . . or	not only . . . but also	

Notice the correlative conjunctions in the following examples.

Connecting Nouns	Either the blanket or the quilt will work.
Connecting Pronouns	Neither she nor I know the story.
Connecting Verbs	Every afternoon, he both calls and e-mails.
Connecting Prepositional Phrases	He's arriving today—whether by car or by bus, I can't say.
Connecting Two Clauses	Not only do they skate, but they also ski.

See Practice 17.1B

Subordinating Conjunctions

Subordinating conjunctions connect two ideas by making one idea dependent on the other.

FREQUENTLY USED SUBORDINATING CONJUNCTIONS				
after	as soon as	if	though	whenever
although	as though	in order that	till	where
as	because	since	unless	wherever
as if	before	so that	until	while
as long as	even though	than	when	

The Dependent Idea The subordinating conjunction always introduces the dependent idea. The subordinating conjunction connects the dependent idea to the main idea.

EXAMPLES   I made the plans **after** **I heard the weather report**.

When **she called yesterday**, I was worried something was wrong.

The examples show that the main idea can come at the beginning or at the end of the sentence. Look at the difference in punctuation. When the dependent idea comes first, it must be separated from the main idea with a comma. If the dependent idea comes second, no comma is necessary.

See Practice 17.1C

See Practice 17.1D

See Practice 17.1E

Conjunctive Adverbs

Conjunctive adverbs are used as conjunctions to connect complete ideas. They are often used as transitions, connecting different ideas by showing comparisons, contrasts, or results.

CONJUNCTIVE ADVERBS	
accordingly	indeed
again	instead
also	moreover
besides	nevertheless
consequently	otherwise
finally	then
furthermore	therefore
however	thus

Notice the punctuation that is used before and after the conjunctive adverbs in the following example. (See Chapter 25 for more about punctuation with conjunctive adverbs.)

See Practice 17.1F

EXAMPLE   This restaurant has great food; **otherwise**, I wouldn't eat here.

PRACTICE 17.1A Supplying Coordinating Conjunctions

Read the sentences. Then, write each sentence, replacing the blank with a coordinating conjunction that makes sense in the sentence.

EXAMPLE   I knew it was getting late, _____ I could not put the book down.

ANSWER   *I knew it was getting late, yet I could not put the book down.*

1. A good athlete must have strength _____ endurance.

2. Get in the car now, _____ you'll have to find another ride.

3. The quarterback delivered the pass quickly _____ accurately.

4. With time _____ patience, you can train your dog.

5. I must study tonight, _____ I have a science test in the morning.

6. The Jacksons drive a small _____ comfortable car.

7. Gina has not called, _____ she has sent me an e-mail.

8. Today is Josh's birthday, _____ we are cooking dinner for him.

9. You can put that plant in the kitchen _____ in the living room.

10. Mom remembered the gift _____ then left it in the car.

PRACTICE 17.1B Writing Sentences With Correlative Conjunctions

Write ten sentences, using each of the correlative conjunctions below.

EXAMPLE   whether . . . or

ANSWER   *I don't know whether I will go to the museum or stay home.*

            Please decide whether you would like cereal or eggs for breakfast.

11. both . . . and

12. either . . . or

13. neither . . . nor

14. not only . . . but also

15. whether . . . or

16. both . . . and

17. either . . . or

18. neither . . . nor

19. not only . . . but also

20. whether . . . or

SPEAKING APPLICATION

Tell a partner about a band you like. Your partner should listen for and name at least one coordinating conjunction and one pair of correlative conjunctions.

WRITING APPLICATION

Write two sentences about the weather. In the first sentence, use a coordinating conjunction. In the second, use a pair of correlative conjunctions.

Read the sentences. Then, write the subordinating conjunction (e.g., *because*, *since*) in each sentence.

EXAMPLE   Unless you notify the book club, you will receive a new book every month.

ANSWER   *Unless*

1. Sheryl might win the spelling bee if she spends some time studying.

2. Jamal went into the diner while everyone else waited outside.

3. Although I like my little brother, he does annoy me sometimes.

4. As soon as I have all the supplies, I will build my own kite.

5. Aunt Jo always takes us out for lunch when she is in town.

6. I can't go to the movies tonight because I have to watch my little sister.

7. I haven't seen Leona since she visited last year.

8. Jerome wants a bicycle so that he can ride to school.

9. When our lost cat was returned to us, we all cried for joy.

10. Even though I have other friends, I really miss Amanda.

Read each pair of sentences. Then, combine the sentences by using a subordinating conjunction. Discuss your sentences with a partner. Your partner should identify the subordinating conjunctions.

EXAMPLE   Jack was very slim. He could lift the barbell over his head.

ANSWER   *Although Jack was very slim, he could lift the barbell over his head.*

11. Anita rushed out of the house. She had to be at school early.

12. The baby began to giggle. I tickled her.

13. The driver stepped on the gas pedal. The car moved forward quickly.

14. Don't come to the concert. You have purchased tickets already.

15. The movers measured the entrance very carefully. They brought the refrigerator inside.

16. Everyone is seated quietly in the room. We can begin the test.

17. Logan decided to try out for the team. He is only a freshman.

18. I blow bubbles with this gum. They pop in my face.

19. You wait patiently. You might see shooting stars cross the sky.

20. We went to the game. A storm was predicted.

SPEAKING APPLICATION

Tell a partner about a career you have considered. Have your partner listen for and name at least one subordinating conjunction (e.g., *because*, *since*).

WRITING APPLICATION

Write two sentences about how you like to spend your free time. Use subordinating conjunctions in both sentences. Write one of the subordinating conjunctions at the beginning of one sentence.

PRACTICE 17.1E Writing Sentences With Subordinating Conjunctions

Read the sentences. Rewrite each, replacing the subordinating conjunction with a different one, adding words as needed. Then, discuss your sentences with a partner who should identify the subordinating conjunctions.

EXAMPLE   I ate a second bowl of cereal because I was still hungry.

ANSWER   I ate a second bowl of cereal *since* I was still hungry.

1. Before you swim, be sure to take a shower.

2. Sara can't come to the concert even though she loves the band.

3. I get tense if I am asked to speak in public.

4. As long as the rain holds off, we will go on a picnic.

5. As Michelle stole the ball, she began racing toward the goal.

6. Dennis broke his glasses after he tripped on the broken sidewalk.

7. When the police officer noticed the open door, she decided to investigate.

8. We all crowded into the back room so that we could surprise Lenore.

9. Although Janette likes pistachios best, she agreed to buy peanuts.

10. Please recycle the paper after you unwrap your presents.

PRACTICE 17.1F Identifying Conjunctive Adverbs

Read the sentences. Then, write the conjunctive adverb in each sentence.

EXAMPLE   Rosa is very smart; indeed, she is the smartest person I know.

ANSWER   *indeed*

11. Consuela wanted to take photography; however, she could not fit it in.

12. Mom is out shopping today; therefore, we'll have to fix our own lunch.

13. Rescue workers helped the frightened passengers; finally, the ordeal was over.

14. I want to get a snack; besides, the concert won't start for at least 15 minutes.

15. Rama had not used the software before; nevertheless, she was willing to try.

16. Jamal might like that group; moreover, he might buy their CDs.

17. The auditorium was filled to capacity; consequently, some people were turned away.

18. Please make sure the thermostat is turned down; otherwise, we will be wasting fuel.

19. They decided not to go to Phoenix; instead, they spent the weekend at the beach.

20. Her test scores were low; furthermore, she had missed several classes.

SPEAKING APPLICATION

Tell a partner about an upcoming concert, parade, or other event. Use at least three subordinating conjunctions. Have your partner listen for and name the subordinating conjunctions you use.

WRITING APPLICATION

Write a biographical paragraph about your favorite film star. Use several subordinating conjunctions in your paragraph.

Test Warm-Up

DIRECTIONS
Read the introduction and the passage that follows. Then, answer the questions to show that you can use and understand subordinating conjunctions in reading and writing.

Diana wrote this paragraph for her science class. Read the paragraph and think about the changes you would suggest as a peer editor. When you finish reading, answer the questions that follow.

What Causes a Lunar Eclipse?

(1) After the sun shines on Earth, it casts a shadow in space. (2) Several times a year, the moon passes through that shadow. (3) This occurs with a full moon. (4) People living on the night side of Earth will observe a lunar eclipse. (5) The moon will seem to disappear. (6) Earth is blocking the sun's light. (7) The eclipse will last as long as the moon moves out of Earth's shadow.

1 The meaning of sentence 1 can be clarified by changing the word ***After*** to —

   A When

   B So that

   C Although

   D Before

2 What is the BEST way to combine sentences 3 and 4?

   F Because this occurs with a full moon, people living on the night side of Earth will observe a lunar eclipse.

   G Before this occurs with a full moon because people living on the night side of Earth will observe a lunar eclipse.

   H As soon as this occurs with a full moon, people living on the night side of Earth will observe a lunar eclipse.

   J If this occurs with a full moon, people living on the night side of Earth will observe a lunar eclipse.

3 What is the BEST way to combine sentences 5 and 6?

   A The moon will seem to disappear in order that Earth is blocking the sun's light.

   B The moon will seem to disappear because Earth is blocking the sun's light.

   C The moon will seem to disappear, Earth is blocking the sun's light.

   D The moon will seem to disappear until Earth is blocking the sun's light.

4 The meaning of sentence 7 can be clarified by changing the phrase ***as long as*** to —

   F since

   G until

   H while

   J whenever

17.2 Interjections

The **interjection** is the part of speech that is used the least. Its only use is to express feelings or emotions.

WRITING COACH

Online
www.phwritingcoach.com

Grammar Practice

Practice your grammar skills with Writing Coach Online.

Grammar Games

Test your knowledge of grammar in this fast-paced interactive video game.

See Practice 17.2A

See Practice 17.2B

> An **interjection** expresses feeling or emotion and functions independently from the rest of a sentence.

17.2.1 RULE

An interjection has no grammatical relationship to any other word in a sentence. It is, therefore, set off from the rest of the sentence with a comma or an exclamation mark.

Interjections can express different feelings or emotions.

JOY	**Wow!** This place is fun.
SURPRISE	**Oh**, I must have called you by accident.
PAIN	**Ouch!** That was sharp.
IMPATIENCE	**Hey!** How long is the line?
HESITATION	I, **uh**, thought you had already left.

Interjections are used more in speech than in writing. They are informal, rather than formal, expressions. When you do see them in writing, they are often included in dialogue. The following chart lists words often used as interjections.

INTERJECTIONS			
ah	gosh	nonsense	ugh
aha	great	oh	uh
alas	heavens	oops	um
boy	hey	ouch	well
darn	huh	psst	what
eureka	hurray	shh	whew
fine	my	terrible	wonderful
golly	never	terrific	wow

PRACTICE 17.2A > Identifying Interjections

Read the sentences. Write the interjection in each sentence. Then, write what emotion the interjection conveys.

EXAMPLE   Wow! Look at that gymnast on the parallel bars!

ANSWER   *Wow — surprise*

1. Hey! Don't touch that cellphone.
2. Gosh, can't you be a little nicer?
3. Darn, my bicycle chain broke.
4. Ouch! That pan is still hot.
5. Whew, that was a close one.
6. Hurray! I won a prize in the sweepstakes!
7. I, uh, think I forgot to bring my lunch.
8. Gee, I never thought I'd see you here.
9. Aha! I have the answer.
10. Fine, take all the crackers you want.

PRACTICE 17.2B > Supplying Interjections

Read the sentences. Rewrite each sentence, using an appropriate interjection in place of the feeling shown in parentheses. Use a comma or an exclamation mark after each interjection.

EXAMPLE   (anger) The stain did not come out of this shirt.

ANSWER   *Darn! The stain did not come out of this shirt.*

11. (surprise) I can't believe the president shook my hand.
12. (impatience) We're going to miss the kickoff.
13. (dislike) That coat is the ugliest thing I've ever seen.
14. (pain) I stubbed my toe on the coffee table.
15. (joy) We are all so happy you got the award.
16. (annoyance) Would you kindly stop talking for just one minute?
17. (anger) You know you're not allowed to do that.
18. (relief) I thought the plane would never land.
19. (joy) I'm leaving for vacation tomorrow.
20. (surprise) I thought you'd forgotten our anniversary.

SPEAKING APPLICATION

With a partner, take turns telling about a memorable experience. Your partner should listen for and name at least two interjections.

WRITING APPLICATION

Write four sentences with interjections. Use commas to punctuate any interjections showing mild emotion, and use exclamation marks with those that show strong emotion.

PRACTICE 1 Writing Sentences With Nouns

Write five sentences, each using one of the following kinds of nouns. Circle those nouns, and underline any other nouns you use.

1. a common noun and a proper noun that name a person

2. a common noun and a proper noun that name a place

3. an abstract noun and a collective noun

4. a single-word compound noun and a hyphenated compound noun

5. a count noun and a non-count noun

PRACTICE 2 Identifying Pronouns

Read the sentences. Then, write the pronoun or pronouns that each sentence contains. Label each pronoun *personal, reflexive, intensive, demonstrative, relative, interrogative, or indefinite.*

1. We heard reports that a hurricane was coming.

2. Whose is that coat, and why is it here?

3. The chef himself made this sandwich for me.

4. Something was making everyone sleepy.

5. She took care of the problem herself.

6. Who wants something from the deli?

7. This is her best movie in years.

8. The house, which needs paint, was once ours.

9. Roger convinced himself that he was right.

10. I myself understand everything that you said.

PRACTICE 3 Using Action and Linking Verbs

Write two sentences for each word below. In the first sentence, use the word as an action verb; in the second sentence, use it as a linking verb.

1. look

2. feel

3. grow

4. sound

5. appear

PRACTICE 4 Identifying Helping Verbs and Main Verbs in Verb Phrases

Read the sentences. Then, write the complete verb phrase in each sentence. Label the parts of each verb phrase *helping* or *main.*

1. Mina has been my friend since kindergarten.

2. The waiter is carrying a large tray of food.

3. I did not see you on the bus this morning.

4. Dad's trip has been postponed until Monday.

5. Peter will never arrive on time.

6. Everyone can sing along.

7. She would not tell me the answer.

8. The hotel was completely renovated last year.

9. The ballgame should be over soon.

10. Have you ever visited Mexico?

Continued on next page ▶

PRACTICE 5 > Revising Sentences With Adjectives and Adverbs

Read the sentences. Then, rewrite each sentence by adding at least one adjective to modify a noun or a pronoun or one adverb to modify a verb, an adjective, or another adverb.

1. Clara knitted a scarf.
2. The day was warm.
3. The child ran up the steps.
4. The nurse spoke to Dad.
5. A vase of flowers sat on the table.
6. The ambulance driver tore through the streets.
7. An alligator crawled onto the road.
8. The man yelled from the other side of the room.
9. The trees stood like soldiers along the stream.
10. Have you eaten in that restaurant?

PRACTICE 6 > Writing Sentences With Prepositions and Adverbs

Write ten sentences describing outdoor activities. In your first five sentences, use the prepositional phrases in items 1–5. In your next five sentences, use the words in items 6–10 as adverbs.

1. beyond the gate
2. after an hour
3. outside the building
4. across the street
5. along the edge
6. beyond
7. after
8. outside
9. across
10. along

PRACTICE 7 > Identifying Conjunctions

Read the sentences. Then, identify each underlined word or pair of words as a *coordinating conjunction*, a *subordinating conjunction*, *correlative conjunctions*, or a *conjunctive adverb*.

1. I saw Karen, <u>but</u> she did not see me.
2. Everyone hurried to class <u>after</u> the bell rang.
3. <u>Both</u> Neil <u>and</u> Fran are away for the summer.
4. I know the answer; <u>therefore</u>, I'll raise my hand.
5. Myra <u>or</u> her brother will walk the dog.

PRACTICE 8 > Revising to Include Interjections

Rewrite the following dialogue, adding interjections to show the speakers' emotions. Use either a comma or an exclamation mark after each interjection.

RAUL: Did you see that tornado yesterday?

AMANDA: Mom and I saw it when we were driving home from the supermarket.

RAUL: I'm glad you are both all right.

AMANDA: It was pretty scary for a few minutes.

RAUL: At least we know what to do in emergencies.

AMANDA: Yes. Mom and I were talking about that.

RAUL: As Mom always says, it's important to have a plan.

BASIC SENTENCE PARTS

While it is important to pair interesting subjects and verbs in your writing, your sentences should also have strong finishes with well-chosen direct objects.

WRITE GUY *Jeff Anderson, M.Ed.*

WHAT DO YOU NOTICE?

Track down the sentence parts as you zoom in on this verse from the poem "Ode to Enchanted Light" by Pablo Neruda.

MENTOR TEXT

> A cicada sends
> its sawing song
> high into the empty air.

Now, ask yourself the following questions:

- What are the subject and verb in this verse?
- What is the direct object of the verb?

The subject is *cicada,* and the verb is *sends.* The noun *song* is the direct object because it receives the action of the verb *sends.* You can figure this out by asking *what* the cicada sends.

Grammar for Writers Strong writing shows how people, things, and events affect one another. To craft dynamic sentences, consider the relationships among your subjects, verbs, and direct objects.

My brother hid my favorite game.

Looks like your game is the direct object of his game.

18.1 The Basic Sentence

There are many kinds of sentences. Some are short; others are long. Some are simple, and others are more complex. In order to be considered complete, a sentence must have two things: a subject and a verb.

The Two Basic Parts of a Sentence

Every sentence, regardless of its length, must have a subject and a verb.

RULE 18.1.1 A complete **sentence** contains a subject and a verb and expresses a complete thought.

The Subject

A sentence must have a **subject.** Most subjects are nouns or pronouns. The subject is usually, but not always, found near the beginning of the sentence.

RULE 18.1.2 The **subject** of a sentence is the word or group of words that names the person, place, thing, or idea that performs the action or is described. It answers the question *Who?* or *What?* before the verb.

EXAMPLES   The **pantry** is full.

Mr. Halpern broke his new mug.

He knows how to fix it.

Glue will fix the mug.

The noun *pantry* is the subject in the first sentence. It tells *what is full*. In the next sentence, the proper noun *Mr. Halpern* tells *who* broke his mug. The pronoun *he* in the third sentence tells *who can fix it*. The noun *Glue* in the fourth sentence tells *what can fix it*.

The Verb

As one of the basic parts of a sentence, the **verb** tells something about the subject.

18.1.3 RULE

> The **verb** in a sentence tells what the subject does, what is done to the subject, or what the condition of the subject is.

EXAMPLES   My sister **won** first place.

Her speech **was presented** at the ceremony.

She **seemed** nervous.

Won tells what *my sister* did. *Was presented* explains what was done with *the speech. Seemed*, a linking verb, tells something about the condition of *she* by linking the subject to *nervous.*

See Practice 18.1A

Using Subjects and Verbs to Express Complete Thoughts

Every basic sentence must express a complete thought.

18.1.4 RULE

> A sentence is a group of words with a subject and a verb that expresses a complete thought and can stand by itself and still make sense.

INCOMPLETE THOUGHT   in the pantry in the kitchen
(This group of words cannot stand by itself as a sentence.)

This incomplete thought contains two prepositional phrases. The phrases can become a sentence only after *both* a subject and a verb are added to them.

COMPLETE THOUGHT   The **pasta is** in the pantry in the kitchen.
                                           subject verb
(This group of words can stand by itself as a sentence.)

See Practice 18.1B   In grammar, incomplete thoughts are often called **fragments.**

PRACTICE 18.1A Finding Subjects and Verbs

Read the sentences. Write the subject and verb of each sentence.

EXAMPLE My injured wrist is bothering me again.

ANSWER *wrist, is bothering*

1. The creation of a television show is a complex process.

2. A very pleased teacher addressed her first-period class.

3. Tomorrow they will begin their long journey.

4. The book describes the causes of World War II.

5. On special occasions Keiko wears a Japanese kimono.

6. Different dogs need different kinds of training.

7. We have enjoyed our time at the Native American pueblo.

8. Over the summer Juan visited several national parks.

9. The reasons for my decision are good ones.

10. Your hospitality has been delightful.

PRACTICE 18.1B Recognizing Complete Thoughts

Read the following groups of words. If a group of words expresses a complete thought, write *complete.* If a group of words expresses an incomplete thought, write *incomplete.*

EXAMPLE To survive the drought.

ANSWER *incomplete*

11. Rodents living underground.

12. If the police do not get here soon.

13. Jamal borrowed two novels from his cousin.

14. The bridge was washed out by the flooding.

15. This afternoon we will go swimming.

16. In the building next to the barbershop.

17. Julio and Felicia decided to mow the lawn.

18. A long report about the American Revolution.

19. Because she was very interested in politics.

20. Mr. Cruz can no longer depend on that old computer.

SPEAKING APPLICATION

With a partner, take turns describing a recent assembly at school. Your partner should listen for and name the subject and verb in each of your sentences.

WRITING APPLICATION

Write three sentences about the beach. Make sure each sentence expresses a complete thought. Underline each subject and circle each verb.

18.2 Complete Subjects and Predicates

Have you ever seen tiles laid on a floor? First, a line is drawn in the center of the room. One tile is placed to the left of the line, and another is placed to the right. Then, more tiles are added in the same way: one to the left and one to the right.

WRITING COACH

Online

www.phwritingcoach.com

Grammar Practice

Practice your grammar skills with Writing Coach Online.

Grammar Games

Test your knowledge of grammar in this fast-paced interactive video game.

Imagine that the first tile on the left is a subject and the first tile on the right is a verb. You would then have a subject and a verb separated by a vertical line, as shown in the example.

EXAMPLE   **Hair** | **fell** .

Now, in the same way that you would add a few more tiles if you were tiling a floor, add a few more words.

EXAMPLE   Blonde **hair** | **fell** on the floor.

At this point, you could add still more words.

EXAMPLE   Margaret's long blonde **hair** | **fell** on the floor in piles.

The centerline is important in laying tiles. It is just as important in dividing these sentences into two parts. All the words to the left of the line in the preceding examples are part of the **complete subject.** The main noun in the complete subject, *hair*, is often called the **simple subject.**

> The **complete subject** of a sentence consists of the subject and any words related to it.

RULE
18.2.1

As in the examples above, the complete subject may be just one word—*hair*—or several words—*Margaret's long blonde hair.*

Look at the example sentences again, plus one with new words added.

EXAMPLES Blonde **hair** | **fell** on the floor.

Margaret's long blonde **hair** | **fell** on the floor in piles.

Margaret's long blonde **hair** | **had fallen** on the floor when it was cut.

All the words to the right of the line in the preceding examples are part of the **complete predicate.** The verb *fell*, or a verb phrase such as *had fallen*, on the other hand, is often called the **simple predicate.**

See Practice 18.2A

> The **complete predicate** of a sentence consists of the verb and any words related to it.

As the examples show, a complete predicate may be just the verb itself or the verb and several other words.

Many sentences do not divide so neatly into subject and predicate. Look at the subjects and predicates in the following sentences.

EXAMPLES **After the movie** , my **friends** **went home** .

With the waves crashing , the **surfers** **jumped into the water** .

In these sentences, part of the predicate comes *before* the subject, and the rest of the predicate follows the subject.

As you have seen, a complete simple sentence contains a simple subject and a simple predicate. In addition, a complete simple sentence expresses a complete thought.

See Practice 18.2B

PRACTICE 18.2A > Identifying Complete Subjects and Predicates

Read the sentences. Rewrite each sentence, and draw a vertical line between the complete subject and the complete predicate. Then, underline the subject once and the verb twice.

EXAMPLE   A terrible tornado was sweeping across the county.

ANSWER   *A terrible tornado | was sweeping across the county.*

1. The woman in blue danced in front of the stage.

2. The two bicycles sat in the garage for months.

3. Heather described her anxieties about the social studies exam.

4. The cherry tree in their backyard has burst into flower.

5. Bernice makes her own jewelry with beads.

6. Small red spots appeared on the little boy's face.

7. Alicia grinned at the children in the park.

8. A large statue of a cowboy stands in the courtyard.

9. Her sister was enjoying the drive.

10. The lawyer's argument did not persuade the judge.

PRACTICE 18.2B > Writing Complete Sentences

Read the items. Each item contains either a complete subject or a complete predicate. Rewrite each item along with the missing part to create complete sentences.

EXAMPLE   _____ drove onto the sidewalk.

ANSWER   *The taxi driver drove onto the sidewalk.*

11. The set for the school play _____.

12. _____ played three songs at halftime.

13. The young basketball coach _____.

14. _____ was hard to fix.

15. My favorite social studies project _____.

16. _____ is much lower now.

17. The local library _____.

18. _____ is a movie I would like to see.

19. The girl and her family _____.

20. _____ might win the chess tournament.

SPEAKING APPLICATION

Tell a partner about a Web site that you have found useful for research. Your partner should listen for the complete subject and complete predicate in each of your sentences.

WRITING APPLICATION

Use sentence 1 as a model, and write three complete sentences of your own. Make sure each of your sentences has a complete subject and a complete predicate.

18.3 Compound Subjects and Compound Verbs

Some sentences have more than one subject. Some have more than one verb.

WRITING COACH

Online

www.phwritingcoach.com

Grammar Practice
Practice your grammar skills with Writing Coach Online.

Grammar Games
Test your knowledge of grammar in this fast-paced interactive video game.

Recognizing Compound Subjects

A sentence containing more than one subject is said to have a **compound subject.**

RULE 18.3.1

> A **compound subject** is two or more subjects that have the same verb and are joined by a conjunction such as *and* or *or.*

EXAMPLES

Parrots and hamsters are small house pets.

compound subject   verb

Singers, dancers, and other artists can learn

compound subject   verb

to perform together.

Recognizing Compound Verbs

A sentence with two or more verbs is said to have a **compound verb.**

RULE 18.3.2

> A **compound verb** is two or more verbs that have the same subject and are joined by a conjunction such as *and* or *or.*

EXAMPLES

The committee may or may not succeed.

subject   compound verb

She plans, organizes, and hosts all the

subject   compound verb

charity events.

Sometimes a sentence will have both a compound subject and a compound verb.

EXAMPLE

Jim and Tara danced and sang at the party.

compound subject   compound verb

See Practice 18.3A
See Practice 18.3B

PRACTICE 18.3A **Recognizing Compound Subjects and
Compound Verbs**

Read the sentences. Write the compound subject and/or the
compound verb in each sentence.

EXAMPLE The dolphins and the trainer work well together
and give an entertaining show.

ANSWER *dolphins, trainer* — *compound subject*
work, give — *compound verb*

1. Toys for dogs and birdseed can be found in Aisle 3.

2. At the skate park Tamesa and Randall got some minor
scrapes.

3. My sister jogs or rides her bike almost every day.

4. The host and the contestants smiled and waved at the
audience.

5. The squirrel chattered loudly and then scampered across
a low branch.

6. Bananas, granola, or fresh peaches taste great with plain
yogurt.

7. The trail winds up the mountain and gradually narrows
near the top.

8. Phoenix and Tucson are both large cities in Arizona.

9. The bear stomped into the river, caught a salmon, and
brought it to her cubs.

10. Balloons or flowers can make a room more festive and
lift everyone's spirits.

SPEAKING APPLICATION

Take turns telling a
partner about an exciting
amusement park ride
you have heard about or
experienced. Your partner
should listen for and name
at least one compound
subject and one compound
verb.

WRITING APPLICATION

Use sentence 2 as a model,
and write two more
sentences that contain
compound subjects. Then,
use sentence 5 as a model
to write two sentences that
contain compound verbs.

PRACTICE 18.3B ▷ **Combining Sentences With Compound Subjects and Compound Verbs**

Read the sentences. Combine each pair of sentences by using compound subjects or compound verbs.

EXAMPLE   The kite dipped suddenly. Then it wrapped itself around a tree.

ANSWER   *The kite dipped suddenly and then wrapped itself around a tree.*

1. Russia traded with the Vikings. France traded with the Vikings.

2. Silent film actors delighted audiences. Silent film actors entertained audiences.

3. Langston Hughes was born in Missouri. He grew up in Kansas and Ohio.

4. Joggers crowd the park every afternoon. Cyclists crowd the park every afternoon.

5. Carlos has a broken leg. He is not able to go hiking with us.

6. The rattlesnake gave a warning. Then it struck Joe's leg.

7. Near the wall, daisies grew in abundance. Bluebonnets grew in abundance.

8. The dentist will clean your teeth. His assistant might clean them instead.

9. Deanna searched the Internet. Deanna found a Web site with some pictures of monarch butterflies.

10. Greeting cards can be found near the front of the store. Wrapping paper can be found near the front, too.

SPEAKING APPLICATION

Take turns telling a partner about a museum you have heard about or visited. Your partner should listen for and name at least one compound subject and one compound verb.

WRITING APPLICATION

Write two sentences with compound subjects and two sentences with compound verbs.

18.4 Hard-to-Find Subjects

It can be difficult to identify simple subjects in certain sentences. These sentences do not follow **normal word order** in which the subject comes before the verb. Sometimes the subject will follow the verb or part of a verb phrase. This is called **inverted word order.** Questions are often presented in inverted word order.

www.phwritingcoach.com

Grammar Practice

Practice your grammar skills with Writing Coach Online.

Grammar Games

Test your knowledge of grammar in this fast-paced interactive video game.

NORMAL WORD ORDER

The **ceremony** **will begin** at 6:00 P.M.
       subject   verb

INVERTED WORD ORDER

When **will** the **ceremony** **begin**?
     verb   subject   verb

Sometimes the subject will not actually be stated in the sentence. It will be understood to be the pronoun *you*. This is often true in sentences that express commands or requests.

The Subject of a Command or Request

When a sentence commands or requests someone to do something, the subject is often unstated.

> The subject of a command or request is understood to be the pronoun *you*.

RULE 18.4.1

COMMANDS OR REQUESTS	HOW THE SENTENCES ARE UNDERSTOOD
Wait!	You wait!
Stop at once!	You stop at once!
Please sit down.	You please sit down.
Tara, take a message.	Tara, you take a message.
Mike, get the groceries.	Mike, you get the groceries.

See Practice 18.4A

Even though a command or request may begin with the name of the person spoken to, the subject is still understood to be *you*.

Finding Subjects in Questions

Questions are often presented in inverted word order. You will usually find the subject in the middle of the sentence.

> **In questions, the subject often follows the verb.**

Some questions in inverted word order begin with the words *what, whom, when, where, why,* and *how.* Others begin with the verb itself or with a helping verb.

EXAMPLES   How **are** the **puppies** this morning?

Did **you** **hold** them yet?

Have **you** **found** owners for them yet?

If you ever have trouble finding the subject in a question, use this trick: Change the question into a statement. The subject will then appear in normal word order before the verb.

QUESTIONS	REWORDED AS STATEMENTS
How is your sister?	Your sister is how today.
What did the manager say?	The manager did say what.
Were the grades posted?	The grades were posted today.
Did she bring the tickets with her?	She did bring the tickets with her.

Not every question is in inverted word order. Some are in normal word order, with the subject before the verb. Questions beginning with *who, whose,* or *which* often follow normal word order.

EXAMPLES   **Who** **has** the keys?

Whose **car** **can go** the fastest?

Which **car** **would handle** the best?

See Practice 18.4B

PRACTICE 18.4A **Identifying Subjects in Commands or Requests**

Read the sentences. Write the subject of each sentence.

EXAMPLE   Just imagine the size of the solar system.

ANSWER   *you*

1. Listen to the lyrics carefully.

2. Jasmine, try to start the car now.

3. After finishing lunch, please clean the dishes.

4. Terri, practice the piano now.

5. Tell me about the marathon, Ernesto.

6. Carmen, choose only the freshest fruits.

7. Just throw those pillows onto the couch for now.

8. Angela, give your sister this book.

9. Please chop the onions while I peel the potatoes.

10. Measure the amount of snow that fell last night.

PRACTICE 18.4B **Finding Subjects in Questions**

Read the questions. Write the subject of each question. If you have trouble finding the subject in a question, change the question into a statement.

EXAMPLE   Has the speaker arrived at the convention center?

ANSWER   *speaker*

11. What did the governor say?

12. Will the fruit stay fresh for three days?

13. Has Mr. Hernandez seen the art exhibit?

14. Why have they blocked off this road?

15. When did the news reach the school?

16. Did the veterinarian cure the cat?

17. Are the actors ready to take the stage?

18. Which train did you take this morning?

19. Whom did the technician call?

20. How is the patient today?

SPEAKING APPLICATION

With a partner, take turns describing an outdoor adventure. Use at least one sentence that is a direction or an order and one that is a question, and have your partner name the subjects.

WRITING APPLICATION

Write one sentence that is a direction or an order and one that is a question. Underline the subject in each sentence.

Finding the Subject in Sentences Beginning With *There* or *Here*

Sentences beginning with *there* or *here* are usually in inverted word order.

> **There or here is never the subject of a sentence.**

There can be used to start a sentence.

SENTENCE
STARTER
There are two choices for new head chef.

There or *here* can also be used as an adverb at the beginning of sentences. As adverbs, these two words point out *where* and modify the verbs.

ADVERB
There is the famous painter.

Here is the first painting he ever sold.

Be alert to sentences beginning with *there* and *here*. They are probably in inverted word order, with the verb appearing before the subject. If you cannot find the subject, reword the sentence in normal word order. If *there* is just a sentence starter, you can drop it from your reworded sentence.

SENTENCES BEGINNING WITH *THERE* OR *HERE*	REWORDED WITH SUBJECT BEFORE VERB
There is a mistake on the exam.	A mistake is there on the exam.
Here comes the instructor of the exam.	The instructor of the exam comes here.

See Practice 18.4C

Finding the Subject in Sentences Inverted for Emphasis

Sometimes a subject is intentionally put after its verb to draw attention to the subject.

> **In some sentences, the subject follows the verb in order to emphasize the subject, or make it stand out.**

In the following examples, notice how the order of the words builds suspense by leading up to the subject.

EXAMPLES

Wandering in the midst of the large crowd **was**
   verb   verb

a lost **puppy**.
     subject

Running through the yard **was** a **group** of
  verb   verb   subject

giggling children.

Hiding under the big leafy bush **was** the
  verb   verb

white **rabbit**.
     subject

You can reword sentences such as these in normal word order to make it easier to find the subject.

INVERTED WORD ORDER	REWORDED WITH SUBJECT BEFORE VERB
Wandering in the midst of the large crowd was a lost puppy.	A lost puppy was wandering in the midst of the large crowd.
Running through the yard was a group of giggling children.	A group of giggling children was running through the yard.
Hiding under the big leafy bush was the white rabbit.	The white rabbit was hiding under the big leafy bush.

See Practice 18.4D

Hard-to-Find Subjects

PRACTICE 18.4C **Identifying Subjects in Sentences Beginning With *Here* or *There***

Read the sentences. Write the subject of each sentence.

EXAMPLE   There might be another solution to that problem.

ANSWER   *solution*

1. There is a fly in the kitchen.
2. Here is the button from your coat.
3. Here comes your biggest fan.
4. There are the missing pieces from the puzzle.
5. Here are your shoes.
6. There are twenty passengers on that bus.
7. There should be a better way.
8. Here is the most difficult question of all.
9. There goes the superhero now!
10. Here comes another group of students.

PRACTICE 18.4D **Identifying Subjects in Sentences Inverted for Emphasis**

Read the sentences. Write the subject of each sentence.

EXAMPLE   From deep in the trench came the squeals of a puppy.

ANSWER   *squeals*

11. Next to the old firehouse is a French bakery.
12. On the top of the building sits an elegant dome.
13. Alongside the elderly lady were two young girls with backpacks.
14. Off the bench sprang an eager backup quarterback.
15. In the middle of the courtyard stood a huge, decorative water fountain.
16. All over the floor lay old photographs from the albums.
17. On that hill once stood a small chapel.
18. Not far from the lake was an old abandoned house.
19. Out of the shadows stepped a dark figure.
20. In a tiny cottage deep in the woods lived a mysterious old man.

SPEAKING APPLICATION

Tell a partner about a scary moment you experienced or imagined. Your partner should listen for one sentence beginning with *here* or *there* and one sentence with inverted word order for emphasis.

WRITING APPLICATION

Use sentence 19 as a model, and write two more sentences with inverted word order. Underline the subject in each sentence.

18.5 Complements

Often, a subject and verb alone can express a complete thought. For example, *Birds fly* can stand by itself as a sentence, even though it contains only two words, a subject and a verb. Other times, however, the thought begun by a subject and its verb must be completed with other words. For example, *Heather collected, The coach told, Our teacher was, Michael feels,* and *Kelly won* all contain a subject and verb, but none expresses a complete thought. All these ideas need **complements.**

RULE 18.5.1

A **complement** is a word or group of words that completes the meaning of a sentence.

www.phwritingcoach.com

Grammar Tutorials

Brush up on your Grammar skills with these animated videos.

Grammar Practice

Practice your grammar skills with Writing Coach Online.

Grammar Games

Test your knowledge of grammar in this fast-paced interactive video game.

Complements are usually nouns, pronouns, or adjectives. They are located right after or very close to the verb. The complements are shown below in blue. The complements answer questions about the subject or verb in order to complete the sentence.

DIFFERENT KINDS OF COMPLEMENTS

Heather **collected** **books**.
subject · verb · complement

The **coach** **told** **us** the **rules**.
· subject · verb · complements

Our **teacher** **was** **tired**.
· subject · verb complement

Michael **feels** **sick**.
subject · verb complement

Kelly **won** the **high jump**.
subject · verb · complement

This section will describe three types of complements: **direct objects, indirect objects,** and **subject complements.** All complements add information about the subjects or verbs in the sentence. They paint a clearer picture that helps the reader understand the writer's thoughts.

Recognizing Direct Objects

Direct objects follow action verbs.

> A **direct object** is a noun or pronoun that receives the action of a verb.

You can find a direct object by asking *What?* or *Whom?* after an action verb.

EXAMPLES

My older **sister** **found** the hidden **passageway**.
    subject verb   direct object

I **called** **Matt** later that night.
subject verb direct object

My friend **Kris** **likes** a relaxing **swim**
    subject verb   direct object
before bedtime.

Passageway, Matt, and *swim* are the direct objects of the verbs in the examples. In the first sentence, *passageway* answers the question *Found what?* In the second sentence, *Matt* answers the question *Called whom?* In the third sentence, *swim* answers the question *Likes what?*

Compound Direct Objects
Like subjects and verbs, direct objects can be compound. That is, one verb can have two or more direct objects.

EXAMPLES

The **cat** **eats** **tuna** and other **food**.
  subject verb direct   direct object
        object

The **board** **chose** **Mrs. Fried**,
  subject verb direct object

Mrs. Kennedy, and **Mrs. Greene** to organize
direct object   direct object
the event.

See Practice 18.5A

See Practice 18.5B

PRACTICE 18.5A > Recognizing Direct Objects

Read the sentences. Write the direct object or the compound direct object in each sentence.

EXAMPLE   Jan told Vince and him about the movie.

ANSWER   *Vince, him*

1. Sari brought a gift to the party.

2. The enthusiastic tourists took many pictures.

3. Jermaine attended a festive parade.

4. He bought pants, shoes, and a baseball cap.

5. In the morning Mom will take me to the soccer match.

6. The new bicycle has ten speeds and special wheels.

7. Please ask Ted and them about the plans for tonight.

8. For his birthday my father got a sweater and a tie.

9. Tyrell twisted his ankle yesterday.

10. The pandas were eating bamboo.

PRACTICE 18.5B > Adding Complements

Read the sentences. Rewrite the sentences, and fill in the blanks with appropriate direct objects. Use both nouns and pronouns.

EXAMPLE   The ship reached ____ very late.

ANSWER   *The ship reached port very late.*

11. Tell ____ about the concert.

12. I want ____ and ____ to join the team.

13. Alicia asked ____ about the science teacher.

14. At the store, get some ____, ____, and ____.

15. I saw ____ in the park this morning.

16. Then she took ____ on a long drive.

17. Last night Terri wrote ____ for class.

18. The boys do not have ____ for the play.

19. The children greeted ____ and ____ warmly.

20. Sara built a ____ and a ____ in woodworking class.

SPEAKING APPLICATION

With a partner, take turns describing how to fix a favorite snack. Your partner should listen for and name at least two direct objects.

WRITING APPLICATION

Use sentence 20 as a model, and write two sentences with compound direct objects.

Distinguishing Between Direct Objects, Adverbs, and Objects of Prepositions

Not all action verbs have direct objects. Be careful not to confuse a direct object with an adverb or with the object of a preposition. If you are unsure if a word or phrase is a direct object, ask yourself who or what is receiving the action of the verb.

RULE 18.5.3

> **A direct object is never an adverb or the noun or pronoun at the end of a prepositional phrase.**

Compare the following examples. Notice that the action verb *drove* has a direct object in only the first sentence.

EXAMPLES

Rich **drove** his **motorcycle**.
subject — verb — direct object

Rich **drove** **slowly**.
subject — verb — adverb

Rich **drove** **through the park**.
subject — verb — prepositional phrase

Each example shows a very common sentence type. The first consists of a subject, a verb, and a direct object. The noun *motorcycle* is the direct object of the verb *drove*.

The second example consists of a subject, a verb, and an adverb. Nothing after the verb in the sentence answers the question *What?* so there is no direct object. *Slowly* modifies the verb and tells *how* Rich drove.

The third example consists of a subject, a verb, and a prepositional phrase. Again, no noun or pronoun answers the question *What?* after the verb. The prepositional phrase tells *where* Rich drove.

Notice also that a single sentence can contain more than one of these three parts.

EXAMPLE

Rich **drove** his **motorcycle** **slowly**
subject — verb — direct object — adverb
through the park.
prepositional phrase

See Practice 18.5C

Finding Direct Objects in Questions

In normal word order, a direct object follows a verb. In questions that are in inverted word order, however, the direct object often appears before the verb and subject.

> **A direct object in a question will sometimes be found before the verb.**

18.5.4 RULE

In the following chart, questions are paired with sentences reworded in normal word order. Compare the positions of the direct objects in each. Direct objects are highlighted in pink, subjects are highlighted in yellow, and verbs are highlighted in orange.

QUESTIONS	REWORDED IN NORMAL WORD ORDER
What sport does she play best?	She does play what sport best?
What does the puppy eat?	The puppy does eat what.
Which car do you like, the red sports car or the black convertible?	You do like which car, the red sports car or the black convertible.
Whom did you meet at the store?	You did meet whom at the store.

In each of the five questions, the direct object appears before, rather than after, the verb. To locate the direct object in a question, put the sentence into normal word order with the subject appearing before the verb. Then, the direct object will be found in its usual position after the verb.

See Practice 18.5D

PRACTICE 18.5C > Distinguishing Direct Object, Adverb, and Object of a Preposition

Read the sentences. Label each underlined word *DO* for direct object, *ADV* for adverb, or *OP* for object of a preposition.

EXAMPLE   Stepping off the ferry, the passengers smiled <u>broadly</u>.

ANSWER   *ADV*

1. In the spring Colin plants <u>peppers</u> in his garden.

2. Near noon we stopped at a roadside <u>diner</u>.

3. Marcus really wants a new <u>pair</u> of in-line skates.

4. In high school my sister played <u>basketball</u>.

5. He leapt <u>suddenly</u> onto the stage.

6. Mr. McNabb changes his <u>mind</u> frequently.

7. I made these <u>candles</u> from a kit.

8. Much to our disappointment, the team played <u>poorly</u>.

9. Rosita has taken her sister to the <u>park</u>.

10. He opened the package <u>eagerly</u>.

PRACTICE 18.5D > Finding Direct Objects in Questions

Read the questions. Write the direct object in each question.

EXAMPLE   Whom did you visit in Spokane?

ANSWER   *Whom*

11. Which shoes did she lose?

12. When will the electrician fix the wiring?

13. What reasons did he give?

14. Which role in the skit do you want?

15. Whom does the host expect?

16. Where did Raphael leave the scissors?

17. When will the workers finish the bridge?

18. What did you order for Gabriel?

19. How many movies did you see this year?

20. What did you write in the e-mail?

SPEAKING APPLICATION

Tell a partner about your favorite television show. Your partner should listen for and name at least two direct objects, one adverb, and one object of a preposition.

WRITING APPLICATION

Write three sentences with direct objects. Make at least one of your sentences a question.

Recognizing Indirect Objects

Sentences with a direct object may also contain another kind of complement, called an **indirect object.** A sentence cannot have an indirect object unless it has a direct object.

> An **indirect object** is a noun or pronoun that comes after an action verb and before a direct object. It names the person or thing to which something is given or for which something is done.

18.5.5 RULE

An indirect object answers the questions *To* or *for whom?* or *To* or *for what?* after an action verb. To find an indirect object, find the direct object first. Then, ask the appropriate question.

EXAMPLE **Grandpa read us a book** before bedtime.
          indirect direct
          object   object

(Read *what?* [*book*])
(Read the book *to whom?* [*us*])

Keep in mind the following pattern: *Subject + Verb + Indirect Object + Direct Object.* An indirect object will almost always come between the verb and the direct object in a sentence.

Compound Indirect Objects

Like a subject, verb, or direct object, an indirect object can be compound.

EXAMPLES **Tara gave** each **dog and cat** a
           subject verb   compound indirect object

treat.
direct object

(Gave *what?* [*treat*])
(Gave a treat *to what?* [*each dog and cat*])

Aunt Sarah offered Kate and me
 subject   verb   compound indirect object

sunglasses and lemonade.
       compound direct object

(Offered *what?* [*sunglasses and lemonade*])
(Offered sunglasses and lemonade to *whom?* [*Kate and me*])

See Practice 18.5E

Distinguishing Between Indirect Objects and Objects of Prepositions

Do not confuse an indirect object with the object of a preposition.

> An indirect object never follows the preposition *to* or *for* in a sentence.

Compare the following examples.

EXAMPLES   Betsy bought **her** a **stereo**.
                      indirect   direct object
                      object

            Betsy bought a **stereo** for **her**.
                      direct object   object of
                                       preposition

In the first example above, *her* is an indirect object. It comes after the verb *bought* and before the direct object *stereo*. In the second example, *her* is the object of the preposition *for* and follows the direct object *stereo*.

EXAMPLES   Brian gave **Nicole** a **letter**.
                      indirect   direct
                      object   object

            Brian gave a **letter** to **Nicole**.
                      direct   object of
                      object   preposition

To find the indirect object in the first example above, you must first find the direct object. Ask yourself what Brian gave. He gave a letter, so *letter* is the direct object. Then, ask yourself to whom Brian gave the letter. He gave it to *Nicole*, so *Nicole* is the indirect object.

Use the same questions in the second example. Again, *letter* is the direct object of *gave*; however, *Nicole* is no longer the indirect object. Instead, it is the object of the preposition *to*.

See Practice 18.5F

PRACTICE 18.5E ▶ Recognizing Indirect Objects

Read the sentences. Write the indirect object in each sentence.

EXAMPLE   The museum gives visitors an educational experience.

ANSWER   *visitors*

1. The zoo veterinarian gave the tiger excellent care.

2. Aunt Polly bought me a ticket to the show.

3. Mrs. Jefferson will give Mark and Terrence their assignment.

4. Would you show us the dance steps?

5. The clerk sold the girls some rings from the display case.

6. For his birthday, order Dad a pair of slippers.

7. The principal handed Rama and me our certificates.

8. I will give the teacher the answers she wants.

9. Did Ira buy his mother a necklace?

10. Pass your cousin the plate of chicken.

PRACTICE 18.5F ▶ Distinguishing Indirect Object and Object of a Preposition

Read the sentences. Write whether the underlined word is an *indirect object* or an *object of a preposition*.

EXAMPLE   The tour guide gave the brochures to the <u>visitors</u>.

ANSWER   *object of a preposition*

11. Tamika gave the CD to her <u>friend</u>.

12. Mom ordered <u>me</u> a new pair of contact lenses.

13. The director read <u>us</u> the stage directions.

14. Have you made a burrito for your <u>brother</u>?

15. Show your <u>mother</u> that funny cartoon.

16. In the lobby, a lady gave a phone number to <u>him</u>.

17. Have you read <u>Jody</u> your poem yet?

18. Jorge told the story to the <u>children</u>.

19. At the concert we handed the <u>usher</u> our tickets.

20. I have saved some mashed potatoes for <u>Jake</u>.

SPEAKING APPLICATION

With a partner, take turns describing a game. Your partner should listen for and name at least two indirect objects.

WRITING APPLICATION

Use sentence 5 as a model, and write three sentences with indirect objects.

Subject Complements

Both direct objects and indirect objects are complements used with action verbs. Linking verbs, however, have a different kind of complement called a **subject complement.** Like direct and indirect objects, subject complements add information to a sentence. However, subject complements give readers more information about the subject of the sentence, not the verb.

> **A subject complement** is a noun, pronoun, or adjective that follows a linking verb and provides important details about the subject.

Predicate Nouns and Pronouns

Both nouns and pronouns are sometimes used as subject complements after linking verbs.

> **A predicate noun** or **predicate pronoun** follows a linking verb and renames or identifies the subject of the sentence.

It is easy to recognize predicate nouns and predicate pronouns. The linking verb acts much like an equal sign between the subject and the noun or pronoun that follows the verb. Both the subject and the predicate noun or pronoun refer to the same person or thing.

EXAMPLES

Rosa **will be** **chair** of the department.
subject   verb   predicate noun

(The predicate noun *chair* renames the subject *Rosa*.)

My first **dog** **was** a **poodle**.
     subject   verb   predicate noun

(The predicate noun *poodle* identifies the subject *dog*.)

The **winners** **were** **they**.
    subject   verb   predicate
                    pronoun

(The predicate pronoun *they* identifies the subject *winners*.)

See Practice 18.5G

See Practice 18.5H

Predicate Adjectives

A linking verb can also be followed by a **predicate adjective.**

> **A predicate adjective** follows a linking verb and describes the subject of the sentence.

RULE 18.5.9

A predicate adjective is considered part of the complete predicate of a sentence because it comes after a linking verb. In spite of this, a predicate adjective does not modify the words in the predicate. Instead, it describes the noun or pronoun that serves as the subject of the linking verb.

EXAMPLES

The **trip** to Washington, D.C., **was** **long**.
subject / verb / predicate adjective

(The predicate adjective *long* describes the subject *trip*.)

The **senator** **seemed** very **anxious**
subject / verb / predicate adjective
to speak to the audience.

(The predicate adjective *anxious* describes the subject *senator*.)

Compound Subject Complements

Like other sentence parts, subject complements can be compound.

> **A compound subject complement** consists of two or more predicate nouns, pronouns, or adjectives joined by a conjunction such as *and* or *or*.

RULE 18.5.10

EXAMPLES

My two favorite **fruits** **are** **pears and apples**.
subject / verb / compound predicate noun

The **sand** **felt** **hot and grainy**.
subject / verb / compound predicate adjective

See Practice 18.5I
See Practice 18.5J

The **batter** **will be** **either he or she**.
subject / verb / compound predicate pronoun

PRACTICE 18.5G ▷ Identifying Predicate Nouns and Predicate Pronouns

Read the sentences. Write the predicate nouns or predicate pronouns in each sentence.

EXAMPLE   At the scene, police were the ones who found evidence of a break-in.

ANSWER   *ones*

1. Ecuador is a small country in South America.
2. Barack Obama became President in 2009.
3. Baseball is my favorite sport in the summer.
4. The Alps are an important part of the beauty of Switzerland.
5. The best singer has never been he.
6. Callie should be the new treasurer of the student council.
7. The border collie is a dog with a great deal of energy.
8. My uncle is a funny guy and also a wonderful chef.
9. In this short story, the main character is a sailor.
10. At the school play, the ushers were Sasha and Riley.

PRACTICE 18.5H ▷ Adding Predicate Nouns and Predicate Pronouns in Sentences

Read the sentences. Then, rewrite the sentences, filling in the blanks with appropriate predicate nouns or predicate pronouns. Use both nouns and pronouns.

EXAMPLE   Darryl was the most talented _____ on the team.

ANSWER   *Darryl was the most talented* **player** *on the team.*

11. The first people to arrive at the meeting were David and _____.
12. Stephanie will always be my _____.
13. Most of the gems inside the bag were _____.
14. My neighbor is the only _____ who knows CPR.
15. The best clothing store in our town is _____.
16. If in trouble, the first person I would turn to is _____.
17. The last thing I expected to see in the room was _____.
18. The country I most want to visit is _____.
19. Melissa studied hard and became a _____.
20. With her grace and athleticism, Li was a great _____.

SPEAKING APPLICATION

With a partner, take turns describing a music video you like. Your partner should listen for and name at least one predicate noun, one predicate pronoun, and one predicate adjective.

WRITING APPLICATION

Write three sentences about your favorite sport. Use at least three predicate nouns or predicate pronouns in your sentences.

394   Basic Sentence Parts

PRACTICE 18.5I Identifying Predicate Adjectives in Sentences

Read the sentences. Write the predicate adjective in each sentence.

EXAMPLE   Those mountains stay snowy for most of the year.

ANSWER   *snowy*

1. A visit to an art gallery can be enjoyable.
2. The beauty of Costa Rica is breathtaking.
3. Maya's sprint times have been remarkable.
4. The governor's words were inspiring to the people of the state.
5. During the ride my baby sister seemed cranky.
6. Most of her school clothing was new.
7. The straw in that basket is very colorful.
8. This water seems quite muddy.
9. Tanya has always been honest about her feelings.
10. The desert looks beautiful in the twilight.

PRACTICE 18.5J Writing Sentences Using Predicate Adjectives

Read the sentences. Rewrite the sentences, and fill in the blanks with appropriate predicate adjectives. Use compound predicate adjectives in some of the sentences.

EXAMPLE   The four-day-old bread looked _____.

ANSWER   *The four-day-old bread looked green and moldy.*

11. After taking a long nap in the afternoon, I felt _____.
12. A good leader should be _____.
13. Because we were so _____, we won the game easily.
14. After the game, Loudon's uniform appeared _____.
15. The air inside the locked cabinet was _____.
16. The carpeting in the room was so _____ that we had to replace it.
17. After she won the contest, Keiko was _____.
18. If you have the flu, you usually feel _____.
19. An ideal study place might be _____.
20. When her name was called as the award winner, Verna seemed _____.

SPEAKING APPLICATION

With a partner, take turns describing the sights and sounds at a carnival. Your partner should listen for and name several predicate adjectives you use.

WRITING APPLICATION

Write a paragraph describing your favorite food. Use at least three predicate adjectives in your description.

Test Warm-Up

DIRECTIONS
Read the introduction and the passage that follows. Then, answer the questions to show that you can use and understand predicate nouns, predicate pronouns, and predicate adjectives in reading and writing.

Anya wrote this story about a store in her town. Read the story and think about the changes you would suggest as a peer editor. When you finish reading, answer the questions that follow.

Party World

(1) I have a part-time job working at Party World on Downey Street. (2) My job isn't very easy, but it's very important. (3) If special balloons are a requirement for a birthday party, then I am the balloon you need to see. (4) The best balloons for a child's party should be colorful. (5) Funny and easy to hold are two other good qualities. (6) My balloon creations are always enjoying the kids.

1 The meaning in sentence 2 can be clarified by changing the predicate adjective *easy* to —

  A long

  B dull

  C difficult

  D boring

2 What change, if any, should be made in sentence 3?

  F Change the predicate noun *balloon* to **machine**

  G Change the predicate noun *balloon* to **person**

  H Change the predicate noun *balloon* to **store owner**

  J Make no change

3 What is the BEST way to combine sentences 4 and 5 to form a compound subject complement?

  A The best balloons for a child's party should be colorful, funny, and easy to hold.

  B The best balloons for a child's party should be colorful, and they should be funny and easy to hold.

  C Colorful and funny balloons are the best ones for a child to hold easily.

  D A child's party should have colorful, funny, and easy to hold balloons.

4 How should sentence 6 be revised?

  F My balloon creations are always in mind of the kids' enjoyment.

  G My balloon creations are always exciting for kids.

  H My balloon creations are always mine for the kids' enjoyment.

  J My balloon creations are always for enjoying the kids.

PHRASES *and* CLAUSES

Use phrases and clauses in a variety of ways to add interest to your writing.

WRITE GUY *Jeff Anderson, M.Ed.*

WHAT DO YOU NOTICE?

Uncover the phrases as you zoom in on lines from the poem "Grandma Ling" by Amy Ling.

MENTOR TEXT

> She smiled, stretched her arms
> to take to heart the eldest daughter
> of her youngest son a quarter century away.

Now, ask yourself the following questions:

- In the second line, how are the words *to take* different from the words *to heart*?
- What is the purpose of the prepositional phrase *of her youngest son* in the third line?

The words *to take* form the infinitive of the verb *take;* infinitives usually use the word *to* before the verb. In the phrase *to heart*, the word *to* is used as a preposition. *To heart* is a prepositional phrase, and the noun *heart* is the object of the preposition. The prepositional phrase *of her youngest son* acts as an adjective modifying the noun *daughter*.

Grammar for Writers Phrases allow writers to provide more information about the nouns and verbs in their sentences. Use phrases to construct lively sentences that flow smoothly.

Your infinitive phrase is very long.

I wrote it to stretch to infinity.

CHAPTER 19

397

19.1 Phrases

Sentences are usually built with more than just a subject and a predicate. **Phrases** play an important role in sentences by adding more information.

RULE

19.1.1

> A **phrase** is a group of words that functions in a sentence as a single part of speech. Phrases do not contain a subject and a verb.

Prepositional Phrases

A **prepositional phrase** has at least two parts, a preposition and a noun or pronoun that is the object of the preposition.

EXAMPLES
behind **trees**
prep   object

near **meadows**
prep   object

The object of the preposition may be modified by one or more adjectives.

EXAMPLES
behind serene tall **trees**
prep   adj   adj   object

near beautiful green **meadows**
prep   adj   adj   object

The object may also be a compound, consisting of two or more objects connected by a conjunction such as *and* or *nor*.

EXAMPLES
behind quiet serene **trees** and **meadows**
prep   adj   adj   object   object

near beautiful green **meadows** and **gardens**
prep   adj   adj   object   object

In a sentence, some prepositional phrases can act as adjectives that modify a noun or pronoun. Other prepositional phrases can act as adverbs that modify a verb, adjective, or adverb.

See Practice 19.1A

Using Prepositional Phrases That Act as Adjectives

A prepositional phrase that acts as an adjective in a sentence is called an **adjective phrase** or **adjectival phrase.**

> An **adjective phrase** or **adjectival phrase** is a prepositional phrase that modifies a noun or pronoun by telling *what kind* or *which one.*

19.1.2

RULE

Unlike one-word adjectives, which usually come before the nouns or pronouns they modify, adjectival phrases usually come after the nouns or pronouns they modify.

ONE-WORD ADJECTIVES	ADJECTIVAL PHRASES
The green meadow started here.	The meadow with two oak trees began there.
The worried forest ranger stopped us.	The forest ranger with the worried face stopped us.

Adjectival phrases answer the same questions as one-word adjectives do. *What kind* of meadow began there? *Which* ranger stopped us?

USES OF ADJECTIVAL PHRASES	
Modifying a Subject	The sound of the hail worried us.
Modifying a Direct Object	It beat against the gutters on the house.

See Practice 19.1B
See Practice 19.1C
See Practice 19.1D

When two adjectival phrases appear in a row, the second phrase may modify the object of the preposition in the first phrase or both phrases may modify the same noun or pronoun.

ADJECTIVAL PHRASES IN A ROW	
Modifying the Object of a Preposition	The skylight on the roof of the house broke.
Modifying the Same Noun	There was the scent of baking in the house.

Using Prepositional Phrases That Act as Adverbs

A prepositional phrase that acts as an adverb modifies the same parts of speech as a one-word adverb does.

RULE

19.1.3

> An **adverbial phrase** or **adverb phrase** is a prepositional phrase that modifies a verb, an adjective, or an adverb. Adverbial phrases point out *where, when, in what way,* or *to what extent.*

Adverbial phrases are used in the same way as one-word adverbs, but they sometimes provide more precise details.

ONE-WORD ADVERBS	ADVERBIAL PHRASES
Bring your books here .	Bring your books into the library .
The class began early .	The class began at exactly 9:00 A.M.

Adverbial phrases can modify verbs, adjectives, and adverbs.

USES OF ADVERBIAL PHRASES	
Modifying a Verb	Rain poured down in heavy sheets . (Poured *in what way?*)
Modifying an Adjective	The sun was cold for early June . (Cold *in what way?*)
Modifying an Adverb	The fire spread slowly for a forest fire . (Slowly *in what way?*)

Adverbial phrases, unlike adjectival phrases, are not always located near the words they modify in a sentence.

EXAMPLE   **During the high tide** , the boats were docked.

Two or more adverbial phrases can also be located in different parts of the sentence and still modify the same word.

See Practice 19.1E

EXAMPLE   **In an instant** , the mice ran **through the kitchen** .   See Practice 19.1F

PRACTICE 19.1A ▷ Identifying Prepositional Phrases

Read the sentences. Then, write the prepositional phrase in each sentence, and underline the object of the preposition.

EXAMPLE   I left the box on the table.

ANSWER   *on the <u>table</u>*

1. In the morning we ate a light breakfast.

2. The shy child was hiding behind the couch.

3. The ice skater performed her routine without any mistakes.

4. The article about the new computer was very interesting.

5. During summer vacation we often play softball.

6. The clerk at the checkout counter operated her cash register very rapidly.

7. I usually do some stretches before my swim.

8. Have you traveled to Austin before, or is this your first trip here?

9. Some audience members near the stage stood up and blocked my view.

10. The young couple from next door came to visit.

PRACTICE 19.1B ▷ Identifying Adjectival Phrases

Read the sentences. Then, write the adjectival phrase in each sentence. One sentence has two adjectival phrases.

EXAMPLE   A flock of sheep grazed in the field.

ANSWER   *of sheep*

11. I bought a jacket with a high collar.

12. The shoes in the closet have never been worn.

13. This is not the highway to the beach.

14. I am reading a good book about pirates.

15. The house beside the river was flooded last spring.

16. The speaker at the podium knew everyone in the room.

17. After five minutes, the sound of the thunder grew louder.

18. When does the train on Track 20 leave for Chicago?

19. High in the tree perched a cat with white stripes.

20. Jane sat with Tom at a table with wobbly legs.

SPEAKING APPLICATION

With a partner, take turns describing a store or a restaurant that you have visited. Your partner should listen for and name a prepositional phrase and an adjectival phrase that you use.

WRITING APPLICATION

Write three sentences about something you are wearing. Use at least one adjectival phrase in each sentence.

Read each prepositional phrase. Then, write a sentence using the phrase as an adjectival phrase. Read your sentences to a partner, and discuss how the adjectival phrases function in the sentences.

EXAMPLE   in the storage closet

ANSWER   *The boxes in the storage closet are filled with books.*

1. with green and white feathers
2. at the fire hydrant
3. for seventh and eighth graders
4. in the top row
5. with a broken arm
6. of giant robots
7. inside the cereal box
8. of delicate lace
9. on the corner of Blair and Sussex streets
10. on the rear windshield

Read each sentence and find an adjectival phrase within it. Then, rewrite the sentence, replacing the adjectival phrase with one of your own.

EXAMPLE   I fixed the top button of my shirt.

ANSWER   I fixed *the top button of my coat.*

11. Helen placed bowls of popcorn around the room.
12. The man inside the booth began to sweat.
13. The doctor gave me a prescription for cold medicine.
14. The prices on the menu are really expensive.
15. Dexter raced the boat with white sails to victory.
16. The gems inside the treasure chest were very valuable.
17. Charlie mimicked every character in the play.
18. I object to the tone of your voice.
19. Everything inside the closet was moth-eaten.
20. The detective suspected the man in the long, dark coat.

SPEAKING APPLICATION

With a partner, take turns describing a highway, a house, or something else being built or repaired. Your partner should listen for and name three adjectival phrases that you use.

WRITING APPLICATION

Write four sentences about a sport you play or watch on television. Use at least three adjectival phrases. Read your sentences aloud to a partner. Have your partner identify each adjectival phrase.

PRACTICE 19.1E > **Writing Sentences With Adverbial Phrases**

Read each sentence and find an adverbial phrase within it. Then, rewrite the sentence replacing the adverbial phrase with one of your own.

EXAMPLE   Dmitri ran for more than three hours.

ANSWER   Dmitri ran *inside the park.*

1. He kept the map safe inside the vault.
2. The dog raced around in circles.
3. After dinner, the party began to break up.
4. The students arranged to take a limousine to the dance.
5. A fierce wind blew outside of our apartment.
6. A scary shadow crept up the walls.
7. We descended the spiral staircase in a hurry.
8. The walls of the house have not been painted in six years.
9. The music echoed throughout the auditorium.
10. In just a minute, the concert will begin.

PRACTICE 19.1F > **Reading and Writing Sentences With Adverbial Phrases**

Read the sentences. Then, rewrite each sentence, adding an adverbial phrase. Try to vary the location of your adverbial phrases. Underline your adverbial phrases. Read your sentences with a partner who should listen for and identify the adverbial phrases you used.

EXAMPLE   Enrique lost ten dollars.

ANSWER   Enrique lost ten dollars *on the train.*

11. We completed the jigsaw puzzle.
12. A small insect buzzed.
13. The babysitter watched the children.
14. The firefighters moved cautiously.
15. We finally located the right street.
16. The soprano shattered the crystal glasses.
17. A tiny deer was prancing.
18. I love watching the sun rise.
19. The snow fell steadily.
20. The passengers had boarded the ship.

SPEAKING APPLICATION

With a partner, take turns describing a time you found something unusual. Your partner should listen for and write three adverbial phrases that you use.

WRITING APPLICATION

Work with a partner to write a brief, two-person dialogue for a scary scene in a movie. You should each use at least three adverbial phrases. Read your dialogue aloud and identify each other's adverbial phrases.

Test Warm-Up

DIRECTIONS
Read the introduction and the passage that follows. Then, answer the questions to show that you can use and understand adjectival and adverbial phrases in reading and writing.

Anita wrote this story about her family's vacation adventure. Read the story and think about the changes you would suggest as a peer editor. When you finish reading, answer the questions that follow.

Swimming With Dolphins

(1) On our family vacation, we all got to do the "Dolphin Dip." (2) In the Florida Keys, that is a special program held at a marine research center throughout the year. (3) We spent 20 minutes with the dolphins. (4) We swam and played. (5) The dolphins were really smart. (6) I jumped up into the air and spun in a circle. (7) A dolphin would copy my actions exactly. (8) My dad took many photographs.

---

1 What is the BEST way to rewrite the ideas in sentence 2?

  A In the Florida Keys throughout the year, that is a special program held at a marine research center.

  B That is a special program in the Florida Keys held throughout the year at a marine research center.

  C That is a special program throughout the year held at a marine research center in the Florida Keys.

  D That is a special program held throughout the year at a marine research center in the Florida Keys.

2 How should sentence 4 be revised to include an adverbial phrase?

  F The whole time, we swam and played.

  G We swam happily and played joyfully.

  H We swam and played inside a large tank.

  J With smiles on our faces, we swam and played.

3 What is the BEST way to combine sentences 6 and 7?

  A If I jumped up into the air and spun in a circle, a dolphin would copy my actions exactly.

  B I jumped up into the air and spun in a circle when a dolphin would copy my actions exactly.

  C Because I jumped up into the air and spun in a circle, a dolphin would copy my actions exactly.

  D If I jumped up into the air and spun in a circle; a dolphin would copy my actions exactly.

4 The meaning of sentence 8 can be clarified by adding which adjectival phrase to the end of the sentence?

  F with the friendly and clever dolphins

  G of us with the dolphins

  H to remind us of the dolphins

  J to keep a record of our trip

Using Appositives and Appositive Phrases

Appositives, like adjectival phrases, give information about nouns or pronouns.

> An **appositive** is a noun or pronoun placed after another noun or pronoun to identify, rename, or explain the preceding word.

19.1.4 **RULE**

Appositives are very useful in writing because they give additional information without using many words.

EXAMPLES

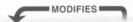
MODIFIES

Our captain **Katie Woo** won the race.

MODIFIES

I admire the author **William Shakespeare**.

An appositive with its own modifiers creates an **appositive phrase.**

> An **appositive phrase** is a noun or pronoun with modifiers. It is placed next to a noun or pronoun and adds information or details.

19.1.5 **RULE**

The modifiers in an appositive phrase can be adjectives or adjectival phrases.

See Practice 19.1G
See Practice 19.1H

EXAMPLES

Uncle Joe, my **favorite** **uncle**, cooks well.
adjective   noun

On the kitchen wall is a platter, an **heirloom**
noun
in my family for years.
adj phrase

Appositives and appositive phrases can also be a compound.

EXAMPLE

Actors, **men** and **women**, performed together.
compound noun

PRACTICE 19.1G **Identifying Appositives and Appositive Phrases**

Read the sentences. Then, write the appositive or appositive phrase in each sentence.

EXAMPLE   I met with John English, publisher of the local newspaper.

ANSWER   *publisher of the local newspaper*

1. Jan painted her room in her favorite color, blue.

2. The magazine article, a brief history of tea, was quite interesting.

3. My brother's car, a very old station wagon, often breaks down.

4. Only the first-prize winner, Cynthia, gets to make a speech.

5. Jim is studying meteorology, the science of atmospheric activity such as the weather.

6. My sister Jane joined her friends in the diner.

7. I admire my friend Carlos, a talented actor.

8. The vegetables carrots and spinach are good sources of vitamins.

9. A popular bunch of musicians, they always draw a large crowd.

10. Author Mark Twain was born in Missouri.

PRACTICE 19.1H **Combining Sentences With Appositive Phrases**

Read the sentences. Combine each pair of sentences by using an appositive phrase.

EXAMPLE   Pedro Salazar is a great athlete. He is the quarterback on our team.

ANSWER   *Pedro Salazar, the quarterback on our team, is a great athlete.*

11. People often use the rose as a symbol of love. It is a beautiful flower.

12. Emily Dickinson was a famous poet. She rarely left her home in her later years.

13. Skiing is a winter sport. Skiing requires special warm clothing.

14. Vermeer is now a famous artist. He had trouble earning a living.

15. Bobcats are large cats found in the wild. They sometimes attack deer.

16. San Antonio is a city with a strong Mexican heritage. The Alamo is in San Antonio.

17. I hope to reach my goal before I am twenty. My goal is to win an Olympic medal.

18. Julie performs in the school musical each year. She is a talented singer.

19. Our hotel is in the French Quarter. That is a famous neighborhood in New Orleans.

20. Victoria ruled at a time of prosperity for her nation. She was Britain's queen for many years.

SPEAKING APPLICATION

With a partner, take turns describing the planets. Include at least three appositive phrases. Your partner should listen for and name three appositive phrases that you use.

WRITING APPLICATION

Write three sentences about different presidents of the United States. Use an appositive phrase in each sentence. Underline each appositive phrase. Read each sentence aloud to a partner. Have your partner identify each appositive phrase you used.

Using Verbals and Verbal Phrases

A **verbal** is any verb form that is used in a sentence not as a verb but as another part of speech.

Like verbs, verbals can be modified by an adverb or adverbial phrase. They can also be followed by a complement. A verbal used with a modifier or a complement is called a **verbal phrase.**

Participles

Participles are verb forms with two basic uses. When they are used with helping verbs, they are verbs. When they are used alone to modify nouns or pronouns, they become adjectives.

> **A participle** is a form of a verb that is often used as an adjective.

19.1.6 RULE

There are two kinds of participles, **present participles** and **past participles.** Each kind can be recognized by its ending.

All present participles end in *-ing.*

EXAMPLES   talking   doing   eating   wanting

Most past participles end either in *-ed* or in *-d.*

EXAMPLES   opened   jumped   played   moved

Other past participles end in *-n, -t, -en,* or another irregular ending.

EXAMPLES   grown   felt   bought   eaten   held

Both present and past participles can be used in sentences as adjectives. They tell *what kind* or *which one.*

PRESENT PARTICIPLES	PAST PARTICIPLES
They scheduled a walking tour.	Chilled water is refreshing.
Answering, he explained what happened.	At the time, she felt concerned.

See Practice 19.1I

See Practice 19.1J

Participle or Verb?

Sometimes, verb phrases (verbs with helping verbs) are confused with participles. A verb phrase always begins with a helping verb. A participle used as an adjective stands by itself and modifies a noun or pronoun.

VERB PHRASES	PARTICIPLES
The boy was racing around the yard.	The racing jockey rode around the track.
Her assistant may have scheduled the meeting earlier.	I spoke at the scheduled meeting.

Participial Phrases

A participle can be expanded into a participial phrase by adding a complement or modifier.

RULE 19.1.7

> A **participial phrase** is a present or past participle and its modifiers. The entire phrase acts as an adjective in a sentence.

Participial phrases can be formed by adding an adverb, an adverbial phrase, or a complement to a participle.

EXAMPLES   The coach, **demonstrating quickly**, explained the play.

The well-known coach, **honored by the victory**, led the team.

The first participial phrase contains the adverb *quickly* added to the participle *demonstrating*. The second includes the adverbial phrase *by the victory* added to the participle *honored*.

A participial phrase can also be placed at the beginning of a sentence. The phrase is usually followed by a comma.

EXAMPLE   **Honored by the victory**, the well-known coach led the team.

See Practice 19.1K
See Practice 19.1L

PRACTICE 19.1I > **Identifying Present and Past Participles**

Read the sentences. Then, write the participle in each sentence, and label it *present participle* or *past participle*.

EXAMPLE   Hurricane Katrina was a devastating storm.

ANSWER   *devastating* — present participle

1. A chirping bird woke me early this morning.

2. Weeping, the child pointed to the small bruise on her knee.

3. Late and worried, the driver checked the time over and over.

4. The grinning hockey player jumped in triumph.

5. The oatmeal, hardening quickly in the pot, would be difficult to remove.

6. The toaster produced burnt toast every morning.

7. The bustling commuters poured out of the subway and raced to their jobs.

8. During her visit to Grandma, my sister fixed a broken chair.

9. There was a moment of silent shock, followed by a great deal of noisy panic.

10. The shovel, lost in the snow, reappeared after the thaw.

PRACTICE 19.1J > **Distinguishing Verbs and Participles**

Read the sentences. Then, write *verb* or *participle* for the underlined word in each sentence.

EXAMPLE   Trusty Toys is a growing business.

ANSWER   *participle*

11. The tired worker took a break.

12. Luis and I are going to the movies tomorrow.

13. Julie is a member of the planning committee.

14. We have been working on our science project.

15. Waiting patiently in the cold, the students chatted together at the bus stop.

16. We should be finished in half an hour.

17. Corey was carefully lifting the heavy suitcase.

18. The winners were not all chosen today.

19. I took three books out of the library, including an Indian cookbook.

20. When was the car's gas tank last filled?

SPEAKING APPLICATION

With a partner, take turns telling about a bad storm. Use two present participles and two past participles. Your partner should listen for and name the participles that you use, and say whether they are present or past participles.

WRITING APPLICATION

Write four sentences about preparing or eating food. In your first sentence, use a present participle. In your second, use the same word as a verb. In your third sentence, use a past participle. In your fourth, use the same word as a verb.

PRACTICE 19.1K > Identifying Participial Phrases

Read the sentences. Then, write the participial phrase in each sentence. Underline the participle.

EXAMPLE   Running swiftly, Cara won the race.

ANSWER   *Running swiftly*

1. Working rapidly, the artist sketched my portrait.

2. The plumber's fee, calculated by the hour, was quite high.

3. Concentrating on his homework, Cal did not hear the phone.

4. The man leaning on the fence is my uncle.

5. The cost, paid in advance, included sales tax.

6. I liked the flowers growing in the garden.

7. The star sang ten songs, including my favorite.

8. Speaking clearly, Anna repeated her request.

9. The senator, elected five years ago, is up for reelection next year.

10. Running down the field, James shouted for his teammate to pass the ball.

PRACTICE 19.1L > Combining Sentences Using Participial Phrases

Read the sentences. Combine each pair of sentences by using a participial phrase.

EXAMPLE   The tree was very old. It towered over the others.

ANSWER   *The tree, towering over the others, was very old.*

11. Ali jogged down the street. Ali met a friend.

12. The child squirmed in front the camera. He had his picture taken.

13. Bob was completely exhausted. He slept for hours.

14. I enjoyed the book. It was written by Maya Angelou.

15. The police officer interviewed witnesses. He obtained valuable information.

16. The case was argued in court. It finally ended in a guilty verdict.

17. The drama club staged a new one-act play. It was chosen from dozens of entries.

18. Zoe was nervous about her audition. She barely ate any of her lunch.

19. The treasure chest held jewels and gold coins. It was found after many years.

20. The hikers were lost in the woods. They were tired and hungry.

SPEAKING APPLICATION

With a partner, take turns describing a race or a contest. Use at least three participial phrases. Your partner should listen for and name the three participial phrases that you use.

WRITING APPLICATION

Tell how to do something by writing four or five short sentences. Then, combine two of the sentences by using a participial phrase. Underline the participial phrase.

Gerunds

Like present participles, **gerunds** end in -*ing*. While present participles are used as adjectives, gerunds can be used as subjects, direct objects, predicate nouns, and objects of prepositions.

> **A gerund is a form of a verb that acts as a noun.**

RULE 19.1.8

USE OF GERUNDS IN SENTENCES	
Subject	Kayaking was a great idea!
Direct Object	Alexis enjoys reading .
Predicate Noun	Her favorite activity is cooking .
Object of a Preposition	Joe never gets tired of driving .

Gerund Phrases

Gerunds can also be part of a phrase.

> **A gerund phrase is a gerund with modifiers or a complement, all acting together as a noun.**

RULE 19.1.9

This chart shows how gerunds are expanded to form gerund phrases.

FORMING GERUND PHRASES	
Gerund With Adjectives	The loud, shrill ringing continued all day.
Gerund With Direct Object	Hearing classical music has inspired many musicians.
Gerund With Prepositional Phrase	The violinist loved playing with her teacher .
Gerund With Adverb and Prepositional Phrase	The conductor amazed the spectators by perfectly directing under such difficult conditions .

See Practice 19.1M
See Practice 19.1N

Infinitives

Infinitives are verb forms that are used as nouns, adjectives, and adverbs. Like participles and gerunds, they can be combined with other words to form phrases.

19.1.10 ▷ An **infinitive** is a verb form that can be used as a noun, an adjective, or an adverb. The word *to* usually appears before the verb.

EXAMPLES   It is necessary **to drive**.

He is the one **to call**.

To study can be difficult sometimes.

Infinitive Phrases

19.1.11 ▷ An **infinitive phrase** is an infinitive with modifiers or a complement, all acting together as a single part of speech.

EXAMPLES   It is important **to drive carefully**.

It is not polite **to beep your horn in traffic**.

They want you **to drive more slowly**.

An **infinitive phrase** can be used in a sentence as a noun, an adjective, or an adverb. As a noun, an infinitive phrase can function as a subject, an object, or an appositive.

USES OF INFINITIVES	
Used as a Subject	To drive carefully is vital.
Used as an Object	He tried to drive carefully.
Used as an Appositive	His mother's suggestion, to drive carefully, saved him.
Used as an Adjective	He has the ability to drive carefully.
Used as an Adverb	It isn't always easy to drive carefully when you're running late.

See Practice 19.1O

See Practice 19.1P

PRACTICE 19.1M Identifying Gerund Phrases

Read the sentences. Then, write the gerund phrase from each sentence, and underline the gerund. Remember to include all modifiers with the phrase.

EXAMPLE   Writing a book was her lifelong dream.

ANSWER   <u>Writing</u> a book

1. Driving too fast is very dangerous.

2. Last night I started reading a new book.

3. You can learn a lot by asking questions.

4. Diving into the pool always gives me a thrill.

5. We will raise money by washing cars.

6. Tonight Mom plans on cooking beans and rice.

7. I love sleeping late in the morning.

8. Is learning a foreign language more difficult for older people?

9. The ringing of the telephone woke me up.

10. Today, using a computer is a vital skill for many jobs.

PRACTICE 19.1N Writing Gerunds and Gerund Phrases

Read the sentences. Then, rewrite each sentence, completing it with a gerund or a gerund phrase.

EXAMPLE   _____ is Jody's favorite activity.

ANSWER   *Playing basketball is Jody's favorite activity.*

11. _____ is a popular sport.

12. For me, the best way to stay healthy is _____.

13. On cold winter days I enjoy _____.

14. That actor is famous for _____.

15. _____ interrupted the mayor's speech.

16. You can win friends by _____.

17. _____ is a good way to begin a sentence.

18. _____ can keep me busy for hours.

19. The idea of _____ is growing more and more appealing.

20. Sculpture is the art of _____.

SPEAKING APPLICATION

With a partner, take turns talking about summer activities. Use at least three gerunds or gerund phrases. Your partner should listen for and name the three gerunds or gerund phrases that you use.

WRITING APPLICATION

Write three sentences about your hobbies. Use a gerund or a gerund phrase in each sentence. Underline each gerund or gerund phrase.

PRACTICE 19.10 ▶ **Identifying Infinitives and Infinitive Phrases**

Read the sentences. Then, write the infinitive phrase from each sentence, and underline the infinitive. Also write *noun, adjective,* or *adverb* to describe each infinitive phrase.

EXAMPLE Stephen tried to work faster.

ANSWER <u>to work</u> faster — noun

1. Celia's dream is to visit Paris.

2. Now is the time to begin the test.

3. To skip a meal is never a good practice.

4. One way to travel through Australia is by train.

5. I hope to win the spelling bee.

6. The best place to go swimming is Sandy Creek.

7. We waited in the rain to hear the speaker.

8. The actress's goal, to win an Oscar, seemed further away than ever.

9. Many of us went to the airport to complain about noise from the planes.

10. Jake was sorry to lose the souvenir bookmark.

PRACTICE 19.1P ▶ **Writing Infinitives and Infinitive Phrases**

Read the sentences. Then, rewrite each sentence, completing it with an infinitive or an infinitive phrase.

EXAMPLE There are five questions _____.

ANSWER *There are five questions to answer.*

11. My plan for the future is _____.

12. _____ is a wonderful opportunity.

13. Some people think golf is not much fun _____.

14. The instructions _____ are not complicated.

15. The goal of the conference is _____.

16. My homeroom teacher asked me _____.

17. The simplest way _____ is on foot.

18. The salesclerk was happy _____.

19. A good pitcher knows how _____.

20. The mayor's promise, _____, brought hope to the residents.

SPEAKING APPLICATION

With a partner, take turns telling about a skill that you want to learn. Use at least three infinitives or infinitive phrases. Your partner should listen for and name the three infinitives or infinitive phrases that you use.

WRITING APPLICATION

Write three sentences about volunteer activities in your community. Use an infinitive or an infinitive phrase in each sentence. Underline each infinitive or infinitive phrase.

19.2 Clauses

Clauses are the basic structural unit of a sentence.

> **A clause** is a group of words with its own subject and verb.

RULE 19.2.1

There are two basic kinds of clauses, **main** or **independent clauses** and **subordinate clauses.**

> **A main** or **independent clause** has a subject and a verb and can stand by itself as a complete sentence.

RULE 19.2.2

As you can see in the examples below, a main clause can be long or short. All main clauses express a complete thought and can stand by themselves as complete sentences.

EXAMPLES   The **window** **rattled**.
              subject   verb

Later that week, **she** **began** using the bike.
              subject   verb

> **A subordinate clause,** also known as a dependent clause, has a subject and a verb but cannot stand by itself as a complete sentence. It is only part of a sentence.

RULE 19.2.3

SUBORDINATE CLAUSES   after **she** **told** her story
              subject verb

while the **audience** **listened**
              subject   verb

After reading a subordinate clause, you will still need more information to have a complete sentence.

Subordinate clauses begin with subordinating conjunctions or relative pronouns.

Some subordinate clauses begin with **subordinating conjunctions,** such as *if, since, when, although, after, because,* and *while.* Others begin with **relative pronouns,** such as *who, which,* or *that.* These words are clues that the clause may not be able to stand alone. Notice how the addition of subordinating words changes the meaning of the main clauses in the examples.

| COMPARING TWO KINDS OF CLAUSES ||
MAIN	SUBORDINATE
They sing this evening.	*when* they sing this evening
This park has a sandpit.	*because* this park has a sandpit
I planted the roses.	the roses *that* I planted

In order to form a complete thought, a subordinate clause must be combined with a main clause.

EXAMPLES

After she presented her data, Tara felt
        subordinate clause   main clause
relieved.

The committee applauded **after Tara presented**
      main clause   subordinate clause
her data.

It was Jake **who was asked to present first**.
   main clause   subordinate clause

When she arrives tonight, Hannah needs to
    subordinate clause   main clause
unpack her suitcase.

See Practice 19.2A
See Practice 19.2B

PRACTICE 19.2A **Identifying Main and Subordinate Clauses**

Read the sentences. Then, write the main and subordinate clauses in each sentence, and label them *main clause* or *subordinate clause.*

EXAMPLE   When I left, May was still singing.

ANSWER   *When I left* — subordinate clause
May was still singing — main clause

1. Before I moved to Iowa, I had never seen snow.

2. Grandma brings a pie whenever she visits.

3. Unless I am mistaken, that woman is Mrs. Lee.

4. He is a great teacher whom I respect very much.

5. Kenneth was relieved when he finished the test.

6. Wait behind the line until the train comes to a complete stop.

7. New Amsterdam, which became New York, was originally a Dutch colonial settlement.

8. If you walk on that road after dark, be careful of potholes.

9. The pants that you bought are too long.

10. Did the person whose entry won first prize ever pick up the award?

PRACTICE 19.2B **Identifying and Using Main and Subordinate Clauses**

Read the clauses. Write *main clause* or *subordinate clause* for each clause. Then, expand each subordinate clause into a complete sentence by adding a main clause.

EXAMPLE   After we ate.

ANSWER   subordinate clause
After we ate, we went for a walk.

11. I enjoy old television shows.

12. If you send a text message.

13. Everyone clapped and whistled.

14. Whenever we eat spaghetti.

15. Unless we leave by four o'clock.

16. That book is a real page turner.

17. Whom I have known since kindergarten.

18. Although I waited for Kay for hours near the park entrance.

19. There was no answer.

20. Study the map carefully.

SPEAKING APPLICATION

With a partner, take turns telling about your weekend plans. Each statement you make should contain one main clause and one subordinate clause. Your partner should listen for and name the clauses.

WRITING APPLICATION

Write three sentences about traveling by car, bus, train, or plane. Each sentence should contain one main clause and one subordinate clause. Underline each main clause, and double underline each subordinate clause. With a partner, discuss the difference between the two types of clauses.

Adjectival Clauses

A subordinate clause will sometimes act as an adjective in a sentence. An adjectival clause, or adjective clause, is a dependent clause and cannot stand on its own.

> An **adjectival clause,** or **adjective clause,** is a subordinate clause that modifies a noun or a pronoun.

Like one-word adjectives and adjectival phrases, **adjectival clauses** tell *what kind* or *which one.*

WHAT KIND?

EXAMPLES   apples **that are juicy and sweet**

WHICH ONE?

the town **where I am from**

Recognizing Adjectival Clauses

Most adjectival clauses begin with the words *that, which, who, whom,* and *whose.* Sometimes an adjectival clause begins with a subordinating conjunction, such as *since, where,* or *when.* In the chart below, the adjectival clauses are hightlighted in pink.

ADJECTIVAL CLAUSES
The manager whom I asked for help met me in her office. (*Which* manager?)
The beach party, which was planned a month ago, is this weekend. (*Which* beach party?)
In the few months since she started training, Tina has become an accomplished lifeguard. (*Which* months?)
The dog is in the pantry closet where I hid the treats. (*Which* closet?)
We visited the museum that shows animals from long ago. (*Which* museum?)
The museum whose exhibits include dinosaurs is located in the center of town. (*Which* museum?)

See Practice 19.2C

Combining Sentences With Adjectival Clauses

Two sentences can be combined into one sentence by changing one of them into an adjectival clause. Sometimes you will need to add a relative pronoun or subordinating conjunction to make the sentence read correctly. In the sentences below, the adjectival clauses are highlighted in pink.

TWO SENTENCES	COMBINED WITH AN ADJECTIVAL CLAUSE
My best friend has written songs based on her life. My friend is a musician.	My best friend, who has written songs based on her life, is a musician.
We visited Wild Animal World. Wild Animal World is my favorite animal park.	We visited Wild Animal World, which is my favorite animal park.
We decided to eat at the rest area. They usually offer the best prices there.	We decided to eat at the rest area, where the best prices are usually offered.
Laura visited her sister. Laura's sister lives on a beach in Florida.	Laura visited her sister, who lives on a beach in Florida.
Delmar goes to karate class on Main Street. He goes to class every week.	Every week, Delmar goes to his karate class, which is on Main Street.

See Practice 19.2D

PRACTICE 19.2C > **Identifying Adjectival Clauses**

Read the sentences. Then, write the adjectival clause in each sentence. One sentence has two adjectival clauses.

EXAMPLE   The employee whom I phoned was not at her desk.

ANSWER   *whom I phoned*

1. The chorus, which meets on Tuesdays and Thursdays, is accepting new members.

2. Aunt Clarice, who was living in Ohio, just moved to Florida.

3. The new student, whom I met in science class, moved here from Atlanta.

4. The wallet that I bought is larger than my last one.

5. The street where I live is not far from here.

6. Someone whose voice is so good should sing in public.

7. Do you remember the day when we last saw each other?

8. What is the name of that excellent relief pitcher who plays for the Cubs?

9. One week after we began the school term, we had already taken two tests.

10. In the time since Sarah left, four people whom she knows arrived at the party and asked for her.

PRACTICE 19.2D > **Combining Sentences Using Adjectival Clauses**

Read the sentences. Combine the pairs of sentences by changing one of them into an adjectival clause.

EXAMPLE   Eudora Welty was a famous writer. She lived in Mississippi.

ANSWER   *Eudora Welty, who lived in Mississippi, was a famous writer.*

11. My sister made me a pair of gloves. She knits beautifully.

12. A beret is a type of cap. It is worn at an angle.

13. The Memorial Day parade lasts for about two hours. It begins on High Street.

14. Barack Obama was born in Hawaii. He became president of the United States in 2009.

15. Newfoundland is Canada's easternmost province. It borders the Atlantic Ocean.

16. The tornado destroyed many homes. It swept through town last night.

17. We visited Gettysburg. That is where President Lincoln gave his famous address.

18. Felice is fluent in three languages. Her name means "happy."

19. My pen pal lives in Peru. I have never met her.

20. Was 1992 a leap year? That is when I was born.

SPEAKING APPLICATION

With a partner, take turns describing a place you have visited. Use at least three adjectival clauses. Your partner should listen for and name the three adjectival clauses that you use.

WRITING APPLICATION

Write three sentences about famous people in history. Use an adjectival clause in each sentence. Underline each adjectival clause. With a partner, discuss the purpose of the adjectival clauses.

Adverbial Clauses

Subordinate clauses can also be used as adverbs. Adverbial clauses or adverb clauses are dependent clauses.

> An **adverbial clause** or **adverb clause** is a subordinate clause that modifies a verb, an adjective, or an adverb.

19.2.6 RULE

Adverbial clauses can answer any of the following questions about the words they modify: *Where? When? In what manner? To what extent? Under what conditions?* or *Why?*

ADVERBIAL CLAUSES	
Modifying Verbs	Put the groceries wherever you find room. (Put *where?*)
	The service will begin when the speaker enters. (Will begin *when?*)
	Jan spoke as if she were joking. (Spoke *in what manner?*)
	I will have tea if you do too. (Will *have under what conditions?*)
Modifying an Adjective	I am happy because I have been shopping all day. (Happy *why?*)
Modifying an Adverb	He knows more than the other officers do. (More *to what extent?*)

Recognizing Adverbial Clauses

> A **subordinating conjunction** introduces an adverbial clause.

19.2.7 RULE

A **subordinating conjunction** always introduces an adverbial clause. In a sentence, the conjunction will usually appear in one of two places—either at the beginning, when the adverbial clause begins the sentence, or in the middle, connecting the independent clause to the subordinate clause. In the examples on the next page, the subordinating conjunctions are highlighted in purple.

Because you came home, I will prepare lunch.

I will prepare lunch **because** you came home.

Whenever you go away, I miss you. I miss you **whenever** you go away.

Common Subordinating Conjunctions

Here are the most common subordinating conjunctions. Knowing them can help you recognize adverbial clauses.

COMMON SUBORDINATING CONJUNCTIONS		
after	even though	unless
although	if	until
as	in order that	when
as if	since	whenever
as long as	so that	where
because	than	wherever
before	though	while

Elliptical Adverbial Clauses

In certain adverbial clauses, words are left out. These clauses are said to be elliptical.

RULE 19.2.8

In an **elliptical adverbial clause,** the verb or the subject and verb are understood rather than stated.

Many elliptical adverbial clauses are introduced by one of two subordinating conjunctions, *as* or *than*. In the following examples, the understood words have been added in parentheses. The first elliptical adverbial clause is missing a verb; the second is missing a subject and a verb.

See Practice 19.2E
See Practice 19.2F

EXAMPLES   My cousin can eat as much **as I** (can eat).

I like this play more **than** (I liked) **that one**.

PRACTICE 19.2E > **Identifying Adverbial Clauses and Recognizing Elliptical Adverbial Clauses**

Read the sentences. Then, write the adverbial clauses. For any of the adverbial clauses that are elliptical, add the understood words in parentheses.

EXAMPLE   My cousin can swim better than I.

ANSWER   *than I (can swim)*

1. I coughed because something tickled my throat.
2. If the weather gets warmer, I will walk to the supermarket.
3. Vic always does stretches before he runs.
4. Whenever I hurry, I make mistakes.
5. Because he broke the law, the man was arrested.
6. Manuel was upset when I arrived late for practice.
7. Although Maria is not a close friend, I always enjoy her company.
8. We left much later than our neighbors.
9. Let's stay at the mall until the last bus leaves.
10. Your guess is as good as mine.

PRACTICE 19.2F > **Combining Sentences With Adverbial Clauses**

Read the sentences. Combine each pair of sentences by changing one of them into an adverbial clause. Use an appropriate subordinating conjunction, and drop or change words as necessary.

EXAMPLE   Charlotte should win the game. Someone else may outscore her.

ANSWER   *Charlotte should win the game unless someone else outscores her.*

11. I brushed my teeth. Then I went to bed.
12. I would love a new bike. However, I cannot afford one.
13. Gregory will mow the lawn. Only rain will prevent him.
14. The chef used potholders. She did not want to burn her hands.
15. You go to the party. Then I will go too.
16. Chet did the laundry. Later, he ironed his shirts.
17. I checked all the television channels. I finally found an old movie.
18. Terry likes children. She volunteers at the day-care center.
19. The bell rings. The dog barks every time.
20. I held the pieces of fabric in place. At the same time, my sister sewed them together.

SPEAKING APPLICATION

With a partner, take turns describing an animal's behavior. Use at least three adverbial clauses. Your partner should listen for and name the three adverbial clauses that you use.

WRITING APPLICATION

Write a short paragraph about a recent news event. Use an adverbial clause in three of your sentences. Underline the adverbial clauses. With a partner, discuss the purpose of the adverbial clauses.

19.3 Classifying Sentences by Structure

All sentences can be classified according to the number and kinds of clauses they contain.

WRITING COACH

Online

www.phwritingcoach.com

Grammar Tutorials
Brush up on your Grammar skills with these animated videos.

Grammar Practice
Practice your grammar skills with Writing Coach Online.

Grammar Games
Test your knowledge of grammar in this fast-paced interactive video game.

The Simple Sentence

The **simple sentence** is the most common type of sentence structure.

RULE 19.3.1

> A **simple sentence** consists of a single independent clause.

Simple sentences vary in length. Some are quite short; others can be several lines long. All simple sentences, however, contain just one subject and one verb. They may also contain adjectives, adverbs, complements, and phrases in different combinations.

Simple sentences can also have various compound parts. They can have a compound subject, a compound verb, or both. Sometimes, they will also have other compound elements, such as a compound direct object or a compound phrase.

All of the following sentences are simple sentences.

TYPES OF SIMPLE SENTENCES	
With One Subject and Verb	The hail fell .
With a Compound Subject	Hail and rain are common.
With a Compound Verb	The floor squeaked and groaned .
With a Compound Subject and Compound Verb	My mother and sister bought the balloons and decorated the room for the party.
With a Compound Direct Object	She opened the gift box and the letter . direct object direct object
With a Compound Prepositional Phrase	You can walk from the subway or from the bus . prep phrase prep phrase

A simple sentence never has a subordinate clause, and it never has more than one main or independent clause.

The Compound Sentence

A **compound sentence** is made up of more than one simple sentence.

> A **compound sentence** consists of two or more main or independent clauses.

RULE 19.3.2

In most compound sentences, the main or independent clauses are joined by a comma and a coordinating conjunction (*and, but, for, nor, or, so,* or *yet*). They may also be connected with a semicolon (;) or a colon (:).

EXAMPLES Linda ran a two-day computer seminar, and ten managers agreed to speak.

All of the managers taught on the first day; two were missing the second day.

See Practice 19.3A
See Practice 19.3B

Notice in both of the preceding examples that there are two separate and complete main clauses, each with its own subject and verb. Like simple sentences, compound sentences never contain subordinate clauses.

The Complex Sentence

Complex sentences contain subordinate clauses, which can be either adjectival clauses or adverbial clauses.

> A **complex sentence** consists of one main or independent clause and one or more subordinate clauses.

RULE 19.3.3

In a complex sentence, the independent clause is often called the **main clause.** The main clause has its own subject and verb, as does each subordinate clause.

In a complex sentence, the main clause can stand alone as a simple sentence. The subordinate clause cannot stand alone as a sentence. Be sure and use a comma to separate the clauses when appropriate.

EXAMPLES

July 4, 1776, is the day that America won its
     main clause   subordinate clause

independence.

Because this day is so important, many
         subordinate clause

towns

have parades and picnics.
      main clause

See Practice 19.3C

In some complex sentences, the main clause is split by a subordinate clause that acts as an adjective.

EXAMPLE

Many people, who have the day

off, participate in games and events.

See Practice 19.3D

The two parts of the main clause form one main clause:
Many people participate in games and events.

The Compound-Complex Sentence

A **compound-complex sentence,** as the name indicates, contains the elements of both a compound sentence and a complex sentence.

RULE 19.3.4

A **compound-complex sentence** consists of two or more main or independent clauses and one or more subordinate clauses.

EXAMPLE

As Joan was leaving for vacation,
      subordinate clause

she remembered to take her ticket, but
      main clause

she forgot her passport that she had renewed
    main clause   subordinate clause

the month before.

PRACTICE 19.3A > Distinguishing Simple and Compound Sentences

Read the sentences. Then, write *simple* or *compound* for each sentence.

EXAMPLE   The zoo gives a student discount, but the museum charges full price.

ANSWER   *compound*

1. The state repaved the highways last year.

2. Sharon and Kayla met at summer camp.

3. I downloaded a song for my sister, but she already had it.

4. The school has a new science lab, and plans for the new auditorium are moving ahead.

5. Either Hugh or Josie will introduce the guest speaker to the class.

6. Please bring sunscreen, towels, and beach chairs.

7. Mom spotted Pell Road and turned right.

8. Terry used binoculars, yet he still could barely see the stage from the fourth balcony.

9. I ate eggs for breakfast; I want something else for lunch.

10. Speak quietly, or you will frighten the kittens.

PRACTICE 19.3B > Combining Simple Sentences to Form Compound Sentences

Read the sentences. Combine the pairs of simple sentences to form compound sentences.

EXAMPLE   Comedies are fine. I prefer action movies.

ANSWER   *Comedies are fine, but I prefer action movies.*

11. My sister sings well. I cannot carry a tune.

12. Our team may win. The other team may beat us.

13. Sue washed the car. Her brother did the laundry.

14. The map is a little dirty. Someone spilled coffee on it.

15. The train arrived at noon. Several passengers got on and off.

16. My study habits have improved. I expect better test scores.

17. The book is rather long. I finished it fairly quickly.

18. I invited Juan to my house. We studied for the test together.

19. The cruise ship stopped first in Juneau. The next stop was Skagway.

20. Louise's dog is a purebred border collie. Mine is a mutt.

SPEAKING APPLICATION

With a partner, take turns telling about a household chore. Use two simple sentences and two compound sentences. Your partner should listen for and identify the simple sentences and the compound sentences.

WRITING APPLICATION

Write four sentences about an event in American history. Use two simple sentences and two compound sentences. Underline the subject and verb in each simple sentence and the subjects and verbs in the clauses of each compound sentence.

PRACTICE 19.3C > Recognizing Complex
Sentences

Read the sentences. Then, label each sentence
complex or *not complex*.

EXAMPLE   Gloria bought pens, pencils, and
paper at the store.

ANSWER   *not complex*

1. Tomorrow is my sister's birthday, but her
party is on Saturday.

2. While officials assessed the storm damage,
the governor declared a state of emergency.

3. Clara brought a housewarming gift to her
new neighbor.

4. Bruce put his backpack on the floor during
lunch, and he forgot it when he left.

5. When the plumber arrived, Fran showed him
the leaking pipe.

6. If you visit the eye doctor, you will take a
vision test.

7. I have a large collection of comics; my
brother's collection is even bigger.

8. The screenplay was finalized, and the filming
began.

9. The athlete from the Ukraine is the one who
earned the gold medal.

10. The real estate agent who sold us our house
has now retired.

PRACTICE 19.3D > Distinguishing Compound
and Complex Sentences

Read the sentences. Then, label each sentence
compound or *complex*.

EXAMPLE   The building that burned was a shoe
store.

ANSWER   *complex*

11. I visit the library often, but I never go by bus.

12. As soon as I got home, I took a shower.

13. The small shop, which was open only on
weekends, sold meat and fish.

14. My dad speaks five different languages, yet
he doesn't travel much anymore.

15. The airport metal detector went off because
I was still wearing my watch.

16. Sam joined the hockey team, and he became
the star player.

17. My grandfather cannot hear well if there is
background noise.

18. Will Jody be ready when the taxi arrives?

19. I like mysteries; Juan prefers science fiction.

20. Answer quickly, before you forget the
question.

WRITING APPLICATION

Write four to five sentences about going to
the dentist. At least two sentences should be
complex sentences. Be sure and punctuate the
sentences correctly. Then, read the sentences
to a partner, and have your partner identify the
complex sentences.

WRITING APPLICATION

Write four sentences about a family tradition.
Use two compound sentences and two
complex sentences. Be sure and punctuate the
sentences correctly.

CHAPTER 20

EFFECTIVE SENTENCES

Use sentences of different lengths and complexity to make your writing more dynamic.

WRITE GUY *Jeff Anderson, M.Ed.*

WHAT DO YOU NOTICE?

Focus on the variety of sentences as you zoom in on these sentences from Act II of *Diary of Anne Frank* by Frances Goodrich and Albert Hackett.

MENTOR TEXT

> Our stomachs are so empty that they rumble and make strange noises, all in different keys. Mr. Van Daan's is deep and low, like a bass fiddle. Mine is high, whistling like a flute.

Now, ask yourself the following questions:

- How and why does the author use sentences of different lengths?
- Why might the author have decided not to combine the second and third sentences?

The author begins with a longer sentence and follows with two shorter sentences. Sentences of different lengths create more variety so that the writing flows. The author may have decided to keep the second and third sentences separated in order to make two distinct points.

Grammar for Writers Writers create flow by using a combination of short and long, simple and complex sentences. If you find too many of one kind of sentence in a text block, look for ways to break them up or combine them for variety.

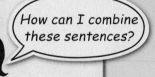

How can I combine these sentences?

I have an extra and and or you can use.

20.1 Classifying the Four Functions of a Sentence

Sentences can be classified according to what they do. Some sentences present facts or information in a direct way, while others pose questions to the reader or listener. Still others present orders or directions. A fourth type of sentence expresses strong emotion.

These four types of sentences are called **declarative, interrogative, imperative,** and **exclamatory.** As well as having a different purpose, each type of sentence is constructed in a different way.

The type of sentence you are writing determines the punctuation mark you use to end the sentence. The three end marks are the **period (.),** the **question mark (?),** and the **exclamation mark (!).**

The **declarative sentence** is the most common type of sentence. It is used to state, or "declare," ideas.

RULE 20.1.1

> A **declarative sentence** states, or declares, an idea and ends with a period.

DECLARATIVE   Space travel is very exciting.

Astronauts train for many years before they can fly into space.

Although it is a dangerous career choice, many people apply to the astronaut training program at NASA.

Interrogative means "asking." An **interrogative sentence** is a question. Interrogative sentences often begin with *who, what, when, why, how,* or *how many*. They end with a question mark.

RULE

20.1.2

An **interrogative sentence** asks a question and ends with a question mark.

INTERROGATIVE

When is the student council election?

Who is running for president?

When will the candidates give their speeches?

RULE

20.1.3

An **imperative sentence** gives an order, or command, or a direction and ends with either a period or an exclamation mark.

The word *imperative* comes from the Latin word that means "commanding." **Imperative sentences** are commands or directions. Most imperative sentences start with a verb. In this type of sentence, the subject is understood to be *you*.

IMPERATIVE

Be careful.

Watch where you step!

Notice the punctuation at the end of these examples. In the first sentence, the period suggests that a mild command is being given in an ordinary tone of voice. The exclamation mark at the end of the second sentence suggests a strong command, one given in a loud voice.

RULE

20.1.4

An **exclamatory sentence** conveys strong emotion and ends with an exclamation mark.

See Practice 20.1A
See Practice 20.1B
See Practice 20.1C
See Practice 20.1D

Exclaim means "to shout out." **Exclamatory sentences** are used to "shout out" emotions such as happiness, fear, delight, or anger.

EXCLAMATORY

What a mess this room is!

I need the key now!

Read the sentences. Then, identify each type of sentence by writing *declarative*, *interrogative*, *imperative*, or *exclamatory*.

EXAMPLE   What did you do in science lab?

ANSWER   *interrogative*

1. Please turn down the volume on your radio.
2. Ginger is a spice popular in Asian cooking.
3. What a dilemma we faced!
4. Which famous American appears on the dollar bill?
5. Lucille Ball was a talented comic performer.
6. How many times has she visited Miami?
7. Stir a cup of water into the mixture.
8. This apple tastes great!
9. I heard thunder in the distance.
10. Don't call before nine in the morning.

Read the sentences. Then, rewrite each sentence, adding the correct end punctuation.

EXAMPLE   Have you had a flu shot this year

ANSWER   *Have you had a flu shot this year?*

11. What a foolish error
12. Please bring a pencil for the test
13. From 1929 until World War II, America suffered through the Great Depression
14. Paula works as a nurse at the health clinic
15. How beautiful Santa Barbara is
16. Clean your room, please
17. What brand of shampoo do you usually use
18. I accept your facts but cannot agree with all your conclusions
19. How will you pay for the meal
20. I asked Don if he knew who the winner was

SPEAKING APPLICATION

With a partner, take turns telling about a beautiful place. Use each of the four types of sentences. Your partner should identify the four types of sentences that you used.

WRITING APPLICATION

Write four sentences about an activity you enjoy. Each sentence should be a different type—declarative, interrogative, imperative, or exclamatory. Be sure to use appropriate end punctuation.

PRACTICE 20.1C > **Writing Four Types of Sentences**

Read the topics. For each topic, write the type of sentence specified in parentheses. Be sure to use the appropriate end punctuation.

EXAMPLE   beautiful scenery (exclamatory)

ANSWER   *What a gorgeous sunset!*

1. a future plan (interrogative)
2. a request to a repair worker (imperative)
3. a movie review (exclamatory)
4. a fact from history (declarative)
5. something that is lost (interrogative)
6. a television newscaster (declarative)
7. a way to save money (imperative)
8. a gift you received (exclamatory)
9. a direction to a child (imperative)
10. a mysterious object (interrogative)

PRACTICE 20.1D > **Revising Four Types of Sentences**

Read the sentences. Rewrite each sentence, changing it to the type of sentence specified in parentheses. Be sure to use the appropriate end punctuation.

EXAMPLE   I sat under the tree. (imperative)

ANSWER   *Don't sit under the tree.*

11. The dog was lost. (interrogative)
12. You can look up the meaning in a dictionary. (imperative)
13. Skiing is exciting. (exclamatory)
14. Is the forest a place of mystery? (declarative)
15. Don't go to the movies today. (interrogative)
16. What a strange noise that was! (declarative)
17. Can I wear jeans to the interview? (imperative)
18. She is a computer genius. (exclamatory)
19. Use the smaller fork for the salad. (declarative)
20. How memorable his speech was! (interrogative)

SPEAKING APPLICATION

With a partner, take turns changing each other's sentence types. Say four sentences that illustrate one of each of the four sentence types. Your partner should change each one to another sentence type. Sentences can be on the subject of your choice.

WRITING APPLICATION

Write four sentences—one declarative, one interrogative, one imperative, and one exclamatory—all about the same natural wonder. Then, turn each sentence into a different type. Be sure to use appropriate end punctuation.

20.2 Combining Sentences

Good writing should include sentences of varying lengths and complexity to create a flow of ideas. One way to achieve sentence variety is to combine sentences to express two or more related ideas or pieces of information in a single sentence.

Look at the example below. Then, look at how the ideas are combined in different ways.

EXAMPLE	I trained for soccer. I trained for tennis.
COMBINED	I trained for soccer and tennis.
	I trained for tennis after I trained for soccer.

Combining Sentence Parts

RULE 20.2.1

> Sentences can be combined by using a **compound subject**, a **compound verb**, or a **compound object.**

EXAMPLE	The sprints are exhausting to run. The marathon is exhausting to run.
COMPOUND SUBJECT	The **sprints** and the **marathon** are exhausting to run.
EXAMPLE	Our team trained hard. Our team won the championship.
COMPOUND VERB	Our team **trained** hard and **won** the championship.
EXAMPLE	Short races require a quick start. Short races require explosive speed.
COMPOUND OBJECT	Short races require a quick **start** and explosive **speed.**

Joining Clauses

A **compound sentence** consists of two or more main or independent clauses. (See Chapter 19 for more information about clauses.) Use a compound sentence when combining related ideas of equal weight.

To create a compound sentence, join two main clauses with a comma and a coordinating conjunction. Common conjunctions include *and, but, nor, for, so, or,* and *yet.* You can also link the two sentences with a semicolon (;) if they are closely related.

> Sentences can be combined by joining two main clauses to create a **compound sentence.**

RULE 20.2.2

EXAMPLE	We went to the planetarium.
	We saw the planets and the stars.
COMPOUND SENTENCE	We went to the planetarium, and we saw the planets and the stars.
EXAMPLE	Sam enjoyed watching the sky.
	Mari enjoyed looking for constellations.
COMPOUND SENTENCE	Sam enjoyed watching the sky, and Mari enjoyed looking for constellations.
EXAMPLE	Lee assembled the telescope.
	Walt turned off the lights in the house.
COMPOUND SENTENCE	Lee assembled the telescope; Walt turned off the lights in the house.
EXAMPLE	Ming knows all of the phases of the moon.
	Jake knows how the moon affects the tides.
COMPOUND SENTENCE	Ming knows all of the phases of the moon, and Jake knows how the moon affects the tides.

See Practice 20.2A
See Practice 20.2B

20.2.3 > **Sentences can be combined by changing one of them into a subordinate clause.**

A **complex sentence** consists of one **main** or **independent clause** and one or more **subordinate clauses.** (See Chapter 19 for more information about clauses.) Combine sentences into a complex sentence to emphasize that one of the ideas in the sentence depends on the other. A subordinating conjunction will help readers understand the relationship. Common subordinating conjunctions are *after, although, because, before, since,* and *unless.* Generally no punctuation is required when a main and a subordinate clause are combined. When the subordinate clause comes first, a comma is needed. (See Chapter 25 for more information on punctuation.)

EXAMPLE   We were frightened. All of the lights went off.

COMBINED   We were frightened because all of the lights
           went off.

See Practice 20.2C

20.2.4 > **Sentences can be combined by changing one of them into a phrase.**

When combining sentences in which one of the sentences simply adds details, change one of the sentences into a **phrase.**

EXAMPLE   The space shuttle will be launched tomorrow.
           It will study asteroids near Earth.

COMBINED   The space shuttle will be launched tomorrow to
           study asteroids near Earth.

EXAMPLE   The space shuttle will launch from Cape Canaveral.
           It will lift off at noon.

COMBINED   The space shuttle will launch from Cape Canaveral
           at noon.

See Practice 20.2D

PRACTICE 20.2A **Combining Sentences Using Compound Subjects, Verbs, and Objects**

Read the sentences. Combine the sentences in each group into a single sentence. Identify each combination as *compound subject, compound verb,* or *compound object.*

EXAMPLE   Sara likes movies. Jo likes them too.

ANSWER   *Sara and Jo like movies. —* compound subject

1. The farmer irrigated his crops. He also weeded them.

2. Margo studies ballet. Olga studies ballet.

3. I put ketchup on my hamburger. I put mustard on it too.

4. Sam phoned me last night. Jewel phoned me last night. April also phoned me last night.

5. Claude likes crosswords. He likes word jumbles. He likes most other word games too.

6. Sam plays soccer. I do too.

7. Yesterday Alexis called. She invited me to her house.

8. We may take a train. We may take a bus. We may take a car.

9. They serve a good breakfast. They serve a bad lunch.

10. Every morning, Liz exercises on her treadmill. Then she swims at the town pool.

PRACTICE 20.2B **Combining Sentences Using Main Clauses**

Read the sentences. Combine each pair into a compound sentence, using the coordinating conjunction in parentheses. Be sure to use the correct punctuation for compound sentences.

EXAMPLE   The supermarket is open. The pharmacy is closed. (but)

ANSWER   *The supermarket is open, but the pharmacy is closed.*

11. We arrived in Milwaukee at noon. Aunt Grace met us at the airport. (and)

12. Many gold seekers went to California by water. Some went overland. (but)

13. The desert is very dry. It gets little rainfall. (;)

14. Bring a towel. Don't forget sunscreen. (and)

15. The earphones may have a loose wire. The entire MP3 player may be broken. (or)

16. My family has a dog. We do not have a cat. (but)

17. The visitors felt special. The governor had greeted them by name. (for)

18. Will you be going downtown? Are you staying home? (or)

19. None of the boys will admit it. Someone sent me this unsigned Valentine card. (yet)

20. Lozenges did not cure my cough. Cough medicine did not make it better. (nor)

SPEAKING APPLICATION

Tell a partner about something you might do after school. Your partner should listen for and identify compound subjects, verbs, or objects.

WRITING APPLICATION

Use sentences 11, 12, and 13 as models, and write three pairs of sentences about a shopping trip. Then, combine each pair by using an appropriate connector.

PRACTICE 20.2C > Combining Sentences Using Subordinate Clauses

Read the sentences. Combine each pair by changing one sentence into a subordinate clause, using the subordinating conjunction in parentheses. Be sure to use the correct punctuation for complex sentences.

EXAMPLE   Louise's shoes were too tight. Louise got blisters. (because)

ANSWER   *Because her shoes were too tight, Louise got blisters.*

1. The company changed its logo. Its products were repackaged with the new design. (after)

2. Thunder startled the horse. The horse nearly threw off its rider. (because)

3. Leo edited the school paper. Rita became the new editor. (until)

4. Ariana sang. Simon played the piano. (as)

5. Mr. Lowell mowed the lawn. Then he painted the house. (before)

6. My favorite team is in the playoffs. They will be more exciting for me this year. (since)

7. I went to northern Arizona. There I saw the Grand Canyon. (where)

8. Helen Keller could not hear or see. Anne Sullivan taught her to speak. (although)

9. In the 1890s, women began wearing loose pants. Bicycle riding became a fad. (when)

10. Hopefully, the library can raise the money. The new wing can be built. (if)

PRACTICE 20.2D > Combining Sentences Using Phrases

Read the sentences. Combine each pair of sentences by changing one into a phrase.

EXAMPLE   Sharla served small sandwiches. They had no crusts.

ANSWER   *Sharla served small sandwiches without crusts.*

11. I read a book. It was about Alaska.

12. I am learning about ecology. That is the study of the environment.

13. The geese flew through the air. The geese maintained a V-shaped formation.

14. Please turn off your cellphone. Do it before entering the museum.

15. Mom and I will play a board game. We will play after dinner.

16. Sheila went to the bank. She made a deposit.

17. My uncle grows zucchini in his vegetable garden. Zucchini is a type of summer squash.

18. Mom ate breakfast. Then Mom left for work.

19. Ralph made an emergency call. The fire department responded promptly.

20. Amy Tan was born in 1952. She grew up in California.

SPEAKING APPLICATION

Tell a partner about something you are studying, using items 11 and 12 as models. Your partner should combine each pair of sentences.

WRITING APPLICATION

Use items 1, 2, and 3 as models, and write three pairs of sentences about a game you like to play. Then, combine each pair by using a subordinating conjunction.

20.3 Varying Sentences

When you vary the length and form of the sentences you write, you are able to create a rhythm, achieve an effect, or emphasize the connections between ideas.

There are several ways you can introduce variety into the sentences you write.

20.3.1
RULE

> **Varying the length of sentences makes writing lively and interesting to read.**

WRITING COACH

Online

www.phwritingcoach.com

Grammar Practice
Practice your grammar skills with Writing Coach Online.

Grammar Games
Test your knowledge of grammar in this fast-paced interactive video game.

Varying Sentence Length

Reading too many long sentences in a row can be just as uninteresting as reading too many short sentences in a row. When you want to emphasize a point or surprise a reader, insert a short, direct sentence to interrupt the flow of several long sentences.

EXAMPLE   In the 1830s, model railroading was not a hobby. However, during that decade the first miniature railroad was built. This first railroad contained a locomotive, several passenger cars, and some track. It was not created for entertainment; it was a model for a locomotive that was being planned. **That first model served its purpose well.**

You can also break some longer sentences into shorter sentences. If the longer sentence contains two or more ideas, you can break up the ideas into separate sentences. However, if a longer sentence contains only one main idea, you should not break it apart.

LONGER SENTENCE   Mathias Baldwin created the first model railroad to help him design a new type of locomotive.

TWO SENTENCES   Mathias Baldwin created the first model railroad. This miniature helped him design a new locomotive.

See Practice 20.3A

Varying Sentence Beginnings

Another way to create variety is by changing from the usual subject–verb order in a sentence.

Sentence beginnings can also be varied by reversing the traditional subject–verb order or starting the sentence with an adverb or a phrase.

EXAMPLES

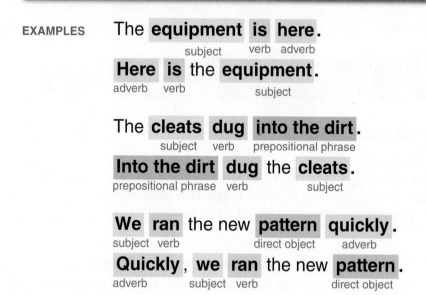

The **equipment is here**.
subject · verb · adverb

Here is the **equipment**.
adverb · verb · subject

The **cleats dug into the dirt**.
subject · verb · prepositional phrase

Into the dirt dug the **cleats**.
prepositional phrase · verb · subject

We ran the new **pattern quickly**.
subject · verb · direct object · adverb

Quickly, **we ran** the new **pattern**.
adverb · subject · verb · direct object

Another way to vary your sentences is to begin them in different ways. For instance, you can start sentences with different parts of speech.

See Practice 20.3B

WAYS TO VARY SENTENCE BEGINNINGS	
Start with a noun.	**Lab experiments**, surprisingly, are fun to conduct.
Start with an adverb.	**Surprisingly**, lab experiments are fun to conduct.
Start with an infinitive phrase.	**To conduct lab experiments**, surprisingly, is fun.
Start with a gerund phrase.	**Conducting lab experiments is**, surprisingly, fun.
Start with a prepositional phrase.	**For an interested student**, lab experiments are fun to conduct.

PRACTICE 20.3A **Varying Sentence Length**

Read the sentences. Rewrite each long compound sentence as two or more shorter sentences.

EXAMPLE   Salmon hatch in rivers, and they swim to the ocean, but they return to the rivers to breed.

ANSWER   *Salmon hatch in rivers. They swim to the ocean, but they return to the rivers to breed.*

1. The waiter brought a bowl of soup, and I ate it, and it was delicious.

2. I spilled juice on my computer keyboard, and now it does not work well, and the letters stick.

3. The tennis star served, and her opponent hit the ball back over the net, but it was a foul.

4. San Diego is a beautiful city, and it has a fine climate, and it also has a wonderful zoo.

5. Maida goes hiking with her brother, and they often hike in the national parks, but they have also hiked the Appalachian Trail.

PRACTICE 20.3B **Varying Sentence Beginnings**

Read the sentences. Rewrite each sentence, changing the beginning as specified in parentheses. If there are two sentences, combine them, using one of the sentences to help you create the specified beginning.

EXAMPLE   Gary and I went out for pizza. (Begin with a prepositional phrase.)

ANSWER   *After school, Gary and I went out for pizza.*

6. I caught a fish. That was surprising. (Begin with an adverb.)

7. Red-winged blackbirds flew toward the lake. (Begin with a prepositional phrase.)

8. Completing the crossword puzzle is my goal. (Begin with an infinitive.)

9. The dancer leaped into the air. (Change the subject-verb order.)

10. My favorite activity is playing baseball. (Begin with a gerund.)

SPEAKING APPLICATION

With a partner, take turns telling about packing a suitcase. Your partner should make suggestions about how to improve your sentences by varying sentence length.

WRITING APPLICATION

Write five sentences about a famous explorer or inventor. Vary your sentence beginnings. Include at least one sentence in which you change the subject-verb order.

20.4 Avoiding Sentence Problems

Recognizing problems with sentences will help you avoid and fix any problems in your writing.

WRITING COACH

Online

www.phwritingcoach.com

Grammar Tutorials
Brush up on your Grammar skills with these animated videos.

Grammar Practice
Practice your grammar skills with Writing Coach Online.

Grammar Games
Test your knowledge of grammar in this fast-paced interactive video game.

Find It / FIX IT

20

Grammar Game Plan

Correcting Fragments

Some groups of words—even though they have a capital letter at the beginning and a period at the end—are not complete sentences. They are **fragments.**

RULE **20.4.1**

> A **fragment** is a group of words that does not express a complete thought.

A fragment can be a group of words that includes a possible subject but no verb. A fragment could also be a group of words that includes a possible verb but no subject. It can even be a group of words that contains no subject and no verb. Fragments can be turned into complete sentences by adding a subject, a verb, or both.

FRAGMENTS	COMPLETE SENTENCES
heard the bell	I heard the bell. (A subject is added.)
the classroom door open	The classroom door is open. (A verb is added.)
in that hall	My locker is in that hall. (A subject and verb are added.)

See Practice 20.4A

Correcting Phrase Fragments A **phrase fragment** cannot stand alone because it does not have both a subject and a verb.

RULE **20.4.2**

> A **phrase fragment** should not be capitalized and punctuated as if it were a sentence.

A phrase fragment can be corrected in one of two ways:
(1) by adding it to a nearby sentence or (2) by adding whatever is needed to make it a complete sentence.

PHRASE FRAGMENT	The explorers left for the Arctic. **on the morning of March 4**
ADDED TO OTHER SENTENCE	The explorers left for the Arctic **on the morning of March 4** .
PHRASE FRAGMENT	They had packed heavy clothing. **along with weatherproof equipment**
COMPLETE SENTENCES	They had packed heavy clothing. They had also packed **weatherproof equipment** .

CHANGING PHRASE FRAGMENTS INTO SENTENCES	
PHRASE FRAGMENT	**COMPLETE SENTENCE**
in the early evening	The flight arrived **in the early evening** .
happy to be home	The travelers were **happy to be home** .
to pick up their luggage	They waited **to pick up their luggage** .

See Practice 20.4B

Correcting Clause Fragments

All clauses have subjects and verbs, but some cannot stand alone as sentences.

> **A subordinate clause** should not be capitalized and punctuated as if it were a sentence.

RULE 20.4.3

Subordinate clauses do not express complete thoughts. Although a subordinate adjective or adverb clause has a subject and a verb, it cannot stand by itself as a sentence. (See Chapter 19 for more information about subordinate clauses and the words that begin them.)

Like phrase fragments, **clause fragments** can usually be corrected in either of two ways: (1) by attaching the fragment to a nearby sentence or (2) by adding whatever words are needed to turn the fragment into a sentence.

CLAUSE FRAGMENT	Jane found the necklace. **that she had lost in gym class**
COMPLETE SENTENCE	Jane found the necklace **that she had lost in gym class**.
CLAUSE FRAGMENT	It was lying on a book. **which was underneath the bench near her locker**
COMPLETE SENTENCE	It was lying on a book, **which was underneath the bench near her locker**.
CLAUSE FRAGMENT	The clasp had broken. **that had held the chain together**
COMPLETE SENTENCE	The clasp **that had held the chain together** had broken.

To change a clause fragment into a sentence by the second method, you must add an independent clause to the fragment.

CHANGING CLAUSE FRAGMENTS INTO SENTENCES	
CLAUSE FRAGMENT	**COMPLETE SENTENCE**
that was overdue	I returned the library book **that was overdue**. The library book **that was overdue** has been returned.
when I got there	The library was almost ready to close **when I got there**. **When I got there**, the library was almost ready to close.
why I was so late	I couldn't figure out **why I was so late**.

See Practice 20.4C
See Practice 20.4D

PRACTICE 20.4A **Recognizing Fragments**

Read the groups of words. Then, write whether each group of words is a *sentence* or a *fragment*.

EXAMPLE   A child reaching for a toy.

ANSWER   *fragment*

1. At the very end of the street.
2. Did they arrive?
3. This highway has no rest stops.
4. A reporter holding a microphone.
5. When we left for Mexico City.
6. Please join us.
7. To say my lines without breaking into laughter.
8. The city with the best restaurants in America.
9. A guard helping the children across the street.
10. We're lost.

PRACTICE 20.4B **Changing Phrase Fragments Into Sentences**

Read the phrase fragments. Then, use each fragment in a sentence.

EXAMPLE   below the ceiling

ANSWER   *Below the ceiling is a shelf with plates on display.*

11. before ten o'clock
12. exhausted by the ordeal
13. a famous inventor
14. to reach school on time
15. between my friend and me
16. should have been informed
17. exercising often
18. buying a new sweater
19. a farmer harvesting his crops
20. a good movie to watch on DVD

SPEAKING APPLICATION

With a partner, take turns creating fragments. Your partner should listen to the fragment and turn it into a sentence.

WRITING APPLICATION

Choose two fragments in Practice 20.4B and write two new sentences.

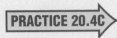

PRACTICE 20.4C Changing Clause Fragments Into Sentences

Read the clause fragments. Then, use each fragment in a sentence.

EXAMPLE   since I heard from her yesterday

ANSWER   *Since I heard from her yesterday, I don't expect Delia to phone today.*

1. if you know the answer

2. before you arrived

3. because I love fruit

4. which you cannot afford to buy

5. since no one can ride that horse

6. after we leave the locker room

7. whom I trust most in the world

8. as long as you keep your promise

9. that I tried hardest to master

10. whose house is closest to mine

PRACTICE 20.4D Changing Fragments Into Sentences

Read the groups of words. If a group of words is a fragment, use it in a sentence. If a group of words is already a sentence, write *sentence*.

EXAMPLE   A new pencil with an eraser.

ANSWER   *I want a new pencil with an eraser.*

11. Around the corner from the deli.

12. Don't give up without a fight.

13. Dreaming of a career as a lawyer.

14. When the cable guy came to the door.

15. The house by the side of the road.

16. A tree fell.

17. The hedge that needs trimming.

18. To put money aside and save it for a rainy day.

19. Are you ready?

20. Unless you think that you can do better.

SPEAKING APPLICATION

With a partner, take turns using fragments 1, 2, and 3 in new sentences.

WRITING APPLICATION

Write two sentences and two fragments about a fictional character. Then, exchange papers with a partner. Identify the two fragments that your partner wrote, and turn them into sentences.

Run-on Sentences

A fragment is an incomplete sentence. A **run-on,** on the other hand, is two or more complete sentences that are punctuated as though they were one sentence.

Find It/ FIX IT

15

Grammar
Game Plan

> **A run-on** is two or more complete sentences that are not properly joined or separated.

20.4.4

RULE

Run-ons are usually the result of carelessness. Check your sentences carefully to see where one sentence ends and the next one begins.

Two Kinds of Run-ons

There are two kinds of run-ons. The first one is made up of two sentences that are run together without any punctuation between them. This is called a **fused sentence.**

The second type of run-on consists of two or more sentences separated by only a comma. This type of run-on is called a **comma splice.**

FUSED SENTENCES	Jimmy ran for the bus he was late.
	I use the gym at school often I like the basketball court.
COMMA SPLICE	I like new cars with sunroofs, they are fun on summer days.
	The new field at the park has lots of rocks, someone needs to get rid of them.

See Practice 20.4E

Find It/ FIX IT

16

Grammar
Game Plan

A good way to distinguish between a run-on and a sentence is to read the words aloud. Your ear will tell you whether you have one or two complete thoughts and whether you need to make a complete break between the thoughts.

Three Ways to Correct Run-ons

There are three ways to correct run-on sentences. You can use end marks, commas and coordinating conjunctions, or semicolons.

Using End Marks
Periods, question marks, and exclamation marks are useful to fix run-on sentences.

RULE

20.4.5

> **Use an end mark to separate a run-on sentence into two sentences.**

Sometimes the best way to correct a run-on is to use an end mark to split the run-on into two shorter but complete sentences. End marks help your reader pause and group your ideas more effectively.

RUN-ON   Last Saturday I saw a new movie, it was really exciting.

CORRECTED   Last Saturday I saw a new movie. It was really exciting.

RUN-ON   Where are you going I can't keep up.

CORRECTED   Where are you going? I can't keep up.

RUN-ON   What did you say I can't hear you.

CORRECTED   What did you say? I can't hear you.

RUN-ON   Where are the new basketballs they were here yesterday.

CORRECTED   Where are the new basketballs? They were here yesterday.

Using Commas and Coordinating Conjunctions
Sometimes the two parts of a run-on are related and should be combined into a compound sentence.

RULE
20.4.6

> **Use a comma and a coordinating conjunction to combine two independent clauses into a compound sentence.**

To separate the clauses properly, use both a comma and a coordinating conjunction. The most common coordinating conjunctions are *and, but, or, for, nor,* and *yet.* Before you separate a sentence into parts, though, be sure each part expresses a complete thought.

RUN-ON	Jim's football uniform is too tight, he needs money to buy a larger size.
CORRECTED	Jim's football uniform is too tight, and he needs money to buy a larger size
RUN-ON	He has grown several inches since last year, his shoes still fit.
CORRECTED	He has grown several inches since last year, but his shoes still fit.

Using Semicolons
You can sometimes use a semicolon to connect the two parts of a run-on into a correct sentence.

RULE
20.4.7

> **Use a semicolon to connect two closely related ideas into one sentence.**

Use a semicolon only when the ideas in both parts of the sentence are closely related.

RUN-ON	My geometry class is scheduled for 1:00, my biology class is scheduled for 1:50.
CORRECTED	My geometry class is scheduled for 1:00; my biology class is scheduled for 1:50.

See Practice 20.4F

PRACTICE 20.4E > **Recognizing Run-ons**

Read the groups of words. Then, write whether each group is a *sentence* or a *run-on*.

EXAMPLE   I went to the post office, I bought stamps.

ANSWER   *run-on*

1. The speech was too long I had to cut it.

2. The hurricane hit the small island, it was quite severe.

3. Well after midnight, I was still awake.

4. I would like to visit Greenland to see the northern lights.

5. The Pacific Ocean was named by Ferdinand Magellan, pacific means "peaceful."

6. Viv lives in a fairy tale she always expects a happy ending.

7. I rode my bicycle to Turner Park, where the music festival was held.

8. Jackson is the capital of Mississippi, it is named for President Andrew Jackson.

9. Kites flew in the sky they were so colorful.

10. Has the mail carrier come, or is she late?

PRACTICE 20.4F > **Correcting Run-ons**

Read the sentences. Rewrite each run-on sentence to correct the problem.

EXAMPLE   Alice went on the school trip, Sylvia did not.

ANSWER   *Alice went on the school trip, but Sylvia did not.*

11. I visited the dentist I had my teeth cleaned.

12. Miranda has a sapphire ring, it is very lovely.

13. New Hampshire was one of the original Thirteen Colonies, Vermont was not.

14. I like baked chicken I had it for dinner.

15. You can go to the six o'clock show, you can go to the eight o'clock show.

16. Agatha Christie wrote mysteries they had clever plots.

17. Vincent Van Gogh was a wonderful painter, his work includes many self-portraits.

18. The washing machine is leaking I cannot find what is wrong with it.

19. Digital cameras can take fine pictures, you can discard the bad ones.

20. The Marfa lights are a mystery, no one knows what causes them.

SPEAKING APPLICATION

Use run-on sentences 11, 12, and 13 as models, and tell your partner about local news. Ask your partner to correct each of your run-on sentences.

WRITING APPLICATION

Write two sentences and two run-ons describing a room in your house. Then, exchange papers with a partner. Identify the two run-ons that your partner wrote, and rewrite them as correct sentences.

Properly Placing Modifiers

If a phrase or clause acting as an adjective or adverb is not placed near the word it modifies, it may seem to modify a different word. Then the sentence may seem unclear or odd.

> **A modifier should be placed as close as possible to the word it describes.**

20.4.8

RULE

A modifier placed too far away from the word it describes is called a **misplaced modifier.**

MISPLACED MODIFIER The soccer club had the most goals **with new uniforms**.

The misplaced phrase *with new uniforms* makes it seem as though the practice had new uniforms.

See Practice 20.4G
See Practice 20.4H

PROPERLY PLACED MODIFIER The soccer club **with new uniforms** had the most goals.

Below is a different type of misplaced modifier that is sometimes called a **dangling modifier.** A dangling modifier at the beginning of a sentence causes the sentence to be unclear.

DANGLING MODIFIER **Sitting on the beach**, the sun felt hot.

In this sentence, *sitting on the beach* should modify a person or people. Instead, it incorrectly modifies *sun.*

CORRECTED **Sitting on the beach**, we felt the hot sun.

PRACTICE 20.4G ▸ **Revising to Correct Misplaced Modifiers**

Read the sentences. Then, rewrite each sentence to correct the underlined misplaced modifier.

EXAMPLE   <u>Rushing for the bus</u>, my lunch was forgotten.

ANSWER   *Rushing for the bus, I forgot my lunch.*

1. <u>Visiting my cousin on Elm Street</u>, my bicycle got a flat tire.

2. The delegates discussed world peace and human rights <u>at the United Nations</u>.

3. I saw a bird through my binoculars <u>that I had never seen before</u>.

4. Gordon will post that photo of Union Station <u>in the morning</u>.

5. Sherry bought a gift for her uncle <u>wrapped in pretty flowered paper</u>.

6. Mary visited her doctor <u>who is sick</u>.

7. Our car got stuck in the middle of the street <u>when it stalled</u>.

8. <u>At an early age</u>, my parents taught me good manners.

9. The judge asked the juror <u>with great seriousness</u> to leave the court room.

10. <u>Making lots of noise</u>, bears hopefully would be scared away from our campsite.

PRACTICE 20.4H ▸ **Recognizing and Correcting Misplaced Modifiers**

Read the sentences. If a sentence has a misplaced modifier, rewrite the sentence so the modifier is properly placed. If a sentence is correct, write *correct*.

EXAMPLE   The dog lost the bone it liked to chew in the alley.

ANSWER   *In the alley, the dog lost the bone it liked to chew.*

11. I saw the dog on the street with a black collar.

12. Pam wore a gray hat on her head that was clearly too small.

13. To get a rebate, you must mail in a form.

14. She stubbed her toe on the table leg wearing sandals.

15. Changing into a bathing suit, I went for a swim.

16. I saw twenty dollars on the floor getting out of bed.

17. In Hollywood, we spotted two movie stars riding around in our old car.

18. Our teacher described traveling through the jungle in our geography class.

19. At the museum I saw the self-portrait of Picasso with my sister.

20. Arriving in the dark, finding the motel gave us trouble.

SPEAKING APPLICATION

With a partner, take turns describing a favorite place. Be sure to use a combination of simple, compound, and complex sentences with modifiers. Your partner should identify the modifiers and correct any misplaced modifiers.

WRITING APPLICATION

Write a brief description of the clothing you are wearing. Include one simple, one compound, and one complex sentence. Then, discuss your sentences with a partner. Your partner should identify the modifiers and correct any misplaced modifiers.

Avoiding Double Negatives

Negative words, such as *nothing* and *not*, are used to deny or to say *no*. Some people mistakenly use **double negatives**—two negative words—when only one is needed.

> **Avoid writing sentences that contain double negatives.**

20.4.9 RULE

In the following examples, negative words are highlighted. The first sentence in each example contains double negatives. The corrected sentences show two ways to correct each double-negative sentence.

DOUBLE NEGATIVES	Mack **didn't** tell **no one** about the party.
CORRECTED SENTENCES	Mack **didn't** tell anyone about the party.
	Mack told **no one** about the party.
DOUBLE NEGATIVES	It seems we **won't** **never** have good weather.
CORRECTED SENTENCES	It seems we will **never** have good weather.
	It seems we **won't** ever have good weather.
DOUBLE NEGATIVES	My sweater **doesn't** fit **no** more.
CORRECTED SENTENCES	My sweater **doesn't** fit anymore.
	My sweater **no** longer fits.
DOUBLE NEGATIVES	**Aren't** you taking **nothing** with you?
CORRECTED SENTENCES	**Aren't** you taking anything with you?
	Are you taking **nothing** with you?
DOUBLE NEGATIVES	We **haven't no** new books here.
CORRECTED SENTENCES	We **haven't** any new books here.
	We have **no** new books here.

See Practice 20.4I
See Practice 20.4J

PRACTICE 20.4I ▷ Using Negatives Correctly

Read the sentences. Then, write the word in parentheses that makes each sentence negative without creating a double negative.

EXAMPLE   I haven't (ever, never) been to Italy.

ANSWER   *ever*

1. I (will, won't) never be taller than my brother.

2. We (do, don't) want anything to spoil the day.

3. He will not do (anything, nothing) to correct the problem.

4. Why hasn't (anybody, nobody) answered yet?

5. Since she moved to Hawaii, my cousin doesn't (ever, never) get home for Thanksgiving.

6. I cannot see (anyone, no one) in this fog.

7. Dean (should, shouldn't) never have gone out in such cold weather.

8. Aren't there (any, no) scrambled eggs left?

9. She is going (anywhere, nowhere) without me.

10. I couldn't read (any, none) of the small print without my glasses.

PRACTICE 20.4J ▷ Revising to Correct Double Negatives

Read the sentences. Then, rewrite each sentence to correct the double negative.

EXAMPLE   I haven't seen none of those movies.

ANSWER   *I haven't seen any of those movies.*
OR
I have seen none of those movies.

11. I can't do nothing about it.

12. There isn't nobody who can replace you.

13. I wouldn't have let no one bother you.

14. There weren't no birds in the nest.

15. Wasn't he never going to stop talking?

16. She didn't eat none of the mashed potatoes.

17. Be sure to tell no one nothing.

18. When I left, I still hadn't seen none of the parade.

19. You ought not to give him nothing.

20. The manager never gave nobody the job.

SPEAKING APPLICATION

With a partner, take turns telling where and when not to use a cellphone. Your partner should identify any double negatives and help correct them.

WRITING APPLICATION

With a partner, write three sentences telling a child how to behave. Include a double negative in each sentence. Then, exchange papers and correct your partner's double negatives.

Grammar Game Plan

Grammar Game Plan

Avoiding Common Usage Problems

This section contains fifteen common usage problems in alphabetical order. Some are expressions that you should avoid in both your speaking and your writing. Others are words that are often confused because of similar spellings or meanings.

(1) accept, except   Do not confuse the spelling of these words. *Accept*, a verb, means "to take what is offered" or "to agree to." *Except*, a preposition, means "leaving out" or "other than."

VERB	Brian **accepted** a part in the play.
PREPOSITION	No one **except** me passed the test.

(2) advice, advise   Do not confuse the spelling of these related words. *Advice*, a noun, means "an opinion." *Advise*, a verb, means "to give an opinion."

NOUN	I took her **advice** to join a club.
VERB	I **advise** new students to join clubs.

(3) affect, effect   *Affect*, a verb, means "to influence" or "to cause a change in." *Effect*, usually a noun, means "result."

VERB	A late start will **affect** your time in a race.
NOUN	What **effect** did the late start have on your race time?

(4) at   Do not use *at* after *where*.

INCORRECT	**Where** is my lunch **at**?
CORRECT	**Where** is my lunch?

(5) because   Do not use *because* after *the reason*. Eliminate one or the other.

INCORRECT	The **reason** he won is **because** he was fast.
CORRECT	He won **because** he was fast.
	The **reason** he won is **that** he was fast.

(6) beside, besides These two prepositions have different meanings and cannot be interchanged. *Beside* means "at the side of" or "close to." *Besides* means "in addition to."

EXAMPLES   My brother and I sit **beside** each other.

No one **besides** us sits on this side of the table.

(7) different from, different than *Different from* is preferred over *different than*.

EXAMPLE   My uniform is **different from** my brother's.

(8) farther, further *Farther* is used to refer to distance. *Further* means "additional" or "to a greater degree or extent."

EXAMPLES   The store is **farther** than the next corner.
After he sang, we needed no **further** auditions.

(9) in, into *In* refers to position. *Into* suggests motion.

POSITION   The groceries are **in** the refrigerator.

MOTION   I put the carrots **into** the vegetable drawer.

(10) kind of, sort of Do not use *kind of* or *sort of* to mean "rather" or "somewhat."

INCORRECT   My mountain bike is **sort of** new.

CORRECT   My mountain bike is **rather** new.

(11) like *Like*, a preposition, means "similar to" or "in the same way as." It should be followed by an object. Do not use *like* before a subject and a verb. Use *as* or *that* instead.

PREPOSITION   The house across the street looks **like** ours.

INCORRECT   This radio doesn't work **like** it should.

CORRECT   This radio doesn't work **as** it should.

(12) that, which, who   *That* and *which* refer to things.
Who refers only to people.

THINGS	There is the book **that** I wanted.
PEOPLE	Where are the people **who** signed up for the trip?

(13) their, there, they're   Do not confuse the spelling of these
three words. *Their,* a possessive adjective, always modifies a
noun. *There* is usually used as a sentence starter or as an adverb.
They're is a contraction of *they are.*

POSSESSIVE ADJECTIVE	The girls wanted to try on **their** uniforms.
SENTENCE STARTER	**There** are cardinals on the new shirts.
ADVERB	The new baseballs are over **there** .
CONTRACTION	**They're** waiting to go to the field.

(14) to, too, two   Do not confuse the spelling of these words.
To plus a noun creates a prepositional phrase. *To* plus a verb
creates an infinitive. *Too* is an adverb and modifies verbs,
adjectives, and other adverbs. *Two* is a number.

PREPOSITION	**to** the station	**to** Dallas
INFINITIVE	**to** understand	**to** receive
ADVERB	**too** strangely	**too** quickly
NUMBER	**two** notebooks	**two** newspapers

(15) when, where, why   Do not use *when, where,* or *why*
directly after a linking verb such as *is.* Reword the sentence.

INCORRECT	To win the race is **why** we trained hard.
CORRECT	We trained hard to win the race.
INCORRECT	In the morning is **when** I like to run.
CORRECT	I like to run in the morning.

See Practice 20.4K
See Practice 20.4L
See Practice 20.4M
See Practice 20.4N

Read the sentences. Then, write the word in parentheses that best completes each sentence.

EXAMPLE   Let's talk (farther, further) about our plans next week.

ANSWER   *further*

1. Everyone (accept, except) me brought a bathing suit to the barbecue.

2. (Their, They're) trying as hard as they can.

3. My best friend gives me good (advice, advise).

4. What (affect, effect) did the weather have on your plans?

5. Your outfit is quite (different from, different than) what you usually wear.

6. I tried to find the television remote but I don't know where (it is, it's at).

7. Will someone (beside, besides) me prepare food for the party?

8. The reason I left early is (because, that) I needed to finish my homework.

9. Pablo was (to, too) exhausted to keep running.

10. She is the politician with (which, whom) I most agree.

Read the sentences. If the underlined word is used correctly, write *correct*. If the word is incorrect, write the correct word.

EXAMPLE   I sat <u>besides</u> the lake in the park.

ANSWER   *beside*

11. <u>There</u> clever remarks made us laugh.

12. Is someone <u>besides</u> Jane going to help me?

13. I walked <u>in</u> the classroom and took my seat.

14. Does music in stores have any <u>effect</u> on shopping habits?

15. The airport was crowded, just <u>like</u> I expected.

16. When I went to the bowling alley, my younger sister went <u>to</u>.

17. Is Saturn <u>farther</u> from the sun than Jupiter?

18. Will your sister <u>except</u> Carl's invitation and go to the party?

19. The reason I struggle with my locker is <u>because</u> my locker door is always getting stuck.

20. What does your doctor <u>advise</u> that you do to get rid of your cold?

SPEAKING APPLICATION

With a partner, take turns talking about runners in a race. Use four sentences, each with a different one of these words: *beside*, *besides*, *farther*, and *further*. Your partner should listen to make sure that you use the four words correctly.

WRITING APPLICATION

With a partner, write four incomplete sentences about a club or a team. In parentheses, give the same choices to complete the sentences as those in Practice 20.4K, sentences 1–4. Then, exchange papers and indicate the correct words to complete your partner's sentences.

PRACTICE 20.4M ▷ **Recognizing and Correcting Usage Problems**

Read the sentences. Then, if a sentence has a usage problem, rewrite it to correct the problem. If a sentence is correct, write *correct*.

EXAMPLE   Jake was to tired to finish the race.

ANSWER   *Jake was too tired to finish the race.*

1. Their are nine justices on the Supreme Court.

2. The biography is sort of interesting.

3. The students went in the computer room.

4. Noon is when we usually eat lunch.

5. The wallpaper looks just as it should look.

6. Please advice me of the problems you encountered.

7. Mom doesn't know where the dog could be at.

8. I have answered all the survey questions except the last one.

9. Our school newspaper is different from other school newspapers.

10. The reason I did poorly on the test is because I did not study enough.

PRACTICE 20.4N ▷ **Avoiding Usage Problems**

Read the pairs of words. For each pair of words, write two sentences that are related in meaning.

EXAMPLE   their, there

ANSWER   *The children have their hearts set on visiting an amusement park.*

They should have fun there.

11. accept, except

12. advice, advise

13. affect, effect

14. beside, besides

15. farther, further

16. in, into

17. like, as

18. their, they're

19. too, two

20. which, who

SPEAKING APPLICATION

With a partner, choose two of the fifteen common usage problems. Explain the rules in your own words to your partner, and give two examples to illustrate.

WRITING APPLICATION

With a partner, write four sentences, each using a different word from the fifteen common usage problems. Then, exchange papers, and make sure your partner has avoided the common usage problems. Correct any errors you find.

Using Parallel Structures

Good writers try to present a series of ideas in similar grammatical structures so the ideas will read smoothly. If one element of a series is not parallel with the others, the result may be jarring or confusing. Parallel structures are important in simple, compound, and complex sentences.

Recognizing the Correct Use of Parallelism

To present a series of ideas of equal importance, you should use parallel grammatical structures.

> **Parallelism** involves presenting equal ideas in words, phrases, clauses, or sentences of similar types.

PARALLEL WORDS	Entering the room, the players felt **nervous**, **excited**, and **energetic**.
PARALLEL PHRASES	The fans in the stands began **clapping their hands** with enthusiasm and **stamping their feet** in rhythm.
PARALLEL CLAUSES	The cheering grew louder **as each player's name was called** and **as each team member ran onto the court**.
PARALLEL SENTENCES	**Every player received** an ovation. **Every player acknowledged** the crowd's applause.

Correcting Faulty Parallelism

Faulty parallelism occurs when a writer uses unequal grammatical structures to express similar ideas.

> Correct a sentence containing faulty parallelism by rewriting it so that each parallel idea is expressed in the same grammatical structure.

Faulty parallelism can involve words, phrases, and clauses in a series or in comparisons.

Correcting Faulty Parallelism in a Series

Always check for parallelism when your writing contains items in a series.

NONPARALLEL STRUCTURES	My after-school job involves **answering phones**,
	                                         gerund phrase
	 taking messages, and **to type up orders**.
	   gerund phrase infinitive phrase

CORRECTION	My after-school job involves **answering phones**,
	                                         gerund phrase
	 taking messages, and **typing up orders**.
	   gerund phrase gerund phrase

NONPARALLEL STRUCTURES	I believed all along **that I would finish the race**
	                                     noun clause
	 but not **coming in first**.
	         infinitive phrase

CORRECTION	I believed all along **that I would finish the race**
	                                     noun clause
	 but not **that I would come in first**.
	            noun clause

Correcting Faulty Parallelism in Comparisons

In writing comparisons, you generally should compare a phrase with the same type of phrase and a clause with the same type of clause.

NONPARALLEL STRUCTURES	We shop **in our neighborhood** rather than
	              prepositional phrase
	 shopping at the mall.
	   gerund phrase

CORRECTION	We shop **in our neighborhood** rather than **at the mall**. prepositional phrase prepositional phrase

NONPARALLEL STRUCTURES	**David** enjoys **building models** as much as
	   subject gerund phrase
	 collecting baseball cards thrills his **friends**.
	      subject direct object

CORRECTION	**David** enjoys **building models** as much as
	   subject gerund phrase
	 his **friends** enjoy **collecting baseball cards**.
	     subject gerund phrase

See Practice 20.4O
 See Practice 20.4P

PRACTICE 20.4O **Revising to Create Parallel Structures**

Read the sentences. Then, rewrite each sentence to correct nonparallel structures. Discuss the new sentences with a partner. Partners may suggest alternate ways to correct some sentences.

EXAMPLE   Sylvia felt tired, frustrated, and filled with anxiety.

ANSWER   *Sylvia felt tired, frustrated, and anxious.*

1. My teacher assigned a chapter to read, a paragraph to write, and to answer questions.

2. I clip articles that interest me, and I may read them again.

3. My friends prefer riding bikes to soccer.

4. The movie featured amazing special effects, exciting characters, and the dialogue was fast-paced.

5. The students met in the library, where ten resolutions were voted on by them.

6. I did poorly on the test more because of running out of time than that I didn't study.

7. I bought a notebook, Jan got pencils, and blank disks were what Evan purchased.

8. If you made your bed and your clothes are put away, you can go to the party.

9. I told my aunt about my friends rather than describing my new teachers.

10. I didn't call because I was out, and my cell phone was left at home.

PRACTICE 20.4P **Writing With Parallel Structures**

Read the sentences. Rewrite the sentences, and fill in the blanks with an appropriate parallel structure. Discuss your sentences with a partner. Your partner should identify and correct any nonparallel structures in your sentences.

EXAMPLE   I enjoy hiking, camping, and _____.

ANSWER   *I enjoy hiking, camping, and swimming.*

11. The wind swept through the valley, blowing over tents, bending trees, and _____.

12. Tell me what you plan to do this afternoon and _____.

13. The jurors filed out of the courtroom, and then _____.

14. I would rather travel by train than _____.

15. To reach the campground, we have to cross a stream, _____ a grove of trees, and to climb a hill.

16. Kim is a terrific dancer, Jin is a talented musician, and Su _____.

17. Jamal described the place where he was born and _____.

18. Here is my list for this afternoon: go to the library, _____, and eat at the sandwich shop.

19. My parents were angry because I stayed out past my curfew and _____.

20. Levi emerged from the water, coughing loudly, spitting out water, and _____.

SPEAKING APPLICATION

Working with a partner, describe how to build something or how to cook something. Your partner should listen for and correct any nonparallel structures you use.

WRITING APPLICATION

Write three sentences that include at least three items in a series. Read your sentences aloud to a partner. Have your partner listen for and correct any nonparallel structures.

Test Warm-Up

DIRECTIONS
Read the introduction and the passage that follows. Then, answer the questions to show that you can use and understand a variety of sentences that use parallel structures in reading and writing.

Anthony wrote this story about one of his family's traditions. Read the story and think about the changes you would suggest as a peer editor. When you finish reading, answer the questions that follow.

Our Apple Picking Adventure

(1) Every fall, my family packs into our van, drives on the highway, and picking apples at a nearby orchard. (2) This year, we had to postpone the trip for a week because of heavy rainstorms and my mother had been sick. (3) Once there, we slogged through mud, climbing over fallen branches, and we battled with others to pick the few good apples left on the trees. (4) By the end of the afternoon, we were tired, wet, and feeling annoyed. (5) Still, we did pick enough apples to make four pies.

---

1 What is the BEST way to revise sentence 1?

A Every fall, my family packs into our van, drives on the highway, and picks apples.

B Every fall, my family packs into our van, goes on the highway to a nearby orchard, and goes apple picking.

C Every fall, my family packs into our van, drives on the highway, and goes apple picking at a nearby orchard.

D Every fall, my family packing into our van, driving on the highway, and picking apples at a nearby orchard.

2 What change, if any, should be made in sentence 2?

F Add a comma after *rainstorms*

G Change *of heavy rainstorms and my mother* to **it had rained heavily and because my mother**

H Change *had been* to **having been**

J Make no change

3 What is the BEST way to revise sentence 3?

A Once there, we slogged through mud, climbed over fallen branches, and to battle with others to pick the few good apples left.

B Once there, we slogged through mud, climbed over fallen branches, and battled with others to pick the few good apples left.

C Once there, to slog through mud, to climb over fallen branches, to battle with others, to pick the few good apples left.

D Once there, we slogged through mud, climbing over fallen branches, and we battled with others picking the few good apples left.

4 What change, if any, should be made in sentence 4?

F Add **feeling** before *tired*

G Delete *feeling* before *annoyed*

H Delete the comma after *tired*

J Make no change

Using Consistent Tenses

Verb tense shows time relationships. Consistent tenses keep writing from being confusing. Review your writing to make sure that verb tenses are consistent.

RULE 20.4.12 > **Verbs in the same sentence should be in the same tense unless there is a logical reason to change tense.**

INCONSISTENT TENSES	She **went** to the park and **finds** her friends, who **are waiting** for her.
CONSISTENT TENSES	She went to the park and found her friends, who were waiting for her.

The first verb, *went*, sets the action in the past. The other actions also happened in the past, not the present.

INCONSISTENT TENSES	Mr. Chin **is promising** a prize to any student who **had told** him the definition of the word.
CONSISTENT TENSES	Mr. Chin is promising a prize to any student who can tell him the definition of the word.

The first verb phrase, *is promising* is in present progressive tense, showing a present action that is in progress. *Had told* is in past perfect tense for no logical reason.

Switching From One Tense to Another
You may switch tense if you use a time word or phrase to explain the tense shift.

EXAMPLE	**Last night**, I stayed up late studying, so **right now** I am struggling to stay awake.

In this case, the shift in tense from past to present shows a logical relationship between parts of the sentence.

See Practice 20.4Q
See Practice 20.4R

PRACTICE 20.4Q > Revising to Eliminate Inconsistent Tenses

Read the sentences. Then, rewrite each sentence so that the verb tense is consistent and logical. Discuss your sentences with a partner. Your partner should identify any inconsistent tenses that remain.

EXAMPLE   When Shira cooked dinner, she uses many pots and pans.

ANSWER   *When Shira cooked dinner, she* used *many pots and pans.*

1. Otto shouted orders that we try to follow.

2. The competitors stand and waited to begin.

3. Today, I read the ad, and tomorrow, I went to the store.

4. I skated all day, and I don't fall even once.

5. When John Adams was president, there are only 16 states in the Union.

6. I will volunteer if you agreed to help me.

7. When the audience claps, Sheralee took a bow and blows her mother a kiss.

8. Save a penny each day, and soon you have many dollars to spend.

9. Maria has taken out the garbage, and she washed the dishes.

10. My brother gets his license yesterday even though he almost fails the parking test.

PRACTICE 20.4R > Writing Sentences With Consistent Tenses

Read the sentences. Then, rewrite each sentence by filling the blank with a clause or verb phrase in the correct tense. Read your sentences to a partner. Your partner should correct any inconsistent verbs in your sentences.

EXAMPLE   I stopped at the store, and I _____.

ANSWER   *I stopped at the store, and I* bought bread and cheese*.*

11. When the electricity in our house went out, the food in our refrigerator _____.

12. I love watching the leaves fall from the trees, but _____.

13. Seven contestants started the race, but _____.

14. When a stranger approached Natalie, she _____.

15. Carlos is staying up all night and _____.

16. Keri knows all of the material, but _____.

17. A strong wind had begun to blow through the trees and _____.

18. When Shelley babysits, she always _____.

19. Liz _____ and used them for her science project.

20. My sister had yelled at me earlier, so _____.

SPEAKING APPLICATION

With a partner, take turns describing two events, one that happened in the past and one that is happening now. Your partner should listen for and write the verbs you use and correct any inconsistent tenses.

WRITING APPLICATION

Write two compound sentences that include at least two verbs in the present tense and two complex sentences that include at least two verbs in the past tense. Read your sentences aloud to a partner. Have your partner listen for and correct any inconsistent verb tenses.

PRACTICE 1 ▷ Using Complete Subjects and Predicates

Each item below contains only a complete subject or a complete predicate. Rewrite each item, making a sentence by adding the missing part indicated in parentheses.

1. The police officer (add a predicate).

2. (add a subject) splashed through the puddles.

3. The new shopping mall (add a predicate).

4. Is (add a subject) dangerous?

5. The star reporter (add a predicate).

6. (add a subject) walked to school.

7. The large ship (add a predicate).

8. (add a subject) smelled wonderful.

9. The pitcher and the catcher (add a predicate).

10. (add a subject) hurried into the building.

PRACTICE 2 ▷ Using Direct Objects

Rewrite each incomplete sentence, supplying a direct object where indicated in parentheses. You may also include the article *a, an,* or *the* or another modifier along with the direct object.

1. Babies require (direct object).

2. I dislike loud (direct object).

3. The chef is making (direct object).

4. In the waiting room, I saw (direct object).

5. Myra decorated (direct object) with sprinkles.

6. Bryce put (direct object) on the shelf.

7. She asked (direct object) and (direct object) for assistance.

8. Val amuses (direct object) with her chatter.

9. The captain showed us (direct object).

10. What causes (direct object) to appear?

PRACTICE 3 ▷ Identifying Indirect Objects

Read the sentences. Then, write the indirect object in each sentence. If there is no indirect object, write *none*.

1. The ticket agent sold him a ticket.

2. The teacher gave the class a test.

3. My sister sewed herself a new skirt.

4. Edith shoveled snow for more than an hour.

5. Don't confuse me with too much information.

6. The opera star sang us the new aria.

7. Marnie offered her friend sound advice.

8. I wish you a good time on your travels.

9. The doctor gave the patient more medicine.

10. Who will toss the seals some fish to eat?

PRACTICE 4 ▷ Identifying Subject Complements

Read the sentences. Then, write the subject complement in each sentence. Also indicate whether it is a *predicate noun,* a *predicate pronoun,* or a *predicate adjective.*

1. The children look happy.

2. The singer with the loudest voice is you.

3. She will be the new star of the show.

4. The flight seemed very turbulent.

5. The puppy is energetic.

6. Louisa May Alcott was a writer.

7. Of all the team's players, the best one is he.

8. Please do not be so noisy at this hour.

9. That loud leopard print is really something.

10. Is Rover a good watchdog?

PRACTICE 5
Using Prepositional Phrases

Read the sentences. Then, rewrite each sentence, supplying the type of prepositional phrase indicated in parentheses.

1. Al bought the DVD. (Add an adjective phrase.)

2. The cat sat patiently. (Add an adverb phrase.)

3. The sound was eerie. (Add an adjective phrase.)

4. Ina brought lemonade. (Add an adverb phrase.)

5. A stranger arrived. (Add an adjective phrase and an adverb phrase.)

PRACTICE 6
Identifying Appositive, Participial, Gerund, and Infinitive Phrases

Read the sentences. Then, write whether the underlined phrase in each sentence is an *appositive phrase*, a *participial phrase*, a *gerund phrase*, or an *infinitive phrase*.

1. Delighted by the puppet show, the children clapped wildly.

2. The Truscotts hope to visit in May.

3. Lance enjoys paddling his canoe up the river.

4. The aardvark, an ant-eating mammal, is found in South Africa.

5. I stood on tiptoe to reach the highest shelf.

6. The acrobat dangling from the rope is one of the Flying Four.

7. Edgar Allan Poe, the author of "The Raven," is also known as the father of the detective story.

8. Listening to quiet music often helps calm people's nerves.

9. Trying not to disturb other library users, David spoke in a whisper.

10. The spacecraft aims to explore Mars.

PRACTICE 7
Recognizing Main and Subordinate Clauses

Read the sentences. Then, write and label the *main clause* and the *subordinate clause* in each sentence.

1. When the teacher asked a question, Sharon raised her hand.

2. The beautician, whose shop is always full, was cutting a customer's hair.

3. I will finish my report on time unless my computer breaks again.

4. A crowd of people waited in the rain for a bus that never came.

5. The straps on your purse ripped because you stuffed too many things into it.

PRACTICE 8
Combining Sentences With Subordinate Clauses

Read the sentences. Combine each pair of sentences by turning one into a subordinate clause. Then, underline the subordinate clause, and indicate whether it is an *adjectival clause* or an *adverbial clause*.

1. The weather is very chilly. You had better wear a warm hat.

2. My dad travels all over the world. He is an airline pilot.

3. I thumbed through the magazine. I finally found the article about the best DVD players.

4. The escalator is quite long. It goes from the basement to the second floor.

5. My cousin Barbara will perform at the birthday party. She is a trained clown.

Continued on next page ▶

Cumulative Review   Chapters 18–20

PRACTICE 9 ▷ Writing Sentences

For each item, write the indicated type of sentence using the words provided.

1. Write a compound sentence using *the librarian* as one of the subjects.

2. Write a declarative sentence using *the kite* as the subject.

3. Write a complex sentence using *has starred* as one of the verbs.

4. Write an exclamatory sentence using the word *enormous*.

5. Write an imperative sentence using *remove* as the verb.

PRACTICE 10 ▷ Combining Sentences

Read the sentences. Combine each pair of sentences by using compound structures. Indicate whether your sentence contains a *compound subject*, a *compound verb*, or a *compound object*, or whether it is a *compound sentence*.

1. Connor is playing soccer. Pierre is playing soccer too.

2. The gardener planted a tree. She also planted some lilies.

3. The chef added the ingredients. He then mixed the ingredients.

4. Darlene lost her umbrella at the movie theater. She also lost her gloves there.

5. The children wanted a new ballfield. The town could not afford one.

PRACTICE 11 ▷ Revising to Correct Fragments and Run-ons

Read each group of words. If it is a fragment, use it in a sentence. If it a run-on, correct the run-on. If it is a sentence that needs no correction, write *correct*.

1. I sat on a park bench the day was so peaceful.

2. A strange creature sitting on a toadstool.

3. Unless the delivery comes by noon.

4. The youngster was pedaling her tricycle.

5. We saw Sandy, she didn't see us.

PRACTICE 12 ▷ Revising to Correct Common Usage Problems

Read the sentences. Then, rewrite each sentence to correct misplaced modifiers, double negatives, and other usage problems.

1. Kay couldn't read none of the letters in the bottom row of the eye doctor's chart.

2. Going without enough sleep effects people's health.

3. I answered every question accept the last.

4. Do we need farther discussion of the issue, or shall we vote?

5. Dressed in sandals and shorts, the rain came as a surprise to me.

6. The reason she could not speak her lines is because her costar made her laugh.

7. There to late to enter their dogs in the dog show.

8. Beside being a wonderful cook, Grandma gives me good advise.

9. Astronomy is where you study the stars, the planets, and other objects in space.

10. A visiting park ranger made a speech describing acid rain in our science class.

CHAPTER 21

USING VERBS

Use the correct tenses of verbs to establish clear, consistent timing of actions in your writing.

WRITE GUY *Jeff Anderson, M.Ed.*

WHAT DO YOU NOTICE?

Think about verbs as you zoom in on these sentences from the story "Flowers for Algernon" by Daniel Keyes.

MENTOR TEXT

> With all due respect for both of these fine scientists, I am well aware of their limitations. If there is an answer, I'll have to find it out for myself.

Now, ask yourself the following questions:

- What does the verb tense in the first sentence tell about the time of the action?
- How does the verb tense change in the second sentence?

In the first sentence, the verb *am* is the present tense of the verb *be*. Therefore, the narrator is speaking about something happening currently. In the second sentence, you can tell the narrator is thinking of doing something in the future because he uses the helping verb *will*, which is embedded in the contraction *I'll*.

Grammar for Writers Writers use verb tenses to show a time of action or state of being in the past, present, or future. Help your writing flow smoothly by changing tenses to show the order of actions and keeping tenses consistent when actions happen at the same time.

My muscles were tense after the race.

But now that's all in the past!

21.1 The Four Principal Parts of Verbs

Verbs have different tenses to express time. The tense of the verb *walk* in the sentence "They *walk* very fast" expresses action in the present. In "They *walked* too far from home," the tense of the verb shows that the action happened in the past. In "They *will walk* home from school," the verb expresses action in the future. These forms of verbs are known as **tenses**.

A verb's **tense** shows the time of the action or state of being that is being described. To use the tenses of a verb correctly, you must know the **principal parts** of the verb.

RULE
21.1.1

> A verb has four **principal parts:** the **present, the present participle,** the **past,** and the **past participle.**

THE FOUR PRINCIPAL PARTS OF *SERVE*			
PRESENT	PRESENT PARTICIPLE	PAST	PAST PARTICIPLE
serve	(am) serving	served	(have) served

The first principal part, called the present, is the form of a verb that is listed in a dictionary. The present participle and the past participle must be combined with helping verbs before they can be used as verbs in sentences. The result will always be a verb phrase.

EXAMPLES   He **serves** the community.

Bill **was serving** his neighbors yesterday.

He **served** his community today.

He **has served** throughout his life.

The way the past and past participle of a verb are formed shows whether the verb is **regular** or **irregular.**

Using Regular Verbs

Most verbs are **regular,** which means that their past and past participle forms follow a standard, predictable pattern.

> **The past and past participle of a regular verb** are formed by adding **-ed** or **-d** to the present form.

21.1.2 RULE

To form the past and past participle of a regular verb such as *chirp* or *hover*, you simply add -ed to the present. With regular verbs that already end in *e*—verbs such as *move* and *charge*—you simply add -d to the present.

PRINCIPAL PARTS OF REGULAR VERBS			
PRESENT	PRESENT PARTICIPLE	PAST	PAST PARTICIPLE
call	(am) calling	called	(have) called
change	(am) changing	changed	(have) changed
charge	(am) charging	charged	(have) charged
chirp	(am) chirping	chirped	(have) chirped
contain	(am) containing	contained	(have) contained
describe	(am) describing	described	(have) described
fix	(am) fixing	fixed	(have) fixed
hover	(am) hovering	hovered	(have) hovered
jump	(am) jumping	jumped	(have) jumped
lift	(am) lifting	lifted	(have) lifted
look	(am) looking	looked	(have) looked
move	(am) moving	moved	(have) moved
play	(am) playing	played	(have) played
save	(am) saving	saved	(have) saved
serve	(am) serving	served	(have) served
ski	(am) skiing	skied	(have) skied
talk	(am) talking	talked	(have) talked
type	(am) typing	typed	(have) typed
visit	(am) visiting	visited	(have) visited
walk	(am) walking	walked	(have) walked

See Practice 21.1A
See Practice 21.1B

PRACTICE 21.1A Identifying Principal Parts of Regular Verbs

Read the sentences. Then, label each underlined verb *present*, *present participle*, *past*, or *past participle*.

EXAMPLE   I <u>watched</u> the football game.

ANSWER   *past*

1. I usually <u>type</u> on the computer instead of writing.
2. We have <u>listened</u> to public radio for years.
3. I am <u>trying</u> to be a good friend.
4. I really <u>like</u> the new school uniforms.
5. I was <u>waiting</u> for you for a long time.
6. Ali <u>planned</u> my surprise party down to the smallest detail.
7. I had <u>expected</u> a longer meeting.
8. Mr. Jameson <u>coaches</u> the Little League team.
9. The band will be <u>playing</u> at Town Hall.
10. Maura has often <u>visited</u> her aunt in Florida.

PRACTICE 21.1B Supplying the Principal Parts of Regular Verbs

Read the verbs. Then, write and label the four principal parts of each verb. Use a form of the helping verb *be* with the present participle and a form of the helping verb *have* with the past participle.

EXAMPLE   explain

ANSWER   *explain* — present
am explaining — present participle
explained — past
has explained — past participle

11. discuss
12. suggest
13. agree
14. remain
15. attempt
16. pause
17. exercise
18. practice
19. play
20. cry

SPEAKING APPLICATION

With a partner, describe in four sentences an activity that you enjoy. In each sentence, use a different principal part of the same verb. Your partner should listen for and identify which principal part you used in each sentence.

WRITING APPLICATION

Write four sentences about someone you have known for a long time. In each sentence, use a different one of the four principal parts of verbs. Label the verbs *present*, *present participle*, *past*, and *past participle*.

Using Irregular Verbs

While most verbs are regular, many very common verbs are **irregular**—their past and past participle forms do not follow a predictable pattern.

> The past and past participle of an **irregular verb** are not formed by adding *-ed* or *-d* to the present tense form.

IRREGULAR VERBS WITH THE SAME PAST AND PAST PARTICIPLE			
PRESENT	PRESENT PARTICIPLE	PAST	PAST PARTICIPLE
bring	(am) bringing	brought	(have) brought
build	(am) building	built	(have) built
buy	(am) buying	bought	(have) bought
catch	(am) catching	caught	(have) caught
fight	(am) fighting	fought	(have) fought
find	(am) finding	found	(have) found
get	(am) getting	got	(have) got *or* (have) gotten
hold	(am) holding	held	(have) held
lay	(am) laying	laid	(have) laid
lead	(am) leading	led	(have) led
lose	(am) losing	lost	(have) lost
pay	(am) paying	paid	(have) paid
say	(am) saying	said	(have) said
sit	(am) sitting	sat	(have) sat
sleep	(am) sleeping	slept	(have) slept
spin	(am) spinning	spun	(have) spun
stand	(am) standing	stood	(have) stood
stick	(am) sticking	stuck	(have) stuck
swing	(am) swinging	swung	(have) swung
teach	(am) teaching	taught	(have) taught
win	(am) winning	won	(have) won

Check a dictionary whenever you are in doubt about the correct form of an irregular verb.

IRREGULAR VERBS WITH THE SAME PRESENT, PAST, AND PAST PARTICIPLE			
PRESENT	PRESENT PARTICIPLE	PAST	PAST PARTICIPLE
bid	(am) bidding	bid	(have) bid
burst	(am) bursting	burst	(have) burst
cost	(am) costing	cost	(have) cost
hurt	(am) hurting	hurt	(have) hurt
put	(am) putting	put	(have) put
set	(am) setting	set	(have) set

IRREGULAR VERBS THAT CHANGE IN OTHER WAYS			
PRESENT	PRESENT PARTICIPLE	PAST	PAST PARTICIPLE
arise	(am) arising	arose	(have) arisen
be	(am) being	was	(have) been
bear	(am) bearing	bore	(have) borne
beat	(am) beating	beat	(have) beaten
begin	(am) beginning	began	(have) begun
blow	(am) blowing	blew	(have) blown
break	(am) breaking	broke	(have) broken
choose	(am) choosing	chose	(have) chosen
come	(am) coming	came	(have) come
do	(am) doing	did	(have) done
draw	(am) drawing	drew	(have) drawn
drink	(am) drinking	drank	(have) drunk
drive	(am) driving	drove	(have) driven
eat	(am) eating	ate	(have) eaten
fall	(am) falling	fell	(have) fallen
fly	(am) flying	flew	(have) flown
forget	(am) forgetting	forgot	(have) forgotten
freeze	(am) freezing	froze	(have) frozen

IRREGULAR VERBS THAT CHANGE IN OTHER WAYS (CONTINUED)			
PRESENT	PRESENT PARTICIPLE	PAST	PAST PARTICIPLE
give	(am) giving	gave	(have) given
go	(am) going	went	(have) gone
grow	(am) growing	grew	(have) grown
know	(am) knowing	knew	(have) known
lie	(am) lying	lay	(have) lain
ride	(am) riding	rode	(have) ridden
ring	(am) ringing	rang	(have) rung
rise	(am) rising	rose	(have) risen
run	(am) running	ran	(have) run
see	(am) seeing	saw	(have) seen
shake	(am) shaking	shook	(have) shaken
sing	(am) singing	sang	(have) sung
sink	(am) sinking	sank	(have) sunk
speak	(am) speaking	spoke	(have) spoken
spring	(am) springing	sprang	(have) sprung
strive	(am) striving	strove	(have) striven
swear	(am) swearing	swore	(have) sworn
swim	(am) swimming	swam	(have) swum
take	(am) taking	took	(have) taken
tear	(am) tearing	tore	(have) torn
throw	(am) throwing	threw	(have) thrown
wear	(am) wearing	wore	(have) worn
weave	(am) weaving	wove	(have) woven
write	(am) writing	wrote	(have) written

See Practice 21.1C

See Practice 21.1D

See Practice 21.1E

See Practice 21.1F

As you can see, there are many irregular verbs. For most of these verbs, you should memorize the different forms. Whenever you are not sure of which form of an irregular verb to use, check a dictionary.

Read the verbs. Then, write and label the four principal parts of each verb. Use a form of the helping verb *be* with the present participle and a form of the helping verb *have* with the past participle.

EXAMPLE   know

ANSWER   *know* — present
          am knowing — present participle
          knew — past
          has known — past participle

1. write
2. hurt
3. burst
4. drink
5. teach
6. sink
7. swim
8. swing
9. lay
10. rise

Read the sentences. Then, choose and write the form of the verb in parentheses that correctly completes each sentence.

EXAMPLE   I have (shook, shaken) the bottle.

ANSWER   *shaken*

11. George (did, done) as much as he could.
12. Yesterday I (ran, run) five miles.
13. I have (spoke, spoken) to him on several occasions.
14. The visitor (rang, rung) the doorbell.
15. The trucker had (drove, driven) hundreds of miles.
16. The fog has finally (rose, risen).
17. She had (began, begun) the project.
18. Have you ever (swam, swum) in an Olympic-sized pool?
19. The owl (came, come) back to our tree.
20. Has the library board (chose, chosen) the new director yet?

SPEAKING APPLICATION

With a partner, share four sentences about going to a restaurant. In each sentence, use a different principal part of the same irregular verb. Your partner should listen for and identify which principal part you used in each sentence.

WRITING APPLICATION

Write two pairs of sentences about school last year. Use only two irregular verbs, one in each pair. One sentence in each pair should use the past form of the verb; the other should use the past participle. Be sure you use the irregular verb forms correctly.

PRACTICE 21.1E > Using Irregular Verbs

Read the sentences. Rewrite each sentence, using the form of the verb in parentheses that correctly completes the sentence.

EXAMPLE   Yesterday Sarah (fall) off her chair.

ANSWER   *Yesterday Sarah fell off her chair.*

1. Last week our teacher (speak) about the effects of the American Revolution.

2. We had (ride) to Audubon Park on the ferry.

3. Yesterday May (sit) at the piano for hours.

4. The new cars have (got) more fuel efficient.

5. The top (spin) for nearly five minutes and finally stopped.

6. At the rally, the politician (shake) my hand.

7. Until this year, Zach had never (fly) in a plane.

8. Have burglars (break) into that apartment?

9. Last week's lunch (cost) less than this week's.

10. Has the ice on the lake (freeze)?

PRACTICE 21.1F > Revising for Irregular Verbs

Read the sentences. Then, if the underlined verb is in the correct form, write *correct*. If it is not, rewrite the sentence with the correct verb form.

EXAMPLE   I <u>drunk</u> a glass of pineapple juice.

ANSWER   *I drank a glass of pineapple juice.*

11. Have you <u>saw</u> this movie?

12. He <u>run</u> over the track at top speed.

13. The doctor has <u>spoke</u> with her patient.

14. My feet <u>sank</u> into the sand.

15. Finally the race <u>begun</u>.

16. Teresa <u>wore</u> long golden earrings.

17. The colony had <u>rose</u> in rebellion.

18. Church bells <u>rung</u> all over London.

19. The dog <u>sprang</u> up at the sound.

20. She had <u>wrote</u> me about the change in plans.

SPEAKING APPLICATION

With a partner, take turns telling about things that have happened in the past month at school. Use at least four irregular verbs, two of them after a form of the helping verb *have.* Your partner should listen for the irregular verbs and make sure they are used correctly.

WRITING APPLICATION

Write four sentences about things you did last summer. In each sentence, use a different irregular verb, two of them after a form of the helping verb *have.*

21.2 The Six Tenses of Verbs

In English, verbs have six **tenses**: the **present**, the **past**, the **future**, the **present perfect**, the **past perfect**, and the **future perfect**.

RULE 21.2.1

> The **tense** of a verb shows the time of the action or state of being.

Every tense has both **basic** forms and **progressive** forms.

Identifying the Basic Forms of the Six Tenses

The chart below shows the **basic** forms of the six tenses, using *stick* as an example. The first column gives the name of each tense. The second column gives the basic form of *stick* in all six tenses. The third column gives the principal part needed to form each tense. Only three of the four principal parts are used in the basic forms: the present, the past, and the past participle.

BASIC FORMS OF THE SIX TENSES OF *STICK*		
TENSE	BASIC FORM	PRINCIPAL PART USED
Present	I stick.	Present
Past	I stuck.	Past
Future	I will stick.	Present
Present Perfect	I have stuck.	Past Participle
Past Perfect	I had stuck.	Past Participle
Future Perfect	I will have stuck.	Past Participle

Study the chart carefully. First, learn the names of the tenses. Then, learn the principal parts needed to form them. Notice also that the last four tenses need helping verbs.

As you have already learned, some verbs form their tenses in a regular, predictable pattern. Other verbs use an irregular pattern. *Stick* is an example of an irregular verb.

See Practice 21.2A
See Practice 21.2B

Conjugating the Basic Forms of Verbs

A helpful way to become familiar with all the forms of a verb is by **conjugating** it.

> A **conjugation** is a list of the singular and plural forms of a verb in a particular tense.

RULE 21.2.2

Each tense in a conjugation has six forms that fit with first-, second-, and third-person forms of the personal pronouns. These forms may change for each personal pronoun, and they may change for each tense.

To conjugate any verb, begin by listing its principal parts. For example, the principal parts of the verb *go* are *go, going, went,* and *gone.* The following chart shows the conjugation of all the basic forms of *go* in all six tenses. Notice that the forms of the helping verbs may change for each personal pronoun and tense.

See Practice 21.2C
See Practice 21.2D
See Practice 21.2E
See Practice 21.2F

CONJUGATION OF THE BASIC FORMS OF GO		
TENSE	SINGULAR	PLURAL
Present	I go. You go. He, she, or it goes.	We go. You go. They go.
Past	I went. You went. He, she, or it went.	We went. You went. They went.
Future	I will go. You will go. He, she, or it will go.	We will go. You will go. They will go.
Present Perfect	I have gone. You have gone. He, she, or it has gone.	We have gone. You have gone. They have gone.
Past Perfect	I had gone. You had gone. He, she, or it had gone.	We had gone. You had gone. They had gone.
Future Perfect	I will have gone. You will have gone. He, she, or it will have gone.	We will have gone. You will have gone. They will have gone.

Conjugating *Be*

The verb *be* is an important verb to know how to conjugate. It is both the most common and the most irregular verb in the English language. You will use the basic forms of *be* when you conjugate the progressive forms of verbs later in this section.

PRINCIPAL PARTS OF *BE*			
PRESENT	**PRESENT PARTICIPLE**	**PAST**	**PAST PARTICIPLE**
be	being	was	been

Once you know the principal parts of *be*, you can conjugate all of the basic forms of *be*.

CONJUGATION OF THE BASIC FORMS OF *BE*		
TENSE	**SINGULAR**	**PLURAL**
Present	I am. You are. He, she, or it is.	We are. You are. They are.
Past	I was. You were. He, she, or it was.	We were. You were. They were.
Future	I will be. You will be. He, she, or it will be.	We will be. You will be. They will be.
Present Perfect	I have been. You have been. He, she, or it has been.	We have been. You have been. They have been.
Past Perfect	I had been. You had been. He, she, or it had been.	We had been. You had been. They had been.
Future Perfect	I will have been. You will have been. He, she, or it will have been.	We will have been. You will have been. They will have been.

PRACTICE 21.2A ▷ **Identifying Present, Past, and Future Tenses of Verbs**

Read the sentences. Then, label each underlined verb *present*, *past*, or *future*.

EXAMPLE   I <u>answered</u> the telephone.

ANSWER   *past*

1. The lighthouse <u>stands</u> in the harbor.

2. A helicopter <u>will fly</u> them to the hospital.

3. We <u>rushed</u> past the scene of the accident.

4. A fence <u>surrounds</u> the Coast Guard station.

5. Emily <u>caught</u> her skirt in the car door.

6. Carl <u>threw</u> the basketball to a teammate.

7. <u>Will</u> you <u>remain</u> behind?

8. The children <u>hurt</u> themselves yesterday.

9. I <u>will</u> not <u>be</u> responsible for your mistakes.

10. The surgeon <u>set</u> the scalpel on the table.

PRACTICE 21.2B ▷ **Identifying Perfect Tenses of Verbs**

Read the sentences. Then, write the verb in each sentence, and label it *present perfect*, *past perfect*, or *future perfect*.

EXAMPLE   I will have finished summer school by next Friday.

ANSWER   *will have finished* — *future perfect*

11. The players have practiced every day after school.

12. Chuck has memorized the names on the list.

13. I have gone to the jazz festival many times.

14. By Monday, I will have attended three graduation parties.

15. The acting company has completed rehearsal.

16. By 5 P.M. I had finished my homework.

17. By 11:30 A.M. I will have finished the exam.

18. I had never considered a different route.

19. By midnight, you will probably have heard spooky noises in the attic.

20. Have you put the dog out?

SPEAKING APPLICATION

With a partner, say one sentence each about your past, present, and future. Use a different tense in each sentence. Your partner should listen for and name the tenses that you use.

WRITING APPLICATION

Use the perfect tenses in sentences 13, 14, and 18 and write three sentences with other verbs in the perfect tense.

Read each sentence. Then, rewrite the sentence, supplying a perfect tense verb to fill the blank. After your sentence, write the specific tense of the perfect verb you used.

EXAMPLE   Before he had lit the campfire, Jon _____ the area thoroughly.

ANSWER   *Before he had lit the campfire, Jon* **had inspected** *the area thoroughly.* (past perfect)

1. The meteorologist _____ residents about the storm for more than a week.

2. I _____ at 5:30 every morning this week.

3. If I average six miles each day, I _____ more than forty miles by the end of the week.

4. Jen left the picnic after she _____ each of her cousins.

5. By halftime, Dan _____ seats at least four times.

6. Before the night is over, our family _____ an impressive meteor shower.

7. After searching inside the dryer, I _____ all four missing socks.

8. The farmer _____ to plant the corn seed earlier, but heavy rains delayed him.

9. The great and powerful Oz _____.

10. By the time the year ends, Danielle _____ every book in the library.

Write a sentence using each verb phrase. With a partner, take turns reading the sentences aloud. Listen for and identify the specific tense of the perfect verb used in the sentence.

EXAMPLE   had not spoken

ANSWER   *Ms. Gordon had not spoken to her sister for ten years.* (past perfect)

11. will have eaten

12. has defeated

13. will have surpassed

14. had expected

15. has measured

16. had intended

17. have captured

18. had never expected

19. will not have spent

20. had climbed

SPEAKING APPLICATION

With a partner, take turns talking about the actions of a young child. Use perfect tense verbs in at least three sentences. Your partner should listen for and name the tense of the perfect tense verbs you used.

WRITING APPLICATION

Write six sentences about a job or career. In each sentence, use a perfect tense verb.

PRACTICE 21.2E > **Forming Verb Tenses**

Read the sentences, which are all in the present tense. Then, rewrite each sentence, changing it to the tense indicated in parentheses.

EXAMPLE   I go to the store every day. (past)

ANSWER   *I went to the store every day.*

1. I collect both stamps and coins. (present perfect)

2. We stay at the lodge during the summer. (future)

3. I wait in the ticket line for hours. (future perfect)

4. He clips quite a few discount coupons from the newspaper. (past perfect)

5. We usually eat breakfast late on Sundays. (past)

6. Josephine teaches many kids how to swim. (present perfect)

7. I see Irma on Friday. (future perfect)

8. A football player catches a pass. (past)

9. The museum is not busy today. (future)

10. The farmer always grows corn. (past perfect)

PRACTICE 21.2F > **Using Verb Tenses Correctly**

Read the sentences. Then, write the verb in parentheses that correctly completes each sentence.

EXAMPLE   I (live, lived) in Wyoming last year.

ANSWER   *lived*

11. That musician (performed, has performed) at our school last month.

12. I (had spoken, speak) to her before last Thanksgiving.

13. I (phoned, will phone) you next Tuesday.

14. Next week the principal (has told, will tell) the students about the plans for the new gym.

15. Until this year, she always (has helped, will help) the school.

16. By tomorrow the electric company (had repaired, will have repaired) the grid.

17. Before now, the lake never (has frozen, freezes).

18. I usually (enjoy, will have enjoyed) her music.

19. By the end of the year, the rock band (has visited, will have visited) all 50 states.

20. All human beings (need, needed) oxygen for survival.

SPEAKING APPLICATION

With a partner, take turns being radio broadcasters describing events in the news. Use perfect tense verbs in at least three sentences. Your partner should listen for and name the perfect tense verbs.

WRITING APPLICATION

Write four sentences about adopting a puppy from a local pet shelter. In each sentence, use a perfect tense verb. At the end of each sentence, name the specific tense of perfect tense verbs you used.

Test Warm-Up

DIRECTIONS
Read the introduction and the passage that follows. Then, answer the questions to show that you can use and understand the function of perfect tense verbs in the context of reading and writing.

Casey wrote this paragraph for her health class. Read the paragraph and think about the changes you would suggest as a peer editor. When you finish reading, answer the questions that follow.

The First Flu Shots

(1) For this report, I was researching the history of flu shots. (2) In the 1930s, American scientists announced that they had finally isolated the virus that caused influenza. (3) Then, doctors began working quickly, and, by the 1940s, they are developing the first flu vaccine. (4) The first flu shots were given to American soldiers. (5) They had been exposed to the flu virus. (6) They are fighting in Europe during World War II. (7) Since that time, millions of people have received flu shots.

1 What change, if any, should be made in sentence 1?

  A Change *was researching* to **research**

  B Change *was researching* to **have researched**

  C Change *was researching* to **will be researching**

  D Make no change

2 What change should be made in sentence 3?

  F Change *are developing* to **had developed**

  G Change *are developing* to **have developed**

  H Change *are developing* to **have been developing**

  J Change *are developing* to **will have been developing**

3 What is the BEST way to combine sentences 5 and 6?

  A They been exposed to the flu virus while fighting in Europe during World War II.

  B They had been exposed to the flu virus while they are fighting in Europe during World War II.

  C They are exposed to the flu virus while fighting in Europe during World War II.

  D They had been exposed to the flu virus while fighting in Europe during World War II.

4 What change, if any, should be made in sentence 7?

  F Change *have received* to **will receive**

  G Change *have received* to **had received**

  H Change *have received* to **will have received**

  J Make no change

Recognizing the Progressive Tense of Verbs

The six tenses of *go* and *be* in their basic forms were shown in the charts earlier in this section. Each of these tenses also has a progressive tense or form. The progressive form describes an event that is in progress. In contrast, the basic forms of a verb describe events that have a definite beginning and end.

> The **progressive tense,** or form, of a verb shows an action or condition that is ongoing.

21.2.3 RULE

All six of the progressive tenses of a verb are made using just one principal part: the present participle. This is the principal part that ends in *-ing*. Then, the correct form of *be* is added to create the progressive tense or form.

Progressive Tenses of *Jog*

PROGRESSIVE TENSE = be + present participle

PRESENT　　I **am jogging** around the track.
　　　　　　　　　　　be　present participle

PAST　　　　I **was jogging** around the track.
　　　　　　　　　　　be　present participle

FUTURE　　I **will be jogging** around the track.
　　　　　　　　　　　be　　present participle

PRESENT PERFECT　　I **have been jogging** around the track since
　　　　　　　　　　　　　　be　　　　present participle

　　　　　five A.M.

PAST PERFECT　　I **had been jogging** around the track, but now
　　　　　　　　　　　　be　　present participle

　　　　　I am running too.

FUTURE PERFECT　　I **will have been jogging** since
　　　　　　　　　　　　　be　　　　　present participle

　　　　　early morning.

Conjugating Progressive Tenses

To create the progressive tenses or forms of a verb, you must know the basic forms of *be*.

RULE 21.2.4

> To conjugate the **progressive** forms of a verb, add the present participle of the verb to a conjugation of the basic forms of *be*.

A complete conjugation of the basic forms of *be* is shown earlier. Compare that conjugation with the conjugation of the progressive forms of *run*. Although the present participle form of the verb does not change, the form of the helping verb does change. It is the form of *be* that tells you whether the action or condition is taking place in the past, present, or future.

CONJUGATION OF THE PROGRESSIVE FORMS OF *RUN*		
TENSE	**SINGULAR**	**PLURAL**
Present Progressive	I am running. You are running. He, she, or it is running.	We are running. You are running. They are running.
Past Progressive	I was running. You were running. He, she, or it was running.	We were running. You were running. They were running.
Future Progressive	I will be running. You will be running. He, she, or it will be running.	We will be running. You will be running. They will be running.
Present Perfect Progressive	I have been running. You have been running. He, she, or it has been running.	We have been running. You have been running. They have been running.
Past Perfect Progressive	I had been running. You had been running. He, she, or it had been running.	We had been running. You had been running. They had been running.
Future Perfect Progressive	I will have been running. You will have been running. He, she, or it will have been running.	We will have been running. You will have been running. They will have been running.

See Practice 21.2G
See Practice 21.2H

PRACTICE 21.2G ▷ **Identifying the Progressive Tenses of Verbs**

Read the sentences. Then, write whether the underlined verb tense in each sentence is *present progressive, past progressive, future progressive, present perfect progressive, past perfect progressive,* or *future perfect progressive.*

EXAMPLE   She <u>has been working</u> all day.

ANSWER   *present perfect progressive*

1. Leticia <u>was studying</u> for the midterm.
2. The morning show <u>will be discussing</u> new movies after the commercial break.
3. I <u>have been shopping</u> there for years.
4. The mechanic <u>is repairing</u> our car.
5. The storyteller <u>had been recounting</u> an interesting tale.
6. Bruce <u>has been telling</u> me all about his adventure.
7. It <u>had been snowing</u> for days.
8. They <u>were explaining</u> the answer to us.
9. By Friday, we <u>will have been living</u> in the new house for six weeks.
10. <u>Are</u> you <u>babysitting</u> tonight?

PRACTICE 21.2H ▷ **Using Progressive Tenses of Verbs**

Read the sentences. Then, rewrite each one as a complete sentence using the tense of the verb in parentheses.

EXAMPLE   Jay _____ home. (*go*, past progressive)

ANSWER   *Jay was going home.*

11. The birds _____ south. (*fly*, present progressive)
12. The columnist _____ for the magazine for two decades. (*write*, present perfect progressive)
13. They _____ company for dinner. (*expect*, past progressive)
14. Up until then, the mail carrier _____ his route. (*walk*, past perfect progressive)
15. I _____ at least one box. (*carry*, future progressive)
16. Before the incident, Uncle Tom _____ a trip to Tampa. (*plan*, past perfect progressive)
17. On their next anniversary, they _____ here for twenty years. (*come*, future perfect progressive)
18. I _____ my name on the list. (*put*, present progressive)
19. By tomorrow, you _____ for your presentation for a week. (*prepare*, future perfect progressive)
20. Jolene _____ foolish again. (*be*, past progressive)

SPEAKING APPLICATION

Tell a partner about events that have happened in the last week and events that will happen next week. Your partner should listen for and identify the verbs you use in a progressive tense.

WRITING APPLICATION

Write six sentences about a traveling circus. Use a different progressive verb tense in each sentence. Then, exchange papers with a partner. Read your sentences aloud. Identify the progressive tenses that your partner has used, and check that they are used correctly.

Identifying Active and Passive Voice

Just as verbs change tense to show time, they may also change form to show whether or not the subject of the verb is performing an action.

RULE 21.2.5

The voice of a verb shows whether or not the subject is performing the action.

In English, most verbs have two **voices: active,** to show that the subject is performing an action, and **passive,** to show that the subject is having an action performed on it.

RULE 21.2.6

A verb is in the active voice when its subject performs the action.

ACTIVE
VOICE

Bob **edited** the paper.

Bill **presented** the project for the group.

In each example above, the subject performs the action, so the verb is said to be in the active voice.

RULE 21.2.7

A verb is in the passive voice when its subject does not perform the action.

PASSIVE
VOICE

The paper **is being edited** by Bob.

The project **was presented** by Bill.

In each example above, the person doing the action becomes the object of the preposition *by* and is no longer the subject. Both subjects—*paper* and *project*—are receivers rather than performers of the action. When the subject is acted upon, the verb is said to be in the passive voice.

See Practice 21.2l

Forming the Tenses of Passive Verbs

A passive verb always has two parts.

> **A passive verb** is always a verb phrase made from a form of *be* plus a past participle.

21.2.8 RULE

The following chart shows a conjugation of the passive forms of the verb *determine* with the pronoun *it*.

CONJUGATION OF THE PASSIVE FORMS OF *DETERMINE*	
TENSE	**PASSIVE FORM**
Present	It is determined.
Past	It was determined.
Future	It will be determined.
Present Perfect	It has been determined.
Past Perfect	It had been determined.
Future Perfect	It will have been determined.

While there are uses for the passive voice, most writing is more lively when it is in the active voice. Think about how to change each sentence below to the active voice. Follow the pattern in the first two examples.

PASSIVE It **is determined** that she is late.

ACTIVE We **have determined** that she is late.

PASSIVE It **was determined** that she is late.

ACTIVE We **determined** that she is late.

PASSIVE It **will be determined** that she is late.

It **has been determined** that she is late.

It **had been determined** that she was late.

It **will have been determined** that she is late.

Using Active and Passive Voices

Each of the two voices has its proper use in English.

RULE 21.2.9

> Use the **active voice** whenever possible.

Sentences with active verbs are less wordy and more forceful than those with passive verbs. Compare, for example, the following sentences. Notice the different number of words each sentence needs to report the same information.

ACTIVE   The teacher **presented** a new project.

PASSIVE   A new project **was presented** by the teacher.

Although you should aim to use the active voice in most of your writing, there will be times when you will need to use the passive voice.

RULE 21.2.10

> Use the **passive voice** to emphasize the receiver of an action rather than the performer of an action.

In the following example, the receiver of the action is the subject *orchestra*. It is the *conductor* (the direct object) who is actually performing the action.

EMPHASIS   The orchestra **was directed** by the conductor.
ON RECEIVER

The passive voice should also be used when there is no performer of the action.

RULE 21.2.11

> Use the **passive voice** to point out the receiver of an action when the performer is unknown or not named in the sentence.

PERFORMER   The sculpture **was created** sometime
UNKNOWN
             in the last century.

See Practice 21.2J

PRACTICE 21.2I ⟩ **Distinguishing Active and Passive Voice**

Read the sentences. Then, write *AV* if the underlined verb is in active voice or *PV* if the verb is in passive voice.

EXAMPLE   A new meeting *was called*.

ANSWER   *PV*

1. Those elm trees <u>were planted</u> by my father.
2. They <u>welcomed</u> the foreign-exchange students.
3. I <u>was comforted</u> by your kind words.
4. The leftovers <u>were heated</u> in the microwave.
5. Roy <u>took</u> our picture by the White House fence.
6. This momentous occasion <u>will be recorded</u> for future generations.
7. The house <u>was covered</u> with moss.
8. She <u>printed</u> the directions for us.
9. A new mayor <u>was elected</u> last November.
10. Clarice <u>was running</u> down the street.

PRACTICE 21.2J ⟩ **Revising to Use Active Voice**

Read the sentences. Then, rewrite each sentence that is in passive voice so that it is in active voice. If a sentence is already in active voice, write *active*.

EXAMPLE   The dinner was cooked by me.

ANSWER   *I cooked the dinner.*

11. This poem was written by Langston Hughes.
12. The designer gown was worn by the model.
13. This garden is shared by several neighbors.
14. She lives in a town by the Mexican border.
15. All the bowling pins were knocked down by Harvey's ball.
16. The Plymouth colony was established by the Pilgrims in 1620.
17. Cassandra was baking a cake.
18. I am informed by Sean about the new schedule.
19. Several questions have been asked by me.
20. Will Lola be chosen by the casting director?

SPEAKING APPLICATION

With a partner, take turns describing an old house or another old building. Use at least two sentences in the active voice and two in the passive voice. Your partner should listen for and name the active and passive verbs that you use.

WRITING APPLICATION

Write an announcement for an activity at your school. Use four sentences, two in the active voice and two in the passive voice.

Moods of Verbs

Verbs in English also use **mood** to describe the status of an action.

RULE 21.2.12

> There are three moods for English verbs: the **indicative mood,** the **subjunctive mood**, and the **imperative mood.**

The **indicative mood** indicates, or states, something. It is also used to ask questions. The **subjunctive mood** describes a wish or a condition that may be contrary to fact.

INDICATIVE MOOD	SUBJUNCTIVE MOOD
Ben **is** in my meeting.	I wish he **were** here for the meeting.
John **has** a new car.	If he **had brought** his car to school, we could have driven together.
I **would like** to run the meeting.	If I **were running** the meeting, I would let everyone speak.

The subjunctive mood can be used to describe situations that are unlikely to happen or not possible. It is often used in clauses that begin with *if* or *that.* In these cases, use the plural form of the verb.

EXAMPLES   If I **were** he, I would drive home before it got dark.
(I am not he, so the situation is not possible.)

Sally wishes that she **were joining** the team today.
(She is not joining until next month, so the situation is not possible.)

The **imperative** mood states a request or command and always uses the present tense. A mild imperative is followed by a period; a strong imperative is followed by an exclamation point.

EXAMPLES   **Write** me when you arrive. Please **don't** forget.
Be careful!

Notice that the subject, *you,* is understood but omitted.

See Practice 21.2K
See Practice 21.2L

PRACTICE 21.2K **Identifying Moods of Verbs**

Read the sentences. Then, write *indicative, subjunctive, or imperative* for the mood of the underlined verb in each sentence.

EXAMPLE   I wish I <u>were</u> an astronaut.

ANSWER   *subjunctive*

1. The country singer <u>wore</u> a sequined suit.

2. <u>Tear</u> this open on the dotted line.

3. If you <u>had watched</u> the game, you would have seen me hit a home run.

4. If Shelley <u>were</u> here at the party, we would have had more fun.

5. Please <u>stay</u> behind the yellow line.

6. In the summer, they often <u>go</u> to the beach.

7. Don't <u>put</u> your elbows on the table.

8. I prefer that she <u>wait</u> until tomorrow.

9. What <u>were</u> those strange creatures?

10. I wish my grandfather <u>were</u> here today.

PRACTICE 21.2L **Writing Sentences to Express Mood**

Read the verbs. Write sentences using the different moods of verbs as indicated below.

EXAMPLE   were (subjunctive)

ANSWER   *If I were you, I'd be careful with that vase.*

11. asked (indicative)

12. were (subjunctive)

13. speak (imperative)

14. visit (indicative)

15. explain (indicative)

16. worked (indicative)

17. wait (imperative)

18. had attended (subjunctive)

19. give (imperative)

20. were (subjunctive)

SPEAKING APPLICATION

With a partner, take turns telling about something you wished for as a child. Use at least one verb in each of the three moods. Your partner should listen for and identify the moods of your verbs.

WRITING APPLICATION

Use sentences 1, 2, and 4 as models, and write three sentences in which you use the same mood as in the sentences.

21.3 Troublesome Verbs

The following verbs cause problems for many speakers and writers of English. Some of the problems involve using the principal parts of certain verbs. Others involve learning to distinguish between the meanings of certain confusing pairs of verbs.

WRITING COACH

Online

www.phwritingcoach.com

Grammar Practice
Practice your grammar skills with Writing Coach Online.

Grammar Games
Test your knowledge of grammar in this fast-paced interactive video game.

(1) ain't   *Ain't* is not considered standard English. Avoid using it in speaking and in writing.

INCORRECT   She **ain't** the first to complete this project.

CORRECT   She **isn't** the first to complete this project.

(2) did, done   Remember that *done* is a past participle and can be used as a verb only with a helping verb such as *have* or *has*. Instead of using *done* without a helping verb, use *did*.

INCORRECT   I already **done** the assignment for school.

CORRECT   I already **did** the assignment for school.

I **have** already **done** the assignment for school.

See Practice 21.3A

(3) dragged, drug   *Drag* is a regular verb. Its principal parts are *drag*, *dragging*, *dragged*, and *dragged*. *Drug* is never correct as the past or past participle of *drag*.

INCORRECT   The letter carrier **drug** the package up the stairs.

CORRECT   The letter carrier **dragged** the package up the stairs.

(4) gone, went   *Gone* is the past participle of *go* and can be used as a verb only with a helping verb such as *have* or *has*. *Went* is the past of *go* and is never used with a helping verb.

INCORRECT   Mike and Tom **gone** to the concert.

We **should have went** along with them.

CORRECT   The group **went** (or **has gone**) to the concert.

Mike and Tom **should have gone** to the concert.

(5) *have, of* The words *have* and *of* often sound very similar. Be careful not to write *of* when you mean the helping verb *have* or its contraction *'ve*.

INCORRECT	Amber should **of** walked home.
CORRECT	Amber should **have** (or **should've**) walked home.

(6) *lay, lie* These verbs look and sound almost alike and have similar meanings. The first step in distinguishing between *lay* and *lie* is to memorize the principal parts of both verbs.

PRINCIPAL PARTS			
lay	laying	laid	laid
lie	lying	lay	lain

Lay usually means "to put (something) down" or "to place (something)." It is almost always followed by a direct object. *Lie* means "to rest in a reclining position" or "to be situated." This verb is used to show the position of a person, place, or thing. *Lie* is never followed by a direct object.

EXAMPLES	The soldier **lays** his mess kit on the ground.
	The children must **lie** down at rest time.

Pay special attention to the past tense of *lay* and *lie*. *Lay* is the past tense of *lie*. The past tense of *lay* is *laid*.

PRESENT TENSE OF *LAY*	I **lay** the book on the shelf.
PAST TENSE OF *LAY*	The athlete **laid** his sneakers on the bench.
PAST TENSE OF *LIE*	The tourist **lay** down in his room.

See Practice 21.3B

(7) *leave, let* *Leave* means "to allow to remain." *Let* means "to permit." Do not reverse the meanings.

INCORRECT	**Leave** me to cook quietly. **Let** the recipe alone.
CORRECT	**Let** me cook quietly. **Leave** the recipe alone.

(8) raise, rise   *Raise* can mean "to lift (something) upward,"
"to build (something)," or "to increase (something)." It is usually
followed by a direct object. *Rise* is not usually followed by a
direct object. This verb means "to get up," "to go up," or "to be
increased."

EXAMPLES   **Raise** the sail to begin the journey.

The kite must **rise** into the sky.

(9) saw, seen   *Seen* is a past participle and can be used as a verb
only with a helping verb such as *have* or *has*.

INCORRECT   I **seen** the sun this morning.

CORRECT   I **saw** the sun this morning.

(10) says, said   A common mistake in reporting what someone
said is to use *says* (present tense) rather than *said* (past tense).

INCORRECT   The chef **says**, "I need it now."

CORRECT   The chef **said**, "I need it now."

(11) set, sit   The first step in learning to distinguish between *set*
and *sit* is to become thoroughly familiar with their principal parts.

PRINCIPAL   set   setting   set   set
PARTS   sit   sitting   sat   sat

Set means "to put (something) in a certain place or position."
It is usually followed by a direct object. *Sit* usually means "to be
seated" or "to rest." It is usually not followed by a direct object.

EXAMPLES   He **set** the hammer on the workbench.

We **have set** the tools safely in the box.

Kris **sat** in the director's chair.

The kitten **has sat** on the fence since it ate.

See Practice 21.3C
See Practice 21.3D

PRACTICE 21.3A **Using *Did* and *Done***

Read the sentences. Then, for each sentence, if *did* or *done* is used correctly, write *correct*. If it is not, write *incorrect*.

EXAMPLE   She done well on the test.

ANSWER   *incorrect*

1. Lara done her homework on time.
2. The volunteers did a lot in the community.
3. My parents have did a lot of work on the house.
4. I haven't done a thing about it.
5. Michael has did his report already.
6. Andrea's done her hair in a new style.
7. I'm not done with you yet.
8. When she finally done the backward somersault, everyone applauded.
9. She'd did a lot for the recycling program.
10. They were done with the assignment before anyone else.

PRACTICE 21.3B **Using *Lay* and *Lie***

Read the sentences. Then, choose and write the correct form of the verb from the pair in parentheses.

EXAMPLE   Yesterday I (lay, laid) in bed until nearly ten o'clock.

ANSWER   *lay*

11. Please ask the cook to (lay, lie) a slice of tomato on my grilled cheese sandwich.
12. My pen was (laying, lying) right there.
13. Last night Mom (laid, lay) the new tablecloth on the dining-room table.
14. I am (laying, lying) the tissues right by my bed.
15. The accountant has (laid, lain) the tax forms on his desk.
16. Sometimes Shane (lays, lies) too long in the sun.
17. It has (lay, lain) there for several months.
18. Where have I (laid, lay) my keys?
19. (Lay, Lie) down and go to sleep.
20. The fox (laid, lay) in wait for the chickens.

SPEAKING APPLICATION

With a partner, take turns telling about something a friend did. Use *did* and *done* two times each. Your partner should listen for the words *did* and *done* and make sure they are used correctly.

WRITING APPLICATION

Write six sentences, each using a different principal part of the verbs *lay* and *lie.* You may use the sentences in Practice 21.3B as models.

Troublesome Verbs

PRACTICE 21.3C Using *Set* and *Sit*

Read the sentences. Then, choose and write the correct form of the verb from the pair in parentheses.

EXAMPLE   She (set, sat) down on the sofa.

ANSWER   *sat*

1. Jack (set, sat) the book on the shelf.

2. We (set, sit) down to a tasty meal every night.

3. I (set, sat) the mouse pad near the keyboard.

4. The workers have finally (set, sat) down for a lunch break.

5. Mae and Jimmy have been (setting, sitting) on the porch for hours.

6. She often (sets, sits) and reads by the creek.

7. Please (set, sit) it down on that chair.

8. Two minutes before show time, everyone had finally (set, sat) down in their seats.

9. The new patio furniture is (setting, sitting) beside the pool.

10. I'm (setting, sitting) on top of the world.

PRACTICE 21.3D Using Troublesome Verbs

Read the sentences. If the underlined verb is used correctly, write *correct*. If it is not, rewrite the sentence using the correct verb.

EXAMPLE   She could <u>of</u> done a better job.

ANSWER   *She could have done a better job.*

11. You should have <u>went</u> with them.

12. They <u>ain't</u> ready yet.

13. My grandmother <u>sat</u> her knitting on the couch.

14. The soldiers <u>raised</u> the flag.

15. Please <u>let</u> your sister alone.

16. I <u>drug</u> the cart across the lawn.

17. I <u>seen</u> a long road stretching ahead.

18. My sister sighed loudly, and she <u>says</u>, "I would love to have a million dollars!"

19. I <u>did</u> my German homework.

20. I <u>could've</u> done better on the test.

SPEAKING APPLICATION

With a partner, take turns telling about things you do in a kitchen or dining room. Use at least two forms of *sit* and two forms of *set*. Your partner should listen for the forms of *sit* and *set* and make sure that they are used correctly.

WRITING APPLICATION

Write five sentences in which you use these words correctly: *done*, *went*, *seen*, *raise*, *said*.

CHAPTER 22

USING PRONOUNS

Match nouns and personal pronouns correctly in your writing to create meaningful sentences.

WRITE GUY *Jeff Anderson, M.Ed.*

WHAT DO YOU NOTICE?

Take note of personal pronouns as you zoom in on these sentences from *An American Childhood* by Annie Dillard.

MENTOR TEXT

> The things in the world did not necessarily cause my overwhelming feelings; the feelings were inside me, beneath my skin, behind my ribs, within my skull. They were even, to some extent, under my control.

Now, ask yourself the following questions:

- How is the personal pronoun *my* used in both clauses in the first sentence?
- How is the personal pronoun *they* used in the second sentence?

In both clauses of the first sentence, *my* is used before nouns (*feelings, skin, ribs,* and *skull*) to show that these things belong to the narrator. *My* is in the possessive case. In the second sentence, *they* is used to refer to the narrator's feelings, which are the subject of the second sentence. *They* is in the nominative case.

Grammar for Writers Selecting the correct case of a personal pronoun allows a writer to express ideas clearly. Use the appropriate personal pronoun cases in your writing to present details accurately.

A pronoun wouldn't wait in line for something, would it?

No, it would just take someone else's place.

22.1 Recognizing Cases of Personal Pronouns

In Chapter 13, you learned that personal pronouns can be arranged in three groups: first person, second person, and third person. Pronouns can also be grouped by their **cases.**

RULE 22.1.1

English has three cases: **nominative, objective,** and **possessive.**

The chart below shows the personal pronouns grouped according to the three cases. The case shows whether a pronoun is being used as a subject, an object, or a possessive.

THE THREE CASES OF PERSONAL PRONOUNS	
NOMINATIVE CASE	**USE IN A SENTENCE**
I, we, you, he, she, it, they	subject of a verb predicate pronoun
OBJECTIVE CASE	**USE IN A SENTENCE**
me, us, you, him, her, it, them	indirect object object of a preposition direct object
POSSESSIVE CASE	**USE IN A SENTENCE**
my, mine, our, ours, your, yours, his, her, hers, its, their, theirs	to show ownership

SUBJECT OF A VERB **She** wanted badly to read the book.

PREDICATE PRONOUN The author is **he**.

INDIRECT OBJECT Please give **me** the telephone.

OBJECT OF A PREPOSITION Please show the letter to **me**.

DIRECT OBJECT A tennis ball hit **her** on the head.

TO SHOW OWNERSHIP That is **my** pencil, not **yours**.

See Practice 22.1A

See Practice 22.1B

PRACTICE 22.1A > **Identifying Cases of Personal Pronouns**

Read the sentences. Then, identify the case of each underlined personal pronoun by writing *nominative*, *objective*, or *possessive*.

EXAMPLE   <u>They</u> told Mr. Finch the news.

ANSWER   *nominative*

1. <u>She</u> designed the team's Web site.

2. Please tell <u>me</u> the location of the nearest post office.

3. <u>Our</u> skit was the funniest of all.

4. Are these slippers <u>yours</u>?

5. At the beach, other friends met <u>them</u>.

6. The leader of the group is <u>he</u>.

7. For <u>us</u>, eating dinner at seven is very late.

8. It was <u>I</u> who answered the phone.

9. <u>Mine</u> is the wool hat with the black dots.

10. The book looks as if <u>it</u> has been read often.

PRACTICE 22.1B > **Identifying Pronoun Cases and Uses**

Read the sentences. Write the case of each underlined pronoun. Then, label it *subject of a verb*, *direct object*, *indirect object*, or *object of a preposition*.

EXAMPLE   <u>He</u> liked the new teacher.

ANSWER   *nominative, subject of a verb*

11. Luis rode with <u>her</u> on the Ferris wheel.

12. <u>We</u> would like a better sound system.

13. Kayla told <u>him</u> about the homework assignment.

14. Serena saw <u>them</u> in the school yard.

15. Yesterday <u>he</u> and Samantha went to the fitness center.

16. The pale blue house on the corner belongs to <u>her</u>.

17. Joanna gave <u>me</u> a small canoe.

18. I used to have a pet caterpillar, but <u>it</u> turned into a butterfly.

19. The winners were Max and <u>I</u>.

20. With <u>it</u> comes a money-back guarantee.

SPEAKING APPLICATION

With a partner, talk about students on a school bus. Use several personal pronouns in different cases. Your partner should listen for and name the personal pronouns and their cases.

WRITING APPLICATION

Write five sentences about students in science class. Underline your pronouns and identify the case of each.

The Nominative Case

Personal pronouns in the nominative case have two uses.

RULE 22.1.2

> Use the **nominative** case for (1) the subject of a verb and (2) a predicate pronoun.

Note that predicate pronouns follow linking verbs. Pronouns that follow linking verbs should be in the nominative case. The linking verbs are highlighted in orange in the examples below.

SUBJECTS	**He** hopes to be in the play.
	Excitedly, **they** dressed for the show.
PREDICATE PRONOUNS	It **was** **I** who called the meeting.
	The best spellers **are** **she** and Joan.

Checking for Errors in the Nominative Case

People seldom forget to use the nominative case for a pronoun that is used by itself as a subject. Problems sometimes arise, however, when the pronoun is part of a compound subject.

INCORRECT	Jessie and **me** played catch.
CORRECT	Jessie and **I** played catch.

To make sure you are using the correct case of the pronoun in a compound subject, isolate the pronoun and the verb in the sentence. *Me played catch* is obviously wrong, so the nominative case *I* should be used instead.

If the sentence is in verb–subject order, rearrange it into subject–verb order, and then isolate the pronoun and verb.

INCORRECT	Are you and **her** going bowling?
REARRANGED	You and **?** are going bowling.
CORRECT	Are you and **she** going bowling?

See Practice 22.1C
See Practice 22.1D

The Objective Case

Personal pronouns in the objective case have three uses.

> Use the **objective** case for (1) a direct object, (2) an indirect object, and (3) the object of a preposition.

DIRECT OBJECT	Frank's reaction to the news upset **me**.
	The teacher lectured **her**.
INDIRECT OBJECT	Tell **him** the results.
	My father gave **me** directions to the mall.
OBJECT OF PREPOSITION	Our sister voted for **her**.
	The children gathered around **me**.

Checking for Errors in the Objective Case

As with the nominative case, people seldom forget to use the objective case for a pronoun that is used by itself as a direct object, indirect object, or object of a preposition. Problems may arise, however, when the pronoun is part of a compound object.

INCORRECT	The children gathered around Sal and **I**.
CORRECT	The children gathered around Sal and **me**.

To make sure you are using the correct case of the pronoun in a compound object, use only the pronoun with the rest of the sentence. *The children gathered around I* is obviously wrong, so the objective case *me* should be used instead.

If the sentence is in verb–subject order, rearrange it into subject–verb order.

INCORRECT	Did my father give Glen and **she** a drink?
REARRANGED	My father gave Glen and **?** a drink.
CORRECT	Did my father give Glen and **her** a drink?

See Practice 22.1E
See Practice 22.1F

The Possessive Case

Personal pronouns in the possessive case show ownership of one sort or another.

RULE

22.1.4

> Use the **possessive** case of personal pronouns before nouns to show possession. In addition, certain personal pronouns may also be used by themselves to indicate possession.

BEFORE NOUNS	The team won **its** tournament.
	Andrew carried **my** package.
BY THEMSELVES	Is this calculator **yours** or **mine**?
	Hers was the longest story.

Find It/ FIX IT

14

Grammar Game Plan

Checking for Errors in the Possessive Case

Personal pronouns in the possessive case are never written with an apostrophe because they already show ownership. Keep this in mind, especially with possessive pronouns that end in *s*.

INCORRECT	These drinks are **our's**, not **their's**.
CORRECT	These drinks are **ours**, not **theirs**.

When the pronoun *it* is followed by an apostrophe and an *s*, the word becomes *it's*, which is a contraction of *it is*. The possessive pronoun *its* does not have an apostrophe.

CONTRACTION	**It's** going to be a long day.
POSSESSIVE PRONOUN	The team loves **its** practices.

To check if you need the contraction *it's* or the possessive pronoun *its*, substitute *it is* and reread the sentence.

INCORRECT	My shoe has lost **it's** heel.
CORRECT	My shoe has lost **its** heel.

See Practice 22.1G

See Practice 22.1H

PRACTICE 22.1C ▷ Identifying Nominative Case Pronouns

Read the sentences. Write the correct pronoun from the choices in parentheses. Then, label the pronoun *subject of a verb* or *predicate pronoun*.

EXAMPLE   Marty and (I, me) ate lunch.

ANSWER   *I— subject of a verb*

1. Apparently (she, her) and Lucy were early.

2. The heads of the student body are Randolph and (I, me).

3. On our street, the Jacksons and (we, us) are the only ones with satellite television.

4. Either Doris or (he, him) will win the prize.

5. (They, them) and their friends chat a lot on their cell phones.

6. The first two people in line were Maurice and (she, her).

7. When the ship sailed into the harbor, (they, them) and the crew cheered.

8. I think the most helpful guidance counselors are Mrs. Kelvin and (he, him).

9. Did (we, us) or the Robinsons arrive first?

10. Before this summer, the best player had been Chester or (I, me).

PRACTICE 22.1D ▷ Using Nominative Case Pronouns in Sentences

Read the sentences. Then, rewrite a completed sentence, using a nominative case pronoun to fill the blank. Vary the nominative case pronouns you use.

EXAMPLE   Entering the room first were Dominic and _____.

ANSWER   *Entering the room first were Dominic and he.*

11. Sam and _____ make up the best doubles team in the city.

12. Can Phil and _____ help you with the project?

13. Standing beneath the birch trees were Carol and _____.

14. My brother and _____ may be a little late.

15. If you ask me nicely, _____ will help you fill out the form.

16. When the car stopped short, Danny and _____ were injured slightly.

17. Flying in a helicopter, Siri and _____ had a great view of the countryside.

18. The coach announced that Derry and _____ would be the starting forwards.

19. Huddled under the blanket are Eugene and _____.

20. When their mother traveled on business, Stella and _____ stayed with their grandmother.

SPEAKING APPLICATION

With a partner, talk about two people you know. Your partner should listen for nominative pronouns and make sure they are used correctly.

WRITING APPLICATION

Using sentences 12, 15, and 20 in Practice 22.1D as models, write three sentences about family members or friends. Underline the nominative case pronouns you use.

PRACTICE 22.1E > Using Objective Case Pronouns

Read the sentences. Write an objective case pronoun to complete each sentence. Then, label each pronoun *direct object, indirect object,* or *object of a preposition.*

EXAMPLE   I gave Darlene and _____ a lift.

ANSWER   *him* — *indirect object*

1. I saw Fred and _____ at the recycling plant.

2. I offered Pam and _____ a helping hand.

3. Ask the baker or _____ for some hard rolls.

4. I am going to town with Saul and _____.

5. Please give Dolores or _____ the message.

6. For my cousin and _____, each football game is more exciting than the last.

7. Rona and I usually walk to school, but sometimes my brother drives _____.

8. Since Mrs. Pai was so helpful, Mom brought Mr. Pai and _____ vegetables from our garden.

9. Did the lifeguard really save Howie and _____ from drowning?

10. I usually go with Paul or my two sisters, but today I am going without Paul or _____.

PRACTICE 22.1F > Using Objective Case Pronouns in Sentences

Read the sentences. Then, rewrite a completed sentence, using an objective case pronoun to fill each blank. Vary the objective case pronouns you use.

EXAMPLE   The best match was between Terry and _____.

ANSWER   *The best match was between Terry and her.*

11. Ms. Hamilton asked _____ four questions on the test.

12. Sandy waited for _____ for over an hour.

13. The coach picked Abby and _____ to be the starting forwards.

14. The child's mother made sure that the seat belt was securely around _____.

15. Give the book to _____ right now, or I'll be late to class.

16. When the boys were injured, the doctor treated _____ right away.

17. Jackson brought his favorite toy with _____.

18. Tomas was hoping that Lorna would ask _____ to go to the dance.

19. The crossing guard helped _____ get across the street safely.

20. The puppy followed closely behind Cindy and _____.

SPEAKING APPLICATION

With a partner, take turns discussing a plan you made with a friend or family member. Your partner should identify objective pronouns you use and make sure they are used correctly.

WRITING APPLICATION

Write five sentences about pets, using objective pronouns. Be sure to use the pronouns correctly. Then, exchange papers with a partner. Your partner should correct any pronoun errors.

PRACTICE 22.1G > Using Possessive Case Pronouns

Read the sentences. Write the correct pronoun from the choices in parentheses.

EXAMPLE   The dog gnawed (its, it's) bone.

ANSWER   *its*

1. Those ballet slippers are (hers, her's).
2. One of (me, my) oldest shirts ripped in the wash.
3. The elephant ate (its, it's) dinner.
4. Is the camera (yours, your's)?
5. That van is (theirs, their's).
6. (Ours, Our's) was a happy ending.
7. That handkerchief is (his, his').
8. The company has changed (its, it's) name.
9. (My, Mine) enemy is plotting against me.
10. (Theirs, There's) is a lovely home.

PRACTICE 22.1H > Writing Sentences With Possessive Case Pronouns

Read the directions. Then, follow the directions to write sentences that contain possessive case pronouns. Underline the possessive pronouns.

EXAMPLE   Write a sentence about a hobby using *her.*

ANSWER   *Sharon placed the stamps in <u>her</u> album.*

11. Write a sentence about twins using *their.*
12. Write a sentence about a cat using *its.*
13. Write a sentence about a picnic using *our.*
14. Write a sentence describing a personal feature using *my.*
15. Write a sentence about a favorite movie using *mine.*
16. Write a sentence about finding something missing using *theirs.*
17. Write a sentence about sports using *your.*
18. Write a sentence about an achievement using *her.*
19. Write a sentence about a popular politician using *his.*
20. Write a sentence about a place using *ours.*

SPEAKING APPLICATION

With a partner, take turns expressing opinions about school uniforms. Use as many different possessive pronouns as you can. Your partner should identify the possessive pronouns you use and make sure they are used correctly.

WRITING APPLICATION

Write three sentences about a sofa, chair, dresser, or other items in your home. Use possessive pronouns in each sentence. Then, exchange papers with a partner. Your partner should correct any pronoun errors.

Test Warm-Up

DIRECTIONS
Read the introduction and the passage that follows. Then, answer the questions to show that you can use and understand nominative, objective, and possessive case pronouns in the context of reading and writing.

Anna wrote this story about trying out for the school chorus. Read the paragraph and think about the changes you would suggest as a peer editor. When you finish reading, answer the questions that follow.

The Trying Tryout

(1) Last September, several of my friends and me tried out for the school chorus. (2) I was really nervous that the first name called would be me. (3) Then, I heard Brooke gasp when the first singers announced to audition were Dee and her. (4) They sang together in almost perfect harmony. (5) It was my turn next. (6) As I opened my mouth to sing, a fly landed right on my tongue, making me cough and choke. (7) I finally regained my composure and started over. (8) In the end, all three of we were selected.

1 What change, if any, should be made in sentence 1?

A Change *several of my friends and me* to **me and several of my friends**

B Change *several of my friends and me* to **several of my friends and they**

C Change *several of my friends and me* to **several of my friends and I**

D Make no change

2 What change, if any, should be made in sentence 2?

F Change *me* to **mines**

G Change *me* to **mine**

H Change *me* to **I**

J Make no change

3 What change should be made in sentence 3?

A Change *Dee and her* to **Dee and she**

B Change *Dee and her* to **Dee and me**

C Change *Dee and her* to **her and Dee**

D Change *were Dee and her* to **was she and Dee**

4 How should sentence 8 be revised?

F In the end, all we were selected.

G In the end, we were selected all.

H In the end, all three of us were selected.

J In the end, all three of they were selected.

Cases of *Who* and *Whom* The pronouns *who* and *whom* are often confused. *Who* is a nominative case pronoun, and *whom* is an objective case pronoun. *Who* and *whom* have two common uses in sentences: They can be used in questions or to begin subordinate clauses in complex sentences.

> **Use *who* for the subject of a verb. Use *whom* for (1) the direct object of a verb and (2) the object of a preposition.**

22.1.5 RULE

You will often find *who* used as the subject of a question. *Who* may also be used as the subject of a subordinate clause in a complex sentence.

SUBJECT OF A QUESTION	**Who** ran the fastest?
SUBJECT OF A SUBORDINATE CLAUSE	I admire the student **who** ran the fastest.

The following examples show *whom* used in questions.

DIRECT OBJECT	**Whom** did she meet at the park?
OBJECT OF PREPOSITION	From **whom** are you getting new skates?

Questions that include *whom* are generally in inverted word order, with the verb appearing before the subject. If you reword the first example in subject–verb word order, you will see that *whom* is the direct object of the verb *did meet: She did meet whom?* In the second example, *whom* is the object of the preposition *from: You are getting the new skates from whom?*

Subordinate clauses that begin with *whom* can be rearranged to show that the pronoun is a direct object.

EXAMPLE	I smiled at the man **whom** my father introduced.
REARRANGED SUBORDINATE CLAUSE	My father introduced **whom**?

See Practice 22.1I
See Practice 22.1J

PRACTICE 22.1I > Identifying the Correct Use of *Who* and *Whom*

Read the sentences. Write the pronoun in parentheses that correctly completes each sentence.

EXAMPLE   I saw (who, whom) you took to the dance.

ANSWER   *whom*

1. (Who, Whom) received the most praise?

2. With (who, whom) did you walk home?

3. Nora is the cheerleader (who, whom) stands behind the others.

4. (Who, Whom) have they chosen for team captain?

5. I know the reporter (who, whom) the newspaper sent to the school cafeteria.

6. The mayor is the elected official in (who, whom) the citizens place the most trust.

7. (Who, Whom) in the play has Drew replaced?

8. Please tell me (who, whom) you would choose as the best speaker.

9. You recommended (who, whom) for the committee?

10. I do not know (who, whom) she is.

PRACTICE 22.1J > Revising to Correct *Who* and *Whom*

Read the sentences. Then, if a sentence uses *who* or *whom* incorrectly, rewrite the sentence with the correct pronoun form. If a sentence has no pronoun error, write *correct*.

EXAMPLE   Who did you meet at the store?

ANSWER   *Whom did you meet at the store?*

11. Who in this crowd ever keeps quiet?

12. Who did she take to the playground?

13. Gail is the one in who I place my faith.

14. I ran into Valerie, whom you saw yesterday.

15. My brother, who needs new gloves, could also use a new winter hat.

16. To who were you talking on the telephone?

17. Of the two, whom is the most efficient?

18. Whom among us has ever been on television?

19. This movie was directed by whom?

20. Please tell me who that is.

SPEAKING APPLICATION

With a partner, take turns asking and answering questions about famous singers. Use *who* or *whom* in each question and answer. Your partner should listen for the pronouns and make sure they are used correctly.

WRITING APPLICATION

Write six sentences about the suspects in a mystery you read or in a movie you saw. Use *who* in three of the sentences and *whom* in the other three. Then, exchange papers with a partner. Your partner should check to make sure you've used the pronouns correctly.

CHAPTER 23

MAKING WORDS AGREE

Present ideas clearly in your writing by making each subject and verb agree and by matching each pronoun to its antecedent, the word or words for which the pronoun stands.

WRITE GUY *Jeff Anderson, M.Ed.*

WHAT DO YOU NOTICE?

Pick out pronouns as you zoom in on this sentence from the story "The Adventure of the Speckled Band" by Arthur Conan Doyle.

MENTOR TEXT

"The metallic clang heard by Miss Stoner was obviously caused by her stepfather hastily closing the door of his safe upon its terrible occupant."

Now, ask yourself the following questions:

- How does the pronoun *her* agree with its antecedent?
- Whose safe was hastily closed? How do you know?

The antecedent of *her* is *Miss Stoner*. *Her* agrees with *Miss Stoner* because it is a singular, feminine pronoun, and *Miss Stoner* is a singular, feminine noun. The possessive pronoun *his* shows that the safe belongs to her stepfather.

Grammar for Writers Creating agreement in number and gender between pronouns and their antecedents is one way writers achieve clarity. An antecedent may be a noun, a group of words, or another pronoun, so keep each situation in mind as you write.

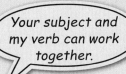

Your subject and my verb can work together.

Just as long as they agree.

23.1 Subject-Verb Agreement

For a sentence to be correct, its subject and verb must match each other, or agree. Subject–verb agreement has one main rule.

RULE 23.1.1

> **The subject and verb in a sentence must agree in number.**

In grammar, the concept of **number** is simple. The number of a word can be either **singular** or **plural.** A singular word indicates *one.* A plural word indicates *more than one.* In English, only nouns, pronouns, and verbs have number.

Singular and Plural Subjects

Most of the time, it is easy to tell whether a simple subject, such as a noun or pronoun, is singular or plural. That is because most nouns are made plural by adding *-s* or *-es* to their singular form.

EXAMPLES

friend	friend **s**
nation	nation **s**
leash	leash **es**
coach	coach **es**

Some nouns form plurals in irregular ways.

EXAMPLES

goose	**geese**
man	**men**
child	**children**
life	**lives**

Pronouns also have different forms to indicate singular and plural. For example, the pronouns *I, he, she, it,* and *this* are singular. *We, they,* and *these* are plural. *You, who,* and *some* can be either singular or plural.

Singular and Plural Verbs

Like nouns, verbs have singular and plural forms. Problems involving number in verbs normally involve the third-person forms in the present tense (*she wants, they want*) and certain forms of the verb *be* (*I am, he is* or *was, we are* or *were*).

The chart shows all the basic forms of several different verbs in the present tense.

SINGULAR AND PLURAL VERBS IN THE PRESENT TENSE		
SINGULAR		**PLURAL**
First and Second Person	**Third Person**	**First, Second, and Third Person**
(I, you) send	(he, she, it) sends	(we, you, they) send
(I, you) go	(he, she, it) goes	(we, you, they) go
(I, you) look	(he, she, it) looks	(we, you, they) look
(I, you) dance	(he, she, it) dances	(we, you, they) dance
(I, you) visit	(he, she, it) visits	(we, you, they) visit
(I, you) work	(he, she, it) works	(we, you, they) work
(I, you) run	(he, she, it) runs	(we, you, they) run
(I, you) discuss	(he, she, it) discusses	(we, you, they) discuss
(I, you) vote	(he, she, it) votes	(we, you, they) vote
(I, you) choose	(he, she, it) chooses	(we, you, they) choose
(I, you) learn	(he, she, it) learns	(we, you, they) learn

Notice that the form of the verb changes only in the third-person singular, when an *-s* or *-es* is added to the verb. Unlike nouns, which usually become plural when *-s* or *-es* is added, verbs with *-s* or *-es* added to them are singular.

The helping verb *be* may also indicate whether a verb is singular or plural. The following chart shows only those forms of the verb *be* that are always singular.

FORMS OF THE HELPING VERB *BE* THAT ARE ALWAYS SINGULAR			
am	is	was	has been

Making Verbs Agree With Singular and Plural Subjects

To check subject–verb agreement, determine the number of the subject. Then, make sure the verb has the same number.

SINGULAR
SUBJECT
AND VERB

Megan likes surfing.

She was at the beach earlier today.

PLURAL
SUBJECT
AND VERB

They like surfing.

Surfers were in the water yesterday.

23.1.2

A prepositional phrase that comes between a subject and its verb does not affect subject–verb agreement.

Often, a subject is separated from its verb by a prepositional phrase. In these cases, it is important to remember that the object of a preposition is never the subject of a sentence.

INCORRECT

The **arrival** of the students **have caused** much excitement at the ceremony.

CORRECT

The **arrival** of the students **has caused** much excitement at the ceremony.

INCORRECT

The **calls** of the bird **was heard** several blocks away.

CORRECT

The **calls** of the bird **were heard** several blocks away.

In the first example, the subject is *arrival*, not *students*, which is the object of the preposition *of*. Because *arrival* is singular, the singular verb *has caused* must be used. In the second example, the subject is the plural *calls*, not *bird*; therefore, it takes the plural verb *were heard*.

See Practice 23.1A
See Practice 23.1B

PRACTICE 23.1A **Making Subjects and Verbs Agree**

Read the sentences. Write the verb in parentheses that agrees with the subject. Then, label the subject *singular* or *plural*.

EXAMPLE   The mice (likes, like) cheese.

ANSWER   *like* — *plural*

1. The index (lists, list) items in alphabetical order.

2. The flag (ripples, ripple) in the wind.

3. Some birds (fly, flies) south in winter.

4. The businessmen (goes, go) to lunch at noon.

5. A box of crackers (sits, sit) on the shelf.

6. The people in our state (votes, vote) for governor next Tuesday.

7. The glow of streetlights and neon signs (makes, make) the nighttime skyline memorable.

8. The size of the pieces of the jigsaw puzzle (decreases, decrease) with the level of difficulty.

9. How many students (are, is) in your class?

10. The papers hidden in a secret drawer of her desk (is, are) missing.

PRACTICE 23.1B **Revising for Subject-Verb Agreement**

Read the sentences. Then, if a sentence has an error in subject-verb agreement, rewrite the sentence correctly. If a sentence has no error, write *correct*.

EXAMPLE   The lions in the cage roars loudly.

ANSWER   *The lions in the cage roar loudly.*

11. It often happens that way.

12. The women belongs to the fitness club.

13. The ballplayers on the bench look bored.

14. The sound of the drums hurt my ears.

15. The tourists on the walk of Old Alexandria like the historical buildings.

16. A sack of groceries are on the counter.

17. The houses across the street from the beach enjoy wonderful views.

18. The students in the library studies for their test.

19. The behavior of the bears in the park often surprise visitors.

20. Her plan to visit several countries in South America sound very interesting.

SPEAKING APPLICATION

With a partner, talk about items found in a cupboard, a pantry, or a kitchen. Use singular and plural subjects and present-tense verbs. Your partner should check that your subjects and verbs agree.

WRITING APPLICATION

Write five sentences about animals in a zoo. Underline your subjects once and verbs twice, and make sure the subjects and verbs agree.

Making Verbs Agree With Collective Nouns

Collective nouns—such as *assembly, audience, class, club*, and *committee*—name groups of people or things. Collective nouns are challenging as subjects because they can take either singular or plural verbs. The number of the verb depends on the meaning of the collective noun in the sentence.

RULE
23.1.3

> Use a singular verb with a collective noun acting as a single unit. Use a plural verb when the individual members of the group are acting individually.

SINGULAR   The **committee** **votes** on the new chair.

PLURAL   The **committee** **have split** their votes on the issue.

SINGULAR   The history **club** **plans** a debate.

PLURAL   The history **club** **were proud** of their individual debating skills.

SINGULAR   The **class** **plants** lettuce and cucumbers.

PLURAL   The **class** **have divided** the lettuce and tomato seeds among the members.

SINGULAR   The soccer **team** **marches** in the parade.

PLURAL   The soccer **team** **have** many different skills.

SINGULAR   The **audience** **roars** after the performance.

PLURAL   The **audience** **have given** their reviews of the show.

See Practice 23.1C
See Practice 23.1D

PRACTICE 23.1C > Making Verbs Agree With Collective Nouns

Read the sentences. Then, write the verb in parentheses that agrees with the subject.

EXAMPLE   The chorus (sounds, sound) lovely.

ANSWER   *sounds*

1. The club (offers, offer) members many advantages.

2. The family often (eats, eat) dinner together.

3. The team (is, are) not likely to reach the finals.

4. The choir (harmonizes, harmonize) well with one another.

5. The class (talks, talk) among themselves.

6. A flock of sheep (needs, need) a shepherd.

7. At weekly meetings, the staff (suggests, suggest) all sorts of ideas to the boss.

8. The jury (disagrees, disagree) with one another about the verdict.

9. At the end of each act, the audience (applauds, applaud).

10. (Does, do) the army recruit on campus?

PRACTICE 23.1D > Revising for Agreement Between Verbs and Collective Nouns

Read the sentences. Then, if a sentence has an error in subject-verb agreement, rewrite the sentence correctly. If a sentence has no error, write *correct.*

EXAMPLE   Our team need someone like you.

ANSWER   *Our team needs someone like you.*

11. The group quarrels among themselves.

12. The troop are seeking new members.

13. The crowd often swells to over a thousand.

14. The company provide jobs to the community.

15. The cast discuss the script with one another.

16. The faculty offers different opinions.

17. Sometimes the herd stampedes.

18. The ship's crew displays different talents.

19. The orchestra rehearse every morning.

20. The swarm descend on the beekeeper.

SPEAKING APPLICATION

With a partner, take turns discussing community organizations. Use at least three collective nouns, such as *club, staff,* and *team.* Your partner should listen for the collective nouns and make sure your verbs agree.

WRITING APPLICATION

Write three sentences in the present tense, using these collective nouns as subjects: *cast, group, company.*

Making Verbs Agree With Compound Subjects

A **compound subject** refers to two or more subjects that share a verb. Compound subjects are connected by conjunctions such as *and, or,* or *nor.*

EXAMPLES   The **museums** and **historical sites** in
compound subject

Chicago **attract** many visitors.
plural verb

Either **Sally** or **Frank** **knows** the way to the
compound subject   singular verb

historical museum.

Neither the **Hancock Observatory** nor the **Art**
compound subject

Institute **disappoints** tourists.
singular verb

A number of rules can help you choose the right verb to use with a compound subject.

Compound Subjects Joined by *And*

RULE 23.1.4

When a compound subject is connected by *and,* the verb that follows is usually plural.

EXAMPLE   **El Paso** and **Dallas** **are** my favorite Texas cities.
compound subject   plural verb

There is an exception to this rule: If the parts of a compound subject are thought of as one person or thing, the subject is singular and takes a singular verb.

EXAMPLES   **Franks and beans** **is** a popular meal when
compound subject   singular verb

camping.

The **strawberries and cream** **is** on the table.
compound subject   singular verb

Compound Subjects Joined by *Or* or *Nor*

> **When two singular subjects are joined by *or* or *nor*, use a singular verb. When two plural subjects are joined by *or* or *nor*, use a plural verb.**

RULE 23.1.5

SINGULAR   A **bicycle** or a **skateboard** **is** a good way to
                        compound subject   singular
                                                      verb
get to the park.

PLURAL   Neither **boys** nor **men** **like** to wear a tie.
                          compound subject   plural verb

In the first example, *or* joins two singular subjects. Although two things make up the compound subject, the subject does not take a plural verb. Either a bicycle or a skateboard is a good way to get to the park, not both of them.

> **When a compound subject is made up of one singular and one plural subject joined by *or* or *nor*, the verb agrees with the subject closer to it.**

RULE 23.1.6

EXAMPLES   Either the **monuments** or the **Alamo**
                            plural subject   singular subject
is interesting to see.
singular verb

Either the **Alamo** or the **monuments**
            singular subject   plural subject
are interesting to see.
plural verb

See Practice 23.1E
See Practice 23.1F

Agreement in Inverted Sentences

In most sentences, the subject comes before the verb. Sometimes, however, this order is turned around, or **inverted.** In other sentences, the helping verb comes before the subject even though the main verb follows the subject.

When a subject comes after the verb, the subject and verb still must agree with each other in number.

EXAMPLE   **Do** the cultural **attractions** in New York City
                plural verb   plural subject

sound exciting to you?

Sentences Beginning With a Prepositional Phrase
In sentences that begin with a prepositional phrase, the object of the preposition may look like a subject, even though it is not.

EXAMPLE   Along the river **were** **throngs** of spectators.
                                plural verb plural subject

In this example, the plural verb *were* agrees with the plural subject *throngs.* The singular noun *river* is the object of the preposition *along.*

Sentences Beginning With *There* or *Here*
Sentences beginning with *there* or *here* are almost always in inverted word order.

EXAMPLES   ·There **were** several **magazines** about sports.
                        plural verb   plural subject

Here **is** the latest **magazine** about sports.
singular verb   singular subject

The contractions *there's* and *here's* both contain the singular verb *is*: *there is* and *here is.* Do not use these contractions with plural subjects.

INCORRECT   Here**'s** the **papers** for the class.

CORRECT   Here **are** the **papers** for the class.

Questions With Inverted Word Order
Many questions are also written in inverted word order.

EXAMPLE   Where **are** the **papers** for the class?
                        plural verb   plural subject

PRACTICE 23.1E > Making Verbs Agree With Compound Subjects

Read the sentences. Then, write the verb in parentheses that agrees with the subject.

EXAMPLE   Kay and Janine (sings, sing) well.

ANSWER   *sing*

1. Either Brad or Ann (takes, take) out the garbage every night.

2. Both chicken and chickpeas (supplies, supply) protein.

3. The rooms and hall (fills, fill) to capacity.

4. Peanut butter and jelly (is, are) traditional in our house.

5. Neither Zack nor Trish (plays, play) tennis.

6. Either the workers or their boss (takes, take) care of the delivery.

7. The doctor or her nurses (administers, administer) flu shots.

8. (Do, Does) Rick or Seth know the answer?

9. Neither the teacher nor his students (arrives, arrive) before nine o'clock.

10. Macaroni and cheese (is, are) the best comfort food.

PRACTICE 23.1F > Revising for Agreement Between Verbs and Compound Subjects

Read the sentences. Then, if a sentence has an error in subject-verb agreement, rewrite the sentence correctly. If a sentence has no error, write *correct*.

EXAMPLE   Phil or Edie often help me.

ANSWER   *Phil or Edie often helps me.*

11. The toaster oven or the microwave often reheat leftovers.

12. The lion and the tiger come from two different continents.

13. Either Anna or Mark attends the meetings.

14. Both the magician and his assistant performs amazing tricks.

15. Neither the coach nor the players spoke to the reporter.

16. Ham and eggs is my favorite breakfast.

17. Either the editors or their publisher respond to readers' letters.

18. Neither Jackie nor Lance write for the magazine anymore.

19. The car and the bike is in the garage.

20. Either the art direction or the costumes was awarded an Oscar.

SPEAKING APPLICATION

With a partner, take turns discussing your favorite foods, using sentences 2 and 4 as models. Use four compound subjects with present-tense verbs. Your partner should listen for the compound subjects and decide if the verbs agree with them.

WRITING APPLICATION

Write four sentences about sports figures and their achievements. Use compound subjects with present-tense verbs. Underline the compound subjects and circle the verbs.

Verb Agreement With Indefinite Pronouns

Indefinite pronouns refer to people, places, or things in a general way.

> When an **indefinite pronoun** is the subject of a sentence, the verb must agree in number with the pronoun.

INDEFINITE PRONOUNS				
SINGULAR			**PLURAL**	**SINGULAR OR PLURAL**
anybody	everyone	nothing	both	all
anyone	everything	one	few	any
anything	much	other	many	more
each	neither	somebody	several	most
either	nobody	someone	others	none
everybody	no one	something		some

Indefinite Pronouns That Are Always Singular

Indefinite pronouns that are always singular take singular verbs. Do not be misled by a prepositional phrase that follows an indefinite pronoun. The singular verb agrees with the indefinite pronoun, not with the object of the preposition.

EXAMPLES

Each of the football team mascots **is** at
singular subject   singular verb

the game.

Either of the cars in the lot **is** in good condition.
singular subject   singular verb

Everyone in the back of the bus **was** singing
singular subject   singular verb

along.

Each of the girls **plays** on the tennis team.
singular subject   singular verb

Indefinite Pronouns That Are Always Plural

Indefinite pronouns that are always plural are used with plural verbs.

EXAMPLES **Both** of my notebooks **are** in the car.
      plural subject   plural verb

          Many of the families **are picnicking** in the
          plural subject   plural verb
          park today.

          Several have decided to join the swim team.
          plural subject   plural verb

          Few are planning to be at home in July.
          plural subject   plural verb

Indefinite Pronouns That May Be Either Singular or Plural

Many indefinite pronouns can take either a singular or a plural verb.

> **The number of the indefinite pronoun is the same as the number of its referent, or the noun to which it refers.**

23.1.9   RULE

The indefinite pronoun is singular if the referent is singular. If the referent is plural, the indefinite pronoun is plural.

SINGULAR   **Some** of the **cheese has** spoiled.

PLURAL   **Some** of the **eggs have** spoiled, too.

In the examples above, *some* is singular when it refers to *cheese*, but plural when it refers to *eggs*.

SINGULAR   **All** of the **money** we collected **is** missing.

PLURAL   **All** of these **cards are** for you.

See Practice 23.1G
See Practice 23.1H

In these examples, *all* is singular when it refers to *money*, but plural when it refers to *cards*.

PRACTICE 23.1G Making Verbs Agree With Indefinite Pronouns

Read the sentences. Then, write the verb in parentheses that agrees with the subject.

EXAMPLE   Both of them (looks, look) happy.

ANSWER   *look*

1. Several of the apples (tastes, taste) bad.

2. Some of the clocks (has, have) the wrong time.

3. More of the music (was, were) played.

4. Most of my questions (have, has) been answered.

5. Few of us (knows, know) the reason.

6. Each of the planets (orbits, orbit) the sun.

7. Neither of the mechanics (works, work) on weekends.

8. None of the residents (is, are) at home.

9. Everything in the closets and attics (was, were) old and dusty.

10. Most of the team members (does, do) different things on weekends.

PRACTICE 23.1H Revising for Agreement Between Verbs and Indefinite Pronouns

Read the sentences. Then, if a sentence has an error in subject-verb agreement, rewrite the sentence correctly. If a sentence has no error, write *correct*.

EXAMPLE   None of the dogs barks a lot.

ANSWER   *None of the dogs bark a lot.*

11. Both of the women play tennis often.

12. More of the workers needs new jobs.

13. Some of the food needs salt.

14. Everything stated in newspaper articles are not always true.

15. Few of the teachers uses the cafeteria.

16. Each of the suggestions have merit.

17. Any of your assistance is welcome.

18. The spices in this meal tastes wonderful.

19. Most of the meal was left over.

20. All of the class members likes to debate with one another.

SPEAKING APPLICATION

With a partner, talk about a board game or another game you have played. Use four indefinite pronouns as subjects with present-tense verbs. Your partner should listen for and confirm that your verbs agree with your subjects.

WRITING APPLICATION

Use sentences 15 and 20 as models, and write four sentences about the results of an imaginary survey. Use indefinite pronouns as subjects with present-tense verbs. Underline your subjects once and verbs twice, and make sure the subjects and verbs agree.

23.2 Agreement Between Pronouns and Antecedents

An **antecedent** is the word or words for which a pronoun stands. A pronoun's antecedent may be a noun, a group of words acting as a noun, or even another pronoun. As with subjects and verbs, pronouns should agree with their antecedents.

Making Personal Pronouns and Antecedents Agree

Person tells whether a pronoun refers to the person speaking (first person), the person spoken to (second person), or the person, place, or thing spoken about (third person). **Number** tells whether the pronoun is singular or plural. **Gender** tells whether a third-person-singular antecedent is masculine or feminine.

Grammar
Game Plan

> **A personal pronoun must agree with its antecedent in person, number, and gender.**

23.2.1 RULE

EXAMPLE   I told **Talie** to bring a jacket with **her**.

In this example, the pronoun *her* is third person and singular. It agrees with its feminine antecedent, *Talie.*

Avoiding Shifts in Person
A personal pronoun must have the same person as its antecedent. Otherwise, the meaning of the sentence is unclear.

INCORRECT   The **students** know **we** must check the answers before handing in tests.
(Who must check the answers? *We* must.)

CORRECT   The **students** know **they** must check the answers before handing in tests.
(Who must check the answers? *The students* must.)

As you can see, a shift in the person of the personal pronoun can make it unclear who is going to check the answers.

Avoiding Problems With Number and Gender

Making pronouns and antecedents agree in number and gender can be difficult. Problems may arise when the antecedent is a collective noun, when the antecedent is a compound joined by *or* or *nor,* or when the gender of the antecedent is not known.

Making Pronouns Agree in Number With Collective Nouns
Collective nouns are challenging because they can take either singular or plural pronouns. The number of the pronoun depends on the meaning of the collective noun in the sentence.

RULE 23.2.2 ▷ Use a singular pronoun to refer to a collective noun that names a group that is acting as a single unit. Use a plural pronoun to refer to a collective noun when the members or parts of a group are acting individually.

SINGULAR   The **audience showed its** approval with applause.

PLURAL   The **audience voted** for **their** favorite songs.

In the first example above, the audience is acting as a single unit when it applauds, so the singular pronoun, *its,* refers to *audience.* In the second example, each member of the audience is voting individually, so the plural pronoun, *their,* refers to *audience.*

Making Pronouns Agree in Number With Compound Nouns

RULE 23.2.3 ▷ Use a singular personal pronoun to refer to two or more singular antecedents joined by *or* or *nor.* Use a plural pronoun with two or more singular antecedents joined by *and.*

Two or more singular antecedents joined by *or* or *nor* must have a singular pronoun, just as they must have a singular verb.

INCORRECT   **Marco** or **John** will bring **their** sandwich.

CORRECT   **Marco** or **John** will bring **his** sandwich.

CORRECT   **Marco** and **John** will bring **their** sandwiches.

Avoiding Problems With Gender

When the gender of a third-person-singular antecedent is not known, you can make the pronoun agree with its antecedent in one of three ways:

(1) Use *he or she, him or her,* or *his or hers.*

(2) Rewrite the sentence so that the antecedent and pronoun are both plural.

(3) Rewrite the sentence to eliminate the pronoun.

Traditionally, the masculine pronouns *he* and *his* have been used to stand for both males and females. Today, using *he or she* and *him or her* is preferred. If any of these corrections seem awkward to you, rewrite the sentence.

Making Personal Pronouns and Indefinite Pronouns Agree

Indefinite pronouns are words such as *each, everybody, either,* and *one.* Pay special attention to the number of a personal pronoun when the antecedent is a singular indefinite pronoun.

> **Use a singular personal pronoun when its antecedent is a singular indefinite pronoun.**

23.2.4 RULE

Do not be misled by a prepositional phrase that follows an indefinite pronoun. The personal pronoun agrees with the indefinite pronoun, not with the object of the preposition.

INCORRECT	**One** of the birds has lost **their** feathers.
CORRECT	**One** of the birds has lost **its** feathers.

INCORRECT	**Everyone** in the group wanted to read **their** book report.
CORRECT	**Everyone** in the group wanted to read **his or her** book report.

See Practice 23.2A
See Practice 23.2B
See Practice 23.2C
See Practice 23.2D

CORRECT	**All** of the students in the group wanted to read **their** book reports.

Read each sentence. Then, rewrite the sentence, filling each blank with a pronoun that agrees with an antecedent in the sentence.

EXAMPLE   Each of the girls wore _____ hair in braids.

ANSWER   *Each of the girls wore* her *hair in braids.*

1. Mr. Blair and his wife signed _____ names.

2. Both boys raised _____ hands.

3. After Max sang, the audience applauded for _____.

4. Since they were running late, neither of the twin girls brought _____ book to class.

5. All students are expected to complete _____ assignments on time.

6. Alicia practiced all week, and _____ won _____ event easily.

7. None of the children changed _____ or _____ behavior despite the scolding.

8. After a noise disturbed _____ nap, the cat yawned and stretched _____ legs.

9. "Brooke and I can vividly recall _____ childhood memories," Nadine said.

10. Neither Walter nor David was willing to share _____ lunch with me.

Read each sentence. Then, rewrite the sentence with the correct pronoun or phrase in parentheses.

EXAMPLE   Both Stan and Lamar had on (his uniform, their uniforms).

ANSWER   *Both Stan and Lamar had on* their uniforms.

11. Neither Marie nor her mom answered (her, their) cell phone.

12. I spoke to the boys, and each agreed to improve (his, their) behavior.

13. Everyone in the girls' club promised that (she, they) would attend the lecture.

14. After casting, the director helped each actor prepare for (their parts, his or her part).

15. Each mouse ran to (its, their) own hole.

16. All members received (his or her, their) music, and (he or she, they) began practicing.

17. Before they study, Arthur and Luis should pick up (his notebook, their notebooks).

18. When they heard the news, Sandra and Blanca were excited about (her, their) father's new job.

19. Each puppy opened (its, their) eyes.

20. Several of my girlfriends said (they were, she was) coming to the field hockey game.

SPEAKING APPLICATION

With a partner, talk about students who excel in the classroom, sports, or other activities. Use several personal pronouns, including *her, his, its,* and *their.* Your partner should identify the personal pronouns and their antecedents, and decide whether they agree.

WRITING APPLICATION

Write six sentences about school supplies. Use compound subjects and indefinite pronouns as subjects, and refer to them with personal pronouns. With a partner, read the sentences aloud and work together to correct any incorrectly identified antecedents.

PRACTICE 23.2C ▷ Revising Sentences for Pronoun-Antecedent Agreement

Read each sentence. Then, rewrite the sentence, changing either the pronoun or the antecedent, so that pronouns and their antecedents agree.

EXAMPLE   After each musician performed their solos, the concert ended.

ANSWER   After *all musicians* performed their solos, the concert ended.

1. If either Bill or Eric calls, please ask them to come for an interview.

2. I invited both Claire and Danica, and I hoped that she would accept.

3. As each boy shouted, "Here," the monitor checked off their names.

4. The teacher reviewed each boy's notebook, and she wrote a personal note to them.

5. Gavin and Joey were the first to arrive, but no one recognized him.

6. Each child's parent is required to sign a permission sheet for them.

7. Neither Erica nor Lori brought in their permission sheet.

8. Everyone was worried, but only one person expressed their concern.

9. Several girls on the track team asked Ms. Warren to be her personal trainer.

10. Because Nadira and Fanny were late, we had to start without her.

PRACTICE 23.2D ▷ Writing Sentences With Correctly Identified Antecedents

Read each sentence beginning. Then, write a complete sentence by adding an ending that includes a pronoun. Be sure you correctly identify the antecedents.

EXAMPLE   Shelby bought two parakeets, and she

ANSWER   Shelby bought two parakeets, and she *brought them home with her.*

11. After the boys ran laps, the coach

12. Each member of the band practiced

13. I couldn't see either of my sisters, but I knew

14. Neither Jake nor Lawrence expects to

15. As the rain continued to fall, every homeowner feared that

16. Everyone Sherry asked gave

17. Each child picked out

18. Both John and Jackson ran the exact same time, so

19. Lucy looked into her brother's eyes and

20. Neither Ellen nor Rachel was willing

SPEAKING APPLICATION

Describe to a partner what happened at lunch one day. Use at least three sentences containing pronouns. Your partner should listen for and correct any problems with pronoun-antecedent agreement.

WRITING APPLICATION

Write six sentences about a practice or rehearsal. Use pronouns in each of your sentences. Read your sentences aloud to a partner. Correct any sentences that have incorrectly identified antecedents.

Test Warm-Up

DIRECTIONS
Read the introduction and the passage that follows. Then, answer the questions to show that you can use and understand sentences that include correctly identified antecedents in the context of reading and writing.

Lucinda wrote this story about a community celebration. Read the story and think about the changes you would suggest as a peer editor. When you finish reading, answer the questions that follow.

Martin Luther King Jr. Day

(1) Each year, our town joins with two nearby communities to celebrate Martin Luther King Jr. Day. (2) First, everyone gathers in their own town and marches to a central location. (3) Members of the Girl Scouts lead the parade, and each one carries a banner that they have made. (4) Then the mayor of each town reads a proclamation passed by their town council. (5) After that, two middle school students come forward, and he takes turns reciting the words of Dr. King's famous "I Have a Dream" speech. (6) It is always a very moving and meaningful celebration.

1 What change, if any, should be made in sentence 2?

A Change *gathers* to **gather**

B Change *their* to **his or her**

C Change *their* to **our**

D Make no change

2 What change should be made in sentence 3?

F Change *lead* to **leads**

G Change *one* to **girl**

H Change *they have* to **he or she has**

J Change *they have* to **she has**

3 What is the BEST way to revise sentence 4?

A Then the three mayors read proclamations passed by their town councils.

B Then the mayor of each town reads a proclamation passed by our town council.

C Then the three mayors read proclamations passed by our town council.

D Then the mayors of all three towns read a proclamations passed by her town council.

4 What change, if any, should be made in sentence 5?

F Change *students* to **student's**

G Change *he takes turns* to **they take turns**

H Change *he takes turns* to **he or she take turns**

J Make no change

USING MODIFIERS

Understanding how to use different forms of adjectives and adverbs as modifiers will help you add variety to your sentences.

CHAPTER 24

WRITE GUY *Jeff Anderson, M.Ed.*

WHAT DO YOU NOTICE?

Focus on modifiers as you zoom in on these sentences from the book *Harriet Tubman: Conductor on the Underground Railroad* by Ann Petry.

MENTOR TEXT

> Harriet felt safer now, though there were danger spots ahead. But the biggest part of her job was over.

Now, ask yourself the following questions:

- What was the author comparing Harriet's feeling to when she wrote that Harriet felt safer?
- What does the superlative adjective *biggest* suggest about the rest of Harriet's job?

The author was comparing Harriet's feelings in the present to her feelings in the past. To compare two things, the *-er* ending is added to most one- or two-syllable adjectives and adverbs. The ending *-est* is used to compare three or more things in the superlative form. *Biggest* is the superlative form of *big* and suggests that Harriet still has parts of her job to do.

Grammar for Writers When writers use modifiers to show forms of comparison, they can craft a complete picture for their readers.

I want to receive a higher score on my next test.

You should try for the highest score.

24.1 Comparisons Using Adjectives and Adverbs

You may recall that adjectives and adverbs are **modifiers.** Adjectives can modify nouns or pronouns. Adverbs can modify verbs, adjectives, or other adverbs. You can use modifiers to make comparisons.

WRITING COACH

Online

www.phwritingcoach.com

Grammar Practice
Practice your grammar skills with Writing Coach Online.

Grammar Games
Test your knowledge of grammar in this fast-paced interactive video game.

Three Forms of Comparison

Modifiers change their form when they show comparison. These different forms are called **forms,** or **degrees, of comparison.**

RULE 24.1.1

Most adjectives and adverbs have three forms, or degrees, of comparison: **positive, comparative,** and **superlative.**

The **positive degree** is used when no comparison is being made. This is the form of a word that is listed in a dictionary. The **comparative degree** is used when two items are being compared. The **superlative degree** is used when three or more items are being compared. When the superlative degree is used, the article *the* is often added.

DEGREE	ADJECTIVE	ADVERB
Positive	My brother has a large bedroom.	My dog runs fast.
Comparative	His bedroom is larger than mine.	My dog runs faster than Sam's dog.
Superlative	My sister has the largest bedroom in our home.	Of all the dogs in the neighborhood, my dog runs the fastest.

Like verbs, adjectives and adverbs change forms in different ways. Some adjectives and adverbs change in regular ways, or according to predictable patterns. As you can see in the chart above, *large* and *fast* form their comparative and superlative degrees regularly, by adding *-er* and *-est* to their positive form.

Regular Modifiers With One or Two Syllables

Most modifiers are **regular**—their degrees of comparison are formed in predictable ways.

> **Use *-er* or *more* to form the comparative degree and use *-est* or *most* to form the superlative degree of most one- and two-syllable modifiers.**

COMPARATIVE AND SUPERLATIVE DEGREES FORMED WITH *-ER* AND *-EST*		
POSITIVE	COMPARATIVE	SUPERLATIVE
deep	deeper	deepest
fast	faster	fastest
friendly	friendlier	friendliest
narrow	narrower	narrowest
sunny	sunnier	sunniest

Use *more* to form a modifier's comparative degree when adding *-er* sounds awkward. Use *most* to form a modifier's superlative degree when adding *-est* sounds awkward.

COMPARATIVE AND SUPERLATIVE DEGREES FORMED WITH *MORE* AND *MOST*		
POSITIVE	COMPARATIVE	SUPERLATIVE
careful	more careful	most careful
complete	more complete	most complete
fun	more fun	most fun
often	more often	most often
quietly	more quietly	most quietly

More and *most* should not be used when the result sounds awkward, however. If you are not sure which form to use, check a dictionary. Most dictionaries list modifiers formed with *-er* and *-est*.

See Practice 24.1A

Regular Modifiers With Three or More Syllables

Modifiers for words with three or more syllables follow the same rules.

RULE 24.1.3

Use *more* and *most* to form the comparative and superlative degrees of all modifiers of three or more syllables. Do not use -*er* or -*est* with modifiers of more than two syllables.

DEGREES OF MODIFIERS WITH THREE OR MORE SYLLABLES		
POSTIVE	COMPARATIVE	SUPERLATIVE
expensive	more expensive	most expensive
flexible	more flexible	most flexible

Adverbs Ending in *-ly*

To modify most adverbs ending in -*ly*, use *more* or *most.*

RULE 24.1.4

Use *more* to form the comparative degree and *most* to form the superlative degree of most adverbs ending in -*ly*.

EXAMPLES   easily, more easily, most easily

peacefully, more peacefully, most peacefully

Using *Less* and *Least*

Less and *least* can show decreasing comparisons.

RULE 24.1.5

Use *less* with a modifier to form the decreasing comparative degree and *least* to form the decreasing superlative degree.

EXAMPLES   cautiously, less cautiously, least cautiously

effectively, less effectively, least effectively

See Practice 24.1B

PRACTICE 24.1A Forming Comparatives and Superlatives of One- and Two-Syllable Modifiers

Read the modifiers. Write the comparative and superlative forms of each modifier.

EXAMPLE   long

ANSWER   *longer, longest*

1. young
2. neat
3. fine
4. hot
5. cloudy
6. hungry
7. careful
8. precious
9. lovely
10. quickly

PRACTICE 24.1B Using Forms of Modifiers

Read the sentences. Then, write each sentence using the form of the modifier in parentheses.

EXAMPLE   Bianca is _____ than I am. (*young*, comparative)

ANSWER   *Bianca is younger than I am.*

11. This box is _____ than that one. (*large*, comparative)

12. Daniela is the _____ runner on the track team. (*swift*, superlative)

13. Which is the _____ item in the museum's gem collection? (*expensive*, superlative)

14. The bus arrived _____ than we expected. (*soon*, comparative)

15. In my opinion, he is the _____ actor performing today. (*talented*, superlative)

16. It is even _____ here than it is on the river. (*foggy*, comparative)

17. She is the _____ of my advisers. (*intelligent*, superlative)

18. Charles is _____ in the evening than he is in the morning. (*tired*, comparative)

19. I spoke _____ than I should have. (*angrily*, comparative)

20. Of the three children, who is the _____ ? (*tall*, superlative)

SPEAKING APPLICATION

With a partner, talk about a favorite sports team. Use comparatives and superlatives of one- and two-syllable modifiers. Your partner should listen for the comparatives and superlatives and decide if they are formed correctly.

WRITING APPLICATION

Write four sentences stating your opinions about different places to live. Use two comparative and two superlative forms of modifiers.

Irregular Adjectives and Adverbs

A few adjectives and adverbs are irregular.

RULE

24.1.6

> **Memorize the comparative and superlative forms of adjectives and adverbs that have irregular spellings.**

The chart lists the most common irregular modifiers.

DEGREES OF IRREGULAR ADJECTIVES AND ADVERBS		
POSITIVE	COMPARATIVE	SUPERLATIVE
bad (adjective)	worse	worst
badly (adverb)	worse	worst
far (distance)	farther	farthest
far (extent)	further	furthest
good (adjective)	better	best
well (adverb)	better	best
many	more	most
much	more	most

When you are unsure about how a modifier forms its degrees of comparison, check a dictionary.

See Practice 24.1C

Using Comparative and Superlative Degrees

Keep these rules in mind when you use the comparative and superlative degrees.

RULE

24.1.7

> **Use the comparative degree to compare *two* people, places, or things. Use the superlative degree to compare *three or more* people, places, or things.**

Usually, you do not need to mention specific numbers when you are making a comparison. Other words in the sentence should help make the meaning clear whether you are comparing two items or three or more items.

EXAMPLES   The lifeguard felt **better** once all

swimmers were safely on the beach.

The lifeguard completed the rowing exercise

in her **best** time this week.

Pay particular attention to the modifiers you use when you are
comparing just two items. Do not use the superlative degree with
fewer than three items.

INCORRECT   Of the two teams, that one was the **best**.

CORRECT   Of the two teams, that one was **better**.

INCORRECT   His was the **fastest** of the two skateboards.

CORRECT   His was the **faster** of the two skateboards.

> Do not make **double comparisons.** Do not use both *-er* and
> *more* to form the comparative degree or both *-est* and *most* to
> form the superlative degree. Also, be sure not to use *-er, more,*
> and *most* with an irregular modifier.

RULE
24.1.8

INCORRECT   Laura finished the assignment the **most**

fastest.

CORRECT   Laura finished the assignment the **fastest**.

INCORRECT   The test was **more worse** than the one the

class took last month.

CORRECT   The test was **worse** than the one the class

See Practice 24.1D   took last month.

Comparisons Using Adjectives and Adverbs

Forming Comparatives and Superlatives of Irregular Adjectives and Adverbs

Read the modifiers. Write the comparative and superlative forms of each modifier.

EXAMPLE   far (distance)

ANSWER   *farther, farthest*

1. much

2. well (adverb)

3. far (extent)

4. bad (adjective)

5. many

6. good (adjective)

7. badly (adverb)

Using Comparatives and Superlatives of Irregular Adjectives and Adverbs

Read the sentences. Then, write each sentence using the form of the modifier in parentheses.

EXAMPLE   The storm was _____ (*bad*, comparative) than predicted.

ANSWER   *The storm was worse than predicted.*

8. The school yard looks _____ than it did before Clean-up Day. (*good*, comparative)

9. He is the _____ dancer in the group. (*good*, superlative)

10. Jared scored the _____ points in last night's basketball game. (*many*, superlative)

11. My _____ friend is my dog. (*good*, superlative)

12. How much _____ is the diner? (*far*, comparative)

13. Milo spends _____ time on the phone than I do. (*much*, comparative)

14. Jamie is the _____ runner on our team. (*fast*, superlative)

15. Sienna did _____ than Cam on the midterm. (*well*, comparative)

16. You sing _____ than I do. (*badly*, comparative)

17. Is Neptune the _____ planet from the sun? (*far*, superlative)

SPEAKING APPLICATION

With a partner, talk about some of your favorite and least favorite things. Use comparative and superlative forms of any of the modifiers in Practice 24.1D.

WRITING APPLICATION

Write five sentences about an athletic competition, each containing a different irregular comparative or superlative modifier. Then, exchange papers with a partner. Your partner should identify the irregular modifiers and the positive forms from which they come.

Making Logical Comparisons

In most situations, you will have no problem forming the degrees of modifiers and using them correctly in sentences. Sometimes, however, you may find that the way you have phrased a sentence makes your comparison unclear. You will then need to think about the words you have chosen and revise your sentence, making sure that your comparison is logical.

> **When you make a comparison, be sure you are comparing things that have clear similarities.**

RULE 24.1.9

Balanced Comparisons

Most comparisons make a statement or ask a question about the way in which similar things are either alike or different.

EXAMPLE Is the **Black Sea** **deeper** than the

Mediterranean Sea?
(Both bodies of water have depths that can be measured and compared.)

Because the sentence compares depth to depth, the comparison is balanced. Problems can occur, however, when a sentence compares dissimilar things. For example, it would be illogical to compare the depth of one sea to the shape of another sea. Depth and shape are not similar things and cannot be compared meaningfully.

ILLOGICAL The girls in his class are taller than her class.
(*Girls* and *class* cannot be logically compared.)

LOGICAL The girls in his class are taller than the girls in

her class.
(Two sets of girls can be logically compared.)

> **Make sure that your sentences compare only similar items.**

RULE 24.1.10

An unbalanced comparison is usually the result of carelessness. The writer may have simply left something out. Read the following incorrect sentences carefully.

INCORRECT **Cooking pasta** is **faster** than **rice**.

The **crowd** on the north side of the field cheers **louder** than the **south side of the field**.

In the first sentence, cooking pasta is mistakenly compared to rice. In the second sentence, people are compared to a place. Both sentences can easily be corrected to make the comparisons balanced.

CORRECT **Cooking pasta** is **faster** than **cooking rice**.

The **crowd** on the north side of the field cheers **louder** than the **crowd** on the south side.

See Practice 24.1E

Other and *Else* in Comparisons

Another common error in writing comparisons is to compare something to itself.

RULE 24.1.11

When comparing one of a group to the rest of the group, make sure your sentence contains the word *other* or *else.*

Adding *other* or *else* can make a comparison clear. For example, in the second sentence below, because *my school* is itself a school, it cannot logically be compared to any *school.* It must be compared to any *other school.*

PROBLEM SENTENCES	CORRECTED SENTENCES
Alia researched and presented her project before anyone.	Alia researched and presented her project before anyone else.
My school was built ten years before any school in the district.	My school was built ten years before any other school in the district.

See Practice 24.1F

PRACTICE 24.1E Making Balanced Comparisons

Read the sentences. Rewrite each sentence, correcting the unbalanced comparison.

EXAMPLE   The temperature indoors is hotter than outdoors.

ANSWER   *The temperature indoors is hotter than the temperature outdoors.*

1. The price of a new home is higher than a car.

2. The traffic at the airport is worse than the highway.

3. My science teacher's tests are harder than my English teacher.

4. The air in the city is more polluted than the country.

5. The recipe for this soup is easier to follow than this stew.

6. This year's festival was better attended than last year.

7. The magazine's readership is much larger than the newspaper.

8. Abby's hair is not as long as Maria.

9. The number of homes on Elm Street is greater than Maple Street.

10. The cold water from the tap in the kitchen is cleaner than the bathroom.

PRACTICE 24.1F Using *Other* and *Else* to Make Logical Comparisons

Read the sentences. Rewrite each sentence, adding *other* or *else* to make the comparisons logical.

EXAMPLE   My sister dances better than anyone in the family.

ANSWER   *My sister dances better than anyone else in the family.*

11. My dad cooks better than anyone in the family.

12. I enjoy football more than any sport.

13. News reporter Aaron Dovetree has worked here longer than anyone.

14. I like sweet potatoes better than any vegetable.

15. I arrived at the party before anyone.

16. Tom plays basketball better than anyone on the team.

17. This tree is taller than any tree in the park.

18. The president gets more press coverage than any politician.

19. Our social studies teacher gives harder tests than anyone on the teaching staff.

20. I find jazz more interesting than any music.

SPEAKING APPLICATION

With a partner, take turns making comparisons about different nations and their customs. Your partner should listen to the comparisons and make sure they are balanced and logical.

WRITING APPLICATION

Write four sentences describing a talented person you know. Make logical comparisons that use *other* and *else* correctly. Use *other* in two of the comparisons; use *else* in the other two.

24.2 Troublesome Adjectives and Adverbs

The common adjectives and adverbs listed below often cause problems in both speaking and writing.

(1) bad and badly *Bad* is an adjective. Use it after linking verbs, such as *are, appear, feel, look,* and *sound. Badly* is an adverb. Use it after action verbs, such as *act, behave, do,* and *perform.*

INCORRECT	Sandy felt **badly** for the losing team.
CORRECT	Sandy felt **bad** for the losing team.

INCORRECT	My car performed **bad** on the road test.
CORRECT	My car performed **badly** on the road test.

(2) good and well *Good* is an adjective. *Well* can be either an adjective or an adverb, depending on its meaning. A common mistake is the use of *good* after an action verb. Use the adverb *well* instead.

INCORRECT	My class danced **good** last evening.
	The report looks **well**.

CORRECT	My class danced **well** last evening.
	The report looks **good**.

As adjectives, *good* and *well* have slightly different meanings, which are often confused. *Well* usually refers simply to health.

EXAMPLES	Maria felt **good** after scoring the only goal.
	The campfire smells **good**.
	My grandmother does not feel **well**.

(3) *fewer and less* Use the adjective *fewer* to answer the question, "How many?" Use the adjective *less* to answer the question, "How much?"

HOW MANY	**fewer** pencils	**fewer** students
HOW MUCH	**less** work	**less** time

(4) *just* When used as an adverb, *just* often means "no more than." When *just* has this meaning, place it right before the word it logically modifies.

INCORRECT   Does she **just** want to try on **one dress**?

CORRECT   Does she want to try on **just** **one dress**?

(5) *only* The position of *only* in a sentence sometimes affects the sentence's entire meaning. Consider the meaning of these sentences.

EXAMPLES   **Only** Adam played the guitar.
(Nobody else played the guitar.)

Adam **only** played the guitar.
(Adam did nothing else with the guitar.)

Adam played **only** the guitar.
(Adam played the guitar and no other instrument.)

Mistakes involving *only* usually occur when its placement in a sentence makes the meaning unclear.

UNCLEAR   **Only** follow the rules from the coach.

BETTER   Follow the rules **only** from the coach.
(not from anyone else)

See Practice 24.2C
See Practice 24.2D

Follow **only** the rules from the coach.
(nothing but the rules)

PRACTICE 24.2A ▷ Using *Bad* and *Badly*, *Good* and *Well*

Read the sentences. Write the word in parentheses that correctly completes each sentence.

EXAMPLE   Emilia writes (good, well).

ANSWER   *well*

1. This chili tastes very (good, well).

2. I feel very (bad, badly) about what happened.

3. I hope to do (good, well) in the contest.

4. Oscar plays basketball (bad, badly).

5. The dancer moves (good, well) even when the music speeds up.

6. The music sounds (good, well).

7. She performed (bad, badly) on the test.

8. The new perfume smells really (good, well).

9. If you eat (bad, badly), your health may be affected.

10. I think the milk turned (bad, badly).

PRACTICE 24.2B ▷ Supplying *Bad* and *Badly*, *Good* and *Well*

Read each sentence. Then, rewrite each sentence, filling in the blank with the correct modifier *bad*, *badly*, *good*, or *well*.

EXAMPLE   After reviewing his notes, Jacques decided he had a _____ presentation.

ANSWER   *After reviewing his notes, Jacques decided he had a **good** presentation.*

11. I felt _____ about forgetting my homework.

12. Since it hadn't been opened in years, the old cellar smelled _____.

13. The color red looks _____ on you.

14. Charles didn't come because he wasn't feeling _____.

15. My young cousins behaved _____ at the family reunion.

16. Most people agree that pizza tastes _____.

17. The gym needs new equipment _____.

18. The violinist performed _____ as the soloist, and she won much praise.

19. When his dog is _____, Josh gives him a treat.

20. To make the team, Tamika needed to do _____ at tryouts.

SPEAKING APPLICATION

Use sentence 3 in Practice 24.2A as a model, and tell a partner two things that you hope to do. Your partner should make sure you've used the modifiers correctly.

WRITING APPLICATION

Write four sentences, each using a different one of these modifiers: *bad, badly, good,* and *well*. Then, exchange papers with a partner. Your partner should make sure you have used the modifiers correctly.

PRACTICE 24.2C > **Using *Fewer* and *Less* Correctly**

Read each sentence. Then, rewrite the sentence, filling the blank with either *fewer* or *less*.

EXAMPLE   When the rain ended, there were _____ than 50 people in the stands.

ANSWER   *When the rain ended, there were* **fewer** *than 50 people in the stands.*

1. During the winter, there are _____ hours of daylight.

2. After the holiday season, Sean will be working _____.

3. The colt stood up when he was _____ than eight hours old.

4. After the sale ended, _____ than six sweaters were left on the shelf.

5. Mom is able to spend _____ time with us since she changed jobs.

6. An incandescent bulb generally burns for _____ hours than a halogen bulb.

7. By shopping at Foodrite Grocery, our family spends _____ money.

8. We cannot go on the trip if _____ than 20 people sign up.

9. My brother is joining his army troop in _____ than six hours' time.

10. Since I went to the dentist, I am feeling _____ pain.

PRACTICE 24.2D > **Using *Just* and *Only* Correctly**

Read each sentence. Then, rewrite any sentences that contain errors in the use of *just* or *only*. If a sentence has no error, write *correct*.

EXAMPLE   Does that pet store only sell fish and birds?

ANSWER   *Does that pet store* **sell only** *fish and birds?*

11. I just want a sandwich for dinner.

12. The committee only gave out three awards this year.

13. When I leave for school, only I carry my books and my lunch.

14. Only Kate's mother and father were in the audience that night.

15. On this farm, they just grow cotton and soybeans.

16. By the time Terri arrived, she only had time to bowl one game.

17. So far, Kevin has only outlined his paper; he has not begun writing.

18. Please put just mustard on my hot dog, not ketchup.

19. The judge instructed the witness to only answer yes or no.

20. My aunt expected only two guests for dinner.

SPEAKING APPLICATION

With a partner, take turns speaking about a recent party. Use *fewer* or *less* and *only* or *just* in at least three of your sentences. Your partner should listen for and correct any misused modifiers.

WRITING APPLICATION

Write four sentences about a special meal you prepared or one you ate. Use one of these words in each sentence: *only, just, less,* and *fewer.*

Test Warm-Up

DIRECTIONS
Read the introduction and the passage that follows. Then, answer the questions to show that you can use and understand troublesome adjectives and adverbs correctly in the context of reading and writing.

Darryl included this paragraph in a report he wrote for social studies. Read the paragraph and think about the changes you would suggest as a peer editor. When you finish reading, answer the questions that follow.

Visit the Philippines

(1) If you want an interesting place to visit, I have just the country for you—the Philippines. (2) The Philippines is an island nation comprised of no less than 7,100 separate islands. (3) However, most of the Filipino people just live on nine of those islands. (4) The country is known for its many fiestas, or celebrations; the Filipinos know how to party good. (5) Even if you miss the fiestas, you should not feel badly, though. (6) You can find something enjoyable and exciting to do in the Philippines almost any day.

1 The meaning of sentence 2 can be clarified by changing the phrase **no less than** to —

  A more than

  B no fewer than

  C just

  D only

2 How should sentence 3 be revised?

  F However, most of the Filipino people live on just nine of those islands.

  G However, fewer of the Filipino people just live on nine of those islands.

  H However, less of the Filipino people just live just on nine of those islands.

  J However, most of the only Filipino people live on nine of those islands.

3 What is the BEST way to revise sentence 4?

  A Insert **less** after **known**

  B Insert **only** after **known**

  C Insert **just** after **known**

  D Change **good** to **well**

4 What change, if any, should be made in sentence 5?

  F Change **badly** to **well**

  G Change **badly** to **good**

  H Change **badly** to **bad**

  J Make no change

Cumulative Review Chapters 21–24

PRACTICE 1 > Identifying Verb Tenses

Read the sentences. For each sentence, write whether the verb tense is *present, past, future, present perfect, past perfect, or future perfect.* Also indicate if the verb is *progressive.*

1. The band is practicing a new march.
2. Mr. Lisi has taught at our school for 10 years.
3. In June, Miriam will have been a postal worker for twenty years.
4. That wholesaler supplies all the restaurants in the area.
5. The public relations department will eventually respond to the complaint.
6. My mother attended a state university.
7. Susanna has been watching that television series for several years.
8. No team from our high school had ever won the state championships before.
9. A group of friends were traveling together.
10. The congressional committee hearing will be airing on television.

PRACTICE 2 > Revising to Use Active Voice

Read the sentences. Then, rewrite each passive voice sentence so that it is in active voice. If a sentence is already in active voice, write *active.*

1. The patient was examined by the doctor.
2. That opera was composed by Giuseppe Verdi.
3. A generous donation to the hospital was made by Mrs. O'Connor.
4. The finest knitwear is designed by her company.
5. The cruise ship is heading for Key West.

PRACTICE 3 > Using Verbs Correctly

Read the sentences. Then, rewrite the sentences to correct any incorrect verb forms. If a sentence has no errors, write *correct.*

1. Yesterday Mom lay the new quilt on the old couch.
2. We have never went to Alabama.
3. The head librarian has asked the town board for more funding for our local library.
4. Sit your package beside the door.
5. At the photo studio yesterday, the photographer says to me, "Smile for the camera."
6. Felicia finally done her science project.
7. The fans have chose a new team mascot for the Cougars.
8. I seen you in the line for concert tickets.
9. Somebody swum across the river yesterday.
10. A talented new performer has arose on the local music scene.

PRACTICE 4 > Identifying Pronoun Cases and Uses

Read the sentences. Write whether each underlined pronoun is in the *nominative, objective,* or *possessive* case. Then, write whether it is used as a *subject,* a *predicate pronoun,* a *direct object,* an *indirect object,* or the *object of a preposition.*

1. I spoke with <u>her</u> before class.
2. The waiter brought <u>us</u> our order.
3. <u>Yours</u> is the silliest-looking hat I have ever seen.
4. Dad always helps <u>me</u> with my math homework.
5. The best singers in our family are Mom and <u>I</u>.

Continued on next page ▶

Cumulative Review 547

Cumulative Review   Chapters 21–24

PRACTICE 5 **Using Pronouns Correctly**

Read the sentences. Then, rewrite the sentences to correct any incorrect pronouns. If a sentence has no errors, write *correct*.

1. I hope the alligator has had it's dinner.

2. Mr. Newman and her traded news.

3. The oldest students in the class are Ray and me.

4. The neighbor gave my sister and I a lift.

5. Whom did you call for more information?

6. Friendship still exists between Shirley and he.

7. Lydia is the one who the teacher praised most.

8. The shed is our's, but the lawn mower is their's.

9. Where did you see Caroline and he?

10. I do not know whom their spokesperson is.

PRACTICE 6 **Revising for Subject–Verb Agreement**

Read the sentences. Then, rewrite the sentences to correct any errors in subject–verb agreement. If a sentence has no errors, write *correct*.

1. Neither Ruby nor I type very quickly.

2. A deck of cards sit on the card table.

3. Each of the spices taste distinctive.

4. The flock flies every which way.

5. None of the answers are correct.

6. Patrick and Maura enjoy Irish step dancing.

7. Bacon and eggs are my favorite breakfast.

8. The coach or his players yells at the umpire.

9. Are the singer or the composer very famous?

10. The team has won another game.

PRACTICE 7 **Revising for Pronoun–Antecedent Agreement**

Read the sentences. Then, rewrite the sentences to correct any errors in pronoun–antecedent agreement. If a sentence has no errors, write *correct*.

1. Each of the girls had their hair in pigtails.

2. They do a dance where you jump in the air.

3. None of the winners received his or her prize.

4. Either the snake or the lizard lost its skin.

5. Everyone kept their boots clean.

6. Several of the factories had closed its doors.

7. Becky and Ella wore braces on her teeth.

8. Neither Gary nor Frank wore their boots.

9. Some of the detectives solved his or her cases.

10. Did everybody have his or her homework?

PRACTICE 8 **Using Modifiers Correctly**

Read the sentences. Then, rewrite the sentences to correct any errors involving modifiers. If a sentence has no errors, write *correct*.

1. Andrea did good at the swim meet.

2. I will ask nothing farther of you.

3. He feels more well but will still visit the doctor.

4. In winter, less fans attend his concerts.

5. Of all the snowstorms, this is the baddest.

6. The ballet company only performs on Fridays.

7. Brian is taller than I am.

8. The music sounds really well.

9. Sheepdogs are more loyal than any dog.

10. Is there a singer more good than she is?

CHAPTER 25

PUNCTUATION

Using punctuation correctly will help you to craft clear, convincing sentences.

WRITE GUY *Jeff Anderson, M.Ed.*

WHAT DO YOU NOTICE?

Note the punctuation as you zoom in on these sentences from the story "Chicoria," retold in English by Rudolfo A. Anaya and adapted in Spanish by José Griego y Maestas.

MENTOR TEXT

> When the maids began to dish up the plates of food, Chicoria turned to one of the servers and said, "Ah, my friends, it looks like they are going to feed us well tonight!"

Now, ask yourself the following questions:

- How are the words that Chicoria speaks set off in this sentence?
- Why do you think the author used an exclamation mark at the end of Chicoria's spoken words?

The comma after *said* signals the beginning of Chicoria's spoken words, and the quotation marks indicate the start and finish of his spoken words. The author used an exclamation mark to show that Chicoria was excited about the food.

Grammar for Writers Whether you are writing fiction or nonfiction, including quotations is a fantastic way to add interest. Using proper punctuation for quotations makes them understandable to readers.

Do you think my paper deserves an A?

There's no question about it!

25.1 End Marks

End marks signal the end or conclusion of a sentence, word, or phrase. There are three end marks: the **period (.)**, the **question mark (?)**, and the **exclamation mark (!)**.

WRITING COACH

Online

www.phwritingcoach.com

Grammar Practice

Practice your grammar skills with Writing Coach Online.

Grammar Games

Test your knowledge of grammar in this fast-paced interactive video game.

Using Periods

A **period** indicates the end of a sentence or an abbreviation.

RULE 25.1.1

Use a period to end a declarative sentence—a statement of fact, idea, or opinion.

DECLARATIVE SENTENCE   This is a beautiful weekend.

RULE 25.1.2

Use a period to end most imperative sentences—sentences that give directions or commands.

IMPERATIVE SENTENCE   Finish practicing the piano.

RULE 25.1.3

Use a period to end a sentence that contains an indirect question.

An **indirect question** restates a question in a declarative sentence. It does not give the speaker's exact words.

INDIRECT QUESTION   Janie asked me if I liked the show.

RULE 25.1.4

Use a period after most abbreviations and initials.

ABBREVIATIONS   Blvd.   Jr.   Gov.   in.   Dr.

INITIALS   Franklin D. Roosevelt   J. K. Rowling

Note: The abbreviation for *inch, in.,* is the only measurement abbreviation that uses a period after it.

When a sentence ends with an abbreviation that uses a period, do not put a second period at the end.

EXAMPLE   Our speaker today is James Young Jr.

> **Do not use periods with acronyms, words formed with the first or first few letters of a series of words.**

25.1.5 RULE

EXAMPLES   UN   United Nations

NASA   National Aeronautics and Space Administration

Using Question Marks

A **question mark** follows a word, phrase, or sentence that asks a question.

> **Use a question mark after an interrogative sentence—one that asks a direct question.**

25.1.6 RULE

INTERROGATIVE SENTENCES

Do turtles lay eggs in water?

What time are you picking me up?

Sometimes a single word or brief phrase is used to ask a direct question. This type of question is punctuated as though it were a complete sentence because the words that are left out are easily understood.

> **Use a question mark after a word or phrase that asks a question.**

25.1.7 RULE

EXAMPLES   I would like to go along with you. When?

I'll meet you for dinner. How about that?

See Practice 25.1A

Using Exclamation Marks

RULE 25.1.8

Use an **exclamation mark** to end a word, phrase, or sentence that shows strong emotion.

EXAMPLES
Look at that classic car**!**

I will not**!**

RULE 25.1.9

Use an exclamation mark after an **imperative** sentence that gives a forceful or urgent command.

IMPERATIVE SENTENCE
Don't burn the eggs**!**

Hurry up**!**

While imperative sentences containing forceful commands often end with an exclamation mark, mild imperatives should end with a period.

MILD IMPERATIVES
Please don't get up**.**

Put the salad in the refrigerator**.**

RULE 25.1.10

Use an exclamation mark after an **interjection** that expresses strong emotion.

INTERJECTIONS
Oh**!** You ruined the surprise.

Stop**!** You are going too fast!

Exclamation marks should not be used too often. Overusing them reduces their emotional effect and makes writing less effective.

See Practice 25.1B

PRACTICE 25.1A Using Question Marks and Periods

Read the sentences. Rewrite each sentence, adding missing question marks and periods.

EXAMPLE   Mom asked if Dr Chavez was available

ANSWER   *Mom asked if Dr. Chavez was available.*

1. Who invented sails for ships
2. Look for the information in an encyclopedia
3. Mrs Young asked whether I had ever been to Portland
4. How many stars are there in a galaxy
5. Send this form to Mr D H Jackson at the mayor's office
6. Is Gov Lopez the woman in the photo
7. Which planet is farthest from the sun
8. Teresa wondered what was wrong with her skateboard
9. The ocean depths hold many fascinating secrets
10. Has the dog really run away Why

PRACTICE 25.1B Using Exclamation Marks and Periods

Read the sentences. Rewrite each sentence, adding missing exclamation marks and periods.

EXAMPLE   Wow What an exciting adventure that was

ANSWER   *Wow! What an exciting adventure that was!*

11. How courageous those mountain climbers are
12. Watch out for that car
13. Please take your seats
14. They'll be here any minute Hurry
15. What a delicious dinner that was
16. Shoot the ball now
17. Ugh That trash smells horrible
18. Whew I'm glad we made it home
19. Tell me the story again
20. What a beautiful morning this is

SPEAKING APPLICATION

Say the following sample sentence three times out loud to your partner, using the different inflections that the three different end marks would give it. Have your partner tell what end mark you are indicating with your voice. *We're not finished yet*

WRITING APPLICATION

Write three sentences using at least one period, one question mark, and one exclamation mark correctly.

25.2 Commas

End marks signal a full stop. **Commas** signal a brief pause.
A comma may be used to separate elements in a sentence or to
set off part of a sentence. Include a comma in your writing when
you want your reader to group information in your sentence.

Using Commas in Compound Sentences

A **compound sentence** consists of two or more main or
independent clauses that are joined by a coordinating
conjunction, such as *and, but, for, nor, or, so,* or *yet.*

RULE 25.2.1

> Use a comma before the conjunction to separate two main or
> independent clauses in a **compound sentence.**

COMPOUND SENTENCE	My puppy has learned to stay in the yard , but I always use his leash on our walks.

Use a comma before a conjunction only when there are complete
sentences on both sides of the conjunction. If the conjunction joins
single words, phrases, or subordinate clauses, do not use a comma.

SINGLE WORDS	Soccer and lacrosse are growing in popularity.
PHRASES	Tony likes both watching soccer and playing football.
SUBORDINATE CLAUSES	I like to play softball because it is good exercise and because it is fun.

In some compound sentences, the main or independent clauses
are very brief, and the meaning is clear. When this occurs, the
comma before the conjunction may be omitted.

EXAMPLE	Gil was here but he left quickly.

See Practice 25.2A

Avoiding Comma Splices

A **comma splice** occurs when two or more sentences have been
joined with only a comma between them.

> **Avoid comma splices by making sure all of your ideas are properly linked.**

INCORRECT   The players arrived in the morning, they gathered on the field.

CORRECT   The players arrived in the morning. They gathered on the field.

Using Commas in a Series

Sometimes, a sentence lists a number of single words or groups of words. When three or more of these items are listed, the list is called a **series.** Separate the items in a series with commas.

> **Use commas to separate three or more words, phrases, or clauses in a series.**

A comma follows each of the items except the last one in a series. The conjunction *and* or *or* is added after the last comma.

SERIES OF WORDS   A gorilla's diet includes roots, stems, leaves, and fruit.

SERIES OF PHRASES   Cleaning my room included sweeping the floor, making the bed, and hanging up the clothes.

There are two exceptions to this rule. If each item except the last one in a series is followed by a conjunction, do not use commas. Also, do not use a comma to separate groups of words that are considered to be one item.

EXAMPLES   We didn't see any birds or insects or spiders.

The sandwich choices are peanut butter and jelly, ham and cheese, or turkey and cheese.

See Practice 25.2B

Using Commas Between Adjectives

Sometimes, two or more adjectives are placed before the noun they describe.

RULE 25.2.4

> **Use commas to separate adjectives of equal rank.**

There are two ways to tell whether adjectives in a sentence are of equal rank:

- If the word *and* can be placed between the adjectives without changing the meaning, the adjectives are of equal rank.

- If the order of the adjectives can be changed, they are of equal rank.

EXAMPLE   She left detailed, precise instructions for me.
(*Detailed and precise instructions* does not change the sentence's meaning. *Precise, detailed instructions* also does not change the meaning.)

RULE 25.2.5

> **Do not use commas to separate adjectives that must appear in a specific order.**

Do not use a comma if adding *and* or changing the order of the adjectives would result in a sentence that makes no sense.

INCORRECT   An experienced and desert guide led our tour.

INCORRECT   A desert experienced guide led our tour.

CORRECT   An experienced desert guide led our tour.

RULE 25.2.6

> **Do not use a comma to separate the last adjective in a series from the noun it modifies.**

INCORRECT   A young, efficient, kind, nurse took care of her.

CORRECT   A young, efficient, kind nurse took care of her.

See Practice 25.2C
See Practice 25.2D

PRACTICE 25.2A > **Using Commas in Compound Sentences**

Read the sentences. Rewrite each sentence, adding commas where they are needed.

EXAMPLE   The fans were getting restless for the kickoff was delayed.

ANSWER   *The fans were getting restless, for the kickoff was delayed.*

1. The courses are organized and the instructors are excellent.

2. It was January yet the days were mild.

3. I know Hector is a good musician but do you think he is ready for the symphony?

4. We stayed an extra day in Phoenix for there were many more sites to see.

5. Will Judy be your partner for the science project or are you paired with someone else?

6. Mr. Garcia loves to entertain so he has a barbecue every weekend in the summer.

7. The runner was exhausted yet he was determined to finish the marathon.

8. The bathroom has been remodeled and it now looks modern and has more storage space.

9. The sign said the store was open until 8:00 P.M. but the doors were locked.

10. Snow fell all night and by morning it had blanketed the hills.

PRACTICE 25.2B > **Using Commas in a Series**

Read the sentences. Rewrite each sentence, adding commas as needed.

EXAMPLE   Jason wrote the script played the main role and directed the other actors.

ANSWER   *Jason wrote the script, played the main role, and directed the other actors.*

11. A second language can be useful in business for travel or in almost any profession.

12. We play soccer at school in the park or in the backyard.

13. Then the boat slowed down changed course and went in a different direction.

14. Staying alert being calm and removing distractions will make you a better driver.

15. We need a screwdriver a pair of pliers and a hammer and nails for this project.

16. Maine New Hampshire Vermont and Massachusetts are famous for fall foliage.

17. The trail starts in the foothills winds up the mountain and stretches along the crest.

18. On the nature hike, Chandra saw birds snakes wildflowers and various insects.

19. The television the CD player and the refrigerator are all new.

20. The raccoon lumbered down the sidewalk across the road and into a drainage opening.

SPEAKING APPLICATION

Read the following compound sentence to your partner without the comma. Then, add the comma by pausing, and have your partner tell how the sentence sounds different. *They wanted to visit the museum but it was closed.*

WRITING APPLICATION

Write three sentences using various types of items in series. Use commas correctly.

Practice   557

PRACTICE 25.2C **Using Commas Between Adjectives**

Read the sentences. Rewrite the sentences, adding commas where necessary. If no comma is needed, write *correct*.

EXAMPLE   On the porch was a large ornate planter with colorful flowers.

ANSWER   *On the porch was a large, ornate planter with colorful flowers.*

1. My friend Serena is a thoughtful kind reliable person.

2. The car already has several minor problems.

3. Four small boys were playing in the sandbox.

4. We heard a low steady hum coming from the cellar.

5. The noisy slow-moving train made its way up the hill.

6. Suddenly, a loud ghastly shriek pierced the night air.

7. Dad bought a beautiful stained-glass lamp for the living room.

8. She stated her demands in a strong forceful voice.

9. Those solid gold bracelets are not for sale.

10. On a damp chilly morning, we started our journey.

PRACTICE 25.2D **Proofreading Sentences for Commas**

Read the sentences. Rewrite each sentence, adding commas where they are needed.

EXAMPLE   The sheep moved on the road in a tight shifting mass.

ANSWER   *The sheep moved on the road in a tight, shifting mass.*

11. I like reading suspenseful well-written mystery novels.

12. What is this coarse sturdy fabric called?

13. I'd like to exchange this dirty torn shirt for one that is new and crisp and clean.

14. The hikers carried simple nutritious snacks and fresh drinking water.

15. To Cassandra, golf is a relaxing challenging pastime.

16. Those birds have made a strong protective nest in which to raise their babies.

17. The rocks at the bottom of the stream were covered with a brown slimy substance.

18. We adopted the dog because he seemed playful smart and affectionate.

19. Terri is a genuine caring and kind girl.

20. A mysterious stranger appeared in the tiny quiet village.

SPEAKING APPLICATION

Say the following two sentences to a partner. Have your partner tell which sentence needs a comma and why.
They noticed faint, eerie music coming from the other room.
The soft jazz music was very soothing.

WRITING APPLICATION

Write two sentences with adjectives that require commas and two with adjectives that do not need commas.

Using Commas After Introductory Words, Phrases, and Clauses

When a sentence begins with an introductory word, phrase, or other structures, that word or phrase is usually separated from the rest of the sentence by a comma.

> **Use a comma after most introductory words, phrases, or dependent clauses.**

See Practice 25.2E

KINDS OF INTRODUCTORY MATERIAL	
Introductory Word	Hey, listen to the great idea I have for our final project.
	Well, I have never seen anything like that.
	Ariel, where are we going?
Introductory Phrase	To save money, we are packing our lunch instead of eating out.
	After practicing for two hours, the team was glad to take a long break.
	To visit China, you will need a passport.
Introductory Adverbial Clause	Although we had missed the introduction, we were able to see the rest of the ceremony.
	When Dominic got on the bus, all of the seats were already taken.
	When Devin arrived, they needed more room at the table.

When a prepositional phrase of only two words begins a sentence, a comma is not absolutely necessary.

EXAMPLES   At night we heard the owls hoot.

In August we go to the beach.

For hours she worked at the computer.

Using Commas With Parenthetical Expressions

A **parenthetical expression** is a word or phrase that is not essential to the meaning of the sentence. These words or phrases generally add extra information to the basic sentence.

> Use commas to set off **parenthetical expressions** from the rest of the sentence.

A parenthetical expression in the middle of a sentence needs two commas. A parenthetical expression at the end of a sentence needs only one.

KINDS OF PARENTHETICAL EXPRESSIONS	
Names of People Being Addressed	Sit down, Brock, while I explain my reasons. Please come straight home, Chung.
Certain Adverbs	The beach, therefore, is easily accessible. His plan will not work, however.
Common Expressions	I understand your actions, of course. They are not old enough to go alone, in my opinion.
Contrasting Expressions	That problem is yours, not mine. These letters, not those, are ready to be mailed.

See Practice 25.2F

See Practice 25.2G

Using Commas With Nonessential Expressions

To determine when a phrase or clause should be set off with commas, decide whether the phrase or clause is **essential** or **nonessential** to the meaning of the sentence. Nonessential expressions can be left out without changing the meaning of the sentence.

> Use commas to set off **nonessential** expressions from the main clause. Do not set off **essential** material with commas.

Appositives and Appositive Phrases

Appositives are often set off with commas, but only when their meaning is not essential to the sentence. In the first example below, the appositive *the Hurricanes* is not set off with commas because it clarifies which team is being discussed.

ESSENTIAL	The team the Hurricanes prepared for the parade.
NONESSENTIAL	The Hurricanes, the winning team, prepared for the parade.

Participial Phrases

Like appositives, participial phrases are set off with commas when their meaning is nonessential. In the first example below, *standing in the room* is essential because it tells which man is the teacher.

ESSENTIAL	The man standing in the room is my teacher.
NONESSENTIAL	My teacher, standing in the room, asked us to be seated.

Adjectival Clauses

Adjectival clauses, too, are set off with commas only if they are nonessential. In the second example below, *which likes to play ball* is nonessential because it adds information about their new dog. The main clause in the sentence is about Bea and her sister being thrilled, not about what their new dog can do.

ESSENTIAL	Bea and her sister wanted a dog that could play ball with them.
NONESSENTIAL	Bea and her sister are thrilled with their new dog, which likes to play ball.

See Practice 25.2H

Using Commas After Introductory Words, Phrases, or Clauses

Read the sentences. Rewrite each sentence, adding the comma needed after the introductory word, phrase, or dependent adverbial clause.

EXAMPLE   As visitors entered the museum they saw a huge dinosaur replica.

ANSWER   *As visitors entered the museum, they saw a huge dinosaur replica.*

1. Why that island is the most beautiful place I've ever seen.

2. Reading about ancient Rome I learned some surprising facts.

3. Yes there is an original sculpture in the hall.

4. When the play was over we all met out front.

5. To preserve the environment humans will have to be diligent.

6. Before the walls can be painted they will need to be cleaned and primed.

7. In every room of the house colorful tapestries decorated the walls.

8. Hey you're blocking my view of the screen.

9. At small booths lining the midway vendors were selling their crafts.

10. Refreshed by our cold beverages we resumed the game.

Proofreading a Passage for Commas

Read the paragraphs. Rewrite the paragraphs, adding commas where they are needed.

EXAMPLE   When we visited New Mexico Aunt Lucy took us to a Native American pueblo.

ANSWER   *When we visited New Mexico, Aunt Lucy took us to a Native American pueblo.*

Driving to Acoma Sky City we saw beautiful scenery and even some wildlife. The pueblo sits on the top of a 367-foot sandstone mesa. This site was chosen because it provided a natural defense against enemies. Why can you imagine how difficult it would be to attack a village that was that high up?

During the one-hour walking tour a tribal member told us stories about the history of Acoma. I was amazed to learn the village was built around 1150 A.D. According to the guide it has been continuously inhabited the entire time. To continue the pueblo life tribal members must stay true to their culture. I think I will remember what I learned on the tour because I was able to see that culture.

SPEAKING APPLICATION

Read the following sentences to a partner. Discuss where to add the comma.
At the fork in the road we turned to the right.
No that's not what I meant.

WRITING APPLICATION

Write one sentence with an introductory word, one with an introductory phrase, one with an introductory clause, and one with a dependent adverbial clause. Use commas correctly in your sentences. Discuss the purpose of the commas with a partner.

PRACTICE 25.2G **Using Commas With Parenthetical Expressions**

Read the sentences. Rewrite each sentence, adding commas as needed to set off parenthetical expressions.

EXAMPLE   He decided therefore to enter the contest.

ANSWER   *He decided, therefore, to enter the contest.*

1. Take the lid off Carmen or the water will boil over.

2. She thought nevertheless that the job would be hers.

3. The fire we believe was a result of bad wiring.

4. The older daughter not the younger one is getting married.

5. Everyone was in good spirits of course.

6. The flight attendant not the pilot greeted the passengers.

7. Gina could you please hand me that paintbrush?

8. The wait at the bus stop however was extremely long.

9. Have you ever gone snowboarding Jared?

10. The debate therefore has been postponed.

PRACTICE 25.2H **Using Commas With Nonessential Expressions**

Read the sentences. Rewrite the sentences, adding commas where needed. If a sentence is punctuated correctly, write *correct*.

EXAMPLE   The first contestant a juggler did not impress the judges.

ANSWER   *The first contestant, a juggler, did not impress the judges.*

11. Charles Dickens a famous British author wrote *A Tale of Two Cities*.

12. The store was hiring only people who had experience.

13. The famous actor Tom Hanks was in that film.

14. This sweater a birthday gift is warm but somewhat scratchy.

15. The song "Neon Moon" was very popular.

16. This stopwatch which was inexpensive is good for timing sprints.

17. This is a painting of George Washington crossing the Delaware River.

18. The woman standing in the back of the room is the high school principal.

19. We took the subway which is pretty fast to the downtown area.

20. The little girl grinning broadly reached out for the balloon.

SPEAKING APPLICATION

Briefly tell a partner about public transportation in your town. Your partner should listen for and name two parenthetical expressions.

WRITING APPLICATION

Write two sentences, one with a nonessential expression and one with an essential phrase or clause. Use commas correctly with the nonessential expression.

Using Commas With Dates and Geographical Names

Dates usually have several parts, including months, days, and years. Commas prevent dates from being unclear.

When a date is made up of three parts, use a comma after each item, except in the case of a month followed by a day.

Notice in the examples that commas are not used to set off a month followed by a numeral standing for a day. Commas are used when both the month and the date are used as an appositive to rename a day of the week.

EXAMPLES   On June 12, 2009, I celebrated my thirteenth birthday with my family.

Monday, October 3, is the date our class is going on a field trip to the history museum.

When a date contains only a month and a year, commas are unnecessary.

EXAMPLES   She will receive her award in May 2015.

Most of the storms we experienced in April 2007 caused severe flooding.

When a geographical name is made up of a city and a state, use a comma after each item except when the state ends a sentence.

EXAMPLES   They lived in Albany, New York, for several years and then moved to Santa Fe, New Mexico.

My family went to San Francisco, California, to visit our many relatives in the area.

See Practice 25.2l

Using Commas in Numbers

Numbers of one hundred or less and numbers made up of two words (for example, *three thousand*) are generally spelled out in words. Other large numbers (for example, 8,463) are written in numerals. Commas make large numbers easier to read.

> **With large numbers of more than three digits, count from the right and add a comma to the left of every third digit to separate it from every fourth digit.**

RULE 25.2.12

EXAMPLES

3,056 miles

782,956 applicants

a population of 1,256,364

> **Use commas with three or more numbers written in a series.**

RULE 25.2.13

EXAMPLES

My book is missing pages 112, 113, and 114.

I think player number 8, 9, or 12 scored the goal.

> **Do not use a comma with ZIP Codes, telephone numbers, page numbers, years, serial numbers, or house numbers.**

RULE 25.2.14

ZIP CODE	02114
TELEPHONE NUMBER	(617) 723-0987
PAGE NUMBER	on page 4529
YEAR	the year 2006
SERIAL NUMBER	504 33 0923
HOUSE NUMBER	1579 Brookdale Road

See Practice 25.2J

PRACTICE 25.2I ▷ Using Commas in Dates and Geographical Names

Read the sentences. Rewrite each sentence, adding commas where they are needed.

EXAMPLE   He will arrive in San Juan Puerto Rico on Tuesday February 17.

ANSWER   *He will arrive in San Juan, Puerto Rico, on Tuesday, February 17.*

1. The new furniture was delivered on Friday March 13 at noon.

2. The family drove to San Francisco California and then to Reno Nevada.

3. The couple was married on Saturday June 25 in Richmond Virginia.

4. The application must be sent to Albuquerque New Mexico by May 21 2012.

5. March 15 is the day we moved to Austin Texas.

6. The Declaration of Independence was approved by Continental Congress on July 4 1776.

7. My mother remembers the May 18 1980 eruption of Mount St. Helens.

8. They moved from Portland Oregon to York Pennsylvania in May 2007.

9. Andrew's ancestors come from Yorkshire England.

10. The reception is scheduled for Saturday May 5.

PRACTICE 25.2J ▷ Using Commas in Numbers

Rewrite each number, adding commas where needed. If no commas are needed, write *correct*.

EXAMPLE   123854 square miles

ANSWER   *123,854*

11. 1500 pages

12. 67000 troops

13. 4876 audience members

14. page 1122

15. a population of 1540967

16. 3000 homes

17. a distance of 13809 miles

18. 1905 Jones Street

19. 31989 students

20. 11277 feet

WRITING APPLICATION

Write four sentences that include the following: a date that requires commas, a date that does *not* require commas, a number that requires commas, and a number that does *not* require commas.

WRITING APPLICATION

Write a brief announcement about an event in your community or at your school. Include at least one date, one geographical name, and one number with at least four digits. Use commas correctly.

Using Commas With Addresses and in Letters

Commas are also used in addresses, salutations of friendly letters, and closings of friendly or business letters.

> **Use a comma after each item in an address made up of two or more parts.**

In the following example, commas are placed after the name, street, and city. There is no comma between the state and the ZIP Code.

EXAMPLE   Please write to Manuela Rosa, 13 Irving Road, Chicago, Illinois 60613.

Fewer commas are needed when an address is written in a letter or on an envelope.

EXAMPLE   Joan Walsh
119 Hastings Boulevard
Oklahoma City, Oklahoma 73146

> **Use a comma after the salutation in a personal letter and after the closing in all letters.**

See Practice 25.2K
See Practice 25.2L

SALUTATION   Dear Aunt Adda,   **CLOSING**   Best wishes,

Using Commas With Direct Quotations

Commas are also used to separate **direct quotations** from other phrases in a sentence.

> **Use commas to set off a direct quotation from the rest of a sentence.**

EXAMPLES   Ted said, "Let's work on our poster now."

"Maybe later, " replied Seth, "because I have to go to my dentist now."

PRACTICE 25.2K ▷ Using Commas in Addresses and Letters

Read the items. Rewrite each item, adding commas where needed. If no commas are needed, write *correct*.

EXAMPLE   Max Jones
515 Poplar Street
New Haven CT 06501

ANSWER   *Max Jones*
515 Poplar Street
New Haven, CT 06501

1. Dear Aunt Teresa

2. 9410 Bryce Avenue

3. I am writing to my friend Sam Meyer 609 Anderson Avenue Austin Texas 78710.

4. Sincerely yours

5. 84 Mimosa Terrace

6. My dearest Stephanie

7. Fondest regards

8. Shawn Wheton
102 Bear Avenue
Hanover PA 17331

9. 902 Fairbanks Lane

10. Kate's address is 2121 Green Spring Road Baltimore Maryland 21201.

PRACTICE 25.2L ▷ Revising a Letter by Adding Commas

Read the letter. Rewrite the letter, adding commas where necessary.

EXAMPLE   The letter was mailed on Tuesday June 2.

ANSWER   *The letter was mailed on Tuesday, June 2.*

Tamesa Glen

1470 Mountain Road

Chapel Hill, NC 27514

June 2 2010

Dear Tamesa

It was good to get your last letter, and I'm glad to hear you are making some new friends in Chapel Hill North Carolina.

All is well with me. I am busy getting ready for our family vacation to New England. We'll be staying in Boston Massachusetts for three nights and in Burlington Vermont for four nights. I'm looking forward to spending time outdoors in Vermont, and I can't wait to see all the old buildings.

I hope you will be able to visit later this summer. How does the week of August 2 through August 8 sound to you?

Your friend

Keiko

WRITING APPLICATION

Use items 3 and 8 as models, and write an address in a sentence and an address for an envelope.

WRITING APPLICATION

Write a brief letter to a friend or relative who lives in a different town. Use commas correctly.

25.3 Semicolons and Colons

The **semicolon (;)** joins related **independent clauses** and signals a longer pause than a comma. The **colon (:)** is used to introduce lists of items and in other special situations.

Using Semicolons to Join Independent Clauses

Sometimes two **independent clauses** are so closely connected in meaning that they make up a single sentence, rather than two separate sentences.

25.3.1 RULE

> **Use a semicolon to join related independent clauses that are not joined by the conjunctions** *and, or, nor, for, but, so,* **or** *yet.*

INDEPENDENT CLAUSES	The winding river has many hazards.
	It is full of snakes and alligators.
CLAUSES JOINED BY SEMICOLONS	The winding river has many hazards ; it is full of snakes and alligators.

A semicolon should be used only when there is a close relationship between the two independent clauses. If the clauses are not very closely related, they should be written as separate sentences with a period or another end mark to separate them or joined with a coordinaring conjunction.

Note that when a sentence contains three or more related independent clauses, they may still be separated with semicolons.

EXAMPLES	We packed our bags ; we packed the car ; we're ready to go on our vacation.
	My dog won first prize in the show ; Larry's dog won second prize ; Noah's dog did not win a prize.

Using Semicolons to Join Clauses Separated by Conjunctive Adverbs or Transitional Expressions

Semicolons help writers show how their ideas connect.

> **Use a semicolon to join independent clauses separated by either a conjunctive adverb or a transitional expression.**

CONJUNCTIVE ADVERBS	*also, besides, consequently, first, furthermore, however, indeed, instead, moreover, nevertheless, otherwise, second, then, therefore, thus*
TRANSITIONAL EXPRESSIONS	*as a result, at this time, for instance, in fact, on the other hand, that is*

EXAMPLE   He arrived late at the train station that morning **;** **as a result** **,** he missed the beginning of the concert.

Remember to place a comma after the conjunctive adverb or transitional expression. The comma sets off the conjunctive adverb or transitional expression, which acts as an introductory expression to the second clause.

Using Semicolons to Avoid Confusion

Sometimes, to avoid confusion, semicolons are used to separate items in a series.

> **Consider the use of semicolons to avoid confusion when items in a series already contain commas.**

See Practice 25.3A
See Practice 25.3B

Place a semicolon after all but the last complete item in a series.

EXAMPLES   The children **,** laughing **;** the clowns **,** singing **;** and the lions **,** roaring **,** all added to the noise at the circus.

Three important dates in Jamestown history are April 30 **,** 1607 **;** September 10 **,** 1607 **;** and January 7 **,** 1608.

Using Colons

The **colon (:)** is used to introduce lists of items and in certain special situations.

> **Use a colon after an independent clause to introduce a list of items.**

The independent clause that comes before the colon often includes the words *the following, as follows, these,* or *those.*

EXAMPLE   I am planning to pack the following supplies for
the trip : a backpack , a tent , and a sleeping bag.

Remember to use commas to separate three or more items in a series.

> **In most cases, do not use a colon after a verb, and never use a colon after a preposition.**

INCORRECT   Tyler always brings : a sandwich , fruit , and juice.

CORRECT   Tyler always brings a sandwich , fruit , and juice.

> **Use a colon to introduce a long or formal quotation.**

EXAMPLE   The sign stated the fire code : "No campfires
allowed from July 1 to September 30."

SOME ADDITIONAL USES OF THE COLON	
To Separate Hours and Minutes	4 : 40 P.M. 7 : 00 A.M.
After the Salutation in a Business Letter	To Whom It May Concern : Dear Dr. Ross :
On Warnings and Labels	Notice : Classes Canceled Danger : No Swimming

See Practice 25.3C
See Practice 25.3D

Read the sentences. Rewrite each sentence, adding any necessary semicolons.

EXAMPLE   Mara decided not to ride her bike to practice it was too far.

ANSWER   *Mara decided not to ride her bike to practice; it was too far.*

1. Training sessions will take place on Thursday, February 26 Tuesday, March 3 and Thursday, March 5.

2. I thought Brent's poem was excellent in fact, it should have won an award.

3. Shakespeare created many great plays he also wrote some memorable sonnets.

4. Jonathan Ryder, brother of the bride Gregory Pope, cousin of the groom and Eric Chavez, friend of the groom, were the three ushers.

5. The team played with a lot of heart nevertheless, they could not win the championship.

6. Paul enjoys hiking Samuel likes fishing.

7. If Jake is not awake by 6:30 A.M., wake him up otherwise, he will miss the bus.

8. Josie failed to take care of her bicycle as a result, it is falling apart.

9. Sarah's favorite sport is basketball Julia enjoys volleyball.

10. Some of the students were asked to serve food others had the task of cleaning up.

Read the sentences. Rewrite each sentence in which semicolons are needed or are used incorrectly. If a sentence is punctuated properly, write *correct*.

EXAMPLE   I caught three fish, however, I threw two of them back.

ANSWER   *I caught three fish; however, I threw two of them back.*

11. The train passes through Columbia, Missouri, Topeka, Kansas, and Ames, Iowa.

12. I arrived two hours before the play's start; nevertheless, the tickets were sold out.

13. A coward dies many deaths, a hero dies but once.

14. Attending the meeting were John, the president, Stu, the treasurer, and Dennis, the secretary.

15. The regular goalie was injured, as a result, Selena got her first chance to start.

16. Our band is performing at Mel's Place on Tuesday October 6, Wednesday October 14, and Tuesday October 20.

17. Joel is a trained engineer; therefore, we asked him to lead our robotics club.

18. If a strange man approaches you, don't talk to him, move away quickly.

19. Melinda opened her arms wide; she embraced the child in a warm hug.

20. If you are passing through Denver; please call my aunt.

SPEAKING APPLICATION

Take turns telling a partner about a trip you have taken. Your partner should listen for a list of places or dates that requires semicolons.

WRITING APPLICATION

Write three sentences that require semicolons. Then, tell a partner why the semicolons are needed.

PRACTICE 25.3C Using Colons

Read the sentences. Rewrite each sentence, adding any necessary colons. If no colon is needed, write *correct.*

EXAMPLE The club offers several activities hiking, skiing, boating, and climbing.

ANSWER *The club offers several activities: hiking, skiing, boating, and climbing.*

1. The Rileys have lived in three different states Missouri, Illinois, and Colorado.

2. The Romance languages include Spanish, Portuguese, French, Italian, and Romanian.

3. Warning Do not allow direct contact with the eyes.

4. The flight is scheduled to leave at 830 A.M.

5. The principal introduced the guest speaker "It is my pleasure to introduce a pillar of the community, Mr. Martin Montoya."

6. He has received acceptance letters from Harvard, Columbia, and Princeton.

7. The following breeds are herding dogs the collie, the kelpie, and the briard.

8. Dad gave me three options finish the paper now, work on it at Grandma's, or stay home.

9. He began the letter "Dear Sir or Madam" and then stated his question.

10. The times of the trains to Denver are as follows 1015 A.M., 1215 P.M., and 430 P.M.

PRACTICE 25.3D Using Colons Correctly in Sentences

Read the sentences. Then, rewrite each sentence, adding necessary colons or removing unneeded ones.

EXAMPLE I arrived at exactly 1234 P.M.

ANSWER *I arrived at exactly 12:34 P.M.*

11. Entering the campsite, Dennis was carrying: a compass, a map, and a canteen.

12. Warning Do not take this medicine on an empty stomach.

13. We put three additional cities on our itinerary Seattle, Vancouver, and Calgary.

14. The restaurant doesn't open until 1000 a.m.

15. We have yet to receive RSVPs from: Aunt Jean, Uncle Benny, and Grandpa Buddy.

16. Caution Icy roads ahead.

17. I distinctly heard her make this statement, "Watch out for flying squirrels!"

18. Here are my classmates whose names begin with S Sam, Stan, Sidney, and Stephen.

19. It's almost 930; are you on your way yet?

20. Note All classes are cancelled tomorrow due to snow.

SPEAKING APPLICATION

With a partner, take turns stating a sentence that contains a list of items. Explain whether or not your list should be introduced by a colon.

WRITING APPLICATION

Write two sentences that provide warnings and two sentences that include a specific time. Check to make sure that you have used colons correctly in your sentences.

Test Warm-Up

DIRECTIONS
Read the introduction and the passage that follows. Then, answer the questions to show that you can use and understand semicolons and colons correctly in the context of reading and writing.

Akiko included this paragraph in her social studies report. Read the paragraph and think about the changes you would suggest as a peer editor. When you finish reading, answer the questions that follow.

Longhorn Caverns

(1) Four of the most interesting cave systems in Texas include: Innerspace Caverns, Natural Bridge Caverns, Caverns of Sonora, and Longhorn Caverns. (2) Longhorn Caverns in Burnet County has a fascinating history. (3) Comanche Indians used to hold tribal councils there long ago. (4) In the 1870s, the outlaw Sam Bass hid successfully in Longhorn Caverns on several occasions, however; he was later killed during a robbery in the town of Round Rock. (5) Today, you can go on a tour of the caverns. (6) If you go, make sure to bring the following items, a flashlight, a camera, and good walking shoes.

---

1 What change, if any, should be made in sentence 1?

  A Replace the colon after *include* with a semicolon

  B Delete the colon after *include*

  C Use semicolons instead of commas in the sentence

  D Make no change

2 What is the BEST way to combine sentences 2 and 3?

  F Replace the period in sentence 2 with a comma

  G Replace the period in sentence 2 with a semicolon

  H Replace the period in sentence 2 with a colon

  J Replace the period in sentence 2 with **and**

3 What change, if any, should be made in sentence 4?

  A Change *occasions, however;* to *occasions; however,*

  B Replace the semicolon with a comma

  C Replace the comma after *occasions* with a colon

  D Make no change

4 What change, if any, should be made in sentence 6?

  F Replace the commas after *flashlight* and *camera* with semicolons.

  G Replace the comma after *items* with a colon

  H Replace the comma after *items* with a semicolon

  J Make no change

25.4 Quotation Marks, Underlining, and Italics

Quotation marks (" ") set off direct quotations, dialogue, and certain types of titles. Other types of titles may be <u>underlined</u> or set in *italics,* a slanted type style.

Find It / FIX IT

6

Grammar
Game Plan

Using Quotation Marks With Quotations

Quotation marks identify the spoken or written words of others. A **direct quotation** represents a person's exact speech or thoughts. An **indirect quotation** reports the general meaning of what a person said or thought.

Both types of quotations are acceptable when you write. Direct quotations, however, generally result in a livelier writing style.

> **Direct quotations should be enclosed in quotation marks.**

RULE
25.4.1

EXAMPLES Stan said, "I decided to try out for the swim team."

"May I finish my project later?" asked Meg.

> **Indirect quotations do not require quotation marks.**

RULE
25.4.2

EXAMPLES My uncle promised that he would watch my game.

The teacher said that my class was going to be the first class to work in the new computer lab.

Using Direct Quotations With Introductory, Concluding, and Interrupting Expressions

Commas help you set off introductory information so that your reader understands who is speaking. Writers usually identify a speaker by using words such as *he asked* or *she said* with a quotation. These expressions can introduce, conclude, or interrupt a quotation.

Find It / FIX IT

18

Grammar
Game Plan

Direct Quotations With Introductory Expressions

Commas are also used to indicate where **introductory expressions** end.

RULE 25.4.3 >

When an **introductory expression** precedes a direct quotation, place a comma after the introductory expression, and write the quotation as a full sentence.

EXAMPLES

My sister begged my mother, "May I go on the hike with my class?"

Nate thought, "I wonder how long the hike will take and how far we will go."

If an introductory expression is very long, set it off with a colon instead of a comma.

EXAMPLE

At the end of the hike, Salim concluded: "The acorn is one of the most important sources of food in the woods."

Direct Quotations With Concluding Expressions

Direct quotations may sometimes end with **concluding expressions.**

RULE 25.4.4 >

When a **concluding expression** follows a direct quotation, write the quotation as a full sentence ending with a comma, question mark, or exclamation mark inside the quotation mark. Then, write the concluding expression. Be sure to use end punctuation to close the sentence.

Concluding expressions are not complete sentences; therefore, they do not begin with capital letters. Notice also that the closing quotation marks are always placed outside the punctuation at the end of direct quotations followed by concluding expressions.

EXAMPLE

"What activities does your camp offer?" inquired Kamilla.

Direct Quotations With Interrupting Expressions

You may use an interrupting expression in a direct quotation, which is also called a **divided quotation.** Interrupting expressions help writers clarify who is speaking and can also break up a long quotation.

> **RULE 25.4.5**
>
> When the direct quotation of one sentence is interrupted, end the first part of the direct quotation with a comma and a quotation mark. Place a comma after the **interrupting expression,** and then use a new set of quotation marks to enclose the rest of the quotation.

EXAMPLES "My grandparents are coming for dinner," explained Jade, "so I want to hurry home after school."

"Do you think," questioned Kyle, "that I could help prepare dinner?"

Do not capitalize the first word of the second part of the sentence.

> **RULE 25.4.6**
>
> When two sentences in a direct quotation are separated by an **interrupting expression,** end the first quoted sentence with a comma, question mark, or exclamation mark and a quotation mark. Place a period after the interrupter, and then write the second quoted sentence as a full quotation.

EXAMPLES "This is Carter's Grove Plantation," the guide said. "It is an fine example of a mid-eighteenth–century mansion."

"What would it have been like to live there?" asked Corrina. "Can you imagine it?"

See Practice 25.4A
See Practice 25.4B

PRACTICE 25.4A > Using Quotation Marks With Direct Quotations

Read the sentences. If the sentence contains a direct quotation, write *D*. If it contains an indirect quotation, write *I*. Then, rewrite each sentence that contains a direct quotation, adding the quotation marks where needed.

EXAMPLE   My older brother is studying graphic design, said Rachel.

ANSWER   *D — "My older brother is studying graphic design," said Rachel.*

1. Marcus asked, Did you ever read anything by James Joyce?

2. The coach told us that a goalie must have especially good reflexes.

3. I like spring better than summer, Hakeem said.

4. Is it true that green chili peppers will help you recover from a cold? asked Darryl.

5. Joel told me that learning to swim was a great experience for him.

6. Emily Dickinson was very talented, Mrs. Hudson explained.

7. The vendor shouted, Get your popcorn here!

8. Gwen asked, Where are the balloons?

9. The little girl kept repeating that she wanted her mommy.

10. Kelsey wonders whether marine biology would interest him.

PRACTICE 25.4B > Punctuating With Interrupting Expressions

Read the sentences. Rewrite each sentence, adding commas and quotation marks where needed.

EXAMPLE   At dusk the guide explained the Sandia Mountains sometimes look pink.

ANSWER   *"At dusk," the guide explained, "the Sandia Mountains sometimes look pink."*

11. This spring said Masako I will plant pansies along the front sidewalk.

12. Be careful what you say Jamal remarked or you might be sorry.

13. Watch your step said the bus driver.

14. Have you ever Mrs. Polk asked seen such beautiful Native American pottery?

15. The doctor said You are healthy.

16. These caves claimed Jaime were once inhabited by ancient peoples.

17. The concert at the park has been canceled announced Clarice.

18. I hope it doesn't rain whined Ramona.

19. Being on time said the teacher is very important.

20. I've always thought said Mom that wolves are beautiful creatures.

WRITING APPLICATION

Write two sentences with direct quotations and two with indirect quotations.

WRITING APPLICATION

Using Sentence 20 as a model, write two more sentences with direct quotations interrupted by expressions.

Using Quotation Marks With Other Punctuation Marks

You have seen that a comma or period used with a direct quotation goes inside the final quotation mark. In some cases, however, end marks should be placed outside of quotation marks.

> **Always place a comma or a period inside the final quotation mark.**

25.4.7 RULE

EXAMPLES   "We are helping to clean up the park**,**" said Neal**.**

Mando added**,** "Our class is meeting by the playground on Saturday morning**."**

> **Place a question mark or an exclamation mark inside the final quotation mark if the end mark is part of the quotation. Do not use an additional end mark outside the quotation marks.**

25.4.8 RULE

EXAMPLES   Retha asked**,** "When may I have a pet**?**"

Dad looked at the footprints and protested loudly**,** "I just finished washing the floor**!**"

> **Place a question mark or exclamation mark outside the final quotation mark if the end mark is part of the entire sentence, not part of the quotation.**

25.4.9 RULE

EXAMPLES   Did I hear you say**,** "I did my homework but forgot to bring it to school"**?**

See Practice 25.4C

Please don't tell me the excuse**,** "I forgot"**!**

Using Single Quotation Marks for Quotations Within Quotations

Double quotation marks are used to enclose the main quotation. The rules for using commas and end marks with **single quotation marks (' ')** are the same as they are with double quotation marks.

Single quotation marks are used to separate a quote that appears inside of another quotation.

25.4.10

> Use **single quotation marks** to set off a quotation within a quotation.

EXAMPLES

"Do you know if it was Katy who called, 'Come back!' as I was leaving?" I asked.

Liam moaned, "I heard someone say, 'Watch out!' as I began to fall."

Punctuating Explanatory Material Within Quotes

Sometimes it is necessary to add information to a quotation that explains the quote more fully. In that case, brackets tell your reader which information came from the original speaker and which came from someone else. (See Section 25.7 for more information on brackets.)

25.4.11

> Use brackets to enclose an explanation located within a quotation to show that the explanation is not part of the original quotation.

EXAMPLES

The principal announced, "Two clubs [the Chess Club and the History Club] worked together to plan the tournament."

"We [the faculty of Central High School] dedicate this plaque to all the student athletes."

See Practice 25.4D

PRACTICE 25.4C > **Using Quotation Marks With Other Punctuation Marks**

Read the sentences. Decide whether the missing punctuation goes inside or outside the quotation marks. Then, rewrite each sentence, adding the proper punctuation for quotations.

EXAMPLE "When did you become interested in gardening" Miguel asked Tina.

ANSWER *"When did you become interested in gardening?" Miguel asked Tina.*

1. "How are we going to get this desk up the stairs" asked Consuela.

2. "The sun sets at 6:45 tonight" he stated.

3. Jim announced, "The movie is starting in ten minutes"

4. Who said, "A penny saved is a penny earned"

5. Donna actually said to me, "You are not welcome here"

6. Did someone say, "This experiment was a disaster"

7. Ami excitedly announced, "I passed the test"

8. Jenny asked, "How many miles is a marathon"

9. Then the host said, "All of our contestants have been fooled"

10. The driver of the boat yelled, "Hold on tight"

PRACTICE 25.4D > **Punctuating Quotations Within Quotations and Explanatory Material**

Read the sentences. Rewrite each sentence, adding single quotation marks or brackets where needed.

EXAMPLE "I heard the boy yell, Watch out! after he threw the ball," said Mason.

ANSWER *"I heard the boy yell, 'Watch out!' after he threw the ball," said Mason.*

11. "Did he really say, My iguana has escaped?" asked Nolan.

12. Tyrell announced to the class, "Ms. Hartin said, Read the first three pages only."

13. "Who said, Let's start with an outline?" asked Mr. Lorenzo.

14. "I heard Mom tell you, The laundry is now your job," said Melissa.

15. The city councilman said, "This intersection 12th St. and Hill Dr. is too dangerous."

16. "Did he say, There's the pin, or There's the pen?" asked Perry.

17. Rosita said, "I thought I heard you say, The milk is sour."

18. "Our highest priority," said Senator Smiley, "is to pass this legislation House Bill 7172"

19. The camp director told us, "No one in the cabin Cabin 12 heard or saw anything."

20. "Then she yelled, Take cover!" said Julio.

WRITING APPLICATION

Write four sentences in which you correctly use punctuation inside and outside quotation marks.

WRITING APPLICATION

Write two sentences including quotations within quotations, and punctuate them correctly.

Using Quotation Marks for Dialogue

A conversation between two or more people is called a **dialogue.** Adding dialogue makes your writing lively because it brings different points of view into your work. It makes your work sound like speech, so dialogue makes your reader feel involved in the scene you describe.

RULE 25.4.12

> When you are writing a **dialogue,** indent to begin a new paragraph with each change of speaker. Also be sure to add quotation marks around a speaker's words. When a new speaker is quoted, be sure to indicate the change to your reader by adding information that identifies the new speaker.

EXAMPLE

"Will you be going with us on the family trip again this summer ? " Noreen asked her cousin .

Gwen hesitated before answering . "I'm afraid so . My parents think I enjoy the experience of traveling with our whole family . "

"You fooled me , too , " Noreen replied . "Maybe the trip will be better this year . I think we're going to places that have large parks . If we're lucky , we might even be able to go on a few rides . "

"Well , at least it can't be any worse , " sighed Gwen . "On the last trip , we waited in line for one hour at three different historic homes in one day ! "

"I remember those lines , " said Noreen . "Didn't you get sunburned while we were waiting? "

Notice that each sentence is punctuated according to the rules discussed earlier in this section.

See Practice 25.4E
See Practice 25.4F

PRACTICE 25.4E Using Quotation Marks in Dialogue

Read the dialogue. Then, rewrite the dialogue. Use proper spacing for quotations and create additional paragraphs where needed. Be sure to use quotation marks and other punctuation correctly.

EXAMPLE   Where have Alisa and Mario gone asked Mom. They went to the nursery answered Dad.

ANSWER   *"Where have Alisa and Mario gone?" asked Mom.*

"They went to the nursery," answered Dad.

This nursery is huge Mario said. Where should we start? I want to look at flowers for the front yard first said Alisa. Okay, said Mario, we can get a flat of marigolds and one of pansies. I know you also want to buy some seeds to start pepper plants and tomato plants said Alisa. Yes Mario replied. That would be great. Look at all the gardening tools over there exclaimed Alisa. They seem to have everything we need here. I don't even need any tools, said Mario. Well, I do, said Alisa. I need some hand tools to plant those flowers. Let's get started said Mario. This will be fun.

PRACTICE 25.4F Revising Dialogue for Punctuation and Paragraphs

Read the dialogue. Then, rewrite the dialogue. Add quotation marks and begin new paragraphs where needed.

EXAMPLE   How did you enjoy your trip to Chicago? asked Malcolm. It was great, but I didn't get to see everything, Nick answered.

ANSWER   *"How did you enjoy your trip to Chicago?" asked Malcolm.*

"It was great, but I didn't get to see everything," Nick answered.

Did you get to spend much time outdoors? Malcolm asked. Oh, yes, said Nick. The weather was great, and we went to the Lincoln Park Zoo and to Navy Pier. How about the Botanic Garden? asked Malcolm. I heard that was worth seeing. No, Nick replied. On the very last day, we had to choose between Navy Pier and the Botanic Garden, and almost everyone in the family chose Navy Pier. What did you do at Navy Pier? asked Malcolm. Oh, there was so much to do there. We spent the whole day. What I remember most is riding the huge Ferris wheel. I hope I get to see Chicago someday, said Malcolm. It sounds pretty exciting.

SPEAKING APPLICATION

With a partner, take turns reciting a brief dialogue. Your partner should listen for and point out each time a paragraph break would be needed.

WRITING APPLICATION

Write a brief dialogue between two friends who are discussing their plans for the weekend. Make sure to punctuate each quotation correctly, and start a new paragraph each time the speaker changes.

Using Quotation Marks in Titles

Quotation marks are generally used to set off the titles of shorter works.

RULE 25.4.13

> Use **quotation marks** to enclose the titles of short written works and around the title of a work that is mentioned as part of a collection.

WRITTEN WORKS THAT USE QUOTATION MARKS	
Title of a Short Story	"The Gift of the Magi"
Chapter From a Book	"The Test Is in the Tasting" from *No-Work Garden Book*
Title of a Short Poem	"Lucy"
Title of an Article	"How to Build a Birdhouse"
Title Mentioned as Part of a Collection	"Uncle Vanya" in *Eight Great Comedies*

RULE 25.4.14

> Use **quotation marks** around the titles of episodes in a television or radio series, songs, and parts of a long musical composition.

ARTISTIC WORKS THAT USE QUOTATION MARKS	
Title of an Episode	"The Nile" from *Cousteau Odyssey*
Title of a Song	"The Best Things in Life Are Free"
Title of a Part of a Long Musical Work	"The Storm" from the *William Tell Overture*

Using Underlining and Italics in Titles

Underlining and **italics** help make titles and other special words and names stand out in your writing. Underlining is used only in handwritten or typewritten material. In printed material, italic (slanted) print is used instead of underlining.

UNDERLINING <u>Treasure Island</u>   ITALICS *Treasure Island*

Underline or **italicize** the titles of long written works and publications that are published as a single work.

25.4.15 RULE

WRITTEN WORKS THAT ARE UNDERLINED OR ITALICIZED	
Title of a Book or Play	*To Kill a Mockingbird, Chicago*
Title of a Long Poem	*Beowulf*
Title of a Magazine or Newspaper	*Newsweek, Chicago Tribune*

Underline or **italicize** the titles of movies, television and radio series, long works of music, and art.

25.4.16 RULE

ARTISTIC WORKS THAT ARE UNDERLINED OR ITALICIZED	
Title of a Movie	*Star Wars*
Title of a Television Series	*Happy Days*
Title of a Long Work of Music	*Moonlight Sonata*
Title of a Music Album	*Pet Sounds*
Title of a Painting	*Christina's World*
Title of a Sculpture	*The Discus Thrower*

Underline or **italicize** the names of individual air, sea, and spacecraft.

25.4.17 RULE

EXAMPLES   *Voyager 2*   the *Mayflower*

Underline or **italicize** words and letters used as names for themselves and foreign words.

25.4.18 RULE

EXAMPLES   Do you know how to spell *Victoria*?

An *obi* is a sash worn with traditional Japanese dress.

See Practice 25.4G
See Practice 25.4H

PRACTICE 25.4G ▷ Underlining Titles, Names, and Words

Read the sentences. Rewrite each sentence, underlining titles, names, and words where needed. You can use italics if you are typing your answers.

EXAMPLE   This year the high school drama club will present Romeo and Juliet.

ANSWER   *This year the high school drama club will present <u>Romeo and Juliet</u>.*

1. My sister is reading The Scarlet Letter, a novel by Nathaniel Hawthorne.

2. An au pair is a person who cares for a family's children in exchange for room and board.

3. I always forget how to spell occasion.

4. The cast gave a good performance in Charlie and the Chocolate Factory.

5. Kimberly is learning to play the koto, a traditional stringed instrument from Japan.

6. The pilgrims had a miserable journey aboard the Mayflower.

7. Remember not to use their when you mean there.

8. Have you ever seen a performance of Hamlet?

9. The Starry Night is one of Van Gogh's famous paintings.

10. Sally Ride, the first American woman to fly in space, was a crew member of the space shuttle Challenger.

PRACTICE 25.4H ▷ Using Underlining and Quotation Marks

Read the sentences. Rewrite each sentence, enclosing the titles in quotation marks or underlining them. You can use italics if you are typing your answers.

EXAMPLE   The collection We'll Always Have Paris includes the short story The Twilight Greens.

ANSWER   *The collection <u>We'll Always Have Paris</u> includes the short story "The Twilight Greens."*

11. My music teacher has composed a long piece called Opus of George.

12. In class we are discussing The Landlady, a short story by Roald Dahl.

13. The poem The Cremation of Sam McGee appears in The Best of Robert Service.

14. The teacher has assigned one chapter, Below the Equator, for homework.

15. That episode was titled Archie Helps Out.

16. Langston Hughes wrote the short poem Refugee in America.

17. Mom is reading Your Child's First Dog, an article in Dog Fancy.

18. The song I'm Yours always puts me in a good mood.

19. The Dying Cowboy is an old American ballad.

20. My brother titled his school newspaper article Baseball Team Needs Help.

WRITING APPLICATION

Write one sentence about a short story you read and one about a movie you saw. Make sure to punctuate the titles correctly.

WRITING APPLICATION

Write a sentence about a ship and one about a spacecraft. You may make up the names if you want, but be sure to use underlining correctly.

25.5 Hyphens

Hyphens (-) are used to combine words and to show a connection between the syllables of words that are broken at the ends of lines.

Using Hyphens in Numbers

Hyphens are used to join compound numbers and fractions.

> Use a **hyphen** when you write two-word numbers from twenty-one through ninety-nine.

RULE 25.5.1

EXAMPLES   twenty-one   thirty-eight

> Use a **hyphen** when you use a fraction as an adjective but not when you use a fraction as a noun.

RULE 25.5.2

ADJECTIVE   The bus is two-thirds full.

NOUN   Two thirds of voters agree with the plan.

Using Hyphens for Prefixes and Suffixes

Many words with common prefixes are no longer hyphenated. The following prefixes are often used before proper nouns: *ante-*, *anti-*, *post-*, *pre-*, and *un-*. Check a dictionary when you are unsure about using a hyphen.

> Use a **hyphen** after a prefix that is followed by a proper noun or adjective.

RULE 25.5.3

EXAMPLES   pre-Civil War   mid-January

> Use a **hyphen** in words with the prefixes *all-*, *ex-*, and *self-* and the suffix *-elect*.

RULE 25.5.4

EXAMPLES   self-employed   governor-elect

Using Hyphens in Compound Words

Compound words are two or more words that must be read together to create a single idea.

RULE
25.5.5

Use a **hyphen** to connect two or more nouns that are used as one compound word, unless a dictionary gives a different spelling.

EXAMPLES   six - year - olds   mother - in - law

Using Hyphens With Compound Modifiers

Hyphens help your reader group information properly.

RULE
25.5.6

Use a hyphen to connect a **compound modifier** that comes before a noun. Do not use a hyphen with a compound modifier that includes a word ending in *-ly* or in a compound proper adjective.

EXAMPLE   In the basket were seven well - fed puppies.

INCORRECT   freshly - baked bread   Native - American art

CORRECT   freshly baked bread   Native American art

A hyphen is not necessary when a compound modifier follows the noun it describes.

MODIFIER
BEFORE NOUN   The never - ending sound of cheering filled the hall.

MODIFIER
AFTER NOUN   The sound of cheering in the hall was never ending.

However, if a dictionary spells a word with a hyphen, the word must always be hyphenated, even when it follows a noun.

EXAMPLE   We plan to visit the park in the off - season.

See Practice 25.5A
See Practice 25.5B

PRACTICE 25.5A ▷ Using Hyphens in Numbers and Words

Read the following items. Write each item, adding hyphens where needed. If an item is already correct, write *correct*.

EXAMPLE   in mid September

ANSWER   *in mid-September*

1. carefully chosen words

2. the post Elizabethan era

3. a two thirds majority

4. twenty two people

5. a well built wall

6. his brother in law

7. a self confident girl

8. a wall that is well built

9. a four story building

10. user friendly instruction manual

PRACTICE 25.5B ▷ Proofreading for Hyphens

Read the sentences. Rewrite each sentence, adding hyphens where needed.

EXAMPLE   The debate team now has twenty one members.

ANSWER   *The debate team now has twenty-one members.*

11. The senator elect is eager to begin serving his state.

12. Our great aunt usually comes to visit in the summer.

13. A low cost plan was presented to the council.

14. We began our cross country trip in New York City.

15. About three quarters of the voters attend the once a month meeting.

16. The famous author illustrator is giving a book signing tomorrow.

17. I returned to my half finished lunch after the fire drill.

18. A well maintained car will usually be reliable.

19. The ex congressman now works in radio.

20. The thirty eight members who voted "yes" made up a two thirds majority.

WRITING APPLICATION

Write three sentences. Include at least three compound nouns or adjectives that need hyphens, and hyphenate them correctly.

WRITING APPLICATION

Write a sentence that contains one hyphenated fraction and one fraction that is not hyphenated.

Using Hyphens at the Ends of Lines

Hyphens serve a useful purpose when they are used to divide words at the ends of lines. They should not, however, be used more often than is necessary because they can make reading feel choppy.

Avoid dividing words at the end of a line whenever possible. If a word must be divided, always divide it between syllables.

EXAMPLE You must not feel that your contri-
bution was insignificant.

Check a dictionary if you are unsure how a word is divided into syllables. Looking up the word *seriously*, for example, you would find that its syllables are *se-ri-ous-ly*.

A hyphen used to divide a word should never be placed at the beginning of the second line. It must be placed at the end of the first line.

INCORRECT His taste in music is quite sophis
-ticated.

CORRECT His taste in music is quite sophis-
ticated.

Using Hyphens Correctly to Divide Words

One-syllable words cannot be divided.

Do *not* divide one-syllable words even if they seem long or sound like words with two syllables.

INCORRECT wh-eel pl-ease shr-ink

CORRECT wheel please shrink

Do *not* divide a word so that a single letter stands alone.

INCORRECT	a-long	i-con	air-y
CORRECT	along	icon	airy

Also avoid placing *-ed* at the beginning of a new line.

INCORRECT	The list of the new team members was post- ed on the wall of the gym.
CORRECT	The list of the new team members was posted on the wall of the gym.

Avoid dividing proper nouns or proper adjectives.

INCORRECT	Jenni-fer	Span-ish
CORRECT	Jennifer	Spanish

Divide a hyphenated word only immediately following the existing hyphen.

INCORRECT	John gave the class an up-to-the-min- ute report each morning.
CORRECT	John gave the class an up-to-the- minute report each morning.

See Practice 25.5C
See Practice 25.5D

PRACTICE 25.5C **Using Hyphens to Divide Words**

Read the following words. Rewrite each word. Then, draw vertical lines between syllables that can be divided at the end of a line. Do nothing to words that cannot be divided.

EXAMPLE   baseball

ANSWER   *base | ball*

1. Daniel

2. highway

3. self-respect

4. steady

5. swallow

6. interrupt

7. stopped

8. panted

9. skillfully

10. intended

PRACTICE 25.5D **Using Hyphens in Words in Sentences**

Read the sentences. If a word has been divided correctly, write *correct.* If not, rewrite the sentence, dividing the word correctly or writing it as one word if it cannot be divided.

EXAMPLE   The wallpaper had dia-mond-shaped patterns.

ANSWER   *The wallpaper had diamond-shaped patterns.*

11. Mr. Ramirez traveled to Cincinnati for a busi-ness meeting.

12. While we were out of town, Terrence water-ed our plants.

13. Several family members have Decem-ber birthdays.

14. Yoko will spend most of her vaca-tion in South Dakota.

15. New York City attracts man-y tourists each year.

16. Tyrell found satisfaction in compl-eting the recycling project.

17. Aisha spends most Saturdays volun-teering at the animal shelter.

18. On the plate sat one lone strawber-ry dipped in yogurt.

19. The outcome of the tourna-ment did not surprise anyone.

20. Miguel wanted to buy a T-shirt, so he bro-ught some extra money with him.

SPEAKING APPLICATION

With a partner, sound out these words and have your partner determine where the syllables break: *shoveling, dismiss, appointment, popular.* Then, check the syllable breaks in a dictionary.

WRITING APPLICATION

Write four sentences. Break each sentence in the middle of a word to show one place it would be correct to divide a word at the end of a line.

25.6 Apostrophes

The **apostrophe (')** is used to show possession or ownership. It is also used in shortened forms of words called contractions. In a contraction, the apostrophe marks the place where letters have been omitted.

Find It / FIX IT

14

Grammar
Game Plan

Using Apostrophes With Possessive Nouns

Apostrophes are used with nouns to show ownership or possession.

> **Add an apostrophe and -s to show the possessive case of most singular nouns and plural nouns that do not end in -s or -es.**

25.6.1 RULE

EXAMPLES   Wayne**'**s brother was the first one in line.

The children**'**s game is in the afternoon.

Even when a singular noun already ends in -s, you can usually add an apostrophe and -s to show possession.

EXAMPLE   The first grade class**'**s play was very funny.

In classical or ancient names that end in -s, it is common to omit the final -s to make pronunciation easier.

EXAMPLE   Zeus**'** thunderbolt is a symbol in Greek mythology.

> **Add an apostrophe to show the possessive case of plural nouns ending in -s or -es. Do not add an -s.**

 25.6.2 RULE

EXAMPLE   The witnesses**'** testimonies were very helpful.

RULE 25.6.3 > Add an apostrophe and -*s* (or just an apostrophe if the word is a plural ending in -*s*) to the last word of a compound noun to form the possessive.

EXAMPLES   My brother-in-law's school

the Girl Scouts' ceremony

See Practice 25.6A

Using Apostrophes With Pronouns

Both indefinite and personal pronouns can show possession.

RULE 25.6.4 > Use an apostrophe and -*s* with indefinite pronouns to show possession.

EXAMPLES   everyone's opinion   everybody's food

RULE 25.6.5 > Do not use an apostrophe with possessive personal pronouns.

POSSESSIVE PERSONAL PRONOUNS		
	SINGULAR	PLURAL
First Person	I, me, my, mine	we, us, our, ours
Second Person	you, your, yours	you, your, yours
Third Person	he, him, his; she, her, hers; it, its	they, them; their, theirs

Some of these pronouns act as adjectives.

EXAMPLES   The cat held a ball of yarn in its paws.

Our car is being repaired.

Others act as subjects, objects, and subject complements.

EXAMPLES   Mine is the red-and-white uniform.

The red-and-gray uniform is his.

See Practice 25.6B

Using Apostrophes With Contractions

Contractions are used in informal speech and writing, especially in dialogue because they create the sound of speech.

> Use an **apostrophe** in a **contraction** to show where one or more letters have been omitted.

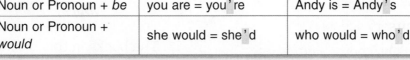

COMMON CONTRACTIONS		
Verb + *not*	is not = isn't	cannot = can't
Noun or Pronoun + *will*	I will = I'll	we will = we'll
Noun or Pronoun + *be*	you are = you're	Andy is = Andy's
Noun or Pronoun + *would*	she would = she'd	who would = who'd

> Avoid using contractions in formal speech and writing.

Contractions may be used in dialogue and in informal speech and writing, but they should be avoided in formal usage.

INFORMAL WRITING   Where's the fire?

FORMAL WRITING   Where is the fire?

Using Apostrophes to Create Plurals

Do not use an apostrophe to form plurals, except in specific instances.

> Use an **apostrophe** and *-s* to create the plural form of a letter, numeral, or a word used as a name for itself.

See Practice 25.6C
See Practice 25.6D

EXAMPLES   There are two 5's in his phone number.

People can confuse *a*'s and *an*'s.

Read each phrase. Write the possessive form of each item.

EXAMPLE   the computer of my mother

ANSWER   *my mother's computer*

1. the tasks of Hercules

2. the thoughts of the men

3. the doors of the nursery school

4. the cellphone of his brother-in-law

5. the clothing of the children

6. the works of the artists

7. the nest of the mice

8. the speech of the governor-elect

9. the coat of her cousin

10. the eyes of the praying mantis

Read the sentences. If all pronouns in a sentence are used correctly, write *correct*. If one or more pronouns are used incorrectly, rewrite the sentence correctly.

EXAMPLE   This pencil is mine, and that one is your's.

ANSWER   *This pencil is mine, and that one is yours.*

11. The books in this backpack are his', not mine.

12. Somebodys' dog was digging in our garden while our's was sleeping inside.

13. The doctor examined the girl and discovered her hand was broken.

14. Ours was the best presentation, even though their's was also excellent.

15. Consider his song idea before you accept hers.

16. It will soon be too late to buy your' mother a gift.

17. Their's is always the first driveway to have it's snow cleared.

18. Is this her scarf, or is it someone else's?

19. Of all the performances, her's was the most impressive.

20. The chair was turned over on it's side.

WRITING APPLICATION

Write three sentences that contain possessive forms of nouns, and punctuate the possessives correctly.

WRITING APPLICATION

Write three sentences that contain the possessive forms of pronouns, and punctuate the possessives correctly. Include at least one personal pronoun and one indefinite pronoun.

PRACTICE 25.6C **Using Apostrophes in Contractions**

Read the sentences. Each sentence contains at least one word group that can be written as a contraction. Write the contractions.

EXAMPLE   Who is going to go to the game?

ANSWER   *Who's*

1. Mom and Dad have not given their permission yet.
2. If you do not want the granola bar, give it to me.
3. Of all the pets we have had, our new parrot is the noisiest.
4. Helen could not remember who was in the movie.
5. We are all in agreement about the chore list.
6. Perry is running across the field.
7. What is the easiest way to get to the mall?
8. If you set the table, I will fix the sandwiches.
9. Where is the key to this lock?
10. Serena wanted to know who would be driving her home.

PRACTICE 25.6D **Proofreading for Apostrophes**

Read the sentences. Rewrite each sentence, adding apostrophes where needed.

EXAMPLE   Ive been waiting here for an hour.

ANSWER   *I've been waiting here for an hour.*

11. I wont be at practice on Tuesday.
12. My niece thinks counting by 2s is fun.
13. Aileen has been ill, but shell be back in school next week.
14. Mrs. Richards suggested that I use fewer *howevers* in my writing.
15. Whats wrong with Cynthia today?
16. The detectives cant seem to solve this case.
17. If you want to get As, youll have to work harder.
18. That little boy shouldnt be crossing the street by himself.
19. His speaking has so many *ums* that it is hard to listen to him sometimes.
20. The play wont be over until at least 10:00.

SPEAKING APPLICATION

With a partner say the following pairs of sentences. Your partner should note how much more casual the second pair sounds.
I will not be late. / I won't be late.
We cannot make a mistake. / We can't make a mistake.

WRITING APPLICATION

Write two sentences with contractions, and make sure each contraction is spelled correctly. Then, write two sentences with plural forms that require apostrophes.

25.7 Parentheses and Brackets

Parentheses and **brackets** enclose explanations or other information that may be omitted from the rest of the sentence without changing its basic meaning or construction.

Parentheses

Parentheses are used to separate information from the rest of a sentence or paragraph.

RULE 25.7.1

Use parentheses to set off explanations or other information that is loosely related to the rest of the sentence.

EXAMPLE   Abraham Lincoln **(**1809–1865**)** led the United States during the Civil War.

RULE 25.7.2

A parenthetical sentence within another sentence should not begin with a capital letter unless the parenthetical sentence begins with a word that should be capitalized.

EXAMPLE   We jumped into the pool **(**the water was freezing**)** and climbed out immediately.

RULE 25.7.3

A parenthetical sentence within another sentence may end with a question mark or exclamation mark if applicable, but it should not end with a period.

INCORRECT   The class trip **(**we all want to go**.)** is planned for the same day as our game**.**

CORRECT   The class trip **(**are you going**?)** is planned for the same day as our game**.**

Parenthetical Sentences That Stand on Their Own

Parenthetical sentences add information to another sentence or a paragraph.

> A **parenthetical sentence** that stands on its own should begin with a capital letter and end with an end mark before the closing parenthesis.

RULE 25.7.4

EXAMPLE   The class trip is planned for the same day as our game**.** **(**Do you think they will change the date**?** **)**

Brackets

Brackets have one major use: to enclose a word or words in a quotation that were not spoken by the person or source that is quoted.

> Use **brackets** to enclose an explanation located within a quote to show that the explanation is not part of the original quote.

RULE 25.7.5

EXAMPLE   Mr. Johnson exclaimed, "This is the first time the baseball team has lost the playoffs since I became coach **[**in 2003**]**."

> Use **brackets** to enclose an explanation that is located within parenthetical text.

RULE 25.7.6

See Practice 25.7A
See Practice 25.7B

EXAMPLE   John Adams **(**the second president of the United States **[**1797–1801**]** **)** was defeated for reelection by Thomas Jefferson.

Parentheses and Brackets

PRACTICE 25.7A Using Parentheses and Brackets

Read the sentences. Rewrite the sentences, adding parentheses or brackets where appropriate.

EXAMPLE   The longer route it follows the river is more scenic.

ANSWER   The longer route *(it follows the river)* is more scenic.

1. Zora Neale Hurston 1891–1960 was influential during the Harlem Renaissance.

2. The entire team all 32 members piled onto the old bus.

3. Principal Yang said, "This fine woman the youth volunteer coordinator can answer your questions."

4. The Earth Day Festival wasn't the weather perfect? was a big success.

5. Queen Elizabeth (she ruled England for 45 years 1558–1603) was the last monarch of the Tudor dynasty.

6. Dr. Gardner stated, "Courses in paleontology the study of dinosaurs are offered at the state college."

PRACTICE 25.7B Proofreading for Parentheses and Brackets

Read the paragraph. Rewrite the paragraph, adding parentheses or brackets where appropriate.

EXAMPLE   The trapping of wild parrots they are sold as pets and loss of habitat have reduced parrot populations.

ANSWER   The trapping of wild parrots *(they are sold as pets)* and loss of habitat have reduced parrot populations.

There are about 372 species a species is the most specific unit of biological classification of parrots. Most parrots have a strong curved bill, very strong legs, and zygodactyl having two toes in the front and two in the back feet. Parrots are usually brightly colored, but some the cockatoo species, to be specific, are white, gray, or black. According to zookeeper Kara Paulson, "Parrots are one of the most diverse bird species in terms of size. Their length can vary from 8 cm 3.2 inches to 1 meter 3.3 feet." Parrots are found mostly in places with tropical climates (areas with warm, moist conditions Brazil and Hawaii, for example).

SPEAKING APPLICATION

With a partner, read the following sentence aloud twice, first without and then with appropriate pauses. *These burritos (they have spinach in them) are delicious.* Discuss which version was easier to understand and why.

WRITING APPLICATION

Write one sentence with information requiring parentheses and one with information requiring brackets.

25.8 Ellipses and Dashes

An **ellipsis** (. . .) shows where words have been omitted from a quoted passage. It can also mark a pause in dialogue. A **dash** (—) shows a strong, sudden break in thought or speech.

Using the Ellipsis

An **ellipsis** consists of three evenly spaced periods, or ellipsis points, in a row. There is a space before the first ellipsis point, between ellipsis points, and after the last ellipsis point. The plural form of the word *ellipsis* is *ellipses*.

> Use an **ellipsis** to show where words have been omitted from a quoted passage. Including an ellipsis shows the reader that the writer has chosen to omit some information.

RULE 25.8.1

QUOTED PASSAGE

"Four score and seven years ago our fathers brought forth on this continent a new nation conceived in liberty and dedicated to the proposition that all men are created equal." –Abraham Lincoln, *The Gettysburg Address,* November 19, 1863

QUOTED PASSAGE WITH WORDS OMITTED

"Fourscore and seven years ago our fathers brought forth . . . a new nation . . . dedicated to the proposition that all men are created equal."

Ellipses in Advertising

Ellipses are commonly used in ads for movies and other media. When you see an ellipsis in an ad, think about what might have been omitted. You might want to find the original review because the ad might be giving a different impression from what the reviewer intended.

ORIGINAL REVIEW

"The news article is neither accurate nor well written and is not recommended reading."

AD WORDING

" . . . accurate . . . well written . . . recommended"

Use an **ellipsis** to mark a pause in a dialogue or speech.

EXAMPLE   "But, in a larger sense, we can not dedicate ... we can not consecrate ... we can not hallow ... this ground."

See Practice 25.8A

It is not necessary to use an **ellipsis** to show an omission at the beginning of material you are quoting. However, if you choose to omit any words *within* material you quote, you must use an ellipsis to show where information has been omitted.

UNNECESSARY   " ... Now we are engaged in a great civil war, testing whether that nation, or any nation, so conceived and so dedicated, can long endure."

CORRECT   "Now we are engaged in a great civil war, testing whether that nation, or any nation so conceived and so dedicated, can long endure."

Use an **ellipsis** to show an omission, pause, or interruption in the middle of a sentence.

EXAMPLE   "But, in a larger sense, we cannot dedicate ... this ground."

Use an **ellipsis** and an end mark to show an omission or a pause at the end of a sentence.

EXAMPLE   "I want to make sure that everyone understood what I just said. We need to. ... "

If you omit words from a source you are quoting, omit the punctuation that accompanies the words unless it is correct in your sentence.

Dashes

Like commas and parentheses, **dashes** separate certain words, phrases, or clauses from the rest of the sentence or paragraph. Dashes, however, signal a stronger, more sudden interruption in thought or speech than commas or parentheses. A dash may also take the place of certain words before an explanation.

Use a dash to show a strong, sudden break in thought or speech.

25.8.6 RULE

EXAMPLE   I can't believe how many goals she scored—Oh, did you see that butterfly?

If the interrupting expression is in the middle of the sentence, use a dash on either side of it to set it off from the rest of the sentence.

EXAMPLE   I read an article—you might have seen it—about the new arena they are building downtown.

Use a dash in place of *in other words, namely,* or *that is* before an explanation.

25.8.7 RULE

EXAMPLES   Dana skateboarded for one reason—pure enjoyment.

To finish her project before the deadline—that is why she is working so hard.

Dashes can also be used to set off nonessential appositives or modifiers.

EXAMPLE   The recycling program—run by the students—has made a real difference in the amount of garbage collected.

See Practice 25.8B

PRACTICE 25.8A > **Using Ellipses**

Read the sentences. For each sentence, tell whether ellipses (or ellipsis points) are used to indicate a *pause* or an *omission*.

EXAMPLE   The text continued, "For thousands of years . . . dogs and men have depended on each other."

ANSWER   *omission*

1. Does this bleak landscape . . . I don't know . . . make you feel melancholy?

2. The speech began, "In our hands is a grand opportunity . . . which we must grasp tightly."

3. According to the review, the book is "a peek into . . . the private lives of nobility."

4. The councilman was famous for this statement: "Progress . . . must never come at the expense of people's dignity."

5. I think . . . to tell you the truth, I'm not sure.

6. It was a day-dreamy kind of day, and . . . my mind was wandering.

7. "Where in this land . . . have we seen no war?" is the first line of the book.

8. Is this . . . the way to the fairgrounds?

9. The letter ended, "And so, my dear friend . . . I will say farewell for now."

10. That painting is so realistic it is as though I can . . . I can . . . actually smell the summer rain.

PRACTICE 25.8B > **Using Dashes**

Read the sentences. Rewrite each sentence, adding dashes where they are needed.

EXAMPLE   There is just one thing I ask of you that you be honest with me.

ANSWER   *There is just one thing I ask of you—that you be honest with me.*

11. The periwinkle I never knew this has many medicinal uses.

12. Hans needed just one more thing to complete his costume a large feather for the hat.

13. Fran told me a story I forget the beginning about a homeless terrier.

14. The software had a bug, and oh, I don't have time to explain.

15. Daffodils at least I think that's what they were adorned every table.

16. June has a reason for waking up so early to have time for a jog in the morning.

17. I'll probably see the hey, Jared, wait up!

18. An entomologist that's someone who studies insects spoke to our science class today.

19. Hydrangeas are interesting plants leafy green shrubs with clumps of tiny white flowers.

20. It's time to wait, don't step there.

SPEAKING APPLICATION

With a partner, read the following two sentences. See if your partner can tell which sentence has an ellipsis and which has a dash.
It was time to go . . . but we lingered by the fire.
Close that—oh, no, the dog has already run off!

WRITING APPLICATION

Write one sentence using punctuation marks, including ellipses, correctly and one sentence using dashes correctly.

CAPITALIZATION

Capitalizing the correct words in your sentences will add a final polish to your writing.

CHAPTER 26

WRITE GUY *Jeff Anderson, M.Ed.*

WHAT DO YOU NOTICE?

Spot the capital letters as you zoom in on this sentence from "Choice: A Tribute to Martin Luther King, Jr." by Alice Walker.

MENTOR TEXT

> In 1960, my mother bought a television set, and each day after school I watched Hamilton Holmes and Charlayne Hunter as they struggled to integrate—fair-skinned as they were—the University of Georgia.

Now, ask yourself the following questions:

- Why is one of the pronouns capitalized?
- Why are certain nouns capitalized while others are not?

The pronoun *I* is always capitalized. The author capitalizes *Hamilton Holmes* and *Charlayne Hunter* because they name specific people. Similarly, because *University of Georgia* is the name of a specific place, the individual nouns in its name are capitalized. Common nouns in the sentence, such as *mother, television set,* and *school,* are not capitalized.

Grammar for Writers Capitalization helps a writer highlight specific people, places, and things for readers. When you use capital letters correctly, you guide readers through your writing.

Should I be capitalized?

Yes, but you should not be.

26.1 Using Capitalization

Capital letters are used for the first words in all sentences and in many quotations. They are also used for the word *I*, whatever its position in a sentence.

The Word *I*

RULE 26.1.1

> The pronoun *I* is always capitalized.

EXAMPLE
I worked for two years as an apprentice before **I** received a promotion.

Sentences

One of the most common uses of a capital letter is to signal the beginning of a sentence. The first word in a sentence must begin with a capital letter.

RULE 26.1.2

> Capitalize the first word in **declarative, interrogative, imperative,** and **exclamatory** sentences.

DECLARATIVE
Strong gusts of wind made it dangerous to walk outside.

INTERROGATIVE
Who found the book I left on the bus this morning?

IMPERATIVE
Think carefully before you respond.

EXCLAMATORY
What an amazing result this is!

See Practice 26.1A
See Practice 26.1B

Sometimes only part of a sentence is written. The rest of the sentence is understood. In these cases, a capital is still needed for the first word.

EXAMPLES
Who? **H**ow so? **I**ndeed!

Quotations

A capital letter also signals the first word in a **direct quotation,** a person's exact words.

> Capitalize the first word in a quotation if the quotation is a complete sentence.

RULE 26.1.3

EXAMPLES   Several people shouted, "**S**top the train!"

"**S**he really wants to go to the concert," Linda confided.

Abby asked, "**D**oes anyone want to play tennis after school?"

> When a quotation consists of one complete sentence in two parts, only capitalize the first part of the quotation.

RULE 26.1.4

EXAMPLES   "**H**ow much longer," asked Bill, "**i**s this meal going to last?"

"**T**he elephant," he said, "**i**s a symbol of wisdom in Asian cultures and is famed for its memory and intelligence."

> If a quotation contains more than one sentence, the first word of each sentence begins with a capital.

RULE 26.1.5

EXAMPLES   "**P**lease distribute these outlines to everyone," said the manager. "**T**hey show the topics we will discuss this afternoon."

"**I**'m finished with the science homework," said Sophie. "**I** will need it for class tomorrow."

See Practice 26.1C
See Practice 26.1D

PRACTICE 26.1A Capitalizing the Word *I* Correctly in Sentences

Read each sentence. Then, rewrite the sentence, correcting any mistakes in capitalization.

EXAMPLE   Silvio and i left the party early.

ANSWER   *Silvio and I left the party early.*

1. If you are going to the mall, can i go with you?

2. Carla picked me for her team even though i've never bowled before.

3. Although i studied hard, i'm not sure i did well on the test.

4. The first ones to arrive were Alex and i.

5. The basket was filled with the peaches i picked.

6. When the polls open, i'll be the first one to vote.

7. The nominative case pronouns include *i* and *we*.

8. Each day, i'm feeling more confident about my language skills.

9. Just he and i were named to the all-star team.

10. Whenever i hear that song, i begin to sing along.

PRACTICE 26.1B Using Capitalization Correctly in Sentences

Read each sentence. Then, rewrite the sentence, correcting any mistakes in capitalization. After the sentence, identify whether it is *declarative, interrogative, imperative,* or *exclamatory*.

EXAMPLE   my mom woke me up before 6:00 this morning.

ANSWER   *My mom woke me up before 6:00 this morning.* (declarative)

11. our house began to shake as the train roared by at 4:00 A.M.

12. the rattling nearly knocked me out of bed.

13. what an incredibly beautiful song!

14. don't waste time; get dressed quickly.

15. where was that loud noise coming from?

16. do your best on the exam.

17. we found our dog Butch under the bed.

18. stay calm, boy, and don't let the noise bother you.

19. when do you think the storm is going to end?

20. i hope we are still driving to seattle tomorrow.

WRITING APPLICATION

Write an e-mail to a friend, discussing upcoming plans. Use *I* or a contraction beginning with *I* at least five times in your e-mail. Make sure you use correct capitalization in your message.

WRITING APPLICATION

Write four sentences about a sports event that you saw live or on television. Make one sentence declarative, one interrogative, one exclamatory, and one imperative. Make sure you use correct capitalization in your sentences.

> **PRACTICE 26.1C** > **Supplying Capitalization**

Read the sentences. Rewrite each sentence, adding the missing capitals.

EXAMPLE   "please clean the table," Yolanda said. "we have visitors on the way."

ANSWER   *"Please clean the table," Yolanda said. "We have visitors on the way."*

1. that arrowhead is thousands of years old.

2. "the decision," Jamal insisted, "is yours."

3. where did you put the new photographs?

4. she and i have been friends for five years.

5. "this assignment is pretty challenging," thought Clarissa.

6. a bus stopped near the corner and let off a little girl.

7. yikes! the cat is tearing up the carpet!

8. consider all the features before you buy a computer.

9. Greta asked, "may Jason and i please have some grapes?"

10. "all the supplies are ready," he said. "we can start painting."

> **PRACTICE 26.1D** > **Proofreading for Capitalization**

Read the sentences. Rewrite each sentence, adding the missing capitals.

EXAMPLE   i lost the ring somewhere. but where?

ANSWER   *I lost the ring somewhere. But where?*

11. what time does the animal shelter open?

12. refer to a dictionary for word origins and spellings.

13. next month? i thought the pool had already been finished.

14. Tamara whispered, "are you awake? i can't sleep."

15. how brave he was!

16. his in-line skates broke the first day he had them.

17. "the yard is clean," she said, "but we still need to mow the grass."

18. "return the book to the library," Julio said. "it is overdue."

19. what? you have to leave already?

20. "we can wait at the subway terminal," said Mr. Romero.

WRITING APPLICATION

Write one declarative sentence, one imperative sentence, and one interrogative sentence. Use capital letters correctly.

WRITING APPLICATION

Use sentences 17, 18, and 20 as models, and write three more sentences with direct quotations, and capitalize them correctly.

Test Warm-Up

DIRECTIONS

Read the introduction and the passage that follows. Then, answer the questions to show that you can use the conventions of capitalization in the context of reading and writing.

Ramon has written this story about a surprising experience he had. Read the story and think about the changes you would suggest as a peer editor. When you finish reading, answer the questions that follow.

Buried Treasure?

(1) While hunting through boxes in the attic, i discovered what appeared to be a treasure map. (2) it was wrinkled and discolored. (3) It had the smell of old paper. (4) According to the map, a treasure was buried inside our hall closet. (5) to get to the treasure, i had to remove years' worth of junk from the closet. (6) When I finished that chore, I found a note taped to the wall. (7) it read, "thanks for the cleaning help—love, mom and dad."

---

1 What change, if any, should be made in sentence 1?

  A Change *hunting* to **hunted**

  B Capitalize *i*

  C Change *discovered* to **discover**

  D Make no change

2 What is the BEST way to combine sentences 2 and 3?

  F It was wrinkled and discolored; It had the smell of old paper.

  G it was wrinkled and discolored, and it had the smell of old paper.

  H It was wrinkled and discolored and smelled like old paper.

  J It was wrinkled, and discolored, and smelled like old paper.

3 How should sentence 5 be revised?

  A To get to the treasure, I had to remove years' worth of junk from the closet.

  B To get to the treasure, i had to remove years' worth of junk from the closet.

  C to get to the treasure, I had to remove years' worth of junk from the closet.

  D To get to the Treasure, I had to remove years' worth of junk from the closet.

4 How should sentence 7 be revised?

  F It read, "Thanks for the cleaning help—love, mom and dad."

  G It read, "Thanks for the cleaning help—love, Mom and Dad."

  H It read, "thanks for the cleaning help—Love, mom and dad."

  J It read, "Thanks for the cleaning help—Love, Mom and Dad."

Using Capitalization for Proper Nouns

An important use of capital letters is to show that a word is a **proper noun.** Proper nouns name specific people, places, or things.

> **Capitalize all proper nouns.**

EXAMPLES   **J**im **T**horpe

Cedar **B**reaks **N**ational **M**onument

Golden **G**ate **B**ridge

Sky **T**ower

Names of People

> **Capitalize each part of a person's full name, including initials.**

EXAMPLES   **B**arbara **A**nn **M**eninger

William **J. T. J**ackson

B. J. Mingle

When a last name has two parts and the first part is *Mac, Mc, O',* or *St.,* the second part of the last name must also be capitalized.

EXAMPLES   **M**ac**G**regor

Mc**G**rath

O'**L**eary

St. **J**ames

For two-part last names that do not begin with *Mac, Mc, O',* or *St.,* the capitalization varies. Check a reliable source, such as a biographical dictionary, for the correct spelling.

See Practice 26.1E

Geographical Places

Any specific geographical location listed on a map should be capitalized.

Capitalize geographical names.

GEOGRAPHICAL NAMES	
Streets	Warren Street, Carlton Avenue, Interstate 10
Cities	Baltimore, London, Memphis, Tokyo
States	Arizona, Florida, Hawaii, Idaho
Nations	Italy, Canada, Kenya, France, Peru, South Korea
Continents	North America, Asia, Africa, Antarctica
Deserts	Sahara, Negev, Mojave
Mountains	Mount Everest, Rocky Mountains
Regions	Great Plains, Appalachian Highlands, Northwest
Islands	Canary Islands, Fiji Islands
Rivers	Mississippi River, Amazon River
Lakes	Lake Michigan, Great Salt Lake, Lake Erie
Bays	Hudson Bay, Baffin Bay, Biscayne Bay
Seas	Black Sea, Mediterranean Sea, North Sea
Oceans	Atlantic Ocean, Arctic Ocean

Regions and Map Directions

Names of regions, such as the South and the Northeast, are capitalized because they refer to a specific geographical location. Map directions that do not refer to a specific geographical location are not capitalized.

Do not capitalize compass points, such as north, southwest, or east, when they simply refer to direction.

REGION   Someday I would like to visit the **S**outheast.

DIRECTION   The train traveled **e**ast for about an hour.

Specific Events and Time Periods

> **Capitalize the names of specific events, periods of time, and documents.**

The following chart contains examples of events, periods of time, and documents that require capitalization.

SPECIFIC EVENTS AND TIMES	
Historical Periods	Age of Enlightenment, Middle Ages, the Renaissance
Historical Events	World War II, Boston Tea Party, Battle of Lexington
Documents	Bill of Rights, Treaty of Paris, Declaration of Independence
Days	Wednesday, Saturday
Months	December, October
Holidays	Thanksgiving, Labor Day
Religious Days	Christmas, Passover, Ramadan
Special Events	Fiddlers' Convention, Boston Marathon, Super Bowl

Names of Seasons
The names of the seasons are an exception to this rule.
Even though they name a specific period of time, the seasons of the year are not capitalized unless they are part of a title or an event name.

SEASONS   In the **f**all, we like to go hiking.

I take most of my vacation in the **s**ummer.

TITLE   Last **w**inter, I read *Driftwood **S**ummer.*

EVENT   It was so hot at the **R**idgewood **F**all Festival

See Practice 26.1F   that it felt like **s**ummer.

PRACTICE 26.1E ▷ Using Capitalization for Names of People

Read the sentences. Write each name, adding the missing capitals.

EXAMPLE   The teacher assigned jeremy mcnabb as allison's lab partner.

ANSWER   *Jeremy McNabb, Allison*

1. The class is studying poetry by walt whitman.

2. Frowning, trina st. paul approached the counter.

3. Mom sent flowers to irene mckinney, who is in the hospital.

4. The letter was addressed to rosa m. garcia.

5. The author walter dean myers was raised by foster parents.

6. She can play music by mozart on the piano.

7. According to sheryl, that story by w. w. jacobs is very suspenseful.

8. Deliver the package to larry o'boyle on the third floor.

9. Have you read anything by julia alvarez?

10. The coach encouraged terri, carlos, and me.

PRACTICE 26.1F ▷ Using Capitalization for Geographical Places, Specific Events, and Time Periods

Read the sentences. Write the name of each geographical place, specific event, and time period, adding the missing capitals.

EXAMPLE   Who is moving into the house on ridgecrest avenue?

ANSWER   *Ridgecrest Avenue*

11. The last two states to be admitted to the united states were alaska and hawaii.

12. Gregory dreams of one day moving to the pacific northwest.

13. The family drove to philadelphia to see a hockey game.

14. My family visited williamsburg, virginia, to learn about the american revolution.

15. The guadalupe river runs through austin, texas.

16. We were amazed by the size of yellowstone national park.

17. The countries of bolivia and peru both border argentina.

18. Are you going to the fall festival next weekend?

19. I just learned that baffin island is part of canada.

20. The scenery on the drive through the san fernando valley was breathtaking.

WRITING APPLICATION

Write three sentences that include people's names, and capitalize them correctly.

WRITING APPLICATION

Write three sentences using at least three different types of geographical names. Make sure to capitalize the names correctly.

Specific Groups

Proper nouns that name specific groups also require capitalization.

> **Capitalize the names of various organizations, government bodies, political parties, and nationalities, as well as the languages spoken by different groups.**

26.1.11 RULE

EXAMPLES   The **P**eace **C**orps helps promote a better understanding of other cultures.

Switzerland's four official languages are **G**erman, **F**rench, **I**talian, and **R**omansch.

John F. Kennedy was the first **B**oy **S**cout to ever become president of the United States.

The proper nouns shown in the chart are groups with which many people are familiar. All specific groups, however, must be capitalized, even if they are not well known.

SPECIFIC GROUPS	
Clubs	Kiwanis Club Rotary Club
Organizations	National Governors Association National Organization for Women
Institutions	Massachusetts Institute of Technology Smithsonian Institution
Businesses	Simon Chemical Corporation Fido's Favorite Pet Foods
Government Bodies	United States Congress Supreme Court
Political Parties	Democrats Republican Party
Nationalities	Chinese, German Nigerian, Iranian
Languages	English, Spanish Korean, Swahili

See Practice 26.1G

Religious References

Use capitals for the names of the religions of the world and certain other words related to religion.

RULE 26.1.12

Capitalize references to religions, deities, and religious scriptures.

The following chart presents words related to five of the world's major religions. Next to each religion are examples of some of the related religious words that must be capitalized. Note that the name of each religion is also capitalized.

RELIGIOUS REFERENCES	
Christianity	God, Lord, Father, Holy Spirit, Bible, books of the Bible (Genesis, Deuteronomy, Psalms, and so on)
Judaism	Lord, Father, Prophets, Torah, Talmud, Midrash
Islam	Allah, Prophet, Mohammed, Quran
Hinduism	Brahma, Bhagavad Gita, Vedas
Buddhism	Buddha, Mahayana, Hinayana

Note in the following examples, however, that the words *god* and *goddess* in references to mythology are not capitalized. A god's or goddess's name, however, is capitalized.

EXAMPLES
In Roman mythology, the **g**od of the sea was **N**eptune.

The **g**oddess **D**iana was the daughter of **J**upiter and was the **g**oddess of the moon.

Specific Places and Items

Monuments, memorials, buildings, celestial bodies, awards, the names of specific vehicles, and trademarked products should be capitalized.

Capitalize the names of specific places and items.

RULE
26.1.13

OTHER SPECIAL PLACES AND ITEMS	
Monuments	Statue of Liberty Washington Monument
Memorials	Winston Churchill Memorial Vietnam Veterans Memorial
Buildings	Houston Museum of Fine Arts Empire State Building the Capitol Building (in Washington, D.C.)
Celestial Bodies (except the moon and sun)	Earth, Milky Way Jupiter, Aries
Awards	Newbery Medal Nobel Peace Prize
Air, Sea, and Space Craft	*Spirit of St. Louis* *Monitor* *Voyager 2* *Metroliner*
Trademarked Brands	Krazy Korn Eco-Friendly Cleanser
Names	Zenox Kermit the Frog the Great Houdini

Capitalize the names of awards.

RULE
26.1.14

Notice that *the* is not capitalized in these examples.

EXAMPLES the Grammy Awards

the Gates Scholarship

the Rookie of the Year Award

See Practice 26.1H   the Good Conduct Medal

PRACTICE 26.1G Using Capitalization for Groups and Organizations

Read the sentences. Write each group or organization, adding the missing capitals.

EXAMPLE   Each state has two representatives in the u.s senate.

ANSWER   *U.S. Senate*

1. Dad recently joined the cedar crest garden club.

2. Mario is a member of the police athletic league.

3. My older sister is attending the university of tennessee.

4. She has always enjoyed the comedy of the british.

5. For more information, contact the national association of broadcasters.

6. Being able to speak portuguese is an advantage in her job.

7. The closest dry cleaner is heights cleaners.

8. Dr. Sanchez is a member of the american medical association.

9. Leila's dad has just started working for the corel corporation.

10. The american kennel club Web site is a good place to start researching dog breeds.

PRACTICE 26.1H Using Capitalization for Religious References and Specific Items and Places

Read the sentences. Write each term that should be capitalized, adding the missing capitals.

EXAMPLE   Crowds of people stood on the steps of the lincoln memorial.

ANSWER   *Lincoln Memorial*

11. The actress won an oscar for her performance.

12. Try clean coat shampoo on your dog.

13. The scriptures of hinduism include the tantras and the agama, among others.

14. The planet venus was named for the Roman goddess of love.

15. In 1985 the space shuttle *atlantis* had its first flight.

16. The tower of london is actually a group of buildings along the Thames River.

17. How many books are there in the new testament?

18. Mom cried when she visited the vietnam veterans memorial.

19. Jan's muslim friend studies the qur'an.

20. One main branch of buddhism is mahayana.

SPEAKING APPLICATION

Read the following sentence aloud to your partner, and have him or her identify each word that should be capitalized.
Scientists used Voyager 2 *to study Triton, a moon of Neptune.*

WRITING APPLICATION

Write three sentences including the following: the name of a specific group or organization, the name of a monument or memorial, and the name of an award.

Using Capitalization for Proper Adjectives

When a proper noun or a form of a proper noun is used to describe another noun, it is called a **proper adjective.** Proper adjectives usually need a capital letter.

Capitalize most proper adjectives.

26.1.15 RULE

In the following examples, notice that both proper nouns and proper adjectives are capitalized. Common nouns that are modified by proper adjectives, however, are not capitalized.

PROPER NOUNS	**K**orean **W**ar
	Cuba
PROPER ADJECTIVES	a **K**orean **W**ar **v**eteran
	a **C**uban **s**andwich

The names of some countries and states must be modified to be used as proper adjectives. For example, something from Kenya is Kenyan, someone from Texas is Texan, a chair from Spain is a Spanish chair, and a building in France is a French building.

Brand Names as Adjectives

Trademarked brand names are considered to be proper nouns. If you use a brand name to describe a common noun, the brand name becomes a proper adjective. In this case, capitalize only the proper adjective and not the common noun.

Capitalize brand names used as adjectives.

26.1.16 RULE

PROPER NOUN	**F**ruit and **R**ice
PROPER ADJECTIVE	**F**ruit and **R**ice **c**ereal

Notice that only the proper adjective *Fruit* and *Rice* is capitalized. The word *cereal* is not capitalized because it is a common noun; it is not part of the trademarked name.

See Practice 26.1l

Using Capitalization for Titles of People

A person's title shows his or her relationship to other people. Whether a title is capitalized often depends on how it is used in a sentence.

Social and Professional Titles

Social and professional titles may be written before a person's name or used alone in place of a person's name.

> Capitalize the title of a person when the title is followed by the person's name or when it is used in place of a person's name in direct address.

BEFORE A NAME
Professor Walsh and **D**ean Smith have approved.

IN DIRECT ADDRESS
Look, **C**orporal, here is the missing weapon!

TITLES OF PEOPLE	
Social	Mister, Madam or Madame, Miss, Ms., Sir
Business	Doctor, Professor, Superintendent
Religious	Reverend, Father, Rabbi, Bishop, Sister
Military	Private, Ensign, Captain, General, Admiral
Government	President, Senator, Representative, Governor, Mayor, Prince, Queen, King

In most cases, do not capitalize titles that are used alone or that follow a person's name—especially if the title is preceded by the articles *a, an,* or *the.*

EXAMPLES
James Goodman, your **a**ttorney, will meet you at the closing.

Tell your **d**octor if you do not feel better soon.

My sister Mary, who is a **p**rivate in the army, will be home on leave soon.

Government Officials

> Capitalize the titles of government officials when they immediately precede the name of specific officials. If no person is named, these titles should be written in lower case.

RULE 26.1.18

EXAMPLES

Congressman **C**lark will throw the honorary first pitch at the new stadium.

Our **c**ongresswoman will throw the honorary first pitch at the new stadium.

Governor **P**aterson is the highest executive authority in the state government.

The **g**overnor is the highest executive authority in a state government.

Note: Certain honorary titles are always capitalized, even if the title is not used with a proper name or direct address. These titles include the First Lady of the United States, Speaker of the House of Representatives, Queen Mother of England, and the Prince of Wales.

Titles for Family Relationships

> Capitalize titles showing family relationships when the title is used with the person's name or as the person's name—except when the title comes after a possessive noun or pronoun.

RULE 26.1.19

BEFORE A NAME

We agree with **U**ncle Bob's position.

IN PLACE OF A NAME

Is **G**randma going to join us?

AFTER POSSESSIVES

Kaitlyn's **u**ncle Bob is the team mascot.

See Practice 26.1J

Notice that the family title *uncle* used in the last example is not capitalized because it is used after the possessive word *Kaitlyn's*.

PRACTICE 26.1I > **Using Capitalization for Proper Adjectives**

Read the sentences. Write the proper adjectives, adding the correct capitalization.

EXAMPLE   Judith is training her dog, an irish setter, in agility.

ANSWER   *Irish*

1. In the living room stood an antique victorian armchair.

2. Who is your favorite character from the arthurian legends?

3. The family usually buys american cars.

4. Does that japanese restaurant serve sushi?

5. Heather was looking for a translated version of that french novel.

6. Doesn't swiss cheese taste good on a turkey sandwich?

7. The professor speaks with a strong german accent.

8. Sometimes these montana winters are harsh.

9. The manhattan skyline looked magical at twilight.

10. Kayla loves studying roman mythology.

PRACTICE 26.1J > **Using Capitalization for Titles of People**

Read the sentences. If the title in each sentence is correctly capitalized, write *correct*. If it is not, rewrite the title correctly.

EXAMPLE   Have you seen superintendent Ferguson this morning?

ANSWER   *Superintendent*

11. Please, colonel, tell us the plan.

12. Has mayor Gomez held elective office before?

13. The queen, Elizabeth, looked over a crowd of her subjects.

14. Excuse me, mr. Jackson, but I need to get through.

15. We took aunt Crystal out for her birthday.

16. The ceremony was conducted by reverend Hill.

17. I really miss my cousin Darius since he moved out of town.

18. Keith told mom you would be late.

19. Paul Rubenstein, the sergeant on duty, will return your call.

20. The president and his family live in the White House.

WRITING APPLICATION

Write three sentences with proper adjectives, and capitalize them correctly.

WRITING APPLICATION

Write two sentences with titles of people, one that requires a capital and one that does not.

Using Capitalization for Titles of Works

Capital letters are used for the titles of things such as written works, pieces of art, and school courses.

> **Capitalize the first word and all other key words in the titles of books, newspapers, magazines, short stories, poems, plays, movies, songs, and artworks.**

26.1.20 RULE

Do not capitalize articles (*a, an, the*), prepositions (*of, to*), and conjunctions (*and, but*) that are fewer than four letters long unless they begin a title. Verbs and personal pronouns, no matter how short, are always capitalized in titles.

EXAMPLE   "**N**ot **W**anted" by Anton Chekhov

> **Capitalize the title of a school course when it is followed by a course number or when it refers to a language. Otherwise, do not capitalize school subjects.**

26.1.21 RULE

EXAMPLES   **S**panish   **B**iology 250   **H**istory II

I have **h**istory in the afternoon.

Using Capitalization in Letters

Several parts of friendly and business letters are capitalized.

> **In the heading, capitalize the street, city, state, and the month.**

26.1.22 RULE

EXAMPLES   **S**econd **S**treet   **B**illings   **M**ontana **A**pril

> **In the salutation, capitalize the first word, any title, and the name of the person or group mentioned. In the closing, capitalize the first word.**

26.1.23 RULE

See Practice 26.1K

SALUTATIONS   **M**y **d**ear **F**rancis,   **D**ear **U**ncle **R**udy,

See Practice 26.1L   **CLOSINGS**   **Y**our **p**artner,   **Y**ours **f**orever,   **L**ove,

PRACTICE 26.1K > **Using Capitalization for Titles of Things**

Read the sentences. Write the titles, adding the correct capitalization.

EXAMPLE   The show *are you afraid of the dark?* ran for five seasons in the 1990s.

ANSWER   *Are You Afraid of the Dark?*

1. Jared has seen *spider-man* several times.

2. The *daily tribune* has an article about the election.

3. Mom reads each issue of *modern housekeeping* from cover to cover.

4. Pablo drew illustrations to go with his poem "ode to the snail on the wall."

5. Hannah is taking sociology 101 and computer science 141 at the community college.

6. For my science report I consulted *the handy weather answer book.*

7. Tamesa read the chapter "rise of the empire" for social studies class.

8. One of Jack London's most famous works is the novel *the call of the wild.*

9. *The boating party,* by Mary Cassatt, will be one of the paintings featured in the exhibit.

10. My five-year-old nephew loves to sing "if you're happy and you know it."

PRACTICE 26.1L > **Using Capitalization for Titles of Things**

Read the sentences. Rewrite each sentence, adding the missing capitals.

EXAMPLE   Consider taking chemistry 101 and also psychology.

ANSWER   *Consider taking Chemistry 101 and also psychology.*

11. "when you wish upon a star" is still one of my mother's favorite songs.

12. Isn't *my fair lady* a musical based on George Bernard Shaw's play *pygmalion*?

13. I really like the characters in *sword of the rightful king.*

14. In biology we are reading the chapter "cells and how they work."

15. Hector's sculpture, *cats napping on rugs,* won first prize at the art show.

16. Mom has renewed her subscription to *the dillsburg journal.*

17. Mr. Tanger teaches algebra II and also calculus.

18. "all summer in a day" is a short story by science-fiction writer Ray Bradbury.

19. Megan enjoyed reading Donald Hall's poem "names of horses."

20. Who starred in the movie *angels in the outfield?*

WRITING APPLICATION

Write the titles of your favorite movie, your favorite television show, your favorite book, and your favorite song. Capitalize each title correctly.

WRITING APPLICATION

Write three sentences with titles of works and school courses, using capitalization correctly.

Using Capitalization in Abbreviations, Acronyms, and Initials

An **abbreviation** is a shortened form of a word or phrase. An **acronym** is an abbreviation of a phrase that takes one or more letters from each word in the phrase being abbreviated.

> In general, capitalize **abbreviations, acronyms,** and **initials** if the words or names they stand for are capitalized.

RULE 26.1.24

INITIALS	**R. U.** Goodman
TITLES	**R**ev. Adam Clayton Powell **J**r.
ACADEMIC DEGREES	Mark Greene, **M.D.**, Ben Casey, **Ph.D.**
ACRONYMS	**NAFTA**, **MIA**

Abbreviations for most units of measurement are not capitalized.

EXAMPLES   **c**m (centimeters)   **g**al (gallons)

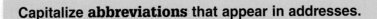

> Capitalize **abbreviations** that appear in addresses.

RULE 26.1.25

Use a two-letter state abbreviation without periods only when the abbreviation is followed by a ZIP Code. Capitalize both letters of the state abbreviation.

EXAMPLE   Albany, **NY** 12207

> Capitalize **acronyms** that stand for proper nouns, such as businesses, government bodies, and organizations.

RULE 26.1.26

Spell out the name of an organization and include its acronym in parentheses the first time you use it. Use only the acronym in later references.

EXAMPLE   Have you heard of the Federal Bureau of Investigation (**FBI**)? The **FBI** protects and defends the United States against foreign threats.

See Practice 26.1M
See Practice 26.1N

PRACTICE 26.1M > **Using Capitalization for Abbreviations**

Read the items. Rewrite each item, adding capitals as needed. If the item is already correct, write *correct*.

EXAMPLE   mrs. Lillian Munson

ANSWER   *Mrs. Lillian Munson*

1. mt. Hood
2. Dan Jones, m.d.
3. Polk's Sporting Goods, ltd.
4. Santa Fe, nm 87501
5. 3366 Fairbanks rd.
6. mr. Kenneth Young jr.
7. 3 ft 5 in.
8. dr. Rosita Jimenez
9. Mary Ellen Morrison, ph.d.
10. a speed limit of 35 mph

PRACTICE 26.1N > **Using Capitalization for Initials and Acronyms**

Read the sentences. Write the initials and acronyms, adding capitals as needed. If a sentence is correct, write *correct*.

EXAMPLE   The Federal Housing Administration, usually referred to as the fha, insures home loans.

ANSWER   *FHA*

11. Mrs. Johnson belongs to the nea (that stands for National Education Association).
12. That medication has not yet been approved by the fda.
13. Arthur w. t. McFearson is my grandfather.
14. The Super Bowl is the biggest event in the nfl each year.
15. Astronauts for nasa have completed years of studying and training.
16. What is the difference between the fbi and the cia?
17. Jaime's mom belongs to the Society of Professional Accountants (spa).
18. I never knew the word *radar* was originally an acronym for *radio detection and ranging*.
19. The Tennessee Volunteers will play in the ncaa tournament this year.
20. That poem about cats is by T. S. Eliot.

WRITING APPLICATION

Write two sentences with abbreviations that require capitals and two with abbreviations that do not need capitals.

WRITING APPLICATION

Write a short paragraph containing two acronyms and two other kinds of abbreviations. (You may make up the acronyms if you wish, but make sure to tell what they stand for.) Use correct capitalization in your paragraph.

PRACTICE 1 Using Periods, Question Marks, and Exclamation Marks

Read the sentences. Then, rewrite the sentences, adding periods, question marks, and exclamation marks where needed.

1. Lou Jr lives on S Congress St in Tucson
2. Where is the central headquarters of the CIA
3. Please be seated
4. What a delicious meal this is
5. She asked if we were comfortable
6. Don't go near that alligator
7. Is he helping with the invitations
8. Oops Did I forget the picnic basket
9. How wonderful our vacation was
10. The coach is taking notes Why

PRACTICE 2 Using Commas Correctly

Read the sentences. Then, rewrite the sentences, adding commas where needed. If a sentence is correct as is, write *correct*.

1. The albatross a large bird is central to the poem.
2. He called "Hey Bella when are you coming?"
3. Before you drop by please give me a call.
4. I asked my friends but no one knew the answer.
5. Her rough chapped hands need lotion of course.
6. The address is 49 Washington Street Newark New Jersey 07102.
7. I left it in my pocket on the table or in my bag.
8. The store had 1224 customers on May 4 2009.
9. I knitted those two blue hats in January 2008.
10. "To get here" Bud explained "take Route 90."

PRACTICE 3 Using Colons, Semicolons, and Quotation Marks

Read the sentences. Then, rewrite the sentences, using colons, semicolons, and quotation marks where needed. If a sentence is correct as is, write *correct*.

1. What poet said, Whatever is, is right?
2. Buy the following items pens, pads, and a ruler.
3. Well, said Shari, the concert starts at 730.
4. The curry was delicious, I love Indian food.
5. Terry asked me for help with the computer.
6. Warning Stay seated until the train stops.
7. Beth asked, Where are you going?
8. How very much I like that poem The Raven!
9. Joe was late, however, we still found good seats.
10. The kosher restaurant served borscht, a soup, knishes, an appetizer, and blintzes, a dessert.

PRACTICE 4 Using Apostrophes Correctly

Read the sentences. Then, rewrite the sentences, adding or removing apostrophes as needed. If a sentence is correct as is, write *correct*.

1. The cat closes it's eyes when its happy.
2. Gregs late and wont help with Kims party.
3. Only three students grades were lower than Cs.
4. Greek mythology tells of Hades' dark regions.
5. This is Alexis's seat, not someone elses.
6. Show me whats ours and whats hers.
7. Theirs is the best stall in the vegetable market.
8. Lana could'nt ever come on Monday's.
9. I wont say hes wrong, but I cant say hes right.
10. The team has its picture in the 2009 yearbook.

Continued on next page ▶

Cumulative Review   Chapters 25–26

PRACTICE 5 ▷ **Using Underlining (or Italics), Hyphens, Dashes, Parentheses, Brackets, and Ellipses**

Read the sentences. Then, rewrite the sentences, adding underlining (or italics if you type your answers on a computer), hyphens, dashes, brackets, parentheses, and ellipses. If a sentence is correct as is, write *correct*.

1. I asked Nino he just moved here from Italy if he would tell us about his childhood.

2. Her brother in law is thirty four years old.

3. Who wrote the novel Friendly Persuasion?

4. The film is set during the Civil War 1861–1865.

5. Her nicely written columns won a Pulitzer Prize.

6. The Titanic, a famous luxury cruise ship, sank after hitting an iceberg.

7. The Preamble says: "We, the people . . . establish this Constitution of the United States."

8. Congress voted on the bill. Click here for a list of members' votes H.R. 301.

9. Becky's dream a modeling career got off to a rocky start.

10. In his speech the librarian said, "She meaning Mrs. Finch is our most generous patron."

PRACTICE 6 ▷ **Using Correct Capitalization**

Read the sentences. Then, rewrite each sentence, using capital letters where they are needed.

1. on sunday, mom heated a can of joy luck soup.

2. in the midwest, we stayed near lake superior.

3. the treaty of ghent ended the war of 1812.

4. w. b. yeats, an irish poet, wrote the poem "the lake isle of innisfree."

5. "the first time i visited doctor rivera," said harry, "was in april of 2004."

6. the planet neptune is named for the roman god neptune, whom the greeks called poseidon.

7. the clark art institute is just west of route 7 at 225 south street in williamstown, massachusetts.

8. was grandmother once a spy for the cia?

9. Katie lives in an apartment building called city towers.

10. novelist pearl s. buck won the nobel prize.

11. former president teddy roosevelt left the republican party to form the bull moose party.

12. my sister takes geology 101 at emory university.

13. the statue of liberty was a gift from the french.

14. what bible text did reverend lee cite on sunday?

15. "i met tom," said nina, "last winter in ohio."

PRACTICE 7 ▷ **Writing Letters With Correct Capitalization and Punctuation**

Write an imaginary business letter with the following information. Use correct capitalization and punctuation.

1. your return address, followed by today's date

2. the addressee (any real city's or town's visitors' information bureau—you can invent the bureau's exact name and address)

3. any appropriate greeting, beginning with *dear*

4. a body of four or five sentences asking about specific tourist sites in the city or town

5. a closing, beginning with *very* or *most*

6. your signature

RESOURCES FOR Writing COACH

WRITING IN THE
Content Areas

Writing in the content areas—math, social studies, science, the arts, and various career and technical studies—is an important tool for learning. The following pages give examples of content area writing along with strategies.

FORMS OF MATH WRITING

Written Estimate An estimate, or informed idea, of the size, cost, time, or other measure of a thing, based on given information.

Analysis of a Problem A description of a problem, such as figuring out how long a trip will take, along with an explanation of the mathematical formulas or equations you can use to solve the problem.

Response to an Open-Ended Math Prompt A response to a question or writing assignment involving math, such as a word problem or a question about a graph or a mathematical concept.

Writing in Math

Prewriting

- **Choosing a Topic** If you have a choice of topics, review your textbook and class notes for ideas, and choose one that interests you.

- **Responding to a Prompt** If you are responding to a prompt, read and then reread the instructions, ensuring that you understand all of the requirements of the assignment.

Drafting

- **State Problems Clearly** Be clear, complete, and accurate in your description of the problem you are analyzing or reporting on. Make sure that you have used technical terms, such as *ratio*, *area*, and *factor*, accurately.

- **Explain Your Solution** Tell readers exactly which mathematical rules or formulas you use in your analysis and why they apply. Clearly spell out each step you take in your reasoning.

- **Use Graphics** By presenting quantitative information in a graph, table, or chart, you make it easier for readers to absorb information. Choose the format appropriate to the material, as follows:

  ✔ **Line Graphs** Use a line graph to show the relationship between two variables, such as time and speed in a problem about a moving object. Clearly label the x- and y-axis with the variable each represents and with the units you are using. Choose units appropriately to make the graph manageable. For example, do not try to represent time in years if you are plotting changes for an entire century; instead, use units of ten years each.

  ✔ **Other Graphs** Use a pie chart to analyze facts about a group, such as the percentage of students who walk to school, the percentage who drive, and the percentage who take the bus. Use a bar graph to compare two or more things at different times or in different categories. Assign a single color to each thing, and use that color consistently for all the bars representing data about that thing.

  ✔ **Tables** Use a table to help readers look up specific values quickly, such as the time the sun sets in each month of the year. Label each column and row with terms that clearly identify the data you are presenting, including the units you are using.

Revising

- **Ensure Accuracy** For accuracy, double-check the formulas you use and the calculations you make.

- **Revise for Traits of Good Writing** Ask yourself the following questions: *How well have I applied mathematical ideas? Does my organizational plan help readers follow my reasoning? Is my voice suitable to my audience and purpose? Have I chosen precise words and used mathematical terms accurately? Are my sentences well constructed and varied? Have I made any errors in grammar, usage, mechanics, and spelling?* Use your answers to help you revise and edit your work.

Writing in Science

Prewriting

- **Choosing a Topic** If you have a choice of topics, look through class notes and your textbook, or conduct a "media flip-through," browsing online articles, or watching television news and documentaries to find a science-related topic.

- **Responding to a Prompt** If you are responding to a prompt, read the instructions carefully, analyzing the requirements and parts of the assignment. Identify key direction words in the prompt or assignment, such as *explain* and *predict*.

- **Gathering Details**
  - ✔ If your assignment requires you to conduct research, search for credible and current sources. Examples of strong sources may include articles in recent issues of science magazines or recently published books. Confirm key facts in more than one source.
  - ✔ If your assignment requires you to conduct an experiment, make sure you follow the guidelines for the experiment accurately. Carefully record the steps you take and the observations you make, and date your notes. Repeat the experiment to confirm results.

Drafting

- **Focus and Elaborate** In your introduction, clearly state your topic. Make sure you tell readers why your topic matters. As you draft, give sufficient details, including background, facts, and examples, to help your readers understand your topic. Summarize your findings and insights in your conclusion.

- **Organize** As you draft, follow a suitable organizational pattern. If you are telling the story of an important scientific breakthrough, consider telling events in chronological order. If you are explaining a natural process, consider discussing causes and the effects that follow from them. If you are defending a solution to a problem, you might give pros and cons, answering each counterargument in turn.

- **Present Data Visually** Consider presenting quantitative information, such as statistics or measurements, in a graph, table, or chart. Choose the format appropriate to the material. (Consult the guidance on visual displays of data under "Use Graphics" on page R2.)

Revising

- **Meet Your Audience's Needs** Identify places in your draft where your audience may need more information, such as additional background, more explanation, or the definition of a technical term. Add the information required.

- **Revise for Traits of Good Writing** Ask yourself the following questions: *How clearly have I presented scientific ideas? Will my organization help a reader see the connections I am making? Is my voice suitable to my audience and purpose? Have I chosen precise words and used technical terms accurately? Are my sentences well constructed and varied? Have I made any errors in grammar, usage, mechanics, and spelling?* Use your answers to revise and edit your work.

FORMS OF SCIENCE WRITING

Lab Report A firsthand report of a scientific experiment, following an appropriate format. A standard lab report includes a statement of the hypothesis, or prediction, that the experiment is designed to test; a list of the materials used; an account of the steps performed; a report of the results observed; and the experimenter's conclusions.

Cause-and-Effect Essay A scientific explanation of the causes and effects involved in natural or technical phenomena, such as solar flares, the digestion of food, or the response of metal to stress.

Technical Procedure Document A step-by-step guide to performing a scientific experiment or performing a technical task involving science. A well-written technical procedure document presents the steps of the procedure in clear order. It breaks steps into substeps and prepares readers by explaining what materials they will need and the time they can expect each step to take.

Response to an Open-Ended Science Prompt A response to a question or writing assignment about science.

Summary of a Science-Related Article A retelling of the main ideas in an article that concerns science or technology, such as an article on a new medical procedure.

Writing in Social Studies

Prewriting

- **Choosing a Topic** If you have a choice of topics, find a suitable topic by looking through class notes and your textbook. Make a quick list of topics in history, politics, or geography that interest you and choose a topic based on your list.

- **Responding to a Prompt** If you are responding to a prompt, read the instructions carefully, analyzing the requirements and parts of the assignment. Identify key direction words in the prompt or assignment, such as *compare*, *describe*, and *argue*.

- **Gathering Details** If your assignment requires you to conduct research, consult a variety of credible sources. For in-depth research, review both primary sources (documents from the time you are investigating) and secondary sources (accounts by those who analyze or report on the information). If you find contradictions, evaluate the likely reasons for the differences.

Drafting

- **Establish a Thesis or Theme** If you are writing a research report or other informative piece, state your main point about your topic in a thesis statement. Include your thesis statement in your introduction. If you are writing a creative piece, such as a historical skit or short story, identify the theme, or main message, you wish to convey.

- **Support Your Thesis or Theme** Organize your work around your main idea.

  ✔ In a research report, support and develop your thesis with well-chosen, relevant details. First, provide background information your readers will need, and then discuss different subtopics in different sections of the body of your report. Clearly connect each subtopic to your main thesis.

  ✔ In a creative work, develop your theme through the conflict between characters. For example, a conflict between two brothers during the Civil War over which side to fight on might dramatize the theme of divided loyalties. Organize events to build to a climax, or point of greatest excitement, that clearly conveys your message.

Revising

- **Sharpen Your Focus** Review your draft for sections that do not clearly support your thesis or theme, and consider eliminating them. Revise unnecessary repetition of ideas. Ensure that the sequence of ideas or events will help reader comprehension.

- **Revise for Traits of Good Writing** Ask yourself the following questions: *How clearly have I developed my thesis or my theme? Will my organization help a reader follow my development of my thesis or theme? Is my voice suitable to my audience and purpose? Have I chosen precise and vivid words, accurately using terms from the period or place about which I am writing? Are my sentences well constructed and varied? Have I made any errors in grammar, usage, mechanics, and spelling?* Use your answers to revise and edit your work.

FORMS OF SOCIAL STUDIES WRITING

Social Studies Research Report
An informative paper, based on research, about a historical period or event or about a specific place or culture. A well-written research report draws on a variety of sources to develop and support a thoughtful point of view on the topic. It cites those sources accurately, following an accepted format.

Biographical Essay An overview of the life of a historically important person. A well-written biographical essay reports the life of its subject accurately and clearly explains the importance of his or her contributions.

Historical Overview A survey, or general picture, of a historical period or development, such as the struggle for women's right to vote. A successful historical overview presents the "big picture," covering major events and important aspects of the topic without getting lost in details.

Historical Cause-and-Effect Essay An analysis of the causes and effects of a historical event. A well-written historical explanation makes clear connections between events to help readers follow the explanation.

Writing About the Arts

Prewriting

Experience the Work Take notes on the subject of each work you will discuss. Consider its mood, or general feeling, and its theme, or insight into life.

✔ For visual arts, consider the use of color, light, line (sharp or smooth, smudged or definite), mass (heavy or light), and composition (the arrangement and balance of forms).

✔ For music, consider the use of melody, rhythm, harmony, and instrumentation. Also, consider the performers' interpretation of the work.

Drafting

Develop Your Ideas As you draft, support your main ideas, including your insights into or feelings about a work, with relevant details.

Revising

Revise for Traits of Good Writing Ask yourself the following questions: *How clearly do I present my ideas? Will my organization help a reader follow my points? Is my voice suitable to my audience and purpose? Have I chosen precise and vivid words, to describe the works? Are my sentences varied? Have I made any errors in grammar, usage, and mechanics?* Use your answers to revise and edit your work.

Writing in Career and Technical Studies

Prewriting

Choosing a Topic If you have a choice of topics, find a suitable one by looking through class notes and your textbook or by listing your own related projects or experiences.

Drafting

Organize Information As you draft, follow a logical organization. If you are explaining a procedure, list steps in the order that your readers should follow. If they need information about the materials and preparation required, provide that information first. Use formatting (such as headings, numbered steps, and bullet points), graphics (such as diagrams), and transitional words and phrases (such as *first*, *next*, and *if… then*).

Revising

Revise for Traits of Good Writing Ask yourself the following questions: *Have I given readers all the information they will need? Will my organization help a reader follow my points? Is my voice suitable to my audience and purpose? Have I chosen precise words, using technical terms accurately? Are my sentences well constructed? Have I made errors in grammar, usage, and mechanics?* Use your answers to revise and edit your work.

FORMS OF WRITING ABOUT THE ARTS

Research Report on a Trend or Style in Art An informative paper, based on research, about a specific group of artists or trend in the arts.

Biographical Essay An overview of the life of an artist or performer.

Analysis of a Work A detailed description of a work offering insights into its meaning and importance.

Review of a Performance or Exhibit An evaluation of an artistic performance or exhibit.

FORMS OF CAREER AND TECHNICAL WRITING

Technical Procedure Document A step-by-step guide to performing a specialized task, such as wiring a circuit or providing first aid.

Response to an Open-Ended Practical Studies Prompt A response to a question or writing assignment about a task or concept in a specialized field.

Technical Research Report An informative paper, based on research, about a specific topic in a practical field, such as a report on balanced diet in the field of health.

Analysis of a Career An informative paper explaining the requirements for a particular job, along with the responsibilities, salary, benefits, and job opportunities.

WRITING FOR
Media

New technology has created many new ways to communicate. Today, it is easy to contribute information to the Internet and send a variety of messages to friends far and near. You can also share your ideas through photos, illustrations, video, and sound recordings.

Writing for Media gives you an overview of some ways you can use today's technology to create, share, and find information. **Here are the topics you will find in this section:**

- **Blogs**

- **Social Networking**

- **Widgets and Feeds**

- **Multimedia Elements**

- **Podcasts**

- **Wikis**

Blogs

A **blog** is a common form of online writing. The word *blog* is a contraction of *Web log*. Most blogs include a series of entries known as posts. The posts appear in a single column and are displayed in reverse chronological order. That means that the most recent post is at the top of the page. As you scroll down, you will find earlier posts.

Blogs have become increasingly popular. Researchers estimate that 75,000 new blogs are launched every day. Blog authors are often called bloggers. They can use their personal sites to share ideas, songs, videos, photos, and other media. People who read blogs can often post their responses with a comments feature found in each new post.

Because blogs are designed so that they are easy to update, bloggers can post new messages as often as they like, often daily. For some people blogs become a public journal or diary in which they share their thoughts about daily events.

Types of Blogs

Not all blogs are the same. Many blogs have a single author, but others are group projects. These are some common types of blog:

- **Personal blogs** often have a general focus. Bloggers post their thoughts on any topic they find interesting in their daily lives.

- **Topical blogs** focus on a specific theme, such as movie reviews, political news, class assignments, or health-care opportunities.

 WEB SAFETY Using the Internet safely means keeping personal information personal. Never include your address (e-mail or physical), last name, or telephone numbers. Avoid mentioning places you go to often.

Never give out passwords you use to access other Web sites and do not respond to e-mails from people you do not know.

Anatomy of a Blog

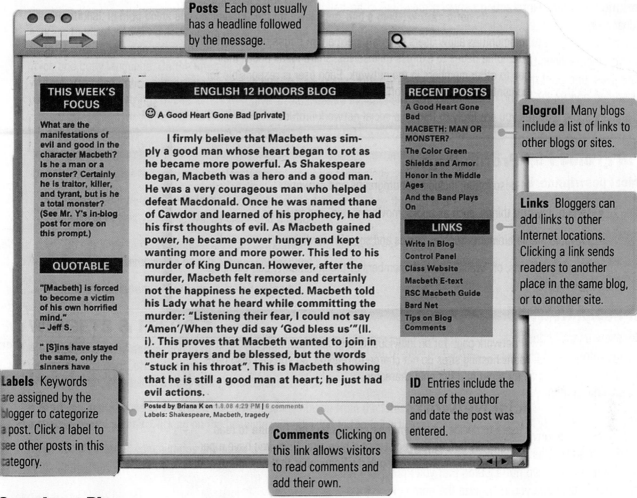

Posts Each post usually has a headline followed by the message.

THIS WEEK'S FOCUS

What are the manifestations of evil and good in the character Macbeth? Is he a man or a monster? Certainly he is traitor, killer, and tyrant, but is he a total monster? (See Mr. Y's in-blog post for more on this prompt.)

QUOTABLE

"[Macbeth] is forced to become a victim of his own horrified mind."
– Jeff S.

" [S]ins have stayed the same, only the sinners have

ENGLISH 12 HONORS BLOG

☺ A Good Heart Gone Bad [private]

I firmly believe that Macbeth was simply a good man whose heart began to rot as he became more powerful. As Shakespeare began, Macbeth was a hero and a good man. He was a very courageous man who helped defeat Macdonald. Once he was named thane of Cawdor and learned of his prophecy, he had his first thoughts of evil. As Macbeth gained power, he became power hungry and kept wanting more and more power. This led to his murder of King Duncan. However, after the murder, Macbeth felt remorse and certainly not the happiness he expected. Macbeth told his Lady what he heard while committing the murder: "Listening their fear, I could not say 'Amen'/When they did say 'God bless us'"(II. i). This proves that Macbeth wanted to join in their prayers and be blessed, but the words "stuck in his throat". This is Macbeth showing that he is still a good man at heart; he just had evil actions.

Posted by Briana K on 1.8.08 4:29 PM | 6 comments
Labels: Shakespeare, Macbeth, tragedy

RECENT POSTS

A Good Heart Gone Bad
MACBETH: MAN OR MONSTER?
The Color Green
Shields and Armor
Honor in the Middle Ages
And the Band Plays On

LINKS

Write In Blog
Control Panel
Class Website
Macbeth E-text
RSC Macbeth Guide
Bard Net
Tips on Blog Comments

Blogroll Many blogs include a list of links to other blogs or sites.

Links Bloggers can add links to other Internet locations. Clicking a link sends readers to another place in the same blog, or to another site.

Labels Keywords are assigned by the blogger to categorize a post. Click a label to see other posts in this category.

Comments Clicking on this link allows visitors to read comments and add their own.

ID Entries include the name of the author and date the post was entered.

Creating a Blog

Keep these hints and strategies in mind to help you create an interesting and fair blog:

- Focus each blog entry on a single topic.

- Vary the length of your posts. Sometimes, all you need is a line or two to share a quick thought. Other posts will be much longer.

- Choose font colors and styles that can be read easily.

- Many people scan blogs rather than read them closely. You can make your main ideas pop out by using clear or clever headlines and boldfacing key terms.

- Give credit to other people's work and ideas. State the names of people whose ideas you are quoting or add a link to take readers to that person's blog or site.

- If you post comments, try to make them brief and polite.

Social Networking

Social networking means any interaction between members of an online community. People can exchange many different kinds of information, from text and voice messages to video images. Many social network communities allow users to create permanent pages that describe themselves. Users create home pages to express themselves, share ideas about their lives, and post messages to other members in the network. Each user is responsible for adding and updating the content on his or her profile page.

Here are some features you are likely to find on a social network profile:

Features of Profile Pages

- A **biographical description**, including photographs and artwork

- **Lists of favorite things**, such as books, movies, music, and fashions

- **Playable media** elements such as videos and sound recordings

- **Message boards**, or "walls," on which members of the community can exchange messages

Privacy in Social Networks

Social networks allow users to decide how open their profiles will be. Be sure to read introductory information carefully before you register at a new site. Once you have a personal profile page, monitor your privacy settings regularly. Remember that any information you post will be available to anyone in your network.

Users often post messages anonymously or using false names, or pseudonyms. People can also post using someone else's name. Judge all information on the net critically. Do not assume that you know who posted some information simply because you recognize the name of the post author. The rapid speed of communication on the Internet can make it easy to jump to conclusions—be careful to avoid this trap.

> You can create a social network page for an individual or a group, such as a school or special interest club. Many hosting sites do not charge to register, so you can also have fun by creating a page for a pet or a fictional character.

Tips for Sending Effective Messages

Technology makes it easy to share ideas quickly, but writing for the Internet poses some special challenges. The writing style for blogs and social networks is often very conversational. In blog posts and comments, instant messages, and e-mails, writers often express themselves very quickly, using relaxed language, short sentences, and abbreviations. However in a face-to-face conversation, we get a lot of information from a speaker's tone of voice and body language. On the Internet, those clues are missing. As a result, Internet writers often use italics or bracketed labels to indicate emotions. Another alternative is using emoticons—strings of characters that give visual clues to indicate emotion.

:-) **smile** *(happy)*   :-(**frown** *(unhappy)*   ;-) **wink** *(light sarcasm)*

> *Use these strategies to communicate effectively when using technology:*
>
> ✔ *Before you click Send, **reread your message** to make sure that your tone is clear.*
>
> ✔ ***Do not jump to conclusions**—ask for clarification first. Make sure you really understand what someone is saying before you respond.*
>
> ✔ ***Use abbreviations** your reader will understand.*

Widgets and Feeds

A **widget** is a small application that performs a specific task. You might find widgets that give weather predictions, offer dictionary definitions or translations, provide entertainment such as games, or present a daily word, photograph, or quotation.

A **feed** is a special kind of widget. It displays headlines taken from the latest content on a specific media source. Clicking on the headline will take you to the full article. Many social network communities and other Web sites allow you to personalize your home page by adding widgets and feeds.

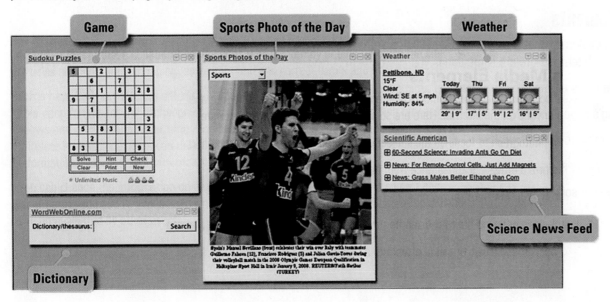

Multimedia Elements

One of the great advantages of communicating on the Internet is that you are not limited to using text only. When you create a Web profile or blog, you can share your ideas using a wide variety of media. In addition to widgets and feeds (see page R9), these media elements can make your Internet communication more entertaining and useful.

GRAPHICS	
Photographs	You can post photographs taken by digital cameras or scanned as files.
Illustrations	Artwork can be created using computer software. You can also use a scanner to post a digital image of a drawing or sketch.
Charts, Graphs, and Maps	Charts and graphs can make statistical information clear. Use spreadsheet software to create these elements. Use Internet sites to find maps of specific places.

VIDEO	
Live Action	Digital video can be recorded by a camera or recorded from another media source.
Animation	Animated videos can also be created using software.

AUDIO	
Music	Many social network communities make it easy to share your favorite music with people who visit your page.
Voice	Use a microphone to add your own voice to your Web page.

Editing Media Elements

You can use software to customize media elements. Open source software is free and available to anyone on the Internet. Here are some things you can do with software:

- **Crop** a photograph to focus on the subject or brighten an image that is too dark.

- **Transform** a drawing's appearance from flat to three-dimensional.

- **Insert** a "You Are Here" arrow on a map.

- **Edit** a video or sound file to shorten its running time.

- **Add** background music or sound effects to a video.

Podcasts

A **podcast** is a digital audio or video recording of a program that is made available on the Internet. Users can replay the podcast on a computer, or download it and replay it on a personal audio player. You might think of podcasts as radio or television programs that you create yourself. They can be embedded on a Web site or fed to a Web page through a podcast widget.

Creating an Effective Podcast

To make a podcast, you will need a recording device, such as a microphone or digital video camera, as well as editing software. Open source editing software is widely available and free of charge. Most audio podcasts are converted into the MP3 format. Here are some tips for creating a podcast that is clear and entertaining:

- **Listen to several podcasts by different authors** to get a feeling for the medium.

- **Make a list** of features and styles you like and also those you want to avoid.

- **Test your microphone** to find the best recording distance. Stand close enough to the microphone so that your voice sounds full, but not so close that you create an echo.

- **Create an outline** that shows your estimated timing for each element.

- **Be prepared** before you record. Rehearse, but do not create a script. Podcasts are best when they have a natural, easy flow.

- **Talk directly to your listeners**. Slow down enough so they can understand you.

- Use software to **edit your podcast before publishing it**. You can edit out mistakes or add additional elements.

Wikis

A **wiki** is a collaborative Web site that lets visitors create, add, remove, and edit content. The term comes from the Hawaiian phrase *wikiwiki*, which means "quick." Web users of a wiki are both the readers and the writers of the site. Some wikis are open to contributions from anyone. Others require visitors to register before they can edit the content. All of the text in these collaborative Web sites was written by people who use the site. Articles are constantly changing, as visitors find and correct errors and improve texts.

You can change the information on a wiki, but be sure your information is correct and clear before you add it. Wikis keep track of all changes, so your work will be recorded and can be evaluated by other users.

Wikis have both advantages and disadvantages as sources of information. They are valuable open forums for the exchange of ideas. The unique collaborative writing process allows entries to change over time. However, entries can also be modified incorrectly. Careless or malicious users can delete good content and add inappropriate or inaccurate information. Wikis may be useful for gathering background information, but should not be used as research resources.

Writing Business Letters

Business letters are often formal in tone and written for a specific business purpose. They generally follow one of several acceptable formats. In block format, all parts of the letter are at the left margin. All business letters, however, have the same parts: heading, inside address, salutation, body, closing, and signature.

The **heading** shows the writer's address and organization (if any).

The **inside address** indicates where the letter will be sent and the date.

A **salutation**, or **greeting,** is punctuated by a colon. When the specific addressee is not known, use a general greeting such as "To Whom It May Concern."

The **body** of the letter states the writer's purpose. In this case, the writer requests that the class participate in the book drive.

The **closing**, "Sincerely," is common, as are "Best regards," "Yours truly," and "Respectfully yours."

Oscar Diego
Community Book Drive
P.O. Box 34535
Middletown, NY 10941

February 10, 2010
Yin Wallenez
English Teacher
Marsden School
1515 Main River Drive
Middletown, NY 10940

Dear Ms. Wallenez:

We are writing to you to encourage you and your class to join in this year's Community Book Drive. We really appreciated your participation last year and hope you will join us again. As you know, the Community Book Drive gathers books for hundreds of children who otherwise could not afford them. Last year we gathered more than 1,500 books!

Participating this year is simple. Just nominate two members of your class to serve as the book drive leaders. They will post flyers about the book drive around the school and other community areas. They will also be responsible for letting the book drive team leaders know when the drop boxes at your school are getting full.

Please let me know if you are interested. I sure hope that your class will be able to make this year's drive as much of a success as the last! Thanks for your time and consideration.

Sincerely,

Oscar Diego

Oscar Diego • Co-Coordinator, Community Book Drive

Writing Friendly Letters

Friendly letters are less formal than business letters. You can use this form to write to a friend, a family member, or anyone with whom you'd like to communicate in a personal, friendly way. Like business letters, friendly letters have the following parts: heading, inside address, salutation, body, closing, and signature. The purpose of a friendly letter might be:

- to share news and feelings
- to send or answer an invitation
- to express thanks

The **heading** includes the writer's address and the date on which he or she wrote the letter. In some very casual letters, the writer may not include his or her address.

The **body** of the letter is the main section and contains the message of the letter.

Some common **closings** for friendly letters include "Best wishes," "Love," and "Take care."

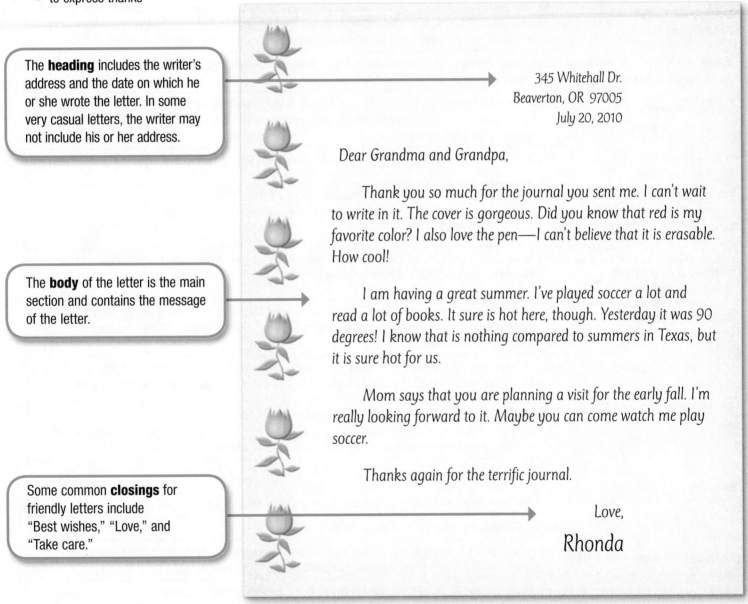

345 Whitehall Dr.
Beaverton, OR 97005
July 20, 2010

Dear Grandma and Grandpa,

Thank you so much for the journal you sent me. I can't wait to write in it. The cover is gorgeous. Did you know that red is my favorite color? I also love the pen—I can't believe that it is erasable. How cool!

I am having a great summer. I've played soccer a lot and read a lot of books. It sure is hot here, though. Yesterday it was 90 degrees! I know that is nothing compared to summers in Texas, but it is sure hot for us.

Mom says that you are planning a visit for the early fall. I'm really looking forward to it. Maybe you can come watch me play soccer.

Thanks again for the terrific journal.

Love,

Rhonda

MLA Style for Listing Sources

Book with one author	London, Jack. *White Fang.* Clayton, DE: Prestwick House, 2007. Print.
Book with two or three authors	Veit, Richard, and Christopher Gould. *Writing, Reading, and Research.* 8th ed. Boston: Wadsworth Cengage, 2009. Print.
Book prepared by an editor	Twain, Mark. *The Complete Essays of Mark Twain.* Ed. Charles Neider. New York: Da Capo, 2000. Print.
Book with more than three authors or editors	Donald, Robert B., et al. *Writing Clear Essays.* 3rd ed. Upper Saddle River, NJ: Prentice Hall, Inc., 1996. Print.
A single work from an anthology	Poe, Edgar Allan. "The Fall of the House of Usher." *American Literature: A Chronological Approach.* Ed. Edgar H. Schuster, Anthony Tovatt, and Patricia O. Tovatt. New York City, NY: McGraw-Hill, 1985. 233–247. Print. [Indicate pages for the entire selection.]
Introduction, foreward, preface, or afterward in a book	Vidal, Gore. Introduction. *Abraham Lincoln: Selected Speeches and Writings.* By Abraham Lincoln. New York: Vintage, 1992. xxi–xxvii. Print.
Signed article in a weekly magazine	Walsh, Brian. "Greening This Old House." *Time* 4 May 2009: 45–47. Print. [For a multi-page article that does not appear on consecutive pages, write only the first page number on which it appears, followed by a plus sign.]
Signed article in a monthly magazine	Fischman, Josh. "A Better Life with Bionics." *National Geographic* Jan. 2010: 34–53. Print.
Unsigned editorial or story	"Wind Power." Editorial. *New York Times* 9 January 2010: A18. Print. [If the editorial or story is signed, begin with the author's name.]
Signed pamphlet	[Treat the pamphlet as though it were a book.]
Audiovisual media, such as films, slide programs, videocassettes, DVDs	*Where the Red Fern Grows.* Dir. Norman Toker. Perf. James Whitmore, Beverly Garland, and Stewart Peterson. 1974. Sterling Entertainment, 1997. DVD.
Radio or TV broadcast transcript	"Texas High School Football Titans Ready for Clash." *Weekend Edition Sunday.* Host Melissa Block. Guests Mike Pesca and Tom Goldman. Natl. Public Radio. KUHF, Houston, 18 Dec. 2009. Print. Transcript.
A single page on a Web site	U.S. Census Bureau: Customer Liaison and Marketing Services Office. "State Facts for Students: Texas." *U.S. Census Bureau.* U.S. Census Bureau, 15 October 2009. Web. 1 November 2009. [Indicate the date of last update if known or use n.d. if not known. After the medium of publication, include the date you accessed the information. You do not need the URL unless it it the only way to find the page. If needed, include it in angled brackets at the end, i.e. <http://www.census.gov/schools/facts/texas.html >.]
Newspaper	Yardley, Jim. "Hurricane Sweeps into Rural Texas; Cities Are Spared." *New York Times* 23 Aug. 1999: A1. Print. [For a multipage article that does not appear on consecutive pages, write only the first page number on which it appears, followed by a plus sign.]
Personal interview	Jones, Robert. Personal interview. 4 Sept. 2006.
Audio with multiple publishers	Simms, James, ed. *Romeo and Juliet.* By William Shakespeare. Oxford: Attica Cybernetics; London: BBC Education; London: HarperCollins, 1995. CD-ROM.
Signed article from an encyclopedia	Askeland, Donald R. "Welding." *World Book Encyclopedia.* 1991 ed. Print. [For a well known reference, you do not need to include the publisher information, only the edition and year, followed by the medium used.]

Commonly Misspelled Words

The list on this page presents words that cause problems for many people. Some of these words are spelled according to set rules, but others follow no specific rules. As you review this list, check to see how many of the words give you trouble in your own writing.

absence	benefit	conscience	excellent	library	prejudice
absolutely	bicycle	conscientious	exercise	license	previous
accidentally	bought	conscious	experience	lightning	probably
accurate	brief	continuous	explanation	likable	procedure
achievement	brilliant	convenience	extension	literature	proceed
affect	bulletin	coolly	extraordinary	mathematics	pronunciation
agreeable	bury	cooperate	familiar	maximum	realize
aisle	buses	correspondence	fascinating	minimum	really
all right	business	courageous	February	misspell	receipt
allowance	cafeteria	courteous	fiery	naturally	receive
analysis	calendar	criticism	financial	necessary	recognize
analyze	campaign	curiosity	foreign	neighbor	recommend
ancient	canceled	deceive	fourth	niece	rehearse
anniversary	candidate	decision	generally	ninety	repetition
answer	capital	defendant	genuine	noticeable	restaurant
anticipate	capitol	definitely	government	occasion	rhythm
anxiety	career	dependent	grammar	occasionally	sandwich
apologize	cashier	description	guidance	occur	schedule
appearance	category	desert	height	occurred	scissors
appreciate	ceiling	dessert	humorous	occurrence	theater
appropriate	certain	dining	immediately	opinion	truly
argument	changeable	disappointed	immigrant	opportunity	usage
athletic	characteristic	distinguish	independence	parallel	valuable
attendance	clothes	effect	independent	particularly	various
awkward	colonel	eighth	individual	personally	vegetable
bargain	column	embarrass	intelligence	persuade	weight
battery	commercial	enthusiastic	judgment	physician	weird
beautiful	commitment	envelope	knowledge	possibility	whale
beginning	condemn	environment	lawyer	precede	yield
believe	congratulate	especially	legible	preferable	

A

address (a´dres´) *n.* the place where a person lives or receives mail

analysis (ə nal´ə sis) *n.* the process of looking at something closely to understand its meaning, structure, or parts

anticipate (an tis´ə pāt´) *v.* to expect or predict; to foresee and then be ready to deal with

argument (är´gyü mənt) *n.* a discussion (written or spoken) which aims to persuade; a set of statements putting forward and backing up an idea or position

aspect (as´pekt´) *n.* a part or feature of something

astonishing (ə stän´ish ing) *adj.* very surprising

C

character (kar´ik tər) *n.* a person (or animal) who plays a part in the action of a story, play, or movie

chronological (krän´ə läj´i kəl) *adj.* described or arranged in the order of time, starting with what happened first

coherence (kō hir´ənts) *n.* the state of having ideas that are clear and logical

coherent (kō hir´ənt) *adj.* well-planned, clear, logical; holding together well

conceivable (kən sēv´ə bəl) *adj.* possible to imagine or grasp mentally

concise (kən sīs´) *adj.* short and clear

conflict (kän´flikt´) *n.* the struggle between people or opposing forces which creates the dramatic action in a play or story

connection (kə nek´shən) *n.* an event or thing that brings together people or ideas; a relationship between people and/or ideas

consequence (kän´si kwens´) *n.* the result of an action

consequently (kän´si kwent´lē) *adv.* as a result

convey (kən vā´) *v.* to make something (for example, an idea or a feeling) known to someone; to communicate

convince (kən vins´) *v.* to make someone believe something is true; to make someone agree through argument

counter-argument (kount´ər är´gyü mənt) *n.* a reason against the original argument

D

defend (dē fend´) *v.* to stand up for, or argue in support of, an idea or stance

detail (dē´tāl´) *n.* a specific fact or piece of information about something

determine (dē tur´mən) *v.* to discover or figure out the facts about something, often by looking at it closely, or doing research or calculations; to decide

develop (di vel´əp) *v.* to explain or build an idea or example bit by bit

device (di vīs´) *n.* the use of words to gain a particular effect in a piece of writing

dialogue (dī´ə lôg´) *n.* a conversation between two or more people in a book, play, or movie

differentiate (dif´ər en´shē āt´) *v.* to notice differences in information

documentation (däk´yü mən tā´shən) *n.* the noting of sources to back up an idea or opinion

E

effect (e fekt´) *n.* the way that something changes because of a separate action

effective (e fekt´iv) *adj.* successful in getting the desired results

element (el´ə mənt) *n.* one of several parts that make up a whole

emotion (ē mō´shən) *n.* a feeling, such as love or joy; feelings generally, as contrasting with reason and logic

emphasize (em´fə sīz´) *v.* to give special importance to

engaging (en gāj´ing) *adj.* charming, interesting; something which draws in and interests (engages) the reader

enhance (en hans´) *v.* to improve, make better

evaluate (ē val´yü āt´) *v.* to look into something carefully to assess and judge it

evidence (ev´ə dəns) *n.* anything that gives proof or shows something to be true

explanation (eks´plə nā´shən) *n.* words used to tell the meaning of something

external (ek stur´nəl) *adj.* on the outside

extraneous (ek strā´nē əs) *adj.* not relevant, unnecessary; unrelated to the subject being discussed

F

fact (fakt) *n.* a piece of information that can be shown to be true

fantasy (fant´ə sē) *n.* imaginative writing that contains things not found in real life

flashback (flash´bak´) *n.* a scene in a story that shows events which happened earlier

foreshadowing (fôr shad´ō ing) *n.* when an author hints at what might happen later in the story

formatting (fôr´mat´ing) *adj.* related to the arrangement of text, images, and graphics on a page

G

genre (zhän´rə) *n.* a type of writing that contains certain features

gesture (jes´chər) *n.* a movement of part of the body (usually hands, arms, or face) to express a meaning or idea

G

hyperbole (hī pur´bə lē) *n.* over-the-top exaggeration

I

idiom (id´ē əm) *n.* an expression, made up of a group of words, where the meaning as a whole is different from what the words mean individually

imagery (im´ij rē) *n.* descriptive language that paints pictures in the mind or appeals to the senses

inconsistencies (in´kən sis´tən sēz) *n.* things that contradict each other

insight (in´sīt´) *n.* a useful, important, deep understanding about a topic

internal (in tur´nəl) *adj.* on the inside

interpret (in tur´prət) *v.* to decide on and explain the meaning of something

issue (ish´ü) *n.* a topic or problem

J

judgment (juj´mənt) *n.* an opinion or conclusion formed after careful thought and evaluation

L

letter (let´ər) *n.* a written or printed message

literary (lit´ar er´ē) *adj.* of or relating to books or other written material

logical (läj´i kəl) *adj.* clear and reasonable; based on logic

M

meter (mēt´ər) *n.* a poem's rhythmic pattern, made by the number of beats in each line

O

opinion (ə pin´yən) *n.* a belief or view that is not necessarily based on facts

option (äp shən) *n.* a possible choice, the freedom or power to make a choice

organized (ôr´gə nīzd´) *adj.* the state of being in order

original (ə rij´i nəl) *adj.* made at the beginning, not copied or reproduced; inventive and unusual; not based on previously existing ideas or creations

P

personification (pər sän´ə fə kā´shən) *n.* a type of figurative language where animals or other non-humans are given human characteristics

perspective (pər spek´tiv) *n.* a way of thinking about something; a point of view

plot (plät) *n.* the sequence of events in a story

point of view (point uv vyü) *n.* the perspective from which a story is told; an attitude, position, standpoint, or way of looking at a situation; an opinion

precise (prē cīs´) *adj.* exact

primary sources (prī´mer ē sôr´səz) *n.* the origin of first-hand knowledge, such as interviews and diaries

propose (prə pōz´) *v.* put forward an idea or plan

puzzling (puz´ling) *adj.* difficult to understand, confusing, or unclear

Q

quotation (kwō tā´shən) *n.* a group of words copied exactly from a speech or piece of writing

R

reader-friendly (rēd´ər frend´lē) *adj.* easy for an audience to read and understand

realistic (rē ə ʹlis tik) *adj.* practical, or dealing with situations in a sensible way

reason (rē´zən) *n.* the ability to think in a clear, rational way

reasoning (rē´zən ing) *n.* the process of reaching a conclusion by looking at the facts

reject (ri jekt´) *v.* to not accept; to refuse (for example an idea or suggestion) because you do not agree

repetition (rep´ə tish´ən) *n.* the act of repeating something that has already been said, done, or written

research (rē´sʉrch´) *v.* to carefully study information on a topic; *n.* the careful study of information on a topic

resolution (rez´ə lü´shən) *n.* what happens to resolve the conflict in the plot of a story

rhetorical devices (ri tôr´i kəl di vī´səz) *n.* strategies and techniques (for example hyperbole) used by writers to draw in or persuade readers

rhythm (rith´əm) *n.* the pattern of stressed and unstressed syllables in spoken or written language, particularly in poetry

S

satisfactory (sat´is fak´tə rē) *adj.* adequate, acceptable; neither especially good nor especially bad

scheme (skēm) *n.* (for a poem) a design or ordered structure

secondary sources (sek´ən der´ē sôr´səz) *n.* books or documents that have second-hand information, which has been derived from primary sources

sensory (sen´sər ē) *adj.* of or relating to the five senses

sequence (sē´kwəns) *n.* when a series of things follows each other in a particular order

setting (set´ing) *n.* the time and place of the action in a story or other piece of writing

strategy (strat´ə jē) *n.* in a piece of writing, a literary tactic or method (such as flashback or foreshadowing) used by the writer to achieve a certain goal or affect

structure (struk´chər) *n.* the way something is organized and put together; *v.* to put together according to a pattern or plan

style (stīl) *n.* a way of doing something; a way of writing

suitable (süt´ə bəl) *adj.* appropriate, right for a particular purpose

summarize (sum´ə rīz´) *v.* to briefly state the main points or main ideas

support (sə pôrt´) *v.* to hold up, to back

suspense (sə spens´) *n.* a feeling of anxiety and uncertainty about what will happen in a story or other piece of writing

sustain (sə stān´) *v.* to keep up, hold up; to affirm or support as true

synthesize (sin´thə sīz´) *v.* to combine, to bring different parts together into a whole

T

technique (tek nēk´) *n.* a special way of doing something

theme (thēm) *n.* a central message, concern, or purpose in a literary work

thesis (thē´sis) *n.* an idea or theory that is stated and then discussed in a logical way

tone (tōn) *n.* a writer's attitude toward his or her subject

transition (tran zish´ən) *n.* the change from one part, place, or idea to another; in writing, the change between sentences, paragraphs, and ideas

V

variety (və rī´ə tē) *n.* a number or range of things which are of a similar type

viewpoint (vyü´point´) *n.* an attitude, position, standpoint, or way of looking at a situation

Spanish Glossary

A

address / dirección *s.* el lugar donde vive una persona o donde se recibe el correo

affect / afectar *v.* tener un efecto en, causar un cambio

analysis / análisis *s.* el proceso de examinar algo detenidamente para entender su significado, su estructura o sus partes

anticipate / anticipar *v.* esperar o predecir; prever y estar preparado para tratar con algo

argument / argumento *s.* razonamiento (escrito o hablado) con el fin de persuadir; una serie de declaraciones que proponen o apoyan una idea o postura

aspect / aspecto *s.* una parte o un atributo de algo

astonishing / asombroso *adj.* muy sorprendente

C

character / personaje *s.* un individuo (humano o animal) que tiene un papel en la acción de un cuento, una obra de teatro o una película

chronological / cronológico *adj.* descrito o arreglado en el orden temporal, empezando con el evento que ocurrió primero

coherence / coherencia *s.* el estado de tener ideas claras y lógicas

coherent / coherente *adj.* bien planeado, claro, lógico; congruente

conceivable / concebible *adj.* que puede ser imaginado o comprendido mentalmente

concise / conciso *adj.* breve y claro

conflict / conflicto *s.* la lucha entre personas o fuerzas opuestas que crea la acción dramática en una obra de teatro o un cuento

connection / conexión *s.* un evento o una cosa que une a las personas o ideas; una relación entre personas y/o ideas

consequence / consecuencia *s.* el resultado de una acción previa

consequently / por consiguiente *adv.* como resultado

convey / expresar *v.* darse a entender algo a alguien (por ejemplo, una idea o sentimiento); comunicar

convince / convencer *v.* hacer que alguien crea algo; persuadir a alguien a través del argumento

counter-argument / contraargumento *s.* una razón contra el argumento original

D

defend / defender *v.* apoyar, discutir para respaldar una idea o postura

detail / detalle *s.* un dato específico o información específica de algo

determine / determinar, decidir *v.* descubrir o deducir los hechos de algo, muchas veces por examinarlo detenidamente o por investigarlo o hacer cálculos; elegir una opción

develop / desarrollar *v.* explicar o exponer poco a poco una idea o ejemplo

device / técnica (literaria) *s.* el uso de palabras para tener un efecto específico en una obra escrita

dialogue / diálogo *s.* una conversación entre dos personajes o más en un libro, obra de teatro o película

differentiate / diferenciar *v.* notar las diferencias

documentation / documentación *s.* la anotación de fuentes para apoyar una idea u opinión

E

effective / efectivo, eficaz *adj.* exitoso en producir los resultados deseados

element / elemento *s.* una de varias partes que forman parte de una totalidad

emotion / sentimiento *s.* una sensación emotiva, como el amor o la alegría; los sentimientos en general, opuestos al razonamiento y la lógica

emphasize / enfatizar *v.* dar importancia especial a algo

engaging / interesante *adj.* encantador, interesante; algo que le atrae y le interesa al lector

enhance / mejorar *v.* hacer mejor, enriquecer

evaluate / evaluar *v.* investigar algo cuidadosamente para analizarlo y valorarlo

evidence / pruebas *s.* cualquier cosa que demuestre o indique que algo es verdadero

explanation / explicación *s.* las palabras que se usan para decir el significado de algo

external / externo *adj.* afuera de

extraneous / superfluo *adj.* irrrelevante, no necesario, no relacionado con el tema tratado

F

fact / hecho *s.* un dato que se puede verificar

fantasy / fantasía *s.* escritura imaginativa que tiene cosas que no se encuentran en la realidad

flashback / flashback *s.* una escena en un cuento que expone los eventos que sucedieron antes

foreshadowing / presagio *n.* cuando un escritor da referencias a lo que puede suceder en el cuento

formatting / formateo *s.* la colocación de texto, imágenes y gráficos en una página

G

genre / género *s.* una clase de escritura que tiene características específicas

gesture / gesto *s.* un moviemiento de una parte del cuerpo (normalmente las manos, brazos o cara) para expresar un significado o una idea

H

hyperbole / hipérbole *s.* exageración excesiva

I

idiom / modismo *s.* una expresión compuesta de un grupo de palabras cuyo significado en conjunto es diferente de lo que significan las palabras individuales

imagery / imágenes *s.* lenguaje descriptivo que crea dibujos en la mente o atrae los sentidos

inconsistencies / inconsecuencias *s.* cosas que se contradicen

insight / perspicacia *s.* el profundo entendimiento útil e importante de un tema

internal / interno *adj.* dentro de

interpret / interpretar *v.* determinar y explicar el significado de algo

issue / cuestión *s.* un tema o un problema

J

judgment / juicio *s.* una opinión o conclusión formada después de una consideración y evaluación cuidadosa

L

letter / carta *s.* un mensaje escrito o impreso

literary / literario *adj.* perteneciente o relativo a los libros u otros materiales escritos

logical / lógico *adj.* claro y razonable; basado en la lógica

M

meter / métrica *s.* el patrón rítmico de un poema, marcado por el tiempo y ritmo de cada verso

O

opinion / opinión *s.* una creencia o perspectiva que no es necesariamente basada en los hechos

option / opción *s.* una elección possible; la libertad o poder de elegir

organized / organizado *adj.* que está ordenado

original / original *adj.* obra producida directamente por su autor sin ser copia, imitación o traducción de otra

P

personification / personificación *s.* un tipo de lenguaje figurado en el que los animales u otros seres no humanos tienen características humanas

perspective / perspective *s.* una manera de pensar; un punto de vista

plot / argumento *s.* la secuencia de eventos en una historia

point of view / punto de vista *s.* la perspectiva de la cual se cuenta una historia

precise / preciso *adj.* exacto

primary sources / fuentes primarias *s.* el origen de información de primera mano, por ejemplo entrevistas y diarios

propose / proponer *v.* plantear una idea o un plan

puzzling / enigmático, confuso *adj.* difícil de entender; confuso, poco claro

Q

quotation / cita *s.* un grupo de palabras copiadas exactamente de un discurso o texto

R

reader-friendly / fácil de leer *adj.* no complicado, fácil de entender y leer

realistic / realista *adj.* Que actúa con sentido práctico o trata de ajustarse a la realidad

reason / razón *s.* la habilidad de pensar de una manera clara y racional

reasoning / razonamiento *s.* el proceso de llegar a una conclusión por examinar los hechos reject / rechazar v. no aceptar, rehusar (por ejemplo una idea o sugerencia) por no estar de acuerdo

reject / rechazar *v.* no aceptar; resistir porque uno no esta de acuedor

repetition / repetición *s.* el acto de repetir algo ya dicho, hecho o escrito

research / investigar *v.* estudiar cuidadosamente la información sobre un tema; investigación *s.* el estudio cuidadoso de la información sobre un tema

resolution / resolución *s.* lo que ocurre para resolver el conflicto en el argumento de una historia

rhetorical devices / técnicas retóricas *s.* estrategias y técnicas (por ejemplo hipérbole) utilizadas por los escritores para atraer o persuadir a los lectores

rhythm / ritmo *s.* el patrón de sílabas tónicas y átonas en el lenguaje oral y escrito, especialmente en la poesía

S

satisfactory / satisfactorio *adj.* adecuado, acceptable, ni especialmente bueno ni especialmente malo

scheme / esquema *s.* (para un poema) un diseño o estructura ordenada

secondary sources / fuentes secundarias *s.* libros o documentos que tienen información de segunda mano que se ha derivado de fuentes primarias

sensory / sensorial *adj.* perteneciente o relativo a los cinco sentidos

sequence / secuencia *s.* cuando una serie de eventos ocurre en un orden determinado

setting / escenario *s.* el lugar y el momento de la acción en un cuento u otra obra escrita

similar / similar *adj.* semejante pero no exactamente igual

strategy / estrategia *s.* en una obra escrita, una táctica o método (como un flashback o el presagio) usado por el autor para lograr un objetivo o efecto específico

structure / estructura *s.* la manera en la que algo está organizado o compuesto; estructurar v. organizar o componer según un patrón o plan

style / estilo *s.* una manera de hacer algo; una manera de escribir

suitable / apropiado *adj.* adecuado, acertado para un propósito particular

summarize / resumir *v.* exponer de una manera breve los puntos o ideas principales

support / apoyar *v.* sostener, respaldar

suspense / suspenso *s.* una sensación de ansiedad e incertidumbre sobre lo que va a pasar en una historia u otra obra escrita

sustain / sostener *v.* mantener, apoyar; afirmar o confirmar como verdadero

synthesize / sintetizar *v.* combinar, unir diferentes partes para formar una totalidad

T

technique / técnica *s.* un método especial de hacer algo

theme / tema *s.* una idea, asunto o propósito principal en una obra literaria

thesis / tesis *s.* una idea o teoría que se expone y que se discute de una manera lógica

tone / tono *s.* la actitud de un escritor hacia su tema o materia

transition / transición *s.* el cambio entre partes, lugares y conceptos; en la escritura, el cambio entre oraciones, párrafos e ideas

V

variety / variedad *s.* un número o rango de cosas que son del mismo tipo o de la misma clase

viewpoint / punto de vista *s.* una actitud, postura o manera de interpretar una situación

Meeting Agenda

Meeting Title: _____

Date: _____

Time: _____

Called by: _____

Attendees: _____

Time	Item	Owner

Cause and Effect Chart

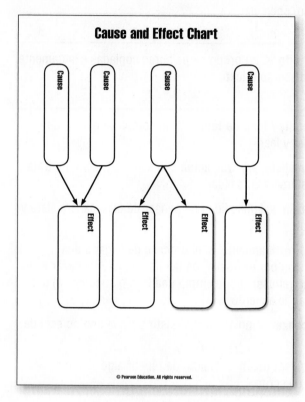

Cluster Diagram

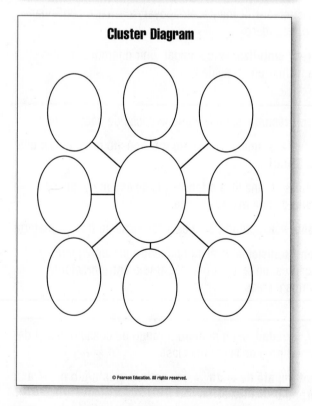

Five Ws Chart

Use these questions as you read, and write important details. Remember, you may not need to answer every question.

Who?
What?
When?
Where?
Why?

Writing Coach Online

Resource Go online for printable versions of these graphic organizers.

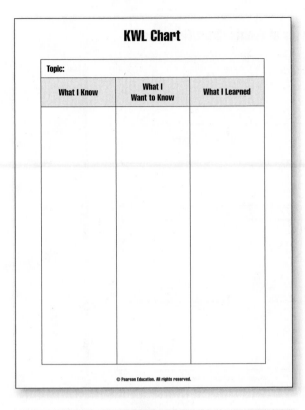

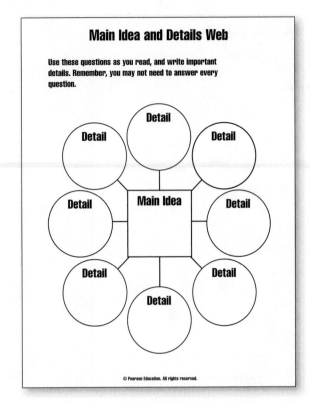

Note Card

Topic:

Source:
-
-
-

Topic:

Source:
-
-
-

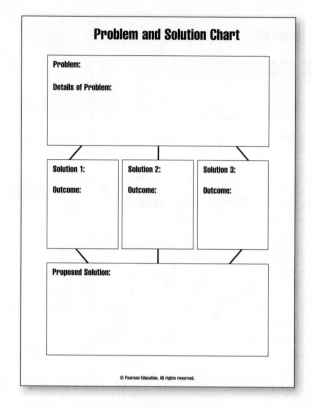

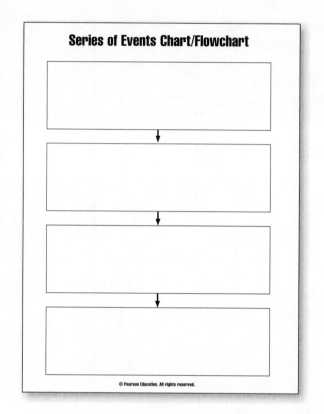

Source Card

Source Number: _____

Source Name: _____

Kind of Source: _____

Author(s): _____

Editor (when applicable): _____

Publisher: _____

Publication Date: _____

Publication Location: _____

Other Information _____

Source Number: _____

Source Name: _____

Kind of Source: _____

Author(s): _____

Editor (when applicable): _____

Publisher: _____

Publication Date: _____

Publication Location: _____

Other Information _____

Outline

Topic   I. _____

  Subtopic   A. _____

    Supporting   1. _____
    details   2. _____
        3. _____
        4. _____

  Subtopic   B. _____

    Supporting   1. _____
    details   2. _____
        3. _____
        4. _____

Topic   II. _____

  Subtopic   A. _____

    Supporting   1. _____
    details   2. _____
        3. _____
        4. _____

  Subtopic   B. _____

    Supporting   1. _____
    details   2. _____
        3. _____
        4. _____

Steps in a Process Chart

Steps	Details
Step 1:	
Step 2:	
Step 3:	
Step 4:	
Step 5:	

Storyboard

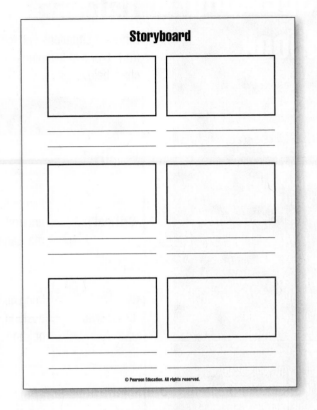

Timeline

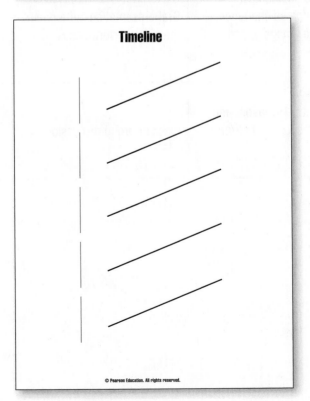

Venn Diagram

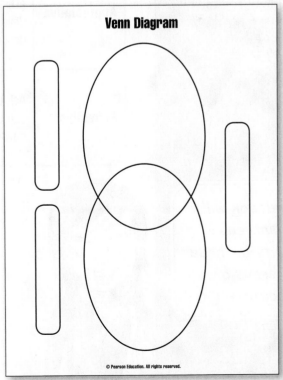

Graphic Organizer Handbook   R27

Listening and Speaking Handbook

Communication travels between people in many forms. You receive information by listening to others, and you convey information through speaking. The more developed these skills are, the more you will be able to communicate your ideas, as well as to comprehend the ideas of others.

If you improve your listening skills, it will become easier to focus your attention on classroom discussions and to identify important information more accurately. If you develop good speaking skills, you will be better prepared to contribute effectively in group discussions, to give formal presentations with more confidence, and to communicate your feelings and ideas to others more easily.

Listening

Different situations call for different types of listening. Learn more about the four main types of listening—critical, empathic, appreciative, and reflective—in the chart below.

Types of Listening		
Type	**How to Listen**	**Situations**
Critical	Listen for facts and supporting details to understand and evaluate the speaker's message.	Informative or persuasive speeches, class discussions, announcements
Empathic	Imagine yourself in the other person's position, and try to understand what he or she is thinking.	Conversations with friends or family
Appreciative	Identify and analyze aesthetic or artistic elements, such as character development, rhyme, imagery, and descriptive language.	Oral presentations of a poem, dramatic performances
Reflective	Ask questions to get information, and use the speaker's responses to form new questions.	Class or group discussions

This handbook will help you increase your ability in these two key areas of communication.

Using Different Types of Questions

A speaker's ideas may not always be clear to you. You may need to ask questions to clarify your understanding. If you understand the different types of questions, you will be able to get the information you need.

- An **open-ended question** does not lead to a single, specific response. Use this question to open up a discussion: "What did you think of the piano recital?"

- A **closed question** leads to a specific response and must be answered with a yes or no: "Did you play a piece by Chopin at your recital?"

- A **factual question** is aimed at getting a particular piece of information and must be answered with facts: "How many years have you been playing the piano?"

Participating in a Group Discussion

In a group discussion, you openly discuss ideas and topics in an informal setting. The group discussions in which you participate will involve, for the most part, your classmates and focus on the subjects you are studying. To get the most out of a group discussion, you need to participate in it.

Use group discussions to express and to listen to ideas in an informal setting.

Communicate Effectively Think about the points you want to make, the order in which you want to make them, the words you will use to express them, and the examples that will support these points before you speak.

Ask Questions Asking questions can help you improve your comprehension of another speaker's ideas. It may also call attention to possible errors in another speaker's points.

Make Relevant Contributions Stay focused on the topic being discussed. Relate comments to your own experience and knowledge, and clearly connect them to your topic. It is important to listen to the points others make so you can build off their ideas. Work to share the connections you see. For example, say whether you agree or disagree, or tell the goup how your ideas connect.

Speaking

Giving a presentation or speech before an audience is generally recognized as public speaking. Effective speakers are well prepared and deliver speeches smoothly and with confidence.

Recognizing Different Kinds of Speeches

There are four main kinds of speeches: informative speeches, persuasive speeches, entertaining speeches, and extemporaneous speeches.

Consider the purpose and audience of your speech before deciding what kind of speech you will give.

- Give an **informative speech** to explain an idea, a process, an object, or an event.

- Give a **persuasive speech** to get your listeners to agree with your position or to take some action. Use formal English when speaking.

- Give an **entertaining speech** to offer your listeners something to enjoy or to amuse them. Use both informal and formal language.

- Give an **extemporaneous speech** when an impromptu occasion arises. It is an informal speech because you do not have a prepared manuscript.

Preparing and Presenting a Speech

If you are asked to deliver a speech, begin choosing a topic that you like or know well. Then, prepare your speech for your audience.

To prepare your speech, research your topic. Make an outline, and use numbered note cards.

Gather Information Use the library and other resources to gather reliable information and to find examples to support your ideas.

Organizing Information Organize your information by writing an outline of main ideas and major details. Then, when you deliver your speech, write the main ideas, major details, quotations, and facts on note cards.

When presenting your speech, use rhetorical forms of language and verbal and nonverbal strategies.

Use Rhetorical Language Repeat key words and phrases to identify your key points. Use active verbs and colorful adjectives to keep your speech interesting. Use parallel phrases to insert a sense of rhythm.

Use Verbal and Nonverbal Strategies Vary the pitch and tone of your voice, and the rate at which you speak. Speak loudly and emphasize key words or phrases. Avoid consistently reading your speech from you notes. Work to maintain eye contact with the audience. As you speak, connect with the audience by using gestures and facial expressions to emphasize key points.

Evaluating a Speech

Evaluating a speech gives you the chance to judge another speaker's skills. It also gives you the opportunity to review and improve your own methods for preparing and presenting a speech.

When you evaluate a speech, you help the speaker and yourself to learn from experience. Listed below are some questions you might ask yourself while evaluating another person's speech or one of your own speeches.

- Did the speaker introduce the topic clearly, develop it well, and conclude it effectively?

- Did the speaker support each main idea with appropriate details?

- Did the speaker approach the platform confidently and establish eye contact with the audience?

- Did the speaker's facial expressions, gestures, and movements appropriately reinforce the words spoken?

- Did the speaker vary the pitch of his or her voice and the rate of his or her speaking?

- Did the speaker enunciate all words clearly?

Listening Critically to a Speech

Hearing happens naturally as sounds reach your ears. Listening, or critical listening, requires that you understand and interpret these sounds.

Critical listening requires preparation, active involvement, and self-evaluation from the listener.

Learning the Listening Process Listening is interactive; the more you involve yourself in the listening process, the more you will understand.

Focus Your Attention Focus your attention on the speaker and block out all distractions—people, noises, and objects. Find out more about the subject that will be discussed beforehand.

Interpret the Information To interpret a speaker's message successfully, you need to identify and understand important information. You might consider listening for repeated words or phrases, pausing momentarily to memorize and/or write key statements, watching non-verbal signals, and combining this new information with what you already know.

Respond to the Speaker's Message Respond to the information you have heard by identifying the larger message of the speech, its most useful points, and your position on the topic.

Index

Grateful acknowledgment is made to the following for copyrighted material:

The Caxton Printers, Ltd.
"How Paul Bunyan Cleared North Dakota (originally titled The Kingdom of North Dakota)" by Dell J. McCormick from *Paul Bunyan Swings His Axe*. Copyright © 1936, The Caxton Printers, Ltd., Caldwell, Idaho. Used by permission.

Dutton Children's Books, A division of Penguin Group (USA), Inc.
From "Anne Frank the Writer" from *Anne Frank: A Hidden Life* by Mirjam Pressler, translated by Anthea Bell. Original text copyright © 1992 by Mirjam Pressler. Translation copyright © 1999 by Macmillan Children's Books. Used by permission of Dutton Children's Books, A Division of Penguin Young Readers Group, A Member of Penguin Group (USA) Inc., 345 Hudson Street, NY, 10014. All rights reserved.

Estate of Howard Moss
"Shall I Compare Thee to a Summer's Day" by Howard Moss from *A Swim Off the Rocks: Light Verse*. Copyright © 1976 by Howard Moss. All rights reserved. Used by permission of Richard Evans.

Gelston Hinds, Jr. o/b/o Amy Ling
"Grandma Ling" by Amy Ling from *Bridge: An Asian American Perspective, Vol. 7, No. 3*. Copyright © 1980 by Amy Ling. Used by permission of the author's husband.

Alfred A. Knopf, Inc., A Division of Random House, Inc.
"April Rain Song" from *The Collected Poems of Langston Hughes* by Langston Hughes, edited by Arnold Rampersad with David Roessel, Associate Editor, copyright © 1994 by The Estate of Langston Hughes. Used by permission of Alfred A. Knopf, a division of Random House, Inc.

Little, Brown and Company, Inc.—Hachette Book Group
"Ode to Enchanted Light" from *Odes to Opposites* by Pablo Neruda. Copyright © 1995 by Pablo Neruda and Fundacion Pablo Neruda (Odes in Spanish). Copyright © 1995 by Ken Krabbenhoft (Odes in English); Copyright © 1995 by Ferris Cook (Illustrations and Compilation). By permission of Little, Brown and Company. All rights reserved.

Louisiana State University Press
"Things" by Lisel Mueller from *Alive Together: New and Selected Poems*. Copyright © 1996 by Lisel Mueller. Used by permission.

National Council of Teachers of English (NCTE)
"Mistakes are a fact of Life: A National Comparative Study" by Andrea A. Lunsford and Karen J. Lunsford translated from *bcs.bedfordstmartins. com/lunsford/PDF/Lunsford_article_Mistakes.pdf*. Copyright © NCTE. Used by permission of National Council of Teachers of English (NCTE).

Harold Ober Associates Incorporated
"April Rain Song" from *The Collected Poems of Langston Hughes* by Langston Hughes, copyright © 1994 by The Estate of Langston Hughes. Used by permission of Harold Ober Associates Incorporated.

New Directions Publishing Corporation
"Old Man" by Jimmy Santiago Baca from *Black Mesa Poems*. Copyright © 1986, 1987, 1988, 1989 by Jimmy Santiago Baca. Used by permission of New Directions.

Pan Macmillan Publishers
From "Anne Frank the Writer" from *Anne Frank: A Hidden Life* by Mirjam Pressler, translated by Anthea Bell. Original text copyright © 1992 by Mirjam Pressler. Translation copyright © 1999 by Macmillan Children's Books.

Robert Siegel (Economy Pictures)
"The Day I Threw the Trivia Bowl" by Robert Siegel from *Guys Write for Guys Read*. Copyright © Robert Siegel. Used by permission of the author.

USA Today-Gannett Co.
"A Few Limits on Teenage Drivers Could Save Their Lives" from *USA TODAY*. Copyright © 2009 USA TODAY a division of Gannett Co. Inc. Used by permission.

Note: Every effort has been made to locate the copyright owner of material reproduced in this component. Omissions brought to our attention will be corrected in subsequent editions.

Image Credits

Illustrations: Monika Melnychuk/i2iart.com

All interior photos provided by Jupiter Images. Except
64: © Glowimages/age fotostock; 90: © Corbis/age fotostock; 118: © Leo Dennis Production/age fotostock; 144: © Pixmann/age fotostock; 203, 227, 228: Courtesy of The Library of Congress.